SUN MICROSYSTEMS PRESS STAROFFICE SERIES

Star**Office** 5.2
Companion

Word processor
Spreadsheet
Drawing program
Database
Presentation program
Scheduler

FLOYD JONES
SOLVEIG HAUGLAND

Sun Microsystems Press
A Prentice Hall Title

PH
PTR

The publisher offers discounts on this book when ordered in bulk quantities. For more information, contact: Corporate Sales Department, Phone: 800-382-3419; Fax: 201-236-7141; E-mail: corpsales@prenhall.com; or write: Prentice Hall PTR, Corp. Sales Dept., One Lake Street, Upper Saddle River, NJ 07458.

Editorial/production supervision: *Patti Guerrieri*
Acquisitions editor: *Gregory G. Doench*
Editorial assistant: *Mary Treacy*
Developmental editor: *Nancy Warner*
Manufacturing manager: *Alexis R. Heydt*
Cover design director: *Jerry Votta*
Cover designer: *Nina Scuderi*
Marketing manager: *Bryan Gambrel*
Sun Microsystems Press:
Marketing manager: *Michael Llwyd Alread*
Publisher: *Rachel Borden*

10 9 8 7 6 5 4 3 2 1

ISBN 0-13-030703-3

Sun Microsystems Press
A Prentice Hall Title

This book is dedicated to mom and dad, who always told
me I could do whatever I wanted, and more.

To Lila. It'll never happen again.

Table of Contents

Preface

StarOffice – Overturning Universal Truths

It used to be that the saying, "You get what you pay for," ranked up there with such indisputable truths as, "What goes up must come down," "Water is wet," and "I had to restart Windows today."

In giving away StarOffice, a powerful, full-featured suite of office software applications, Sun Microsystems has made the saying, "you get what you pay for," not only disputable, but just plain false. StarOffice's applications for working with documents, spreadsheets, slide presentations, Web sites, graphics, and databases, and for managing schedules, appointments, and email, make StarOffice a legitimate replacement for any office product on the market.

StarOffice is free. It provides a user-friendly, flexible, and completely integrated work environment. It provides a comprehensive set of tools that let you, for example, create a Web site start-to-finish (along with graphics, animations, and image maps) and upload the files to a Web server. It supports an obscene number of file formats. It needs less storage space than Microsoft Office.

What goes up must come down. Water is wet. StarOffice is free.

(And yes, I really *did* have to restart Windows today.)

Microsoft Office Compatibility

StarOffice is particularly strong in its ability to open Microsoft Office file formats and save the documents back as Microsoft Office files. It even boasts an AutoPilot that automatically converts entire directories of Word, Excel, and PowerPoint documents and their templates to StarOffice formats, from which you can save back to the original Microsoft formats.

What It Runs On

StarOffice runs on Windows, Linux, and Solaris. Even though MacOS isn't currently supported, you can set StarOffice to display dialog boxes that look exactly like Macintosh dialog boxes.

About this Book

This is a book that lets you find what you need quickly and get it done. This isn't a book for "dummies," with epic-length procedures for cutting and pasting. On the other hand, we don't include extensive details on technical concepts like ODBC and LDAP.

We wrote the book that we would want: all the important stuff, but nothing too basic or technically impractical for the intermediate user (and with a little humor along the way). We also talked to hundreds of new StarOffice users, so we were able to document what people really need to do using StarOffice to do it.

We made certain assumptions before starting this book. We assume that you are familiar and comfortable with the operating system you're using, and that you have previously used products like StarOffice, such as a word processor, spreadsheet, or presentation tool.

Reading Is Fundamental

If you're like most intermediate users, you already know enough to be dangerous, which means you'll probably just dive in and try to do things in StarOffice without any help. Sometimes that strategy works, other times it doesn't. If it doesn't, read the relevant sections in this book. We also indexed the living daylights out of this book, so use the Index, too, particularly a little entry we like to call "troubleshooting."

What Now?

Download and install StarOffice 5.2 if you haven't already. See Chapter 1, *Installation*, on page 3 for more information.

Go through Chapter 3, *Taming the StarOffice Environment*, on page 91. It gives you an overview of the StarOffice work environment and shows you lots of useful things that will help you no matter which StarOffice applications you're using.

Use the tutorials. We've included something for those of you who like to plunge in quickly and get your hands dirty without reading all the procedures ahead of time. At the beginning of most major parts of the book, there's a section called *Quick Start* that contains a *Guided Tour*. The guided tour leads you through specific steps that will help you get to know a lot of the features for each product, including features you probably won't come across while just exploring, as well as few of the product's "gotchas" that we want you to know ahead of time.

Don't panic!

Acknowledgements

We'd like to thank the friends who donated their time to reading and commenting on drafts of the book, in return for nothing but a t-shirt and chance at fame through appearing in the examples: Caron Newman, Carlene Bratach, Paul Bratach, Barry Fish, Takane Aizeki, Scott Hudson, Bryan Basham, Greg Anderson, Arnaud Insinger, Patrick Born, Steve "Shewi" Osvold, and Dan "Born in the spring of increased gyration" Batten. May the road rise up to meet you, may your hard drives fragment slowly, and your applications be robust and user friendly.

Thanks to Simon "Dread Pirate" Roberts for his generosity with his technical expertise and his equipment of every kind and variety.

Thanks to Rob Reiner, for being such a darned fine film maker, and to Peter van der Linden, for proving that computer books can be good reading.

Thanks to Patti Guerrieri, her team of tireless eyes, and the technical reviewers, who cranked out the invaluable proofs and technical changes to us as fast as we could type them in.

Thanks to Floyd for daydreaming during that staff meeting and coming up with the idea for writing this book in the first place, and to Greg Doench and Rachel Borden, for shepherding us through the book-writing process. And thanks to SolBean for taking it by the horns and hanging on till the buzzer.

Also big thanks to Deb Scott, Jari Paukku, Dave Nelson, Bryan Gambrel, Leila Chucri, Sarah Bate, Nancy Warner, Mary Treacy, Jimbo Rose, Kimbo Lee, Trish Pate, Dena Steward, the SES team, eBeth Duran, Mark Leiker, Michael Bohn, John Will, Jeff "Big Daddy" Chacon, Anthony "Duke" Reynoso, the McCulloughs (for all the babysitting), and of course, both sets of Ma and Pa.

And to everyone else we forgot or owe money to. You know who you are.

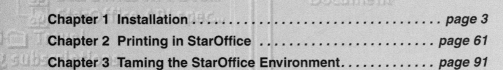

Getting Started

Installation

Installation Checklist

StarOffice is an integrated work environment, not a bunch of separate applications, so you'll install everything using the instructions in this chapter. The installation process isn't excessively complex, but we've provided a checklist to help you make sure you've done everything, in the right order.

Note – If you're going to stick the CD in the drive without following the checklist, at least read *Operating System-Specific Notes* on page 8 before you start. There are some Linux and Solaris errors, in particular, that you will encounter if you don't take the precautions covered in that section.

---

1   Get the software – *Buying a CD or Downloading the StarOffice Software* on page 5

2   Review the installation documentation provided on the CD – *Reading the StarOffice Install and Migration Documentation* on page 6

3   Check that your system meets hardware and software system requirements – *System Requirements* on page 7

4   Review notes on your operating system – *Operating System-Specific Notes* on page 8

5   Install StarOffice – *Installing StarOffice: Single-User* on page 9 or *Installing StarOffice: Multi-User* on page 18

6   Start StarOffice – *Starting StarOffice* on page 46

7   Enter Internet information – *Entering Information in the Internet Setup AutoPilot* on page 47

8   Register StarOffice – *Registration* on page 52

9   Set up printers – *Printing in StarOffice* on page 61

10   To see what you can do with StarOffice now that you've installed it – *Taming the StarOffice Environment* on page 91. You can also check out the *Quick Start* section of each part in this book, which has a tutorial and feature overview.

This chapter also includes information on installing the standalone StarOffice Impress presentation file player, on page 53. However, unless you're heading off to Munich with your laptop tomorrow morning to give a presentation to your CEO, you can wait on installing it until you need it.

Buying a CD or Downloading the StarOffice Software

You can download the software for free from Sun's Web site, or you can buy the CD. Unless you have an exceptionally powerful Internet connection, we **strongly** recommend that you invest the $15 to $40 and buy the CD. The software is about 100 MB, which would take a while to download, and it's much handier to have the CD around.

Note – StarOffice Schedule Server, the multi-user server software for the calendar part of StarOffice, isn't included in the download; only in the CD. In addition, the stand-alone StarOffice Impress presentation player is a separate download from the same site; it's not included in the main StarOffice download.

You can still use Schedule on your local computer without Schedule Server, in a multi-user or single-user environment. You just need Schedule Server if you want users to be able to see each others' schedules.

Obtaining a StarOffice CD

You can buy the packaged CD, with a bit of documentation, from Amazon. Search for StarOffice in the Software category. At the time this book was published, it was $40.

`http://www.amazon.com`

You also can buy it from Sun for $10 plus shipping. Obviously, ordering it from Sun is cheaper. The only advantage to ordering it from Amazon is if you're ordering other stuff at the same time and find it more convenient, or if you want rushed shipping.

1   Open your browser, such as Netscape Navigator, and type the following URL, then press Enter:

    `http://www.sun.com/staroffice/`

2   In the Downloads section, click the StarOffice 5.2 link.

3   Click the link for ordering the small CD kit.

4   Follow the subsequent directions.

Downloading the StarOffice Software

These directions were correct at the time of publication; if they're not now, go to `http://www.sun.com` and follow the directions posted there.

1   Open your browser, such as Netscape Navigator, and type the following URL, then press Enter:

    `http://www.sun.com/staroffice/`

2   In the Downloads section, click the StarOffice 5.2 link.

3   Click the download link for StarOffice 5.2.

4   Follow the subsequent instructions.

5   If you downloaded the software, untar or unzip it, depending upon your operating system.

- To untar, use a terminal window. Navigate to the directory where you downloaded the software to and type `tar xvf filename`

- To unzip, use File Manager to go to the directory where you downloaded the software. Double-click the `.zip` file or files.

  In Windows, you need WinZip (shareware) to do this. With WinZip, double-clicking launches WinZip, from which you can extract the downloaded software. (To get WinZip, go to `http://www.winzip.com`.)

Reading the StarOffice Install and Migration Documentation

The CD (and the downloaded software) contain detailed information about updating from the previous version, and about the installation. Print and read the information for your operating system. The information is included in the `documentation` directory.

The information is in PDF format, so you'll need Adobe Acrobat Reader to read it. It is included in `/documentation/acrobat` and is also available for free at `http://www.adobe.com`.

The `MIGRATION.PDF` file contains valuable information about updating from 5.1 to 5.2 and also describes the StarOffice directory structure.

The `INDEX.TXT` file lists the contents of the CD or downloaded software.

It's also a good idea to read the `readme` file in the *operating_system*/office52 directory.

System Requirements

Make sure you've got the necessary hardware, memory, and other requirements before you get started. This was correct as of publication date of this book, but check your StarOffice documentation and the information on the Web site, as well. Check out the general and technical FAQs. There's a lot of good, up-to-the-minute information there about system requirements, features, and so on. The StarOffice Web site is `http://www.sun.com/staroffice`

StarOffice Requirements

Table 1-1 lists the information for every type of supported system.

Note – These are the "official" requirements; however, StarOffice is a bit of a resource hog and while it will run adequately with 64 MB of RAM, you'll probably be happier with 128 MB or more.

Table 1-1   StarOffice System Requirements

System requirement	Linux	Solaris Sparc	Solaris Intel	Microsoft Windows
Operating system	Linux kernel 2.0.x or higher; glibc2 v 2.1.1 on Intel x86-compatible hardware	Solaris operating environment 8, 7, 2.6, and 2.5.1	Solaris operating environment 8, 7, 2.6, and 2.5.1	Microsoft Windows 95, 98, NT, 2000
Processor/ hardware		85-MHz SPARC processor; 233-MHz Pentium recommended	85-MHz SPARC processor; 233-MHz Pentium recommended	90-MHz Pentium or higher; 233-MHz Pentium recommended
Hard disk space for StarOffice: Single-user	180-250 MB (depending on options selected) 20 MB during installation for temporary files	180-250 MB (depending on options selected) 20 MB during installation for temporary files	180-250 MB (depending on options selected) 20 MB during installation for temporary files	180-250 MB (depending on options selected) 20 MB during installation for temporary files
Hard disk space for StarOffice: Multi-user	Client: 2-4 MB Server: 230 MB	Client: 2-4 MB Server: 230 MB	Server: 2-4 MB Client: 230 MB	Server: 2-4 MB Client: 230 MB
Swap space for installation process	80 MB	80 MB	80 MB	80 MB
RAM	64 MB or more (minimum, 32 MB)	64 MB or more (minimum, 32 MB)	64 MB or more (minimum, 32 MB)	64 MB or more (minimum, 32 MB)
CD-ROM drive	Required if you will be using a CD to install	Required if you will be using a CD to install	Required if you will be using a CD to install	Required if you will be using a CD to install

Note – Before installing StarOffice 5.2 under Solaris, you must install a Sun Microsystems operating system patch. StarOffice won't work without this patch. Refer to the `index.txt` file on the CD-ROM for more information.

StarOffice Schedule Server System Requirements

Depending on the operating system, the installation will need 20 to 40 MB of free disk space for your Schedule installation directory. In addition, another 2 MB will be needed for every user who runs a schedule on this server. For more information, see *Schedule Server Features* on page 843 and *StarOffice Schedule Features* on page 874.

Updating From 5.1 to 5.2

If you've already got StarOffice 5.1 installed, be sure you've read the `MIGRATION.PDF` document on the CD or in the downloaded software. The `MIGRATION.PDF` file contains valuable information about updating from 5.1 to 5.2 and also describes the StarOffice directory structure. In addition, page 12 of the June 2000 version provides detailed information about the directory that files from 5.1 are copied to in 5.2.

- If you want your current files to be automatically migrated to version 5.2, just install 5.2 according to the instructions in *Installing StarOffice: Single-User* or *Installing StarOffice: Multi-User*. When you have the option to import personal data during the installation process, select the option and specify the 5.1 StarOffice path, such as `C:\office51`.

- If you want to manually copy or move the files, install StarOffice 5.2 as usual but don't import personal data. Then copy the 5.1 files to the appropriate 5.2 files, according to the information provided in `MIGRATION.PDF`.

Operating System-Specific Notes

Be sure to read these notes before you start the install.

Windows In Windows, at the time this book was produced, StarOffice 5.2 does not run when there are mutations or other special characters in the login-name/user-name or in the system directories. When you have these characters (ASCII > 127, e.g. ä, ü, é, etc.) in your login-name/user-name, StarOffice 5.2 won't function. A patch is available for this problem at the following site. Just follow the StarOffice Patches link once you access the site.

`http://supportforum.sun.com`

Solaris Before installing StarOffice 5.2 under Solaris you must install a Sun Microsystems operating system patch. StarOffice won't work without this patch. Refer to the INDEX.TXT file on the CD or in the downloaded software for more information.

Linux You **must** mount your CD-ROM drive with Execute rights to be able to run the setup script from the CD. If you don't, a message stating "Permission denied" will appear.

Mount it with the command:

`mount -o exec /dev/cdrom /cdrom`

or add in the file `/etc/fstab` `"exec"` for the CD.

Installing StarOffice: Single-User

The installation is pretty straightforward—just stick the CD in the drive and go. You'll probably get a couple puzzling windows, asking if you want to install a Java Runtime Environment (you definitely do) or Adabas (only if you're into relational databases). We walk you through each step of the way, in the following procedure.

1   Be sure you've read the operating system-specific notes on page 5.

2   In a Linux or Solaris environment, be sure you're logged in as the user who will be running StarOffice.

3   Insert the StarOffice CD in your CD-ROM drive and use your file manager or a terminal window to see its contents. (If you had to download the software, go to the directory you downloaded it to.) Figure 1-1 shows how the CD would look in the file manager of a Solaris computer.

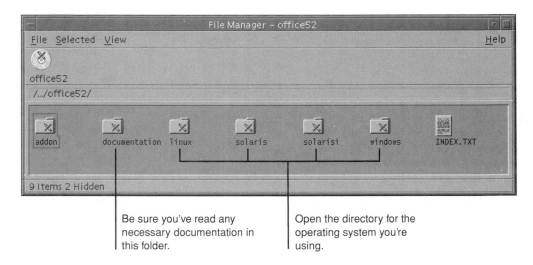

Be sure you've read any necessary documentation in this folder.

Open the directory for the operating system you're using.

Figure 1-1   StarOffice CD contents

4   The CD has a separate directory for each operating system—go to the directory for the type of system you're using, then to the office52 subdirectory.

5   Double-click the setup or setup.exe file. (If you're in a terminal window, type **./setup** or **./setup.exe**)

Note – If a message states that you need to install patches, navigate to the office52/platform/patches directory on the CD and follow the instructions in the readme and installation information documents.

---

6   The window in Figure 1-2 will appear. Click Next.

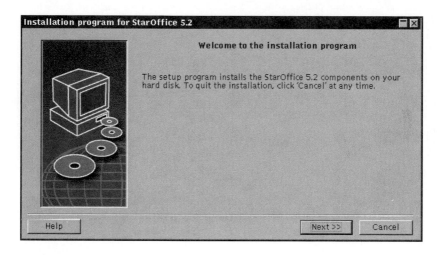

Figure 1-2   Introductory window of StarOffice installation

7   The window in Figure 1-3 will appear. It contains operating system-specific information about the StarOffice Installation (your window might look different). Read the displayed information carefully, then click Next.

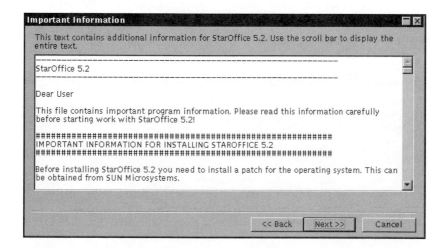

Figure 1-3   Installation information

8   The window in Figure 1-4 will appear, displaying the license agreement. Review it and, if you agree to the terms, click Accept.

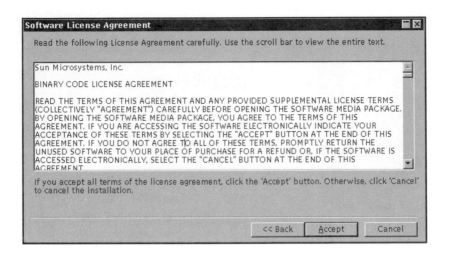

Figure 1-4   License agreement

9   If you currently have StarOffice installed, the window in Figure 1-5 will appear.

- If you want to automatically migrate your StarOffice files created with the older
  version to the directory where you're installing 5.2, select the Import personal
  data option and enter the path to your old StarOffice directory. Click Next.

- If you want to manually copy the files over later, don't mark the option. See
  Updating From 5.1 to 5.2 on page 8 after installation. Click Next.

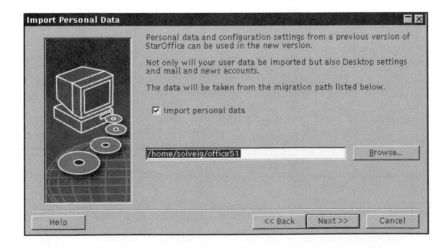

Figure 1-5   Specifying existing StarOffice user data location

10 The personal data window in Figure 1-6 will appear. This information will appear in general options windows in StarOffice; you can enter it now, or choose Tools > Options > General and enter it later.

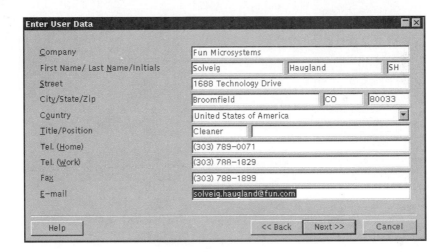

Figure 1-6   Personal information window

11 The installation type window shown in Figure 1-7 will appear.

- If you won't be synchronizing a PalmPilot with StarOffice's calendar module, Schedule, select the Standard Installation and click Next.

- If you need to install the PalmPilot synchronization software, select Custom Installation and click Next.

Note – The Minimal Installation really isn't a good idea. It's not that much less disk space, and it leaves out a lot of things, including the entire StarOffice Image program (you wouldn't be able to open any GIF or JPG files), and pretty much all the templates, help files, and example files.

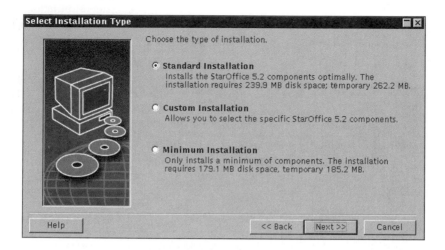

Figure 1-7   Selecting installation type

12 The window in Figure 1-8 will appear. Enter the directory, new or existing, where you want to install StarOffice. Click Next.

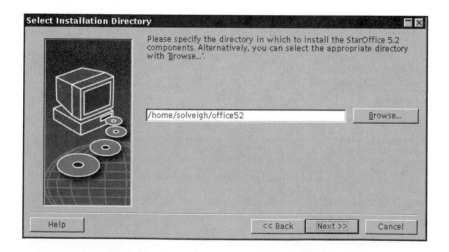

Figure 1-8   Selecting installation location

13 If you selected Custom Installation, a window will appear that allows you to specify the components you want. Expand the StarOffice 5.2 Program Modules item and go to the Schedule component. Under that, select PalmPilot integration, then click Next.

Select the PalmPilot
Integration module and be
sure the icon is fully colored,
not dimmed or white.

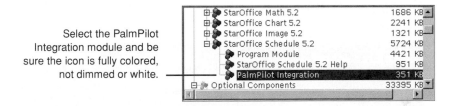

Figure 1-9   PalmPilot Integration install option

14   The window in Figure 1-10 will appear. Click Complete to begin copying files.

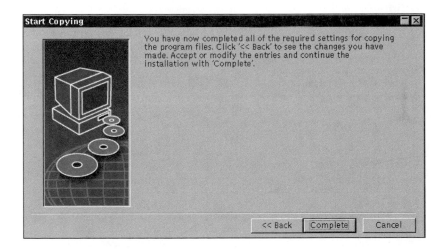

Figure 1-10   End of installation options

15   The installation process will continue for quite a while; a progress bar will show how much of the process is complete and approximately how much time is left.

The installation program sits for quite a while on the last item, Registration of the components. Even though it looks like it's done, it's not until you get the window in Figure 1-13.

16   The window in Figure 1-10 might appear after you click Complete. StarOffice needs Java software in order to run some of its features, and provides the JRE 1.1.8 (Java Runtime Environment), which provides everything Java programs need to run on your computer.

Other JRE or JDK sources might be listed in the window; however, StarOffice can be pretty picky so it's best to install the one provided. Click Install. In Solaris and Linux the install will run with no further prompting; in Windows, a few windows will appear that will guide you through the installation process.

When the install is complete, select the Java 1.1.8 that is added to the list in the window and click OK.

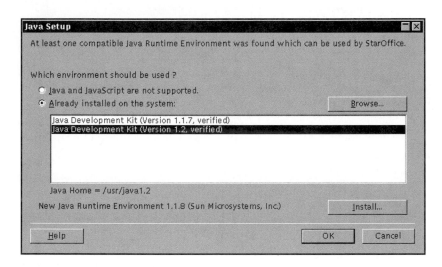

Figure 1-11   Java setup

Note – If the Java install doesn't work, or StarOffice doesn't recognize the installed JRE, see *Installing Java Separately* on page 57.

---

17   If the window in Figure 1-12 appears, and asks if you want to replace files already on your system, choose to do so. Click Replace All.

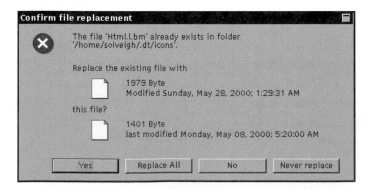

Figure 1-12   File replacement confirmation

18   The window in Figure 1-13 will appear, stating that the installation is complete. Click Complete as instructed.

Figure 1-13   Installation complete

19 Another window will appear, allowing you to install the Adabas database. See Table 34-1 on page 993 for information; it's StarOffice's relational database.

If you want to install it, follow the windows as prompted. (It's pretty simple, but you can refer to the documented procedure in *Installing Adabas* on page 29 if you want.)

Note – A message will appear, stating that a StarOffice icon will be created for your desktop but you need to restart to see it. On Linux, this might or might not happen. If it doesn't, create your own if you're feeling up to it. You can also see the information in *Starting StarOffice* on page 46.

What's Next

Start StarOffice (see *Starting StarOffice: Single-User* on page 46), then enter some basic Internet setup information (*Entering Information in the Internet Setup AutoPilot* on page 47) and complete the steps in *Registration* on page 52.

If you're on Linux or Solaris, then go to *Printer Setup* on page 62 to get your printers set up and named the way you want them. If you're on Windows, StarOffice is hooked up to the same printer setup windows that you use for all your other applications, so you don't need to do anything.

After you're all done with those, you can start getting to know StarOffice. See *Taming the StarOffice Environment* on page 91 for some extremely useful tips that will make working in StarOffice a lot easier.

Troubleshooting

If you got any error messages about already having StarOffice installed, check for the following files on your system:

- .sversionrc in the Solaris or Linux home directory
- .sversion.ini in the Windows directory

Open the files; they contain the path and version number of StarOffice if it is currently installed. If the version number is 5.2, you need to uninstall StarOffice first (see *Removing StarOffice* on page 58).

For more information about these files, see *Secret Install Files* on page 60.

Depending on how your system is set up, you might not have the correct permissions to the directory where you're trying to install. Make sure you can read, write, and execute in the StarOffice directory and in your system temporary directory.

Installing StarOffice: Multi-User

Complete the steps in this section to install StarOffice in a multi-user system.

Before You Begin

Be sure that the computers are set up and networked appropriately. Refer to SETUP.PDF, as well.

Complete the following procedures in this section, in the order they're included:

- *Planning the Installation* on page 18
- *Installing StarOffice on the Server* on page 21
- *Installing Adabas* on page 29 (optional)
- *Installing Schedule Server* on page 33 (optional)
- *Making the Installed Files Available and General Troubleshooting* on page 37
- *Installing StarOffice on Each Client* on page 38
- *Viewing Where Data Is Stored* on page 44

Planning the Installation

This section tells you what to expect and how to plan what computers you'll install StarOffice on.

Installation Overview

You'll be installing StarOffice on the server, then running a setup file that gets installed on the server, to install StarOffice on clients.

The **files installed on the server** include the following:

- Program and help files, including the setup file used to run the client install
- A share directory containing shared resources such as templates, and configuration settings for items like printers
- A SdlSrv directory, separate from the StarOffice directory, containing files for services and user calendars (a separate, optional install)

The **files installed on the client** include the following:

- Program and help files, including the soffice file used to start StarOffice on the client
- A user directory containing files created by the user on that client (includes modified templates, client-specific configurations, etc.)

An options window in StarOffice determines where the program looks by default for your files. For multi-user systems, it's useful to specify other locations for certain files, using the path setup window. (Choose Tools > Options > General > Paths.)

StarOffice Configuration Planning

The only special configuration considerations for StarOffice are for the Schedule Server (see the next section). Otherwise, just pick a server machine and clients that meet the system requirements listed in *System Requirements* on page 7. Also, make sure the location where you installed StarOffice on the server is accessible to client machines via the network.

If you want a computer to be the data server to multiple clients, and to have a client installation on it, as well, run the server installation, then client installation, on it.

Note – If you want to install StarOffice, single-user, on several computers, run the server install (*Installing StarOffice on the Server* on page 21). Then run the client install on each computer (*Installing StarOffice on Each Client* on page 38), but select the Local installation option, not the smaller client installation.

Schedule Server Configuration Planning

In order to have a multi-user scheduling system, you'll need to install the Schedule Server. (See *StarOffice Schedule Server Overview* on page 843 for more information the Schedule Server in general.)

Use one of the following basic configuration setups:

- Combination workstation/Schedule server computer – Install a StarOffice client and Schedule Server. Follow the steps in *Installing StarOffice on Each Client* on page 38, then *Installing Schedule Server* on page 33.

- Standalone server computer – If the server computer is the StarOffice server computer, install the StarOffice server installation and Schedule server. Follow the steps in *Installing StarOffice on the Server* on page 21, then *Installing Schedule Server* on page 33.

  If the server computer is designated only as the Schedule Server computer, install the Schedule program module and the Schedule Server. Follow the steps in *Installing the Schedule Server Software* on page 33, then *Installing the Schedule Program Module* on page 36.

Note – *Don't install Schedule in the same directory with StarOffice or the standalone application.* This will make both programs unusable.

Figure 1-14 illustrates two options.

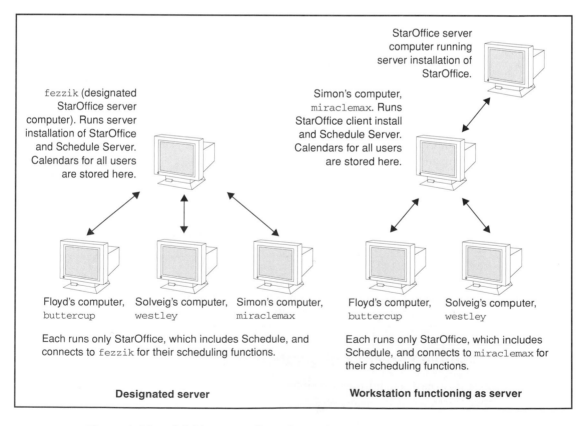

fezzik (designated StarOffice server computer). Runs server installation of StarOffice and Schedule Server. Calendars for all users are stored here.

StarOffice server computer running server installation of StarOffice.

Simon's computer, miraclemax. Runs StarOffice client install and Schedule Server. Calendars for all users are stored here.

Floyd's computer, buttercup

Solveig's computer, westley

Simon's computer, miraclemax

Floyd's computer, buttercup

Solveig's computer, westley

Each runs only StarOffice, which includes Schedule, and connects to fezzik for their scheduling functions.

Each runs only StarOffice, which includes Schedule, and connects to miraclemax for their scheduling functions.

Designated server

Workstation functioning as server

Figure 1-14   Multi-user configuration options

You must continually run both programs on the server computer. If, in Figure 1-14, Simon shuts down his computer, Floyd and Solveig won't be able to use Schedule.

Installing StarOffice on the Server

Complete the server installation in a directory with sufficient disk space (see *System Requirements* on page 7) and to which all users have read/write access.

1   Be sure you've read the operating system-specific notes on page 5.

2   If you've got a previous version of StarOffice installed, first check for the following files on your system:

- `.sversionrc` in the Solaris or Linux home directory
- `.sversion.ini` in the Windows directory

Open the files; they contain the path and version number of StarOffice if it is currently installed. If the version number is 5.2, you need to uninstall StarOffice first (see *Removing StarOffice* on page 58).

For more information about these files, see *Secret Install Files* on page 60.

3   Insert the CD in the server's CD-ROM drive. In Solaris and Linux, you'll probably need to mount the CD-ROM, typically with a command like `mount /mnt/cdrom`

4   In a Linux or Solaris environment, be sure you're logged in as the user who will be running StarOffice.

5   In a terminal window, navigate to the directory on the CD for your operating system, then to the `office52` subdirectory; for example, go to `/linux/office52/`.

6   Type the appropriate command and press Enter:
   `./setup -net` (Linux or Solaris) or **`./setup.exe -net`** (Windows)

If a message states that you need to install patches, navigate to the `office52/`*`platform`*`/patches` directory on the CD and follow the instructions in the readme and installation information documents.

7   The window in Figure 1-15 will appear. Click Next.

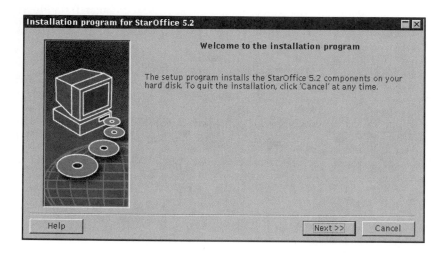

Figure 1-15   Introductory window of StarOffice installation

8   The window in Figure 1-16 will appear. Read the displayed information carefully; it contains operating system-specific information about the StarOffice Installation. Click Next.

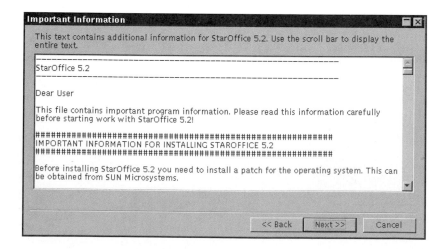

Figure 1-16   Installation information

9   The window in Figure 1-17 will appear, displaying the license agreement. Review it and, if you agree to the terms, click Accept.

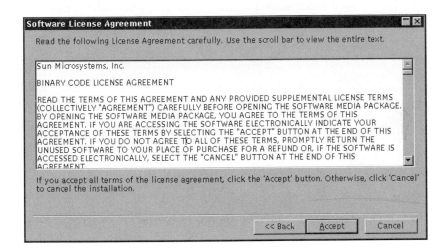

Figure 1-17   License agreement

10   If you currently have StarOffice installed, the window in Figure 1-18 will appear.

- If you want to automatically migrate your StarOffice files created with the older version to the directory where you're installing 5.2, select the Import personal data option and enter the path to your old StarOffice directory. Click Next.

- If you want to manually copy the files over later, don't mark the option. See *Updating From 5.1 to 5.2* on page 8 when you've finished installation.

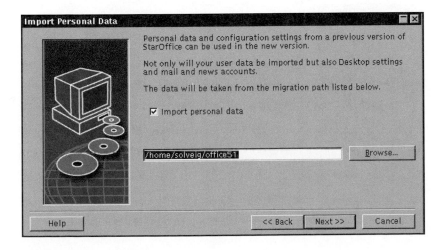

Figure 1-18   Specifying existing StarOffice user data location

11 The personal data window (Figure 1-19) will appear. Leave it blank and let users fill in their own information later using Tools > Options > General.

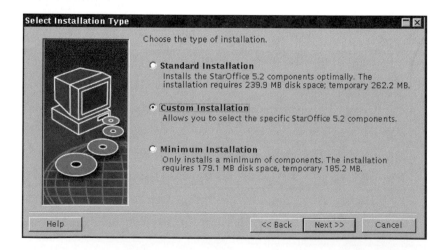

Figure 1-19   Personal information window

12 The installation type window (Figure 1-20) will appear; select Custom Installation and click Next.

Figure 1-20   Selecting installation type

Note – The Minimal Installation really isn't a good idea. It's not that much less disk space, and it leaves out a lot of things, including the entire StarOffice Image program (you wouldn't be able to open any GIF or JPG files), and pretty much all the templates, help files, and example files.

13 The window in Figure 1-21 will appear. Enter the directory, new or existing, where you want to install StarOffice. Click Next.

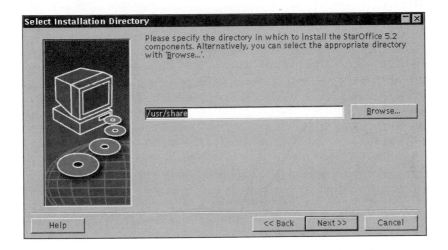

Figure 1-21   Selecting installation location

Note – If you let StarOffice create the installation directory for you, it will assign fairly restrictive access rights to it. You'll need to apply the appropriate rights to it after installation so you can access the installed setup program.

14 The window in Figure 1-22 will appear. Expand the + symbol next to the items listed to locate the module you want to select or deselect.

It's a good idea to install all of StarOffice; it's an integrated suite of applications, so many features depend on files not included in that particular program.

Any component with a white icon is deselected; any full-color component is selected. Any faded-color component has parts that aren't selected.

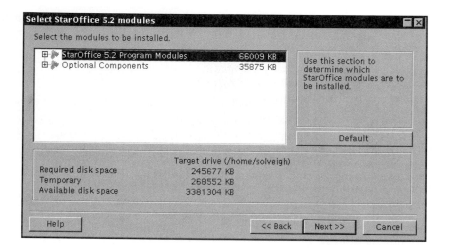

Figure 1-22   Selecting components to install

Note – If any users will by synchronizing their PalmPilots with StarOffice Schedule, be sure to select the PalmPilot Integration module, shown in Figure 1-23. It's not installed by default.

Select the PalmPilot Integration module and be sure the icon is fully colored, not dimmed or white. ———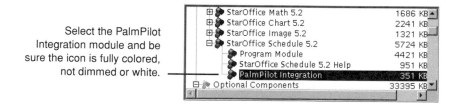

Figure 1-23   PalmPilot Integration install option

15 Expand the + symbol next to the items listed to locate the module you want to install. Most items are selected; select or double-click an item to make its icon white if you don't want to install it.

16 The window in Figure 1-24 will appear. Click Complete to begin copying files.

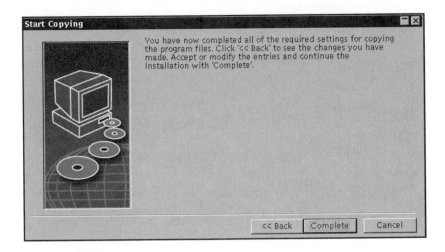

Figure 1-24   End of installation options

17 The installation process will continue for quite a while; a progress bar will show how much of the process is complete and approximately how much time is left.

The installation program sits for quite a while on the last item, Registration of the components. Even though it looks like it's done, it's not until you get the window in Figure 1-27.

18 The window in Figure 1-25 might appear after you click Complete. StarOffice needs Java software in order to run some of its features, and provides the JRE 1.1.8 (Java Runtime Environment), which provides everything Java programs need to run on your computer.

Other JRE or JDK sources might be listed in the window; however, StarOffice can be pretty picky so it's best to install the one provided. Click Install. In Solaris and Linux the install will run with no further prompting; in Windows, a few windows will appear that will guide you through the installation process.

When the install is complete, select the Java 1.1.8 that is added to the list in the window and click OK.

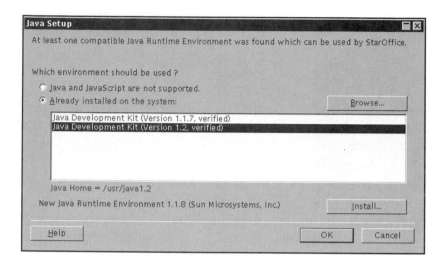

Figure 1-25   Java setup

Note – If the Java install doesn't work, or StarOffice doesn't recognize the installed JRE, see *Installing Java Separately* on page 57.

---

19   If the window in Figure 1-26 appears, and asks if you want to replace files already on your system, choose to do so.

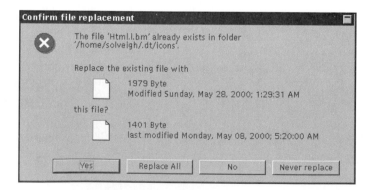

Figure 1-26   File replacement confirmation

20   The window in Figure 1-27 will appear, stating that the installation is complete. Click Complete as instructed.

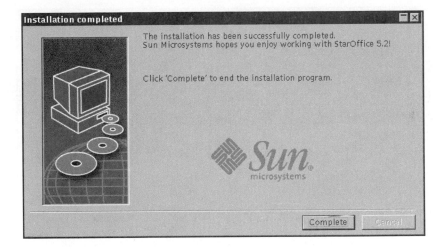

Figure 1-27   Installation complete

21   Another window will appear, allowing you to install the Adabas database. See Table 34-1 on page 993 for information; it's StarOffice's relational database.

If you want to install it, follow the windows as prompted. (It's pretty simple, but you can refer to the documented procedure in *Installing Adabas* on page 29 if you want. You need to install it only on the server, if you're using a multi-user system.

Note – A message will appear, stating that a StarOffice icon will be created for your desktop but you need to restart to see it. On Linux, this might or might not happen. If it doesn't, create your own if you're feeling up to it. You can also see the information in *Starting StarOffice* on page 46.

Installing Adabas

Adabas is StarOffice's relational database tool; see Table 34-1 on page 993 for information. That installation starts automatically after each full installation. You need to install it only on the server, if you're using a multi-user system.

The SETUP.PDF file contains additional information about Adabas.

To install it, follow these steps on the server computer.

1   The window in Figure 1-28 automatically appears after StarOffice installation. Click Next.

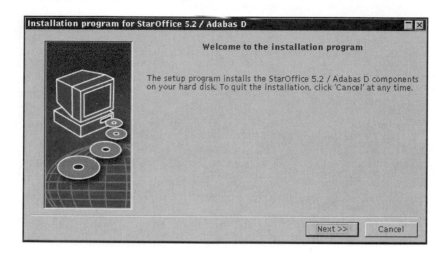

Figure 1-28   Adabas installation welcome window

2   The README file will be displayed (Figure 1-29). Review it, then click Next.

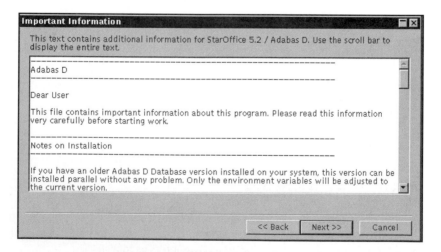

Figure 1-29   Adabas installation Important Information window

3   The License Agreement window will appear (Figure 1-30). Review it, and if you will comply with the terms, click Agree.

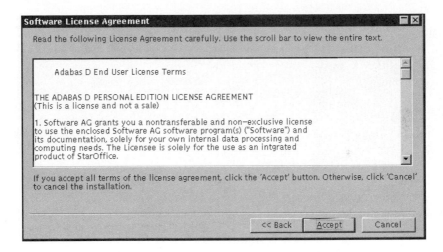

Figure 1-30   Adabas software licensing agreement window

4   The installation location window will appear (Figure 1-31). Accept the default or enter another location, then click Next.

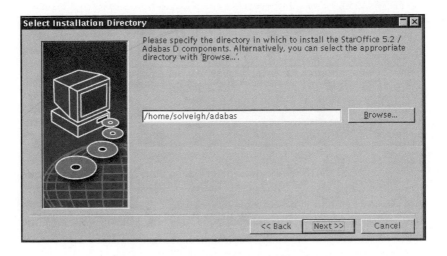

Figure 1-31   Adabas installation location window

Note – If you let StarOffice create the installation directory for you, it will assign fairly restrictive access rights to it. You'll need to apply the appropriate rights to it after installation so you can access the installed setup program.

5   Click Complete to start the installation process (Figure 1-32).

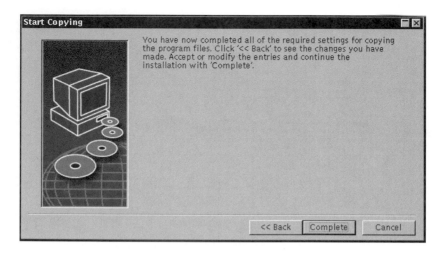

Figure 1-32   Adabas begin installation window

6   The window in Figure 1-33 will appear at the end of the process to indicate the installation is complete.

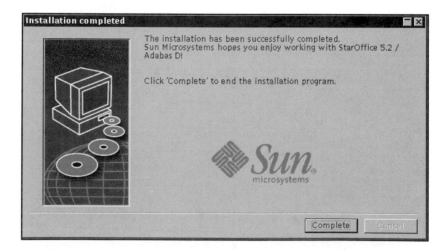

Figure 1-33   Adabas installation completion window

Installing Schedule Server

The Schedule Server lets users view and, where you set up the rights, edit each others' schedules. You can read about Schedule Server in *StarOffice Schedule Server Overview* on page 843.

Before you begin, review *Schedule Server Configuration Planning* on page 19.

Note – Schedule Server is available only on the CD version of StarOffice, not in the download version.

Installing the Schedule Server Software

Follow these steps on the computer which will be the server for Schedule Server.

1   If you're installing on a Windows NT or UNIX computer, you must log in with administrator or root access.

2   Insert the CD in the CD-ROM.

3   Locate the directory for Schedule for your platform, `platform/sserver`, and double-click the `setup` or `setup.exe` file.

4   The first installation window will appear (Figure 1-34). Read the information displayed, then click Next.

Figure 1-34   Initial Schedule Server installation window

5   The second installation window will appear (Figure 1-35). Review all the information in the displayed README document, then click Next.

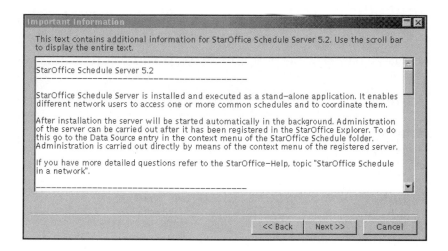

Figure 1-35   Schedule Server README file

6   The next installation window will appear (Figure 1-36). Review the license
agreement, then click Accept.

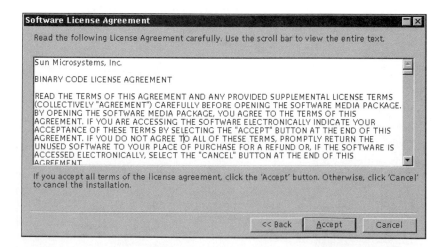

Figure 1-36   Schedule Server license agreement

7   In the window in Figure 1-37, select the directory to install Schedule in.

Note – *Don't install Schedule in the same directory with StarOffice*. This will make both
programs unusable.

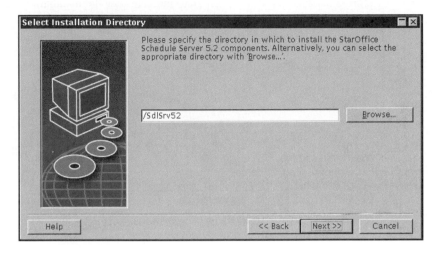

Figure 1-37   Schedule Server location window

Note – If you let StarOffice create the installation directory for you, it will assign fairly restrictive access rights to it. You'll need to apply the appropriate rights to it after installation so that users will be able to read and write their calendar data.

---

8   The Start Copying window will appear (Figure 1-38). Click Complete to begin copying files.

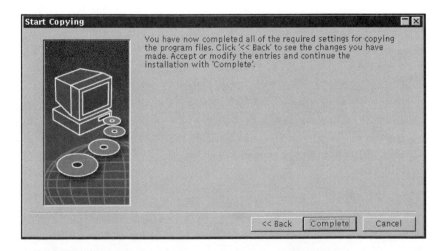

Figure 1-38   Schedule Server Start Copying window

9   A progress bar appears on your screen to indicate how the installation's going. The StarOffice Schedule Server Setup window (Figure 1-39) will appear shortly before the end of the installation. Select the HTTP port and the Administration port for the server; you can typically accept the default values unless other services already occupy those ports. Select the Start Administration Service option, then click OK.

If this isn't the first Schedule Server you're installing, make sure each port is different than the ports you entered for the previous ones.

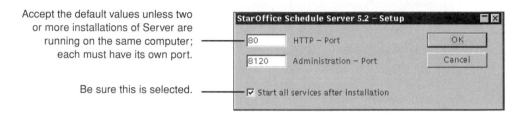

Accept the default values unless two or more installations of Server are running on the same computer; each must have its own port.

Be sure this is selected.

Figure 1-39   Entering the HTTP port and administration port

Note – The HTTP port is used by the Web administration windows to administer the services; the Administration port is used for the administration itself. The port by which users access the Schedule Server and their calendars is created by default and displayed in the Schedule Server administration window (see Figure 28-5 on page 849). Users and administrators enter it in the Data Source Properties window to log into the server (see Figure 28-9 on page 853). The default for the first Server is 4243.

---

10   When copying is completed, a window will appear, stating that the installation is done. Click Complete.

Installing the Schedule Program Module

Note – You can just install the program module; however, it's probably simpler to just run a client install on the Schedule Server computer, if you've already done the -net server install on that computer or another computer.

A version of StarOffice, either the entire program (a full or client installation) or the program module, needs to be running on the computer where you installed Schedule Server. If the Schedule Server computer is **different** than your standard StarOffice server, complete the *Installing StarOffice: Multi-User* on page 18 again. Choose the Custom Installation, then unmark all options except the program module for Schedule Server, as shown in Figure 1-40.

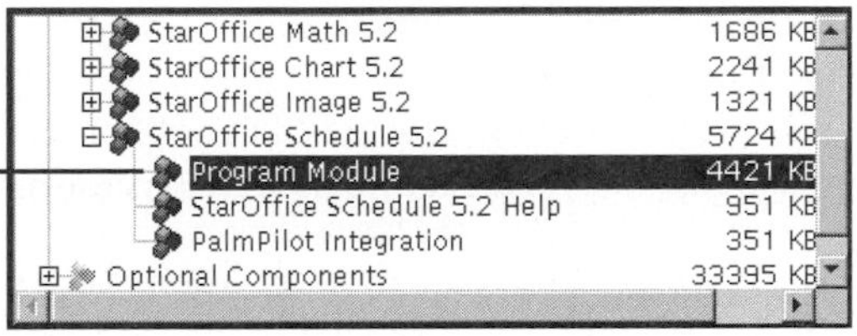

Select the Program Module item and be sure the icon is fully colored, not dimmed or white.

Figure 1-40   Schedule Program Module installation option

Note – *Don't install the program module in the same directory as Schedule Server.* This will make both programs unusable.

Removing Schedule Server

If you want to remove Schedule Server, run **./setup** or **./setup.exe** in the service subdirectory of the installed Schedule Server directory. Then select the Deinstallation option in the Setup dialog.

Making the Installed Files Available and General Troubleshooting

You need to make sure the location where you installed StarOffice on the server is accessible to client machines via the network.

A perfect installation program would interact correctly with the operating system to make sure all the files and directories in the installed StarOffice directory have the appropriate permissions. However, that isn't the StarOffice installation program. StarOffice sets appropriate permissions for the files automatically, but you'll probably have to fuss with the directory permissions. All client machines will need read and execute permissions so that you can run the setup file on the server to do the client installation, and so that users can get at the files they need (including templates, icons, etc.).

Check the access permissions on all the directories where you installed StarOffice (soffice52, typically). The StarOffice directory and all subdirectories need to have read and execute permission for any users accessing StarOffice (group and other, for example, in Solaris). If they don't, use the appropriate procedures for your operating system to set the permissions.

Note – In Solaris, and on most Linux computers, you can run the following command to assign read and execute rights to group and other for all directories within the stated directory. As with all operations that affect permissions, this should be completed only by an experienced system administrator.

```
find office52 -type d -exec chmod go+r {} \;
```

This means, starting with the office52 directory and continuing through all subdirectories, apply read and execute permissions for group and other.

The same guidelines apply to the SdlSrv52 directory, if you installed the Schedule Server. Clients need to be able to read and execute in all directories, and write to the file where their schedules are stored, in SdlSrv52/user/store/*server_name*.

Depending on how your system is set up, users might not automatically have read, write, and execute permissions on their temporary directory, and that they can copy files into that directory. Check those permissions, as well, before beginning the client install.

Finally, take a look at the files in the share directory on the server. Any modifications or new files users make are generally saved in their own user folder, and aren't available to other users. If you want users to be able to create new or modified versions of those files, such as templates, and share them on the server, set the permissions appropriately and let users know where to save their new templates or other files. However, note that with this approach, users can permanently change shared resources if they modify the original instead of making a copy.

You might encounter problems in Windows if you install StarOffice in the root directory and the number of files in the root directory exceeds 256. Solaris and Linux installations might fail if the home directory on the server isn't available.

Installing StarOffice on Each Client

Complete this procedure **on each client computer**, or have each user complete it.

1   In a Linux or Solaris environment, log into the client computer as the user who will be running StarOffice there.

1   On the client computer, navigate to the office52/program directory **on the server where you installed StarOffice**. (You don't need the CD for the client installation.)

2   Double-click the setup file or setup.exe file, or run either of the following commands:
     ./setup or **./setup.exe**

Note – If you have problems accessing the file, be sure that the correct access rights are set on the server computer for the client user, especially if you let StarOffice create the installation directory.

---

3   A welcome window will appear. Click Next.

4   The window in Figure 1-41 will appear. Click Next.

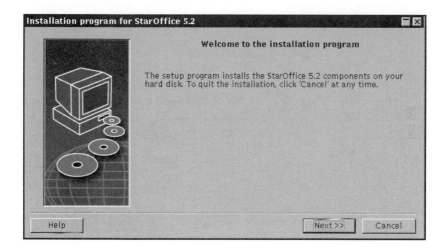

Figure 1-41   Introductory window of StarOffice installation

5   The window in Figure 1-42 will appear. Read the displayed information carefully; it
        contains operating system-specific information about the StarOffice Installation.
        Click Next.

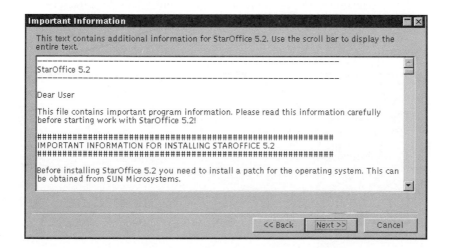

Figure 1-42   Installation information

6   The window in Figure 1-43 will appear, displaying the license agreement. Review it
        and, if you agree to the terms, click Accept.

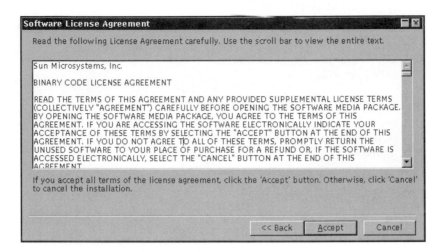

Figure 1-43   License agreement

7   If you currently have StarOffice installed, the window in Figure 1-44 will appear.

- If you want to automatically migrate your StarOffice files created with the older version to the directory where you're installing 5.2, select the Import personal data option and enter the path to your old StarOffice directory. Click Next.

- If you want to manually copy the files over later, don't mark the option. See *Updating From 5.1 to 5.2* on page 8 when you've finished installation.

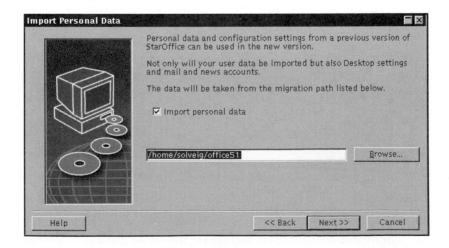

Figure 1-44   Specifying existing StarOffice user data location

8   The personal data window will appear (Figure 1-45). This information will appear in general options windows in StarOffice; you can enter it now, or choose Tools > Options > General and enter it later.

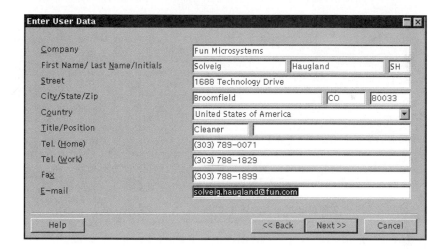

Figure 1-45   Personal information window

9   The installation type window (Figure 1-46) will appear. Select Standard Workstation Installation. Click Next.

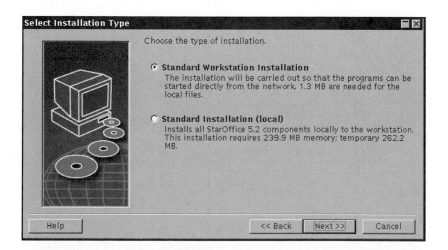

Figure 1-46   Installation type window

10 The installation location window will appear (Figure 1-47). Enter a new or existing directory on the client and click Next.

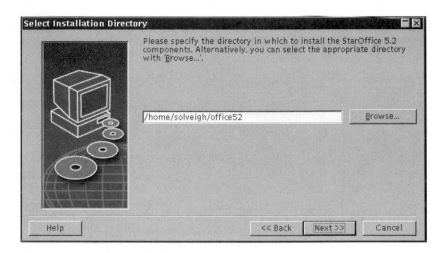

Figure 1-47   Installation type window

11   The window in Figure 1-48 will appear. Click Complete to begin copying files.

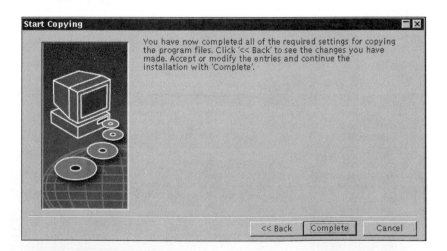

Figure 1-48   End of installation options

12   The window in Figure 1-49 might appear after you click Complete.

13   StarOffice needs Java software in order to run some of its features, and provides the JRE 1.1.8 (Java Runtime Environment), which provides everything Java programs need to run on your computer.

Other JRE or JDK sources might be listed in the window; however, StarOffice can be pretty picky so it's best to install the one provided. Click Install. In Solaris and Linux the install will run with no further prompting; in Windows, a few windows will appear that will guide you through the installation process.

When the install is complete, select the Java 1.1.8 that is added to the list in the window and click OK.

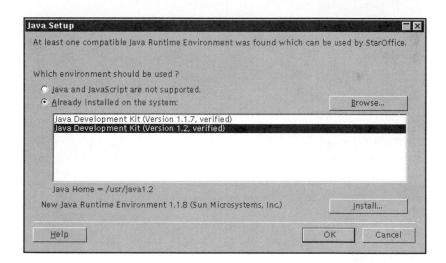

Figure 1-49   Java setup

Note – If the Java install doesn't work, or StarOffice doesn't recognize the installed JRE, see *Installing Java Separately* on page 57.

---

14 If the window in Figure 1-50 appears, and asks if you want to replace files already on your system, choose to do so.

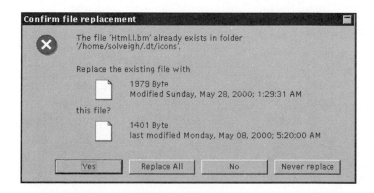

Figure 1-50   File replacement confirmation

15 The window in Figure 1-51 will appear, stating that the installation is complete. Click Complete as instructed.

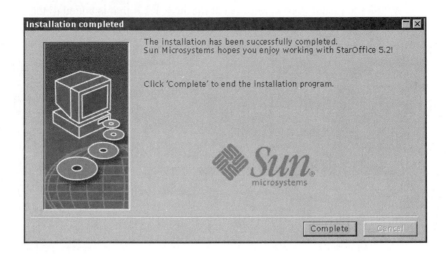

Figure 1-51   Installation complete

Note – A message will appear, stating that a StarOffice icon will be created for your desktop but you need to restart to see it. On Linux, this might or might not happen. If it doesn't, create your own if you're feeling up to it. You can also see the information in *Starting StarOffice* on page 46.

Viewing Where Data Is Stored

You can use a couple different sources to see where your data ended up, and where StarOffice is looking for it.

The MIGRATION.PDF document on the CD contains information about where files are stored.

In addition, the Paths window within the StarOffice general options is very useful, in order to see where each client installation looks for files. Choose Tools > Options > General > Paths; the window in Figure 1-52 will appear. Scroll through the list to see where each type of file is stored. In this illustration, the server computer is neepneep.

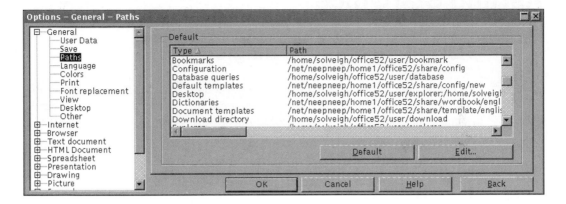

Figure 1-52   File paths window

In the help topic for this window, a table provides more information about each item listed, and specifies whether the default is the client or the server.

If both the server and client are listed, it means that files of that type such as templates that are provided by StarOffice are stored on the server, but new or modified files of that type are stored locally.

Note – Refer to *Changing Paths to Folders* on page 112 if you want to change where the client looks for files. Be sure that, if you change from the client to the server, the files on the server have permissions that allow the client to access them. In addition, all files might not be installed on the client, so exercise caution when switching from server to client.

What's Next

Start StarOffice (see *Starting StarOffice: Multi-User* on page 46), then enter some basic Internet setup information (*Entering Information in the Internet Setup AutoPilot* on page 47) and complete the steps in *Registration* on page 52.

If you're on Linux or Solaris, then go to *Printer Setup* on page 62 to get your printers set up and named the way you want them. If you're on Windows, StarOffice is hooked up to the same printer setup windows that you use for all your other applications, so you don't need to do anything.

After you're all done with those, you can start getting to know StarOffice. See *Taming the StarOffice Environment* on page 91 for some extremely useful tips that will make working in StarOffice a lot easier.

Starting StarOffice

Starting StarOffice: Single-User

A program item will be added to your desktop; choose StarOffice 5.2 to start. You also can locate the executable StarOffice file (`setup` or `setup.exe`) in the directory where you installed, and double-click it. (The program item won't appear until you restart the computer.)

Starting StarOffice: Multi-User

You don't need to start anything on the server except, if you're using it, Schedule Server (which was started automatically).

Start StarOffice on each client, either with the program item added to the desktop or running the `setup` or `setup.exe` file in the **client's** StarOffice directory. (The program item won't appear until you restart the client.)

Troubleshooting

The following cover a few common problems.

Trouble starting or running StarOffice on client If you have any problems starting a client, with messages such as "Cannot determine current directory" or "Cannot initialize gallery," check the file access rights on the server. All clients must be able to read and execute in all directories within the installed StarOffice directory on the server.

StarOffice not starting, or claiming it's still running In Solaris, killing StarOffice doesn't always bring down the underlying process, just the interface. When you try to start it again, the operating system thinks StarOffice is still running, so nothing happens. If you kill StarOffice, use a command like `ps -ef` to list processes, then kill any that correspond to the `soffice.bin` file or the server installation of StarOffice.

The following command searches for all processes containing `soffice`:

```
ps -ef | grep soffice
```

It also might have started and you just can't see it. StarOffice likes to hang out up at the very top of your screen, sometimes. If you see a horizontal line that looks like the bottom of a window, drag it down. If it won't move, hold down the Alt key, then drag it.

Cannot find file *filename* Start StarOffice in a terminal window. Navigate to the StarOffice directory (`office52`) on your computer (not the server computer) and type **`./soffice`**

Starts fullscreen Hold down the Alt key and drag the application down.

Entering Information in the Internet Setup AutoPilot

After you install StarOffice and start it for the first time, you'll be prompted to specify where connectivity and mail information should come from. (To enter the information later, click Cancel, then choose File > AutoPilot > Internet when you're ready to use it.)

The autopilot is a sort of "top ten" Internet connectivity settings you need to enter; these settings and more are available through various windows when you choose Tools > Options in StarOffice. It's a good idea to enter this information now if you want to get started with browsing the Internet and using mail and Schedule right away. But if you don't know the information you'll need to enter, like proxies, mail servers, and so on, you can enter it all later. The instructions are in on page 357 and *Setting Up Mail and News* on page 933.

Note – The simplest way to get through this one is just to select the automatic import option, if one appears, then just click Next through to the end.

---

1 Start StarOffice.

2 The first AutoPilot window will appear (Figure 1-53). Click Next.

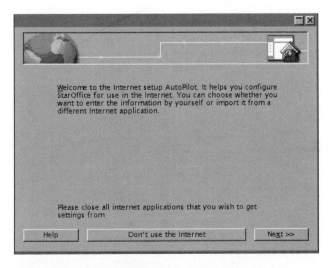

Figure 1-53   First Internet setup AutoPilot window

3 The next window (Figure 1-54) will appear. Select whether to take settings from a current application (quicker) or enter information manually. Click Next.

If you select an item from the list, skip to Step 9.

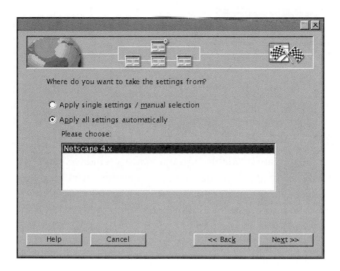

Figure 1-54   Second Internet setup AutoPilot window

4   If you chose to enter settings manually, ask your system administrator or Internet service provider for the proxies and ports to enter (Figure 1-55). You can also check your browser for the proxies and ports you use; choose Edit > Preferences > Advanced > Proxies.

Depending on your ISP provider, it might not be necessary to always use a proxy. For example, no proxy is required for AOL or CompuServe.

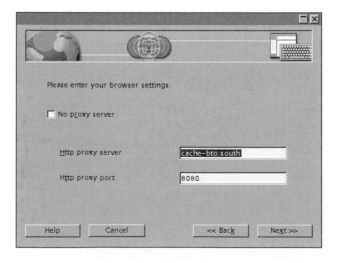

Figure 1-55   Browser settings window

5   In the window in Figure 1-56, decide whether to use existing email settings from another application, to enter them manually in the next window, or to enter no settings.

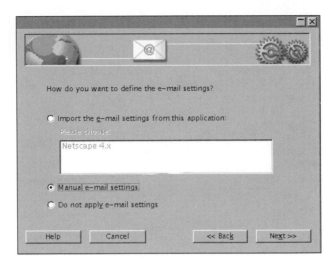

Figure 1-56   Choosing source of email settings

6   If you chose to enter settings manually, see *Setting Up Mail and News* on page 940 for information on how to enter the settings in the window in Figure 1-57.

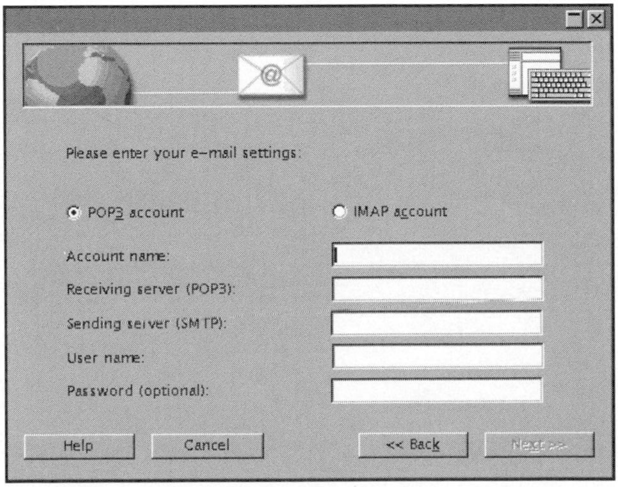

Figure 1-57   Email settings window

7   In the window in Figure 1-58, decide whether to use existing news settings from another application, to enter them manually in the next window, or to enter no settings.

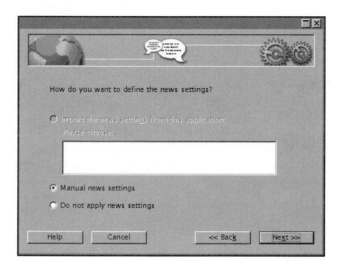

Figure 1-58   Choosing source of news settings

8   If you chose to enter settings manually, enter the account name and news server to use, in the window in Figure 1-59.

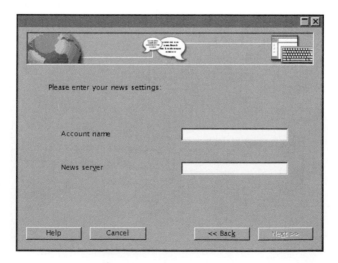

Figure 1-59   News settings window

9   The confirmation window will appear (Figure 1-60). Click Next.

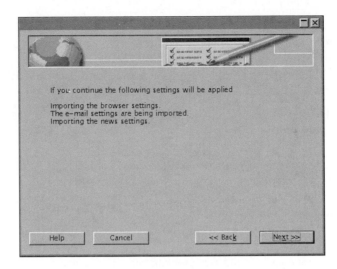

Figure 1-60   Confirmation window

10   The last autopilot window will appear (Figure 1-61). Click OK.

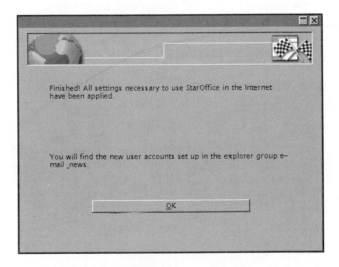

Figure 1-61   Last Internet setup AutoPilot window

Registration

When you start StarOffice, you can register at that time, or ask to be prompted to later. Registering isn't required, but as a registered user, you will receive technical support if problems with your software arise. You will also always receive the latest information and news pertaining to StarOffice. Furthermore, only registered StarOffice users have access to the knowledge database on the Sun Web site.

In a multi-user system, it's a good idea for every user to register who wants to individually get this information.

Note – If you obtained your copy of StarOffice from the SDLC (Sun Download Center), you are already registered. If you are a current StarOffice 5.x user who received a media key with the product and you need a registration key, refer to the following newsgroup to obtain registration information:

`news://starnews.sun.com/staroffice.com.support.announce`

Your registration as a StarOffice user can only be completed online. To register as a StarOffice user you have the following two options:

- Choose Help > Registration. You will automatically be sent to a Web site containing a registration form.

- After you start StarOffice, a dialog appears where you will be asked if you want to register as a StarOffice user. In this dialog, select the Register now option. You will automatically be sent to the registration form.

If a message states that the Web site can't be resolved:

- Activate online access by clicking Internet Online/Offline icon in the function bar and set up proxies; see *Proxy Options* on page 374.

- Or go to the same Web site using a different browser.

Once you register, you will receive a user name and password from us which you can use at any time to change your registration data. Sun Microsystems will only store your submitted data for internal purposes and will not forward it to third parties.

Installing StarOffice Player for Impress Presentations

The player lets you run presentations without installing all of StarOffice. This is generally for use on laptops you take to deliver presentations and is not necessary for standard StarOffice use.

If you install the player and StarOffice on the same computer, **don't** install them in the same directory.

1   Locate the file `soplayer` on the CD or in your downloaded files. Double-click it.

2   The welcome window shown in Figure 1-62 will appear; click Next.

Figure 1-62   Player installation welcome window

3   The README for the player is displayed (Figure 1-63). Read it, then click Next.

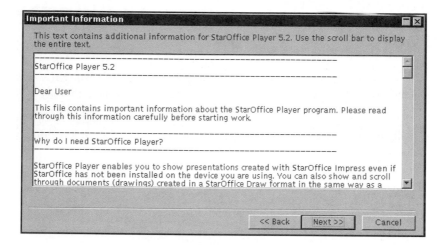

Figure 1-63   Player README file

4   The license agreement window will appear (Figure 1-64); read it, then click Accept if you agree to the conditions.

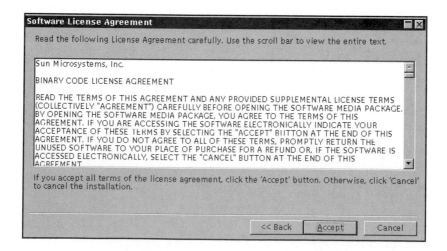

Figure 1-64   Player license agreement window

5   The installation directory window will appear (Figure 1-65); accept the default or enter a new one, then click Next. Don't install the player in the same location as StarOffice.

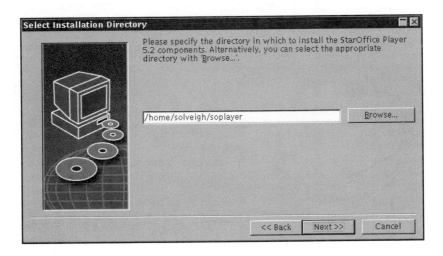

Figure 1-65   Player installation directory window

6   The last window will appear (Figure 1-66); click Complete to begin the installation process.

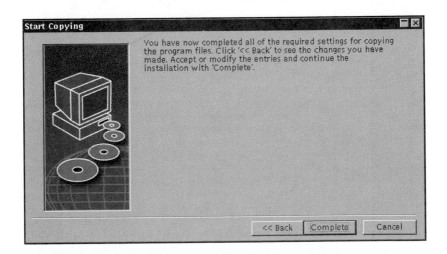

Figure 1-66   Begin-installation window

7   The window in Figure 1-67 will appear when the installation is done. Click Complete.

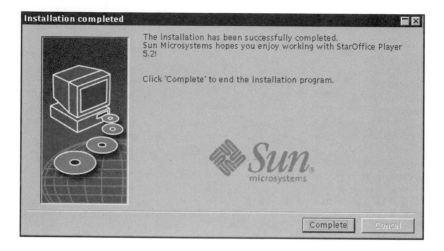

Figure 1-67   Last player installation window

Installing Additional Components

If you didn't install all of StarOffice, you can run the install again and select them.

Note – You must select everything you did before, in addition to the new components you want to install this time.

The process is pretty simple.

1   Insert the CD-ROM in the drive, if you're using the CD.

2   Start the installation the same way you did before, with the `setup` or `setup.exe` file.

3   In the Installation program for StarOffice 5.2 window, select the Modify installation option. Click Next.

4   In the Select StarOffice 5.2 modules window, click the + sign next to the Program Modules and Optional Components items. Make sure that everything you currently have installed, as well as everything else you want, has a colored icon to its left, not dimmed or white.

Note – It's a good idea to just install everything. Double-click on the Program Modules and Optional Components items until the icons for both are colored.

5   Click Complete. Continue the installation

Installing Java Separately and Monitoring Java

You definitely need Java installed for StarOffice to run well—don't even think about doing without it. Once you get it installed, you can also use a couple of monitoring windows if you just check in on how Java processing is running, what the garbage collector is up to, etc.

Installing Java Separately

The normal installation process prompts you with a Java window and lets you select an existing installation or install the JRE 1.1.8 (Java Runtime Environment) provided with StarOffice. Install the JRE 1.1.8.

However, if this doesn't work, follow these steps to install Java after you've finished the StarOffice installation. (In a multi-user environment, install it on the server as well as the clients.)

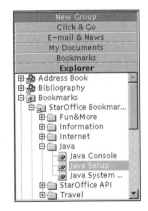

1   In Explorer, expand Bookmarks, then StarOffice Bookmarks, then the Java item.

2   You'll see three bookmarks, including Java Setup. Double-click Java Setup.

3   A window will appear, similar to the Java window in the installation. If a JRE 1.1.8 installation is listed, select it and click OK. If not, click Install and install it. Then select it when the Java window reappears, and click OK.

4   If StarOffice continues to cause problems, reinstall. This time, StarOffice should recognize the JRE you just installed and allow you to select it from the list in the Java installation window.

If all else fails, download `jdk118_v1` from `http://www.blackdown.org`, and run the entire installation process again.

Monitoring Java Processing

There's no reason in normal day-to-day use for you to need these features. But if you want to check up on your Java processing, here's how. Just use the Java Console and Java System... bookmarks to open the console and monitor windows shown in Figure 1-68.

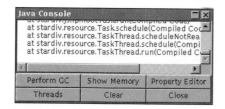 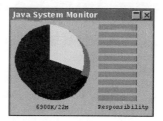

Figure 1-68   Java Console and Java System Monitor

Repairing Damaged StarOffice Programs

If you suddenly start having problems with particular applications, or if StarOffice just won't start, the files might be damaged. StarOffice has a built-in "file repair kit" that can help.

1   In Linux or Solaris, click the StarOffice icon on your taskbar and choose SOSetup. In Windows, choose Start > Programs > StarOffice 5.2 > StarOffice Setup.

    You also can locate the StarOffice `office52` directory and double-click the `setup` or `setup.exe` file.

2   Select the Repair option.

3   Click Complete to run the installation.

Removing StarOffice

To remove StarOffice, follow these steps.

Multi-User Uninstall

For clients, complete the single-user uninstall. For the server, delete the StarOffice directory from the server computer.

Single-User Uninstall

1   Click the StarOffice icon on your taskbar and choose SOSetup, or locate the `setup` or `setup.exe` file in your installed `office52` directory. (In Windows, you can choose Start > Programs > StarOffice 5.2 > StarOffice Setup.)

2   Select Deinstallation and click Next.

3   Select Delete all files if you want to delete configuration files and files you've created, in addition to the program files. Click Complete.

Note – This won't delete the .`Xpdefaults` file, if you created one, or other StarOffice preferences files that are outside the `office52` directory. (See *Multi-User Print Setup* on page 62, *Secret Install Files* on page 60, and *Getting the StarOffice Icon off Your HTML Files* on page 381.)

Help With StarOffice

With this book, you've got a good foundation of information on the way StarOffice is supposed to work, as well as many of the ways it doesn't work, and what to do about it. But if you encounter problems, we recommend that you use the following resources.

Index   Check the **troubleshooting** entry in the index of this book. We tried to get everything that's a bit unusual into that entry. For example, the Permission Denied error on Linux is indexed under **troubleshooting**.

The Knowledge Database   Sun Microsystems maintains a StarOffice troubleshooting area on its web site, called the Knowledge Database, for registered StarOffice users. At publication time this site was:

`http://www.sun.com/staroffice/knowledgedatabase`

The Support Forum   You also can double-click the Support Forum icon in the StarOffice desktop, which takes you to this site:

`http://www.sun.com/supportforum/staroffice`

Unfortunately, StarOffice doesn't maintain an error log, so you can't check it to find out what might be causing problems.

Secret Install Files

Note – This is techy information for people who want or need to fiddle with their configuration files; ignore this information if you just want to get on with using StarOffice.

StarOffice has a registry-type file that tracks where and how StarOffice is installed:

* .sversionrc in the Solaris or Linux home directory
* .sversion.ini in the Windows directory

The contents look something like this:

```
[Versions]
;StarOffice 5.1a=/home/solveigh/Office51a
StarOffice 5.1=/home/solveigh/Office
StarOffice Player 5.2=/home/solveigh/soplayer
Adabas=/home/solveigh/adabas
StarOffice 5.2=/home/solveigh/office52
```

If you install StarOffice 5.2, then attempt to do another installation on the same computer, StarOffice will complain and say no, sorry, it's already installed—remove it first (see page 58) if you want to reinstall.

You can run the install again if you comment out—put a semicolon in front of—the current installation location of StarOffice. For example, if you had the file shown previously on your system, and you wanted to also install StarOffice in /home/solveigh/apps/office52, you'd first put a semicolon in front of the /home/solveigh/office52 line, then install StarOffice again:

```
[Versions]
;StarOffice 5.1a=/home/solveigh/Office51a
StarOffice 5.1=/home/solveigh/Office
StarOffice Player 5.2=/home/solveigh/soplayer
Adabas=/home/solveigh/adabas
;StarOffice 5.2=/home/solveigh/office52
```

Keep in mind that this will almost certainly mess up the StarOffice icons that the installation adds to your task bar or Start menu. When you start StarOffice, be sure to do so by typing **./soffice** in a terminal window, in the appropriate office52 directory.

In Linux or Solaris, both installations might have to share the same printer setup file, depending on how the system is set up. See *Single-User Print Setup* on page 62 or *Multi-User Print Setup* on page 62.

Note – Make a backup of any files you edit.

chapter 2

Printing in StarOffice

61

Printer Setup

Use the information in this section for printer and fax setup in Linux and Solaris operating environments. For printing procedures and additional information, see the subsequent sections in this chapter.

Note – This section applies only to Solaris and Linux users. Windows users should simply use their standard operating system printer setup windows, then continue to *Basic Printing and Faxing for StarOffice Documents* on page 75.

Solaris and UNIX users should also refer to the section titled *Setting up Printers, Fax Machines and Fonts under Unix* in the SETUP.PDF file. It contains valuable, detailed information about printers, fonts, and other items.

Getting Started

It's a good idea to review this section to understand how printer setup works and the files that are involved.

Printer Information Storage Location

File configuration information is stored in on the server in a multi-user system, or on each client in single-user systems, in office52/share/xp3/Xpdefaults.

Single-User Print Setup

If you had a default printer set up before you installed StarOffice, you should be able to print to it right now with no additional setup. When you installed StarOffice, it automatically detected your default printer, and lists it as the Generic Printer in the Print window when you choose File > Print.

To change the Generic Printer to a different printer, see *Quick Printer Setup: Modifying the Generic Printer* on page 65. To change the name to something more descriptive, see *Changing the Displayed Name of a Printer* on page 72.

Multi-User Print Setup

Log onto the server and set up printers that you want all clients to be able to access. See *Adding a New Printer* on page 66 and other procedures as necessary in this section.

If you want to make sure users can't change the printers you set up in Xpdefaults, make sure that file is write-protected. The error message window shown in Figure 2-1 will then appear when users start the Printer Setup program from their desktops.

Figure 2-1   Printer setup write access denied

Users won't be able to do anything but view the list of printers available, as shown in Figure 2-2.

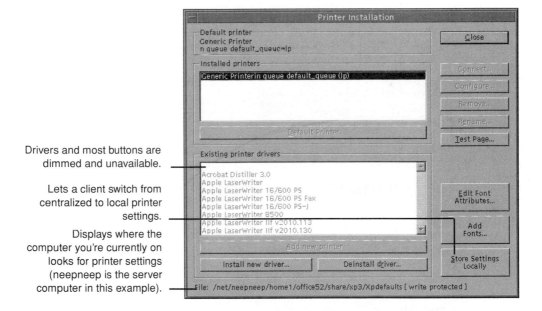

Drivers and most buttons are dimmed and unavailable.

Lets a client switch from centralized to local printer settings.

Displays where the computer you're currently on looks for printer settings (neepneep is the server computer in this example).

Figure 2-2   Write-protected printer setup window for clients

As stated in the message, each user can click the Store Settings Locally button to store printer settings locally. This will copy the current settings on the server in the Xpdefaults file to an .Xpdefaults (note the dot) file on the client's home directory.

The change to the Printer Installation window caused by clicking the Store Settings Locally button is shown in Figure 2-3.

The button name changes to Match Local Settings. If you install additional printers on the server, the user can click Match Local Settings to add the new printers to his or her .Xpdefaults file. (The button won't point the client back to the printer configuration file on the server, however.)

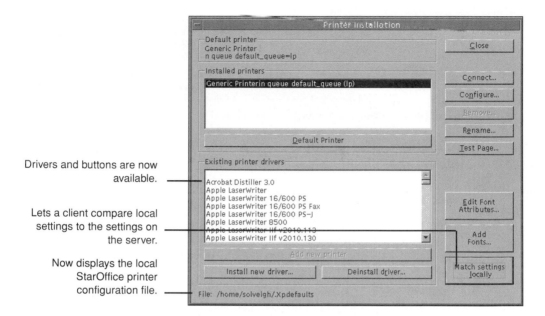

Drivers and buttons are now available.

Lets a client compare local settings to the settings on the server.

Now displays the local StarOffice printer configuration file.

Figure 2-3   Printer Installation window for client storing files locally

Starting the Printer Setup Program

Figure 2-4 shows the Printer Setup program window. Set up printers first from the server. Log in as root and:

- Double-click the Printer Setup icon on the StarOffice desktop
- Or go to the office52/program directory on the server and run the spadmin program.

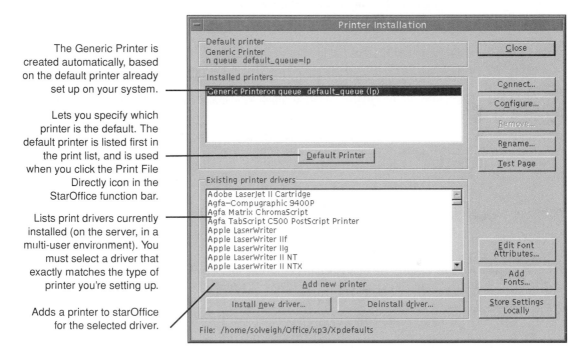

The Generic Printer is
created automatically, based
on the default printer already
set up on your system.

Lets you specify which
printer is the default. The
default printer is listed first in
the print list, and is used
when you click the Print File
Directly icon in the
StarOffice function bar.

Lists print drivers currently
installed (on the server, in a
multi-user environment). You
must select a driver that
exactly matches the type of
printer you're setting up.

Adds a printer to starOffice
for the selected driver.

Figure 2-4   Printer Installation window

Note – If you're on a client in a multi-user StarOffice environment, most of the fields in
the window might appear dimmed and you won't be able to change them. Click the Save
Settings Locally if you want to do any local printer setup.

Quick Printer Setup: Modifying the Generic Printer

StarOffice automatically sets itself up with a Generic Printer that prints to your computer's
default printer. If it isn't printing correctly, or is printing to the wrong printer, follow these
steps to specify the right printer.

Note – Whatever you do, don't delete the Generic Printer. (It makes the gremlins angry
and when they're angry, they try to make your system crash.) You'll need it in order to just
open, much less print, files that were created with older versions of StarOffice, or otherwise just think that they need a Generic Printer in order to just exist on your system. This
doesn't make much sense, but it's true nonetheless. In addition, the Generic Printer is
what's used to print to a file (PostScript).

1   Start the Printer Setup program (Figure 2-4).

2   In the Installed Printers list, select Generic Printer.

3   Click Connect to open the Connect window.

4   Select the correct printer from the Existing queues list, then click OK.

5   In the Printer Installation window, click Rename if you want to change the name "Generic Printer" to something more descriptive.

Note – StarOffice is inconsistent in how soon it displays your new printer in the Print window. If it doesn't show up, restart StarOffice.

Adding a New Printer

Note – In Solaris, StarOffice only offers direct support for PostScript printers. Other printers have to be set up as described in the *Setting up Printers under Unix* section of the SETUP.PDF file included on the StarOffice CD.

1   Open the Printer Installation window (Figure 2-4).

2   Select the correct driver from that window.

    It's a good idea to walk over to the printer you're setting up and check exactly what kind of printer it is. Then select a driver with exactly the same name from the driver list.

3   Click the Add new printer button.

    A new entry will appear in the Installed printers list, with the name of the selected driver.

4   Select the new printer in the Installed printers list, and click Connect.

5   In the Connect window (Figure 2-5), select the printer to connect to from the Existing queues list, then click OK. The only queues that show up here are the ones already set up for your system; in Solaris, for instance, they must be set up in Print Manager.

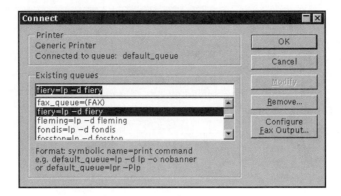

Figure 2-5   Selecting a printer

6   To make sure the printer is working, click the Test Page button in the Printer Installation window.

Note – StarOffice is inconsistent in how soon it displays your new printer in the Print window. If it doesn't show up, restart StarOffice.

Setting Up General Printer Options

The Configure button lets you open the Printer Properties window, where you can set options like duplex printing, input trays, paper size and orientation, device information, and margins. (For duplex printing, see *Setting Up a Duplex Printer* on page 69.) You don't have to enter information in this window; default values are set up for each window, and document-specific windows let you specify much of the same information. Those windows generally override anything you set here.

Note – For detailed information on how StarOffice portrait and landscape printing really works, see *Specifying Portrait or Landscape Orientation* on page 82, as well as the printing procedure for each application.

---

1   Open the Printer Installation window (Figure 2-4).

2   Select a printer from the Installed printers list, or set up a new printer, then click Configure.

3   Enter the appropriate information in the Paper, Device, and Additional settings tabs of the Printer properties window (Figure 2-6 through Figure 2-8).

When you've finished, click OK.

Select the paper size you want as the default.

Select the page orientation you want as the default. (Document-specific page settings generally override whatever you set here.)

All options aren't available for all printers; make the appropriate selection here.

If you want to print using a scale other than 100%, enter the scale here.

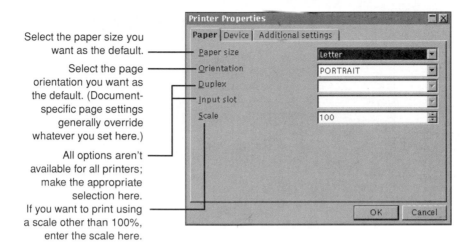

Figure 2-6   Entering printer paper options

Select an item; the corresponding options are listed in the Current value list.

Select a new value for the item if necessary.

Select the type of color or grayscale you want to print with (that the printer supports).

Enter the color depth you want to use (that the printer supports).

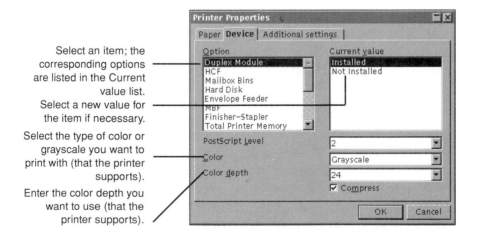

Figure 2-7   Entering printer device options

Note – If you're using the generic printer driver, to support older PostScript printers select Level 1 under PostScript. Otherwise select Level 2. If your printer can only issue black and white output, set Grayscale under Color; otherwise set Color. If conversion under Grayscale leads to poor results, you can always set Color under Color and leave the conversion to the printer or PostScript emulator.

Enter the margins you
want for the printer.
Document-specific
margins override these
settings.

Click Default values to
enter default margins for
all four fields (shown).

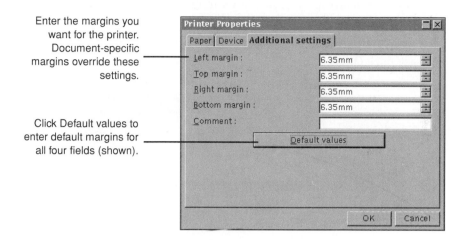

Figure 2-8   Entering printer margins

Setting Up a Duplex Printer

Follow these steps to set up StarOffice to print to a duplex-enabled printer (one that can print on both sides of a sheet of paper). You must already have a printer capable of duplex printing; if it isn't, setting it up as duplex in StarOffice won't help.

1   Open the Printer Installation window (Figure 2-4 on page 65).

2   Select the correct driver from that window and click Add new printer.

It's a good idea to walk over to the duplex-enabled printer you're setting up and check exactly what kind of printer it is. Then select a driver with exactly the same name from the driver list, as shown in Figure 2-9.

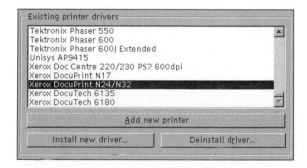

Figure 2-9   Selecting a printer driver for a duplex printer

3   Select the newly added printer driver from the Installed Printers list and click
Connect.

4   In the Connect window (Figure 2-10), select the queue for the duplex-enabled printer
and click OK.

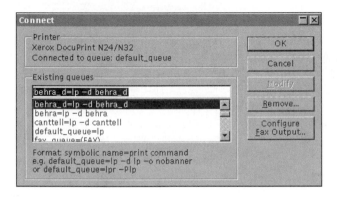

Figure 2-10   Selecting a queue (the duplex-enabled printer)

5   In the Printer Installation window, click Configure, then in the Printer Properties
window, click the Device tab. Under the Option list, select Duplex Module and in the
Current Value list, select Installed.

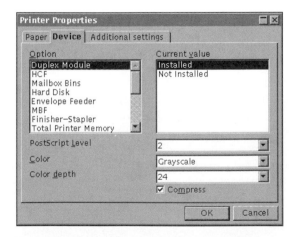

Figure 2-11   Enabling duplex printing in printer options

6   Click the Paper tab of the Printer Properties window. Select paper size and
orientation.

Note – The paper size you select is important; if you're having printing problems, check the paper size. If you're in the United States, for example, make sure you select Letter or Legal in the Printer Properties window. (Choose File > Print, select a printer, and click Properties. In the Paper tab, select the right paper size from the Paper size list.)

7 From the Duplex list, select the appropriate duplex option.

Note – Tumbling has no effect on landscape-oriented pages, only portrait.

Tumbling means that when printed the pages are flipped vertically (tumbled), so that turning the page up leaves both sides correctly oriented (as in a legal notepad). The tumbling options are illustrated in Figure 2-12.

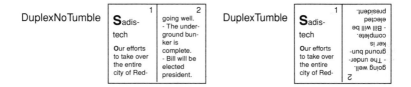

Figure 2-12 Duplex tumbling options

The None option turns off duplexing so that each page is printed on a different sheet of paper. The Ignore option prints the page the same was as DuplexNoTumble (standard duplex printing).

8 Click OK to close the window and save changes.

Note – To turn the duplex feature on and off on the fly in Solaris and UNIX, choose File > Print and select the printer. Click the Properties button and in the Printer Properties window, click the Paper tab. From the Duplex list, select None. You'll need to do this each time you print if you want to do it more than once; the settings you make in this window generally apply only to one print job.

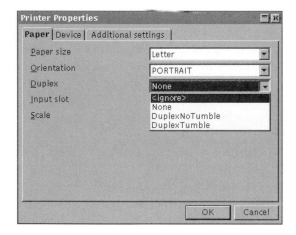

Figure 2-13   Selecting additional duplex printing options

Changing the Displayed Name of a Printer

1   Open the Printer Installation window (Figure 2-4).

2   Select the printer, such as Generic Printer, in the Installed printers list.

3   Click Rename.

4   Enter a new name in the Install window and click OK.

Making a Printer Your Default Printer

Your default printer is the one a document is printed to when you click the Print File Directly icon in the function bar.

1   Open the Printer Installation window (Figure 2-4).

2   Select the printer you want and click the Default Printer button.

Note – You can't remove a printer if it's your default printer.

Removing a Printer

If you don't want a printer in the list of available printers anymore, follow these steps.

1   Open the Printer Installation window (Figure 2-4).

2   If the printer is your default printer, select a different printer in the list and click Default Printer. You can't remove your default printer.

3   Select the printer you want to remove and click Remove. Click Yes when prompted.

Installing Drivers

Operating systems support printers by use of software modules called drivers. A driver is a printer-specific program that lets your applications print to a particular printer—there's a different driver for every type of printer.

Most systems come with many printer drivers already installed. If you need to install a new one for use with StarOffice, however, follow these steps. You can also use this procedure to install a fax driver.

1   Open the Printer Installation window (Figure 2-4).

2   Click the Install new driver button.

3   In the Driver Installation window, click Browse and select the directory containing the driver or drivers.

4   In the Installable drivers list, select one or more drivers to install, then click OK.

Setting Up Faxing Capabilities

You can fax documents directly from StarOffice, if you have a fax modem and have installed a fax driver. To fax, see *Faxing in StarOffice* on page 79.

1   Set up a printer as described in *Adding a New Printer* on page 66.

2   During step 5 of that procedure, follow the instructions, then click Configure Fax Output to display the Configure Fax window (Figure 2-14). Enter the required fax command and its parameters. Use the variables TMP and PHONE if necessary.

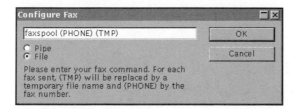

Figure 2-14   Configure fax window

Font Maintenance

Each operating system handles fonts differently. Extensive font installation and maintenance instructions are beyond the scope of this book; see the setup instructions included with StarOffice for detailed information about fonts on your operating system.

Note – Fonts are covered in the section titled *Setting up Printers, Fax Machines and Fonts under Unix* in the SETUP.PDF file. You can also refer to *Replacing Fonts* on page 146.

The Printer Installation window provides you with the mechanism for installing and modifying fonts for use when you print StarOffice documents.

Adding Fonts

1   Open the Printer Installation window (see page 65).

2   Click the Add Fonts button.

3   In the Font Path window (Figure 2-15), select the path where the fonts are stored and follow the instructions in the window.

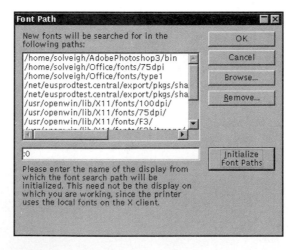

Figure 2-15   Setting font paths

Editing Font Attributes

1   Open the Printer Installation window (see page 65).

2   Click the Edit Font Attributes button.

3   In the Fonts window (Figure 2-16), make the required changes to the font.

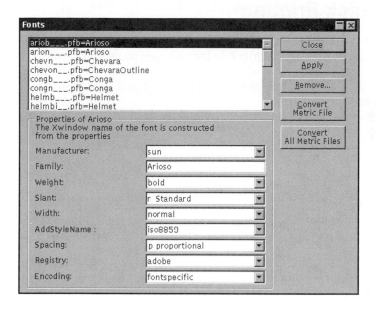

Figure 2-16   Editing font attributes

Basic Printing and Faxing for StarOffice Documents

This section contains the basics. For more advanced stuff, such as printing brochures and margins troubleshooting, see *Advanced Setup and Printing for StarOffice Documents* on page 80.

If you have a printer set up when you install StarOffice, you can print without doing anything else. When you install StarOffice, it automatically detects your default printer, names it Generic Printer, and lets you select it in the Print window.

Before you begin, add any printers you want, configure them, and set printer options. If you're using Linux or Solaris, follow the directions in the previous section, *Printer Setup* on page 62. If you're using Windows, refer to your operating system documentation.

Qulck Printing

You can print one copy of your entire document directly to the default StarOffice printer by clicking the Print File Directly icon on the function bar.

To specify your default StarOffice printer, see *Making a Printer Your Default Printer* on page 72.

Printing Using the Print Window

1   Choose File > Print.

2   In the Print window (Figure 2-18), enter the appropriate options.

3   Click Properties if you need to set printer-specific options. These options are covered in *Setting Up General Printer Options* on page 67.

4   Click Options to enter application-specific printing options. See the printing information for the application you're using for more information.

5   Select what to print: All (the entire document), Range (a range of slides or pages), or Selection (the currently selected text or graphics). Use dashes to form ranges, and use commas or semicolons to separate pages or ranges (1, 3, 4, 6-10).

Note – StarOffice defaults to Selection, rather than All or Range, if anything in the document is selected. Check this each time you print.

---

6   Enter the number of copies and, if it's two or more, choose whether to collate.

7   Click OK to print. A message will appear, stating the name of the printer that the document is being printed to.

If you have problems printing, check to be sure the margins and orientation are set correctly, especially in Draw and Impress. (Choose Format > Page and select the Page tab.) In addition, make sure you've selected the right paper format, such as Letter.

Make a selection here appropriate for the country where you're located (User format can cause problems; select a different format for best results.)

Paper format
Letter 8.5 x 11 in ⚪ Portrait ⚪ Landscape
Width   8.50"   Paper source
Height 11.00" [From printer settings]

Figure 2-17   Selecting the right paper format

If all else fails, close StarOffice and restart it.

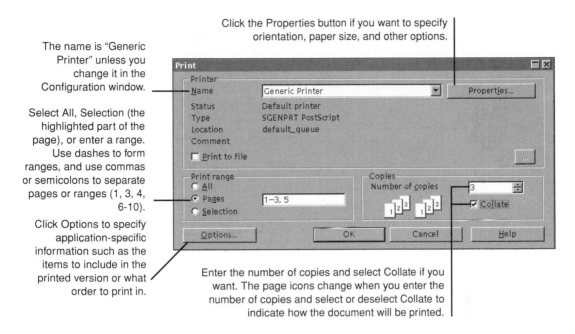

The name is "Generic
Printer" unless you
change it in the
Configuration window.

Select All, Selection (the
highlighted part of the
page), or enter a range.
Use dashes to form
ranges, and use commas
or semicolons to separate
pages or ranges (1, 3, 4,
6-10).

Click Options to specify
application-specific
information such as the
items to include in the
printed version or what
order to print in.

Click the Properties button if you want to specify
orientation, paper size, and other options.

Enter the number of copies and select Collate if you
want. The page icons change when you enter the
number of copies and select or deselect Collate to
indicate how the document will be printed.

Figure 2-18   Specifying options using the Print window (Solaris)

Printing to a PostScript or PDF File

You can save StarOffice in a variety of formats, so distributing soft copy of StarOffice documents isn't too much trouble, in general. However, if you have imported graphics, if you want to post the file on the Web, or for other reasons need a standard cross-platform format, it's a good idea to print your document to a file.

Two formats are most common:

*   PostScript – Many Solaris and Linux users can read PostScript files; a common file-reading application is GhostScript.
*   Adobe's Acrobat PDF – A very widely used, portable file format with low storage size requirements. In order to turn PostScript files into PDF files, you need the Adobe Acrobat product.

Note – If you're on a network in Solaris, you can use the following command to see if Distiller is available: `which distill` If you have distiller, you can create PDFs from PostScript files by typing `distill` *filename*`.ps`

This section shows you how to print a document or book to a PostScript file. Once in a PostScript file, a document can be turned over to a print shop or turned into a Portable Document Format (PDF) file for Web or other electronic delivery.

You don't need an actual PostScript printer to print to a PostScript file. You just need the printer driver installed on your system. There's a lot of good information on PostScript print drivers on the Adobe Web site: http://www.adobe.com

---

Note – If you're using Windows, you can install the HP LaserJet 4V/4MV PostScript printer and set the Print to File option for it. (See your Windows documentation if you need help installing printers.) This is a pretty good print driver for producing PostScript files. If your PostScript files end up in grayscale and you want to print in color or display the document electronically with color (as in a PDF file), go to http://www.Adobe.com and find the instructions for installing their PostScript printer driver.

Follow these steps to print a PostScript file. Once you've created it, refer to the documentation from Adobe if you want to create a PDF file.

1   Install the PostScript printer driver according to the installation instructions that were included with it.

2   Choose File > Print to print the document.

3   Select the PostScript printer in your list of printers, and select the Print to file option, as shown in Figure 2-19. (In Solaris and Linux, all printers are PostScript.)

To print to a file, select the Print to file option and enter the path and the file name, with a .ps extension.

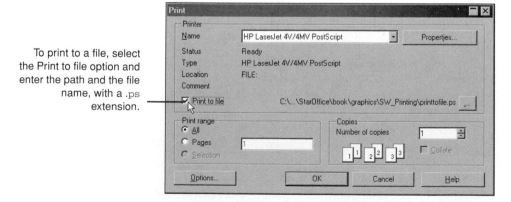

Figure 2-19   Specifying options using the Print window

4   When you select the Print to file option, a window is displayed to let you name and select the path for the PostScript file that will be printed. When you name the file, be sure to give it a .ps file extension.

5   Click OK to print.

A message will appear, stating the name of the printer that the document is being printed to. This is fine; the document will still be printed to a file.

Faxing in StarOffice

If you have a fax modem connected to your computer, you can fax your current StarOffice document directly from your computer. To set up faxing in Solaris or Linux, see *Setting Up Faxing Capabilities* on page 73; in Windows, use the tools provided with your operating system.

Creating a Cover Letter Using Autopilot

You can use Autopilot to create a Writer fax cover sheet, with the number, recipient's address from your address book, and other elements. Choose File > Autopilot > Fax and enter information as prompted. The fax will be saved in a file in the location you specify in the last window.

The fax is also created as a template by default in the `user/template/` directory; you'll see it in the Document Templates window, in the Standard category.

Figure 2-20 on page 80 shows a fax cover sheet in Writer, created using Autopilot, with the address book displayed.

Creating the Faxable Document Without Autopilot

If you're not faxing using a cover sheet created in Autopilot, specify the number in the document. (You don't have to, though; if you don't specify a fax number in the document, a dialog will prompt you to enter it.) Precede and follow the fax number with the characters @ @. A valid entry, for example, would be @ @9077890071@ @. If you don't want these characters to be displayed in the document, make them the background color, such as white.

You also can enter a field command that takes the fax number from the current database. (For more information on mail merges and databases, see *Mailings* on page 321.)

Faxing Any Document

Typically, you should be able to just choose File > Print and select the fax driver in the Name list. Refer to the documentation included with your fax modem for more information. Some fax software, however, requires you to enter the phone number; refer to your fax software documentation for more information.

Figure 2-20   Fax cover sheet created using Autopilot

Advanced Setup and Printing for StarOffice Documents

StarOffice enables—perhaps requires is a better word—you to do a fair bit of tweaking in order to get the printed results you want. This section is a somewhat miscellaneous but useful grouping of system-wide printing issues. Be sure to at least skim through this information before you start, so you'll know where to come back to when StarOffice resists your attempts to switch orientation, or flashes warnings at you.

Managing Print Warnings

If your document doesn't match some of the restrictions or parameters for printing, the occasional warning will appear.

Setting Up Paper Size and Orientation Notifications

You can choose whether an error message should pop up when your document settings and printer settings don't match. You can have a warning for neither, one or both. The warning window is covered in the next section, *Selecting an Option in the Print Warning Window*.

The warning window also appears if you don't have these options marked, when the paper size and orientation match but the image is just too big for the output—for example, if you've drawn a rectangle that goes outside any of the page margins you've set for the document. But it doesn't hurt to have this additional level of protection; it can save you some frustration while you're trying to track down why your document isn't printing correctly.

1   Choose Tools > Options > General > Print.

2   Select the Paper size and/or Paper orientation options, then click OK.

- Paper size (legal versus standard, for example) – If the current printer does not have the required paper size for the document, an error message will appear.

- Paper orientation (landscape versus portrait) – If the printer cannot print using the orientation you've specified for the document, an error message will appear.

Selecting an Option in the Print Warning Window

If you set up the notification described in *Setting Up Paper Size and Orientation Notifications*, or if a slide won't fit the page setup options you've specified, the window in Figure 2-21 will appear when necessary.

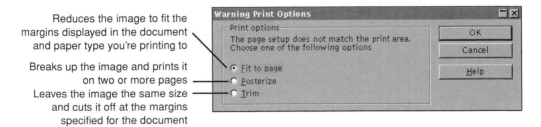

Reduces the image to fit the margins displayed in the document and paper type you're printing to

Breaks up the image and prints it on two or more pages

Leaves the image the same size and cuts it off at the margins specified for the document

Figure 2-21   Print Options warning window

Note – If you select Fit to page, the warning window won't appear again for this document.

Specifying Portrait or Landscape Orientation

There are a lot of places you can set page orientation (portrait or landscape). It can get a little confusing, so we've provided Table 2-1 to show you (all in one place) where you can go to set document and printer margins.

Table 2-1   Orientation-setting windows

Window	Navigation	Book section
Print Options (for Page Preview mode) These settings are used only if you print using the Print icon in the Page Preview window.	In Calc, Writer, and Web with Print Layout on, choose File > Page Preview. Click the Print options page view icon.	Calc: *Controlling Pagination and Formatting* on page 601 Writer and Web: *Using Page Preview* on page 467
Page Style Overrides any setting in the Printer Properties window.	In Writer, Web, Draw, Calc, and Impress, choose Format > Page.	Calc: *Setting Page and Sheet Printing Options* on page 601 Writer and Web: Figure 5-32 on page 212 Draw: *Page Setup* on page 739 Impress: *Specifying Landscape or Portrait Orientation* on page 725
Printer Properties (Determines the orientation for StarOffice Image but nothing else.	In Linux and Solaris, open the Printer Installation window (double-click the Printer Setup icon in the StarOffice desktop), then click Configure. On all platforms, choose File > Printer Setup, select a printer and click Properties. Select the Paper tab.	*Setting Up General Printer Options* on page 67

Setting Margins

You can set the margins for each printer in Printer Setup (Figure 2-8 on page 69). However, most of the same windows that let you set orientation let you set margins, as well (for most applications, choose Format > Page and click the Page tab). Those settings generally override anything in the Printer Setup window.

The margin information for printers sets the maximum possible area for printing; margin information for documents can set margins within those bounds, but not outside. Keep track of the margin options for both, when you print.

If you're using headers and footers, keep in mind that those need to be within the printer margins, as well.

Note – In Draw and Impress, the margin settings occasionally go crazy and provide defaults for new documents that just aren't usable. Be sure to check margins in all documents, but in Draw and Impress in particular, if you're having problems getting the results you want.

Fitting Multiple Pages Onto One Sheet

StarOffice provides brochure printing, handout printing, and page preview features. Use the following cross-references to find the information you need.

Table 2-2   Printing multiple pages on one sheet

Feature	Application	Navigation	Book Section
Brochure printing	Web, Writer, Impress, Draw	File > Print > Options	*Printing Brochures* on page 350
Handouts (similar to Page Preview)	Impress (Draw files are easily adaptable to Impress files)	Click the Handout icon on the right side of the work area	*Creating Slide Handouts* on page 703
Page Preview (similar to Handouts)	Calc, Writer, Web	Calc: File > Page Preview Writer: File > Page Preview Web: File > Page Preview when Print Layout is activated	Calc: Figure 22-3 on page 602 Writer: *Printing More than One Page on a Sheet of Paper* on page 349 Web: *Using Page Preview* on page 467

Note – The Tile feature, available in many Print Options windows, seems to be (to put it tactfully) an unimplemented feature.

Fitting a Document Onto One Page

StarOffice provides different ways for you to "scrunch" data that overflows one page so that it will print using only one sheet of paper.

Table 2-3   Information for fitting a document onto one page

Feature	Application	Navigation	Book Section
Setting image size Lets you specify how large the image should be, and at which edge or corner the image should be printed.	Image	File > Page Setup	*Page Setup* on page 836
Page Setup	Calc	Calc: Format > Page > Sheet	*Setting Page and Sheet Printing Options* on page 601
Fit to size	Draw, Impress	File > Print > Options	Draw: *Printing Options Setup* on page 801 Impress: *Setting Printing Options* on page 726
Scale	Printer setup	File > Print, click Properties, then click the Paper tab	*Setting Up General Printer Options* on page 67

Note – In Draw or Impress, you'll be prompted if a slide won't fit onto the page. See *Selecting an Option in the Print Warning Window* on page 81.

Using a Different Scale

To print a document larger or smaller than it is, use the Scale field in the printer setup window. (See *Setting Up General Printer Options* on page 67.)

Printing Left or Right Pages, or in Reversed Order

If your printer prints pages backwards, instead of starting at 1, you can print from Web and Writer in reversed order.

You can also print only the left, or only the right, pages from Writer.

1 Choose Tools > Options > *application* > Print, or by choosing File > Print > Options.

Note – If you use the first navigation option, all subsequent documents will have the settings you apply in step 2. If you use the second navigation method, the settings will apply only to the document you're currently working with.

---

2 Select the Left pages, Right pages (Writer only), or Reversed options.

Printing Brochures

In Impress, Draw, Web, and Writer, you can print a a document so that it can be made into a brochure. When the pages of the printed brochure are folded in half and stapled, there are two slides on each side of each page, and they're in the correct order for a brochure. Two pages are printed on each sheet of paper. (You'll need to change the paper size in Page Setup to fit the document onto Letter-size paper; see the procedure for tips on setting margins.)

Note – It works well in Draw and Impress, but it's less useful in Web and Writer.

How Brochure Printing Works

Here's how brochure printing works for an eight-page brochure, if you're not using a duplex printer.

- Select Brochure and print Right or Front only to a single-sided printer – StarOffice prints pages 8, 1, 6, and 3, in that order, on two sheets of paper.
- Select Brochure and print Left or Back only to a single-sided printer – StarOffice prints pages 2, 7, 4, and 5, in that order, on two sheets of paper.
- Select Brochure and print both front and back to a tumbled duplex printer – StarOffice prints 8, 1, 2, 7, 6, 3, 4, and 5, on two sheets of paper.

Figure 2-22 shows what the output would look like for a portrait document printed in Draw or Impress.

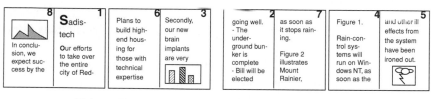

Right, or Front   Left, or Back

Figure 2-22   Brochure output for a portrait document in Draw or Impress

Figure 2-23 shows what the output would look like for a landscape document, such as a presentation.

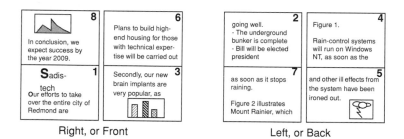

Right, or Front   Left, or Back

Figure 2-23   Brochure output for a landscape document in Draw or Impress

Figure 2-24 shows the way that Writer and Web do brochure printing.

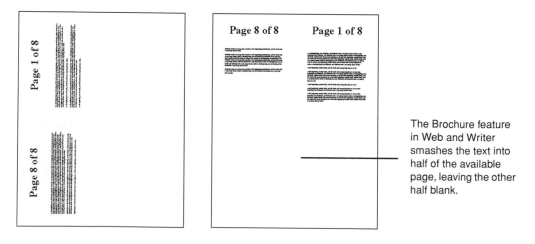

The Brochure feature in Web and Writer smashes the text into half of the available page, leaving the other half blank.

Figure 2-24   Brochure output in Web and Writer, landscape and portrait

The fun thing about printing brochures is that it works two or three different ways, among four applications. Both applications print the pages in the same order, as shown in Figure 2-22 and Figure 2-23, but the page dimensions are different. The brochure is one-fourth the size of the original document. StarOffice shrinks the font and page dimensions so that you only print on half of a Letter-sized piece of paper, as shown at right, but doesn't turn the page 90 degrees, as it should. Page setup can make it smaller, but can't improve the situation.

If at this point you think, "I'm not going to bother with brochure printing in Web and Writer," you have our sympathies.

Before You Begin

Note on brochures in Web You're better off having a duplex-capable printer, or else you're printing two copies of every brochure. StarOffice's Web team left off the options that let you print only the front, or only the back, pages for a brochure. See *Setting Up a Duplex Printer* on page 69 for more information.

Setup for Draw and Impress You'll need to modify the page size, then adjust the content as necessary to fit within the smaller page size.

If you print without changing the margins, you'll end up with only 2/3 of the contents of the odd pages. Choose Format > Page and select the Page tab. From the Paper format list, select User paper size and enter dimensions in the Width and Height fields below it. Figure 2-25 illustrates the settings for a portrait document printed on Letter-size paper.

For a **portrait** document, width should be half the long side of the paper you're printing to. For **landscape**, width should be the same as the short side.

For a **portrait** document, height should be the same as the short side of the paper you're printing to. For **landscape**, height should be half the long side.

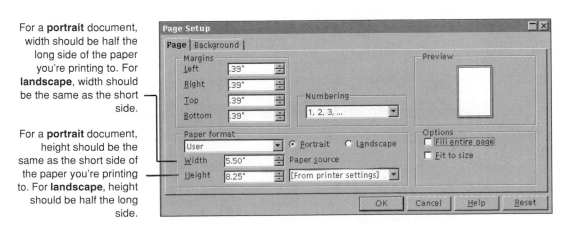

Figure 2-25   Draw and Impress: Page setup for a brochure

Printing the Brochure on a Duplex Printer

1   Choose File > Print.

2   Be sure your document margins and size are set up correctly, according to the setup instructions earlier in this section.

3   Be sure your duplex printer is set up correctly, according to Table 2-4. See *Setting Up a Duplex Printer* on page 69 for more information.

Table 2-4   Duplex printing settings

Application	Orientation	Duplex setting
Writer, Web	Portrait	DuplexNoTumble
	Landscape	DuplexTumble
Draw and Impress	Portrait	DuplexTumble
	Landscape	DuplexTumble

4   In the Print window, click the Properties button. In the printer setup window, set the orientation to landscape or portrait, and select the correct paper size.

Note – It usually doesn't matter what you put in this window, but it does for brochures. The orientation and paper size must match what you specified in the page setup window for the document.

5   In the Print window, click Options.

6   Select the Brochure option and, if you're using Writer, Draw, or Impress, select the Front (or Right) option.

7   Click OK, then click OK again to print.

Printing the Brochure on a Single-Sided Printer

1   Choose File > Print.

2   Be sure your document margins and size are set up correctly, according to the setup instructions earlier in this section.

3   In the Print window, click the Properties button. In the printer setup window, set the orientation to landscape or portrait, and select the correct paper size.

Note – It usually doesn't matter what you put in this window, but it does for brochures. The orientation and paper size must match what you specified in the page setup window for the document.

4   In the Print window, click Options.

5   Select the Brochure option and, if you're using Writer, Draw, or Impress, select the Front (or Right) option.

6   Click OK, then click OK again to print.

7   Put the printed pages into the printer, correct side up, and choose File > Print again.

Note – If your printer prints cover sheets for every print job, add an extra sheet of paper on **top** of the sheets, or turn off cover sheets.

---

8   Click Properties again and make sure that the orientation and paper size are still correct.

9   Click Options again. In the Printer Options window, select Brochure again.

- If you're using Web, select Reversed
- If you're using Writer, Draw, or Impress, select Left (or Back)

10   Click OK, then click OK again to print.

11   If you're using Web, you now have two copies of the brochure. The odd sheets of paper (not pages) go together, and the even sheets of paper go together.

Setting Up Pages for DocuTech 135 Signature Printing

If you're producing bound documents through a print shop, and the print shop has a Xerox DocuTech 135 printing machine, here's a trick that can ultimately save paper, give you a standard book size, and potentially reduce the time it takes to print and bind documents.

Using this trick only if it's acceptable that your bound documents be 7 inches wide by 8.5 inches tall (legal-size paper turned landscape and either cut in half or folded).

This trick also involves printing the document to a PostScript file. See *Printing to a PostScript or PDF File* on page 77.

If you really want to impress the folks at the print shop, make your total page count divisible by 4.

1   Create left and right page styles using the **Letter 8.5 x 11 in** page format with **Portrait** orientation (Page Style window, Page tab).

2   Set the left and right page margins to the settings shown in Figure 2-26.

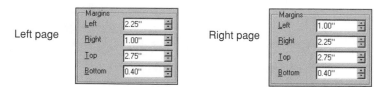

Figure 2-26   Setting left/right page margins for DocuTech signature printing

3   Print the document to a PostScript file using your PostScript printer driver.

4   Give the file to the print shop, and tell them you want it printed in one of the following ways:

-    Signature using legal-size paper; saddle-stitch binding. (This means folded in half and bound on the fold. Only use this if your document is less than 100 pages.)

-    Signature using legal-size paper; two-up binding (cut in half). (For spiral binding or perfect binding.)

Setting Up Colors for Commercial Printing

If you'll be printing high-quality color copies of a document, you should probably switch color models from RGB (red-green-blue, the model used by your monitor) to CMYK (cyan-magenta-yellow-black, the model used by commercial printers).

Both palettes are included in StarOffice, though RGB is the default. Follow these steps to switch to CMYK.

1   Choose Format > Area.

2   In the Area window, click the Colors tab.

3   Click Open.

4   Select CMYK from the Color sample list.

5   Click the Load Color List icon.

6   In the `config` folder, select the `cmyk.soc` file and click Open.

7   Assign CMYK colors to the document.

Taming the StarOffice Environment

About this Chapter

Because StarOffice is an integrated software suite, it crams a lot of features into a single interface, and it takes a lot of toolbars, windows, and options to control it all. This chapter is a loosely organized mish-mash of tasks and information to help you control and set up the StarOffice environment. Some of the tasks are simple, some are more advanced, and they're all interspersed. But if you take a little time to peruse this chapter, you'll pick up some good tips that will help you better understand how StarOffice works.

The StarOffice Work Area

Figure 3-1 displays the major parts of the StarOffice work area. The Explorer window isn't expanded as shown here when you start StarOffice for the first time. Click the arrow icon on the left side of the work area to expand Explorer, as shown in Figure 3-1. Beamer (a file-viewing window) isn't displayed by default. See *Beamer* on page 104.

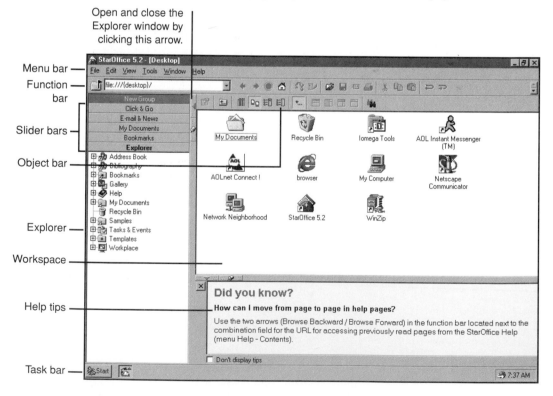

Figure 3-1   The StarOffice work area

About the StarOffice Desktop

StarOffice is a completely integrated office suite. All of its applications and features run inside its environment. For example, if you want to write a document in StarOffice Writer, you don't launch Writer as a separate, standalone application. You launch it from within StarOffice. The same holds true for all other StarOffice applications.

The Learning Curve

Because of this high level of integration, StarOffice can seem like its own operating system—which means it takes some getting used to. Just as it took you some time to get comfortable with your current operating system, it will take a little time to feel comfortable with the StarOffice environment.

StarOffice has a lot of configuration options—more than you'll probably ever use. For example, StarOffice lets you set the exact vertical and horizontal pixel spacing between the desktop icons. (To get to this setting, by the way, select Tools > Options > General > Desktop.)

You don't need to understand every single feature to be proficient with StarOffice.

Windows Note – The StarOffice desktop simulates aspects of the Windows desktop and tools, but it doesn't fully synchronize with it. For example:

- If you want your Windows task bar shortcuts to be identical in StarOffice, you have to add them to StarOffice. (See *Adding Shortcuts to the Task Bar* on page 123.)
- While StarOffice displays your Windows desktop icons, you can organize them differently in StarOffice. For example, if your Windows desktop organizes icons by Type, you can set your StarOffice desktop to organize them by title, type, size, or modification date.

StarOffice Vocabulary

Some of StarOffice's options have different names than you might expect. For example, in order to "wrap" text in a spreadsheet cell, you need to select an option called "Line Break." In order to make the options clearer, we refer to them by their more conventional names. Instead of the four different terms that StarOffice uses to describe the background of a presentation, for example, we just say "background," then direct you to the option with the non-traditional name.

The Workspace and Task Bar

The workspace, shown in Figure 3-1, is where the StarOffice applications run. All open files have a corresponding icon in the task bar. See Figure 3-2. Bring open files into the workspace by clicking their corresponding icon.

Figure 3-2   Task bar showing open files and folders

Note – When you double-click an item in the Explorer window to open it in the workspace, the new item or document will replace the last icon in the task bar, closing the previously open item or document. To open a new item or document without closing and replacing the last open item, hold down the Ctrl key while you double-click on the new item in the Explorer window.

The Toolbar

Toolbar icons, shown in Figure 3-3, are more than they seem. If a toolbar icon has a green arrow, that means there are more options for you to select by clicking and holding the left mouse button down on the icon.

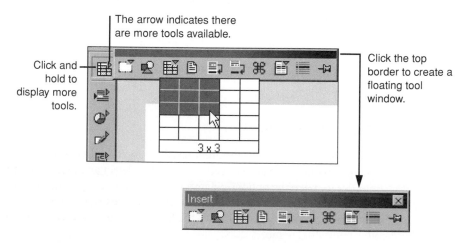

Figure 3-3   The toolbar

The toolbar icons with green arrows can display different icons on the main toolbar. For example, the Insert button on the toolbar displays the Insert Table icon if a table was the last thing you inserted.

Note – When you use the drawing tools, you can double-click the icons to repeat drawings without clicking the icon multiple times. For example, if you want to draw more than one rectangle, double-click the rectangle icon and draw one rectangle after another. To stop drawing rectangles, click in an open area of the workspace.

You can also add and remove toolbar icons by right-clicking the toolbar, choosing Visible Buttons, and selecting or deselecting tools.

The Context-Sensitive Object Bar

The object bar is context sensitive, which means it shows the tools you can use depending on the task you're trying to perform. For example, as Figure 3-4 illustrates, if the cursor is in a paragraph, the object bar displays tools for basic text and paragraph formatting. If your cursor is in a table, it shows tools for working with tables.

However, when you're in a table and want to format text, you can replace the table object bar with the text formatting object bar by clicking the arrow at the far right of the object bar, as shown in Figure 3-4.

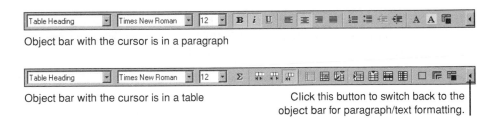

Object bar with the cursor is in a paragraph

Object bar with the cursor is in a table   Click this button to switch back to the object bar for paragraph/text formatting.

Figure 3-4   The context-sensitive object bar

Viewing Hidden Icons

If your monitor is small, if you've resized StarOffice, or if the display settings in your operating system make it so you can't see all available icons in the function bar, option bar, or toolbar, a small set of arrows is displayed to let you view these icons (see Figure 3-5).

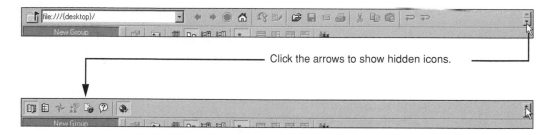

Figure 3-5   Viewing hidden icons

If you don't want to click arrows all the time to display hidden buttons, remember (or set up) keyboard shortcuts to the buttons you want to use often. For example, press Ctrl+Shift+E to show the Explorer window, and press F11 to show and hide the Stylist.

For information on viewing available shortcut keys or setting up your own keyboard shortcuts, see *Assigning Shortcut Keys* on page 100.

Showing Inactive Menu Items

A certain software design tendency has been in vogue recently that has caused confusion and frustration among many users (which isn't good, because frustration leads to anger, anger leads to hate, and it all goes downhill from there).

We're speaking of the practice of hiding inactive menu items. The way it works is that when you're not allowed to perform a certain action at a given point, the menu item you would use to perform the action is hidden rather than turned gray.

This practice causes confusion, because if you expect to be able to do something but don't see the menu item for it, you may assume that the software is broken or was installed incorrectly. On the other hand, if you see the menu item grayed out, you'll probably assume, correctly, that you must not be able to use that feature for some reason.

Fortunately, StarOffice resolves this dilemma nicely and lets you change inactive menu items from hidden (the default) to gray, saving you from a lot of frustration.

1   Choose Tools > Options > General > View.

2   Select the Inactive Menu Items option.

3   Click OK.

Viewing inactive menu items is also useful for seeing features that are available in StarOffice. If the menu items are hidden, you may never know that certain features exist.

The Application-Sensitive Menu

The StarOffice menus are application sensitive. That means StarOffice knows which application is open and can change menus accordingly. For example, when you're working in StarOffice Writer, the Insert menu is different than when you're working in StarOffice Calc, as shown in Figure 3-6.

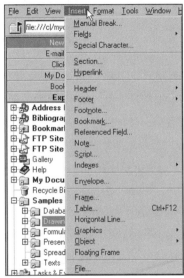

StarOffice Writer Insert menu

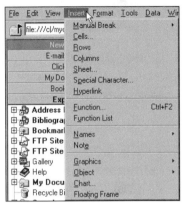

StarOffice Calc Insert menu

Figure 3-6   The Insert menu for Writer and Calc

Right-Clicking: Just Do It

Get right-click happy in StarOffice. Some of the best shortcuts and most efficient ways of doing things happen through right-click menus.

You can click the right mouse button just about anywhere in StarOffice to bring up a context-sensitive menu. Sometimes a right-click is the only way to access some features, like *Update*, which refreshes the Explorer window.

Lefties If you've configured your left mouse button to act as the right mouse button, left-click to bring up context menus.

Note – If you use StarOffice online help, the term "context menu" means the right-click menu.

Simulating the Look and Feel of Other Operating Systems

StarOffice can simulate the look and feel of many operating systems, such as Macintosh, XWindows, and OS/2. This is useful if you're working on one system, such as a PC, and you're more accustomed to, or prefer working in, another operating environment, such as Macintosh.

1   Choose Tools > Options > General > View.

2   In the View window, select the operating system you want to simulate in the Look & Feel field.

3   Click OK.

Controlling Mouse Pointer Positioning

When you open a window in StarOffice (for example, the Tools > Options window), you can have StarOffice automatically position the mouse pointer relative to the window: centered or on the active button.

1   Choose Tools > Options > General > View.

2   In the View window, select the option you want in the Mouse positioning field.

3   Click OK.

Customizing Menus

StarOffice lets you manipulate its menu bar by creating, changing, and reorganizing menu items.

You won't necessarily be considered a nerd for using this functionality, but it is getting into advanced user territory. Most users aren't likely to use or need this functionality, so we won't go into detailed procedures for customizing your menus. Instead, the information presented here is meant merely to help guide you if you are feeling adventuresome and want to change a menu or two.

Each StarOffice application has its own set of menus. If you want to modify menus for a specific application, make sure the application is active when you begin.

1   Choose Tools > Configure.

2   Select the Menu tab (see Figure 3-7).

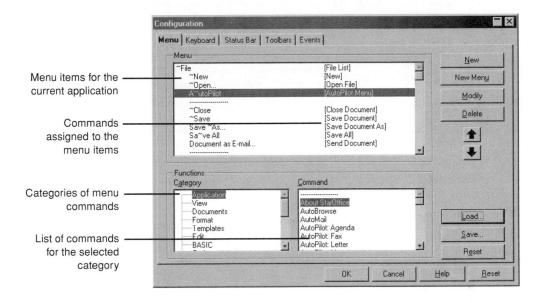

Figure 3-7   The Menu Configuration window

Menus are stored in configuration (.cfg) files. By default they're in the Office52\user\config folder. When you create, modify, and save menus, you're making changes to a .cfg file.

Table 3-1 describes elements of this window. It's provided to help guide you through making menu changes.

Table 3-1   Elements of the Menu Configuration window

Field/Button	Description
Menu	Displays the contents of the entire menu bar for the active application.
~ (the tilde symbol)	In the names of menu items, the tilde (~) precedes a letter that will be underlined as a menu keyboard shortcut.
---------------------	The separator line, available in the Command field, draws a physical line between menu items. Use this to separate logical groups of commands (such as cut, copy, and paste).
Category	This field is how StarOffice organizes commands. The list provides general categories that house commands, which appear in the Command field when you select a category.

Table 3-1   Elements of the Menu Configuration window (continued)

Field/Button	Description
Command	This field displays the commands, or actions, that you can assign to menu items. If you don't see the command you want to use, select a different category in the Category field.
New button	Inserts a new item below the selected menu item.
New Menu button	Inserts a new menu item below the selected menu item. New menus display inside of existing menus and have fly-out submenus. To rename the new menu item, right-click it.
Modify button	Replaces the selected menu item with the selected command.
Delete button	Deletes the selected menu item. You can't delete top-level menu items, such as File and Edit.
⬆ ⬇	Moves the selected menu item up or down in the list.
Load button	Lets you select another configuration file to edit and/or load as the StarOffice configuration, which includes settings for menus, keyboard shortcuts, the status bar, toolbars, and events.
Save button	Lets you save the active configuration file.
Reset button	Resets the menu to that of the previously saved .cfg file. Any unsaved changes are lost.

Assigning Shortcut Keys

StarOffice lets you assign actions to keyboard keys, or combinations of keys. A number of these shortcut keys are set up by default, such as the F9 key to recalculate StarOffice Calc spreadsheets or the F11 key to launch the Stylist.

Each StarOffice application has its own set of shortcut keys. For example, in Writer, the F12 key turns numbering on and off; in Calc, the F12 key lets you define a cell group.

You can also assign shortcut keys to run any macros you create. For example, if you create a macro that inserts the text "Java™" (or any other product name with a trademark or registration mark), you can assign that macro to a shortcut key that automatically inserts that text when you press the key.

If you want to modify shortcut keys for a specific application, make sure the application is active when you begin. This procedure is the same for assigning a new shortcut as it is for replacing an existing shortcut.

1   Choose Tools > Configure.

2   Select the Keyboard tab (see Figure 3-8).

3   In the Keyboard list, select the key or key combination you want to use.

4   In the Category list, select the category containing the command you want to assign.

Any macros you've created will be stored in one of the macro categories.

The commands for the category you select are displayed in the Command list.

5   Select the command you want to assign to the keyboard shortcut.

6   Click the Assign button.

The name of the command is inserted next to the shortcut in the Keyboard list.

7   Click OK.

For more guidance on this window, see Table 3-2.

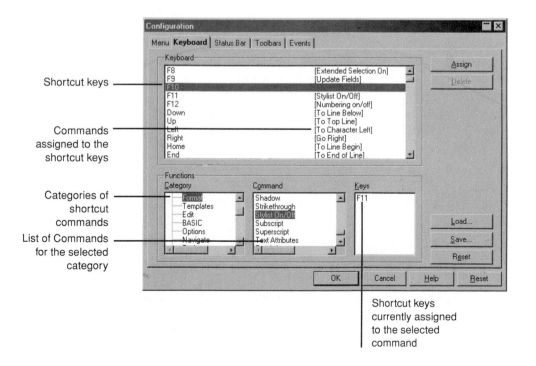

Figure 3-8   The Keyboard Configuration window

Note – Even if you don't want to assign or modify shortcut keys, the Keyboard tab is a great reference for viewing the shortcuts you can use.

Keyboard shortcuts are stored in configuration (`.cfg`) files. By default they're in the `Office52\user\config` folder. When you assign, modify, and save shortcut key settings, you're making changes to a `.cfg` file.

Table 3-2 describes elements of the Keyboard Configuration window. It's provided to help guide you through making shortcut key changes.

Table 3-2   Elements of the Keyboard Configuration window

Field/Button	Description
Keyboard	Lists all available keys and key combinations and the respective commands assigned to them.
Category	This field is how StarOffice organizes commands. The list provides general categories that contain commands, which appear in the Command list when you select a category.
Command	Lists the commands, or actions, that you can assign to keys. If you don't see the command you want to use, select a different category in the Category field.
Keys	Displays the key or key combination assigned to the selected command. If this field is empty, no key or key combination is assigned to the command.
Delete button	Deletes the command assigned to the selected shortcut key.
Load button	Lets you select another configuration file to edit and/or load as the StarOffice configuration, which includes settings for menus, keyboard shortcuts, the status bar, toolbars, and events.
Save button	Lets you save the active configuration file.
Reset button	Resets the keyboard shortcuts to their previously saved settings. Any unsaved changes are lost.

Organizing and Managing Your Files

Explorer and Beamer are two windows on the StarOffice desktop that help you organize and view the contents of your work environment. The simplest explanation is that Explorer contains folders that hold subfolders, files, and other elements, and Beamer displays the contents of a selected Explorer folder.

You can turn Explorer and Beamer on and off with their respective buttons in the function bar.

Explorer | | Beamer

Explorer

Explorer is StarOffice's filing cabinet. It displays the current folder structure of your system, whether you're working off of a network or a hard drive. (If you're working on a network and want to be sure you see the current file structure, see *On a Network – Staying Current in Online Mode* on page 111.)

Explorer also helps you organize other elements of your system, from Email, to common tasks, to Internet bookmarks. Explorer uses slider bars to organize different groups of information. To view a group in Explorer, click its slider bar (see Figure 3-9). StarOffice comes with the following default groups:

* E-mail & News – Lets you organize Email and newsgroup information.

* Click & Go – Provides shortcuts to StarOffice applications.

* My Documents – Displays your default work folder, as specified in Tools > Options > General > Paths > My documents.

* Bookmarks – Displays your default favorite places on the Internet folder, as specified in the Tools > Options > General > Paths > Bookmarks.

* Explorer – Displays your system's entire folder structure and many useful StarOffice folders. You can maintain your system folders directly from this window.

Sliders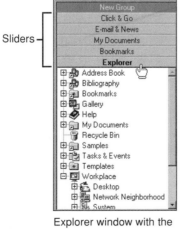

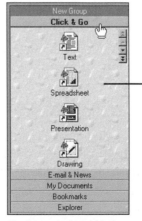

You can set separate background colors and images for each group in Explorer. Right-click in the section and follow the steps in *Adding Wallpaper to the Workspace* on page 124.

Explorer window with the
Explorer slider selected

Explorer window with the
Click & Go slider selected

Figure 3-9   The Explorer window

Note – If you're using StarOffice on a network in a multi-user situation, some of the files, such as Gallery items or Templates, might be stored on the server rather than on your local machine. If one of the procedures in this book tells you to look for files in a specific folder, such as `office52/user/...`, but you don't see the file(s) you need in that folder, the file(s) might be stored in a network location instead. To see where files are stored, choose Tools > Options > General > Paths, and scroll down the list of paths.

Changing How Group Items Are Displayed Right-click a group's slider bar and select Large Icons, Small Icons, or Hierarchical.

Hierarchical shows folders in a tree view with (+) and (-) symbols to let you expand and contract folders. To display files as well as folders in Hierarchical view, right-click the group slider and select Display Documents. The Explorer group must be in Hierarchical view to display Gallery thumbnails in Beamer.

Rearranging and Renaming Sliders To rearrange sliders, click and drag a slider to a new position. To rename a slider, right-click a slider bar and choose Rename Group.

Creating Groups In Explorer, drag the folder that you want to create a new group for onto the New Group bar at the top of Explorer. The name of the folder becomes the name on the group's slider.

You can also right-click the New Group bar, choose Create New Group as Folder, and type the name of the group on the new slider that is added.

Adding Items to a Group You can then add items to a group by opening the group, right-clicking in the open area below the group's slider, and choosing the item you want to add.

Removing Groups Right-click the slider of the group you want to remove, and select Remove Group.

Showing Hidden Files and Folders If you want to see all files and folders, especially hidden files and folders, right-click in Explorer and choose Show > Hidden Objects. This also lets you see hidden files and folders in the Open and Save As windows. If you want to see all items in right-click menus, right-click in the Explorer window and choose Show > All Properties.

Beamer

StarOffice Beamer is a window that displays the contents of a selected item in Explorer. In addition to displaying files and subfolders of an Explorer folder, Beamer displays other elements such as thumbnail previews of graphic and sound files in the StarOffice Gallery, and database table fields.

Figure 3-10 illustrates the versatility of StarOffice's integrated environment. Beamer displays the files of a Web site (connected online through FTP to the service provider that hosts the Web site). The work area displays the contents of a folder on the hard drive. Files can be dragged from the hard drive to the FTP site to upload the Web files and vice versa.

Beamer displaying the files of a Web site

The workspace, displaying files to be uploaded to the Web site by dragging them into Beamer

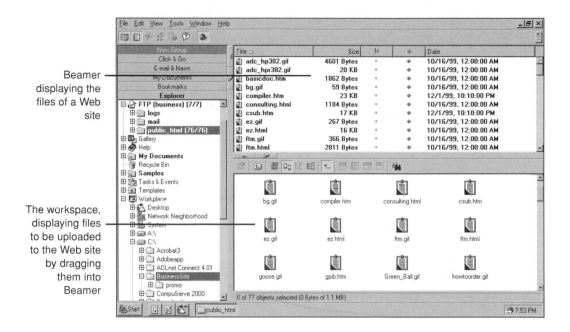

Figure 3-10   Beamer displaying the files on a Web site

Double-clicking an item in Explorer displays the contents of that item in the work area, replacing the previously opened item. (To prevent that, hold down the Ctrl key while you double-click). Single-clicking an item displays the contents of the item in Beamer, assuming the Beamer window is open.

Beamer and Gallery

With a full installation, StarOffice includes a library (called the Gallery) of stock art, sounds, and animated GIF files. A Gallery folder near the top of the Explorer group provides a way to view thumbnail sketches in Beamer. The Gallery is composed of links to source files.

Viewing Thumbnails

1   Open the Beamer window (by clicking its button on the Function bar).

2   Click the Explorer slider (see Figure 3-11).

3   If the Explorer group doesn't show its contents in hierarchical view (as a tree structure with folders and subfolders), right-click the Explorer slider and choose Hierarchical.

4 Expand the Gallery folder in Explorer and click a category (or "theme").

Figure 3-11 Viewing flag thumbnails

Previewing Thumbnail Files

Thumbnails provide a convenient way to preview sounds and GIF animations (since a thumbnail of a picture is really a preview itself). To preview a sound or GIF file, double-click it. To quit the preview and return to thumbnail view, double-click the object again.

Using Thumbnails

You can drag thumbnails from Beamer into any open document. To insert a file into a document as a link to the source file rather than as a copy of the file (links make the document size much smaller), hold down Ctrl+Shift while you drag the thumbnail into the document. You can also drag thumbnails onto the task bar to open the source files.

In Figure 3-12, a custom GIF file that was added to the Gallery is dragged from Beamer directly into an HTML document. See Customizing the Gallery, next.

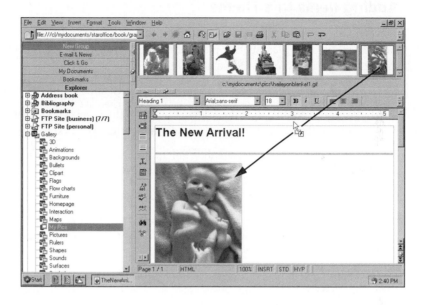

Figure 3-12   Dragging a thumbnail into an HTML document

 Tip There is also a `gallery` subfolder in the `Office52\share` or `Office52\user` folders. Items in this folder can't be viewed as thumbnails in Beamer, but they serve as the source files for the thumbnails.

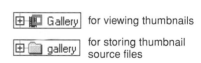

for viewing thumbnails

for storing thumbnail source files

Customizing the Gallery

This section shows you how to customize and maintain the Gallery.

Adding Themes

You can add your own themes (categories) to the Gallery to display your own graphics, sounds, and animations.

1   Right-click the Gallery folder and select New Theme.

2   In the Properties of the New Theme window, click the General tab.

3   Type the name of the theme and click OK.

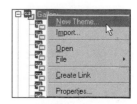

When you select the new theme in the Explorer window, Beamer shows a blank area until you add items to your theme.

Adding Items to a Theme

You can add your own pictures, sounds, and animations to themes you've created, and you can mix all types of files, such as pictures, sounds, and animated GIFs, in a single theme. (You can't add items to StarOffice default themes.)

1   Make sure Beamer is open. If it's not, click the Beamer button in the function bar.

2   In Explorer, double-click the folder containing the item(s) you want to add to the Gallery so that the contents of the folder appear in the workspace.

3   In the Explorer window, click the Gallery theme to which you want to add an item. If the selected theme is empty, Beamer shows a blank area.

4   Drag the file(s) from the work area to the Beamer.

If the thumbnail doesn't appear, right-click the theme folder and select Update. If it still doesn't appear, it probably means the Gallery doesn't support the type of file you're trying to add.

If you want to delete items from the Gallery, right-click the thumbnail you want to delete and select Delete. You can only delete Gallery items in themes you created.

Beamer and Databases

Beamer can display the contents of a database. This is useful for doing database searches and setting up mail merges.

1   Make sure Beamer is open. If it's not, click the Beamer button in the function bar.

2   In Explorer, select the database table you want to view. The table is displayed in Beamer.

Figure 3-13 shows more of Beamer's power and flexibility. Once the contents of a database table are displayed, you can, for example, drag database fields into a document or Email to create a mail merge.

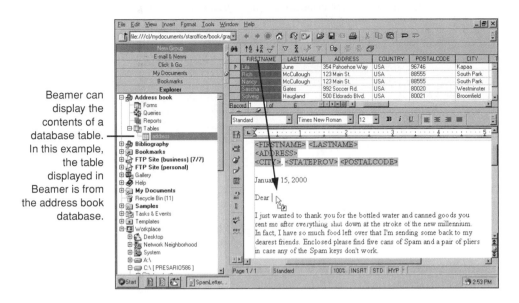

Beamer can display the contents of a database table. In this example, the table displayed in Beamer is from the address book database.

Figure 3-13   Beamer displaying the contents of a database table

Sorting and Resizing Columns in Beamer and the Work Area

When you're displaying files in Beamer or the work area, you can sort the files in ascending or descending order by category. Click the category heading by which you want to sort. Click again to reverse the order.

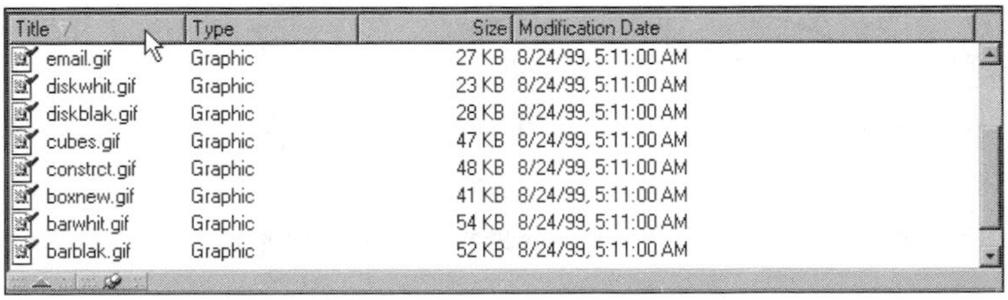

Title	Type	Size	Modification Date
email.gif	Graphic	27 KB	8/24/99, 5:11:00 AM
diskwhit.gif	Graphic	23 KB	8/24/99, 5:11:00 AM
diskblak.gif	Graphic	28 KB	8/24/99, 5:11:00 AM
cubes.gif	Graphic	47 KB	8/24/99, 5:11:00 AM
constrct.gif	Graphic	48 KB	8/24/99, 5:11:00 AM
boxnew.gif	Graphic	41 KB	8/24/99, 5:11:00 AM
barwhit.gif	Graphic	54 KB	8/24/99, 5:11:00 AM
barblak.gif	Graphic	52 KB	8/24/99, 5:11:00 AM

Figure 3-14   Sorting items in Beamer

You can resize the column widths in Beamer or the work area. Position the mouse pointer over a heading's divider line until the pointer changes. Then click and drag to the desired width, or double-click to resize to the longest item width in that column.

Title	Type	Size	Modification Date
email.gif	Grap...	27 KB	8/24/99, 5:11:00 AM
diskwhit.gif	Grap...	23 KB	8/24/99, 5:11:00 AM
diskblak.gif	Grap...	28 KB	8/24/99, 5:11:00 AM
cubes.gif	Grap...	47 KB	8/24/99, 5:11:00 AM
constrct.gif	Grap...	48 KB	8/24/99, 5:11:00 AM
boxnew.gif	Grap...	41 KB	8/24/99, 5:11:00 AM
barwhit.gif	Grap...	54 KB	8/24/99, 5:11:00 AM
barblak.gif	Grap...	52 KB	8/24/99, 5:11:00 AM

Figure 3-15   Resizing columns in Beamer

Using the StarOffice Recycle Bin

StarOffice acts so much like its own operating system that it even has its own Recycle Bin. When you delete a folder, a file, a shortcut icon, or anything else from the StarOffice work area, StarOffice sends it to its own Recycle Bin rather than to your operating system's Recycle Bin.

This means that even non-StarOffice files and folders you delete in the Explorer window are sent to the StarOffice Recycle Bin rather than to your operating system's Recycle Bin.

You can see the Recycle Bin in the Explorer window. By default, deleted items in the Recycle Bin are stored in `Office52\User\Store\Trash`.

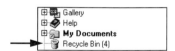

Undeleting Items From the StarOffice Recycle Bin

When you undelete, or restore, items from the Recycle Bin, they are put back in the location from where they were deleted.

1   In the Explorer window, open the Recycle Bin (double-click) or single-click to view it in Beamer.

If the Beamer window is open, you just need to single-click to view the Recycle Bin contents in Beamer.

2   Select the item(s) to be restored, right-click the selected item(s), and choose Restore.

You can also restore items by navigating in the Explorer window to the `Office52\User\Store\Trash` folder (or wherever you've set the Recycle Bin path) and moving the deleted items to another location in the file system.

Emptying the Recycle Bin

Emptying the Recycle Bin permanently deletes the items in it.

1   Right-click the Recycle Bin.

2   Choose Empty Recycle Bin.

You can also delete specific items from the Recycle Bin by selecting them and pressing the Delete key.

You can also choose to have items deleted directly without being sent to the Recycle Bin, or you can have the Recycle Bin automatically delete items it's held onto for a certain number of days. To set these options, right-click the Recycle Bin icon, choose Properties, and in the Options tab select the options you want.

Changing the Recycle Bin Path

By default, items deleted from the StarOffice work area are stored in `Office52\User\Store\Trash`. You can change the default path of this folder.

1   Choose Tools > Options > General > Paths.

2   In the list of paths, select Recycle Bin.

3   Click the Edit button.

4   In the Select Path window, navigate to the folder you want to use.

5   Click the Select button.

6   Click OK in the Options window.

Windows Note – Because the Windows Recycle Bin is not associated with a path in the file system, you can't set the StarOffice Recycle Bin to use the Windows Recycle Bin.

On a Network – Staying Current in Online Mode

If you use StarOffice on a network, stay in Online mode to ensure you see network directories and files in real time.

Clicking the Internet Online/Offline button on the function bar toggles between Online and Offline mode. When the button is pressed in, Online mode is active.

If you're running StarOffice on a standalone computer, switching to Offline mode is useful when you want to prevent automatic modem connections that might result from mistakenly clicking on a hyperlink to an Internet site.

StarOffice must be in online mode to access the Internet, though in offline mode you can
see any cached Web pages from previous online sessions.

Changing Paths to Folders

When you save, open, or insert a file, StarOffice opens the Save As, Open, and Insert
windows with a default folder selected. StarOffice uses two different default folders: one
for opening and saving files and one for inserting graphics. You can change either of these
default folders to make it easier to get to the folders you commonly use.

You'll find this feature extremely useful, especially if you spend a lot of time working in a
specific directory. For example, if you're going to be inserting a lot of graphics from a
specific folder, it's a hassle to click through a bunch of folders in the Insert window to
reach the folder you want. By resetting the graphics path to the folder you want, the Insert
window opens to that folder automatically. And if it doesn't, you can just click the Default
Directory button in the Insert window to show your folder.

1   Choose Tools > Options > General > Paths (see Figure 3-16).

2   In the list of paths, select the Graphics folder to change its default, or select the My
     Documents folder to change its default.

3   Click Edit.

4   In the Select Path window, navigate to the folder you want to use as your work folder
     and click Select.

5   Click OK.

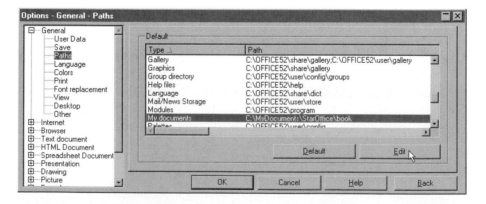

Figure 3-16   Changing default paths

Another benefit of changing the My Documents path is when you're working on a
network. In the Explorer window, under the Explorer group, the Workplace item
sometimes lists everyone's home directory, showing you more folders than you normally

want to see—especially if all you want to see is your home directory. By changing My Documents to your home directory, you can view only your home directory by clicking the My Documents slider in the Explorer window.

In the Paths window (Figure 3-16) you can change other system paths. Many are StarOffice system-level paths and should be left alone. You may want to change others at some point, such as the Download path. Download is the default folder for storing files downloaded from the Internet. And StarOffice crashes and you lose your work, check the path to the Backup copies to see where a possible backup copy may exist.

Note – If you want to revert back to the StarOffice default path for an item, select it in the Paths window and click the Default button.

Getting Help

This section describes some of the more useful ways of finding help for StarOffice.

Finding What You Need in this Book

One of the best things about StarOffice is that many of its features are shared. For example, you can insert spreadsheets and OLE objects in Writer, Impress, and other programs; drawing tools are available in Draw, Impress, Writer, and so on.

This means you have hundreds of features at your fingertips. However, it also means you might not be sure where to look for information on the topic. We generally cover major features like inserting objects in only one or two places. We use a lot of cross-references, but we don't cross-reference everything.

If you're looking for information on a feature in the chapter for your program and you can't find it, don't assume it's not in the book. It's probably just in another section. First and foremost we recommend you use the index. But in general, a lot of features are covered in the Writer section and in this Environment chapter. Draw and Impress share a lot of features, too, so if you can't find information in one, look in the other.

Help Agent

Help Agent is StarOffice's context-sensitive online help system. Wherever you are in StarOffice (the context), Help Agent displays help for that specific context. *Turning Off the Always-Present Help Agent* on page 117 shows you how to turn off Help Agent if it becomes annoying (because it

pops up constantly). But Help Agent can be useful—when you display it on your own terms—when you need it. Launch Help Agent with its button on the function bar.

You can also start the Help Agent by clicking the Help button in most windows in StarOffice.

Searching Help

In the main help window (Help > Contents) or in the Help Agent, you can click the Search Help button to search the help index or to search for specific text in help.

Writing Your Own Comments in Online Help

StarOffice lets you add your own comments in the main help system. Use comments to supplement the help system, especially when you find the answer to a problem that wasn't covered in online help. You can add only one comment per help topic, though the comment can be as long as you want it.

1   Launch online help and open the help topic to which you want to add a comment.

2   In the Online Help button bar, click the Write Comments button.

3   In the Comments window (see Figure 3-17), enter the comment you want to add and click OK.

    A Comment icon is displayed next to the help topic name.

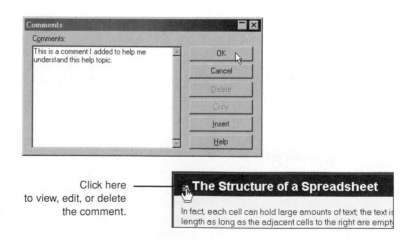

Figure 3-17   Adding your own notes to online help

Bookmarking Help Topics

If there's a help topic you know you'll be referencing a lot, create a bookmark for it to let you jump to it quickly.

1   Open the help topic you want to bookmark.

2   In the Online Help button bar, click the Insert Bookmark button.

A bookmark for the topic is displayed in the Help > Bookmark folder in Explorer, as shown in Figure 3-18. To jump to a bookmark, double-click it in Explorer.

Figure 3-18   Bookmarks into online help

Web Sites

Sun Microsystems maintains a StarOffice troubleshooting area on its Web site, called the Knowledge Database, for registered StarOffice users:
`http://www.sun.com/staroffice/knowledgedatabase`

You can also find answers in StarOffice newsgroups:
`news://starnews.sun.com`
See *Setting Up Newsgroup Accounts Manually* on page 948 for information on connecting to these newsgroups.

Also check the Web site of StarOffice guru Werner Roth:
`http://www.wernerroth.de/en/staroffice`

Turning Off Annoying Features

This section shows you how to turn off features that you don't want to use, or that you simply find annoying.

Turning Off the Integrated Desktop

StarOffice is such an integrated software package that it assimilates your operating system environment into its own environment. (If you're a Trekkie, images of the Borg are almost inescapable.) The effects of this assimilation differ among operating systems.

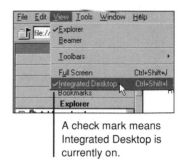

A check mark means Integrated Desktop is currently on.

If you don't want to use StarOffice as your pseudo-operating system, choose View > Integrated Desktop to remove the check mark from the menu option. If you don't see that menu item, or if Integrated Desktop is already deselected, choose View > Full Screen to get out of Full Screen mode.

You can turn Integrated Desktop or Full Screen back on with the same procedure.

Turning Off Help Tips

StarOffice help tips appear by default at the bottom of the desktop. If you don't want to view the help tips, here's how to turn them off:

1   Click the Don't display tips option under the help tips window (see Figure 3-19).

2   Click the Close button in the upper left of that window.

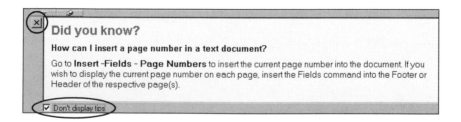

Figure 3-19   Turning off help tips

To turn the help tips back on:

1   Choose Tools > Options > General > Other.

2   Select the Show Tips option.

3   Click OK.

You must restart StarOffice to redisplay the help tips.

Turning Off the Always-Present Help Agent

StarOffice offers its own context-sensitive help system called the Help Agent (which is actually a useful feature, but it can be distracting if it pops up constantly). In theory it's similar to the Microsoft Office Assistant (the paper clip). By default, just about every time you start to perform a new task, the Help Agent window launches with information specific to the task you're trying to perform (assuming you close the window each time it launches).

StarOffice lets you turn off the Help Agent for all topics.

1   Choose Tools > Options > General > Other.

2   In the Help Agent section of the window, deselect the Start automatically option (see Figure 3-20).

3   Click OK.

You can reset Help Agent to its default behavior by selecting the Reset to default start settings option and clicking OK.

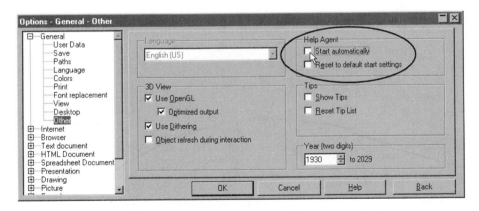

Figure 3-20   Turning off the Help Agent

Turning Off Auto Completion as You Type

As you type in a text or HTML document, StarOffice tries to guess what you're typing and inserts the rest of the words automatically. Most of the time the words StarOffice completes aren't the words you really want. To turn this feature off:

1   With a text or HTML document open, select Tools > AutoCorrect/AutoFormat.

2   Select the Word Completion tab.

3   Deselect the Complete Words option and click OK.

If you want to take the time to change the way StarOffice completes words by default, you can actually make this feature productive for you by limiting the words you want StarOffice to complete. For example, if in your business correspondence you use words that are tricky to spell or you're typing product names with trademark or copyright symbols over and over, you can limit Word Completion to those words.

See Figure 3-21 for tips on making Word Completion an asset rather than an annoyance.

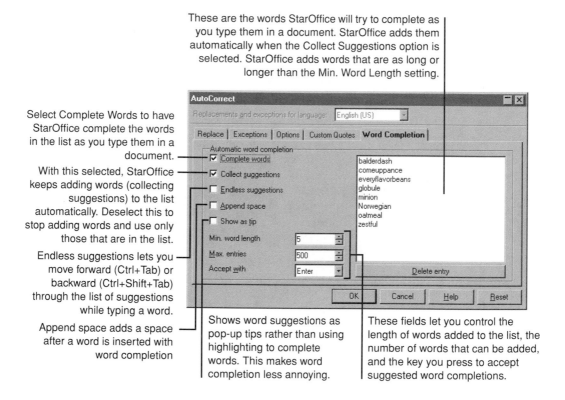

Figure 3-21   Setting Word Completion to be useful instead of annoying

Word completion works only on single words. If you want to insert more than one word automatically into a document, see *Creating and Inserting Predefined Text and Templates* on page 167.

Moving or Resizing StarOffice in Solaris

Sometimes when you start StarOffice in the Solaris environment, the window opens with the title bar hidden beyond reach at the top of the screen, making it impossible for you to minimize, maximize, or drag the window into view.

To move the window, hold down the Alt key while you drag the window down.

If StarOffice is full-screen and you want to minimize or resize it, choose View > Full Screen or View Integrated Desktop to remove the check mark next to either option.

Opening a File So It Doesn't Replace the Current Document

If you have a file open in StarOffice, and you double-click a file or folder in either the Explorer or Beamer window to open it, the new file or folder replaces the previously open file or folder. If the current file hasn't been saved, a dialog box appears and gives you the opportunity to open the new document in its own window (by clicking the "New Task" button).

If you have more than one file or folder open, the new file or folder you double-click to open replaces the file or folder that is currently open when you double-click.

This also happens when you double-click a bookmark or click a hyperlink in a document that opens another document.

There are a few ways to prevent this from happening:

• Hold down the Ctrl key while you double-click.

• Choose File > Open to open a new file.

• Set up hyperlinks and bookmarks to open in a new blank window automatically. See *Linking to a File, Site, or Event* on page 433.

Rearranging the Environment

You can change many aspects of the StarOffice environment to make it look, feel, and behave the way you want. Following are the more useful tips that affect the overall work environment.

Controlling Tooltips

StarOffice lets you control the display of its tooltips—the pop-up labels that display when the mouse pointer hovers over a button or menu item (see Figure 3-22). Tooltips are an excellent way to discover StarOffice features and capabilities without having to consult a manual or the StarOffice help system.

Basic tooltips display by default. You can also show more detailed (extended) tips, or turn tips off altogether. The following example shows a Tip and an Extended Tip for the same button.

Tips

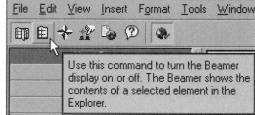
Extended Tips

Figure 3-22   Tips and Extended Tips

Controlling Tooltips Select Help > Tips, or Help > Extended Tips. This either adds or removes the check mark next to the menu item, depending on the current setting. A check mark means the feature is on.

If both Tips and Extended Tips are checked, Extended Tips display.

Making Windows Anchored or Floating

Many windows in StarOffice can be anchored to the StarOffice desktop (docked) rather than floating (undocked), as shown in Figure 3-23.

Docking a Window Hold down the Ctrl key and drag the undocked window from its title bar to the edge of the screen where you want it docked.

Undocking a Window Hold down the Ctrl key and double-click either the top of the docked window or an open area inside the window.

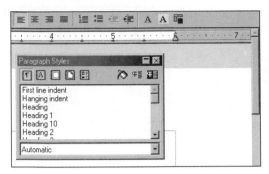 

Undocked Stylist window in Writer   Docked Stylist window in Writer

Figure 3-23   Undocked and docked windows

Showing and Hiding Docked Windows

A docked window has an arrow icon to let you show and hide the window.

Click the arrow to show and hide the docked window.

Figure 3-24   Showing and hiding a docked window

Preventing the Workspace From Running Under Docked Windows

When a docked window is open, the workspace may run under the window, preventing you from seeing the entire workspace. A docked window has a Stick Pin icon to let you bring the edge of the workspace to the outside edge of the docked window, preventing the workspace from running under the window (see Figure 3-25).

Icons are shown here running under the docked window.

Click the stick pin to prevent the desktop icons from running under the docked window.

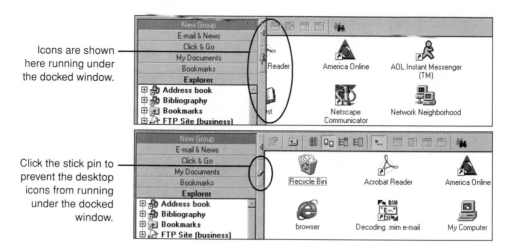

Figure 3-25   Preventing the workspace from running under docked windows

Collapsing Windows

You can collapse and expand many floating windows in StarOffice by double-clicking their title bars, as shown in Figure 3-26. This feature is useful when you want to work back and forth between a window and a document; for example, when you're making index entries.

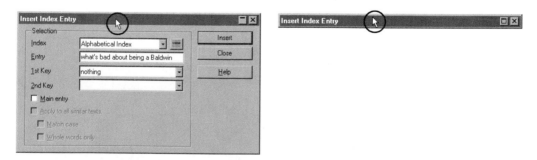

Figure 3-26   Collapsing and expanding windows

Adding Shortcuts to the Task Bar

You can add shortcuts to the StarOffice task bar for single-click access to programs, files, and folders.

1   In the Explorer window or Beamer, locate the icon for the program, file, or folder for which you want to create a shortcut.

2   Drag the icon to the empty space between the StarOffice Start button and desktop icon.

To remove a task bar shortcut, right-click it and select Remove.

Changing the Desktop Contents

The default desktop view StarOffice uses depends on the platform you're on. For example, on Solaris, the contents of the Click & Go group are displayed in the workspace; and on Windows, the icons on your Windows desktop are displayed. You can change what's displayed in the work area; for example, you can display the contents of one of your system folders on the desktop.

1   In StarOffice, navigate to the group of items you want to appear in your StarOffice work area; for example, the Click & Go group or a file folder in the Explorer window.

2   If you want to display an Explorer window group (such as Click & Go) in the StarOffice work area, right-click a blank area of the group and select Desktop.

If you want to display the contents of a folder in the work area, right-click the folder and select Desktop.

The group appears in the StarOffice work area.

You can change the contents of your work area by right-clicking the desktop icon and selecting a desktop from a list of those you've created.

Changing the work area contents

Note – You can also click and hold down the desktop icon to select an item from the current desktop, or to move through subfolders as you do by clicking and moving through the Start menu.

Adding Wallpaper to the Workspace

StarOffice lets you use pictures and graphics as background wallpaper for the StarOffice workspace. This is particularly useful when, for example, you're working nonstop on a very long book, and the only way you get to see your family is if you put a picture of them in the background of your workspace.

1   Right-click an empty spot on the workspace and select Properties.

2   In the Background tab of the Properties window, select Graphic in the As field.

3   Click Browse.

4   In the Find Graphics window, navigate to the folder containing the graphic you want to use.

    StarOffice full install includes a graphics library in `Office52\share\gallery`.

5   Select the graphic you want to use.

    Select the Preview option to view the selected graphic, as shown in Figure 3-27.

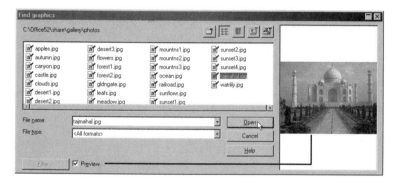

Figure 3-27   Finding the graphic you want to use as wallpaper

6   Click Open.

7   In the Properties window, select the Preview option and set the positioning of the graphic, as shown in Figure 3-28.

8   Click OK.

When you position the graphic in the Properties window, you have the following three options:

Position This option lets you position the graphic relative to the workspace, as shown in Figure 3-28.

Area This option stretches the graphic to fit within the entire workspace.

Tile This option duplicates the graphic multiple times to fill the entire workspace.

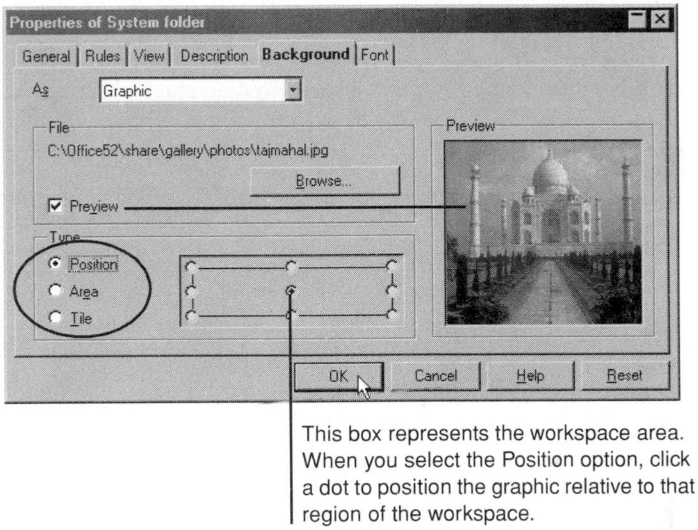

This box represents the workspace area. When you select the Position option, click a dot to position the graphic relative to that region of the workspace.

Figure 3-28   Positioning the graphic in relation to the workspace

Changing the Desktop Font

StarOffice uses your default operating system font for its own desktop environment. If you want to change the StarOffice desktop font without changing your default operating system font, use the StarOffice font replacement feature.

This procedure lets you change the font of all text that appears in the StarOffice environment, such as under icons, in menus, in help topics, and in windows.

Before you use this procedure, you have to locate your operating system's font settings to see which font is used. If you need help finding it, see your operating system's documentation.

Windows Note – In Windows, the system font is usually MS Sans Serif. You can double-check this by right-clicking the Windows desktop, choosing Properties, clicking the Appearance tab, clicking the menu bar in the picture of the Active Window, and looking in the Font field at the bottom of the Display Properties window.

1   In StarOffice, select Tools > Options > General > Font replacement.

2   Select the Apply replacement table option, as shown in Figure 3-29.

3   In the Font field, select the name of your operating system's default font.

4 In the Replace with field, select the name of the font you want to use as StarOffice's desktop font.

5 Click the green check mark button. The font substitution information is displayed in the main area of the window.

6 Select the check box in the Always column and the Screen column.

7 Click OK.

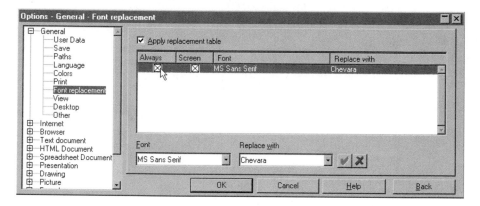

Figure 3-29 Changing the StarOffice desktop font

Note – While this procedure is used to make a cosmetic font change to your StarOffice desktop, it is a font replacement nonetheless. That means that if you're working with a document that happens to use the same font as the system font you're replacing, the font replacement will also be used in the document. For more information, see *Replacing Fonts* on page 146.

To revert back to the default desktop font, see *Removing Font Replacement* on page 147.

Previewing Fonts Before You Select Them

When you select a font from a drop-down list, StarOffice lets you see the font names in their actual fonts. To turn this feature on:

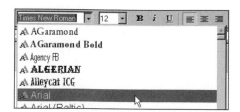

1 Choose Tools > Options > General > View.

2 Mark the Preview in fonts lists option.

3 Click OK.

Customizing Colors Used in StarOffice

The colors offered by StarOffice, whether for background color or font color, are based on a standard color palette (Figure 3-30). You can add to and modify this standard palette.

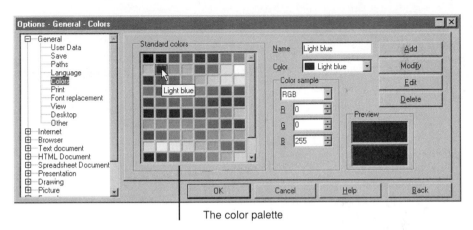

The color palette

Figure 3-30   Customizing colors used in StarOffice

There are two color formats used in StarOffice: RGB and CMYK. Use RGB (red, green, blue) colors in documents that will be viewed online. Use CMYK (cyan, magenta, yellow, black) colors in documents that will be printed to paper in color. Professional print shops that do color separations need colors to be CMYK.

Adding a Color

1   Choose Tools > Options > General > Colors.

2   Click the Add button.

3   In the Name field, type a name for the new color.

4   In the Color Sample area, select RGB or CMYK values and enter values that create the color you want, as displayed in the Preview area.

5   Click OK.

Editing a Color

1   Choose Tools > Options > General > Colors.

2   In the color palette, select the color you want to edit.

3   Either change its values manually in the Color Sample area, or click Edit and select a different color, and Click OK.

Working With Documents

This section provides useful tips for working with StarOffice documents.

Previewing Templates

StarOffice includes templates to help you create resumes, memos, fax cover sheets, budgets, calendars, slide presentations, newsletters, HTML documents, envelopes, and numerous other types of documents.

To get a better idea of what templates look like:

1   In the Explorer window, expand the Templates folder (by clicking the "+" sign next to it) and double-click the template category you want to view. The folder opens in the workspace.

2   In the workspace, select the template you want to preview.

3   In the object bar, click the Preview button. The template is displayed in the lower half of the workspace, as shown in Figure 3-31.

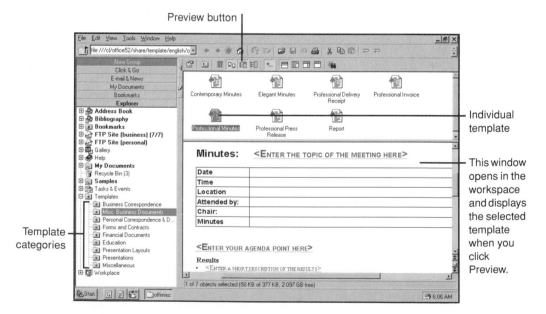

Figure 3-31   Previewing templates

You can also preview thumbnails of templates:

1   Choose File > New > From Template.

2   In the New window, click the More button.

3   Select the Preview option, as shown in Figure 3-32.

4   Select a template category in the Categories list, and select a template in the Templates list. The template is displayed in the Preview area.

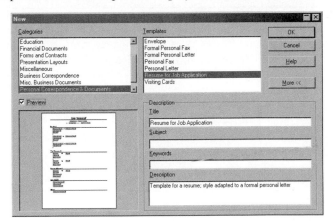

Figure 3-32   Viewing template thumbnails

If you click OK at this point, a new document is created based on the selected template.

Using Automatic File Extensions

When you save a document, you can have StarOffice add the file extension automatically. You should use this feature most of the time, especially if you can't remember the StarOffice extensions. Incorrect file extensions you type manually can make it difficult to track down files later.

In the Save As window, select the Automatic file name extension option before clicking Save (see Figure 3-33). StarOffice adds the extension automatically.

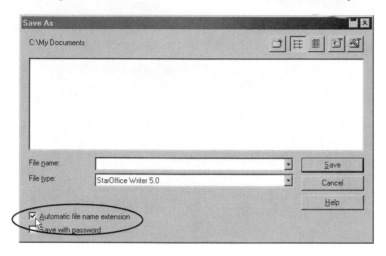

Figure 3-33   Adding file extensions automatically

Password-Protecting Documents

You can assign passwords to documents to keep unauthorized people from opening them. When you password-protect a document, you're prompted to enter the password when opening it.

1   In the Save As window, select the Save with password option.

2   When you click Save, the Enter Password window is displayed, as shown in Figure 3-34.

3   Type in a password, type the password again in the Confirm field, and click OK.

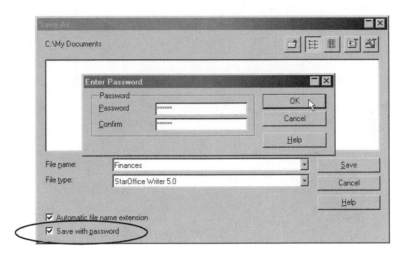

Figure 3-34   Password-protecting a document

Note – If you forget the password, you're out of luck. You can't open or print the document without it. You may want to write down document passwords somewhere, or store them in a text file in an obscure folder on your system.

To turn password protection off for a document, open the document, choose File > Save As, and deselect the Save with password option.

Changing File Paths in Dialog Boxes

In any dialog box or window that lets you navigate through your system folders (for example, the Save As window), you don't have to navigate solely by clicking the Up One Level and Default Directory buttons, or by double-clicking folders. You can also enter the path you want directly in the File name field and press Enter (see Figure 3-35).

Solaris Note – In Solaris, you can type the tilde symbol (~) in the File name field and press Enter to reach your home directory.

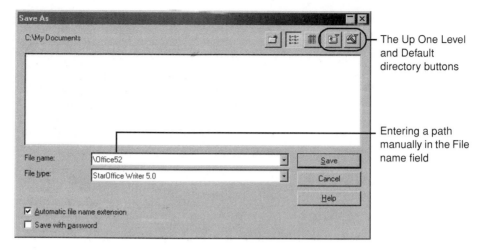

The Up One Level
and Default
directory buttons

Entering a path
manually in the File
name field

Figure 3-35   Navigating by typing a path directly in the File name field

Setting Document Save Options

StarOffice lets you set document save options such as automatically creating backup
copies of files, saving documents automatically at specific time intervals, and
remembering such details as which windows were open and where the cursor was last
positioned when you were last working in the document.

1   Select Tools > Options > General > Save (see Figure 3-36).

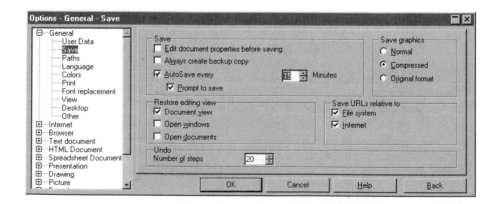

Figure 3-36   Setting Save options

2   Set Save options. Some options are self-explanatory. Table 3-3 describes those that
are not.

Table 3-3   Selected Save options

Option	Description
Document view	This option lets you open a document to the place where you were when you saved and closed it previously (for example, your cursor position, highlighted cell, and so on).
Open windows	If you close StarOffice with dialog boxes still open, this option automatically opens those dialog boxes next time you launch StarOffice.
Open documents	If you have documents open when you close StarOffice, this option automatically opens those documents when you launch StarOffice.
Save graphics	The following options apply to graphics that are inserted in documents as copies rather than links. Normal – Graphics are saved in standard format. Compressed – Raster (pixel) graphics are compressed in a StarOffice compression format. Vector graphics are not compressed. Original format – Saves the graphic as the original format. Any other computer that opens the file must support the formats of inserted graphics.
Save URLs relative to	This option determines how path names in file systems and Internet URLs are stored. Keep these options checked unless you have a specific reason not to. When you save a document, for example, in one folder (My Documents), and that document has a link to a document in another folder (public), you can save the path (the URL) from one document to another relatively or absolutely. Absolutely means that a path to a document, for example, is exactly `C:\My Documents\public`. If you moved the two folders as a group to another location, the link would be broken, because the path would no longer be `C:\My Documents\public`. Saving documents with relative paths, however, ensures that you could move the `My Documents\public` set of folders to a different location and the links will still work correctly.
Undo	The Number of Steps field lets you set how many steps to keep in memory for the Undo feature. If you set the number to 10, for example, you can undo up to your past 10 actions. The more steps you add, the more RAM that is used. The maximum number of steps is 100.

Working With Documents Side by Side

As you open different documents in StarOffice, you normally switch between them by clicking their icons in the task bar and working on them individually. But StarOffice gives you a few options for viewing multiple documents at once in the work area.

These features are particularly useful when you want to drag and drop, copy, cut, and paste information between documents.

Arranging Documents Vertically or Horizontally

StarOffice can arrange your open documents so they're all visible next to each other vertically or horizontally. This is a great feature, but if you have more than two documents open, the screen can get crowded.

StarOffice simply reduces the size of the document windows, as shown in Figure 3-37. Each has its own option bar, toolbar, and status bar, and you can minimize and maximize the windows.

1   With the documents open you want to view side-by-side, choose Window > Vertically (or Horizontally).

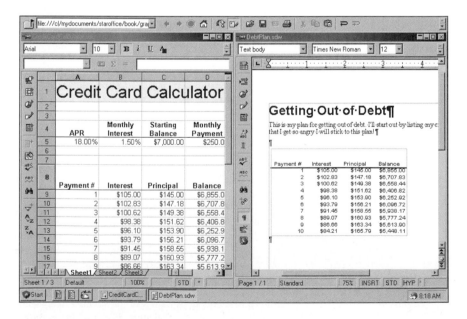

Figure 3-37   Documents arranged vertically

2   To get out of vertical or horizontal mode, simply resize or maximize the windows.

Combining Document Icons

Instead of arranging separate document windows, this procedure combines documents and displays them side-by-side in a single window, combining their icons on the task bar into a single icon.

Viewing the Documents Together In the task bar, drag the icon of one open document onto the icon of the other open document, as shown in Figure 3-38.

Figure 3-38   Dragging one document's icon onto another document icon

Both documents display in the work area. Each has its own scroll bars, but they share a single toolbar, object bar, status bar, and task bar icon, all of which change when you switch between documents. The menu bar also changes when you switch between documents.

For example, say you have a Writer document and a Calc spreadsheet side-by-side. When you're working with the Writer document, the object bar and toolbar show buttons that are unique to Writer. When you click in the spreadsheet, the toolbar and object bar change to show buttons that are unique to Calc.

The now single task bar icon changes names depending on which document the cursor is in.

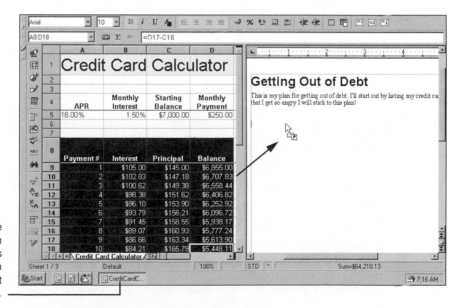

Figure 3-39   Working between documents that have a combined icon

Figure 3-39 illustrates a powerful StarOffice feature: you can drag elements of one document into another document. In the example, selected cells in Calc are dragged into a Writer document.

You can still work with each file as if each is separate, and you can save each file separately.

Viewing the Documents Separately Again Click and hold the icon for the combined documents and drag to an open area of the task bar, as shown in Figure 3-40.

Figure 3-40   Separating documents that have a combined icon

Controlling How StarOffice Changes Text

As you type in StarOffice, a lot of interesting—and unexpected—things can happen. For example, words are capitalized automatically, spelling is changed, words are completed, fractions are reformatted, and internet URLs turn into hyperlinks. Any of these automatic changes can be helpful or annoying, depending on what you want to happen. The good thing is that you can control exactly how StarOffice makes automatic changes.

The place to control these changes is in the AutoCorrect window. With a document open, choose Tools > AutoCorrect. With a text or HTML document open, the menu option is called AutoCorrect/AutoFormat.

The following procedures cover different aspects of the AutoCorrect window.

Correcting and Formatting as You Type

If you make consistent typos such as "teh" instead of "the," or if you want to create an automatic copyright symbol "©" by typing "(C)", you can have StarOffice apply those changes automatically as you type.

1   With a document of some type open, choose Tools > AutoCorrect. (With a text or HTML document open, the menu item is AutoCorrect/AutoFormat.)

2   In the AutoCorrect window, select the Replace tab, which displays the current text replacement settings, as shown in Figure 3-41.

3   In the Replace field, type the typo or character you want to replace with something else.

4   In the With field, type the replacement word or character.

5   Click the New button.

6   When you're finished creating replacements, click OK.

To enter a special character, such as a © symbol, close the AutoCorrect window, insert the special character in a document (Insert > Special Character), copy it, open the AutoCorrect window, and paste the character into the Replace or With fields.

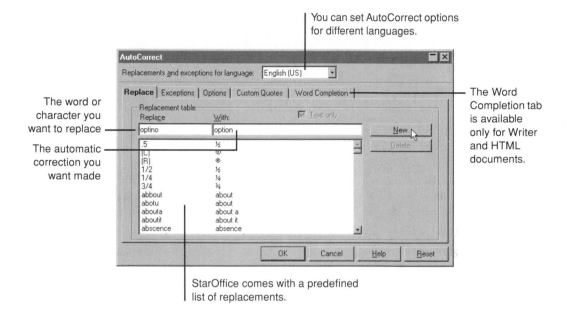

Figure 3-41   The AutoCorrect window

To delete a replacement, select it in the list and click the Delete button.

If you use spreadsheets, you should delete the line that replaces .5 with 1/2.

Controlling Capitalization

By default, StarOffice tries to capitalize the first letter after a period and a space. For example, if you use "attn." as shorthand for "attention," StarOffice capitalizes the first letter of the next word in the sentence.

StarOffice also changes words that begin with two capital letters by changing the second capital to lowercase. This feature is designed for fast typists who sometimes don't let go of the Shift key quickly enough before typing the second letter of a word. But there may be certain words that you do want to begin with two capital letters. For example, if you type the name of a software company called "MSmonopoly," StarOffice changes the second letter to lowercase to make "Msmonopoly." (Since this rule applies only to words that begin with two capitals, StarOffice won't change words that begin with three or more capitals, such as "MSMonopoly," because it assumes since you haven't let go of the Shift key by the third letter, you intentionally want capital letters.)

To stop this behavior altogether, see Activating and Deactivating Automatic Changes, next. However, if you want StarOffice to make the changes automatically in some cases but not in others, use this procedure to add exceptions to those rules. StarOffice comes with a default set of predefined exceptions to prevent automatic first-letter capitalizations.

1   With a document of some type open, choose Tools > AutoCorrect. (With a text or HTML document open, the menu item is AutoCorrect/AutoFormat.)

2   In the AutoCorrect window, select the Exceptions tab.

3   Type an exception you want to add in either the Abbreviations or Words with TWo INitial CApitals fields, and click New to add it to the list, as shown in Figure 3-42.

4   When you're finished, click OK.

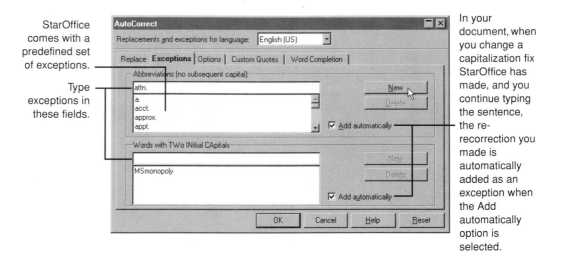

StarOffice comes with a predefined set of exceptions.

Type exceptions in these fields.

In your document, when you change a capitalization fix StarOffice has made, and you continue typing the sentence, the re-recorrection you made is automatically added as an exception when the Add automatically option is selected.

Figure 3-42   Controlling automatic capitalization by creating exceptions

To delete an exception, select it in the list and click the Delete button.

Activating and Deactivating Automatic Changes

This procedure shows you how to activate and deactivate the specific types of automatic text changes StarOffice makes.

1   With a document of some type open, choose Tools > AutoCorrect. (With a text or HTML document open, the menu item is AutoCorrect/AutoFormat.)

2   In the AutoCorrect window, select the Options tab.

3   Select or deselect the types of automatic corrections you want StarOffice to make.

    See Table 3-4 for descriptions of the options.

4 When you're finished, click OK.

StarOffice gives you clues about the functionality of some options by the way it names them. For example, TWo INitial CApitals illustrates the types of words that feature will change automatically; and the Automatic *bold* and _underline_ option shows you the characters you need to type on the keyboard to automatically bold or underline words.

An option is activated if there's an "x" in its check box.

Table 3-4 Options for automatic text changes StarOffice can make

Option	Description
Use replacement table	Uses the replacements listed in the Replace tab of the AutoCorrect window.
Correct TWo INitial CApitals	This is a great feature for fast typists. It automatically sets a second letter from capital to lowercase when you don't let go of the Shift key quickly enough after typing a first capital letter. You can set exceptions to this rule in the Exceptions tab of the AutoCorrect window.
Capitalize first letter of every sentence	After you type a period and a space, this feature automatically changes the next letter to a capital if you type it lowercase. You can set exceptions to this rule in the Exceptions tab of the AutoCorrect window.
Automatic *bold* and _underline_	Automatically turns a word bold if you type an asterisk before and after the word, and underlines a word if you type an underscore character before and after the word.
URL recognition	If you type a group of characters that StarOffice thinks is a link to a Web site (a URL), such as `http://www.sun.com`, this feature automatically converts the group of characters into a hyperlink. Instead of turning this feature off, you can remove URL hyperlinking in your document on a case-by-case basis by pressing Ctrl+Z to undo the automatic hyperlink after it happens, or by dragging through the hyperlink to select it and choosing Format > Default.
Replace 1st... with 1st...	If you type 1st, 2nd, 3rd, 4th, etc., this option automatically makes the letters after the number superscript, such as 1st, 2nd, 3rd, 4th.
Replace 1/2... with $\frac{1}{2}$...	When you type a fraction (two numbers separated by a forward slash), this feature changes the fraction to a special character. Only fractions that have corresponding special characters for the current font are converted. Most standard fonts have only three special characters for the fractions 1/4, 1/2, and 3/4.

Table 3-4   Options for automatic text changes StarOffice can make (continued)

Option	Description
Replace dashes	When you type a dash with a space on either side of it, this option converts the dash from a hyphen to a longer en dash.
Ignore double spaces	This option lets you type only a single space between characters.
Apply Numbering - Symbol:	This option works only when you use the "Standard," "Text body," or "Text body indent" paragraph styles. If you type a number followed by a period, a space (or tab), and some text, then press Enter, this option autonumbers the paragraph as if you clicked the numbering icon in the object bar. If you type a hyphen followed by a space (or tab) and some text, then press Enter, the hyphen is converted to a long dash bullet character. If you type a + or a * character followed by a space (or tab) and some text, the paragraph becomes bulleted as if you clicked the bullets icon in the object bar. You can change the bullet character used for the + or * symbol by selecting the name of this option in the AutoCorrect window and clicking the Edit button.
Apply border	With this option, typing certain characters in succession and pressing Enter automatically creates a border line under the paragraph. The following character combinations illustrate the respective types of borders they create. --- becomes === becomes *** becomes ~~~ becomes ### becomes You can modify the border by clicking in the paragraph just above the line, choosing Format > Paragraph, and changing the setting on the Borders tab. To remove a border added with this option, click in the paragraph just above the line and choose Format > Default.

Table 3-4   Options for automatic text changes StarOffice can make (continued)

Option	Description
Create table	With this option activated, you can create a table from the keyboard by typing a '+' to signify column borders, typing successive '-' characters to signify column widths, and pressing Enter at the end of the line. For example, typing +----------------------+---------------------------+------------+ and pressing Enter creates a three-column table.
Apply styles	This option is for applying heading formats automatically, and works only when you use the "Standard" paragraph style. When you begin a paragraph with a capital letter and don't end the sentence with a period, pressing Enter twice at the end of the line automatically changes the line to the Heading 1 paragraph style. The extra paragraph below the heading is removed. If you press the Tab key twice before typing the heading text, pressing the Enter key twice at the end of the line automatically changes the line to the Heading 2 paragraph style. Three tabs creates a Heading 3, and so on.
Remove blank paragraphs	With this option activated, choose Format > AutoFormat > Apply (or Apply and Edit Changes) to remove all blank paragraphs from your document. If you're using StarOffice's direct cursor, this option is indispensable.
Replace custom styles	With this option activated, choose Format > AutoFormat > Apply (or Apply and Edit Changes) to convert any custom styles applied in your document to their equivalent default StarOffice styles.
Replace bullets with:	This option works only on paragraphs using the "Standard" paragraph style. The paragraphs must begin with a '*', '+', or '-', be followed by a space (or tab) and some text. With this option activated, choose Format > AutoFormat > Apply (or Apply and Edit Changes) to convert these paragraphs into bulleted paragraphs with a bullet character of your choice. To change the bullet character used, select the name of this option in the AutoCorrect window and click the Edit button.
Replace "standard" quotes with „custom" quotes	With this option activated, choose Format > AutoFormat > Apply (or Apply and Edit Changes) to convert single and double quote marks to the quote characters that are set in the Custom Quotes tab of the AutoCorrect window.

Table 3-4   Options for automatic text changes StarOffice can make (continued)

Option	Description
Combine single line paragraphs if length greater than %	This option works only on paragraphs using the "Standard" paragraph style. With this option activated, choose Format > AutoFormat > Apply (or Apply and Edit Changes) to combine adjacent, single-line paragraphs into a single paragraph. The single-line paragraphs must be at least as wide (with relation to the total page width) as the percentage set for this option. To change the percentage on this option, select the option name in the AutoCorrect window and click the Edit button.
	If you activate this option while you have existing text in the document, none of the existing text is affected. Only the text you type after you activate the option is affected.

Controlling Quote Marks

The most common use of this feature is to control the type of quotation marks used in a document. More specifically, use this feature to switch back and forth between using straight quotes and curly quotes (called "smart quotes" in other applications).

This feature also lets you substitute single and double quotes with any other characters you want.

1   With a document of some type open, choose Tools > AutoCorrect. (With a text or HTML document open, the menu item is AutoCorrect/AutoFormat.)

2   In the AutoCorrect window, select the Custom Quotes tab.

3   Set the options for using quotes.

    Use Figure 3-43 for guidance.

4   Click OK.

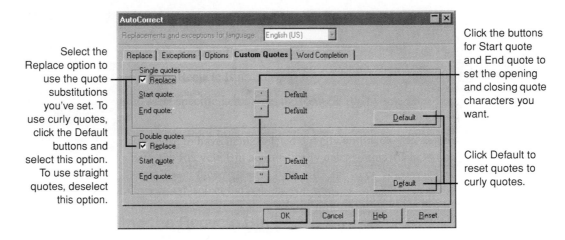

Select the Replace option to use the quote substitutions you've set. To use curly quotes, click the Default buttons and select this option. To use straight quotes, deselect this option.

Click the buttons for Start quote and End quote to set the opening and closing quote characters you want.

Click Default to reset quotes to curly quotes.

Figure 3-43   Setting quote options

Controlling Word Completion

See *Turning Off Auto Completion as You Type* on page 117. This procedure is in the Turning Off Annoying Features section, but it also shows you ways to make automatic word completion more of a help than a hindrance.

Customizing Spelling and Language Options

StarOffice's Spelling and Language options lets you customize the way spell check behaves; manage the words used for spell check by letting you add, edit, and remove dictionaries; and set global hyphenation options.

Customizing Spell Check

Whether you use spell check manually (Tools > Spellcheck > Check) or automatically (by clicking the AutoSpellcheck icon in the toolbar to underline misspelled words), you can set the rules for spell check.

1   Choose Tools > Options > General > Language.

2   In the Check Spelling area of the Options window, select the options you want, as shown in Figure 3-44.

3   Click OK.

The Check special regions option applies to parts of a document such as headers and footers.

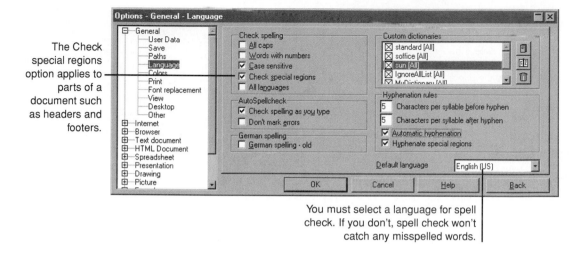

You must select a language for spell check. If you don't, spell check won't catch any misspelled words.

Figure 3-44   Setting Spelling and Language options

Turning Automatic Spell Check On and Off

The automatic spell checking feature places a squiggly line under misspelled words (words the StarOffice dictionary doesn't recognize).

1   Choose Tools > Options > General > Language.

2   Select the Check spelling as you type option to turn on automatic spell check, as shown in Figure 3-44.

3   Click OK.

The Check spelling as you type option affects all documents you work with in StarOffice. You can, however, turn automatic spell check on and off while working in a document by clicking the AutoSpellcheck button on the toolbar.

Adding a Custom Dictionary

StarOffice performs spell check against a system dictionary (or more than one dictionary if you installed support for more than one language). It also checks spelling against custom dictionaries. StarOffice lets you add and modify custom dictionaries.

The main reason to use a custom dictionary is to speed the spell check process. If you're going to use terms in your documents that a spell check would normally catch (such as product names, unique spellings of common words, and so on), you can add these words to a custom dictionary so that spell check will recognize them.

1   Choose Tools > Options > General > Language.

2 In the Custom Dictionaries area, click the New button.

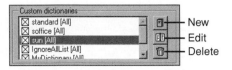

3 In the New Dictionary window, type the name of the dictionary, select the applicable language, and click OK.

4 In the Options window, select the new dictionary and click the Edit button.

5 In the Edit Custom Dictionary window (Figure 3-45), add the dictionary terms you want. When you're finished, click Close.

6 To use the custom dictionary in spell checks, click the box next to it in the custom dictionaries list to put an 'x' next to it.

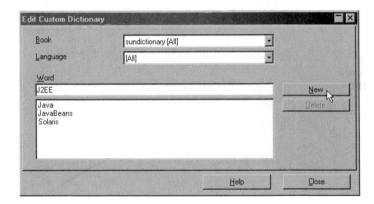

Figure 3-45   Adding terms to a dictionary

Setting Hyphenation Rules

StarOffice's Language options let you set default global hyphenation rules for StarOffice documents. The settings are only default, which means they can be overridden by modifying individual paragraph formats in text, HTML, and presentation documents.

1 Choose Tools > Options > General > Language.

2 In the Hyphenation rules section of the Options window, set the rules you want.

Use Figure 3-46 for guidance.

3 Click OK.

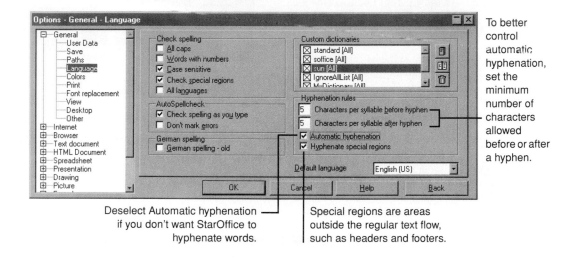

To better control automatic hyphenation, set the minimum number of characters allowed before or after a hyphen.

Deselect Automatic hyphenation if you don't want StarOffice to hyphenate words.

Special regions are areas outside the regular text flow, such as headers and footers.

Figure 3-46   Setting default hyphenation rules

Once hyphenation has occurred throughout a text, HTML, or presentation document, you can change the hyphenation of individual occurrences by choosing Tools > Hyphenation and moving among hyphenated words.

Replacing Fonts

StarOffice has a feature called Font Replacement that can serve multiple purposes. With Font Replacement you can:

- Change the desktop font used in StarOffice (see *Changing the Desktop Font* on page 125).

- Convert one font to another in documents you view and print in StarOffice; for example, if you want to view a document with TrueType fonts but print it using postscript fonts.

- Replace a font you don't have installed on your system that is used in a document with a font you do have installed.

This procedure covers the second and third of these situations, since the first situation is covered earlier in this chapter.

1   In StarOffice, select Tools > Options > General > Font Replacement.

2   Select the Apply replacement table option.

3   In the Font field, select the name of the font you want to replace.

4   In the Replace with field, select the name of the font you want to use as the replacement.

5   Click the green check mark button, as shown in Figure 3-47. The font substitution information is displayed in the main area of the window.

6   Select or deselect the check boxes in the Always and Screen columns for the type of font replacement you want.

   •   Always – Select this option to apply the replacement regardless of whether or not the font is installed on your system. If you want to use a replacement only if the font isn't available on your system, deselect this option.

   •   Screen – Select this option if you want the font replacement to appear in the screen only, and not in the printout of the document. Deselect this option if you want the font replacement to print out as well.

7   Click OK.

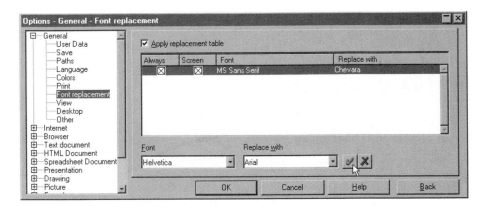

Figure 3-47   Setting up Font Replacement

Removing Font Replacement

Use this procedure to delete a font replacement.

1   Select Tools > Options > General > Font Replacement.

2   In the list of replacements, select the replacement you want to remove and click the red X button.

3   Click OK.

If you want to leave font substitution information intact but disabled, deselect the Apply replacement table option and click OK.

Setting Default Zoom View for Documents

When you create a new document, the blank starting page (whether it's a text document, a spreadsheet, or a slideshow presentation), opens in a standard zoom view, or scale. If you want new document pages to appear larger or smaller in the work area, change its default scaling percentage.

1   Select Tools > Options > General > View.

2   In the View window, change the percentage in the Scaling field.

3   Click OK.

Opening Corrupt Documents

Once in a while (but not too often) a file will become corrupt, resulting in a couple of possible things happening when you try to open the corrupt file: a message telling you the file is corrupt, or StarOffice crashing.

Use this procedure to open a corrupt file, which will recover most if not all of the data.

1   Choose File > Open.

2   In the Open window, select the corrupt file.

3   Press Ctrl+Alt+L.

4   Click OK in the message box that appears.

5   Click the Open button to open the file.

6   Choose File > Save As, and give the file a new name.

You can then open the new file normally.

Converting Microsoft Office Documents

The easiest way to convert a single Microsoft Word, Excel, or PowerPoint document to a StarOffice format is simply to open it in StarOffice and save it as a StarOffice Writer, Calc, or Impress document. You can even get tricky and, for example, open a Word 95 document in Writer and save it as a Word 97 document.

While StarOffice can also open documents created in many other applications, it has an automated tool called the AutoPilot for converting Microsoft Word, Excel, and PowerPoint documents and templates to StarOffice documents and templates. One of the most powerful AutoPilot features is that it can convert entire folders of Microsoft Office documents and templates to StarOffice documents and templates in one shot.

1   Select File > AutoPilot > Microsoft Import.

2   Read the first window of Microsoft Office Import AutoPilot, then click Continue.

3   At the top of the next window, click the button for Word, Excel, or PowerPoint and set the appropriate options, as shown in Figure 3-48.

Set options for each of those applications as appropriate. Click Continue.

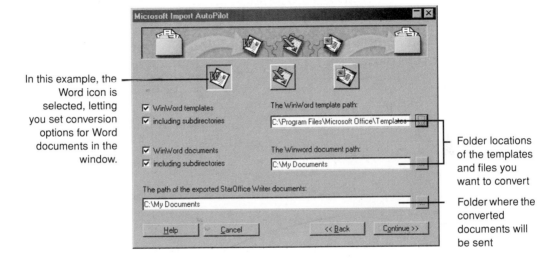

In this example, the Word icon is selected, letting you set conversion options for Word documents in the window.

Folder locations of the templates and files you want to convert

Folder where the converted documents will be sent

Figure 3-48   Second window of the Microsoft Office Import AutoPilot

4   In the next window, review the current settings in the Summary area, as shown in Figure 3-49.

You can also change the default names of the StarOffice template folders that will be created for storing the Word, Excel, and PowerPoint templates that are converted to StarOffice templates.

This area lists the options you've set.

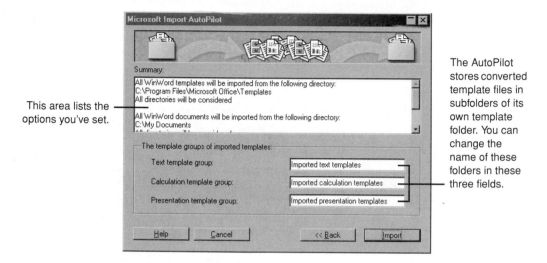

The AutoPilot stores converted template files in subfolders of its own template folder. You can change the name of these folders in these three fields.

Figure 3-49   Third window of the Microsoft Office Import AutoPilot

5   Click the Import button to run the conversion.

StarOffice Writer

Getting Started With Writer

Quick Start

This section contains the following information to help you get started quickly:

- A checklist that points you to common tasks for quick reference
- Feature overview
- Multiple ways of starting Writer
- An overview of the Writer work area
- A guided tour

See 3, *Taming the StarOffice Environment*, on page 91 for general tips that can make working with StarOffice a lot easier.

Quick Start Checklist

If you need to create a document quickly, the following sections should be particularly helpful:

- Starting a document based on a template – *Creating a Writer Document From a Template* on page 165
- Adding headers and footers – *Inserting Headers and Footers* on page 268
- Adding page numbers – *Page Numbering* on page 284
- Formatting paragraphs – *Paragraph Formatting* on page 184
- Adding graphics – *Inserting a Graphic File* on page 228, *Inserting a StarOffice Gallery Image* on page 229, and *Tips for Adjusting Inserted Objects* on page 256
- Printing and creating PDF files – 11, *Printing in StarOffice Writer*, on page 347

StarOffice Writer Features

Writer is every bit as powerful as any word processing application on the market, and in many ways it's superior. Following are some of the features that set Writer apart:

Document Filters Writer has a huge number of filters for opening documents created in other formats. Its filter for Microsoft Word is particularly good.

Graphics Support You can insert graphics of just about every conceivable format, including Adobe Photoshop PSD.

Conversion From Microsoft The AutoPilot (wizard) lets you convert Microsoft Office documents (even entire directories of them) with a few clicks.

Book Creation Writer offers superior features for creating multi-file books.

Table Features You can perform calculations in Writer tables, and create charts to illustrate the table data. Charts update dynamically when table contents change. Another indispensable table feature is repeatable table headings: type it once, and when a table breaks to a new page the heading appears on the next page automatically.

Text Selection Writer lets you select nonconsecutive blocks of text.

Version Control You can store versions of a Writer document as it moves through a lifecycle, letting you revert back to an earlier version if necessary. Writer also offers a full set of editing aids that display changes made to a document.

With the conditional sections feature, you can select any parts of your document and assign conditional names to those parts. You can then hide or password-protect those conditional sections, letting you show and hide sections to create different versions of the same document. (See *Using Sections* on page 337 for practical ways to use this feature.) Sections also support content reuse, letting you insert links to sections in other documents, and those sections are updated automatically when the source sections change.

Mail Merge When you're creating a mail merge, StarOffice lets you drag database fields from a database and drop them into a Writer document.

Table of Contents Hyperlinking For easy troubleshooting of tables of contents, or to let readers jump to sections in a document automatically, Writer lets you set up hyperlinks in table of contents entries.

Starting Writer

You can start Writer in a number of ways:

- Start > Text Document
- File > New > Text Document
- From the Click & Go slider in the Explorer window (clicking the Text shortcut)
- With a task bar shortcut (see *Adding Shortcuts to the Task Bar* on page 123)

The Writer Work Area

Use tooltips to get to know Writer. There are tooltips for almost all StarOffice fields and icons. Just position your mouse over anything you want to know the name of. You can turn tooltips on and off by choosing Help > Tips.

Clicking the Help button in a window or pressing F1 is the quickest way to get help for that window. If only general help appears, click in a field in the window.

Figure 4-1 shows the major components of the Writer environment.

The **function bar** displays the path of the open file and lets you access global functions.

In addition to showing global StarOffice commands, the **menu bar** shows commands specific to the active application.

The **object bar** lets you apply formatting to selected text.

The **ruler** lets you view page dimensions and set tab stops. Right-click the ruler to change the unit of measurement shown on the ruler.

The **toolbar** lets you access commonly used word processing features.

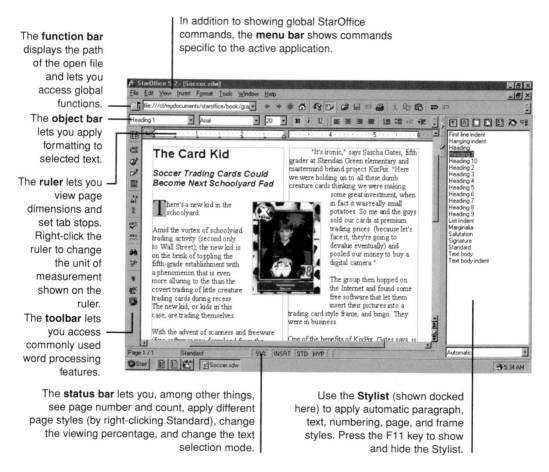

The **status bar** lets you, among other things, see page number and count, apply different page styles (by right-clicking Standard), change the viewing percentage, and change the text selection mode.

Use the **Stylist** (shown docked here) to apply automatic paragraph, text, numbering, page, and frame styles. Press the F11 key to show and hide the Stylist.

Figure 4-1   The Writer work area

Guided Tour

Use this tutorial to give you a brief introduction to the Writer environment.

1 Launch Writer.

2 Type the following in the document: `Gift Ideas for the Boss`

3 Press the F11 key to display the Stylist.

4 Hold down the Ctrl key, put the mouse pointer on the Stylist title bar, drag the window into the right edge of the Writer work area, and release the Ctrl key and mouse button. The Stylist docks to the Writer work area, as shown in Figure 4-2.

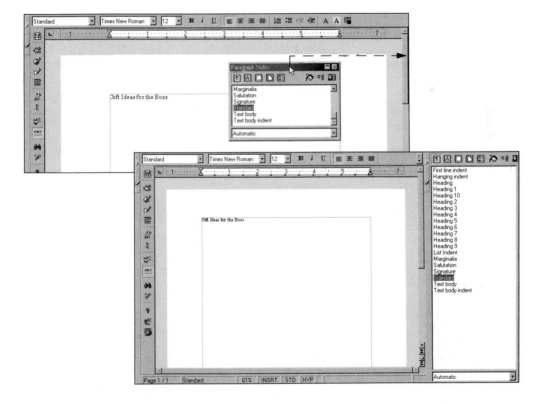

Figure 4-2   Docking a window

5 In the Stylist, make sure the Paragraph Styles icon is selected to display the paragraph styles.

6   Right-click the zoom percentage box in the status bar and select a percentage that displays the document in a comfortable size for you.

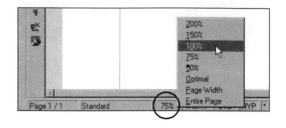

7   Click in the text you typed. In the Stylist, double-click Heading 1. The text you typed changes.

8   Press the End key to jump to the end of the line, and press Enter.

9   Type the following four paragraphs (pressing Enter at the end of each):

```
Following are the top three gift ideas for the boss:

New crystal ball

Replacement case of spearmint Euphoria Gum

Machiavelli's Essential New Age Guide to Dealing With
Smart Aleck Minions
```

10 Select the last three paragraphs by dragging through them.

11 In the object bar, click the bullets icon. If you don't see the icon, use Figure 4-3 for guidance.

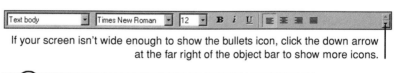

If your screen isn't wide enough to show the bullets icon, click the down arrow at the far right of the object bar to show more icons.

Figure 4-3   Showing more icons

The last three sentences become a bulleted list.

12 With the bulleted paragraphs still highlighted, click the Increase Indent icon in the object bar. The list indents to the right.

13 Click in the `Gift Ideas for the Boss` heading paragraph, and select Format > Paragraph.

14   In the Paragraph window (Figure 4-4), on the Indents & Spacing tab, change the
Bottom spacing to .25 (don't forget the decimal point in front).

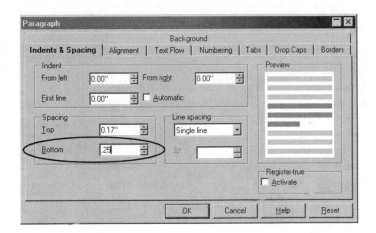

Figure 4-4   The Paragraph window

15   Click OK. The space increases between the heading paragraph and the first body
paragraph.

16   Select the entire heading paragraph and select Format > Character.

17   In the Character window (Figure 4-5), on the Font tab, change the color to Red.

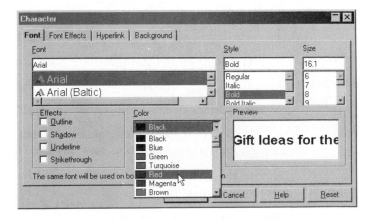

Figure 4-5   The Character window

18   Click OK. The paragraph font color changes to Red.

19   Click at the end of the last bulleted paragraph and press Enter. Another bullet is
displayed.

20   Click the Bullets icon to end the bulleted list, or just press Enter again.

In the next steps you'll insert a table. You may need to adjust your zoom percentage to see more of the page.

21   In the toolbar click and hold down the Insert icon. Another set of icons is displayed.

22   Move the pointer to the table icon. A small table picture is displayed below the icon. Move the pointer into the table picture so that two columns and four rows are selected (Figure 4-6), and release the mouse button.

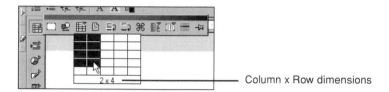

Column x Row dimensions

Figure 4-6   Inserting a two-column, four-row table

A two-column, four-row table is inserted into the document.

23   In the two heading row cells, type the following:

```
Gift      Price
```

Notice the table headings have their own paragraph format.

24   Type the gift names in the remaining cells of the Gift column, and type their prices in the Price cells. (After you enter the last price, click below the table.)

```
Crystal Ball              $45

Euphoria Gum              $18

Machiavelli's Guide       $120
```

Because you added dollar signs, StarOffice automatically adds .00 to the end of the numbers.

In the final steps you'll insert a header that includes the date and page number.

25   Select Insert > Header > Standard. A header text box is displayed.

26 In the main toolbar, click and hold down the Insert Fields icon, and select Date. The current date is displayed in the header.

27 Press the Tab key twice.

28 Click and hold down the Insert Fields icon again, and select Page Numbers. The page number is displayed in the right side of the header.

Post-Tutorial Tip

When you applied the Heading 1 paragraph style to your heading earlier in the exercise, the heading took on automatic format properties (font, font size, font color, and spacing between the heading and the first body paragraph). Let's say that after you made these changes to the heading (increasing the space between paragraphs and changing the font color to red), you wanted all your Heading 1 paragraphs to have the new formats. Simply highlight the entire paragraph, then click and drag it onto the Heading 1 item in the Stylist, as shown in Figure 4-7.

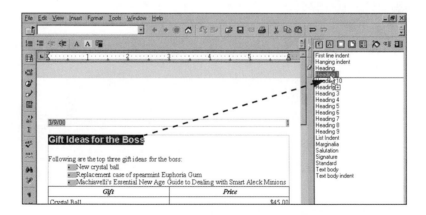

Figure 4-7   Updating a style by dragging and dropping

Writer Setup Options

StarOffice lets you control hundreds of options—probably more than you will ever need to control. Choose Tools > Options > Text document to view the Writer options.

We don't go through each window of options one by one, for the following reasons:

* The important settings are covered in procedures throughout the book.

* Many are self-explanatory.

* The default settings for these options are generally well chosen.

However, the options aren't in an obvious place in any of the menu bars or object bars—you need to choose Tools > Options > Text document—so we've pointed them out here to make sure you're aware of them (see Figure 4-8). It's also helpful to know what types of functions these options do control, so if you want to know that before you start using this program, open the options now to get an idea of their scope before continuing.

The options are default values used for each new Writer document.

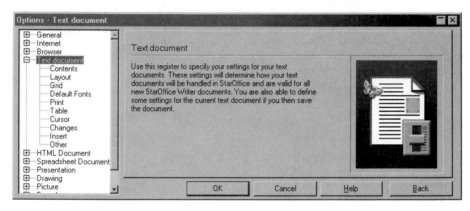

Figure 4-8   Location of Writer setup options

Keyboard Shortcuts

Table 4-1 lists some of the more useful keyboard shortcuts that can save you time while working with Writer documents.

Table 4-1   The more useful Writer keyboard shortcuts

Pressing this...	Does this
F5	Opens/Closes Navigator window (whether it's docked or undocked).
F11	Opens/Closes the Stylist window (whether it's docked or undocked).
Home	Moves the cursor to the beginning of the line.
End	Moves the cursor to the end of the line.
Ctrl+Home	Jumps to the beginning of the document.
Ctrl+End	Jumps to the end of the document.
F9	Updates fields (such as cross-references, dates, and page numbers).
Ctrl+Enter	Creates a manual page break.
F12	Applies numbering to selected paragraphs. Also removes numbering.
Shift+F12	Applies bullets to selected paragraphs. Also removes bullets.
Shift+Enter	Creates a soft return. In a paragraph, a soft return drops the cursor to the next line (properly indented in a bulleted or numbered list) without creating a new paragraph.
Ctrl+b	Applies/Removes bold formatting in selected text.
Ctrl+i	Applies/Removes italic formatting in selected text.
Ctrl+u	Applies/Removes underlining in selected text.
Ctrl+z	Undo. Reverses the previous change you made.
Ctrl+Space	Creates a nonbreaking space to keep items together on the same line.
Ctrl+a	Selects all contents of the document.

Creating a New Document

You can create a new Writer document in a number of ways:

- From scratch
- Using AutoPilot, the Writer "wizard"
- Using a template
- Using an existing Writer document (by using File > Save As)

Creating a Document From Scratch

You can create a new, empty Writer document in a number of ways:

- Start > Text Document
- File > New > Text Document
- From the Click & Go slider in the Explorer window (clicking the Text shortcut)
- With a task bar shortcut (see *Adding Shortcuts to the Task Bar* on page 123)

Using AutoPilot to Create a Document

The StarOffice AutoPilot is a powerful tool that guides you through the creation of four types of Writer documents: a letter, a fax, an agenda, or a memo. AutoPilot formats your document based on the elements you choose to include in the document (such as a logo, subject line, date, agenda topics, and owners, etc.). The AutoPilot for the letter and fax even let you set up mail merge fields from a database. (For more information on mail merges, see 9, *Mailings*, on page 321.)

AutoPilot also lets you save the document as a template.

The best way to see how AutoPilot creates documents is to experiment with it. If you're not sure what a specific option is in an AutoPilot window, select the option and see how it appears in the document after you click the Create button.

1 Choose File > AutoPilot > (Letter, Fax, Agenda, or Memo).

2 Follow the instructions and explanations in AutoPilot (Figure 4-9). You don't have to go through every window; you can click the Create button at any time.

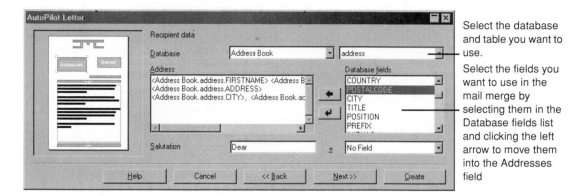

Figure 4-9   Setting up mail merge fields in a letter with AutoPilot

Creating a Writer Document From a Template

You can create new documents from templates. For more information on templates, see *Using Templates* on page 220.

1   Choose File > New > From Template.

2   In the New window (see Figure 4-10), select a template category from the Categories list. Categories correspond to template folders within the `Office52` folder.

3   Select the template you want in the Templates list.

If you want to preview the template and see a description of it, click the More button and select the Preview option.

4   Click OK. A new Writer document opens with the template formatting and styles.

When you save the document, it saves as a Writer document (not as a template) by default.

When you create a document from a template using this procedure, you can look at the document properties (File > Properties, General tab) to see the name of the template the document is based on.

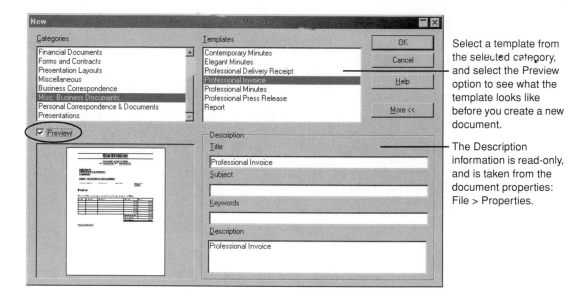

Select a template from the selected category, and select the Preview option to see what the template looks like before you create a new document.

The Description information is read-only, and is taken from the document properties: File > Properties.

Figure 4-10   Creating a new document from a template

If your template is located in a folder other than one of the StarOffice template folders (Office52\share\template*language**template_folder* or Office52\user\template*template_folder*), you won't be able to select the template in the New window. You have to move the template to one of the template folders so you can select it in the New window.

Note – If you don't want to use any of the existing templates, use the AutoPilot to create a specific type of document. See *Using AutoPilot to Create a Document* on page 164.

Writer Tips

The following sections provide tips to help you get the most out of Writer.

Displaying a Vertical Ruler

By default, Writer displays a horizontal ruler in documents. You can also turn on a vertical ruler. This is particularly useful for lining up objects in a document such as graphics.

1   Choose Tools > Options > Text document > Layout.

2   Select the Vertical ruler option.

3 Click OK.

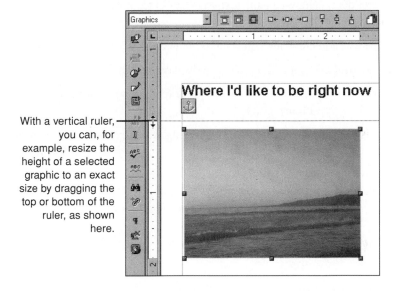

With a vertical ruler, you can, for example, resize the height of a selected graphic to an exact size by dragging the top or bottom of the ruler, as shown here.

Figure 4-11 Displaying a vertical ruler

Changing the Unit of Measurement

You can change the unit of measurement shown on the ruler by right-clicking the ruler. However, this doesn't change the unit of measurement shown in formatting and other windows throughout Writer. To change the overall Writer unit of measurement:

1 Choose Tools > Options > Text document > Layout.

2 Change the unit of measurement in the Meas. units field, and Click OK.

Creating and Inserting Predefined Text and Templates

If there's a set of boilerplate text you use frequently that you don't want to retype every time you use it, such as an Email signature, trademarked term, or company letterhead heading, create an AutoText entry for it in Writer. When you do this, you can insert it quickly—either with a keyboard shortcut or by selecting it from a list of AutoText items.

AutoText entries can be formatted and can include graphics, tables, and fields.

Creating AutoText Entries

1   In a Writer document, create the text you want to turn into AutoText. Apply formatting and include graphics if desired.

2   Select the text and elements you want to include.

3   Click the AutoText tool in the toolbar to display the AutoText window.

4   Select the category (below the Name field) in which you want to store the new AutoText (see Figure 4-12).

Categories are simply containers for organizing AutoText items. If you want to create your own categories for storing AutoText items, see *Adding New AutoText Categories* on page 169.

5   Type a Name and Shortcut for the new AutoText.

6   Click the AutoText button, and select New.

The new AutoText name is displayed in its respective category.

7   Click Close.

8   Test your AutoText entry to see if it works. See *Inserting AutoText Entries in Your Document* on page 170.

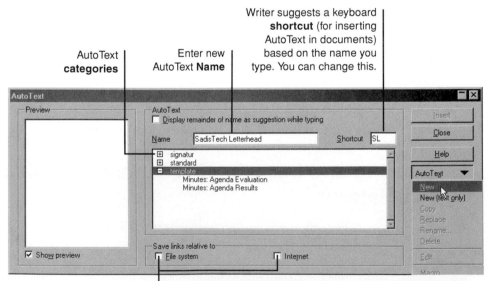

Figure 4-12   The AutoText window

Editing Existing AutoText Items

1   With Writer active, click the AutoText tool in the toolbar.

2   Select the name of the AutoText you want to edit.

3   Click the AutoText button and select Edit. The AutoText window closes and the AutoText opens in a new Writer document.

4   Make edits to the AutoText in Writer.

5   Select the edited AutoText.

6   Click the AutoText tool in the toolbar.

7   In the AutoText window, select the name of the AutoText you edited.

8   Click the AutoText button and select Replace.

9   Click Close.

Adding New AutoText Categories

The AutoText categories are simply storage containers for organizing AutoText. Writer comes with three predefined categories: signature, standard, and template. You can add your own categories for storing AutoText you create.

1   With Writer active, click the AutoText tool in the toolbar.

2   In the AutoText window (see Figure 4-13), click the Categories button.

3   In the Categories window, type the name of the category you want to add.

4   Click New.

5   Click OK.

Type the name of the **new** category and click New.

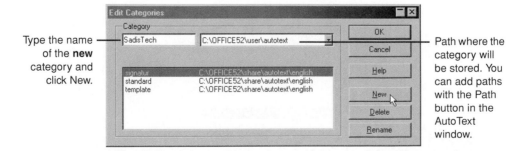

Path where the category will be stored. You can add paths with the Path button in the AutoText window.

Figure 4-13   Adding a category

Moving AutoText to Different Categories

To move AutoText items from one category to another, drag the AutoText item you want to move into the new category, as shown in Figure 4-14.

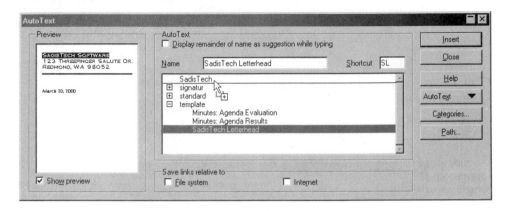

Figure 4-14   Dragging AutoText into another category

Inserting AutoText Entries in Your Document

See the previous procedures for information on creating, editing, and organizing AutoText.

1   In your open document, click where you want to insert the AutoText.

2   Click and hold the AutoText tool in the toolbar, choose the category of the AutoText, and select the AutoText name, as shown in Figure 4-15.

If you know the shortcut for the AutoText you want to insert, you can also type it (for example, "SL") and press the F3 key.

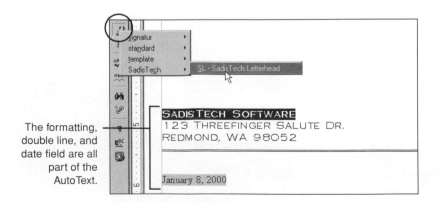

Figure 4-15   AutoText inserted from the toolbar

About the Direct Cursor Feature

The direct cursor feature, which we don't recommend you use, lets you click in any blank area of a page to insert empty paragraphs and tabs up to the point where you click. Activate direct cursor by clicking its tool on the toolbar.

The reason we don't recommend using it is because creating spacing by inserting a bunch of empty paragraphs and tabs runs counter to good paragraph style control. (See *Power Formatting With Styles* on page 201.) Also, if you forget to turn the feature off, you could accidentally add paragraphs and tabs where you didn't really want to, and you'd have to take another step to undo it.

But if you do use direct cursor, make sure to use it with nonprinting characters turned on (also on the toolbar) so you can see the results.

You can set specific options for the behavior of direct cursor by choosing Tools > Options > Text document > Cursor.

Selecting Nonconsecutive Blocks of Text

Writer lets you select nonconsecutive blocks of text for cutting, copying, deleting, and formatting.

1   In the status bar, click the box that says STD until it reads ADD, as shown in Figure 4-16.

     Choosing ADD changes the text selection mode.

2   Select nonconsecutive blocks of text.

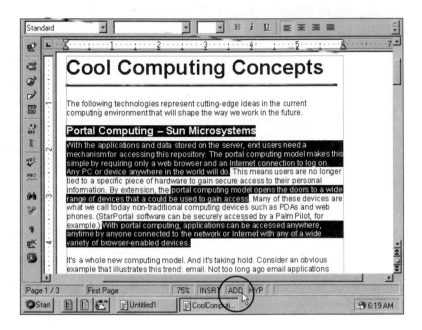

Figure 4-16   Selecting nonconsecutive blocks of text

After you perform an action on nonconsecutive text selections, such as deleting, cutting, or pasting, selection mode returns to STD automatically.

Working With Non-Writer Documents

One of StarOffice's greatest strengths is its ability to open documents that were created in other word processing applications—in fact, in a multitude of other applications. In particular, StarOffice is good at opening and converting documents that were created in Microsoft Office.

If you want to view the file types StarOffice can convert, choose File > Open. In the Open window, click the File type field and scroll through the list of formats.

In addition to opening documents of other formats into Writer, you can also insert them into existing Writer documents, where they take on the Writer format automatically. See *Inserting Other Documents* on page 254.

To see which kinds of document formats Writer can save to, make sure Writer is active and choose File > Save As. Click the File type field and scroll through the list of formats.

Turning Writer Documents Into HTML

You can turn a Writer document into HTML (Hypertext Markup Language) for Web delivery. Though StarOffice tries to simulate in HTML the layout of the original document, some aspects of the original layout may not translate to HTML.

There are two ways to convert to HTML: using Save As to create a single HTML document, or using Send to create multiple HTML documents out of a single Writer document.

Using Save As

Using Save As to convert a document to HTML creates a single HTML file.

1   With the Writer document open, choose File > Save As.

2   In the File type field, select HTML (StarOffice Writer).

3   Name the file and click Save.

Using Send

Using Send lets you create multiple HTML files out of a single document. A separate HTML document is created each time Writer encounters a specific paragraph format that you designate.

1   With the Writer document open, Choose File > Send > Create HTML Document.

2   In the Name and path window, enter a file name for the document.

     The name you enter will be the main table of contents page that will link to all other HTML pages that are created. The file names of all generated HTML files will begin with the file name you enter and end with a number.

3   Click the Style button to select the paragraph style in the Writer document that will be used to create a separate HTML file each time Writer encounters that paragraph style.

4   Click Save.

     The result is an HTML page that lists hyperlinks to other HTML pages that were created, as shown in Figure 4-17.

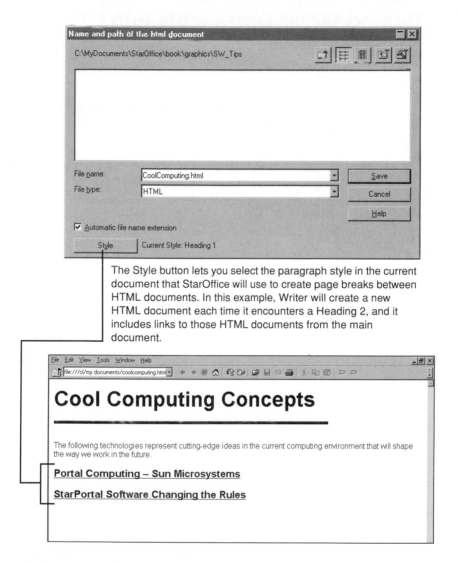

The Style button lets you select the paragraph style in the current document that StarOffice will use to create page breaks between HTML documents. In this example, Writer will create a new HTML document each time it encounters a Heading 2, and it includes links to those HTML documents from the main document.

Figure 4-17   Converting to HTML using Send

Sending a Document as Email

Instead of launching Mail, creating a new mail message, and attaching a Writer file to it, you can send an open Writer file as an Email attachment or as the contents of an Email message.

You can also select part of a Writer document and send only that as an Email.

1   With the document you want to mail open, choose File > Send > Document as E-mail.

2   In the Send Mail window, select whether you want the file sent as an attachment, as the content of the Email body, or whether you want just the selected part of the document sent (see Figure 4-18).

3   Click OK.

If you select Use
selection (which
is activated only
if you've
selected part of
the document),
the selection is
inserted in the
Email body.

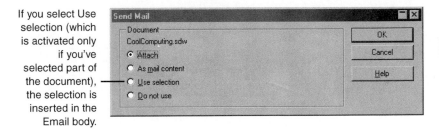

Figure 4-18   Sending a Writer document as Email

If the document is unsaved, StarOffice displays the Save As window. Save the file.

Mail launches with the document either as an attachment or as the contents of the Email message, depending on which option you selected.

Formatting Documents

IN THIS CHAPTER

Basics of Formatting

This section provides information for basic text formatting techniques in Writer you perform manually by selecting text and applying different attributes to it.

Why Bother With Manual Formatting?

You may be used to formatting text manually, one piece at a time. But if you're interested in maintaining style consistency and saving yourself time and headaches, we strongly encourage you to use styles. See *Why You Should Use Styles* on page 202.

It's important, however, to understand manual formatting because:

- You can format paragraphs manually, making them look and behave the way you want, then create a style for them.

- Formatting text manually helps you understand the text properties and formatting possibilities.

- You may actually create a document more quickly when the document is one or two pages and uses formatting you don't plan to reuse.

Character vs. Paragraph Formatting

A concept that's helpful to understand is the difference between paragraph formatting and character formatting.

- Character formatting applies to text within a paragraph. For example, when you want to make a word in the middle of a paragraph red, you apply character formatting to the word.

- A paragraph in Writer is any amount of text that has a hard return at the end of it (by pressing Enter). So technically, a paragraph can be as short as a single letter, or even blank.

    When you apply formatting to a paragraph, everything in the paragraph is affected. For example, if you change a paragraph to double spacing, every line in the paragraph is double-spaced.

Character Formatting

For simple, quick-and-dirty character formatting such as changing font and font size, and applying bold, italic, and underline, use the object bar (Figure 5-1). For more advanced character formatting options, see *Using the Character Formatting Window* on page 181.

Quick Character Formatting

This section shows you quick character formatting tricks, especially those you might not be familiar with.

Using the Object Bar

Using the object bar to apply character formatting is fairly straightforward (see Figure 5-1). You can change font, font size, and apply or remove bold, italic, and underline formatting.

If the cursor is in a table, the object bar changes. See *Formatting and Using Tables* on page 233. (Use the arrow that will be displayed at the far right of the object bar if you want to switch from the table object bar to the text formatting object bar.)

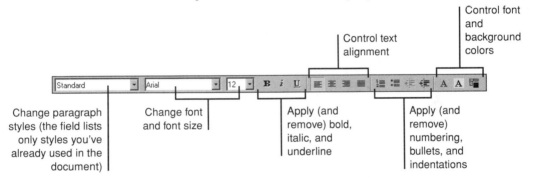

Figure 5-1   Writer object bar

Note – You can also select the text you want to format and right-click to choose different formatting options.

Quick Font and Character Background Color

There are two other object bar tools for character formatting you might not be as familiar with, as shown in Figure 5-2: font color and highlighting. The colors are from the standard StarOffice color palette.

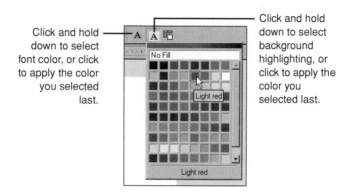

Click and hold down to select font color, or click to apply the color you selected last.

Click and hold down to select background highlighting, or click to apply the color you selected last.

Figure 5-2   Setting font and background colors

Inserting Special Characters

To insert a character you can't enter directly from your keyboard:

1   Click in the text where you want to insert the special character.

2   Choose Insert > Special Character.

3   Select the character you want to insert, as shown in Figure 5-3.

4   Click OK.

Different fonts have different special characters you can use. But for the sake of style and consistency, it's usually best to keep the special character font and the text font the same.

StarOffice also comes with a special characters font called Starbats, which is similar to Wingdings and ZapfDingbats.

When using any special characters in documents that may be opened by different users, those special characters may not be the same if those users don't have that particular font installed—especially if they're on a different platform.

Select the font — for the special character.

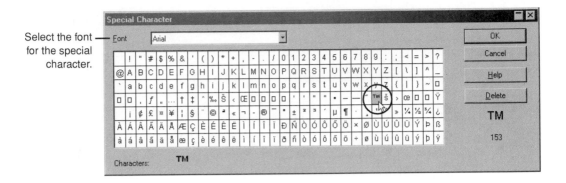

Figure 5-3   Inserting special characters

Note – If you commonly use a word with a special character, such as a product name with a trademark symbol, you can set up an AutoText entry for it. See *Creating AutoText Entries* on page 168.

Using the Character Formatting Window

This section describes the more advanced character formatting options of the Character format window.

1   Select the text you want to format.

2   Choose Format > Character. The Character window is displayed.

3   Apply the character formats you want and click OK.

When selecting text to apply character formatting, be aware of selecting spaces at the beginning or end of the selection, because the spaces get formatted, too. For example, if you're applying a fixed-width font (such as `courier`) to some selected text and you've selected the space after the text, the space will become fixed-width and may make the spacing seem too big. To avoid this, select a word by double-clicking it. To select more than one word, double-click the first word and drag through the other words you want to select.

Figure 5-4 describes character formatting options on each of the tabs in the Character window.

Displays the current font and list of available fonts you can apply.

Select the effects you want to apply.

All colors from the standard StarOffice color palette are available.

Adjust font style and size.

Displays the selected text and shows what it looks like as you apply formatting.

Select the language you want to use in spell checking.

Lets you apply more effects. Blinking makes the text blink (in Writer only).

Control exact point spacing between characters when you select Expanded or Condensed.

Pair kerning puts characters closer together to improve text appearance.

You can make the text superscript or subscript.

Set the relative font size for superscript or subscript text. Deselect Automatic to further raise and lower the super or sub.

The underlining and strikethrough fields are activated when you select those effects on the Font tab. Select the Individual words option if you don't want spaces underlined.

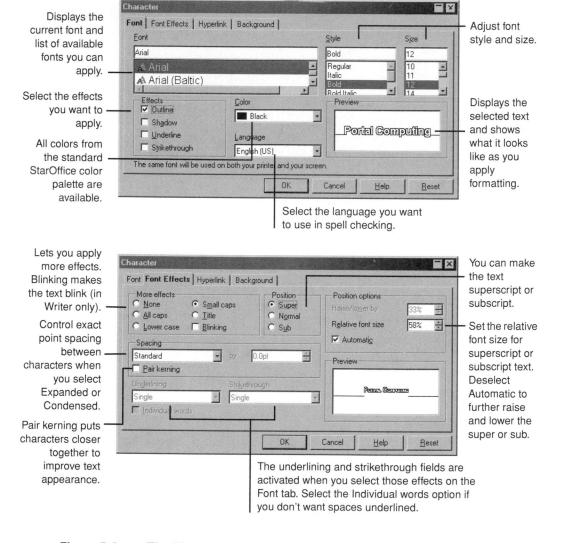

Figure 5-4   The Character window, Font and Font Effects tabs

---

Note – Pair kerning also supports non-English characters (ligatures) such as æ. Your printer driver must support ligatures to display and print them correctly.

About the Hyperlink Tab The Hyperlink tab (Figure 5-5) isn't for character formatting per se. It's for linking text to such things as an Internet address, an Email address, a StarOffice macro, a network file, or, heaven forbid, a hard-coded path to a file on your hard drive. (If you set up a hyperlink that points to a file on your computer's hard drive, others won't be able to get to the file when they click the hyperlink.)

The actual result to the text is that it changes to show that it's a hyperlink, similar to how linked words appear on a Web page.

If you link to a file, especially if the file isn't in a standard format like HTML or PDF, the person clicking the link must have the software installed to open the file. If you're working on a stand-alone computer but you plan on uploading the current file to a network, you can manually enter a relative path to a file on the network (for example, /net/sounds/cartman.wav), so that when you upload the file to the network the link will work.

Shows the text you've selected

The Name you enter will be displayed in the Navigator window under the "Hyperlink" item.

Select the window in which the hyperlink target will open. We recommend _blank.

Type the URL to link to an Internet site or network file, or click Browse to set the path to the file you want opened when the text is clicked.

Click Events to assign a macro to the selected text.

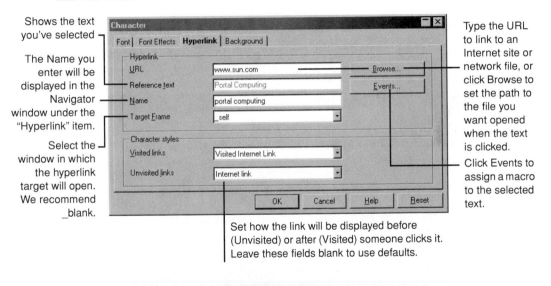

Set how the link will be displayed before (Unvisited) or after (Visited) someone clicks it. Leave these fields blank to use defaults.

You can select a background color for the selected text from the standard StarOffice color palette. To remove a background color, select No Fill.

Name of selected color.

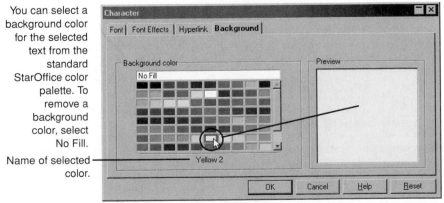

Figure 5-5   The Character window, Hyperlink and Background tabs

Paragraph Formatting

Unlike character formatting where the text you want to format must be highlighted, paragraph formatting only requires that the cursor be somewhere in the paragraph you want to format.

For quick paragraph formatting such as justification, numbering, bulleting, indenting, setting tabs, and applying a background color, use the object bar and ruler. For more advanced paragraph formatting options, see *Using the Paragraph Format Window* on page 187.

Quick Paragraph Formatting

Using the object bar and ruler for paragraph formatting is fairly straightforward. Following are a few quick paragraph formatting tricks you might not be aware of.

Quick Indenting

If you want to tweak paragraph indentations for one or more paragraphs without going into the Paragraph window, change them on the ruler.

1   Select the paragraph(s) you want to indent.

2   On the horizontal ruler, click and drag the bottom triangle to set the left indent.

The bottom triangle moves the top triangle as well.

3   Click and drag the top triangle to set the indent for the first line, as shown in Figure 5-6.

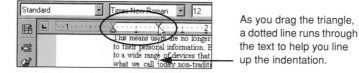

As you drag the triangle, a dotted line runs through the text to help you line up the indentation.

Figure 5-6   Setting the indent from the ruler

Quick Tab Setting

You can insert and move tab settings on the horizontal ruler for one or more paragraphs.

1   Select the paragraph(s) for which you want to insert or adjust the tab settings.

2   Click the tab button to the left of the ruler repeatedly to select the type of tab you want to insert (left, right, decimal, or centered).

3   Click the place on the ruler where you want the tab to be, as shown in Figure 5-7.

Click the tab icon repeatedly until you see the kind of tab you want to insert, then click on the ruler to place the tab.

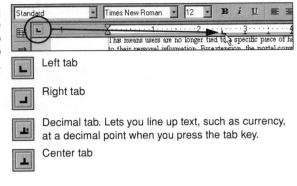

Left tab

Right tab

Decimal tab. Lets you line up text, such as currency, at a decimal point when you press the tab key.

Center tab

Figure 5-7   Setting tabs on the ruler

To adjust a tab setting, drag the tab marker along the ruler. To remove a tab setting, drag it off the ruler.

For areas on the ruler where you haven't inserted a custom tab stop, Writer uses its default tab settings, which are defined in Tools > Options > Text document > Layout, in the Tab stops area of the window.

Using Columns

You can change the number of columns for a selected block of text.

1   Select the text you want.

2   Choose Format > Columns.

3   In the Columns window, set the options you want. See Figure 5-8.

4   Click OK.

Portal Computing

With the applications and data stored on the server, end users need a mechanism for accessing this repository. The portal computing model makes this simple by requiring only a web browser and an Internet connection to log on. Any PC or device anywhere in the world will do. This means users are no longer tied to a specific piece of hardware to gain secure access to their personal information. By extension, the portal computing model opens the doors to a wide range of devices that a could be used to gain access. Many of these devices are what we call today non-traditional computing devices such as PDAs and web phones. (StarPortal software can be securely accessed by a Palm Pilot, for example.) With portal computing, applications can be accessed anywhere, anytime by anyone connected to the network or Internet with any of a wide variety of browser-enabled devices.

It's a whole new computing model. And it's taking hold. Consider an obvious example that illustrates this trend: email. Not too long ago email applications were sold in shrink-wrapped boxes and installed locally on individual computers.

When you create a column this way, the columns become a section. If you ever want to use Writer's document comparison tools, be aware that the comparison tool doesn't currently recognize, and therefore can't compare, text in sections.

Select a preset
column style, or
select the Amount of
columns you want for
the page style. The
number of columns
must be set to more
than one to activate
most options in the
window.

Set the amount of
Spacing, or "gutter",
you want between
columns.

In the Preview area,
see the effects of the
column options you
select.

You can also apply the
column options to the
entire page by selecting
the page style.

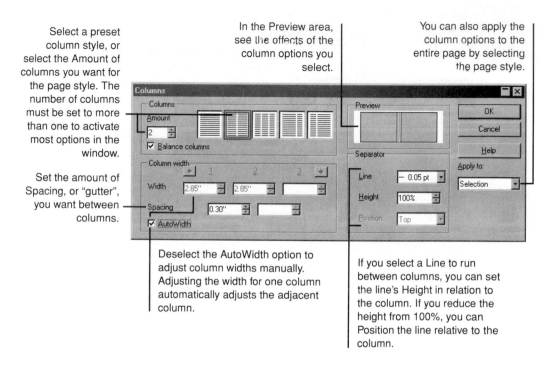

Deselect the AutoWidth option to
adjust column widths manually.
Adjusting the width for one column
automatically adjusts the adjacent
column.

If you select a Line to run
between columns, you can set
the line's Height in relation to
the column. If you reduce the
height from 100%, you can
Position the line relative to the
column.

Figure 5-8   Setting column options

You can also start with a blank multiple-column area by selecting an empty paragraph and
setting columns as described in this procedure.

Setting Paragraph Background Color

You can set paragraph background color from the object bar. The colors are from the
standard StarOffice color palette, as shown in Figure 5-9.

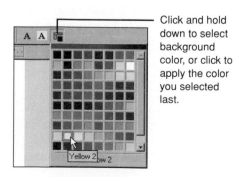

Click and hold
down to select
background
color, or click to
apply the color
you selected
last.

Figure 5-9   Setting background color for a paragraph from the object bar

Changing Default Fonts

When you create a new Writer document from scratch (see page 164), Writer uses its Standard template for the new, blank document. The Standard template has its own paragraph formatting styles defined. For example, standard body text is set to a certain font, as are headings, bulleted and numbered lists, figure captions you insert, and text in indexes you generate.

This procedure shows you how to change the default font that the Writer standard template uses for these paragraph styles when you create a new, blank document.

If you've set another template to be used when creating new documents from scratch (see *Assigning a Different Template Than the Standard Template for New Documents* on page 221), the default settings you apply in this procedure won't apply. They apply to Writer's Standard template only.

1   Select Tools > Options > Text document > Default Fonts.

2   Change fonts for the respective types of paragraphs (see Figure 5-10).

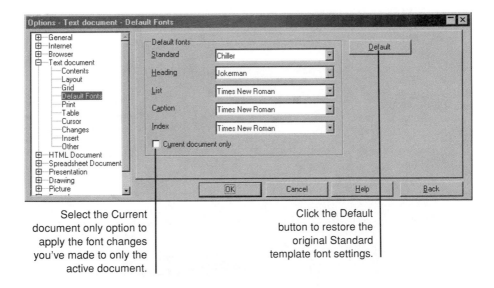

Select the Current
document only option to
apply the font changes
you've made to only the
active document.

Click the Default
button to restore the
original Standard
template font settings.

Figure 5-10   Changing the default fonts used by Writer's Standard template

Using the Paragraph Format Window

This section describes the more advanced paragraph formatting options of the Paragraph format window.

Note -- The Paragraph format window doesn't let you change the font for a paragraph. To change a paragraph font style manually, you must select the entire paragraph and use character formatting (see *Character Formatting* on page 178). Changing font attributes this way differs from using styles, because the paragraph style definition includes font settings—which is yet another reason why using styles is a good idea. See *Why You Should Use Styles* on page 202 and *Paragraph Styles* on page 205.

You can also access many of the following manual paragraph formatting options with right-click menus.

1   Click in the paragraph you want to format.

2   Right-click and choose Paragraph. The Paragraph window is displayed.

3   Apply the paragraph formats you want and click OK.

Figure 5-11 through Figure 5-18 describe paragraph formatting options on each of the tabs in the Paragraph window.

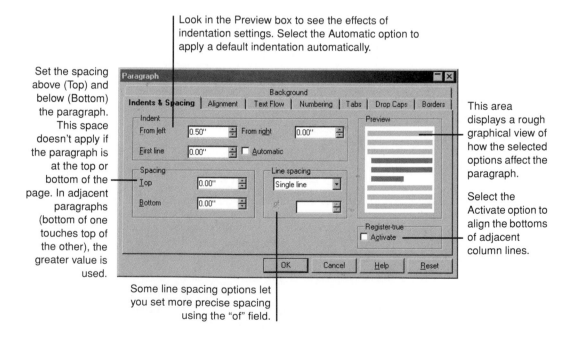

Look in the Preview box to see the effects of indentation settings. Select the Automatic option to apply a default indentation automatically.

Set the spacing above (Top) and below (Bottom) the paragraph. This space doesn't apply if the paragraph is at the top or bottom of the page. In adjacent paragraphs (bottom of one touches top of the other), the greater value is used.

This area displays a rough graphical view of how the selected options affect the paragraph.

Select the Activate option to align the bottoms of adjacent column lines.

Some line spacing options let you set more precise spacing using the "of" field.

Figure 5-11   The Paragraph window, Indents & Spacing tab

When you select Justify to stretch text to the left and right sides of the page, you can align the last line separately. For example, if the last line is short, select Left justification to avoid stretching it across to the right.

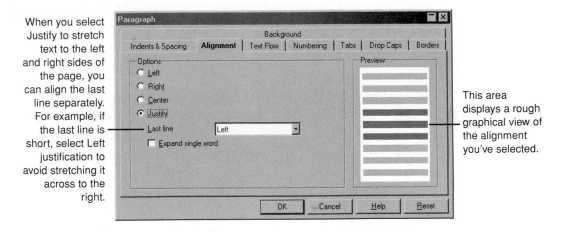

This area displays a rough graphical view of the alignment you've selected.

Figure 5-12   The Paragraph window, Alignment tab

Select the Automatically option to hyphenate end-of-line words. You can prevent Writer from getting too hyphenation happy by controlling the number of characters that must be present at the end and beginning of a line, and by limiting the number of consecutive lines that can be hyphenated.

Select the Break option to select either a Page or Column break for the selected paragraph. Select Before to move the paragraph to the next page or column; select After to move the next paragraph to the next page or column.

You can set the minimum number of paragraph lines that must appear on the previous page (orphan) or following page (widow) when a paragraph crosses pages. Selecting the orphan or widow options deactivates the Don't separate lines option, and vice versa.

The Keep with next paragraph option lets you, for example, keep a heading with the text that follows it if a page break occurs.

When you select the Page and Before options to move a paragraph to a new page, you can select the With page style option and apply a page style for the new page (choose from the list of currently defined page styles).

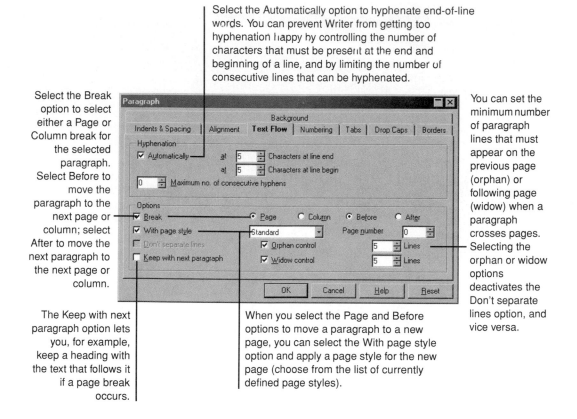

Figure 5-13   The Paragraph window, Text Flow tab

You can apply currently defined numbering/ bulleting styles to the selected paragraph(s). You either have to know what the numbering styles look like, or you have to apply the styles to find out. When you define your own styles, you'll know what they look like (see the tip on page 204).

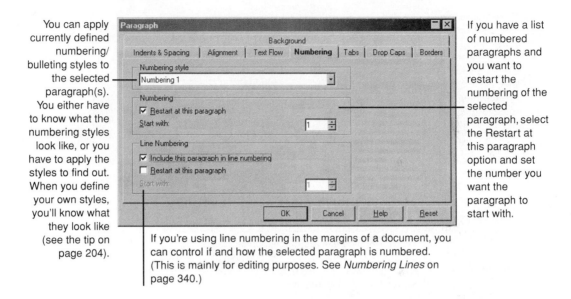

If you have a list of numbered paragraphs and you want to restart the numbering of the selected paragraph, select the Restart at this paragraph option and set the number you want the paragraph to start with.

If you're using line numbering in the margins of a document, you can control if and how the selected paragraph is numbered. (This is mainly for editing purposes. See *Numbering Lines* on page 340.)

Figure 5-14   The Paragraph window, Numbering tab

Enter the new tab Position (measured from the edge of the text frame, not from the edge of the entire page), and select the Type. The Decimal type lines up tabbed paragraphs to the decimal character you specify (for example, for currency amounts).

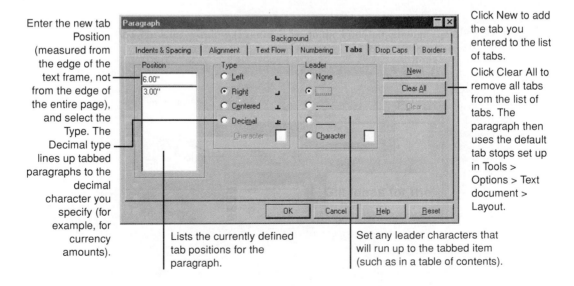

Click New to add the tab you entered to the list of tabs.

Click Clear All to remove all tabs from the list of tabs. The paragraph then uses the default tab stops set up in Tools > Options > Text document > Layout.

Lists the currently defined tab positions for the paragraph.

Set any leader characters that will run up to the tabbed item (such as in a table of contents).

Figure 5-15   The Paragraph window, Tabs tab

Select the Show drop caps option to use a drop cap for the selected paragraph. Selecting this box activates the remaining fields.

Select the Whole word option to use the entire first word of the paragraph as a drop cap. If you don't select this option, you can set a specific number of characters to use for the drop cap.

This area displays a rough graphical view of how the selected drop cap options will look.

You can enter drop cap Text that is different than the beginning paragraph text. You can apply a Character style to the drop cap from the current list of character styles. (See *Character Styles* on page 208.)

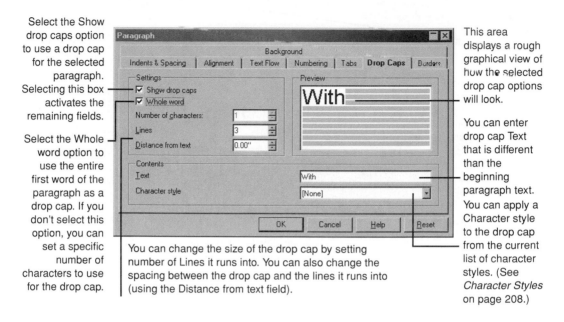

You can change the size of the drop cap by setting number of Lines it runs into. You can also change the spacing between the drop cap and the lines it runs into (using the Distance from text field).

Figure 5-16   The Paragraph window, Drop Caps tab

Click one of the Presets boxes to apply that border style. Click the empty first box to clear all line (not shadow) settings.

Select a Line Style for the border.

Click a Shadow style Position box to apply that shadow angle to the line. Click the first box to clear shadow settings.

The gray box in the Frame area represents the entire paragraph. You can add or remove lines relative to the paragraph by clicking above, below, or to either side of, the gray box. Click Spacing to set the spacing between the lines and the text.

You can change the size of the selected shadow's width.

You can choose a shadow color and a border line color from the standard StarOffice color palette.

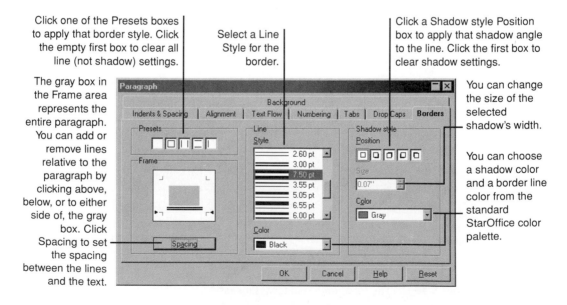

Figure 5-17   The Paragraph window, Borders tab

In the As field, select whether you want Color or a Graphic for the paragraph background. Selecting a color is straightforward, so this window shows options for using a graphic.

Clicking Browse brings up the Search graphic window for selecting the graphic you want to use. In the Search graphic window, select the Link option to activate the Link field in this window. To keep the size of your document smaller, use the Link option for graphics.

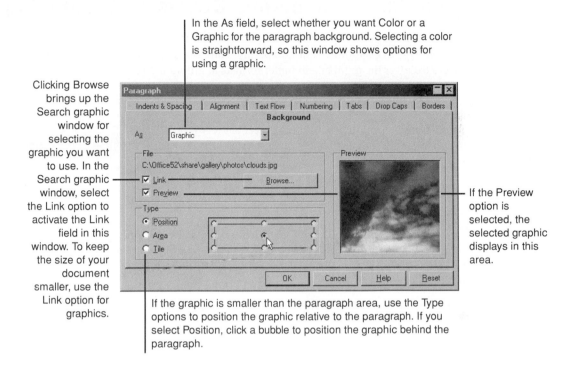

If the Preview option is selected, the selected graphic displays in this area.

If the graphic is smaller than the paragraph area, use the Type options to position the graphic relative to the paragraph. If you select Position, click a bubble to position the graphic behind the paragraph.

Figure 5-18   The Paragraph window, Background tab

Using Borders and Backgrounds

The following tips pertain to using text borders and backgrounds.

Putting a Box Around Text   To put two paragraphs within a box, such as a heading and a paragraph, add a soft return (Shift+Enter) between the paragraphs and format the heading and body text manually.

Using Background Colors and Graphics   Using a dark or detailed graphic or color can wash out text. However, using a dark graphic or color with white font can produce nice results.

Since a graphic, if it's large, can fill the entire dimensions of a paragraph, the text runs into the edges of the graphic. A background color behaves the same way. If you want to create space between the text and the edges of the graphic or color, try using a text frame inside the paragraph. See *Frames* on page 248.

Using Basic Numbering, Bullets, and Outlining

This section describes how to format quickly with numbers, bullets, and outlining. It also shows you how to customize your numbering, bulleting, and outlining so that you have more control over the number and bullet formats at different levels of indentation.

Quick Numbering and Bulleting

The numbering and bullet tools in the object bar lets you insert plain numbering and bullets quickly. You can highlight existing paragraphs and apply numbering or bulleting to them, or begin a new numbered or bulleted list by clicking the appropriate button in an empty paragraph.

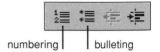

numbering bulleting

If you want to use more interesting numbers or bullets, use this procedure. The quickest way to apply numbering and bulleting is to set up numbering and bulleting styles, especially if you're going to use the same kinds again and again. See *Power Formatting With Styles* on page 201.

1   Highlight the paragraphs you want to bullet, or position the cursor where you want to begin a new list.

2   Choose Format > Numbering/Bullets.

3   In the Numbering/Bullets window (Figure 5-19), select the numbering or bullets you want to use in the Bullets, Numbering style, or Graphics tabs. (It's a good idea not to select the Link option. See the note in Figure 5-19.)

4   Click OK.

If you select the Link graphics option and send the file to someone, they won't be able to see the bullets if they don't have the bullet graphics to link to or if the path to the graphics is different than it is on your system.

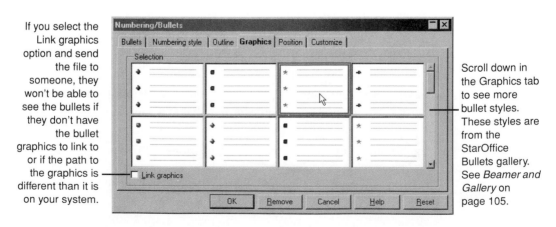

Scroll down in the Graphics tab to see more bullet styles. These styles are from the StarOffice Bullets gallery. See *Beamer and Gallery* on page 105.

Figure 5-19   Predefined bullet styles in the Graphics tab

If you're starting a new bulleted or numbered list, type the text at the first list item and press Enter. The new paragraph takes on the number or bullet format. If you press Enter at a numbered or bulleted paragraph that doesn't have text with it, the bullet or number is removed from the paragraph.

To restart numbering, see Figure 5-13 on page 190.

Quick Outlining

This procedure shows you how to create a basic outline format based on a predefined set of outlining styles.

1   Position the cursor where you want to begin outlining.

2   Choose Format > Numbering/Bullets.

3   In the Outline tab, select the style of outlining you want to use, as shown in Figure 5-20.

4   Click OK. The window closes and the first-level number appears in the text.

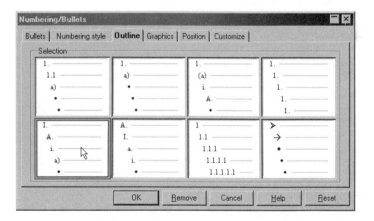

Figure 5-20   Predefined outline styles

As you press Enter at the end of a line, you stay at the same numbering level and the numbering increments. To move in a level, press the Tab key. To move out a level, press Shift+Tab.

Customizing Numbering, Bullets, and Outlining

There are many aspects to customizing numbering, bulleting, and outlining. Besides changing font and characters, perhaps the most important reason for customization is setting up different tiers, or indented levels, as Figure 5-20 shows.

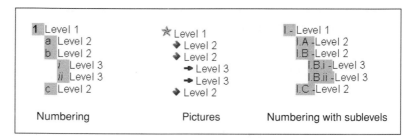

Figure 5-21   Numbering/Bullet levels

1   Position the cursor where you want to begin numbering or bullets, or highlight the text you want to number or bullet.

2   Choose Format > Numbering/Bullets. The Numbering/Bullets window is displayed.

3   Select the Customize tab.

4   In the Level box, select a level number.

Levels correspond to the level of indentation. The higher the level number, the greater the indentation.

5   In the Numbering field, select the type of numbering or bullet you want the level to be.

6   Set any appropriate options for the level (such as Before, After, or Character Style). See Figure 5-22 and Figure 5-23 for more information.

7   Set up any other levels you want to customize.

8   When you're finished, click OK.

9   Begin using your custom numbering/bulleting (see page 200).

Writer uses default position and spacing for each level. If you want to fine-tune the position and spacing of the levels, see *Fine-Tuning the Position and Spacing of Levels* on page 199.

Numbering is where you determine whether the selected level number is going to be a number or a bullet. The format area displays different options depending on the numbering you choose.

When you select a level number, every option you set in the Format area of the window applies to that level. If you select the 1-10 level item, the options you set apply to all 10 possible levels.

The Preview area displays a rough graphical view of the options you apply to the different levels.

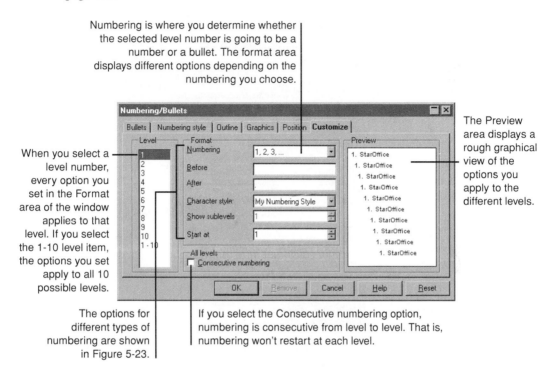

The options for different types of numbering are shown in Figure 5-23.

If you select the Consecutive numbering option, numbering is consecutive from level to level. That is, numbering won't restart at each level.

Figure 5-22   The Numbering/Bullets window, Customize tab

The Format area of the Numbering/Bullets window displays different options depending on your selection in the Numbering field. The pictures in Figure 5-23 illustrate these different options.

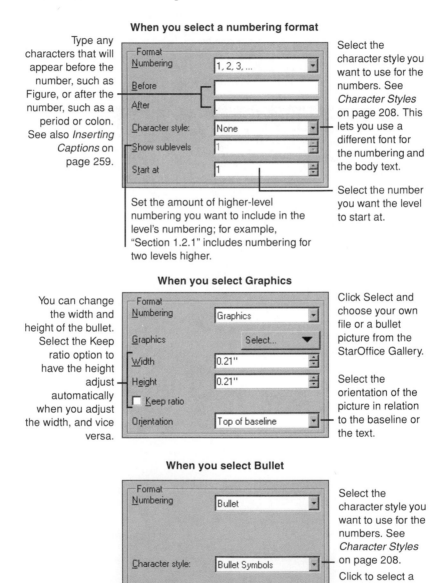

When you select a numbering format

Type any characters that will appear before the number, such as Figure, or after the number, such as a period or colon. See also *Inserting Captions* on page 259.

Select the character style you want to use for the numbers. See *Character Styles* on page 208. This lets you use a different font for the numbering and the body text.

Set the amount of higher-level numbering you want to include in the level's numbering; for example, "Section 1.2.1" includes numbering for two levels higher.

Select the number you want the level to start at.

When you select Graphics

You can change the width and height of the bullet. Select the Keep ratio option to have the height adjust automatically when you adjust the width, and vice versa.

Click Select and choose your own file or a bullet picture from the StarOffice Gallery.

Select the orientation of the picture in relation to the baseline or the text.

When you select Bullet

Select the character style you want to use for the numbers. See *Character Styles* on page 208.

Click to select a bullet from the Special Characters.

Figure 5-23   Format options for different Numbering selections

You can also mix numbers and bullets when setting your levels, as Figure 5-24 illustrates.

Figure 5-24   Mixing bullets and numbers

Fine-Tuning the Position and Spacing of Levels

You can change the default position and spacing Writer uses for numbers and bullets.

1   Click in the numbered or bulleted paragraph you want to change.

2   Choose Format > Numbering/Bullets.

3   In the Numbering/Bullets window, select the Position tab.

4   Select a level in the Level box, and adjust its settings. Select and adjust all levels you want to change.

5   When you're finished, click OK.

Figure 5-25 describes the options in the Position tab.

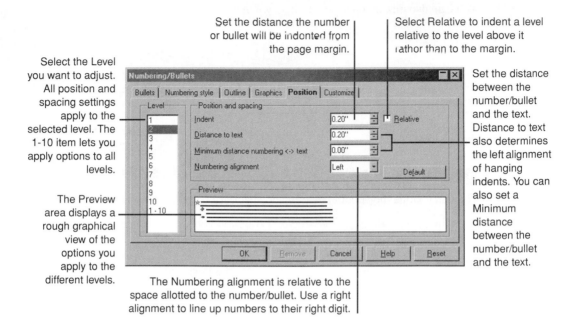

Set the distance the number or bullet will be indented from the page margin.

Select Relative to indent a level relative to the level above it rather than to the margin.

Select the Level you want to adjust. All position and spacing settings apply to the selected level. The 1-10 item lets you apply options to all levels.

Set the distance between the number/bullet and the text. Distance to text also determines the left alignment of hanging indents. You can also set a Minimum distance between the number/bullet and the text.

The Preview area displays a rough graphical view of the options you apply to the different levels.

The Numbering alignment is relative to the space allotted to the number/bullet. Use a right alignment to line up numbers to their right digit.

Figure 5-25   The Numbering/Bullets window, Position tab

Saving Numbering/Bullet Customizations

The customization only applies to the paragraphs that use it. For example, if you create and use a customized numbering hierarchy in one place in a document, you can't click the numbering button in the object bar and continue using the customized numbering system at another point in the document. You'd either have to copy the first line of the customized numbering style and paste it elsewhere in the document, or recreate the numbering system in the Numbering/Bullets window for a different part of the document. To save your customization, create a new numbering style. See *Creating a Numbering Style* on page 210.

Cross-Referencing Paragraph Numbering

If you want to cross-reference the autogenerated numbers/text of a paragraph, such as "Figure 5-1" in a caption paragraph style, you need to number those paragraph formats in a different way. See *Outline Numbering* on page 278.

Changing Indent Levels With the Tab Key

As you press Enter at the end of a numbered or bulleted paragraph, you stay at the same numbering level. To move in a level, press the Tab key. To move up a level, press Shift+Tab. If you're using numbering, the numbering increments according to the level.

Power Formatting With Styles

In the previous sections we talked about formatting characters and paragraphs manually, which is how most people format: selecting text and either clicking quick-formatting tools on the object bar and ruler or choosing a Format menu item to set specific formatting options.

There are legitimate reasons to use only manual formatting (such as quick formatting of short documents whose styles you don't plan to reuse). However, to get the most out of Writer and to work more quickly with more consistency, use styles and templates.

About Writer Styles

Paragraphs, text, pages, and other elements have certain characteristics: for example, a heading (like the one just above this paragraph) that is 16-pt. bold Helvetica with a 3/4-inch left indent. A style is simply a name given to this set of characteristics, such as *Heading 2*.

Figure 5-26 illustrates the five types of styles in Writer.

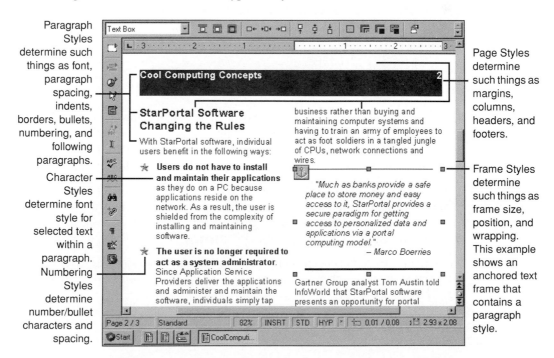

Figure 5-26   The five types of styles in Writer

Why You Should Use Styles

Following are the reasons why you should use styles. Any one of these reasons alone justifies using them.

Instant Formatting With a double-click you can transform a plain text paragraph into one with a different font, font size, font color, indentation, spacing, alignment, and background color. All paragraphs that are given that style are identical.

Automation When you end a paragraph and press Enter, the next paragraph can become another style automatically. For example, pressing enter at the end of a heading can put you directly into a body paragraph style. Also, when you modify a style, all paragraphs with that style are updated automatically. Automation is good! It doesn't mean "cookie-cutter"; it means you work more quickly, efficiently, and consistently.

Maintaining Consistency Using styles ensures your documents will maintain a consistent style.

Running Headers and Footers If you want the main headings in your document to appear automatically in the header or footer of the document, your main headings need to be styles.

Table of Contents Generation Writer uses heading styles to generate tables of contents automatically. Using styles for figure and table captions also lets you build lists of figures and tables.

How Styles Work in Writer

The Stylist should be your closest companion in Writer. To show it (and hide it), press the F11 key. By default it is displayed as a floating window, but we recommend docking it to an edge of the Writer work area (see *Making Windows Anchored or Floating* on page 120). When you dock it, it stays docked when you press the F11 key to show it.

Behind the scenes, styles also use styles in Writer. For example, if a paragraph style uses numbering or bullets, you'll select the numbering style to use within the paragraph style. Also, in numbering styles, you can assign a character style to use for the numbering or bullet characters.

Styles apply only to the document in which you create them. To make styles in one document available to other documents, see *Loading Styles From Another Document* on page 221.

About the Stylist

The Stylist is the control center for viewing, applying, adding, modifying, and deleting styles. Figure 5-27 and Table 5-1 describe the elements of the Stylist.

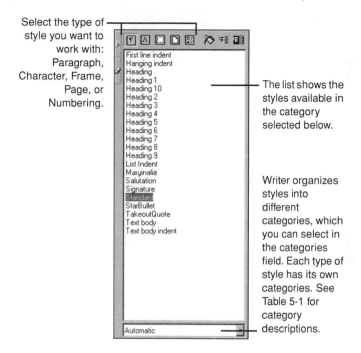

Select the type of style you want to work with: Paragraph, Character, Frame, Page, or Numbering.

The list shows the styles available in the category selected below.

Writer organizes styles into different categories, which you can select in the categories field. Each type of style has its own categories. See Table 5-1 for category descriptions.

Figure 5-27   The Stylist

The following table describes style categories, found in the drop-down list at the bottom of the Stylist.

Table 5-1   Writer Stylist categories

Category	Description
All	Shows all defined styles for each style type.
Applied Styles	Shows all the styles you've used in your document so far. Since these applied styles are also displayed in the object bar, take advantage of this by selecting a different category in the Stylist. This lets you see styles for two categories at once.
Custom Styles	Shows the styles you've created beyond the default styles provided by Writer. The styles you create remain in this category even if you assign them to a different category.

Table 5-1 Writer Stylist categories (continued)

Category	Description
Hierarchical	Displays styles in a hierarchical tree view. If a style has a plus sign next to it (+), click the plus sign to view the styles that were created based on that style.
The following categories apply only to paragraph styles	
Automatic	Allows the category to change based on where the cursor is located in the document. For example, if the cursor is in a body paragraph, the Text Styles category is shown. If the cursor is moved to within a header, the Special Styles category is shown.
Text Styles	Shows styles that are related to heading and body text.
Chapter Styles	Shows styles that are related to chapter-level text, such as titles and subtitles.
List Styles	Shows an ungodly and confusing amount of hanging indent paragraph styles without bullets. Use this category only if you want to get dizzy. Instead, create your own numbered and bulleted list paragraph styles and store them in a category other than this one.
Index Styles	Shows styles that are related to indexes and tables of contents.
Special Styles	Shows styles that are used in special regions such as headers, footers, and tables.
HTML Styles	Shows styles that are used in HTML documents. Use this category when you're working in Writer/Web.
Conditional Styles	Shows the paragraph styles that have conditions. For example, a paragraph style that behaves differently in a table than it does in regular body text.

The Style Catalog You can also create, modify, and delete styles using the Style Catalog (Format > Styles > Catalog).

Tips for Using Styles

With the Stylist docked, make sure you have tooltips turned on (Help > Tips) to help you select the style type you want. When the mouse pointer hovers over a style type button, its name is displayed. (If the Stylist is a floating window, the name of the selected style category is displayed in the window's title bar.)

Writer comes with a predefined set of styles: paragraph, character, numbering, page, and frame. These defaults are designed to get you going, but ultimately you'll want to modify the defaults or create your own styles. If you find you're not using a lot of the default styles (especially the paragraph and character styles), and since you can't delete them, stay in the Custom Styles category of the Stylist. This will help you more quickly find the styles you do want to use, which also makes using styles less intimidating, because you're not swimming in a sea of unfamiliar styles names you had no part in creating. And since it's good practice not to go too overboard creating a multitude of possible styles (you should only create the ones you'll really use), the Custom Styles category should give you plenty of room to store all the styles you need.

You don't have to have all your styles perfect before you start using them. You'll want to make adjustments to them as you work. The great thing about styles is that you can change them when you want, and all of the paragraphs that use them are updated automatically.

Paragraph Styles

This section describes how to create paragraph styles. If you're not clear about the technical difference between paragraphs and characters, review the difference between paragraph and character formatting on page 178.

For information on applying styles, see page 217; for modifying styles, see page 218; for deleting styles, see page 219; for changing the category of styles, see page 219.

Creating a Paragraph Style

Creating a paragraph style is fairly easy. In fact, if you know how to format paragraphs manually (see *Paragraph Formatting* on page 184), you know 90 percent of creating a paragraph style.

1   In the Stylist, click the Paragraph Styles button.

2   Select the category in which you want to put the new style.

3   If you want to create a new style based on an existing style, select the style you want to base it on before you right-click.

4   Right-click in the Stylist and select New. The Paragraph Style window is displayed.

5   Set the formatting options for the paragraph. (See the field descriptions in *Character Formatting* on page 178 and *Paragraph Formatting* on page 184 for more information.)

6   In the Organizer tab, type a name for the style.

     Use a name that will help you remember what the style either looks like or is used for.

7   Set the options in the Condition tab, if applicable. (See Figure 5-28.)

8   Click OK.

Figure 5-28 shows paragraph style options on the Organizer and Condition tabs.

Enter the name of the new paragraph style. Use a name that will help you remember what the style either looks like or is used for.

Select the next paragraph style that will be used when you press Enter at the end of this paragraph style. This is one of the most important paragraph style settings.

Select the AutoUpdate option to update all paragraphs of this style when the style is modified.

In the Based on field, select the paragraph style whose base paragraph settings you want to use for the fields you don't change.

If you select a Category other than Custom Styles for the new style, the new style will be put in Custom Styles anyway.

Select the Conditional style option if you want to set conditions for the style.

The Applied Styles column shows the styles you have applied to the listed contexts.

Select the context in which you want the paragraph to behave differently, select a style to use when the paragraph is in that context, and click Assign.

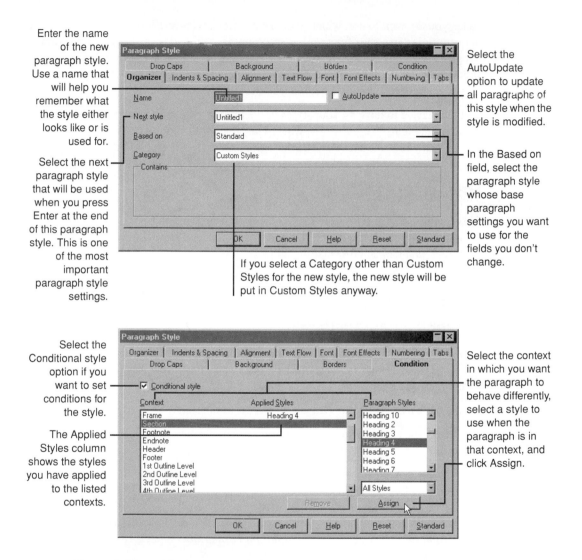

Figure 5-28   The Paragraph Style window, Organizer and Condition tabs

About Conditional Paragraphs StarOffice lets you can create different conditions for how a paragraph style is used. For example, you can have the Text Body paragraph style take on different characteristics when it's used in different places (under different conditions): in headers, body text, tables, and so on. There's no compelling reason why you'd want to use this feature over creating separate paragraph formats. There is, however a compelling reason *not* to use this feature: it can be a maintenance nightmare. As the following section on Using Conditions shows, this feature adds an unnecessary layer of complexity when you're simply trying to modify a paragraph style.

Using Conditions When you want to modify a paragraph style, look first to see if it has a Condition tab with condition settings. Here's why: Because conditional paragraphs can take on different paragraph style characteristics when they're used in different contexts, modifying them can get confusing. For example, suppose a body text paragraph is a 10 pt. regular (not bold) font in a body paragraph, and it has a conditional setting that makes it appear as a 12 pt. italic font in a text box. If you want to change the text box font, you may be thrown by the fact that the font definition for a text body paragraph doesn't match what is shown in the text box. You might then be tempted to make a wholesale change to the text body font to see if that fixes the seeming font disparity. If you do that, the font for all text body paragraphs change, but the text in the text box remains the same because the condition remains the same.

Creating a Paragraph Style Using Drag and Drop

You can also create a style by drag and drop. This method doesn't let you set Organizer or Condition tab options.

1   In your document, format the paragraph manually (see *Paragraph Formatting* on page 184 and *Character Formatting* on page 178).

2   In the Stylist, click the Paragraph Styles button and select a paragraph style category to which you want to add the style.

3   In the document, select the paragraph you want to add, click and hold on the selection, and drag the pointer into the Stylist, as shown in Figure 5-29.

     Make sure you don't drag onto the name of an existing style, because you will overwrite the style.

4   In the Create Style window, type a name for the style and click OK.

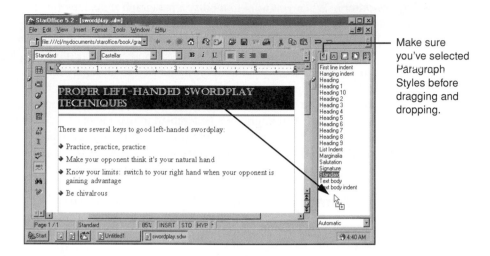

Make sure
you've selected
Paragraph
Styles before
dragging and
dropping.

Figure 5-29   Creating a paragraph style using drag and drop

Cross-Referencing Paragraphs that Have Numbering If you want to cross-reference the autogenerated numbers/text of a paragraph, such as "Figure 5-1" in a caption paragraph style, you need to number those paragraph formats in a different way. See *Outline Numbering* on page 278.

Character Styles

This section describes how to create character styles. If you're not clear about the technical difference between characters and paragraphs, see *Character vs. Paragraph Formatting* on page 178.

For information on applying styles, see page 217; for modifying styles, see page 218; for deleting styles, see page 219; for changing the category of styles, see page 219.

Creating a Character Style

Creating a character style is fairly easy. In fact, if you know how to format characters manually (see *Character Formatting* on page 178), you know 90 percent of creating a character style.

1   In the Stylist, click the Character Styles button.

2   At the bottom of the Stylist, select the category in which you want to put the new style.

3   If you want to create a new style based on an existing style, select the style you want to base it on before you right-click. For more information on this, see Figure 5-30.

4   Right-click in the Stylist and select New. The Character Style window is displayed.

5   Set the formatting options for the character style.

See the field descriptions in *Character Formatting* on page 178 for more information.

6   In the Organizer tab, type a name for the style.

Use a name that will help you remember what the style either looks like or is used for.

7   Click OK.

The character style doesn't include hyperlink properties, which are offered in the Character window (Format > Character). You must set hyperlink properties on a case-by-base basis. See Figure 5-5 on page 183 for details.

Figure 5-30 shows the options in the Organizer tab.

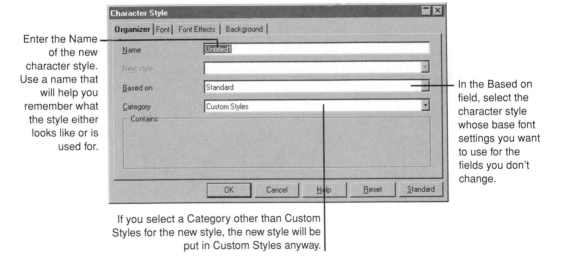

Enter the Name of the new character style. Use a name that will help you remember what the style either looks like or is used for.

In the Based on field, select the character style whose base font settings you want to use for the fields you don't change.

If you select a Category other than Custom Styles for the new style, the new style will be put in Custom Styles anyway.

Figure 5-30   The Character Style window, Organizer tab

Creating a Character Style Using Drag and Drop

You can also create a style by drag and drop. This method doesn't let you set Organizer tab options.

1   Format the characters manually (see *Character Formatting* on page 178).

2   In the Stylist, click the Character Styles button and select a character style category to which you want to add the style.

3   In the document, select the text you want to add, click and hold on it, and drag the pointer into the Stylist.

Make sure you don't drag onto the name of an existing style, because you will overwrite the style.

4   In the Create Style window, type a name for the style and click OK.

Numbering (and Bullet) Styles

You can save custom numbering or bulleted lists by creating styles for them. Numbering Styles (which can include bullet styles) let you quickly apply custom numbering to any part of your document.

This section describes how to create numbering styles.

For information on applying styles, see page 217; for modifying styles, see page 218; for deleting styles, see page 219; for changing the category of styles, see page 219.

Creating a Numbering Style

Creating a numbering style is fairly easy. In fact, if you know how to format with numbers and bullets manually (see *Using Basic Numbering, Bullets, and Outlining* on page 194), you know 90 percent of creating a numbering style.

1   In the Stylist, click the Numbering Styles button.

2   Right-click in the Stylist and select New. The Numbering Style window is displayed.

3   Set the numbering options for the numbering style.

4   In the Organizer tab, type a name for the style.

Use a name that will help you remember what the style either looks like or is used for.

5   Click OK.

Note – You can also use a numbering style as part of a paragraph style, so that when you apply a paragraph style in the document, the numbering or bullets appear automatically. See *Creating a Paragraph Style* on page 205.

Creating a Numbering Style Using Drag and Drop

You can also create a numbering style by drag and drop.

1   Format the numbering/bullets manually (see *Using Basic Numbering, Bullets, and Outlining* on page 194 and *Customizing Numbering, Bullets, and Outlining* on page 196).

2   In the Stylist, click the Numbering Styles button.

3   In the document, select the first line of the custom numbering you want to add, click and hold on it, and drag the pointer into the Stylist.

You don't have to select the number/bullet in that paragraph; just the text.

Make sure you don't drag onto the name of an existing style, because you will overwrite the style.

4   In the Create Style window, type a name for the style and click OK.

Page Styles

Page styles control such elements as margins, headers, footers, columns, and which page styles follow each other.

For information on applying styles, see page 217; for modifying styles, see page 218; for deleting styles, see page 219; for changing the category of styles, see page 219.

Creating a Page Style

1   In the Stylist, click the Page Styles button.

2   Select the category in which you want to put the new style.

3   Right-click in the Stylist and select New. The Page Style window is displayed.

4   Set the options you want for the page.

    If you need help setting options, refer to the following figures.

5   Click OK.

Figure 5-31 shows page style options on each of the tabs in the Page Style window.

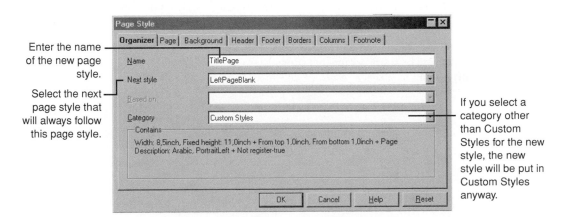

Enter the name of the new page style.

Select the next page style that will always follow this page style.

If you select a category other than Custom Styles for the new style, the new style will be put in Custom Styles anyway.

Figure 5-31   The Page Style window, Organizer tab

Page Layout determines the flow of the document: if the style applies to all pages, if you want to use mirrored facing pages, or if the page style is for a right or left page in the document flow.

Preview shows a rough graphical representation of the options you set.

If you select Mirrored in the Page layout field, Left and Right margins become Inner and Outer.

If you adjust the page Width and Height manually, the Paper format becomes User (custom).

If you're using multiple columns and you want text rows in adjacent columns to line up on their baselines in this page style, select Activate; then select a Reference paragraph style, such as body text, that will always register-true in this page style.

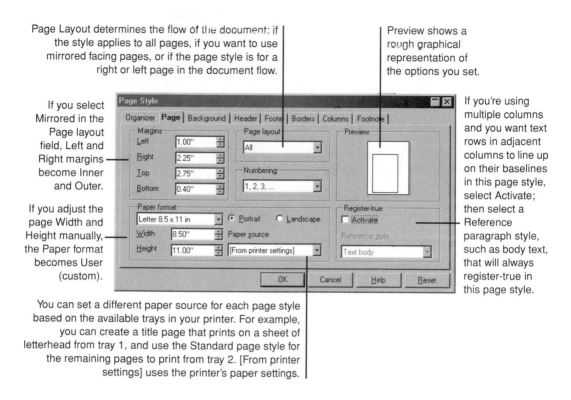

You can set a different paper source for each page style based on the available trays in your printer. For example, you can create a title page that prints on a sheet of letterhead from tray 1, and use the Standard page style for the remaining pages to print from tray 2. [From printer settings] uses the printer's paper settings.

Figure 5-32 The Page Style window, Page tab

About the Next Style Field As you create custom styles, you may need to wait to set this field until all the page styles you want to use are created.

About the Page Layout Field If your document seems to skip pages in the page numbering or starts documents at page zero, try setting the Page Layout field (in the Page tab) to All.

In the As field, select whether you want Color or a Graphic for the page background. Selecting a color is straightforward, so this window shows options for using a graphic.

Clicking Browse brings up the Search graphic window for selecting the graphic you want to use. In the Search graphic window, select the Link option to activate the Link field in this window. To keep the size of your document smaller, use the Link option for graphics.

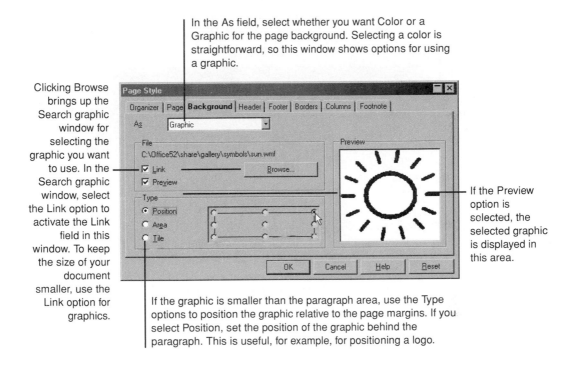

If the Preview option is selected, the selected graphic is displayed in this area.

If the graphic is smaller than the paragraph area, use the Type options to position the graphic relative to the page margins. If you select Position, set the position of the graphic behind the paragraph. This is useful, for example, for positioning a logo.

Figure 5-33   The Page Style window, Background tab

If you want the page style to have a header, select the Header on option to activate the other fields.
Set the Spacing between the header and the rest of the page; set the Height of the header text box, or select AutoFit height to adjust the header height to the text you enter.
You can only increase the size of the left and right header margins.
In the Preview area, see the effects of the header options you select.
Click More to set border and background color/graphic options for the header (same options as Background and Borders tabs).
If you want to use different header information on left and right pages, don't select the Same content left/right option.
Page Style
Organizer
Page
Background
Header
Footer
Borders
Columns
Footnote
Headers
Header on
Spacing
0.20"
Height
0.20"
AutoFit height
Left margin
0.00"
Right margin
0.00"
Same content left/right
Preview
More...
OK
Cancel
Help
Reset

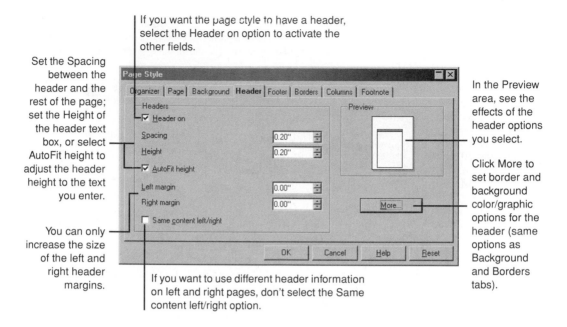

Figure 5-34 The Page Style window, Header tab

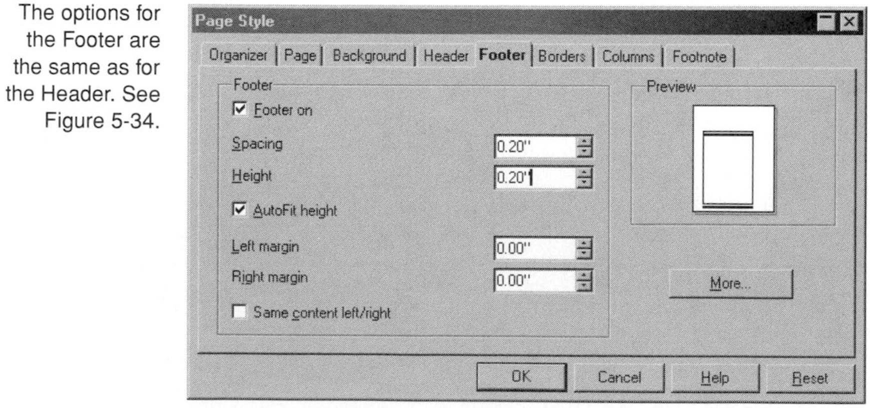

The options for the Footer are the same as for the Header. See Figure 5-34.
Page Style
Organizer
Page
Background
Header
Footer
Borders
Columns
Footnote
Footer
Footer on
Spacing
0.20"
Height
0.20"
AutoFit height
Left margin
0.00"
Right margin
0.00"
Same content left/right
Preview
More...
OK
Cancel
Help
Reset

Figure 5-35 The Page Style window, Footer tab

Click one of the Presets boxes to apply that border style. Click the empty first box to clear all line (not shadow) settings.

Select a line style for the border.

Click a Shadow style Position box to apply that shadow angle to the line. Click the first box to clear shadow settings.

The gray box in the Frame area represents the entire page. You can add or remove lines relative to the page by clicking above, below, or to either side of the gray box.

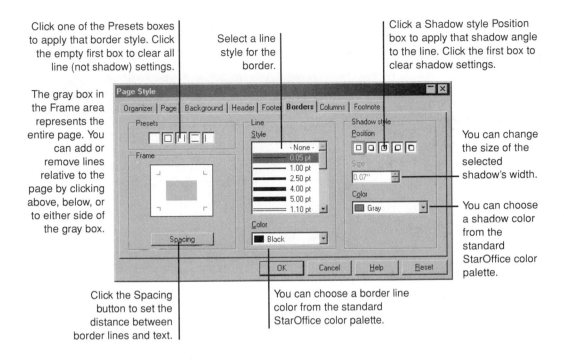

You can change the size of the selected shadow's width.

You can choose a shadow color from the standard StarOffice color palette.

Click the Spacing button to set the distance between border lines and text.

You can choose a border line color from the standard StarOffice color palette.

Figure 5-36   The Page Style window, Borders tab

Select a preset column style, or select in Amount the columns you want for the page style.

Set the amount of pacing, or "gutter," you want between columns.

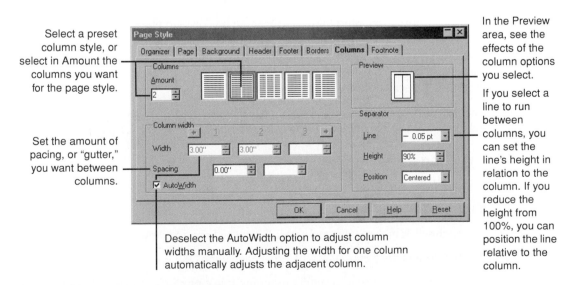

In the Preview area, see the effects of the column options you select.

If you select a line to run between columns, you can set the line's height in relation to the column. If you reduce the height from 100%, you can position the line relative to the column.

Deselect the AutoWidth option to adjust column widths manually. Adjusting the width for one column automatically adjusts the adjacent column.

Figure 5-37   The Page Style window, Columns tab

Select No larger than page area if you want unlimited
footnote space on a page. Or you can limit the Maximum
footnote height from the bottom of the page.

Distance from
text is the
distance from the
footnote line to
the bottom of the
body text.

Set options for
the line that will
divide the
footnotes from
the body text.

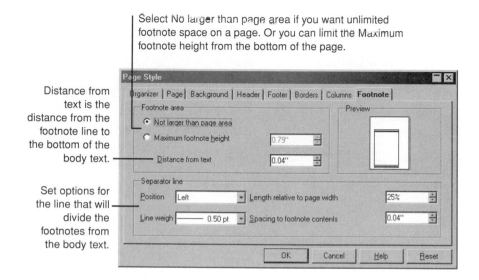

Figure 5-38   The Page Style window, Footnote tab

About Footnote Settings Footnote settings apply to footnotes you insert by choosing
Insert > Footnote.

Frame Styles

Frames are boxes you insert into a document to hold paragraphs and graphics around
which you want to wrap the body text of your document. Frame styles let you use a
consistent format for frames you commonly use. Frame styles control such attributes as
frame size, position, wrapping, borders, backgrounds, and number of columns. You can
even assign macros to run when the frame is selected.

For information on applying styles, see page 217; for modifying styles, see page 218; for
deleting styles, see page 219; for changing the category of styles, see page 219.

Creating a Frame Style

1   In the Stylist, click the Frame Styles button.

2   Select the category in which you want to put the new style.

3   Right-click in the Stylist and select New. The Frame Style window is displayed.

4   Set the options you want for the frame, and click OK.

Creating a frame style is similar to setting frame properties when you insert one in a
document. See *Tips for Adjusting Inserted Objects* on page 256.

Applying Styles

1   Select the paragraph, character, page, or frame to which you want to apply a style.

2   In the Stylist, select the type of style you want to apply, select a category, and double-click the name of the style you want to use.

Applying Paragraph Styles

As you apply styles in the document, the object bar displays styles you've applied so far. You can then apply styles from the object bar as well.

Applying Character Styles

You get more control over selecting words by double-clicking them. For example, you don't have to take time pinpointing the cursor to avoid selecting spaces before or after a word.

To select a series of words, double-click the first word, and as you drag through the remaining words you want to select, each word is selected in full. Again, this lets you drag quickly without having to avoid selecting the space after the last word.

You can also select nonsequential words by double-clicking. See *Selecting Nonconsecutive Blocks of Text* on page 171.

Removing Numbers and Bullets

Remove numbering or bulleting in a paragraph by clicking in the numbered or bulleted paragraph (or highlighting multiple paragraphs) and clicking the Numbering or Bullets icons in the object bar.

Applying and Overriding Page Style Flows

In a page style, the Next style field on the Organizer tab forces a page to be followed by a specific page: for example, a left page is followed by a right page and vice versa. So if you apply a page style to a page by double-clicking the page style in the Stylist, all subsequent pages will follow the Next style rules begun by the page style you've applied.

You can break the flow of page styles by creating a manual break. For example, you can break a left/right page flow at the end of a section by manually inserting a blank page with no headers or footers. Here's how:

1   Click in the exact place in the document where you want to create a break.

   If you're breaking at a heading, click at the very beginning of the heading.

2   Choose Insert > Manual Break.

3   Select Page Break, and in the Style field, select the page style you want to use for the new page.

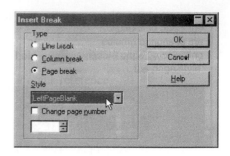

4   If you want the page to restart at a page number other than what is used in the regular page flow, select the Change page number option and set the page number the new page will begin with.

For a practical example of changing page numbering, see *Chapter-Page Numbering* on page 286.

5   Click OK.

You can also use this technique to switch between portrait and landscape page styles.

Applying Frame Styles

To apply a frame style, you must first insert a frame. See *Inserting Text Boxes* on page 249.

After you insert a frame, the frame styles appear in the Stylist. Double-click a frame style to apply it to the frame you inserted.

Modifying Styles

1   In the Stylist, select the style type containing the style you want to modify.

2   Select the category the style belongs to.

3   Right-click the style and select Modify.

If you're modifying a paragraph style, check to see if the paragraph style has a Condition tab with conditional settings. See the caution on using conditions on page 207.

4   Change settings for the style. If you need formatting guidance, see the previous formatting sections.

5   Click OK.

6   If a style doesn't update automatically in the document, select the name of the style in the Stylist and click the Update Style button at the top of the Stylist.

About Updating Paragraphs   If you try to update a paragraph but the paragraph font doesn't change, you may have applied a character style to the paragraph that is overriding the paragraph style. To fix this, select the entire paragraph and choose Format > Default. This removes the character style override and lets the paragraph use its own style.

Modifying Styles Using Drag and Drop

You can also modify paragraph, character, and numbering styles by drag and drop:

1   Format the paragraph, characters, or numbering manually (with the object bar or from the Format menu).

2   In the Stylist, select the type of style you're modifying and select the category the style belongs to.

3   In the document, select the modified paragraph, characters, or numbering; click and hold on it; and drag the pointer into the Stylist and onto the name of the style you want to modify.

The character style doesn't include hyperlink properties, which are offered in the Character window (Format > Character). You must set hyperlink properties on a case-by-base basis. See Figure 5-5 on page 183 for details.

Deleting Styles

Default StarOffice styles cannot be deleted. This procedure applies to custom styles you've created.

Before you delete a style, select it in the Stylist, right-click it, select Modify, and select the Organizer tab. Look at the style selected in the Based on field (if applicable). When you delete the style, if it was used in the document, the parts of the document that were assigned that style become the style shown in the Based on field.

1   In the Stylist, select the style you want to delete.

2   Right-click it, and select Delete.

3   Click Yes in the confirmation window.

Changing Style Categories

You can reorganize the styles you create by moving them into different categories. However, you can't change the categories of default Writer styles.

1   In the Stylist, select the style whose category you want to change.

2   Right-click it, and select Modify.

3   Select the Organizer tab.

4   In the Category field, select the new category you want to use.

5   Click OK.

All styles you create are custom, and therefore put in the Custom Styles category. Changing a style from the custom category to another category simply puts your custom style in an additional category.

Using Templates

Up to this point in the chapter we've progressed from manually setting specific formatting characteristics to grouping those characteristics into specific styles. Styles are containers for characteristics. This section takes the progression a step further by talking about templates, which are containers for styles.

A template is a document that was created with specific styles that can be used as a model for creating a specific type of document. For example, StarOffice installs with templates to help you create resumes, memos, fax cover sheets, budgets, calendars, newsletters, HTML documents, envelopes, and a bevy of other types of documents.

Templates are even more than containers for styles. They can also contain predefined text, graphics, pagination, work environment settings (toolbars, keyboard shortcuts, etc.), and other elements that will always be used in a new document of that type.

To take a look at the templates StarOffice provides, see *Previewing Templates* on page 128.

Creating a Document From a Template

See *Creating a Writer Document From a Template* on page 165.

If you want to just use the styles from a template, see *Loading Styles From Another Document* on page 221.

About the Standard Template

When you start a new Writer document, Writer bases the new document on a template called Standard, which has a standard set of styles and some behind-the-scenes functionality. If you don't like the default style settings provided by the Standard template (for example, if you want to use a different font size for the Text body or heading styles), you can have Writer use another template for new documents.

If all you want to do is start new documents with different font faces than those provided by the Standard template, there's an easy way to change the default standard fonts. See *Changing Default Fonts* on page 187.

Assigning a Different Template Than the Standard Template for New Documents

1   Start a new Writer document.

2   Modify the styles you want to change, and add any new styles you want.

3   Choose File > Save As, and save the document as a Writer template.

4   Open the Explorer and Beamer windows.

5   In the Explorer window, select the folder containing the template you created.

6   In the Beamer window, select the new template you created, right-click it, and choose Set Default Template > Text Document.

The new template will now be used whenever you start a new Writer document.

Switching Back to the Standard Template for New Documents

If you switched from the Standard template to another template for creating new documents (see previous procedure), use this procedure to switch back to the Standard template.

1   Open the Explorer and Beamer windows.

2   In the Explorer window, select Click & Go slider.

3   Right-click the Text icon and choose Reset Default.

The Reset Default menu item is only available if another document is being used as the default template.

The Standard template will now be used whenever you start a new Writer document.

Loading Styles From Another Document

If you want a document to use styles from another document or a template, you can load all styles or individual styles.

This procedure isn't the same as using a template to create a document. See *Creating a Writer Document From a Template* on page 165.

Loading All Styles

1   Start a new document or open the document into which you want to load different styles.

2   Choose Format > Styles > Load.

3   In the File type field, select whether you want to load styles from a Writer document (files ending in .sdw) or a Writer template (files ending in .vor).

4   At the bottom of the window, select the types of styles you want to load, as shown in Figure 5-39.

Select the Overwrite option to replace the style definitions for styles with the same name. If you don't select Overwrite, style settings with the same name won't be overwritten in the open document.

If you're loading styles from a template, you can also click the Templates button at the bottom of the window to select a template.

If you don't see the styles update automatically in the Stylist, click one of the other style buttons in the Stylist, then click the button of the styles you want to see.

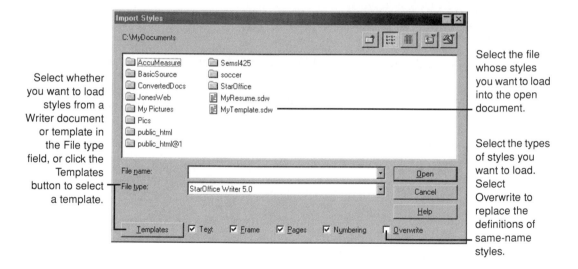

Select whether you want to load styles from a Writer document or template in the File type field, or click the Templates button to select a template.

Select the file whose styles you want to load into the open document.

Select the types of styles you want to load. Select Overwrite to replace the definitions of same-name styles.

Figure 5-39   Loading styles from the Import Styles window

Loading Individual Styles

If you want to load individual styles from one document into another (rather than loading all styles), use the template Organizer.

1   With Writer active, choose File > Templates > Organize.

You can also choose Format > Styles > Catalog, and click the Organizer button.

2   In the Document Templates window (Figure 5-40), below each list box, select whether you want to view Document Templates or Documents.

One list box will be used to copy styles from a document into the document listed in the other list box.

3   In one list box, double-click the file whose styles you want to use, then double-click the Styles icon below it. The styles used in the document are displayed.

4   In the other list box, double-click the name and the Styles icon of the document into which you want to load the styles.

5   Drag the style(s) you want to use from one document to the other.

Use Figure 5-40 for guidance on using the Document Templates window.

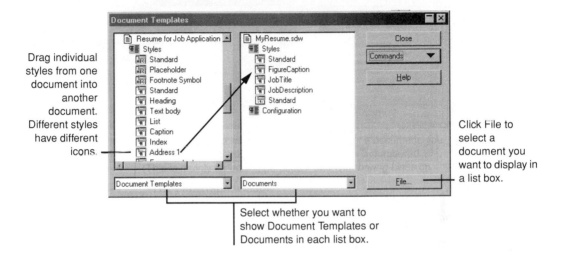

Drag individual styles from one document into another document. Different styles have different icons.

Click File to select a document you want to display in a list box.

Select whether you want to show Document Templates or Documents in each list box.

Figure 5-40   Loading styles from one document to another in the Document Templates window

Creating a Template

Creating a template isn't much more than formatting a document, adding boilerplate content to it, and saving it as a template.

If all you want to use a template for is to automatically insert boilerplate stuff like a company logo and address for a letterhead, you can also use the AutoText feature. See *Creating and Inserting Predefined Text and Templates* on page 167.

1   Create a document, adding any styles, formatting, graphics, tables, and any other content you want to use for a template.

2   Choose File > Templates > Save.

3   In the Document Templates window, enter new name for template.

4   Select a template category in which you want to store the template. (To create your own template category, see *Creating a Template Category* on page 225.)

5   Click OK. The template is ready to use.

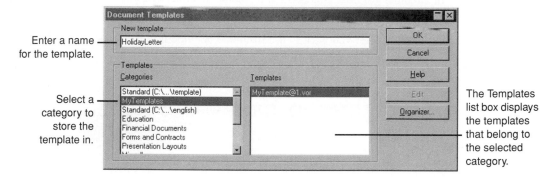

Enter a name for the template.

Select a category to store the template in.

The Templates list box displays the templates that belong to the selected category.

Figure 5-41 Creating a new template in the Document Templates window

Editing Templates

If you edit one of StarOffice's default templates, you may notice it uses a handful of automated fields. For help on fields, see 7, *Headers, Footers, and Fields*, on page 267.

1 With Writer active, choose File > Templates > Organize.

2 In the Document Templates window, select Document Templates in the field at the bottom of the window.

3 Double-click the folder containing the template you want to edit.

4 Select the template you want to edit.

5 Click the Commands button and choose Edit.

6 Modify and save the template.

If you want to edit a template that isn't stored in a StarOffice template folder, you can edit it by choosing File > Templates > Edit and double-clicking the template you want.

Importing and Exporting Templates

Importing and exporting templates is simply a way of moving template files into and out of the StarOffice template folders.

This procedure shows you how to import and export templates using the Organizer. You can also import and export templates in the Explorer window by moving them into and out of the subfolders of the StarOffice template folder.

Importing a Template

1 With Writer active, choose File > Templates > Organize.

2   In the Document Templates window, choose Document Templates in the field at the bottom of the window.

3   Select the template folder into which you want to import the template.

4   Click the Commands button and choose Import Template.

5   Locate and double-click the template you want to import. (Template files have a .vor extension.)

Exporting a Template

1   With Writer active, choose File > Templates > Organize.

2   In the Document Templates window, select Document Templates in the field at the bottom of the window.

3   Double-click the category containing the template you want to export.

4   Select the template you want to export.

5   Click the Commands button and choose Export Template.

6   In the Save As window, navigate to the folder to which you want to export the template.

7   Click Save.

Importing Microsoft Office Templates

See *Converting Microsoft Office Documents* on page 148.

Organizing Templates

In addition to letting you edit, import, and export templates, and share styles between documents, the Document Templates Organizer lets you create template categories.

Creating a Template Category

This procedure shows you how to create a template category using the Organizer. You can also create a category by adding a new subfolder to the StarOffice template folder in the Explorer window.

1   With Writer active, choose File > Templates > Organize.

     You can also choose Format > Styles > Catalog, and click the Organizer button.

2   Select Document Templates in the field at the bottom of the window.

3   Select any of the template folders.

4   Click the Commands button and choose New.

5   A new *Untitled* folder is displayed with the name highlighted. Type the name of the new template category.

Moving Templates to Different Categories

This procedure shows you how to move templates to different categories using the Organizer. You can also move templates to different categories in the Explorer window by moving them around between the subfolders of the StarOffice template folder.

1   With Writer active, choose File > Templates > Organize.

You can also choose Format > Styles > Catalog, and click the Organizer button.

2   Select Document Templates in the field at the bottom of the window.

3   Double-click the folder containing the template you want to move.

4   Hold down the Shift key and drag the template you want to move into another category folder.

If you don't hold down the Shift key while you drag, you copy the template rather than move it.

Deleting Templates and Template Categories

1   With Writer active, choose File > Templates > Organize.

You can also choose Format > Styles > Catalog, and click the Organizer button.

2   Select Document Templates in the field at the bottom of the window.

3   Select the category folder or template you want to delete.

4   Click the Commands button and choose Delete.

5   Click Yes in the confirmation window.

Adding Objects to Documents

Graphics and Drawings

You can insert raster graphics (pixels) and vector graphics (line drawings) into Writer documents. For more information on raster and vector graphics, see 26, *StarOffice Draw: Creating Vector Graphics*, on page 731, and 27, *StarOffice Image: Creating Raster Graphics*, on page 805.

For information on adjusting inserted graphics within the flow of a text document, such as anchoring, moving, and wrapping text around, see *Tips for Adjusting Inserted Objects* on page 256.

Inserting a Graphic File

You can insert any raster file, such as a GIF or JPG, into a Writer document.

1   Click the location in the document where you want to insert the picture.

2   Click and hold the Insert tool on the toolbar, and click the Insert Graphics tool.

    You can also choose Insert > Graphics > From File.

3   Select the file you want, then click Open.

4   Select the Preview option if you want to see the graphic before you insert it.

5   Select the Link option, as shown in Figure 6-1, if you want to be connected to the original file. The picture in the document will be updated when the picture file is updated. It also helps keep your document file size down. However, changing the location of the inserted file will break the link.

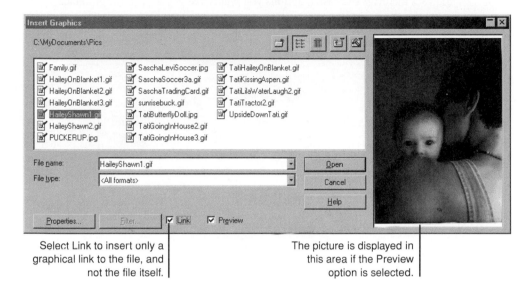

Select Link to insert only a graphical link to the file, and not the file itself.

The picture is displayed in this area if the Preview option is selected.

Figure 6-1   Inserting a picture

Inserting a StarOffice Gallery Image

You can drag and drop images from the StarOffice Gallery into a Writer document. See *Beamer and Gallery* on page 105.

Inserting a Graphical Horizontal Line

1   Click where you want to insert the graphical horizontal line.

2   Choose Insert > Horizontal line.

3   Select the line you want to use, and click OK.

Editing Graphics

For information on editing the content of raster graphics, see 27, *StarOffice Image: Creating Raster Graphics*, on page 805.

Cropping and Resizing Inserted Pictures

After you insert a picture, you can crop it directly in Writer without having to modify the picture in Image.

1   Double-click the image.

2   In the Graphics window, click the Crop tab.

3   Set the crop and resize options you want. See Figure 6-2 for guidance.

4   Click OK.

Click the down arrows for a negative crop.

Select Keep size to make the cropped area the full size of the original image. Select Keep scale to make the cropped image size proportional to the whole.

Crop lines display in the crop area.

Change the image width and height by unit of measurement or by percentage. Even after you've resized the image, you can return it to its original size by clicking that button.

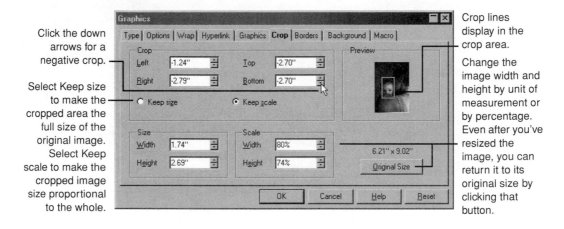

Figure 6-2   Cropping and resizing an image

Creating and Adjusting Drawings

You can use Writer's vector drawing tools to add line drawings to your documents.

1   Click and hold down the Show Draw Functions button on the toolbar to display the drawing tools you can use.

2   Click the icon of the shape you want to draw.

The pointer turns into cross hairs, and the object bar displays Draw options.

3   Draw the object where you want it to display in the document, as shown in Figure 6-3.

4   With the drawing selected, set the color and line options you want.

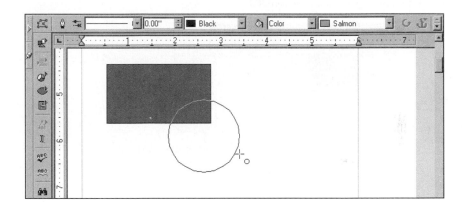

Figure 6-3   Inserting drawings in documents

For detailed information on creating and adjusting drawings, see 26, *StarOffice Draw: Creating Vector Graphics*, on page 731.

Inserting an Empty StarOffice Draw Image

You can insert an empty Draw image and begin creating a new one.

See *Inserting an Empty Image* on page 681.

Tables

Writer gives you a lot of flexibility for inserting tables and formatting tables. Perhaps the most powerful table feature is the ability to perform basic calculations in cells, and to create charts based on table contents.

For information on creating charts, see *Charts* on page 243.

This section shows you how to insert and format tables.

Inserting Tables

There are two ways to insert tables in Writer. The first way is a quick method of inserting basic rows and columns. The second way gives you more control over table formatting, even letting you choose from a handful of preset table formats.

Inserting a Quick Table

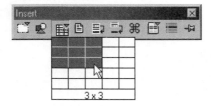

This method of inserting a table gives you only a basic table with a single-line border around all cells. If you want to insert a table with more formatting, see the next procedure.

1   Click the location in the document where you want to insert the table.

2   Click and hold the Insert tool on the toolbar.

3   Click the Insert Table tool. A small grid is displayed below the Insert Table tool.

4   Move the pointer through the grid and select the number of rows and columns you want the table to be. The grid expands as you move the pointer into its borders, and the table dimensions display at the bottom of the grid.

The row count includes a table header row and borders by default. If you want to change these and other defaults, choose Tools > Options > Text document > Insert, or Tools > Options > Text document > Table.

Inserting a Table With More Formats

You can also insert tables in a way that gives you control over every aspect of a table's appearance.

1   Choose Insert > Table.

2   In the Insert Table window, enter a table name.

The table name is used to identify the table when Navigator is used.

3   Set the number of columns and rows, and set the header options.

4   To apply preset formatting to the table, click the AutoFormat button.

5   In the AutoFormat window, click the More button.

6   Set the elements you want to AutoFormat.

Figure 6-4 describes options in the Insert Table and AutoFormat windows.

Type a name for
the table that will
identify it when
you use Navigator.

If you select the
Header option, the
number or rows
you set includes a
header row.

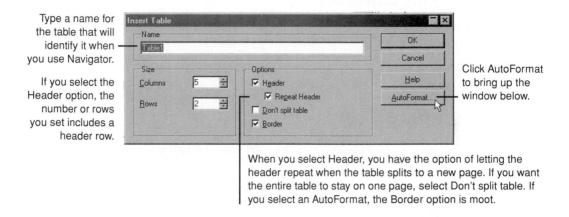

Click AutoFormat
to bring up the
window below.

When you select Header, you have the option of letting the
header repeat when the table splits to a new page. If you want
the entire table to stay on one page, select Don't split table. If
you select an AutoFormat, the Border option is moot.

When you select a
Format, it is
displayed in the
Preview area.

Select the
Formatting options
you want. See the
effects of selecting
and deselecting
options in the
Preview area.

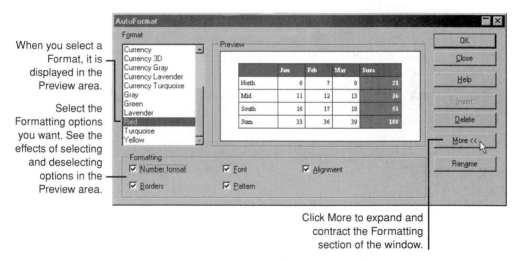

Click More to expand and
contract the Formatting
section of the window.

Figure 6-4   Inserting a table and applying a predefined AutoFormat

If your table runs to the bottom of the page and disappears, deselect the Don't split option.
If that doesn't work, try deselecting the Repeat Header option as well.

Formatting and Using Tables

Use this section to help you format cells, perform calculations, and modify tables after
you've inserted them.

Using the Object Bar

When you click inside a table, the object bar changes to show the table formatting tools in Figure 6-5.

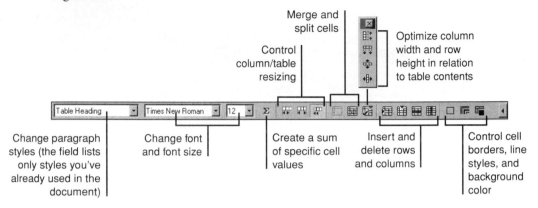

Figure 6-5   The object bar when the cursor is in a table

To switch back to the text formatting tools in the object bar, click the large left-pointing arrow at the right side of the object bar.

If you simply want to apply (or remove) bold, italicize, or underline table text formatting, use the following keyboard shortcuts instead of switching to the text formatting object bar.

Bold – Ctrl+B

Italic – Ctrl+I

Underline – Ctrl+U

You can use these shortcuts in combination with each other to make selected text ***bold italic***, for example.

Changing Column Widths

Position the mouse pointer on top of a table cell border. When the pointer changes to a double arrow, click and drag to the new width.

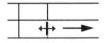

Making Column Widths Equal

1   Select the columns you want to make equal
widths.

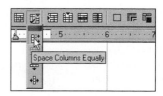

2   In the object bar (which now shows table tools),
click and hold down the Optimize button, then
click the Space Columns Equally button.

You can change the default column width used when
you insert a table. Choose Tools > Options > Text document > Table, and make the change
in the Insert area of the Options window.

For more precise control over column and table width, see *General Table Formatting* on
page 240.

Number Formatting in Cells

You can assign different number formats to specific cells, so that when you type in a value
or perform a calculation, the value automatically becomes a dollar amount, a percentage, a
date, or whichever format you've chosen. You can also change number-formatted cells
back to regular text format using this procedure.

1   Select the cell(s) you want to format.

2   Right-click and choose Number Format. You can also choose Format > Number
Format.

3   Select a numbering format category and set options for it.

Use Figure 6-6 for guidance.

4   Click OK.

When you select the
Currency category, you can
choose which country
currency format to use.

Sot values for numbers that
can use decimals, leading
zeros, negative values, or
thousand separators.

When you select
a type of number
in the Category
list, you can
choose among
different Format
options.

You can change
the language for
category types
that use text
such as month
names.

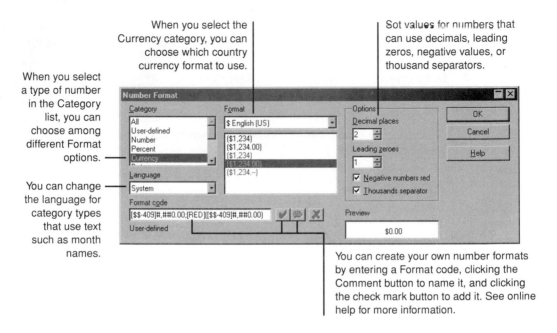

You can create your own number formats
by entering a Format code, clicking the
Comment button to name it, and clicking
the check mark button to add it. See online
help for more information.

Figure 6-6   Setting number format options

Performing Calculations in Writer Table Cells

One of the most impressive features of Writer tables is the ability to perform calculations in cells like the ones you can create in a spreadsheet application.

1   Click in the cell you want to contain the solution to the formula.

2   Press the F2 key to display the formula box (just above the object bar).

You can also click the sum button to bring up the formula box and have Writer insert a sum formula automatically, based on the table contents.

If a sum is all you want, and the correct cells are used in the formula, just press Enter here and you're done.

3   Enter a formula. Be sure to begin the formula with an equals sign, and click cells to include a reference to their contents in the formula. If you need help with structuring your formula and using cell references, see Chapter 18, *Calculating and Manipulating Data*, on page 521.

You can also click and hold down the Formula button in the formula bar for help inserting certain formula elements.

4   Click the Apply button or press Enter to calculate the formula.

When you change numbers in the cells that were referenced in the formula, the calculated amount changes. If for some reason it doesn't change, click in the calculated cell and press the F9 key.

If you want to include more sophisticated tables in your Writer docs, you can insert parts of or entire Calc spreadsheets. See *Spreadsheets* on page 244.

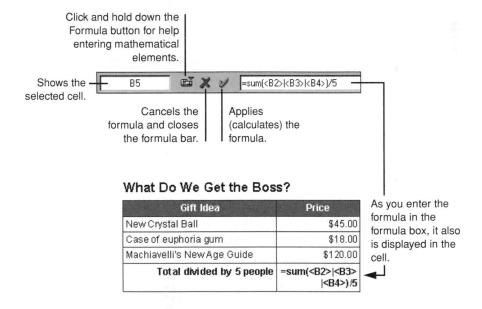

Figure 6-7   Performing calculations in Writer tables

The syntax for cell references is different in a Writer table than it is in a Calc spreadsheet. In a Writer table, cell references must be opened and closed by the less-than and greater-than symbols. For example, a reference to cell B4 would need to be entered as <B4>. If you're building a formula, and you click a cell to add it to the formula, this syntax is used automatically.

Also, as shown in Figure 6-7, you can use a pipe symbol "|" instead of a plus symbol "+". You can't do that in Calc.

Making Calculations in Body Text

You can also make one-time calculations outside of cells in the body text of your document, though this isn't particularly useful if any of the numbers in your formula changes, because the calculated amount won't adjust automatically.

1   Enter the formula in your text followed by an equals sign. For example:

```
(45+15+120)/5=
```

2   Copy the formula.

3   Press F2, and paste the formula into the formula box.

4   Press Enter. The solution to the formula is displayed in the text as a field.

Inserting Columns and Rows

You can insert rows and columns into a table after you've already created it.

1   Click in a row or column next to where you want to make the insertion.

     The new rows or columns you insert will share the same formatting as the selected row or column.

2   Right-click, and choose Row > Insert, or Column > Insert. (There are also Insert Row and Insert Column buttons on the object bar.)

3   In the Insert window, set the number of rows or columns you want to insert, and designate whether you want to insert them before or after the selected area in the table.

4   Click OK.

To adjust the default column widths when columns are inserted, choose Tools > Options > Text document > Table, and make the adjustment in the Insert section of the Options window.

Repeating the Heading Row

The first row of a table is always the header row, whether or not you apply some kind of a table heading paragraph format to it. To make the header row repeat when the table breaks to a new page:

1   Click in the table, right-click, and choose Table.

2   In the Text Flow tab, select the Repeat heading option.

3   Click OK.

If you want more than one heading row to repeat, select the cells in the heading and choose Format > Cell > Split. Then, in the Split Cells window, set the number of rows you want the heading row to be, select the Horizontally option, and click OK.

Deleting Columns, Rows, and Entire Tables

1   Select the first cell(s) in the row(s) or column(s) you want to delete.

2   Right-click the selection and choose Row > Delete, or Column > Delete.

     There are also Delete Row and Delete Column buttons on the object bar.

Be careful when you delete columns and rows. If you select a column for deletion, but you right-click and choose Row > Delete, all selected rows are deleted rather than the column. That means if you select an entire column, you will delete the entire table by right-clicking and choosing Rows > Delete.

Changing Row Height

You can change the space between cell text and top and bottom of the cell by changing the row height. Increasing the row height also lets you to see the effects of the vertical alignment of the cell contents.

1   Select the rows you want to change.

2   Right-click and choose Row > Height. You can also choose Format > Row > Height.

3   In the Row Height window, set the new size.

4   Select the Fit to size option if you want the row height to adjust automatically with the amount and size of text entered.

Changing Vertical Alignment

When you increase the space above and below cell text by increasing the row height, you can vertically align the text to display at the top, middle, or bottom of the cell. To do this, select the cells you want to align, right-click, and choose Cell > (Top, Center, or Bottom).

	Gift Idea	Price
Top aligned ———	New Crystal Ball	$45.00
Center aligned ———	Case of euphoria gum	$18.00
Bottom aligned ———	Machiavelli's New Age Guide	$120.00

Figure 6-8   Vertical alignments

Protecting Cell Contents

You can keep the contents of certain cells from being edited directly by protecting them, effectively making them read-only.

1   Select the cells you want to protect.

2   Right-click, and choose Cell > Protect.

To make a cell writable again, select it, right-click, and choose Cell > Unprotect.

Merging and Splitting Cells

You can merge multiple cells so that they become a single cell, and you can split a single cell into multiple cells.

1   Select the cells you want to merge or split.

2   Click the Merge or Split button on the object bar, or right-click and choose Cell > (Merge or Split).

General Table Formatting

Use this procedure for more overall table formatting, such as changing table width, alignment, space above and below the table in the document, determining whether the table breaks to a new column or page or whether the heading repeats, and tweaking table borders and background.

For quick border and background color formatting, use the object bar.

1   Click in the table. If you want to change specific cell borders or background, select the cells you want to modify.

2   Right-click and choose Table.

You can also choose Format > Table.

3   Make modifications to the table in the Table Format window.

Use Figure 6-9 through Figure 6-13 for guidance.

Adjust the overall width of the table. This width relates to the information on the Columns tab. Select Relative to make the table width a percentage of the page width.

The Name field is used to identify the table when you use Navigator. Use a descriptive name.

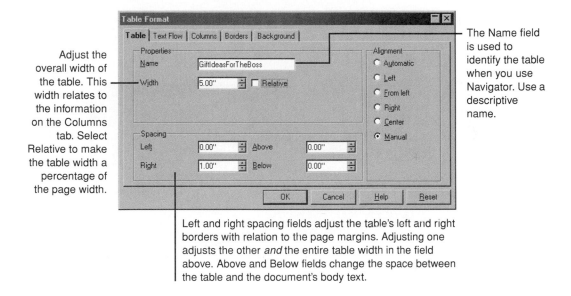

Left and right spacing fields adjust the table's left and right borders with relation to the page margins. Adjusting one adjusts the other *and* the entire table width in the field above. Above and Below fields change the space between the table and the document's body text.

Figure 6-9   The Table Format window, Table tab

The Width field is important, because it controls the total width of the table. If the table width is less than the page width, you won't be able to manually widen the table in Writer.

Select Break if you want the table to break to a new column or page. Select Before to move the table to the next page or column; select After to move the next body text to the next page or column.

When you select the Page and Before options to move a table to a new page, you can select the With page style option and apply a page style for the new page (choose from the list of currently defined page styles).

The Keep with next paragraph option lets you, for example, keep the table with the table caption that follows it if a page break occurs.

Set the Vertical alignment for cell text with relation to the top and bottom of the cell.

Select Don't split table to keep the entire table on a page; select Repeat heading to have the table heading repeat if the table splits to another page.

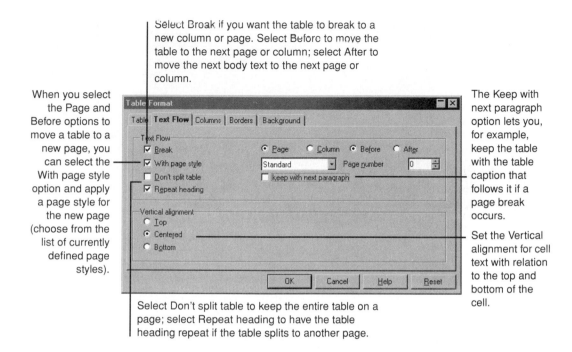

Figure 6-10   The Table Format window, Text Flow tab

Select Fit to table width to have the existing table expand proportionately by the Remaining Space amount. Remaining space is the amount of space the table can expand to the Width field in the Table tab.

If you select the Adjust columns proportionally option, adjusting the Column width of one column automatically adjusts the width of the other columns. Width adjustment stops when the Remaining space is zero.

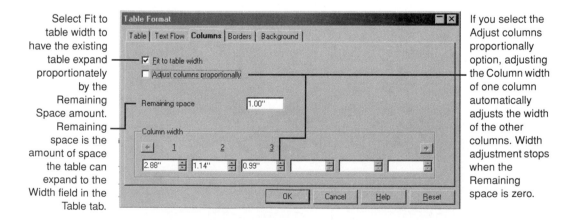

Figure 6-11   The Table Format window, Columns tab

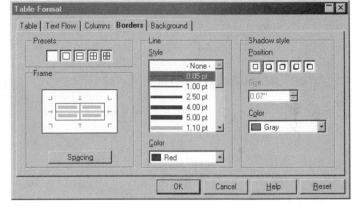

Setting cell borders is similar to setting paragraph borders. If you need help, see Figure 5-17 on page 192.

Figure 6-12   The Table Format window, Borders tab

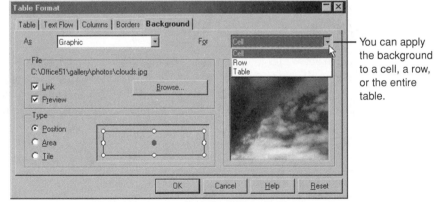

Setting cell background is similar to setting paragraph background. If you need help, see Figure 5-18 on page 193.

You can apply the background to a cell, a row, or the entire table.

Figure 6-13   The Table Format window, Background tab

Charts

The StarOffice Chart tool lets you create charts based on information in Writer tables. StarOffice Chart uses a wizard to help you set options for the chart.

Creating and Modifying Charts

The process for creating and modifying charts in Writer is the same as it is for creating them in Calc. See *Charts* on page 552.

Updating Charts

You can choose whether you want to update charts automatically or manually when Writer table contents change.

Automatically Updating Charts

Follow this procedure to update charts automatically when the tables they were based on change.

1   Choose Tools > Options > Text document > Other.

2   Select the Update charts automatically option.

3   Click OK.

Manually Updating Charts

You can set Writer to update charts manually when the contents of tables change. A good reason to do this is if you're making frequent changes to tables and you don't want charts to update until you're finished making changes. Constant chart updates take up memory and processing power and potentially slow down the table editing process.

1   Choose Tools > Options > Text document > Other.

2   Deselect the Update charts automatically option.

3   Click OK.

4   When you change the contents of a table, click somewhere in the table and press the F9 key.

Spreadsheets

When you insert a Calc spreadsheet into Writer, you literally insert a spreadsheet. Whether you copy part of a spreadsheet and paste it into Writer or insert the entire spreadsheet through OLE (Object Linking and Embedding), you can double-click the spreadsheet and edit it as if you're working in Calc.

The inserted spreadsheet is standalone, has no links to the original spreadsheet, and cannot be saved as a separate spreadsheet file.

For information on adjusting inserted spreadsheets within the flow of a text document, such as anchoring, moving, and wrapping text around, see *Tips for Adjusting Inserted Objects* on page 256.

Inserting Part of a Spreadsheet

1   With both Writer and the desired Calc spreadsheet open, select the cells in the spreadsheet you want to insert in Writer.

2   Press Ctrl+C or choose Edit > Copy to copy.

3   Switch to your Writer document, and click where you want to insert the spreadsheet.

4   Choose Edit > Paste Special.

5   In the Paste Special window, select Calc Spreadsheet and click OK.

The spreadsheet is displayed in the Writer document as an object with green resize handles, as shown in Figure 6-14. You can edit the spreadsheet in Writer after you insert it. See *Editing Inserted Calc Spreadsheets* on page 246.

You can also use this procedure to insert spreadsheets from other spreadsheet applications. In the Paste Special window, select the appropriate spreadsheet type.

Figure 6-14   Inserting part of a Calc spreadsheet

If your Calc and Writer documents are displayed side by side, you can also select cells in a spreadsheet and click and drag them into the Writer document.

Inserting a Whole Spreadsheet

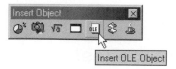

In addition to inserting part of a Calc spreadsheet into Writer, you can insert an entire spreadsheet. This usually works best if you're inserting into a landscape page. This is a hit-and-miss procedure, though, because if your spreadsheet is wider than the Writer page, or if it has more rows than can fit on a page, the results won't be good. Instead, consider converting a spreadsheet to a Writer table. See *Converting a Calc Table to a Writer Table* on page 248.

To insert a whole spreadsheet:

1   Click in Writer where you want to insert the spreadsheet.

2   In the toolbar, click and hold down the Insert Objects tool, and click the Insert OLE Object tool.

3   In the Insert OLE Object window (Figure 6-15), select the Create from file option.

4   Click the Search button, and double-click the spreadsheet you want to insert.

5   Click OK.

You can also insert a blank spreadsheet by selecting the Create new option in the Insert OLE Object window.

Figure 6-15   Inserting a whole Calc spreadsheet

Editing Inserted Calc Spreadsheets

If you inserted only selected cells from a Calc spreadsheet, only this data—not any other data in the original spreadsheet—is brought into Writer.

1   In Writer, double-click the Calc spreadsheet object.

The object's resize handles turn black, and the spreadsheet becomes an editable Calc spreadsheet, with spreadsheet tabs, scroll bars, menus, tools, a formula bar, and the Calc object bar (see Figure 6-16).

2   Make changes to the spreadsheet (this doesn't change the original spreadsheet).

3   Click outside of the spreadsheet to get out of edit mode.

The cells that were displayed in the spreadsheet window when you got out of edit mode now display. To change the cells that are displayed, double-click to get back into edit mode, and use the scrollbars to view the correct cells.

When you edit an inserted Calc spreadsheet, you have all the controls available when you're working in Calc itself, such as inserting graphics, shown here.

Editing the object doesn't affect the original spreadsheet.

Figure 6-16   Editing an inserted Calc spreadsheet

Updating Automatically as the Spreadsheet Changes

This feature works in Windows only. You can insert a Calc spreadsheet into Writer so that when you edit the spreadsheet file itself, the changes automatically appear in the spreadsheet object in Writer. The drawback to using this method is that the spreadsheet object pasted into Writer is displayed as a basic, unformatted table.

1   In Calc, select the cells you want to insert into Writer.

2   Press Ctrl+C or choose Edit > Copy to copy.

3   Switch to your Writer document, and click where you want to insert the spreadsheet.

4   Choose Edit > Paste Special.

5   In the Paste Special window, select DDE link, and click OK.

DDE stands for Dynamic Data Exchange.

Deleting a DDE Linked Spreadsheet

If you use the previous procedure to insert a Calc spreadsheet into Writer, you can't delete the table by simply selecting its cells and deleting rows or columns. You have to click in the paragraph above or below the table, drag through it so that the whole thing is selected, and press Delete.

Converting a Calc Table to a Writer Table

If you want to put the contents of a spreadsheet in a Writer document, but the spreadsheet is too big to fit on the Writer pages, use this procedure to convert the spreadsheet to a Writer table that will span multiple pages.

1   Select the contents of the spreadsheet.

2   In Writer, click where you want to insert the table, and choose Edit > Paste Special.

3   In the Paste Special window, select the Unformatted text option, and click OK.

The text of the spreadsheet is pasted into the Writer document.

4   Select the text that was just pasted into Writer, and choose Tools > Text <-> Table.

5   In the Convert Text to Table window, select the Tabs option, as shown in Figure 6-17.

6   Select any other options or formatting you want.

7   Click OK.

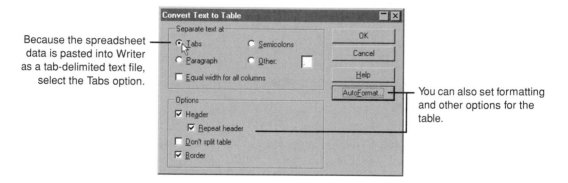

Figure 6-17   Converting tab-delimited text to a Writer table

Frames

There are two types of frames in Writer: text boxes and floating frames.

Text boxes are mainly containers that hold text that you want the body text of a document to wrap around, though you can also insert anything in a text box, even another frame.

Floating frames hold an entire, open file inside of a frame, whether it's a graphic, a slide presentation, a web page, or a spreadsheet. When you insert a floating frame, StarOffice lets you work with that file within Writer as if you were working with the file in its native

StarOffice application. Menus, the toolbar, and the object bar all change to let you work with the file in the floating frame.

For information on adjusting inserted frames within the flow of a text document, such as anchoring, moving, and wrapping text around, see *Tips for Adjusting Inserted Objects* on page 256.

Inserting Text Boxes

You can insert a basic, single- or multiple-column text box quickly by drawing it into your document, or you can use more precise control over the text boxes you insert. The following procedures show you each way.

Drawing a Quick Text Box

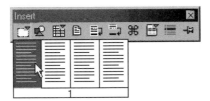

1   In the toolbar, click and hold down the Insert tool.

2   Click and hold down the Insert frame manually tool, and select the number of columns you want to insert. The pointer changes to cross hairs.

3   Click and drag to draw the text box in the location where you want to anchor it.

You can apply more precise formatting to the text by selecting it, right-clicking, and choosing Frame.

Inserting a Text Box With More Control

Use this procedure if you want more up-front control over the properties of the text box you want to insert.

1   Click where you want to insert the text box.

2   Choose Insert > Frame.

3   In the Frame window, set the options you want. Except for the Columns tab, which is fairly straightforward, the options are described in *Tips for Adjusting Inserted Objects* on page 256.

Inserting a Floating Frame

A floating frame is much more than a text box. It can contain an entire file of any type that StarOffice can open.

1   Click where you want to insert the floating frame.

2   In the toolbar, click and hold down the Insert Object tool, and click the Insert Floating Frame tool.

3   In the Frame Properties window, click the ⌷...⌷ button to select the file.

4   Set the remaining properties for the window.

     Use Figure 6-18 for guidance.

5   Click OK.

Enter a Name that will identify the
frame when you use Navigator.

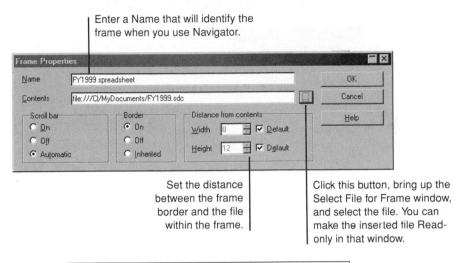

Set the distance
between the frame
border and the file
within the frame.

Click this button, bring up the
Select File for Frame window,
and select the file. You can
make the inserted file Read-
only in that window.

The contents of a
floating frame can be
edited inside Writer
as if you were editing
the file in its native
StarOffice
application. You can
also save the file
inside the floating
frame. In this
example, a
spreadsheet file is in
the floating frame.

Figure 6-18   Inserting a floating frame

Mathematical Formulas

StarOffice has a tool called Math that lets you insert and build formulas in a document.

For information on adjusting inserted formulas within the flow of a text document, such as anchoring, moving, and wrapping text around, see *Tips for Adjusting Inserted Objects* on page 256.

Inserting and Building Formulas

When you insert a formula, you have to build it using Math's formula notation language. Math makes entering the formula notation easier with formula tools that insert notation automatically. Use the formula tools to help you learn the formula language.

1   Click where you want to insert the formula.

2   In the toolbar, click and hold down the Insert Objects tool, and click the Insert Formula tool.

3   Enter the formula in the Commands window (Figure 6-19). To use the formula tools, choose View > Selection, or right-click in the Commands window.

   As you build the formula, it is displayed inside the document.

4   When you're finished, press the Esc key to close the Commands window.

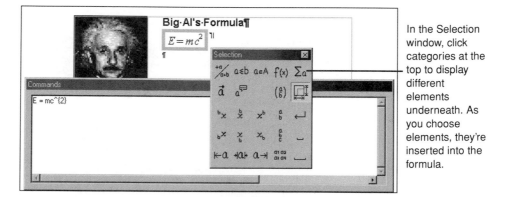

In the Selection window, click categories at the top to display different elements underneath. As you choose elements, they're inserted into the formula.

Figure 6-19   Inserting a formula

Changing the Formula Format

You can change the font, spacing, and alignment of formulas you create.

Changing Font Face

You can change the font face for individual elements of a formula.

1   With the formula Commands window active, select Format > Fonts.

2   In the Font Types window, click the Modify button to select a different font for a specific element of the formula.

3   Click OK.

As you assign a different font to a formula element, that font becomes available for selection in the field next to the element.

Changing Font Size

You can change overall font size for the entire formula, and you can adjust the relative font sizes of parts of the formula.

1   With the formula Commands window active, select Format > Font Size.

2   In the Font Sizes window, changing the Base size changes the font for the entire formula.

3   Adjust the relative percentage sizes of parts of the formula.

4   Click OK.

Changing Spacing Between Formula Elements

1   With the formula Commands window active, select Format > Spacing.

2   In the Spacing window, click the Category button and choose the item you want to adjust.

3   As you make adjustments in the left side of the window, a preview area displays the effects of your changes.

4   Click OK.

To return to the spacing defaults, click the Default button in the Spacing window.

Changing Alignment of Formula Elements

You can set the elements in a formula to be aligned left, center, or right relative to the width of the formula box in your document.

1   With the formula Commands window active, select Format > Alignment.

2   Select Left, Centered, or Right, and click OK.

Inserting Special Characters in Formulas

You can insert special characters into your formula.

1   In the Commands window, click in the formula where you want to insert a special character.

2   Choose Tools > Symbols > Catalog, or click the Symbols tool on the toolbar.

3   In the Symbols window, select the symbol you want, and click Insert.

4   Click Close.

Creating and Importing Formula Files

You can create standalone formula files in StarOffice Math, then import them into a Writer document.

Creating a Formula File

1   Choose File > New > Formula. The Math environment is displayed.

2   Create a formula in the Commands window.

3   Choose File > Save As. In the Save As window, the File type should say Math 5.0.

4   Name the file, set the path to the folder you want, and click Save.

Importing a Formula File Into Writer

1   Insert a formula in Writer. See *Inserting and Building Formulas* on page 252.

2   With the Commands window active, choose Tools > Import Formula.

3   Select the formula file, and click Insert.

Documents

Writer lets you insert, or import, entire text documents into the flow of a Writer document. The documents you insert can be in a wide range of non-Writer formats. You can also insert parts of other Writer documents.

The inserted document uses the page formatting of the document you insert it into; but if you insert another Writer document, it brings all of its styles with it.

Inserting Other Documents

1   In Writer, click where you want to insert the document.

2   On the toolbar, click and hold down the Insert tool, then click the Document tool.

3   At the bottom of the Insert window, select the File type of the document you want to insert, then find and select the document.

4   Click Insert. The document is brought into Writer.

Inserting Parts of Writer Documents

See *Inserting Sections As Links* on page 338.

Scanning Images Into Writer

Typically when you scan an image, especially if it's just one picture, the scanner includes all the empty space around the image as part of the scan. This can make a scanned object take up a lot of space when you scan it into Writer. But Writer lets you crop pictures, which is perfect for handling scanned images.

If you want to save images you scan, we recommend scanning them into Image and saving them. You can then insert them into Writer. (Or you can scan them into Writer, then copy and paste them into Image.)

For information on adjusting scanned images within the flow of a text document, such as anchoring, moving, and wrapping text around, see *Tips for Adjusting Inserted Objects* on page 256.

1   Make sure your scanner and software are properly installed and configured, and that the scanner is turned on and plugged into the computer.

2   In Writer, click where you want to insert the scanned image.

3   Choose Insert > Graphics > Scan > Request. Use the scanner software that launches to scan the image. After the scan, you may need to close the scanner software. The scanned image is displayed in Writer.

4   If you need to crop the image, double-click it.

5   In the Graphics window, click the Crop tab and crop the image.

Make sure the Keep scale option is selected. Click the down arrows next to the Left, Right, Top, and Bottom fields to crop negatively, which is what you need to do for this procedure, as shown in Figure 6-20.

6   Click OK. The resize handles on the image now surround only the cropped area.

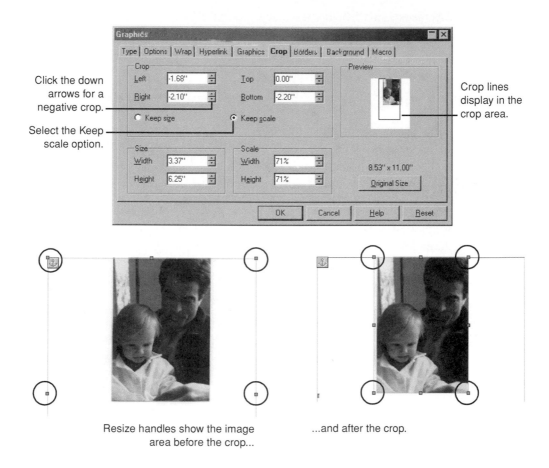

Figure 6-20   Scanning and cropping an image

Tips for Adjusting Inserted Objects

When you insert an object, you can change how it is displayed and affects the flow of the document. For example, you can change its size and position, determine how text wraps around it or how much space there is between the object and the body text, anchor it to a paragraph or in the middle of a sentence as a character, set hyperlink properties, and apply borders and backgrounds.

You can access these controls by selecting and right-clicking an object to see menu options, or by double-clicking it to change settings in a window. These tips don't apply to tables.

The following are some of the more useful tips for adjusting inserted objects.

Anchoring an Object

Objects are anchored to keep them at an exact point in a document. As the document changes, the object moves or remains in place as the document changes, depending on the anchoring options you set. When you select an object, an anchor icon is displayed, showing you where the object is anchored.

You can move this anchor by dragging it to a different place in the document, which also moves the object.

In the toolbar, click the Nonprinting Characters tool to show paragraph symbols and help you more accurately anchor an object.

Moving Objects

You can move objects in a document just by clicking and dragging them.

Creating Space Around Objects

If you want to increase or decrease the space between an object and the document's body text:

1   Click the object. For some objects, like floating frames, you may need to position the cursor over the object until the cursor changes to cross hairs with arrows before you click.

2   Choose Format > Object. (If the object is a graphic, choose Format > Graphics.)

     You can also double-click the object.

3   In the window that is displayed, select the Wrap tab.

4   In the Spacing area of the window, adjust the top, bottom, left, and right spacing as desired.

5   Click OK.

Manually Resizing Objects

If you want to manually resize an object by clicking it and dragging its resize handles, you can maintain their exact proportions as you resize by holding down the Shift key while you drag from a corner resize handle.

Lining Up Objects on a Grid

You can exercise more control over your alignment of objects in a document by using a grid to line things up, as Figure 6-21 illustrates.

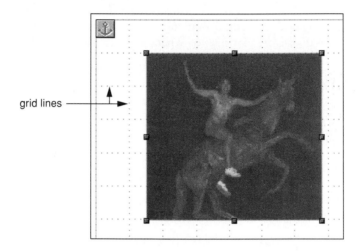

grid lines

Figure 6-21   Using a grid to align objects

To set grid options for your documents:

1   Choose Tools > Options > Text document > Grid.

2   In the Options window, set the grid options, as described in Figure 6-22.

3   Click OK.

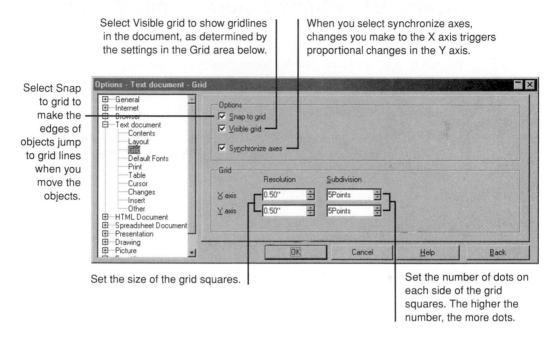

Select Visible grid to show gridlines in the document, as determined by the settings in the Grid area below.

When you select synchronize axes, changes you make to the X axis triggers proportional changes in the Y axis.

Select Snap to grid to make the edges of objects jump to grid lines when you move the objects.

Set the size of the grid squares.

Set the number of dots on each side of the grid squares. The higher the number, the more dots.

Figure 6-22   Setting grid options

Inserting Captions

Use the following procedure to insert captions for illustrations, drawings, tables, and any other objects you insert.

There are a couple of ways you can insert captions: using Writer's caption tool, or creating your own autonumbered paragraph formats. There are benefits and drawbacks to each:

Using Writer's Caption Tool The benefit is that you can insert captions automatically whenever you insert an object in Writer. One drawback is that the caption is inserted directly above or below the object, and you have to manually change the spacing between each object and its caption. Another drawback is that you can edit the caption title directly. It's not created as an non-editable field.

Using AutoNumbered Paragraph Formats One benefit is that you can't edit the caption title or number. It's all one non-editable field. Another benefit is that it's easier to control the spacing between the paragraph format and the object. The drawback is that you have to manually apply the paragraph format to get the caption title and number. It's not inserted automatically when you insert an element like a graphic.

With either method you can generate a list of figures, tables, or lists of any other elements.

Inserting Captions Automatically With the Caption Tool

You can have Writer insert captions automatically when you insert objects into Writer.

1   Choose Tools > Options > Text document > Insert.

2   Select the Automatic option, and click the ellipses button.

3   In the Caption window, select the box next to each StarOffice object for which you want to generate an automatic caption, and set the caption options for each, as shown in Figure 6-23.

4   Click OK in the Caption window.

5   Click OK in the Options window.

If you want to use chapter-number numbering for the captions (such as "Illustration 3-5"), make sure you've defined a top-level paragraph, such as Heading 1, as the level 1 outline number with an auto-generated chapter number. See *Outline Numbering* on page 278. Also, in the Caption window (Figure 6-23), set the Level field to None. For some reason this creates the number format correctly.

Each type of caption has a corresponding paragraph style that you can modify. But in the paragraph format for each type of caption (Graphic, Illustration, and so on), be sure **not** to assign a numbering style on the Numbering tab. That will mess up your automatic caption numbering.

To stop automatic captioning, simply deselect the Automatic option in the Options window.

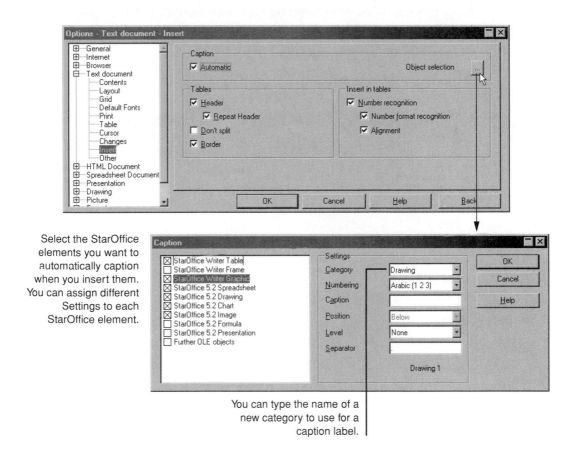

Figure 6-23   Setting automatic caption options

Inserting Captions Manually With the Caption Tool

If you don't want to insert captions automatically you can insert them manually.

1   If you want to use chapter-number numbering for the captions (such as "Illustration 3-5"), make sure you've defined a chapter paragraph that uses an auto-generated chapter number.

See *Outline Numbering* on page 278.

2   Select the inserted object you want to insert a caption for.

3   Choose Insert > Caption.

4   Set options for the caption in the Caption window. See Figure 6-24.

5   If you want to use chapter-number caption numbering, click the Options button, set the options you want, and click OK. See Figure 6-24.

6   Click OK in the Caption window.

Each type of caption has a corresponding paragraph style that you can modify.

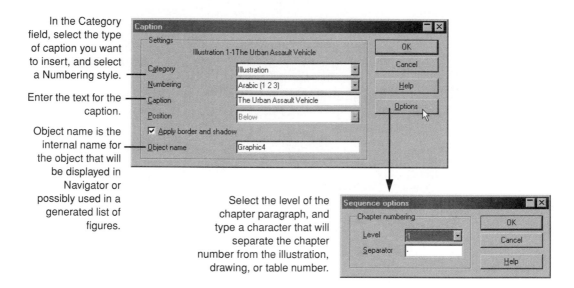

In the Category field, select the type of caption you want to insert, and select a Numbering style.

Enter the text for the caption.

Object name is the internal name for the object that will be displayed in Navigator or possibly used in a generated list of figures.

Select the level of the chapter paragraph, and type a character that will separate the chapter number from the illustration, drawing, or table number.

Figure 6-24   Setting caption options

Caption Numbering With Paragraph Formats

You can create a numbered paragraph style specifically designed for captions (figure, table, or whatever kind of caption you want to create). For example, if you insert a picture into your document, you can apply the caption paragraph format you created below the picture, and it will automatically insert **Figure #:** as the paragraph numbering, letting you type the caption after it.

For example, use the Before and After fields (shown in Figure 6-25) to get the following numbering (which, as you can see, also includes letters):

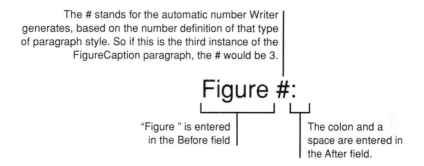

The # stands for the automatic number Writer generates, based on the number definition of that type of paragraph style. So if this is the third instance of the FigureCaption paragraph, the # would be 3.

Figure #:

"Figure " is entered in the Before field

The colon and a space are entered in the After field.

Figure 6-25 Example of setting up caption numbering

Captions Without a Chapter Number This procedure deals with paragraph and numbering styles. It's for straight caption numbering without including a chapter number. For more information, see *Paragraph Styles* on page 205 and *Numbering (and Bullet) Styles* on page 210.

1 Create a *numbering* style and name it; for example, "FigureCaption."

See Figure 6-25 for an example of setting up the numbering style for figures.

2 Create a *paragraph* style called, for example, "FigureCaption."

3 In the numbering properties for the paragraph style, select the "FigureCaption." numbering style. Then, whenever you apply the FigureCaption paragraph style, the numbering appears like this automatically.

Create a different kind of paragraph and numbering format for each type of caption you want to use, such as tables, illustrations, and so on.

Captions Using a Chapter Number This procedure shows you how to create a paragraph style that includes a chapter number in the caption number, such as "Figure 4-2."

This procedure involves using outline numbering. For more information, see *Outline Numbering* on page 278.

1 Create a *paragraph* style called, for example, "FigureCaption."

Do **not** assign a numbering style on the Numbering tab of the paragraph style.

2 After you create the paragraph style, choose Tools > Outline Numbering.

3   In the Outline Numbering window (Figure 6-26), select Level 1, make sure the paragraph style is the chapter-level style (such as Heading 1) that will be the first style used in the document, and make sure it's set up to generate a chapter number (in the Number field).

4   Select any other level in the Outline Numbering window, and assign your caption paragraph to it.

If you skip a level or more from Level 1, assign a numbering style to each level between Level 1 and the level of your caption.

Select a character style for the autonumber, such as "Strong Emphasis".

Set the Show sublevels field to 2.

In the Before field, type the text you want to appear before the autonumber, such as "Figure" followed by a space.

In the After field, type the character you want to appear after the autonumber, such as a colon followed by a space.

Make sure the Start at field is set to 1.

Figure 6-26 on page 265 illustrates these settings.

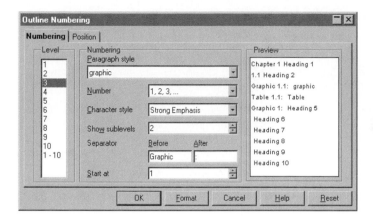

Figure 6-26   Setting up caption numbering to include the chapter number

Headers, Footers, and Fields

Using Headers and Footers

Headers and footers, the text areas that appear at the top and bottom of a page, contain information that runs from page to page, such as page number, date, the title of the current page heading, copyright information, and notes about confidential and proprietary information.

Usually when you enter information into headers and footers, the information repeats automatically as new pages are created. If you are using alternating left and right pages, each can have its own headers and footers, so that all right-page headers and footers are the same, as are all left-page headers and footers.

Inserting Headers and Footers

While you can insert headers and footers on the fly (Insert > Header) or (Insert > Footer), you must customize their height, width, spacing from the document body, background, and borders through the document's page styles (see *Page Styles* on page 211).

When you insert headers and footers, as shown in Figure 7-1, they don't run beyond the margin settings of the document. Instead, they automatically adjust the main text area of the document. You cannot extend the width of headers and footers beyond the document's page width.

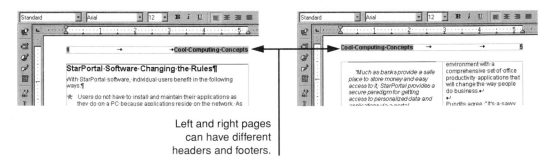

Left and right pages
can have different
headers and footers.

Figure 7-1   Left and right headers

Adding Content to Headers and Footers

Since headers and footers are text boxes, you can include anything in a header or footer that you can include in the main document. Most often you'll probably want to include such information as date, page number, author, filename, and section headings. Instead of typing this type of information in manually, you can insert fields that contain this information.

Inserting Fields Into Headers and Footers

Fields contain information such as page numbers, dates, and section headings that are generated automatically by Writer. For more information on fields, see Using Fields below.

1   Click in the exact spot in the header or footer where you want to insert a field.

2   In the toolbar, click and hold down the Insert Fields tool, and choose the field you want to insert. (You can also choose Insert > Fields.)

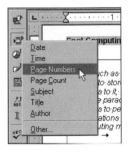

If you don't see the field you want, choose Other, and select the field you want to use in the Fields window. For definitions of the fields in this window, see Table 7-1 on page 271.

Formatting Headers and Footers

Writer provides the following default header and footer paragraph styles: Header, Header left, Header right, Footer, Footer left, and Footer right. The left and right styles are used when your document is set up to alternate between left and right pages. You can format headers and footers manually, or you can change any of their styles. If you need help with formatting, see 5, *Formatting Documents*, on page 177.

Removing Headers and Footers

You can remove headers and footers on the fly by choosing Insert > Header (or Insert > Footer) and selecting the page style that has a check mark next to it. You can also turn headers and footers off within each page style (see *Page Styles* on page 211).

Using Fields

Fields are bits of information, such as page numbers, dates, document headings, cross-references, index markers, database fields, and a host of other information that Writer generates or that you can insert. For example, you can insert a field into a document that shows the date that the document was last modified, or you can insert page numbering to show the current page number along with the total page count, as shown in Figure 7-2.

You can insert fields into any part of a document where you can enter text, and the field text takes on the properties of the paragraph style it's inserted into. You can also apply character formats to fields.

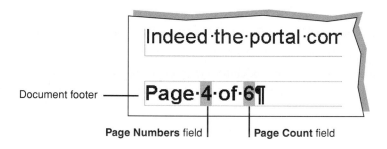

Document footer ──────

Page Numbers field   **Page Count** field

Figure 7-2   Page Numbers and Page Count fields

Headers and Footers on page 283 shows specific uses of fields in long documents and books.

Inserting Fields

1   Click in the exact spot in the document where you want to insert a field.

2   In the toolbar, click and hold down the Insert Fields tool, and choose the field you want to insert. (You can also choose Insert > Fields.)

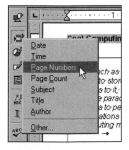

If you don't see the field you want, choose Other, and select the field you want to use in the Fields window. For definitions of the fields in this window, see Table 7-1 on page 271.

The "Other" Fields

When you click and hold on the Insert Fields tool in the toolbar, then choose Other (or choose Insert > Fields > Other), the Fields window is displayed (Figure 7-3) to let you select another type of field.

Each tab in the Fields window has a Type list. When you select a field type, related options display in the right area of the window.

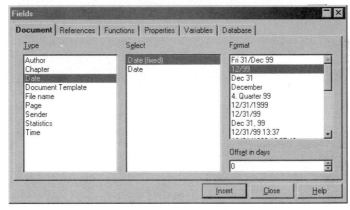

In this example, you can select a fixed or current date, then select the format for the date as you want it to display in the document.

Figure 7-3   The Fields window

You can leave the Fields window open, and switch back and forth between it and your document. The following table describes the fields available in the Fields window.

Table 7-1   Descriptions of "Other" fields

Field	Description
Document tab	
Author	The author of the document, as identified in Tools > Options > General > User Data. Select the Fixed content option if you don't want the name of the author to change when someone else opens the document.
Chapter	Think of this as "chapter-level heading" instead. Use this to display the current document heading in the header or footer (called running heads). In the Level field, set the level of heading you want to display. Levels map directly to chapter numbering styles. See *Outline Numbering* on page 278.
Date	Inserts the current date, based on the computer's date setting. Select Date (fixed) if you want the date to remain what it was when you inserted it. Select Date if you want the date to update each time the document is opened.
Document Template	Inserts basic information about the template the document is based on.

Table 7-1   Descriptions of "Other" fields (continued)

Field	Description
File Name	Lets you insert the name of the file in different ways. Select the Fixed content box if you want to display the original file name if it's later changed.
Page	Inserts a page number. Select the As Page Style format to use the default numbering format set up in the current page style. Otherwise, select the numbering style you want to use.
Sender	Inserts select information about the person sending the document, as defined in Tools > Options > General > User Data.
Statistics	Gives you the count of the number of different elements in the document: words, characters, pages, graphics, etc.
Time	Inserts the time, based on the computer's clock. Select Time (fixed) if you want the time to remain what it was when you inserted it (further testing needs to be done to see if this makes time stand still). Select Time if you want the time to update each time the document is opened. You can enter a positive or negative offset number to adjust the inserted time relative to the current time. You can also select Additional Formats in the Format list and define your own time format.
References tab	
Set Reference	Use this for cross-referencing. In Writer, you don't cross-reference existing content. You must put (set) a reference in the spot you want to cross-reference. Click where you want to reference, enter the name of the reference point (usually the name of a heading, figure, or table you want to cross-reference), and click Insert. The reference names you've entered display in the Selection list, where you can cross-reference them using Insert Reference (next).
Insert Reference	When you want to cross-reference something (either in the current document or in another file that's part of a master document), select Insert Reference, select the item you want to cross-reference (in the Selection list), select the format for the cross-reference, and click Insert. (For more information, see *Cross-Referencing* on page 296.) You can also use above/below, which inserts the words *above* or *below* if the reference occurs before or after the insertion point. For example, "See Water Ballet for Dogs above." But for heaven's sake, if you use above/below, make sure the reference is physically on the same page as the cross-reference. If it's not, you may have your poor readers looking randomly up at the sky or down at the floor trying to find the reference.

Table 7-1   Descriptions of "Other" fields (continued)

Field	Description
Bookmarks	You can also cross-reference bookmarks you've inserted using Insert > Bookmark. When you insert bookmarks in an HTML document, Writer creates an <A NAME=*bookmarkname*> reference for internal page jumps. However, bookmarks in a Writer document are not converted to <A NAME=> references if you convert the document to HTML.
Functions tab	
Conditional Text	Insert text depending on a condition. Under Condition, enter x eq 1, for example. Under Then, enter text that is inserted if x=1. Under Else, enter text that is inserted otherwise. X can be determined with the field types "Set variable" or with an input field for a new variable.
Input Field	Inserting form fields for text input. You can add a remark. When you click the Insert button, the dialog Input Field appears, where you can enter and edit the desired text.
Execute Macro	Insert a text field that automatically executes an assigned macro following a double-click. You can choose the desired macro with the Macro button. After choosing the macro, you can enter the necessary remarks in the text field Remark.
Placeholder	Insert a placeholder in the document. You determine the placeholder type under Format. Enter the description in the Text field Placeholder. If you click the placeholder in the document, you can insert the object that is represented by the placeholder.
Hidden Text	Insert text that is hidden if a condition is met. In order to hide such text on screen, deselect the option Hidden Text under Tools > Options > Text document > Contents.
Hidden Paragraph	Hide a paragraph if the condition entered under Condition is true. These fields can be used, for example, to suppress empty paragraphs during printing. To hide such paragraphs on screen, deactivate the menu command View > Hidden Paragraphs or the option Hidden Paragraphs under Tools > Options > Text document > Contents. The conditions for "Hidden Text" and "Hidden Paragraph" can now be formulated in a similar manner. In earlier document formats, up until StarWriter 4.0, the reversed logic was valid for "Hidden text". When saving and loading older formats, the logic for "Hidden text" is therefore automatically reversed.

Table 7-1   Descriptions of "Other" fields (continued)

Field	Description
DocInformation tab	
Created	Lets you insert the name of the author who created the document, and the time and date the document was created. Select the Fixed content option to keep this information from changing when other people open and change the document.
Description	Inserts the document description, taken from the Comment field of the document properties (File > Properties, Description tab).
Document Number	Inserts the number of times the document has been saved.
Editing Time	Inserts information about time spent editing the document.
Info	Inserts the information from the selected Info field, taken from the Info fields of the document properties (File > Properties, User Defined tab).
Keywords	Inserts the keywords assigned to the document, taken from the Keywords field of the document properties (File > Properties, Description tab).
Modified	Inserts the name of the author who last modified the document, or the time and date the document was last modified.
Most Recent Print	Inserts the name of the author who last printed the document, or the time and date the document was last printed.
Subject	Inserts the subject of the document, taken from the Subject field of the document properties (File > Properties, Description tab).
Title	Inserts the title of the document, taken from the Title field of the document properties (File > Properties, Description tab).
Variables tab	
Set Variable	Lets you create and insert a variable in a document that can be used as a trigger for conditions. For example, you can create a variable to trigger certain sections of the document to be hidden if the variable is a certain value.
Show Variable	Inserts the value of a selected variable in the document.
DDE Field	Lets you insert a Dynamic Data Exchange (DDE) link to another document.
Insert Formula	Lets you enter a formula and insert the results in the document.
Input Field	Lets you select a predefined variable and turn it into a hyperlink that brings up a window to let you change its value.

Table 7-1   Descriptions of "Other" fields (continued)

Field	Description
Number Sequence	Lets you insert a number, as well as incorporate the chapter number (set up in Tools > Outline Numbering), for a drawing, graphic, illustration, table, or for text in general.
Set Page Variable	For use with the Show Page Variable. Lets you set a marker in the document from which to begin page counting. Be sure to select "on". You can also enter an offset, positive or negative, with relation to the marker. An offset of -1 would be as if the marker were inserted 1 page earlier. See the next description for how you might use this.
Show Page Variable	Inserts the number of pages from the Set Page Variable marker to where this variable is inserted. One way to use this would be to set a marker (using Set Page Variable) in a document at the beginning of a topic, and at the end of the topic (say it's five pages later), type, "The past <#> pages described the three major factors to overcome in order to successfully build a summer home in a fire swamp", where <#> is the inserted Show Page Variable.
User Field	Lets you create a variable that will be the same wherever you insert it and change universally when you change it in one place. For example, say you want to insert the text "Microsoft" throughout a document. If you know the value of that variable is going to change, like from "Microsoft" to "Monopoly", a user field lets you change it in one place and it updates everywhere. To help automate the changing of its value, select the first instance of a user variable in the document, and insert an Input field so that all you have to do to change the value of the field is click on it and make the change in the window that appears.
Database tab	
Any Record	Lets you set a condition on database records to determine which records are used in a mail merge. Click the Help button in this window for more details. TRUE is the default condition, which means all selected records will be included.
Database Name	Inserts into the document the name of the database selected in the Database selection area.
Form letter field	Lets you insert database fields in a document to set up a mail merge.

Table 7-1   Descriptions of "Other" fields (continued)

Field	Description
Next record	Inserts a Next record marker between mail merge groupings in a document to print consecutive records on the same page. The records you want to include must be selected in the Beamer window.
Record number	Inserts in the document the number of the record that's selected in the Beamer window.

Editing Fields

You can't edit a field by typing in it. You have to either replace it with another field or double-click it to open the Edit Fields window and redefine the field. Refer to Figure 7-1 for help on types of fields.

Turning Off the Gray Background

Any time you insert a field or any other element that's generated by Writer, it is displayed with a nonprinting gray background by default. If you don't want to see the gray background on-screen, choose View > Field Shadings.

However, we recommend leaving field shading on, because it helps you distinguish between what you enter as text and what is generated by Writer.

chapter

8

Books and Longer Documents

Overview

If you're creating long documents, you're likely to want to use elements like cross-references, running heads, tables of contents, indexes, and other lists, like lists of figures. Writer has some decent tools for doing all this. If your long documents are getting a little too long and difficult to manage, Writer has a master document feature that lets you group multiple files into a single book, where you can create a single table of contents, an index (and other lists), create cross-references between book files, and use continuous page numbering. In this chapter, the terms *book* and *master document* are synonymous.

Creating a master document means you'll need to stretch your mental muscles and apply your existing knowledge of Writer styles (see *Power Formatting With Styles* on page 201) and headers and footers (see *Using Headers and Footers* on page 268). This knowledge is particularly useful when it comes to troubleshooting your master documents.

This chapter shows you first how to create and maintain a master document, then how to perform tasks that are common to long documents and books.

Note – When working with long documents, you might want to keep file size to a minimum. In that case, when you insert graphics, select the Link option. This puts an image of a graphic in the document without inserting the entire graphic file. The drawback to this is that Writer always has to know where those graphic files are. So when you send or move the files, you must also send or set new links to the graphics files.

Outline Numbering

This feature is one of the most confusing and non-intuitive in StarOffice; and if it didn't play such an important part in how other features in StarOffice work, you'd be wise to ignore it altogether.

However, outline numbering is essential if you want to:

- Cross-reference paragraph numbers

  Even if you set up numbering in a paragraph style, if you don't use outline numbering, you can't cross-reference the generated number or generated text, such as "Chapter 1", "Figure 2-7", or a number such as "1.1.2" preceding an outlined item.

- Number graphics, tables, and other inserted elements, using the chapter number and the number of the element in the document, such as "Figure 5-1"

- Set up running headings in document headers and footers

Automatic numbering for paragraphs isn't a new concept we're just presenting in this book. In fact, *Paragraph Formatting* on page 184 talks about just that. Outline numbering is different than paragraph numbering, because Writer keys off of outline numbering to enable the features in the previous list.

Before we show you how to set up outline numbering, we need to note a few limitations.

Outline Numbering Limitations

- Only one paragraph style can be used as *the* chapter paragraph, even though you'll see 10 paragraph style levels in the Outline Numbering window.

- Of the paragraph styles listed **in the Outline Numbering window**, Writer uses the first of those paragraph styles it encounters in the document or book as the chapter-level heading.

  For example, if you want to use a Heading 2 as a running head in the header or footer of a document or book, but a Heading 1 appears before a Heading 2 as the first paragraph style in the document, Writer sees the Heading 1 as the chapter paragraph and you can't use the Heading 2 for running heads.

  To fix this problem you'd have to unassign Heading 1 from the list of paragraph styles in the Outline Numbering window so that it's not one of the paragraphs assigned to use outline numbering.

- If you want to use a page numbering format that uses chapter-page (such as 3-1, where 3 is the chapter number), or if you want to number inserted objects like graphics using a numbering format such as "Figure 2-7", you must assign a number format (in the Outline Numbering window) to the level that will serve as the chapter number. But because only one paragraph style can be the chapter paragraph, you can only set up a running head that displays the contents of the chapter-numbered paragraph. Make sure the paragraph style you want to use for the outline numbering is set as the Level 1 paragraph style in the Outline Numbering window.

Simplicity Is a Virtue

But the aforementioned limitations, it turns out, are good for a couple of reasons: one, they discourage using chapter-page numbering (such as 3-5 for chapter 3, page 5), which makes it difficult for readers to find page numbers; and two, you're forced to keep your headers and footers simple (yet helpful) by using only one running head.

Figure 8-1 shows different outline autonumbering styles for the chapter paragraph.

Notice the headers in each example. The second example has a running head, which is the text of the chapter title. But in the first example, because the chapter number includes only an auto-generated number, there's no title text to display as a running head.

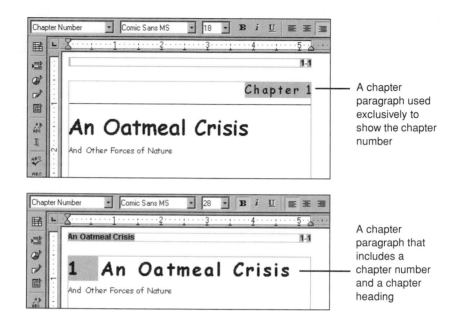

A chapter paragraph used exclusively to show the chapter number

A chapter paragraph that includes a chapter number and a chapter heading

Figure 8-1   Different automatic outline numbering styles for a chapter paragraph

Setting Up Outline Numbering

It may be helpful to review *Outline Numbering Limitations* on page 279 before using this procedure.

1   Decide which heading level you want to use as your chapter number.

2   Choose Tools > Outline Numbering.

3   In the Outline Numbering window, select Level 1.

4   In the Paragraph style field, select the paragraph style you want to use for the chapter.

   The paragraph style you select doesn't have to be set up with a chapter autonumber. This can simply be the paragraph style you want to use in running heads.

5   If the paragraph style you select as
     the Level 1 style isn't the style of the
     first paragraph in the document or
     book, unassign from the Outline
     Numbering window any styles that
     appear before the Level 1 style in the
     document.

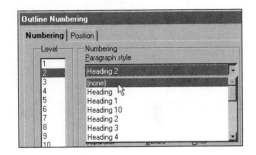

     To do this, select the levels for the
     styles you want to remove, and in the
     Paragraph styles field, select None.

6   If you want the paragraph style to include an automatic chapter number, select a
     Number format and set appropriate numbering options. See Figure 8-2.

7   Click the Position tab (also Figure 8-2), and set any applicable options, especially if
     you want to indent the chapter paragraph style or set the amount of spacing between
     the chapter number and the chapter text.

     Position changes to the outline numbering style override (but don't replace) the
     indents and spacing of the paragraph style itself.

8   Click OK.

The Show sublevels field is extremely important when you want to use hierarchical
outline numbering or figure/table numbering that includes the chapter number. For
example, assign the Graphic and Table styles to whichever outline levels you want, and set
the sublevel of each to a value of 2. That means the Figure/Table paragraph numbering
will pick up the level 1 chapter number and generate its own number, such as
"Figure 1-5".

You can change the default paragraph style used for the selected level.

The word "Chapter" and a space, as entered in the Before field, appear before the chapter number (1).

Select the heading level that you want to contain the chapter number.
Select the type of numbering you want the chapter headings to use.
You can have the numbering itself use a predefined character style.

Preview displays the name of the paragraph style assigned to each level. If you set a numbering format for a level, that number is also displayed, along with any text you've entered before or after the number.

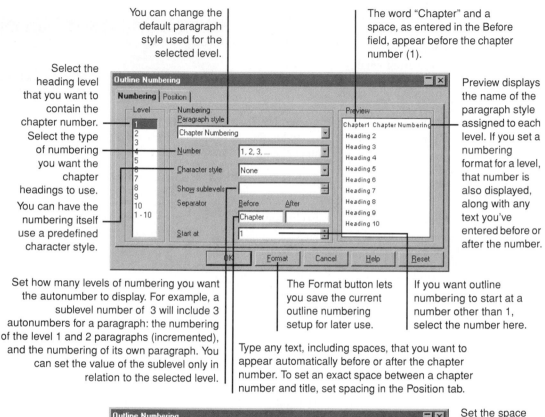

Set how many levels of numbering you want the autonumber to display. For example, a sublevel number of 3 will include 3 autonumbers for a paragraph: the numbering of the level 1 and 2 paragraphs (incremented), and the numbering of its own paragraph. You can set the value of the sublevel only in relation to the selected level.

The Format button lets you save the current outline numbering setup for later use.

If you want outline numbering to start at a number other than 1, select the number here.

Type any text, including spaces, that you want to appear automatically before or after the chapter number. To set an exact space between a chapter number and title, set spacing in the Position tab.

Set the distance the number will be indented from the page margin.

Set the space between the number and the text. Space to text also determines the left alignment of a hanging indent. You can also set a Minimum space between the number and the text.

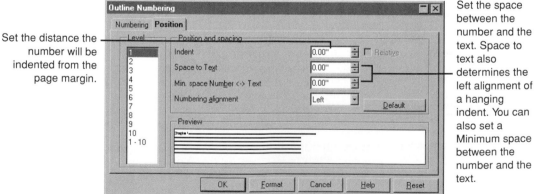

Figure 8-2   Setting outline numbering options

Saving Different Outline Numbering Versions

StarOffice lets you save different versions of outline numbering that you can switch between. If you want to save the current combination of outline settings to revert back to later:

1 In the Outline Numbering window, click the Format button, and choose Save As, as shown in Figure 8-3.

2 In the Save As window, type a name for the configuration, and click OK.

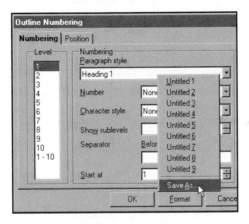

Figure 8-3   Saving an Outline Numbering configuration

The saved format is available to all documents.

To select a saved outline numbering versions later, click the Format button, choose the format, and click OK to apply it to the document.

Headers and Footers

Headers and footers are essential for longer documents and books. At the very least they hold page numbers. But the more reader-friendly approach is to also include such information as the name of the publication and the current main heading in the document (a running head), as shown in Figure 8-4. In fact, the headers of this book show those very things.

For more information on headers and footers and the types of information you can insert in them, see 7, *Headers, Footers, and Fields*, on page 267.

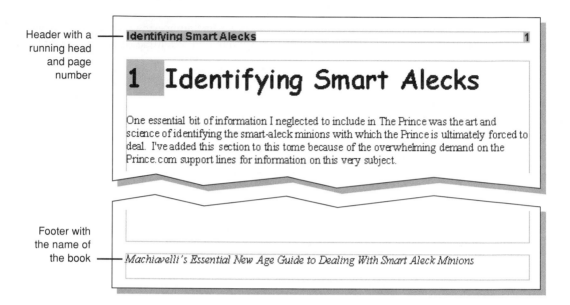

Header with a running head and page number

Footer with the name of the book

Figure 8-4   Header and footer on a right page

Figure 5-34 on page 214 and Figure 5-35 on page 214 show how to set up headers and footers for the page styles you'll use in your books and longer documents. Those settings merely ensure that the header and/or footer text boxes will be displayed on your pages. This section shows you how to put the stuff you want in those headers and footers.

To get the most flexibility with headers and footers, use alternating left/right page styles (see *Applying and Overriding Page Style Flows* on page 217 and the Next style field in Figure 5-31 on page 211). That way you can have separate headers and footers that contain different information. For example, you could display the page number and name of the book on all left pages, and show the page number and the name of the current main heading (a running head) on all right pages. Another possibility is putting the name of the publication on the left and right footers, and putting the running head and page number in the left and right headers.

Page Numbering

This section shows you a few common page numbering techniques that should cover 95 percent of your page numbering needs: regular ol' page numbering, transitioning from one numbering style to another (for example, lowercase Roman numerals to regular Arabic numbers), and using a chapter-page numbering style, such as 3-1.

Regular Ol' Page Numbering

Simplicity is a beautiful thing. Here's how to insert regular page numbers in your headers and footers.

1   Click in the header or footer where you want to insert the page number.

2   In the toolbar, click and hold down the Insert Fields tool, and choose Page Numbers.

3   If you're using alternating headers and footers in a document (as determined in the page style), insert the page number on the alternate page(s).

Use alternating headers and footers, for example, in left and right page styles, if you want the page number to be on the far left and far right sides of your pages.

If you want to use a *page # of #* format, insert Page Number and Page Count fields in the header or footer, as shown in Figure 7-2 on page 270.

Transitioning to a Different Numbering Style

This procedure shows you how to transition from one numbering scheme, such as lowercase Roman numerals for front matter (title page, table of contents, preface), to another numbering scheme where the body of the document starts.

This isn't a quick procedure. Some work with page styles is involved. If you need help with page styles, see *Page Styles* on page 211.

For troubleshooting purposes, you should also be aware of the general effects of applying page styles to a document. See *Applying and Overriding Page Style Flows* on page 217.

1   Create different page styles for the sections that will use different page numbering.

For example, create alternating PrefaceLeft and PrefaceRight page styles that use a lowercase Roman numeral numbering scheme for a Preface section (as shown in Figure 8-5), and create Left and Right page styles for the main part of the document or book that use a regular Arabic numbering scheme.

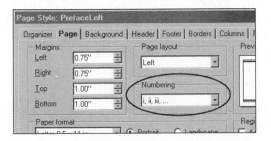

Figure 8-5   Setting a numbering scheme for a page style

2   Apply the beginning page styles to the document.

For example, apply a Title page style to the first page of the document, which is followed by alternating PrefaceLeft and PrefaceRight page styles.

3   Click at the beginning of the heading you want to begin the main body section, at which you will restart numbering.

4   Choose Insert > Manual Break.

5   In the Insert Break window, select Page break.

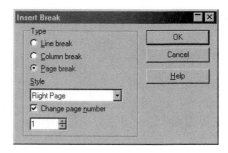

6   In the Style field, choose the page style you want to begin the main body of the document.

7   Select the Change page number option.

The number 1 appears by default. If you want the main body to start with a number other than 1, change the value.

8   Click OK.

The flow of alternating PrefaceRight and PrefaceLeft pages is overridden, and the new flow of alternating Right and Left page styles begins with its new numbering scheme.

Chapter-Page Numbering

This procedure shows you how to set up page numbering that shows the chapter number and restarts the page number when a new chapter starts. For example, the first page of Chapter 3 would be numbered 3-1.

This style is easier on the author, because changes in one chapter don't throw off the page numbering for the rest of the document; but its baaaaaaad for the reader who's trying to find pages in the document. (It's your conscience.) We present this section because, unfortunately, this page numbering style is still widely used.

If you want to use this procedure, you have to be okay with the fact that each chapter heading (the Heading 1 style, for example) will start on a new page and have an automatically generated chapter number. You also have to be okay with the fact that the only type of running head you'll be able to use is the chapter-level heading. For more information on that, see Using Running Heads next.

1   Make sure you've set up outline numbering in the document so that a paragraph style uses an automatically generated chapter number.

See *Setting Up Outline Numbering* on page 280.

2   Position the cursor in the header or footer where you want to insert page numbering.

3   Press Ctrl+F2 to display the Fields window.

4   On the Document tab, in the Type list, select Chapter.

5   In the Format list, select Chapter number without separator, as shown in Figure 8-6.

This option inserts only the automatically generated chapter number without any Before or After text. If you want to show Before or After text in the page numbering, such as "Chapter," select Chapter number in the Format list.

6   Click Insert.

Keep the Fields window open.

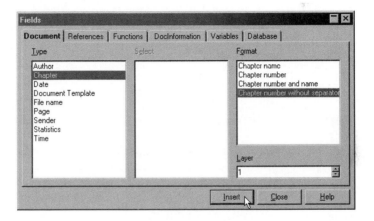

Figure 8-6   Inserting the "chapter" number

7   In the header or footer, insert a separator character after the chapter number you just inserted.

8   In the Fields window, select the Type called Page, select Page Numbers in the Select list, and select a page number style in the Format list.

9   Click Insert.

You can close the Fields window.

10 If you're using more than one set of headers and footers in the document, copy and paste the page numbering to all pertinent headers or footers.

11 Edit the paragraph that is set as the chapter paragraph. For example, if you're using Heading 1 as your chapter paragraph, select the Heading 1 paragraph style in the Stylist, right-click, and choose Modify.

12 In the Paragraph Style window, click the Text Flow tab, and set the options shown in Figure 8-7.

13 Click OK.

Select Break, Page, and Before. — Select With page style and select a page style the paragraph will start on.

Change the page number to 1.

Figure 8-7   Restarting page numbering

With this type of page numbering set up, when Writer sees a Heading 1 (or whichever is the chapter heading), it puts the heading at the top of a new page and restarts the page numbering, as shown in Figure 8-8.

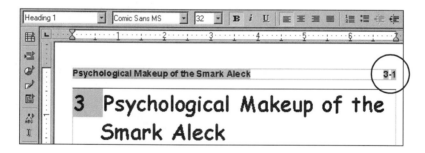

Figure 8-8   Chapter-page numbering

Using Running Heads

Running heads show the current text of a certain paragraph, like a heading. For example, you can have the contents of the current Heading 1 display on each page. Each new instance of a Heading 1 changes the running head text starting at that point until another Heading 1 appears in the document. This very book uses running heads in the header: chapters on the left pages, and Heading 1 titles on the right pages.

1   Set up outline numbering so that the paragraph style you want to use for the running head is selected as Level 1 in the Outline Numbering window.

See *Outline Numbering* on page 278.

2   Click in the header or footer where you want to insert the numbering.

3   Press Ctrl+F2 to bring up the Fields window.

4   On the Document tab, in the Type list, select Chapter.

5   In the Format list, select Chapter name.

6   Click Insert.

7   If you're using more than one set of headers and footers in the document, copy and paste the running head to all pertinent headers or footers.

Books (Master Documents)

A master document looks just like any other Writer document. The difference is that a master document is made up of separate Writer files, as shown in Figure 8-9.

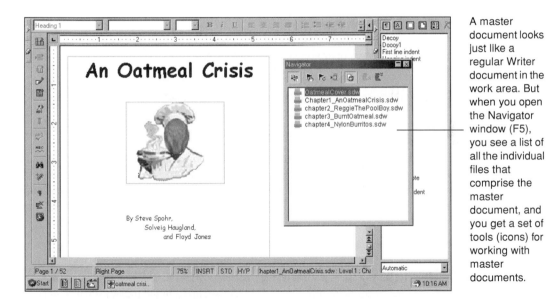

A master document looks just like a regular Writer document in the work area. But when you open the Navigator window (F5), you see a list of all the individual files that comprise the master document, and you get a set of tools (icons) for working with master documents.

Figure 8-9   A master document

When you create a master document, all the files you include are displayed in a single read-only document (meaning you can't edit it directly), as if all of your files were really a single file. The read-only document is composed of links to the individual documents. The master document lets you rearrange the order of files, lets you add a master table of contents and index, and allows cross-referencing between its files.

Master Document Principles

There are a few principles involved with master documents that will help you plan, work with, and troubleshoot master documents.

- When you add a file to a master document, the master document automatically imports the styles for that file. However, any additions or changes to styles in the master document itself do not affect the source file styles.

  What does this mean? You can create separate styles, such as page styles, to be used for only the master document. However, if you change or add a style to a master document, and you want that change or addition in the source file as well, you have to make the change in both places.

- Often when you work with master documents you'll do a lot of fine-tuning. For example, you may decide to use different fonts or page layouts along the way. Master documents have their own styles that are separate from the styles of the individual documents it contains. So you can fine-tune a master document by modifying its own styles.

  You can then load the styles from the master document into its source documents if you want to update their styles to match the master document. See *Loading Styles From Another Document* on page 221.

  If you want to keep master document styles different than the styles of the source documents, you can use and maintain different templates for each.

- A Writer file can be used in multiple master documents.

- When put in a master document, source files behave exactly the way you've set them up. For example, if page numbering in your source files is set up to be continuous, page numbering will increment between files in the master document. So if Chapter 1 ends at page 56, Chapter 2 will start numbering at 57 in the master document—unless the page numbering in the Chapter 2 source file is set to restart page numbering.

  Any paragraphs styles with autonumber properties are also incremented in a master document. For example, if you have a "Chapter Number" paragraph style with a numbering format that automatically displays "Chapter #" (where # is an autonumber), outline numbering will be consecutive in the master document (Chapter 1, Chapter 2, and so on), as shown in Figure 8-10.

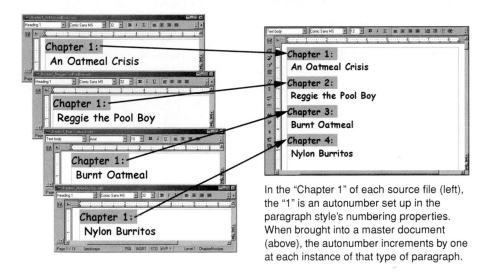

In the "Chapter 1" of each source file (left), the "1" is an autonumber set up in the paragraph style's numbering properties. When brought into a master document (above), the autonumber increments by one at each instance of that type of paragraph.

Figure 8-10   Autonumbers increment in a master document

Creating a Master Document

You can create a master document from an existing file, or you can create one from scratch. The only minor advantage to creating a master document from an existing file is that the file is added to the master document automatically, saving you a step.

Creating a Master Document From Scratch

1   Choose File > New > Master document.

    A blank document appears, along with the Navigator window in master document view. Navigator shows an item called Text.

2   Add the files you want to include in the master document. In the Navigator window, click and hold down the Insert button, and choose File.

3   In the Insert window, find and double-click the first file you want to add.

4   Add the rest of the files the same way.

    As you add files, their contents display in the document.

5   Delete the Text item. Select it, right-click, and choose delete.

6   After you add the files, you can rearrange them in the master document by selecting one and clicking the Move Up or Move Down button in Navigator.

7   If you want to use all the styles from your documents, load them into the master document. If you need help doing this, see *Loading Styles From Another Document* on page 221.

8   Save the master document.

The Insert button in the docked Navigator window

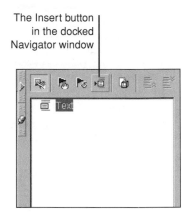

Select a file and click the Move Up or Move Down button.

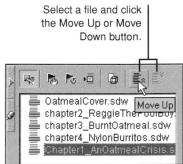

Creating a Master Document From an Existing File

1   With a Writer document open that you want to include in the master document, choose File > Send > Create Master Document.

2   In the Name and Path window, navigate to the location where you want to store the master document file, type in a file name, and click Save.

    A blank Writer master document is displayed in the work area, and Navigator opens in master document mode. Navigator displays a new file named after the source file, with a number appended to the end of the name.

3   Follow the steps in the previous procedure for adding and rearranging files in the master document.

4   Delete the blank document that Writer used to start the master document. Select the file in Navigator, right-click, and choose Delete.

Master Document Headers and Footers

While you can't edit the body of the master document, you can edit the headers and footers. This lets you create the custom headers and footers you may need for the master document. Headers and footers are associated with page styles, so changing page styles also changes the headers and footers used.

Using Page Styles in a Master Document

You can create your own styles for a master document to use a different layout for the book than what is used in the source files. StarOffice also comes with a couple of book templates you can borrow page styles from. For more information on templates, see *Using Templates* on page 220.

If you want to change a page style for a given page, click in the header or footer and apply the page style (you can't click in the body of the master document, because it's read-only). This tip also comes with a warning, because the page style you apply uses its own header and footer settings, as well as its own Next Style for the page style that will follow it. This could cause a chain reaction that requires you to modify a lot of page styles to get the flow you want.

Editing Source Files

In order to change the content of the master document, you must edit the source files that make up the master document. Edit source files by double-clicking them in the master document Navigator window. You can also open them the way you normally open files.

You have to save the changes you make in the source files for the master document to pick up the changes.

Updating the Master Document

There are different aspects to updating a master document. The main aspect has to do with updating the links to the content of the files so that the most current content is displayed in the master document. The other aspect of updating master documents is updating styles if you change styles in the source files.

The master document has to be updated when its files change. Updating a master document refreshes the links to the source files, displays the files in their current state, and updates generated information (like page numbering, the table of contents, and the index).

Updating Links Automatically

When you open a master document you previously saved, Writer asks you if you want to update all links. Writer is asking you if you want to update the master document to reflect the current state of all its document files. You can set the automatic link update options in

Tools > Options > Text document > Other, in the Update Links area. If you select Always, when you open the master document, Writer updates the links to the files without prompting you.

If you select On request, Writer prompts you to update the links whenever you open the master document. If you select Never, Writer opens the master document without updating the links, and you need to update them manually.

Updating Links Manually

With the master document open, you can manually update individual pieces of the master document, or you can update the whole thing. Select a master document file in Navigator, click and hold down the Update button in Navigator, and select one of the following options:

- Selection – Updates the selected item, whether it's a file or a section of the table of contents.
- Indexes – Updates all generated lists (table of contents, index, list of figures, etc.).
- Links – Updates all files without updating indexes.
- All – Updates all files and indexes.

Updating Styles

If you edit styles in your source documents, you'll need to reload them into the master document, and vice versa. For information on updating styles in master documents, see *Master Document Principles* on page 289.

Navigator

Navigator is a tool used throughout StarOffice. In Writer, Navigator serves three main purposes:

- Navigator holds and lets you maintain files in a master document (as described in the Books (Master Documents) section starting on page 289).
- Navigator lets you locate and jump to different parts of your document quickly.
- Navigator lets you drag and drop hyperlinked references from one part of a document into another part, or from one document to another.

Launching Navigator

When you create a master document, Navigator launches automatically in master document mode. Otherwise, press the **F5** key to open and close the Navigator window, or choose Edit > Navigator.

The Navigator window can be floating or docked. (See *Making Windows Anchored or Floating* on page 120.) In this section, Navigator is shown docked.

Master Document Navigator   When a master document is open, you can switch between the master document Navigator and the regular Navigator by clicking the Toggle button, as shown in Figure 8-11.

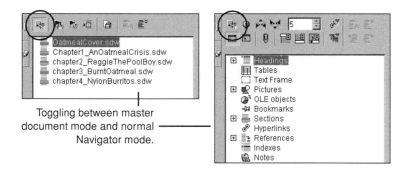

Figure 8-11   Navigator in master document view and regular view

Navigating

If you're in normal Navigator mode, the Navigator window displays all the parts of your document: Headings, tables, pictures, bookmarks, and so on, as shown in Figure 8-12. These different parts are displayed in a hierarchical tree view that lets you expand and contract groups of things. You can also customize the way Navigator displays its contents.

Navigator also offers a variety of ways you can jump to different parts of your document.

The Navigation button brings up a window (below) to let you select the type of item you want to jump to in the document.

Jumps to the previous or next instance of the Navigation item you selected.

Jumps to the page number you enter.

These buttons let you rearrange and change the levels of headings.

The Outline Level button lets you show a specific number of Heading levels.

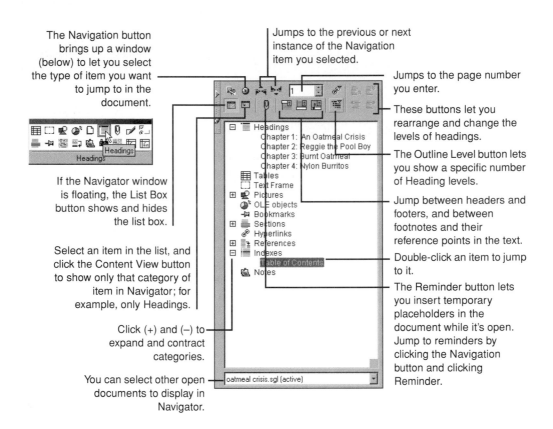

If the Navigator window is floating, the List Box button shows and hides the list box.

Select an item in the list, and click the Content View button to show only that category of item in Navigator; for example, only Headings.

Click (+) and (–) to expand and contract categories.

You can select other open documents to display in Navigator.

Jump between headers and footers, and between footnotes and their reference points in the text.

Double-click an item to jump to it.

The Reminder button lets you insert temporary placeholders in the document while it's open. Jump to reminders by clicking the Navigation button and clicking Reminder.

Figure 8-12   Navigator

If you just want to jump from item type to item type (for example, from heading to heading), click the Navigation button at the bottom of the vertical scroll bar, and select the type of item you want to jump to. Then click the up and down arrow buttons above and below the Navigation button to jump to the previous or next instances of the item.

Cross-Referencing

Cross-referencing information is essential to long documents. You want to be able to tell readers where related material is located in the document, and you want to be able to use heading titles and page numbers. While setting up cross-referencing is a little clunky in Writer, it works.

You can only set cross-references in a single document. StarOffice 5.2 doesn't let you cross-reference between files in a master document.

The basic principle behind cross-referencing in Writer is that you have to set a cross-reference marker that can be pointed at, or referenced. When you want to insert a cross-reference to an item, you have to locate its marker and insert a reference to it.

Set the Reference Marker

1   Select the exact text in a document you want to reference.

2   Press Ctrl+F2 (or choose Insert > Fields > Other) to bring up the Fields window.

3   Click the References tab.

4   In the Type list, select Set Reference.

5   Type a name for the reference in the Name field. Make it a name you can recognize later.

6   Click Insert. The name you typed is displayed in the Selection list. This is the marker name you'll point to later to reference the item.

You can leave the Fields window open while you perform the next steps.

Create a Cross-Reference to the Marker

7   Click in the document where you want to insert a cross-reference. (Enter any necessary text, such as *See* and *on page*, in front of where you want to insert the cross-reference.)

8   In the Fields window, click the References tab.

9   In the Type list, select Insert Reference.

10   In the Selection list, select the reference you want to insert.

11   In the Formats list, select Reference to insert the name of the reference, or select Page to insert the page number to the reference. (You have to insert each separately.)

12   Click Insert.

Adding a Hyperlink Cross-Reference

In a long document (not a master document), you can create a cross-reference as a hyperlink, so that when you click on it you jump to that part of the document.

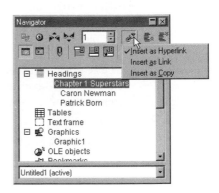

1   Open Navigator (press the F5 key).

2   In the Navigator window, click and hold down the Drag Mode button, and select Insert as Hyperlink.

3   At the bottom of the Navigator window, make sure the active document is selected in the drop-down list.

4   In the list of items, expand (click the "+" next to) the item, such as Headings, containing the item you want to insert into the document as a hyperlink.

5   Drag the item from the Navigator window into the document where you want it to appear.

People reading the document online must open the document in StarOffice for the hyperlinks to work.

Creating a Table of Contents

You can insert a table of contents into a single long document or into a master document. There are different procedures for each.

A table of contents is easiest to create if you've used styles for headings rather than just selecting plain text and manually making it big and bold. See *Power Formatting With Styles* on page 201 for more information on styles.

Note – In StarOffice, a table of contents is a type of "index." Index is the all-encompassing term for tables of contents, indexes, lists of figures, and so on. Debate the terminology all you want, but just know that any type of list with associated page numbers is created through a menu item called "Indexes" off the Insert menu.

Inserting a Table of Contents Into a Document

Use this procedure for inserting a table of contents into a single document rather than a master document. The procedure for inserting a table of contents into a master document follows this one.

Make sure you've used paragraph styles for the headings in your document, such as Heading 1 or any that you've created. Also mark any special text you want to include in the table of contents (see *Marking Special Table of Contents Entries* on page 302).

1   Click in the document where you want to insert the table of contents.

2   Choose Insert > Indexes > Indexes.

3   In the Insert Index window, set the options you want.

For guidance, use Figure 8-13 on page 300, Figure 8-14 on page 301, and *Using the Codes* on page 302.

4   When you're finished, click OK.

Writer inserts a table of contents, though it is very basic looking. To format the paragraph styles in the table of contents, see *Formatting and Editing a Table of Contents* on page 303.

Enter the title you want to use for the table of contents. Select Outline to include default headings in the table of contents, subject to the level limit set in the Evaluation level field.

Select Index marks to include special table of contents entries you've marked.

If you want to edit the table of contents entries directly after you generate the table, deselect the Protected option.

You can limit the number of heading levels shown in the table of contents.

Select Additional styles to include other-than-default paragraph styles in the table. Click the ellipsis points button to set the additional styles.

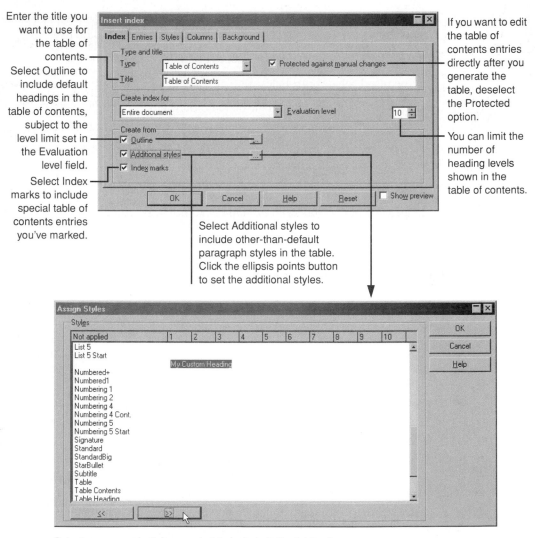

Select a paragraph style you want to include in the table of contents, and click the arrows at the bottom of the window to assign the style to a table of contents level (based on the numbers at the top of the window). Click OK when you're finished.

Figure 8-13   Setting table of contents options in the Insert Index window

Select a table of contents heading level you want to define.

In the boxes in the Structure area, enter the codes and text that define the selected level of your table of contents. See *Using the Codes* on page 302.

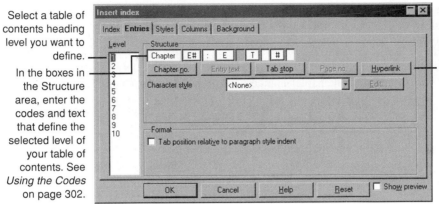

You can type codes in manually or click the buttons in this row to insert codes. (If a button is grayed, its code has already been used.)

In this example, the word "Chapter" and the colon ":" are text entries.

Level 1 entry
Level 2 entries

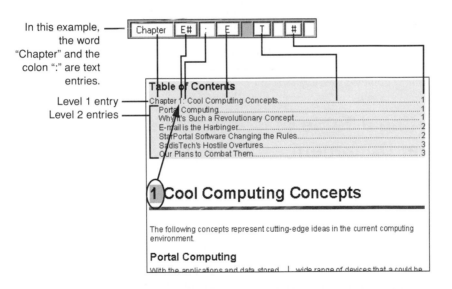

Insert hyperlink codes before and after the part of the table of contents line you want to hyperlink. Click hyperlinked entries to jump to that part of the document.

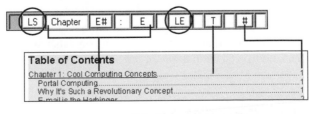

The tab and page number codes (T and #) are outside of the hyperlink codes and are therefore not hyperlinked.

Figure 8-14   Defining what's in each level of a table of contents

Using the Codes

When you select a table of contents level in the Entries tab (see Figure 8-14), you can customize the way that level in the table of contents is displayed. Do this by working with the table of contents codes. Here's what each of the codes means:

*   <E#> – If the paragraph level (for example, Heading 1) uses outline numbering, this tag inserts the full chapter number definition, whether it's *1*, *Chapter 1*, or whatever.

    See *Outline Numbering* on page 278.

*   <E> – Inserts the text of the heading.

*   <T> – Inserts a tab with leader dots. The tab distance and leader dots are defined in the paragraph styles used for table of contents entries, such as Contents 1, Contents 2, and so on.

*   <#> – Inserts the page number.

*   <LS> and <LE> – Opening and closing tags that enclose the part of the table of contents entry you want to hyperlink to its respective section of the document.

In addition to mixing and matching codes, you can enter text along with them such as *Chapter* or *page*. Figure 8-14 shows how the codes, and the extra text typed in, map to the actual table of contents that is generated.

Inserting a Table of Contents Into a Master Document

1   With the master document open, make sure Navigator is open (press the F5 key), and toggle to the master document view.

2   In the Navigator window, select the file you want to put the table of contents before.

3   In Navigator, click and hold down the Insert button, and choose Table of Contents.

4   Set the options for the table of contents. If you need help setting options, see *Inserting a Table of Contents Into a Document* on page 298.

5   Click OK.

As in a single document, all parts of a table of contents have their own paragraph formats that you can modify. Click in a line of the table of contents, and the name of the style is highlighted in the Stylist under paragraph styles, as shown in Figure 8-16 on page 304.

Marking Special Table of Contents Entries

There may be instances where you want to include certain parts of a document in a table of contents. For example, say you're creating a table of contents that contains entries for Heading 1 and Heading 2 items only, but there's a single item at the Heading 4 level that is an extremely important section, and you want to include it in the table of contents as well. You can mark that item as a special entry for inclusion in the table of contents.

1   In your document, select the text you want to include in the table of contents.

    In a master document, you need to select the text in the source file.

2   Choose Insert > Indexes > Entry.

3   In the Insert Index Entry window (Figure 8-15), select Table of Contents in the Index field.

    The text you selected in the document shows up in the Entry field automatically.

4   In the Level field, set the level of the item as it will appear in the table of contents.

5   Click Insert.

6   The Insert Index Entry stays open for you to select and insert more text in the document.

7   When you're finished inserting special table of contents entries, click Close.

If you select Apply to all similar texts, all text that matches what's in the Entry field will be marked and included in the table of contents. That's why you should *not* use this feature for table of contents entries. It's meant to be used for index entries.

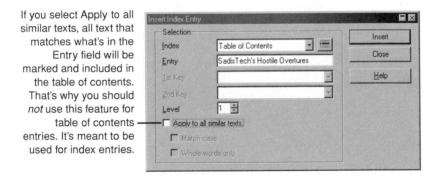

Figure 8-15   Marking special entries for inclusion in a table of contents

When you generate the table of contents, be sure that in the Insert Index window, on the Index tab, you select the Index marks option. If you don't, your special table of contents entries won't be included in the index.

Formatting and Editing a Table of Contents

A table of contents is typically a big block of read-only text that you can't edit directly (though you can change this effect in the first tab of the Insert Index window, shown in Figure 8-13 on page 300). Best practices are to regenerate the table of contents to change the text inside of it; because if you change just the table of contents entry, the heading used to generate it is still incorrect, and if you regenerate the table of contents for some reason, the incorrect heading will reappear.

In terms of formatting, you can change the formatting of the table of contents entries without regenerating the table of contents.

Basic Table of Contents Formatting

Each level in a table of contents has its own paragraph style. For example, level 1 headings by default are associated with the "Contents 1" paragraph style, which uses plain ol' vanilla formatting. To change the formatting of table of contents levels, modify their associated paragraph formats.

You can tell which paragraph style is associated with a level by clicking in a line of the table of contents. The paragraph style used for it will be highlighted in the Stylist, as shown in Figure 8-16.

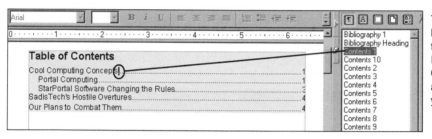

The cursor is in a level 1 entry in the table of contents. In the Stylist, Contents 1 is the associated style you must modify.

Figure 8-16   Identifying styles used for table of contents levels

For more information on modifying paragraph styles, see *Paragraph Styles* on page 205.

Advanced Table of Contents Formatting

Instead of using and modifying the default paragraph table of contents styles, you can assign other paragraph styles to table of contents entries. Using this procedure you can also change the number of columns used for the table of contents, and you can add background color or graphics to the table of contents.

1   Click in the table of contents, right-click, and choose Edit Index.

2   In the Insert Index window, select the Styles tab. See Figure 8-17.

The Levels list displays the table of contents title and the 10 possible table of contents levels, with the paragraph styles that are assigned to those levels (in parentheses).

The Paragraph styles list displays all the paragraph styles defined in the document.

3   In the Levels list, select the item you want to assign a different paragraph format to.

4   In the Paragraph styles list, select the paragraph style you want to assign to the selected level.

You can't assign Writer's default Heading # styles to levels, but you can assign them to the table of contents title.

5   Click the Assign button.

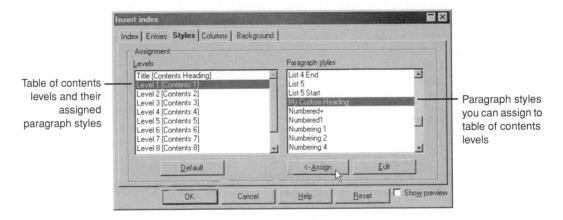

Table of contents
levels and their
assigned
paragraph styles

Paragraph styles
you can assign to
table of contents
levels

Figure 8-17   Assigning paragraph styles to table of contents levels

6   Set column options in the Columns tab, and set background color or graphic options in the Background tab.

These settings are similar to those used in defining page styles. If you need more information, see Figure 5-37 on page 215 for column information and Figure 5-33 on page 213 for background information.

7   Click OK.

Fixing Page Flow After You Insert a Table of Contents

When you insert a table of contents above the content of your document, you may need to paginate your document so that the table of contents is by itself on one (or more) pages, and the body of your document starts on a new page. Figure 8-14 on page 301 shows a table of contents that is sitting right above the body of the document.

In a master document, you must use this procedure on the individual source files.

1   Click at the beginning of the body of the document and press Ctrl+Enter to break the body to a new page.

2   If you're using left and right page styles, and the table of contents ends on a right page, you may also need to click at the end of the table of contents and create a page break so that an empty left page is created.

This lets you start the body of the document on a right page. See *Applying and Overriding Page Style Flows* on page 217.

3   After you change pagination, update the table of contents (next).

Editing a Table of Contents

Editing a table of contents involves tasks like including or excluding certain types of paragraph styles that are displayed, altering the way entries are displayed, associating levels with other-than-default paragraph formats, and making other fundamental changes to a table of contents.

If your basic table of contents setup is just as you want it, and you've simply added new content to your document, you only need to update the table of contents, not edit it. See Updating a Table of Contents, next.

To edit a table of contents:

1   Click in the table of contents.

2   Right-click, and choose Edit Index.

3   In the Insert Index window, make the changes you want.

If you need help, see Figure 8-13, Figure 8-14, and Figure 8-17.

4   Click OK.

Updating a Table of Contents

If the contents or page count of a document changes after a table of contents has been generated, update the table of contents using this procedure.

However, if you need to make more fundamental changes to the table of contents structure, you need to edit the table of contents. See the previous procedure.

1   Click in the table of contents.

2   Right-click and choose Update Index.

Removing a Table of Contents

You can't remove a table of contents by selecting it and deleting it. To remove a table of contents, click in it, right-click, and choose Remove Index.

Creating an Index

There are professional indexers in the world. Their work can dramatically increase the quality of a book. Conversely, a poor index can cause a lot of reader frustration. So assuming you do not aspire to be a professional indexer, we'll leave you with perhaps the most useful advice a professional indexer is likely to give you to create a decent index: pretend you're a reader.

Stepping into the reader's shoes helps you anticipate what information the reader will want to find in the index. If a section in your document or book contains important information on creating a file, which words might the target reader look for in the index to get to that information? "Creating a file" is an obvious choice. But might they also look under the word "File"? What about "Generating"? "Adding"? "Starting"? Or what about "Document" in addition to "File"? Or even more specifically, "Text document" or "Spreadsheet"? The index terms you use may not even appear in the text of a document or book.

The index entries you insert are up to you. But looking at your index from a reader's perspective helps ensure that the index will be more useful than it otherwise would be.

Marking Index Entries

For Writer to generate an index with related page numbers, you must mark the items you want to index right where they appear in the document.

1   Select the text you want to use as the index entry. You can also just click inside the word you want to index.

2   Choose Insert > Indexes > Entry.

3   In the Insert Index Entry window, select Alphabetical Index in the Index field.

4   Set the remaining options for the entry. Use Figure 8-18 for guidance.

5   Click Insert.

     The Insert Index Entry window stays open for you to mark other index entries in the document.

When you insert an index entry, the selected word gets a gray background (if View > Field Shadings is activated).

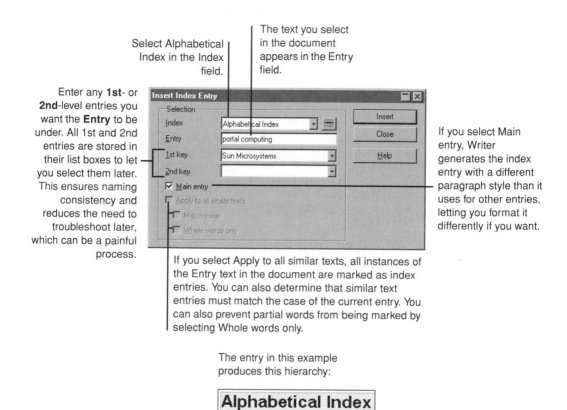

Select Alphabetical Index in the Index field.

The text you select in the document appears in the Entry field.

Enter any **1st**- or **2nd**-level entries you want the **Entry** to be under. All 1st and 2nd entries are stored in their list boxes to let you select them later. This ensures naming consistency and reduces the need to troubleshoot later, which can be a painful process.

If you select Main entry, Writer generates the index entry with a different paragraph style than it uses for other entries, letting you format it differently if you want.

If you select Apply to all similar texts, all instances of the Entry text in the document are marked as index entries. You can also determine that similar text entries must match the case of the current entry. You can also prevent partial words from being marked by selecting Whole words only.

The entry in this example produces this hierarchy:

Figure 8-18   Making index entries

Inserting an Index Into a Single Document

Use this procedure for inserting a table of contents into a single document rather than a master document. The procedure for inserting a table of contents into a master document follows this one.

You don't have to insert all your index entries before you generate an index. You can go back and make additional entries, then update the index.

1   Click in the document where you want to insert the index.

2   Choose Insert > Indexes > Indexes.

3   In the Insert Index window, select Alphabetical Index in the Type field.

4   Set the options in the Index tab. Use Figure 8-19 for guidance.

5   Set options in the remaining tabs. If you need guidance, *Inserting a Table of Contents Into a Document* on page 298 contains similar information.

6   Click OK.

Select Alphabetical Index in the Type field, and enter the title that you want for the generated index. You can generate the index based on entries in the entire document or in only the current chapter.

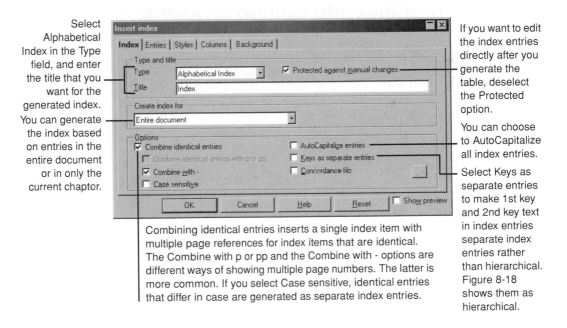

If you want to edit the index entries directly after you generate the table, deselect the Protected option.

You can choose to AutoCapitalize all index entries.

Select Keys as separate entries to make 1st key and 2nd key text in index entries separate index entries rather than hierarchical. Figure 8-18 shows them as hierarchical.

Combining identical entries inserts a single index item with multiple page references for index items that are identical. The Combine with p or pp and the Combine with - options are different ways of showing multiple page numbers. The latter is more common. If you select Case sensitive, identical entries that differ in case are generated as separate index entries.

Figure 8-19   Setting index options in the Insert Index window

All parts of an index have their own paragraph formats you can modify. Click in a line of the index, and the name of the style is highlighted in the Stylist under paragraph styles.

Inserting an Index Into a Master Document

1   With the master document open, make sure Navigator is open (press the F5 key), and toggle to the master document view in Navigator.

2   In the Navigator window, select the last file of the master document.

3   In Navigator, click and hold down the Insert button, and choose Index.

4   Set the options for the Index. See the previous section if you need help setting options.

5   Click OK.

6   If you want to move the index to a different place in the master document, select the index item in the Navigator (master document view), and click one of the Move buttons to position the index where you want.

All parts of an index have their own paragraph formats that you can modify. Click in a line of the table of contents, and the name of the style is highlighted in the Stylist under paragraph styles.

Formatting and Editing an Index

The principles and procedure for formatting and editing an index are the same as that for formatting and editing a table of contents. See *Formatting and Editing a Table of Contents* on page 303.

Updating an Index

The procedure for updating an index is the same as that for updating a table of contents. See *Updating a Table of Contents* on page 306.

Tips for Troubleshooting Indexes

Indexes never end up perfect the first time. In order to fix an index, you really should fix the index entries rather than editing the index itself, then update the index. Unfortunately, there's no streamlined way to jump from an index item to the index marker in the document to fix it. You have to hunt and peck through the document(s), which can be really time-consuming. Use the following tips to help with the troubleshooting process.

- Choose View > Field Shadings. This shows the gray background of index entries.

- To locate index entries in a document, use the Navigation tool. (Click the little dot button at the bottom of the vertical scroll bar, click Index entry, and use the up and down arrows above and below the button to jump to the previous or next entry.) If you  click the lower arrow to move to the next entry, the cursor is in the perfect position to use the next tip.

- You can click in an index entry and choose Edit > Index Entry to bring up the Edit Index Entry window (Figure 8-20), which lets you change, delete, and move to previous and next index entries.

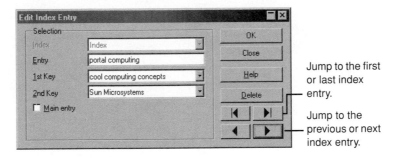

Jump to the first or last index entry.

Jump to the previous or next index entry.

Figure 8-20   Troubleshooting an index

Creating Lists of Figures and Other Lists

If you've used captions in your document for figures, tables, and other elements (see *Inserting Captions* on page 259), you can create lists of these elements.

Inserting a List Into a Single Document

1   Click where you want to insert the list.

2   Choose Insert > Indexes > Indexes.

3   In the Insert Index window, select the Type of list you want to generate.

- If you used your own paragraph styles for captioning, select User-Defined.

- If you used Writer's caption tool to enter captions, select Illustration Index or Index of Tables.

4   Enter a Title for the list.

5   Set options in the Index tab. Use Figure 8-21 for guidance.

6   Set options in the remaining tabs. If you need guidance, the information in *Inserting a Table of Contents Into a Document* on page 298 contains similar information.

7   Click OK.

To generate a list based on caption paragraph styles you've created, select User-Defined in the Type Field, select the Styles option (only), click the ellipsis button, and set the paragraph style you want to generate the list with.

Select a paragraph style you want to include in the list, and click the arrows at the bottom of the window to assign the style to level 1 (based on the numbers at the top of the window). Click OK when you're finished.

If you select Illustration Index or Index of Tables, select the Caption option, and select the type (category) of captions you want to list.

Select Object names to list the objects by the internal names assigned to them (such as Graphic 1).

In the Display field, select the information you want included in the list.

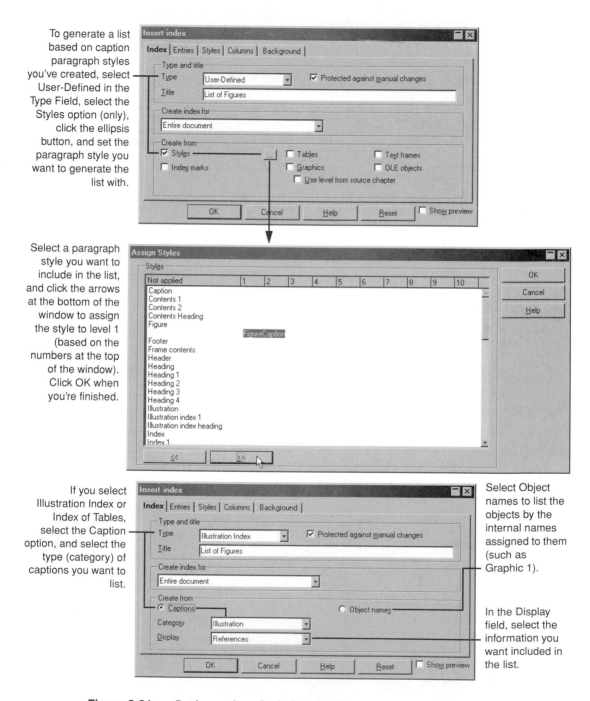

Figure 8-21   Setting options for index-type lists

The list title and items have their own paragraph styles you can modify, just like tables of contents and indexes.

You can also generate lists of objects you've inserted in a document. In the Insert Index window, select the type called Table of Objects, and select the types of StarOffice objects you want to list (such as StarOffice Chart, StarOffice Calc, and so on).

Inserting a List in a Master Document

You can insert one or more lists in a master document.

1   With the master document open, make sure Navigator is open (press the F5 key), and toggle to the master document view in Navigator.

2   In the Navigator window, select the last file of the master document.

3   In Navigator, click and hold down the Insert button, and choose User-Defined Index.

4   In the Type field, select the type of caption list you want to create.

5   Set the options for the list. See the previous section if you need help setting options.

6   Click OK.

7   Select the list item in the Navigator (master document view), and click the Move Up or Move Down buttons to move the list to the desired location in the master document.

All parts of a list have their own paragraph formats that you can modify. Click in a line of the table of contents, and the name of the style is highlighted in the Stylist under paragraph styles.

Formatting and Editing Lists

The principles and procedures for formatting and editing lists are the same as those for formatting and editing a table of contents. See *Formatting and Editing a Table of Contents* on page 303.

Updating Lists

The procedure for updating lists is the same as that for updating a table of contents. See *Updating a Table of Contents* on page 306.

Bibliographies

Writer lets you store bibliography information for different publications you'll reference in your documents. Once bibliography information is stored, you can insert bibliography references in your document, then generate a formatted bibliography at the end of a document.

Because StarOffice uses the default bibliography database table, called *biblio*, to generate bibliographies, use only this table to store bibliography information in a database. The only alternative to store bibliography information in a database is to store it inside individual documents. The procedure for that is included in this section.

Entering Bibliography Information

You can enter bibliography information in the StarOffice Bibliography database, or you can enter and store bibliography information in individual documents.

Using the Bibliography Database

You can add to and change the bibliography database by choosing Edit > Bibliography Database and entering information in the appropriate fields.

You can also edit the Bibliography database directly using the following procedure:

1   Open the Explorer and Beamer windows.

2   In the Explorer window, expand the Bibliography item, and expand the Table item.

3   Select the bibliography table (it's called *biblio* by default), as shown in Figure 8-22.

4   In the Beamer window, make any necessary additions or changes to the database.

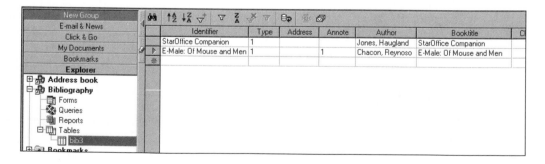

Figure 8-22   Adding to the bibliography database

The bibliography database includes sample data that you can delete. To delete these samples, open the database, click the gray box next to the first record you want to delete (the entire row becomes highlighted), hold down Shift, click the gray box next to the last item you want to delete (are records in between become highlighted), and press Delete.

Storing Bibliography Information in an Individual Document

Bibliography entries stored in a document are *not* stored in the StarOffice bibliography database. There isn't a compelling reason to store bibliography information this way. Storing it in the bibliography database ensures that all documents have access to the information. However, if for some reason your bibliography database becomes inaccessible or corrupted, use this procedure as a workaround.

1   Click in the document where you want to insert a bibliography reference.

2   Choose Insert > Indexes > Bibliography Entry.

3   In the Insert Bibliography Entry window, select the From document content option.

4   Click New.

5   In the Define Bibliography Entry window, enter bibliography information. See Figure 8-23.

    The Short name you enter will be used in bibliography drop-down lists.

6   Click OK.

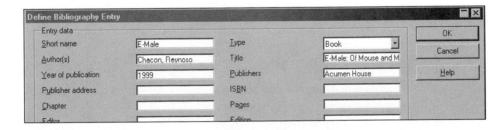

Figure 8-23   A portion of the Define Bibliography Entry window

Inserting Bibliography References in a Document

You can insert references to bibliography items that are stored either in the bibliography database or within a document itself.

See *Entering Bibliography Information* on page 314.

1   Click in the document where you want to insert a bibliography reference.

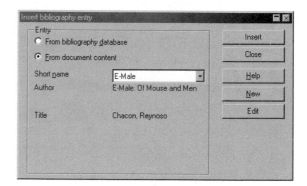

2   Choose Insert > Indexes > Bibliography Entry.

3   In the Insert Bibliography Entry window, select whether you want to insert a bibliography reference from the bibliography database or from the document content.

If you select the From document content option, you have to have already created and inserted the bibliography reference using the procedure in *Storing Bibliography Information in an Individual Document* on page 315 in order to see any items in the drop-down list.

4   In the Short name field, select the bibliography entry you want to insert.

5   Click Insert.

Writer inserts a bracketed reference containing the bibliography item's short name. You can change this reference to show an endnote number rather than the short name. To do this, when you generate the bibliography, be sure in the Insert Index window, on the Index tab, to select the Number entries field.

Generating a Bibliography

You can generate a bibliography for a single document or a master document.

Inserting a Bibliography Into a Single Document

1   Make sure you've inserted bibliography references in the document.

     See *Inserting Bibliography References in a Document* on page 316.

2   Click in the document where you want to insert the bibliography.

3   Choose Insert > Indexes > Indexes.

4   In the Insert Index window, select Bibliography in the Type field.

5   Enter a Title for the bibliography.

6   Select the Number entries option if you want to change all the bibliography references in the document to numbers, as shown in Figure 8-24.

     These numbers will correspond with numbered bibliography entries in the generated list.

7   Set options in the remaining tabs. If you need guidance, the information in *Inserting a Table of Contents Into a Document* on page 298 contains similar information.

8   Click OK.

     Figure 8-24 on page 318 illustrates the procedure.

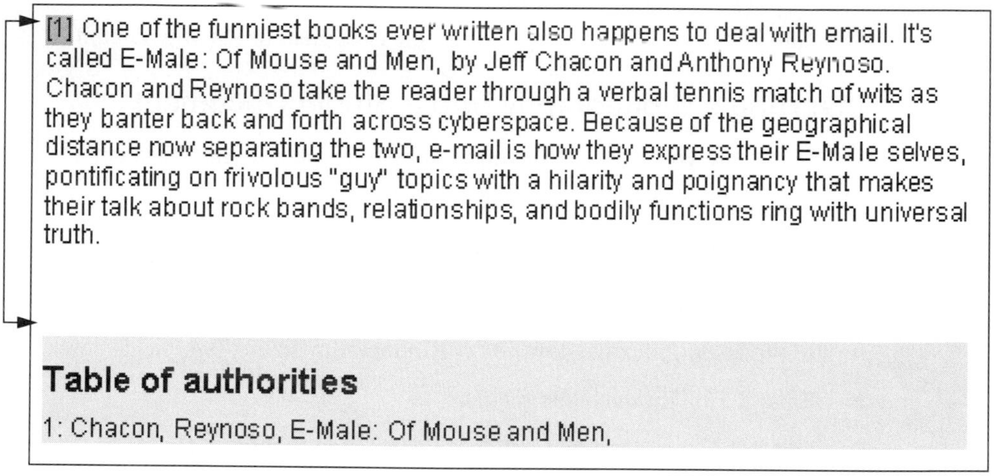

[1] One of the funniest books ever written also happens to deal with email. It's called E-Male: Of Mouse and Men, by Jeff Chacon and Anthony Reynoso. Chacon and Reynoso take the reader through a verbal tennis match of wits as they banter back and forth across cyberspace. Because of the geographical distance now separating the two, e-mail is how they express their E-Male selves, pontificating on frivolous "guy" topics with a hilarity and poignancy that makes their talk about rock bands, relationships, and bodily functions ring with universal truth.

Table of authorities

1: Chacon, Reynoso, E-Male: Of Mouse and Men,

Figure 8-24   A bibliography reference and a generated bibliography

Inserting a Bibliography Into a Master Document

1   With the master document open, make sure Navigator is open (press the F5 key), and toggle to the master document view in Navigator.

2   In the Navigator window, select the last file of the master document.

3   In Navigator, click and hold down the Insert button, and choose User-Defined Index.

4   In the Type field, select Bibliography.

5   Select the Number entries option if you want to change all the bibliography references in the document to numbers.

     These numbers will correspond with numbered bibliography entries in the generated list.

6   Set options in the remaining tabs. If you need guidance, the information in *Inserting a Table of Contents Into a Document* on page 298 contains similar information.

7   Click OK.

8   Select the bibliography item in the Navigator (master document view), and click the Move Up or Move Down buttons to move the bibliography to the desired location in the master document.

All parts of a list have their own paragraph formats that you can modify. Click in a line of the table of contents, and the name of the style is highlighted in the Stylist under paragraph styles.

Formatting and Editing Bibliographies

The principles and procedures for formatting and editing bibliographies are the same as those for formatting and editing a table of contents. See *Formatting and Editing a Table of Contents* on page 303.

Updating Bibliographies

The procedure for updating a bibliography is the same as that for updating a table of contents. See *Updating a Table of Contents* on page 306.

Mailings

About Mailings, Databases, and Mail Merges

Mailings, for the purposes of this book, have to do mostly with setting up mail merges in Writer to do mass mailing, which includes Email.

Databases

In order to do mail merges in StarOffice, the databases containing all the contacts you want to include in the mail merge must be set up in StarOffice. If you're groaning at the implications of this, you're in good company. It involves not only the possibility of importing non-StarOffice databases into StarOffice, but also setting up and maintaining databases effectively. For example, if you want to be able to filter out certain contacts in a mail merge, you have to do things like filter a database, create a query for a database, or set up and maintain a check box field in a table.

In , , on page 985, we show you how to import non-StarOffice databases, perform filtering, set up queries, and add fields to databases. We'll also show you how to perform basic filtering and set up queries in this chapter. But we don't cover strategies for setting up and maintaining databases. We explain why we don't in *The Database Tirade* on page 990.

While databases themselves can seem a bit ominous, the good news is that once you get the databases you want into StarOffice, doing mail merges is easy.

If you don't have any existing databases to import, that's fine, because StarOffice comes with a default address book you can fill up and use in mail merges.

Mail Merges

A mail merge involves inserting the names of database fields into your document. For example, in the heading of a letter, the inserted database fields would look something like this:

<PREFIX> <FIRSTNAME> <LASTNAME>
<TITLE>
<COMPANY>
<ADDRESS>
<CITY>, <STATEPROV> <POSTALCODE>

Dear <FIRSTNAME> <LASTNAME>,

These fields form a link to your database, pull the information out of it, and put it into your document. In Writer, you can drag and drop these fields from your database into your document.

A single group of information in a database is called a record. A record can include a lot of information, such as a person's first name, last name, address, phone number, Email address, spouse's name, children's names, and whether or not you've already sent them a Christmas card.

If you do a mail merge using a one-page letter, all the relevant information in a single record is inserted onto the page. A new page is created for each record used in the database.

You can send mail merges directly to your printer, or you can send them to files, where you can open them and print them out later.

Merging to a Document

1   Open or create the document you want to use for a mail merge.

2   Open the Explorer and Beamer windows. (Click their buttons on the function bar.)

3   In Explorer, expand the database you want to use, and select the table or query containing the fields you want to use in the mail merge. (See *Getting Nerdy With Queries* on page 326 for basic information on setting up a query. It's really not that tough.)

4   The contents of the query or table display in Beamer.

5   Perform any filtering to include or exclude records during the mail merge. If you're setting up a mail merge from a query, this filtering information is probably already set up. If you're setting up a mail merge from a table, see Basic Filtering, next.

You can also select a group of records to include in a merge. Hold down Ctrl and click the box next to each record you want to include, or click the first record of a range you want to select, hold down Shift, and click the last record of the range.

6   In Beamer, click and drag the headings of the database fields you want to use into the document, as shown in Figure 9-1, and add any necessary punctuation and paragraph breaks between fields.

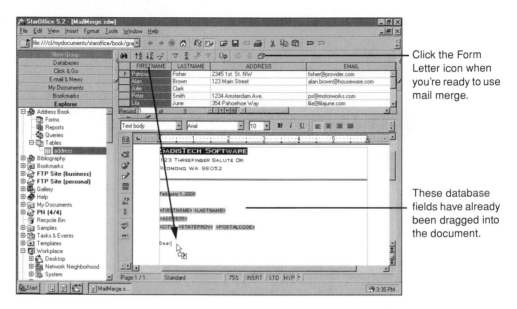

Click the Form Letter icon when you're ready to use mail merge.

These database fields have already been dragged into the document.

Figure 9-1   Dragging database fields into a document for mail merge

At this point, you don't actually have to do the merge right away. You can save and close the document. It will be ready for the merge next time you open it, which you perform with the following steps.

7   Click the Form Letter icon in Beamer's object bar, shown in Figure 9-1, (or choose File > Form Letter).

8   In the Form Letter window, set the options you want for the merge.

Use Figure 9-2 for guidance.

9   Click OK.

StarOffice also comes with templates that have mail merge fields already set up that are connected to the StarOffice Address Book. If you don't want to set up your own fields, start a new document using one of these templates. To do this, choose File > New > From Template, and select the template you want to use. In the New window, click the More button to preview selected templates before you choose which one you want to use.

Select the records you want to use in the merge. The Selected records option is available only if you select specific records in Beamer. Select From to set a range of records.

Select whether you want to send the merge to your printer, to an Email (Email addresses in the records will be used to send the document), or to a file. Each option has its own settings, which are fairly self-explanatory. The ones that aren't are explained next.

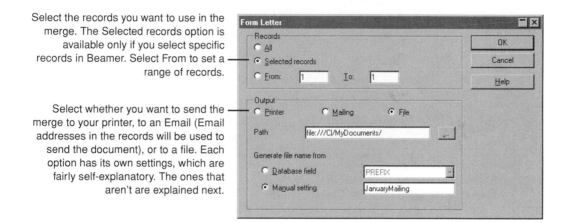

Figure 9-2   Setting mail merge options in the Form Letter window

If You Merge to a Printer Select the Single print jobs option if you want each print job (letter) to be printed on a new sheet of paper.

If You Merge to Email (Mailing) To use this option, you have to have Email set up in StarOffice. The Email is sent through StarOffice's Email tool. When choosing the Mailing option for a mail merge, you can select a format (HTML, RTF, and StarOffice) for the Email that will be used in addition to text format, which is always used. Only use formats that your recipients can read. For example, in order to read an Email in StarOffice format, the recipient must be reading Email in StarOffice. If the recipient isn't reading the message in StarOffice, he or she will see the message in text format only. If you included graphics within the message itself, they won't display, not even as attachments.

Also, be careful about sending a document that has graphics in it. If you inserted the graphics using the Link option, your recipients won't be able to see the graphics if the link points to a location that only you can access, like your own hard drive or a folder on the network that only you have access to.

If You Merge to a File A separate file is created for each letter. After you set the folder to which the files will be printed, you can choose whether the files will be named according to a database field or according to what you type in the Manual setting field.

Basic Filtering

Before you push the final button to do a mail merge, you can do some basic filtering on the database to include and/or exclude specific records.

1   With Beamer displaying the database, click the Default
     Filter icon in the object bar to bring up the Filter
     window.

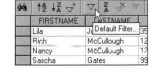

2   In the Filter window, set the filtering conditions.

     Use Figure 9-3 for guidance.

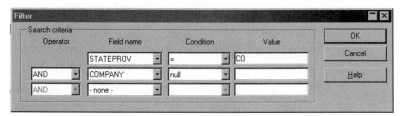

This filter setting will produce the following results: the record will be included in
the merge if its STATEPROV value equals CO; and it will be included if the
COMPANY field is empty (null). All other records will be excluded.

Figure 9-3   Basic record filtering

Getting Nerdy With Queries

Queries help you focus in on specific information in your database. For example, in a huge
database with lots of fields, you can create a query that shows just first names and Email
addresses; or you can create a query that just shows mailing label information.

When you create a query, it is displayed under the Queries
item of your database (in the Explorer window). When you
select it, its contents display in Beamer. Creating a mail merge
by selecting a query is great, because you see only the fields
and records you want to use.

Once you create a query, you can use it for mail merges the
same way you do a database table: select the query in the Explorer window, open the
Beamer window, and drag fields from the query (in the Beamer window) into the
document to set up a mail merge.

To create a query:

1   Expand your database in the Explorer window.

2   Right-click the Queries item in the Explorer window, and choose New > Query >
     AutoPilot.

3   The first window of the AutoPilot lists all the tables of the database. Select the table
     you want, and click Next.

4   In the second AutoPilot window, move the fields you want to use for the query from the left side of the window to the right side of the window, and click Next.

5   Use the third AutoPilot window to filter the specific records you want to include in the query. The filtering options are identical to those shown in Figure 9-3. Click the Preview button in this window to see what the results of the filtering will be. Click Next.

6   The fourth AutoPilot window lets you set sorting options for the records. Click Next.

7   In the final window, name the query and click Finish. The query is displayed in Explorer, and you can select it to display it in Beamer.

Fixing Problems With Empty Fields

If some records in the database don't have certain fields filled in, those empty fields will create extra spaces and blank lines in the mail merge. Use the following merge fields as an example.

<PREFIX> <FIRSTNAME> <LASTNAME>
<COMPANY>
<ADDRESS>
<CITY>, <STATE> <POSTALCODE>

If a record doesn't have a Mr., Ms., Dr., or whatever in the Prefix field, the merge will show an empty space before the first name. Also, if the record doesn't have any company information entered, there will be an empty paragraph between the name and the address.

Here's how to make the merge remove the empty space and the blank line. (You can use the techniques in these procedures to tighten up other parts of mail merges.)

Fixing the Empty Space Problem

This procedure shows you how to fix empty space on a line caused by empty fields. A prime example of this issue is when a database record doesn't have a prefix (Mr., Ms., Dr.) for one of your contacts. So we use a <PREFIX> field as an example in this procedure.

1   Don't put a space between the Prefix and the First name fields, so that it looks like this: <PREFIX><FIRSTNAME>

2   Click between the two fields, and press Ctrl+F2 to bring up the Fields window.

3   Click the Functions tab.

4   In the Type list, select Hidden Text.

5   In the Condition field, type PREFIX.

6   In the Text field, press the space bar to enter a space.

7   Click Insert.

The condition you just entered means that if a prefix exists in a record, it will be printed with a space after it. If there's no prefix in the record, the line will begin with the first name.

Fixing the Empty Line Problem

This procedure shows you how to fix empty lines caused by empty fields. A prime example of this is when a database record doesn't have company information for one of your contacts, so we use a <COMPANY> field as an example.

1   Click in front of the <COMPANY> field.

2   Press Ctrl+F2 to bring up the Fields window.

3   Click the Functions tab.

4   In the Type list, select Hidden Paragraph.

5   In the Condition field, enter COMPANY EQ " " (which translated means, "if COMPANY equals nothing").

6   Click Insert.

The condition you just entered means that if there's nothing in the company field, create a hidden paragraph. That brings the address information just beneath the name information in the mail merge.

Merging to an Envelope

If you set up your mail merge for envelopes the same way you set it up for your letters (that is, using the same table or query, the same filtering, and the same print options), the envelopes will print in the same order as your letters, making them easy to collate with your letters.

1   Configure your printer so that the paper type is set to the envelope size you need.

2   With a Writer document open, choose Insert > Envelope.

3   In the Envelope window, set the merge fields and other options for the envelope. Use Figure 9-4 and Figure 9-5 for guidance.

    In the Format tab, the Format field defaults to C65. You'll probably need to change this, especially in the United States where the standard business envelope is Env. 10.

4   Click New doc to create a new file for the envelope.

5   Choose File > Form Letter.

6   In the Form Letter window, set the options you want for the merge. Use Figure 9-2 on page 325 for guidance.

If you print the envelopes to a file, **a separate file is created for each envelope**.

7   Click OK.

If you're merging directly to your printer, you can print a full stack of envelopes without manually feeding the printer. Each contact will print on its own envelope.

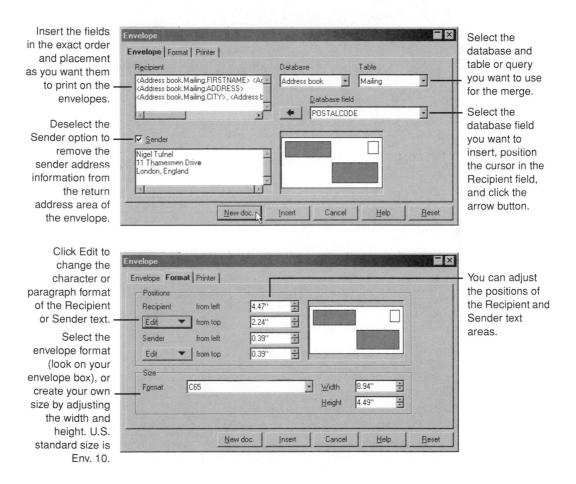

Insert the fields in the exact order and placement as you want them to print on the envelopes.

Deselect the Sender option to remove the sender address information from the return address area of the envelope.

Select the database and table or query you want to use for the merge.

Select the database field you want to insert, position the cursor in the Recipient field, and click the arrow button.

Click Edit to change the character or paragraph format of the Recipient or Sender text.

Select the envelope format (look on your envelope box), or create your own size by adjusting the width and height. U.S. standard size is Env. 10.

You can adjust the positions of the Recipient and Sender text areas.

Figure 9-4   The Envelope window, Envelope and Format tabs

Set the options for how the envelope will be fed through the printer.

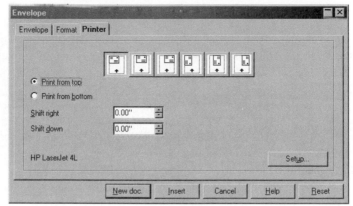

Figure 9-5   The Envelope window, Printer tab

Merging to Labels

1   Choose File > New > Labels.

2   In the Labels window, set the merge fields and other options for the labels. Use Figure 9-6 through Figure 9-8 for guidance.

3   Click New Document to create a new file for the labels.

4   Choose File > Form Letter.

5   In the Form Letter window, set the options you want for the merge. Use Figure 9-2 on page 325 for guidance.

6   Click OK.

Select the Address option to print your
address rather than a mail merge. This
would be useful for printing return
address labels and business cards.

Insert the fields
in the exact order
and placement
as you want them
to print on the
labels.

Select whether
you want the
labels to print on
Continuous
paper or on
individual
Sheets.

Select the
Database and
Table or query
you want to use
for the merge.

Select a
database field
you want to
insert, position
the cursor in the
Label text field,
and click the left
arrow button.

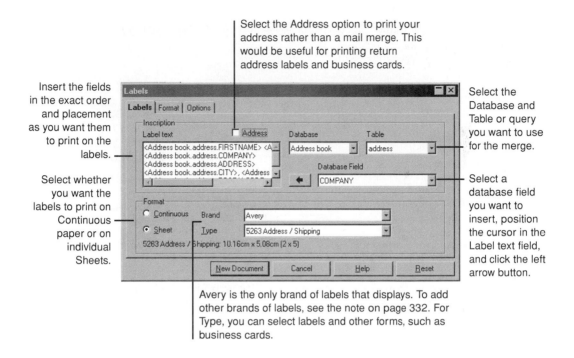

Avery is the only brand of labels that displays. To add
other brands of labels, see the note on page 332. For
Type, you can select labels and other forms, such as
business cards.

Figure 9-6   The Labels window, Labels tab

If the type of
labels you have
doesn't match
any of the
choices on the
Labels tab, you
can adjust the
label sizes in this
window to match
your labels.

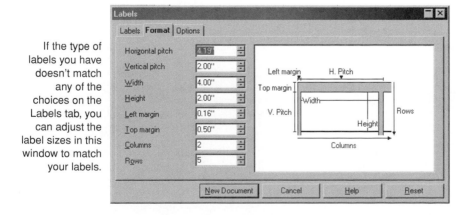

Figure 9-7   The Labels window, Format tab

If you want to print a single label, select the option and set the column and row location of the label. The available coordinates are based on the type of labels you've selected.

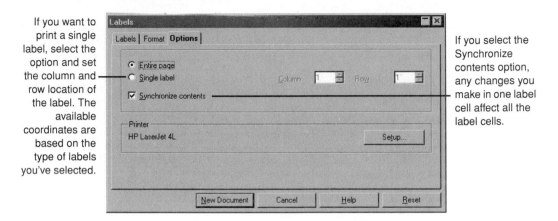

If you select the Synchronize contents option, any changes you make in one label cell affect all the label cells.

Figure 9-8   The Labels window, Options tab

Note – You can also add label definitions that aren't installed with StarOffice. In the `Office52/share/config` folder, open the `labels.ini` file. It contains directions for adding label definitions to the file.

chapter

10

Version Control and Editing Tools

Note About Version Control

There are two different aspects to keeping track of different versions of a document.

- The most common aspect is keeping track of incremental changes in a document so that, if necessary, you can revert back to a previously saved version of the document.

- The second aspect has to do with maintaining two or more distinct versions of a document. One document contains all versions, but different parts of the document can be turned on or off, depending on the audience the document is aimed at. For example, a software company could have a marketing document on a certain software product that contains not only generic information about the product, but also information that is specific to three software platforms. Using conditional text, you can print three different versions of the document, each targeted to a specific software platform audience.

  Using another example, with a wink to our colleagues at Sun, you can create a single classroom instruction guide, but print one with instructor notes and one without.

  In this chapter we'll refer to this second aspect of version control as using *sections*.

Maintaining Incremental Versions of a Document

There truly is no substitute for a good version control software product, where you can check content into and out of a database that controls the process with strict rules and security. Just short of that, however, Writer lets you save incremental versions of a document.

As you work on a document, you can save snapshots of it as it develops. Versioning lets you view prior versions of a document, make visual comparisons between the current version and prior versions, accept or reject those changes, or revert back to a prior version.

Saving Versions of a Document

You must save a document before you can create versions for it. That is, if you start a new document, you can't create versions until you save the document.

To create a version:

1   With the document open, choose File > Versions.

2   In the Versions window (Figure 10-1), click the Save New Version button.

3   In the Insert Version Comment window, type a description of the version, and click OK.

The version is added to list with a time and date stamp, your name (as taken from Tools > Options > General > User Data), and the version description.

When you click the Save New Version button, a window opens and lets you enter a comment about the version.

Select a version and click one of the buttons to the right.

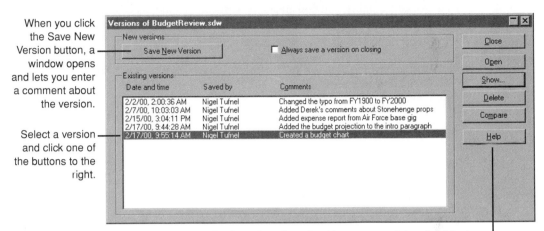

For the selected version: You can open it (read-only), show the full comment on it, delete it, and compare it to the current open version, where you can accept or reject all or part of the changes made between the current and previous version.

Figure 10-1   Maintaining versions of a document

To delete a version (you're not prompted to confirm a deletion), select it in the list and click the Delete button.

Opening Versions

You can open a version in read-only mode to view it. While you can't edit previous versions of a document, you can compare the working version with a previous version, which lets you reject any changes made between the two versions. See Comparing Versions of a Document

In order to open a prior version of a document, a prior version has to have been created. See *Saving Versions of a Document* on page 334.

To open a prior version:

1   With the source document open, choose File > Versions.

2   In the Versions window (Figure 10-1), select the version you want to view, and click the Open button.

You can also open read-only versions of a document from the Open window (File > Open) by selecting the version you want from the Versions field.

Comparing Versions of a Document

This procedure shows you how to compare different versions of the same document, which is different than comparing two separate documents (see *Comparing Separate Documents* on page 340).

When you compare versions, StarOffice automatically turns on change marks (Edit > Changes > Show). You can change the way these change marks look in Tools > Options > Text document > Changes.

Note – StarOffice doesn't currently support comparing content that's in special regions, such as headers, footers, footnotes, frames, fields, and sections. And since manually inserted columns are tagged as sections, content in columns can't be compared. Yes, this is a drag. If you want to use columns *and* compare documents to prior versions, consider making your page styles multi-column instead.

To compare different versions of a document:

1   With the source document open, choose File > Versions.

2   In the Versions window (Figure 10-1), select the version you want to compare to the open document.

3   Click the Compare button.

The Accept or Reject Changes window appears, and the document shows change marks that differentiate the two versions. You can accept and reject changes (see *Accepting or Rejecting Changes* on page 342), or close the Accept or Reject Changes window and view the changes in the document itself.

The change marks that are displayed are in relation to the current version. For example, if you compared the current version to Version 3, the change marks show how Version 3 differs from the current version.

To see what the change marks mean, go to Tools > Options > Text document > Changes.

To get the Accept or Reject Changes window back, choose Edit > Changes > Accept or Reject.

Reverting to Prior Versions of a Document

Sometimes people just need to start over. If you create many versions of a document, then decide that you want to go back and use one of the older versions, either to replace the current version or as the starting point for a new document, use this procedure.

1   With the document open, choose File > Versions.

2   In the Versions window (Figure 10-1 on page 335), select the version you want to revert back to.

3   Click the Compare button.

4   In the Accept or Reject Changes window, click the Reject All button.

    This rejects all the changes made up to the current version.

5   Close the Accept or Reject Changes window.

6   Either save the document as the current document (**which overwrites the current version**), or choose File > Save As to save the document as another document.

Using Sections

Sections are blocks of text that you name. Sections can be protected (made read-only), and they can be hidden. Hiding sections means you can maintain many production versions of a document all within a single document, by showing and hiding specific sections.

Sections are also great for reusing information. For example, if you create a lot of legal contracts, you can create small, reusable sections, each of which can be inserted into a new contract document, and linked so that when the individual sections change, they're updated in the long contract document automatically.

Also, when you change the number of columns for a specific block of text using Format > Columns, those columns are turned into a section automatically.

Note – If you want to visually compare documents with Writer's change tools, know that StarOffice doesn't currently support comparing content that's in special regions, such as headers, footers, footnotes, frames, fields, and sections. So if you use sections, you won't be able to compare the content inside sections.

This procedure shows you how to create a section, then hide it, and show it again.

Creating Sections

1   Select the text you want to make a section.

2   Choose Insert > Section.

3   In the Insert Section window (Figure 10-2), type a meaningful name for the section in the New Section box.

4   Select the Protected option to make the section read-only, or select the Hidden option to hide the section in the document. See the next procedure for using links.

5   Click Insert.

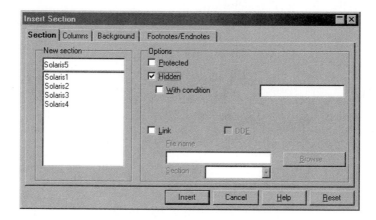

Figure 10-2   Creating and hiding a section

Inserting Sections As Links

You can insert a section from another document as a link, which means when the section in the source document changes, the link to it changes, as well. The source document must have sections defined in order for this procedure to work.

1   Position the cursor where you want to insert the section, and choose Insert > Section.

2   In the Insert Section window, select the Link option.

3   Click the Browse button.

4   In the Insert window, select the document containing the sections you want to link to, and click Insert. The document is added to the File name field.

5   In the Section field, select the section in the source document you want to link to.

6   In the New section field, name the section as you want it to be labeled in the current document.

7   Click OK.

You can also insert a link as a DDE link. For more information, select the DDE option and click the Help button.

If a document uses links, make sure you update it in case the source files have changed. Update the links by choosing Tools > Update > Links. You can also determine how links are updated in the Options window by choosing Tools > Options > Text document > Other. If you choose the Always option in this window, links are updated automatically when you open the document. If you choose the On request option, you're prompted to update links every time you open the document. If you choose the Never option, links are not updated when you open the document. You must update them manually using Tools > Update > Links.

If you want to see where the source of a link is, choose Format > Sections, and in the Edit Sections window, select the section that is the link to view its details.

Modifying and Deleting Sections

After you create sections, you can go back and change their behavior.

1   Choose Format > Sections.

2   In the Edit Sections window, select the section you want, as shown in Figure 10-3.

3   Select the options for the section.

If you delete a section, you just delete the section identifier, not the content in the document itself. If you delete a section that is a link, the text remains in the document, but the link to the source document is broken.

4   Click OK.

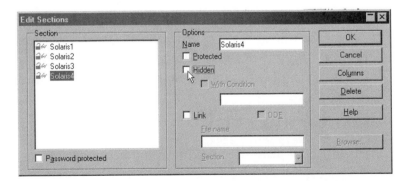

Figure 10-3   Changing section options

Using the Automated Editing Tools

Writer offers a number of tools to let you compare documents and show the effects of changes made to documents.

Comparing Separate Documents

This procedure shows you how to compare two separate documents, which is different than comparing different versions of the same document (see *Comparing Versions of a Document* on page 336).

Note – StarOffice doesn't currently support comparing content that's in special regions, such as headers, footers, footnotes, frames, fields, and sections. And since manually inserted columns are tagged as sections, content in columns can't be compared. Yes, this is a drag. If you want to use columns *and* compare documents, consider making your page styles multi-column instead.

To compare two separate documents:

1   Open the document you want to use as the basis for the comparison.

2   Choose Edit > Compare Document.

3   In the Insert window, select the document you want to compare to the open document, and click Insert.

The Accept or Reject Changes window appears. You can either use it to accept or reject changes (see *Accepting or Rejecting Changes* on page 342) or close it to view the visual differences.

The change marks that are displayed are in relation to the starting document. For example, if you started with Document A, then selected Document B to compare it to, the change marks show how Document B differs from Document A.

To see what the change marks mean, go to Tools > Options > Text document > Changes.

Numbering Lines

You can add line numbers beside lines in Writer. Line numbers are good references for quickly referencing locations in a document; for example, an edit being delivered over the phone.

1   Choose Tools > Line Numbering.

2   In the Line Numbering window (Figure 10-4), select the Show numbering option, and customize any of the options for displaying line numbering.

3   Click OK.

To remove line numbering, deselect the Show numbering option.

You can further control line numbering through paragraph styles, which let you restart line numbering at specific paragraph styles or let you not include paragraph styles in line numbering. See Figure 5-14 on page 191.

Set the line numbering style and the relative position of the numbering to the body of the document.

Set the interval of lines to be numbered. If you set it to 1, every line will be numbered. If you set it at 5, every fifth line will be numbered.

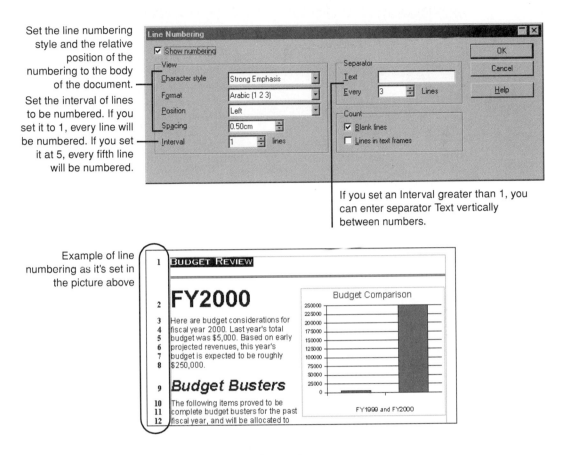

If you set an Interval greater than 1, you can enter separator Text vertically between numbers.

Example of line numbering as it's set in the picture above

Figure 10-4   Setting line numbering options

Using Change Bars and Other Editing Marks

You can show the effects of changes to a document in many different ways, such as displaying change bars in the margins next to text and automatically formatting text in different ways when it is deleted, inserted, or if the text attributes simply change.

Setting Up Change Bars and Editing Marks

1   Set up the options for change bars and edits. Choose Tools > Options > Text document > Changes.

2   Set the options you want.

     Use Figure 10-5 for guidance.

3   Click OK.

The editing marks don't show up in your document right away. You must complete the next procedure to show them.

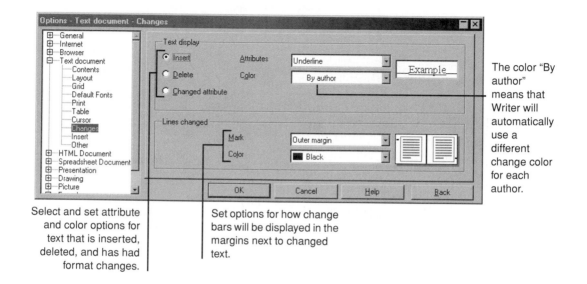

Select and set attribute and color options for text that is inserted, deleted, and has had format changes.

Set options for how change bars will be displayed in the margins next to changed text.

The color "By author" means that Writer will automatically use a different change color for each author.

Figure 10-5   Setting document change options

You can't assign change formats to specific authors. StarOffice randomly assigns different colors and styles when a different author edits the content.

Showing Change Bars and Editing Marks

1   Choose Edit > Changes > Record to keep track of the changes.

2   Choose Edit > Changes > Show to display the changes made.

You can turn off the Show option at any time, and as long as the Record option is selected, changes will be tracked. But if you turn off the Record option, changes to the document will no longer be recorded.

Accepting or Rejecting Changes

Writer gives you the opportunity to accept or reject changes made to a document. When you accept a change, the content becomes a normal part of the current document. When you reject a change, the change returns to its previous state in the document.

In order to accept or reject changes, Writer needs to know that changes have occurred, which means that the Record feature needs to be activated while you work with documents (Edit > Changes > Record).

To accept or reject changes:

1   Choose Edit > Changes > Accept or Reject.

2   In the Accept or Reject Changes window (Figure 10-6), you can select one or more items in the list to accept or reject.

You can modify the list of changes by clicking the Filter tab (Figure 10-7) and setting the criteria for which changes will be shown in the List tab.

3   In the List tab, click the appropriate button at the bottom of the window.

Whether you accept or reject changes, the items you accept or reject are removed from the Accept or Reject Changes window.

4   Close the window when you're finished.

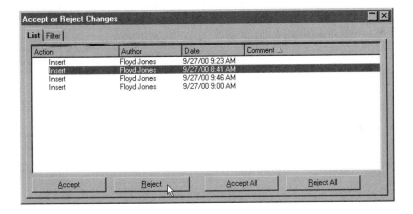

Figure 10-6   Accepting and rejecting changes

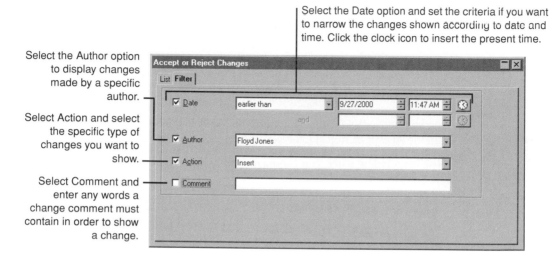

Select the Date option and set the criteria if you want to narrow the changes shown according to date and time. Click the clock icon to insert the present time.

Select the Author option to display changes made by a specific author.

Select Action and select the specific type of changes you want to show.

Select Comment and enter any words a change comment must contain in order to show a change.

Figure 10-7   Filtering the list of changes

Note – Rejecting changes is a great way to perform a selective undo. When you use undo, in order to undo something five steps back, you have to undo the previous four steps as well. With the accept/reject feature, you can pinpoint the exact action you want to undo (reject). While each change is given a generic description, you can pinpoint the change you want to reject like this: With the Accept or Reject Changes window open, select the change, and the change is highlighted in the document. Then click the Reject button.

Using Notes

Notes are a way to insert comments in a document, with a flag that shows that a note is there, but without showing the text itself. Notes are a great way for authors and reviewers to communicate with one another.

Inserting Notes

1   Click in the document where you want to insert a note.

2   Choose Insert > Note.

3   In the Insert Note window (Figure 10-8), enter the appropriate information.

4   Click OK. The note will be indicated with a yellow rectangle at the point in the text where you inserted the note.

The initials currently entered in the User Data window (Tools > Options > General > User Data) are displayed here and will be printed above the note if you print notes with this document.

Enter the note in the Text field.

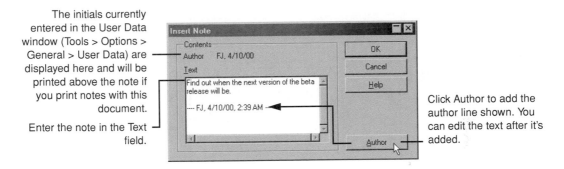

Click Author to add the author line shown. You can edit the text after it's added.

Figure 10-8   Inserting a note

Viewing and Editing Notes

1   Double-click the yellow note indicator.

2   The Edit Note window is like the Insert Note window, except that you can browse from note to note using the arrows.

3   You can change the note, or add your own comments below the current note. If you're adding to a current note, your initials from the Tools > Options > General > User Data window will replace the ones currently identifying the note.

Printing Notes

The Print Options window lets you choose whether to print notes, and where. See *Setting Printing Options* on page 348 for more information.

Showing and Hiding Note Indicators

To show or hide note indicators in StarOffice, choose Tools > Options > Text document > Contents and select or deselect the Notes option.

Printing in StarOffice Writer

Setting Printing Options

The printing options you set using this procedure apply to all Writer documents you work with.

1   Choose Tools > Options > Text document > Print.

You can also choose File > Print and go into the print options to see the window in Figure 11-1.

2   Select what you want to print.

Select Left pages and Right pages to print those pages. The only reason you'd deselect one is if you wanted to print double-sided: printing all left pages, for example, lets you flip them over and print the right pages on the back.

Select Reversed to reverse the order of the page printing to last page first, especially if your printer prints with pages facing up. Select Brochure to enable the brochure printing options. See *Printing Brochures* on page 350 for more information.

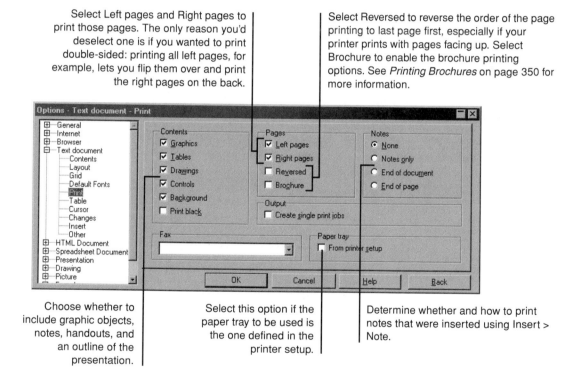

Choose whether to include graphic objects, notes, handouts, and an outline of the presentation.

Select this option if the paper tray to be used is the one defined in the printer setup.

Determine whether and how to print notes that were inserted using Insert > Note.

Figure 11-1   Selecting printing options

Specifying Landscape or Portrait Orientation

To specify whether a document should be portrait or landscape, choose Format > Page and select the Page tab.

You *can* also set orientation in the Printer Options window. (Choose File > Printer Setup, click Properties.) However, all testing indicates that the setting in the Printer Setup window is completely irrelevant; sometimes it changes to reflect what you've set in the Page Setup window, but if you make any changes there, it doesn't affect printing.

See also *Specifying Portrait or Landscape Orientation* on page 82 for more information on the ways you can set orientation throughout StarOffice.

Printing Notes

The Print Options window lets you choose whether to print notes in the page. See *Using Notes* on page 344.

You can choose one of the following note printing options:

*   None – Notes aren't printed.
*   Notes only – Only the notes are printed, not the page content.
*   End of document – The notes are printed on one or more separate sheets of paper, at the end of the document.
*   End of page – The notes for each page are printed on one or more separate sheets of paper, after each page on which there are notes.

If the yellow note flag is showing when you print, it won't show on the printed copy.

Notes are printed like the example in Figure 11-2.

The author line is printed only if added by note inserter.

Author and date of last change are printed here.

```
Page: 1 Line: 2 Author: SH 3/18/00
This is similar to the link on the previous page.
----SH, 3/18/00, 1:17 PM----

Page: 1 Line: 13 Author: FJ 3/19/00
Check this before sending in final files.
----SH, 3/18/00, 2:24 PM----
This works, I tested it myself, you meddling fishwife.
----FJ, 3/19/00, 4:17 AM----
```

Figure 11-2   How notes are printed

Printing More than One Page on a Sheet of Paper

StarOffice lets you squeeze many pages of a document onto a single sheet of paper for compressed printing.

1   With a Writer document open, choose File > Page Preview.

2   In the Page Preview object bar, click the Print
    Options Page View icon.

3   In the Print Options window, set the options you
    want.

    Use Figure 11-3 for guidance.

4   Click OK.

5   In the Page Preview object bar, click the Print
    Page View icon to print the document according
    to the options you set for compressed printing.

The rows and columns
you set represent the
number of pages that will
print on a single sheet.

You can set extra spacing
around the edge of the
printed sheet.

You can increase the
horizontal spacing
between columns and the
vertical spacing between
rows.

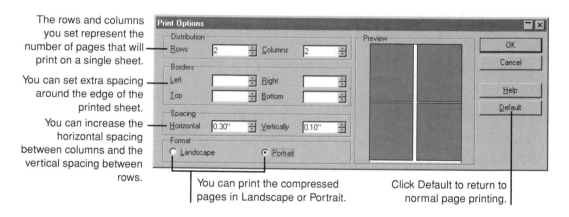

You can print the compressed
pages in Landscape or Portrait.

Click Default to return to
normal page printing.

Figure 11-3   Setting options for compressed printing

Printing Brochures

In Writer and other StarOffice applications, you can print a brochure so that, when the
pages are folded in half and stapled, there are two slides on each side of each page, and
they're in the correct order for a brochure. The size of each slide is reduced, if necessary,
to fit.

Here's how brochure printing works for an eight-page brochure:

- Select Brochure in the Printing options window and print Front side (or Right Pages) only – Writer prints pages 8 and 1 on the first page, and 6 and 3 on the next page.

- Select Brochure and print Back side (or Left Pages) only, and flip the two pages over to print on their back sides – Writer prints pages 2 and 7 on one page (the back side of the 8 and 1 page), and 4 and 5 on the next page (the back side of the 6 and 3 page).

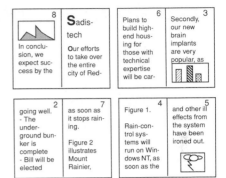

In this example, we're using an 8-page document. You can use brochure printing on any number of pages, as long as the total page count is divisible by 4.

Follow these steps to print a brochure:

1   Set up left and right page styles, especially if you want to set up page numbers to print at the outside edge (right side for right pages, left side for left pages). See *Page Styles* on page 211.

   StarOffice reduces the content somewhat to make the page fit, but might not fully adjust the width of the page if it's too wide. You may have to experiment to get the correct margin settings. You also may need to use larger-than-usual fonts because of the automatic page shrinkage. Again, you may have to experiment.

2   Choose File > Print.

   In the Print window, changing orientation doesn't affect printing; choosing another paper size, such as Legal, will affect how much the pages are compressed.

3   In the Print window, click Options.

4   In the Options window, select All. (For some printers, this option is on the main Print window.)

5   Select the Brochure option and the Front side (or Right Pages) option. Deselect the Back side (or Left Pages) option.

6   Click OK, then click OK again to print.

7   After the pages print, put the printed pages back into the printer with the blank side facing in the correct direction, and choose File > Print, and click the Options button.

8   In the Options window, select Brochure and Back side (or Left Pages), deselect the Front side (or Right Pages) option, then print again.

Printing to PostScript and PDF

This chapter shows you how to print a document or book to a PostScript file. Once in a PostScript file, a document can be turned over to a print shop or turned into a Portable Document Format (PDF) file for web or other electronic delivery. In order to turn PostScript files into PDF files, you need the Adobe Acrobat product.

You don't need an actual PostScript printer to print to a PostScript file. You just need the printer driver installed on your system. There's a lot of good information on PostScript printer drivers on the Adobe Web site: http://www.adobe.com.

1   Make sure you have a PostScript printer driver installed on your system.

If you're running StarOffice on Linux or Solaris, you can use the generic printer driver installed with StarOffice. If you're on Windows, see the note on page 353.

2   When you select File > Print to print the document, select the PostScript printer in your list of printers, and select the Print to file option, as shown in Figure 11-4.

3   When you select the Print to file option, a window is displayed to let you name and select the path for the PostScript file that will be printed. When you name the file, be sure to give it a .ps file extension.

4   Print the document.

If you have Adobe Acrobat installed, distill the PostScript file to create a PDF file. If you're on a network, Acrobat Distiller may be installed on your system. If you're on a UNIX network, for example, type which distill in a terminal window. If a path is returned showing where the program resides, you can create a PDF file. To do so, in the terminal window, change to the directory containing the PostScript file. Then type distill my.ps (where my.ps is the name of the PostScript file) and press Return.

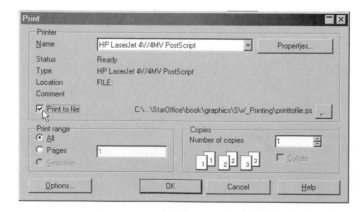

Figure 11-4   Setting options for printing to a PostScript file

---

Windows Note – If you're on Windows, you can install the HP LaserJet 4V/4MV Post-Script printer and set the Print to File option for it. (See your Windows documentation if you need help installing printers.) This is one of the best printer drivers available for producing PostScript files. If you have color in your document and for some reason your Post-Script driver isn't producing full-color PostScript files, and you want to print in color or display the document electronically with color (as in a PDF file), go to http://www.Adobe.com and find the instructions for installing Adobe's PostScript printer driver.

Setting Up Pages for DocuTech 135 Signature Printing

If you're producing bound documents through a print shop, and the print shop has a Xerox DocuTech 135 printing machine, here's a trick that can ultimately save paper, give you a standard book size, and potentially reduce the time it takes to print and bind documents.

Use this trick only if it's acceptable that your bound documents be 7 inches wide by 8.5 inches tall (legal-size paper turned landscape and either cut in half or folded).

This trick also involves printing the document to a PostScript file. See *Printing to PostScript and PDF* on page 352.

1   Create left and right page styles using the **Letter 8.5 x 11** page format with **Portrait** orientation (Page Style window, Page tab).

2   Set the left and right page margins to the settings shown in Figure 11-5.

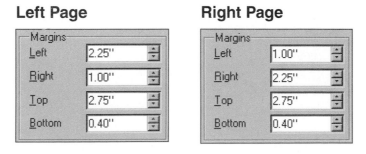

Figure 11-5   Setting left/right page margins for DocuTech signature printing

3   Print the document to a PostScript file using your PostScript printer driver.

4   Give the file to the printer, and tell them you want it printed in one of the following ways:

- Signature using legal-size paper; saddle-stitch binding. (This means folded in half and bound on the fold. Only use this if your document is less than 100 pages.)

- Signature using legal-size paper; two-up binding (cut in half). (For spiral binding or perfect binding.)

If you really want to impress the folks at the printer, make your total page count divisible by four.

StarOffice Web

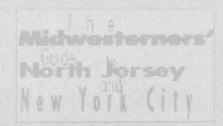

StarOffice Web Setup

The Setup Steps You Really Need to Do

Eventually, you're going to read this whole setup chapter and get to know how StarOffice really works, inside and out (there are some lovely LDAP and MIME options you can set). But until you have time for that, here's what you need to get up and browsing, and avoid the problems that the person in the next cube will be encountering.

1   Enter proxy information.

The simplest (if more time-consuming) way to do this, if you've already got a browser running on your system, is to run the Internet setup AutoPilot (choose File > AutoPilot > Internet Setup). Just choose to import all settings from your browser, and you're set.

If you prefer the manual approach, enter proxies according to the information in *Proxy Options* on page 374.

2   Set up URLs to be relative or absolute (it can cause you a lot of annoyance if they're not set up the way you expect); see *URL Options* on page 379.

3   Shut off HTML- and Web-specific annoying features; see *AutoFormat Options* on page 379.

4   If you want to double-click HTML files and have them open in something other than StarOffice, see *Getting the StarOffice Icon Off Your HTML Files* on page 381.

5   In order to be able to actually get online and to use the Internet-related tools on the StarOffice toolbars, see *Enabling Internet Connectivity* on page 384 and *Displaying the Hyperlink Bar* on page 384.

Once you've entered all the setup options that affect your system, see *Quick Start* on page 386.

Note – We really do recommend that you at least skim this section sometime soon so that if you have browsing problems you know what kinds of options you can change.

Browser Options

There are more setup options for browser connections than for nearly anything else in StarOffice. For most of the options, it's fine to leave the default values. However, it's a good idea to take a look to see whether you want to change anything.

Setting up your StarOffice browser is pretty similar to setting up Netscape: just a proxy here and a cache setting there, and you're pretty much set.

To set the options in this section, choose Tools > Options > Browser, then select the option that corresponds to the title, such as Cache.

Cache Settings

Define the cache settings in the window shown in Figure 12-1. The StarOffice Web browser can load Internet pages and graphics from the Internet or intranet by using an HTTP protocol, from the cache in memory and from temporary files on your hard disk. The data will be compared and only new and modified objects will be requested from the Internet (which is slower) or intranet.

Information about network drives is stored in the cache, as well.

The `store` folder of your StarOffice installation is used as a hard disk drive cache. Make sure that the drive it's on has enough free memory. Completely loaded FTP documents are not cached. Data that was stored in the cache when loaded from HTTP pages will be saved in a common file.

Enter the number of documents that the browser caches in the main memory. Documents saved in the memory will be displayed much faster than documents loaded for the first time.

Enter the amount of memory (in kilobytes) to be used by the browser for storing HTTP documents in the hard drive. The oldest saved data will be the first data to be overwritten by the cache.

Clearing the memory cache removes the documents from the internal clipboard of the Web browser. Clearing the hard drive cache frees up some hard disk space.

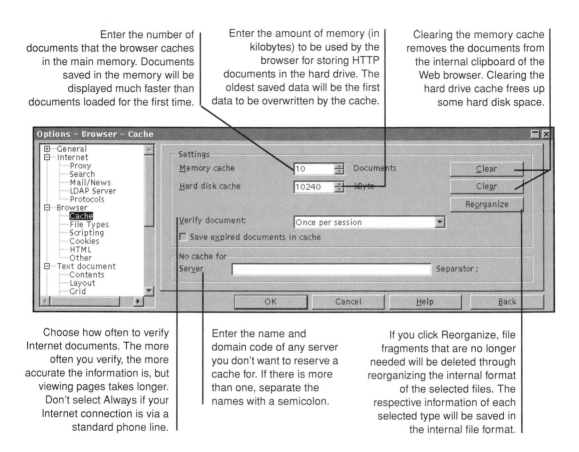

Choose how often to verify Internet documents. The more often you verify, the more accurate the information is, but viewing pages takes longer. Don't select Always if your Internet connection is via a standard phone line.

Enter the name and domain code of any server you don't want to reserve a cache for. If there is more than one, separate the names with a semicolon.

If you click Reorganize, file fragments that are no longer needed will be deleted through reorganizing the internal format of the selected files. The respective information of each selected type will be saved in the internal file format.

Figure 12-1   Cache options

File Type (MIME) Settings

Unless you're interested in hard-core tweaking, you can leave the settings as is and skip to the next section.

You can use the window shown in Figure 12-2 to determine how files that you download are managed. The Internet server sends a *MIME type* with each file; your browser looks at the type, then decides how to handle it on the basis of the entries in this window (Figure 12-2). StarOffice can display, reproduce, execute, or store the file locally.

When you're prompted to select a filter from the Filter window in StarOffice, this indicates you've downloaded a file that StarOffice doesn't have an entry for in this window, and it doesn't know what to do with it.

Note – StarOffice Web, in some environments, changes a preferences file so that when you double-click HTML files in your file manager, they open in StarOffice. You can't do a thing about it in this window, but it's covered in *Getting the StarOffice Icon Off Your HTML Files* on page 381.

MIME stands for Multipurpose Internet Mail Extension. This refers to a fixed specification regarding the transfer of multimedia mail in the Internet. This specification defines, among other things, the formal composition of message contents, how to deal with accents and special characters in message headers (generally, the Internet can only decipher 7-bit character coding), and how to create the necessary extensions in order to view the message.

Mime types are also very important in the Web to display multimedia files on as many computer systems as possible. They are organized according to pattern type/subtype. An X indicates that the respective type is only defined locally. Types without local limitations should be able to be defined and used internationally.

This list box contains the registered data type, listing MIME type, extension, clipboard ID, application, and filter. Select a file to view or modify; to assign a new type, edit fields below it, then click Add.

Select the application to open when the selected file type is downloaded from the Internet. Select Other and in the Filter list specify if other or unknown file types should be stored on your computer or handled in another way.

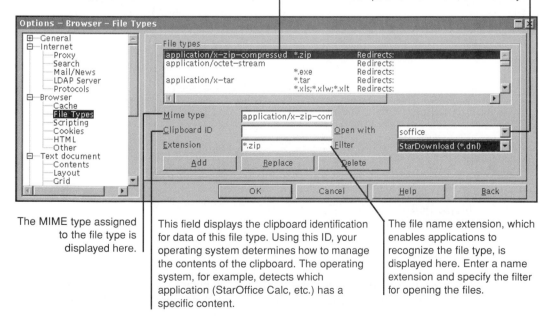

The MIME type assigned to the file type is displayed here.

This field displays the clipboard identification for data of this file type. Using this ID, your operating system determines how to manage the contents of the clipboard. The operating system, for example, detects which application (StarOffice Calc, etc.) has a specific content.

The file name extension, which enables applications to recognize the file type, is displayed here. Enter a name extension and specify the filter for opening the files.

Figure 12-2   File type options

Scripting Options

Use this window to determine whether JavaScript and StarOffice Basic Scripts should be executed. Leave the default values as they are unless you have a specific reason to not run scripts from one of the URLs in the list, or to not run JavaScript. Set up options in the window shown in Figure 12-3.

The StarOffice Basic Scripts enable you to define which URLs are trustworthy enough to allow scripts from this source to be executed without any confirmation process.

Note – If you restrict the list of trusted URLs or select the Never execute StarOffice Basic Script option, you might receive an error message saying "Missing access right" when you try to use AutoPilot or load a template, because they use Basic scripts.

Lists the locations from which scripts will be run, if you marked the From list option.

Unmark this option if you specifically don't want to allow JavaScript scripts to be run.

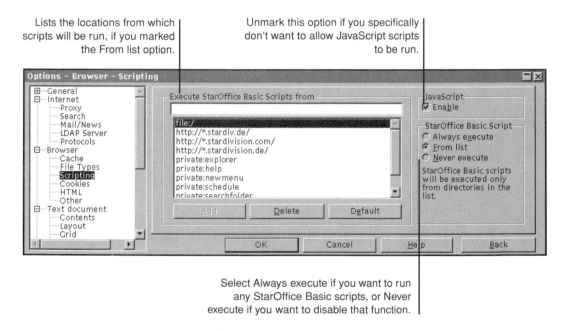

Select Always execute if you want to run any StarOffice Basic scripts, or Never execute if you want to disable that function.

Figure 12-3   Scripting options

Cookie Options

Cookies are files that are downloaded to your computer to store information like how long it's been since you visited a site, or your ID for a Web page like Yahoo! You can control whether to use them when you're accessing the Internet with the StarOffice browser. Cookies are stored in the HTTP cache in the /user/store folder. The window is shown in Figure 12-4.

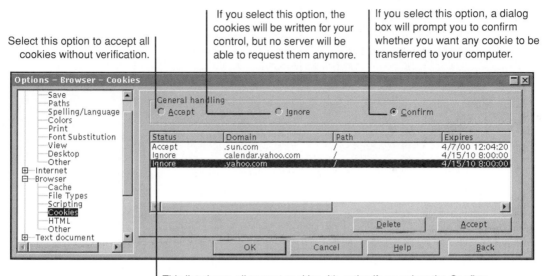

Figure 12-4   Cookie options

HTML Options: Font Size, Import, and Export

Choose Tools > Options > Browser > HTML to define the basic settings for HTML pages, both the pages you view online and those you edit. The window is shown in Figure 12-5.

About Exporting Formats

You can select from several options what format you want to export HTML pages in. The Explorer option is self-explanatory; here's more specific information on the Netscape selections:

Netscape Navigator 3.0   Selecting this option includes the Netscape 3 extensions multicol and Spacer when exporting.

Netscape Navigator 4.0   This entry activates the Netscape 4 extensions for HTML export. You will be able to export the same things as with Netscape 3.0. You can also export special styles. However, unlike the StarOffice Writer export format, special attributes such as drop caps, small caps, paragraph backgrounds, and character spacing cannot be exported.

Enter the point size for each of the preset sizes in HTML. This affects Web pages you browse, not HTML styles in documents you create.

Select this option to override font settings in HTML pages you open with the settings in the Font sizes section at the left.

If you select this option, any tags unrecognized by StarOffice will be marked with notes (see page 421).

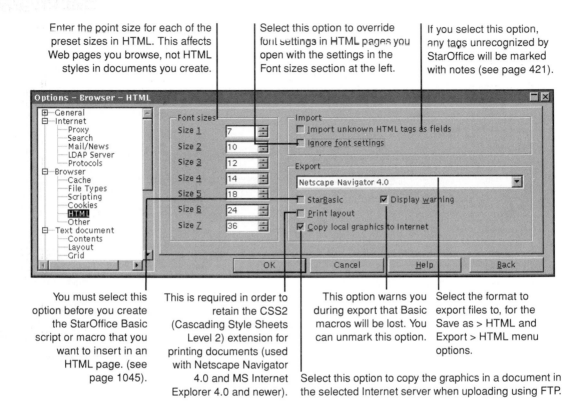

You must select this option before you create the StarOffice Basic script or macro that you want to insert in an HTML page. (see page 1045).

This is required in order to retain the CSS2 (Cascading Style Sheets Level 2) extension for printing documents (used with Netscape Navigator 4.0 and MS Internet Explorer 4.0 and newer).

This option warns you during export that Basic macros will be lost. You can unmark this option.

Select the format to export files to, for the Save as > HTML and Export > HTML menu options.

Select this option to copy the graphics in a document in the selected Internet server when uploading using FTP.

Figure 12-5   HTML options

Other Options: Setting a Home Page, Browser Connection Information, and Java Options

Use the window in Figure 12-6 to set the properties for your browser connection. You can define the settings for Java, for your homepage, for the ID of the StarOffice Browser, etc.

Note – We recommend that you leave all security- and Java-related settings as they are.

Browser identification This field contains the text that your browser uses to identify itself when sending requests to servers on the Internet. The StarOffice Web browser identifies itself as Mozilla/3.0, the name used by most Web browsers.

Some Web servers ask your browser to identify itself. This can produce a variety of results. For example, if a Netscape Navigator is detected (it answers as Mozilla), it will only be sent pages conforming to the HTML Standard, whereas a Microsoft Internet Explorer will be offered a different page specifically for this browser.

Disabling Java If Java is not installed, JavaScript cannot run either. (This is a little odd, but it's the way StarOffice implements the two.) If Java is installed, it is possible to disable Java while still enabling JavaScript (see the JavaScript option in Figure 12-3 on page 362). You really should keep Java enabled; if you don't, all sorts of problems can crop up in applications or features that don't seem even remotely related to Java.

Note – There are three Java-related links within Explorer. In Explorer, expand Bookmarks, then StarOffice Bookmarks. The links let you see the Java Console window, install Java (JRE 1.1.8), and see the Java System Monitor. The first and third items aren't necessary, but they're kind of interesting if you want to see what's going on (it's also interesting to come up with possible reasons why StarOffice thought this feature was necessary).

See *Installing Java Separately and Monitoring Java* on page 57 for more information on installing Java, and the three Java bookmarks,

Disabling security checks If you unmark the Enable security checks option, Java will not run any security checks for *external codes* (for example, applets), i.e. files not defined in the classpath.

If the check is disabled, **applets can also read from and write to all drives**. JavaScript can access the entire Java Runtime Environment through the LiveConnect interface, so this creates a security loophole for JavaScript as well.

If you have to disable the security check, do so only when one of the following conditions applies:

- If you know for sure what the applet, Java program, or JavaScript is going to do.
- If you are logged in as a guest under Windows NT or UNIX and the operating system therefore prevents you from reading or destroying security sensitive data.

JDBC and Java When searching for Java (as well as JDBC) driver classes, the value you enter in the Class path field is no longer evaluated. You need to include any additional paths to be used with Java and JDBC in the classpath; see Figure 12-6. (The CLASSPATH contains .zip and .jar files or directories with Java class files.)

If you deselect these, special Java-enabled features in StarOffice won't run and applet security and other external sources won't be checked. We recommend you keep these options selected.

This allows you to define if and how Java applications should access your network. Host means they will access the network as the host computer.

Add other Java classes or libraries to the StarOffice environment. Java classes that are called through the CLASSPATH are not subject to any security check. Separate the paths with a colon; include a backslash after all directories.

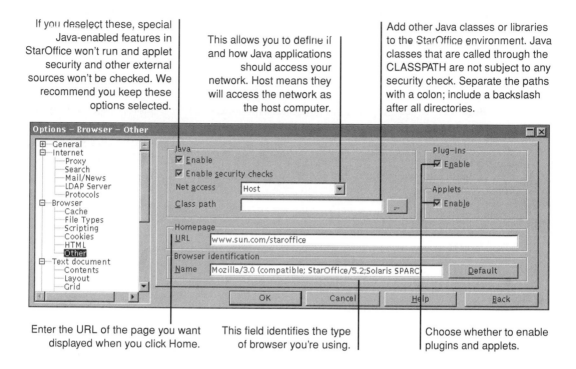

Enter the URL of the page you want displayed when you click Home.

This field identifies the type of browser you're using.

Choose whether to enable plugins and applets.

Figure 12-6   Other options

External Browser Options

If you'll be using a browser other than the one included with StarOffice, you can use the window in Figure 12-7 to set the properties for it.

Note – This seems like another feature from StarOffice's overly excitable designers. We think, if you want to use a browser instead of StarOffice Web, just go ahead and start it and use it, and don't fuss about with setting it up here.

It's probably useful occasionally: if you run a lot of presentations, for instance, with links to external Web sites, and you want to make sure Netscape is used to display those sites rather than StarOffice, you can use this window to make it happen.

The logic used to set up this window is a little on the loopy side; here's the basic gist of what you can do. (The exact option names you see might be different, depending on the options you chose if you ran the Internet AutoPilot.)

- If you activate the Use external browser option, all browsing will be done with that browser except any servers you add to the Addresses list.

- If you don't activate the Use external browser option (but do enter the path to one), all browsing will be done with StarOffice Web except any servers you add to the Addresses list.

If you use an external browser in either case, its own cache and other browser settings will apply, not the ones you've set up for StarOffice Web.

You can't use Netscape as an external browser if you're running StarOffice on Windows.

Note – If you choose to use an external browser and the path to the browser executable file isn't correct, StarOffice won't notify you of this—you just won't be able to get to the Internet. If the browser path is incorrect, you won't even be able to access the servers on the list of servers to access using StarOffice Web.

Review the window in Figure 12-7, then follow the appropriate procedure to enter browsing options.

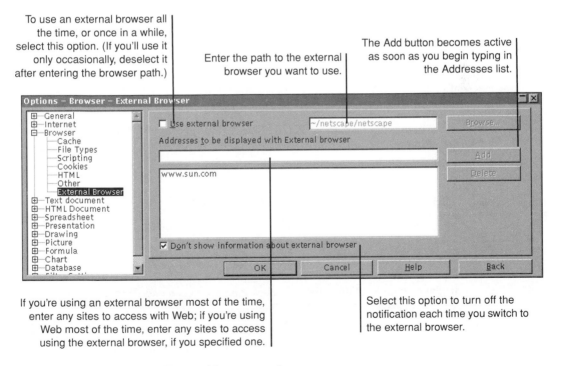

To use an external browser all the time, or once in a while, select this option. (If you'll use it only occasionally, deselect it after entering the browser path.)

Enter the path to the external browser you want to use.

The Add button becomes active as soon as you begin typing in the Addresses list.

If you're using an external browser most of the time, enter any sites to access with Web; if you're using Web most of the time, enter any sites to access using the external browser, if you specified one.

Select this option to turn off the notification each time you switch to the external browser.

Figure 12-7   External browser options

Note – When you install StarOffice, all your HTML files get associated with StarOffice, rather than your browser (or whatever application they were associated with before). Double-clicking an HTML file now starts StarOffice. Selecting an external browser in this windows doesn't change that effect; however, you can switch your system back by following the directions in *Getting the StarOffice Icon Off Your HTML Files* on page 381.

To Use StarOffice Web All the Time

You don't need to make any entries in this window; the default settings make Web your default browser.

To Use StarOffice Web Most of the Time

1   Select the Use external browser option.

2   Enter the path to your browser that you want to use for occasional files or sites.

3   Deselect the Use external browser option.

4   The list title will change to Addresses to be displayed with External browser. Type any sites you want to access using StarOffice Web in the Addresses list, and click Add after each one. Type file:/// preceding the path and filename to access local files using the external browser.

5   A message stating that the external browser uses its own browser settings will pop up each time you switch to the external browser. Select the Don't show information about external browser option to turn it off.

To Use an External Browser Most or All of the Time

1   Select the Use external browser option.

2   Enter the path to your browser.

3   Type any sites you want to access using StarOffice Web in the Addresses to be displayed with StarOffice list, and click Add after each one. Type file:/// to access local files using StarOffice Web.

4   A message stating that the external browser uses its own browser settings will pop up each time you switch to the external browser. Select the Don't show information about external browser option to turn it off.

Note – If a Java installation wasn't found during installation, the message "No Java Installation Found" might appear. See the installation for information on installing Java and making StarOffice recognize the installation.

HTML Document Options

Several setup options windows let you determine how objects and other elements are displayed, and let you set grid options.

All options are included here except print options (see *Printing Options* on page 465).

Note – Most of these options affect both the Web pages you browse and HTML documents you edit. The options are generally for display only, such as the option to set the size of HTML styles 1 through 7, and are not applied permanently.

To set all of the options in this section, choose Tools > Options > HTML Document, then select the option that corresponds to the title, such as Contents.

Contents Options

The window in Figure 12-8 lets you pick what parts of each HTML page are shown by default.

Note – You can choose to hide graphics here by deselecting the Graphics and objects option. You can load graphics on a page by page basis by right-clicking and choosing Load Graphics.

Choose what to show. Selecting Field codes displays inserted fields' name and type as well as contents in pages.

You can change these settings easily in a page using the View menu.

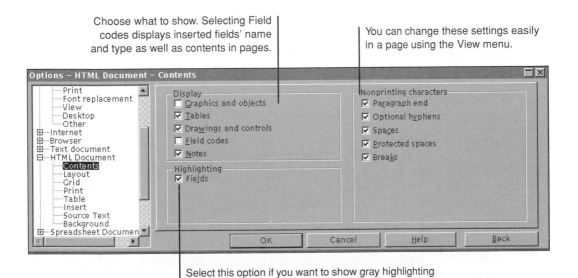

Select this option if you want to show gray highlighting with fields you insert by choosing Insert > Fields.

Figure 12-8   Contents display options

Layout Options

The window in Figure 12-9 enables you to control a variety of display and layout options, including handle size and unit of measurement.

Note – The Smooth scroll option is supposed to make scrolling speed consistent when you select text and drag the mouse down below the border of the window. However, scrolling works the same way whether the option is marked or not.

Select Text boundaries to display page margins as thin lines; select Table boundaries to enclose table cells with a line; select Section boundaries to display lines around sections.

Select Guides to display lines projecting from each object axis when you move objects.

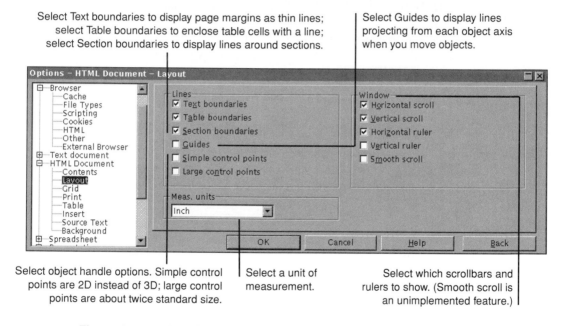

Select object handle options. Simple control points are 2D instead of 3D; large control points are about twice standard size.

Select a unit of measurement.

Select which scrollbars and rulers to show. (Smooth scroll is an unimplemented feature.)

Figure 12-9   Setting layout options

Grid Options

You can set the dimensions for a grid, which you can display, and snap objects to. (Snapping to the grid means objects you create, insert, or move will be aligned with the closest gridpoint.) Use the Grid window, shown in Figure 12-10.

The grid, when displayed, is a set of very faint dots, one at each point where the X and Y grid axes intersect. If you selected Visible grid and it doesn't seem to be visible, take a closer look at the work area—it's just that the dots are light and far apart. You can't darken the grid display, but you can increase the number of dots by increasing the number of points in the Subdivision fields. This adds more dots to each line.

Aligns all objects with the grid automatically.

Select this option to display the grid.

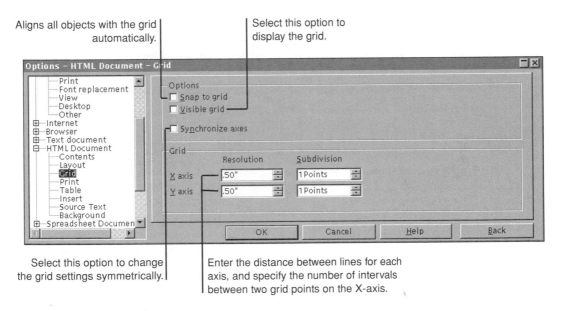

Select this option to change the grid settings symmetrically.

Enter the distance between lines for each axis, and specify the number of intervals between two grid points on the X-axis.

Figure 12-10   Setting standard grid options

Table Options

Use the window in Figure 12-11 to set the default values for tables.

Enter the default measurement for moving rows and columns.

Enter the default measurement rows and columns in new tables.

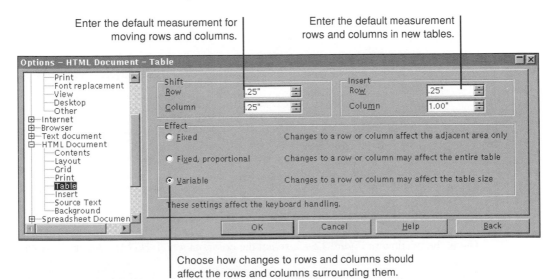

Choose how changes to rows and columns should affect the rows and columns surrounding them.

Figure 12-11   Setting table options

Insert Options

Using the window in Figure 12-12, specify rules for how objects are inserted in HTML documents. The table options affect the default table format when you choose Insert > Table. The Insert in tables options affect how numbers are evaluated inside tables, if you format them using one of the formats available when you choose Format > Number Format.

Note – Hard formats in a table will not be influenced by the entries you make here. If you, for example, defined a centered orientation for text cells, this setting will also apply to text or numbers. The cell contents orientation, therefore, will depend on the prior settings, which will be active even when you're making modifications.

Specify what elements a table should have by default when you choose Insert > Table. (You also can specify these preferences when you insert the table.)

Select this option to have numbers in cells recognized as numbers rather than standard text. It lets you perform calculations.

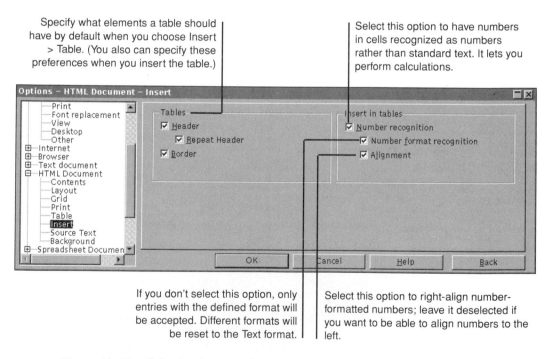

If you don't select this option, only entries with the defined format will be accepted. Different formats will be reset to the Text format.

Select this option to right-align number-formatted numbers; leave it deselected if you want to be able to align numbers to the left.

Figure 12-12   Selecting insert options

Source Text Options

Using the window in Figure 12-13, select the colors in which HTML source is displayed.

Note – If you're writing macros and wondering if these selections affect the colors that macros are displayed in, in the macro IDE—they don't.

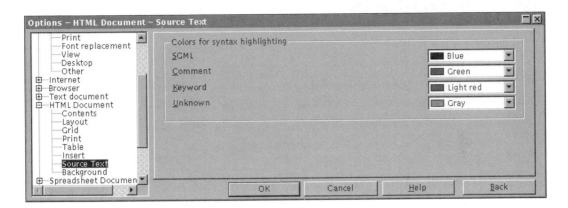

Figure 12-13   Selecting colors for HTML source

Background Options

Using the window in Figure 12-14, you can select a background color for pages. This background isn't applied to Web pages, only to HTML documents stored on your system.

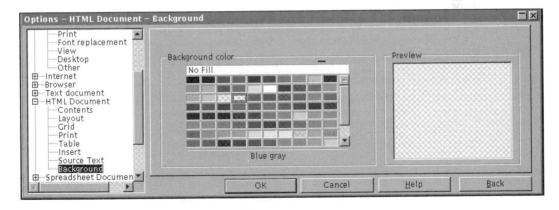

Figure 12-14   Setting a default background for all local HTML documents

Internet Options

The Internet options control general Internet connectivity and affect other applications as well, such as StarOffice Mail.

To set all of the options in this section, choose Tools > Options > Internet, then select the option that corresponds to the title, such as Proxy.

For information on Mail and News options, see *StarOffice Mail and Address Book* on page 931.

Proxy Options

Use the window shown in Figure 12-15 to define the settings for the proxy server. Default settings for your current proxies are often read from your system and set up automatically, so you might not need to change anything.

Proxies The proxy server can be manually or automatically set up to access the Internet over an interconnected network. A proxy is a computer in the network acting as a kind of clipboard for data transfer. Whenever you access the Internet from a company network and request a Web page that has already been read by a colleague, the proxy will be able to display it much more quickly as long as it's still in memory. All that needs to be checked in this case is that the page stored in the proxy is the latest version. If this is the case, the page won't have to be downloaded from the much slower Internet but can be loaded directly from the proxy.

Figuring out your proxy names and ports Ask your system administrator or Internet service provider for the proxies and ports to enter. You can also check your browser for the proxies and ports you use. In Netscape, choose Edit > Preferences > Advanced > Proxies. In Internet Explorer, choose Tools > Internet Options > Connections. Depending on the provider, it may or may not be necessary to always use a proxy. For example, no proxy is required for AOL or CompuServe.

Server names Always enter server names without the protocol prefix (`http`, `ftp`, etc.). For example, enter `starnews.stardivision` rather than `http://starnews.stardivision`.

See *Using FTP: File Transfer Protocol* on page 401 for information on setting up FTP through StarOffice.

Select Manual if you use a proxy; select
None If you want to set up a connection
directly on your computer to an Internet
provider that doesn't use a proxy.

Enter the proxy, if any, for
URLs starting with http://
No proxy is required for
AOL or CompuServe.

Enter the name of the FTP
server to use for FTP
connections.

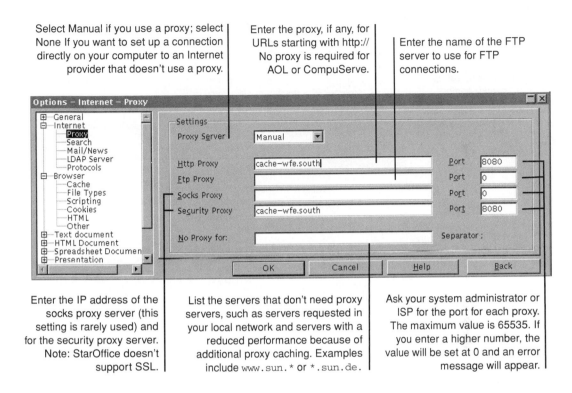

Enter the IP address of the
socks proxy server (this
setting is rarely used) and
for the security proxy server.
Note: StarOffice doesn't
support SSL.

List the servers that don't need proxy
servers, such as servers requested in
your local network and servers with a
reduced performance because of
additional proxy caching. Examples
include `www.sun.*` or `*.sun.de`.

Ask your system administrator or
ISP for the port for each proxy.
The maximum value is 65535. If
you enter a higher number, the
value will be set at 0 and an error
message will appear.

Figure 12-15   Proxy options

Search Options

StarOffice lets you use any of several popular search engines to search the Internet straight from StarOffice, without having to go to a particular search engine site. See *Using Web's Search Engine Connections* on page 393 for information on how to search and selecting the search engine to use.

Several search engines are already set up for you; you probably don't need to change these settings unless you need to do some tweaking, or want to add a search engine to the list.

Note – If you're wondering "Why should I set up a search engine here when I can just go to the search engine site or use one of the search engines already set up in StarOffice?" the answer is "No good reason. Besides, doing the setup is a pain in the neck." It's just the overly excitable StarOffice feature designers at work again. (You might want to modify how StarOffice searches for words or phrases in existing search engines, but that's all.)

1   Choose Tools > Options > Internet > Search (Figure 12-16).

2   Enter the appropriate information.

Lists the currently set up search engines.

Enter or change the title of the search engine; this name will appear in StarOffice.

Enter the URL that appears in front of the keyword when you search on this engine's site (search for any word, then copy everything from the URL up, without the keyword).

Choose how to search for words if you enter more than one. **And:** both scott and hudson; **Or:** scott or hudson; **Exact:** scott hudson.

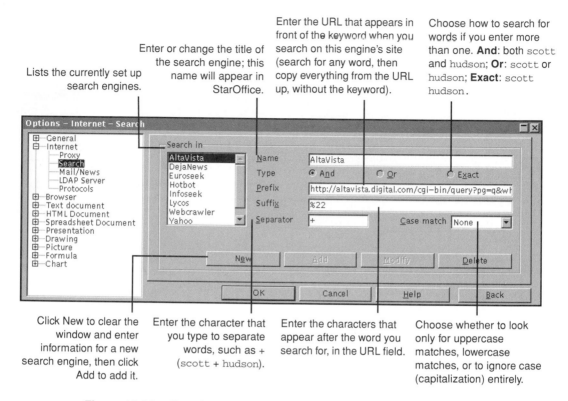

Click New to clear the window and enter information for a new search engine, then click Add to add it.

Enter the character that you type to separate words, such as + (scott + hudson).

Enter the characters that appear after the word you search for, in the URL field.

Choose whether to look only for uppercase matches, lowercase matches, or to ignore case (capitalization) entirely.

Figure 12-16   Search options

This setup makes you do things the hard way—you can't just enter a URL and get on with your life. Here are some guidelines for figuring out what the prefix (the codes the engine puts in front of what you're searching for), suffix (the code after the keyword), and the separator (what goes between multiple keywords) are for each new search engine.

1   Activate the search engine and perform a search with at least two words.

2   Copy the URL from the URL field in the Function bar and paste it into a blank document.

3   Change the conditions for the search in the search engine, if it offers you the choice.

4   Again, copy the contents of the URL field.

5   Compare the URLs with the sample URLs that you can copy from the fields of this dialog. You should then be able to recognize the prefix, suffix, and separator for various conditions.

LDAP Options

Unless you're an ardent LDAP fan, you don't need to bother with this window.

About LDAP The Lightweight Directory Access Protocol allows simpler access in the Internet and Intranet to directories on other computers. The LDAP server provides the clients the desired information, which depending on the record may contain text, graphics, sound files, URLs, and other information. The directories must be hierarchically ordered and can contain files as well as addresses, lists, and other data. It represents a simplified version of the X.500 protocol and is adapted to the TCP/IP protocol.

What's cool about LDAP and StarOffice If your company stores email addresses on an LDAP server, the Mail program in StarOffice recognizes and fills in addresses after you start typing in the To field of a new email. That way, you don't have to fill up your Address Book database with everyone in the company in order to get email address recognition. You can also search LDAP through the Address Book interface.

Go to the Options > Internet > LDAP Server window (Figure 12-17). The list displays the pre-configured LDAP servers, currently Bigfoot and Switchboard. It also displays the LDAP servers that you have included.

Select a server to modify it, or click New to set up a new one.

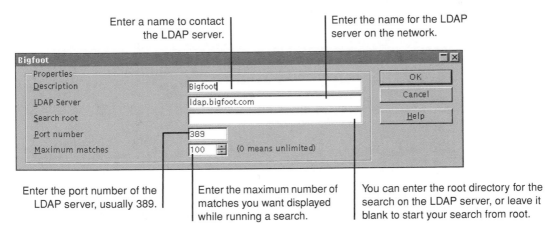

Enter a name to contact the LDAP server.

Enter the name for the LDAP server on the network.

Enter the port number of the LDAP server, usually 389.

Enter the maximum number of matches you want displayed while running a search.

You can enter the root directory for the search on the LDAP server, or leave it blank to start your search from root.

Figure 12-17   LDAP options

Protocol Options

Use the window in Figure 12-18 to define the protocols, the DNS server (domain name service), and further properties related to the Internet connection. The StarOffice install looks at existing settings for other Internet applications and uses them as defaults, so as with other windows, you probably don't need to change these.

DNS server The DNS server is used to convert the entire computer name that you set in a URL (such as www.sun.com) into a 32-bit IP (Internet protocol) address. The 32-bit IP addresses are displayed in four decimal numbers. Each decimal number is between 0 and 255 and represents the first, second, third, and last 8 bits of the entire 32 bits. We strongly recommend that you choose the Automatic option; it lets you use the DNS server from your ISP. If you select Manual, you need to enter the IP address of the DNS server that you want to use.

Enter the maximum number of Internet connections at one time to HTTP servers. 4 is typical; higher numbers don't necessarily increase data transfer speed.

Enter the maximum number of Internet connections at one time to FTP servers.

Select this option if you want to submit your email address to the visited server while browsing with an HTTP protocol.

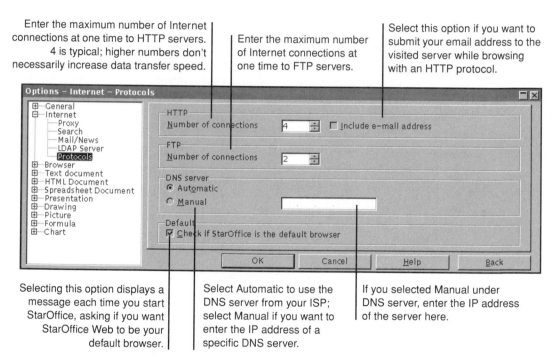

Selecting this option displays a message each time you start StarOffice, asking if you want StarOffice Web to be your default browser.

Select Automatic to use the DNS server from your ISP; select Manual if you want to enter the IP address of a specific DNS server.

If you selected Manual under DNS server, enter the IP address of the server here.

Figure 12-18   Protocol options

Note – If you don't have a browser installed, you might get a message saying StarOffice couldn't load the plugin manager and you need to run a repair option. You don't need to do this, since the repair program won't find any plugins. StarOffice will run without plugins, but some browser functions might not be available, and you might not be able to open some email attachments.

URL Options

The Options > General > Save window contains two fields that control how URLs are saved: relative to the file system or Internet, or absolute. It's important that you set them correctly for how you want to use StarOffice, and that you know the impact of changing the settings.

This determines whether the full path to a file or Web site, such as `C:\book\reviewers\fezzik.sdw`, is saved (absolute), or if only the path from the linking file to the linked file is saved (relative). For a file in the same directory, for example, only `fezzik.sdw` would be saved.

- Relative addressing is more convenient if the files you link to are part of the same set of subfolders and unlikely to change location.
- Relative addressing is possible only if the source document and the link are located on the same drive.

Choose Tools > Options > General > Save. Select or deselect the Relative to file system and Relative to Internet options, in the Save URLs relative to section of the window.

If you change your options from relative to absolute, this changes URLs previously saved as relative when you edit and save files containing relative links. This works the same way in reverse.

If you plan to put a page online as part of your Web site, make sure that both options are set to Relative. If the options are set to absolute and you enter a relative link to a file, like `fezzik.html`, an absolute URL will be entered automatically. The automatic absolute URL is *currentpath/filename*.

Note – Tool tips always display the absolute path, even if only the relative path is saved. In HTML files, you can choose View > HTML Source to see what's actually saved in the link's HTML code.

AutoFormat Options

StarOffice doesn't have a helpful paperclip buddy, but it does have a few features that you'll probably want to turn off. This section covers the Web-relevant and particularly annoying features; for full coverage, see *Turning Off Annoying Features* on page 115.

Controlling Automatic URL Recognition

By default StarOffice underlines and turns blue any recognizable URL: a Web site, FTP address, document, etc. As soon as that happens, the text is "hot" and StarOffice will take you to the link if you click on the text. You can't edit the text except by placing the cursor to the right or left and using the arrow keys.

To turn off this feature, open a new HTML document (File > New > HTML Document). Then choose Tools > AutoCorrect/AutoFormat. The AutoCorrect window is shown in Figure 12-19. Select the Options tab, then unmark both boxes next to the URL Recognition item.

If you want recognition to occur when you're typing, but not with the command Format > AutoFormat > Format Document, leave the box selected in the [T] column and leave the box in the [M] column blank.

Deselect URL Recognition, and any other options you don't want occurring automatically. Most of the features are more intrusive than helpful.

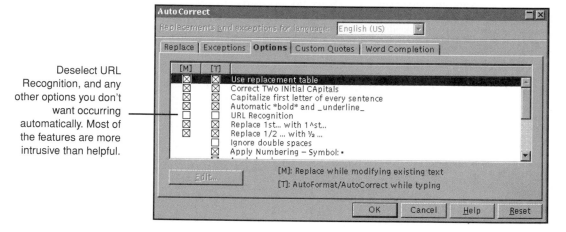

Figure 12-19   Turning off AutoFormat options

Note – In Writer and other StarOffice applications, the AutoCorrect window is called the AutoFormat window.

Turning Off Automatic Formatting

The AutoCorrect window lets you control numerous additional autoformatting options. The ones we found particularly annoying are shown here; for more information about these or other options, see the online help or *Turning Off Annoying Features* on page 115.

Options Tab Options

- Capitalize first letter of every sentence
- Automatic *bold* and _underline_ (sometimes you just want to emphasize words with asterisks instead of bold)

Word Completion Tab Options

*   Complete words (automatically completes a word you've half-typed if it thinks it knows what you're going to type)

Getting the StarOffice Icon Off Your HTML Files

One of the less endearing things about StarOffice is that when you install it, all existing HTML documents, and any new ones you create, automatically get associated with StarOffice. In Solaris, for example, this means that double-clicking any HTML file in File Manager automatically opens StarOffice, and the nice little right-click option of Edit, which lets you edit the HTML source in a text editor, goes away.

The settings for external browser in Figure 12-7 on page 367 and Figure 12-2 on page 361 don't affect this.

You can get around this in a couple different ways, covered in the following sections.

Save Files With `.htm` or `.HTML` Extensions

StarOffice only attaches itself to files with lowercase .html extensions; it doesn't care about anything else. Anything with an extension such as `.htm`, `.HTML`, `.Html`, or other legal variation will retain the usual browser association; when you double-click a file with one of those extensions, it'll open in whatever application it opened in before you installed StarOffice.

This applies to files you create in StarOffice, a text editor, or any HTML editor.

If you're saving the file in StarOffice, this mean you need to unmark the Automatic file name extension option in the Save or Save as window.

Change Settings for Application/File Association

Follow the directions for your operating system.

Windows

In Windows Explorer, choose View > Folder Options, and in the File Types tab, change the application associated with .html documents.

Solaris and Linux

1   Locate the `·/.dt/types/StarOffice52.dt` file.

2   Always take appropriate cautions when editing system configuration files; back up this file before you continue.

3   Remove the HTML data below from the `StarOffice52.dt` file, then log out of your computer and log in again. (You have to restart your operating system; it's not enough to restart StarOffice.)

```
DATA_ATTRIBUTES StarOffice_HTML
{
    ACTIONS Open
    ICON Html
}

DATA_CRITERIA StarOffice_HTMLA
{
    DATA_ATTRIBUTES_NAME StarOffice_HTML
    MODE !d
    NAME_PATTERN *.html
}

ACTION Open
{
    ARG_TYPE StarOffice_HTML
    TYPE MAP
    MAP_ACTION StarOffice
}
```

4   If completing this section doesn't work, look for any other .dt files, such as `Old-StarOffice52.dt`, and rename them with `.old` after the .dt. For example, rename `Old-StarOffice52.dt` to `Old-StarOffice52.dt.old`.

Understanding Target Frames

Throughout StarOffice Web, when you're creating a bookmark or setting up a hyperlink, you can choose the **target frame**. It's shown at right in the hyperlink bar1.

Overview

If you're not used to that phrase or option, it can be confusing (if you are, it's even more confusing). Typically, the option refers to framesets (see *Using Frames* on page 413). But in StarOffice, it's not just that. The option controls whether this URL will open in the same window within StarOffice (closing and replacing your current document), or in a different window. Usually it's the same window, which can be a little annoying since it means your current document suddenly disappears and is replaced by the new one. (For information on how to get around that when you're browsing and using StarOffice in general, see *Making Files Open in Their Own Separate Windows* on page 401.)

StarOffice thinks of itself as a browser, which is why it uses the term "target frame." In general StarOffice use, a "frame" is a document, or work area, designated by the file name that appears in the task bar (Figure 12-20). The figure shows three frames, each of which you could click to see the corresponding document fill the work area.

Counting desktop, there are five frames in the task bar.

Current frame.

Figure 12-20   StarOffice task bar and icons for three separate "frames"

What You Should Do

If you had the files in Figure 12-20 open and you then double-clicked a file in Beamer, or entered a URL in the browser field and went to that, it would open in the same frame where the `kyles_mom.html` file is now, closing that file.

If you actually want StarOffice to act like this, select `_self` when you get a chance to select a target frame for a file. If you want it to open in a new separate frame and leave all current files well enough alone, select `_blank` instead.

Enabling Internet Connectivity

For browsing or if you use StarOffice on a network, stay in Online mode to access the Internet, and to ensure you see network directories and files in real time.

Click the Online mode button at the far right of the function bar to switch between Online and Offline mode. When the button is pressed in, Online mode is active. If you're running StarOffice on a standalone computer, switching to Offline mode is useful when you want to prevent automatic modem connections. When, for example, you click a hyperlink, if you have email set up in StarOffice to poll for mail periodically, you'll get error messages at the set polling interval.

Displaying the Hyperlink Bar

The Hyperlink Bar, which contains the icons you can use to browse, create bookmarks, insert hyperlinks, and so on, sometimes isn't displayed by default. Choose View > Toolbars > Hyperlink Bar to display it.

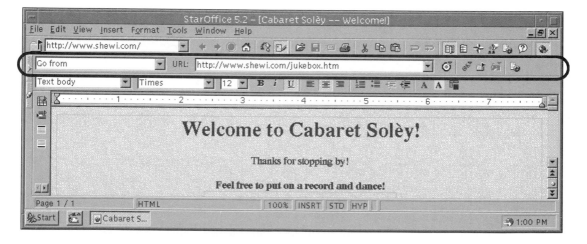

Figure 12-21 Hyperlink bar

Browsing

Quick Start

This section contains the following information to help you get started quickly:

*   A checklist for quickly browsing or making a Web page
*   Feature overview
*   How to start the StarOffice Web browser and make a new Web page
*   A five-minute tutorial

Note – Writer and Web are fairly similar: many features, such as styles and templates, are nearly identical. See *StarOffice Writer* on page 151 if you can't find the information you need in the chapters for StarOffice Web.

See *Taming the StarOffice Environment* on page 91 for general tips that can make working with StarOffice a lot easier.

Quick Start Checklist

If you have to make a Web page tonight for a presentation tomorrow morning at 8:00, these are the sections that will probably do you the most good right now:

*   Create a file – *Creating a New HTML Document Based on a Template* on page 406
*   Add links – *Adding Hyperlinks to StarOffice Documents* on page 431
*   Add graphics – *Adding and Formatting Graphics* on page 424
*   Add objects – *Inserting Spreadsheets and Other Objects* on page 441
*   Print it – *Printing in StarOffice Web* on page 463

StarOffice Web Features

StarOffice Web includes both a browser and a WYSIWYG (what you see is what you get) Web page or HTML document editor.

Note – StarOffice Web's browser doesn't support Secure Sockets Layer, or SSL, the security mechanism widely used on the Internet. This means, for example, that you can't use StarOffice as your browser to purchase items through your favorite online store if it requires you to check out using SSL.

StarOffice Web features include, but aren't limited to:

Browsing and bookmarks Web has the usual browsing capabilities, and it lets you import Netscape and Internet Explorer bookmarks as well as make your own new ones.

Powerful file-creation features The Impress AutoPilot provides templates and samples that let you quickly and easily pick attributes like an introduction page, formatting, and backgrounds.

Text formatting Full Writer text entry and formatting.

On-the-fly editable HTML source While some WYSIWYG editors don't let you edit the source code, Web lets you view it, edit it, and save it all in the same window. Web also comes with modifiable color coding that makes HTML more readable.

Insert hyperlinks in any StarOffice document You can link to FTP sites, Web sites, other local documents, even to a command that creates a new StarOffice document.

Insert files using OLE, and graphics You can insert a variety of files, as well as files such as spreadsheets and graphs, and include any graphics by inserting graphics or using Draw's graphics tools. All Draw tools are available in Impress.

Active content You can add applets, scripts, plugins, and hyperlinks to StarOffice Basic macros.

Forms and fields You can add a variety of buttons, dropdown lists, and so on, linking them to a site or to a database.

FTP account setup Web includes a simple, easy way to set up an FTP account (file transfer protocol) to transfer files to another computer.

Note – We don't include information about guidelines to follow when developing Web pages, such as keeping graphics use low or having frame and non-frame versions. That information is beyond the scope of this book.

Starting StarOffice Web

Be sure you've enabled online connectivity using the Internet Online/Offline icon in the function bar.

Browsing Just open StarOffice and enter the URL you want to go to in the Load URL field (where the URL is shown in the figure at right). Then press the Enter key. If you get  errors, check the setup options described in *StarOffice Web Setup* on page 357, particularly proxies.

Creating a new HTML document Choose File > New > HTML Document, or Start > More > HTML Document.

The Web Work Area

The StarOffice Web editor work area is shown in Figure 13-1.

The text for the currently selected hyperlink and its URL are shown here in the hyperlink bar; the upper field shows where the file saved.

The current **object bar** is for text formatting; the graphics, table, or other object bars will appear depending upon what elements you're working with.

The **hyperlink bar** contains the Target Frame, Hyperlink (for hotlinks), Link (for bookmark links), and Find icons.

Most of the text formatting capabilities from Writer are available on the toolbar and from the Format menu; different styles are available for HTML documents.

The **Insert icon** and corresponding tearoff menu let you insert different objects. You can print headers and footers on each page. The **Text Animation icon** lets you add a scrolling or blinking text marquee.

The **Picture icon** shows or hides graphics. The **Show HTML Source icon** is present only in true HTML files, not in Writer files saved as HTML.

You can insert, paste, or link graphics to your page.

The **task bar** shows an icon for each open file— referred to as separate **frames** sometimes in Web.

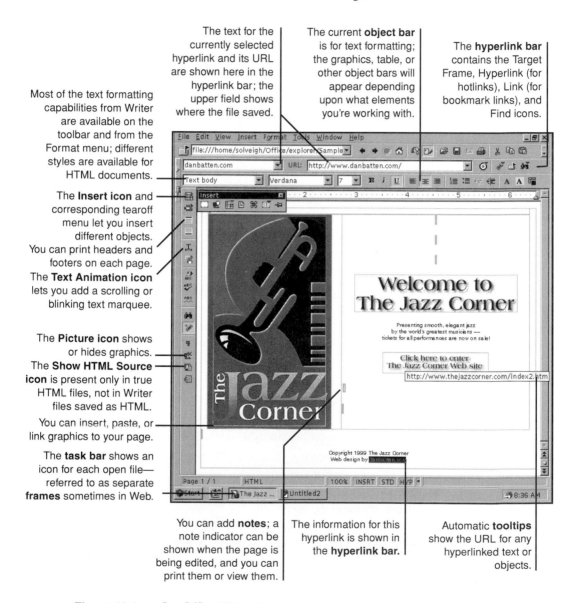

You can add **notes**; a note indicator can be shown when the page is being edited, and you can print them or view them.

The information for this hyperlink is shown in the **hyperlink bar.**

Automatic **tooltips** show the URL for any hyperlinked text or objects.

Figure 13-1   StarOffice Web editor work area

Guided Tour

This should take about ten to fifteen minutes, and demonstrates the browser and editor.

Before You Begin

1   Choose View > Toolbars > Hyperlink Bar and be sure it's marked.

2   Click the Internet Online/Offline icon in the function bar.

Browser

1   Type the URL of a Web site in the Load URL field at the top left of the work area. (If you want a suggestion, `http://www.bulwer-lytton.com` is a fun site.)

2   Press Enter.

3   If Explorer isn't showing, choose View > Explorer.

4   Click the Bookmarks slider.

5   When the Web page appears, click and hold down the mouse on the Bookmark icon to the left of the Load URL field.

6   Drag the icon down to the Bookmarks area.

7   Select the bookmark, then click and hold down the mouse on Target Frame.

8   A list of options will appear; select _blank. This will make the bookmarked Web page open in a new document in StarOffice, instead of replacing the current document.

HTML Editor

1   Choose File > Autopilot > Web Page.

2   Select a template from the list.

3   Click Style and select a Style from the list.

4   Click Create.

5   Save the file, then close the document.

6   Choose File > New > HTML Document.

7   Choose Insert > Graphic.

8   Navigate to `share/gallery/photos` and select `forest1.jpg`.

Note – If you're in a multi-user system, the template folders are typically on the server, not among your own local files.

---

9   Click the Properties button in the Insert Graphics window. Reduce the size of the graphic approximately by half, but keep the same proportions. Then choose how you want the text to wrap (in the Wrap tab), and name the graphic (in the Options tab).

10   Click OK to close the Graphics window.

11   Click Open.

12   Above the graphic, type the following heading: The Three Terrors of the Fireswamp

13   Click in the text and assign it the Heading 1 style, in the Apply Style list at the left side of the object bar. (If the object bar isn't displayed, choose View > Toolbars > Object Bar.)

14   Click the Text Animation icon on the toolbar.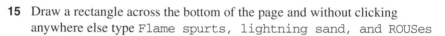

15   Draw a rectangle across the bottom of the page and without clicking anywhere else type Flame spurts, lightning sand, and ROUSes

16   Click once on the text; the text frame will appear with a thin border. Double-click to make the text frame change from a thin border to a thick border and to make the text selectable. Select the text and use the object bar to make it 36 points high.

17   In order to change the color, right-click on the text and choose Character. In the Character window, select Magenta and click OK.

18   Click outside of the text frame. Then click on it again once to make the thin text frame border appear. Right-click the text frame choose Text. In the Text window, select the Text Animation tab. In the Effects list, select Scroll Back and Forth, and click the right-pointing arrow. Click OK.

19   Below the animated text marquee, type the following: Additional Information

20   Select the text you just typed and click the **Hyperlink Dialog** icon (not the Hyperlink icon) in the hyperlink bar.

21   In the Hyperlink window, type the following URL in the Target field, then click Apply, and click Close:

     http://us.imdb.com/Title?0093779

22   Save the file.

23   Click the hyperlink to the Web site. Notice that it opens the Web site but closes the file you were working on. Close the Web site and reopen the file.

24   This time, hold down the Ctrl key while clicking the hyperlink. The Web site will come up in its own window this time.

25   Save this document and note its location.

26 Choose File > Save As under a different name in the same directory. Change the Heading 1 text to blue and save the file again.

27 Choose File > New > Frameset.

28 In the file that appears, right-click in it and choose Split Horizontal.

29 Right-click in the new upper section and choose Properties.

30 In the Floating Frame window, click the Properties tab, then click the browse icon to the right of the Contents field.

31 Select the first file and click OK.

32 Right-click in the lower frame and choose Properties.

33 Click the browse icon for the Contents field again and select the second file. Click OK.

Basic Browsing

You've probably already noticed the Load URL field at the top of the StarOffice object and function bars. You can browse from any application, all the time—just enter the URL, and you're on your way.

Note – StarOffice Web's browser doesn't support Secure Sockets Layer, or SSL, the security mechanism widely used on the Internet. This means, for example, that you can't use StarOffice as your browser to purchase items through your favorite online store if it requires you to check out using SSL.

Setup

Check the settings in the Browser and HTML Documents options windows; see on page 357 and *HTML Document Options* on page 369.

Enable online connectivity using the Internet Online/Offline icon in the function bar; see page 384.

Browsing

To use bookmarks to access the Internet, see *Working With Bookmarks* on page 394.

To enter the URL directly, use either of the following methods:

•   Choose File > Open and enter the URL in the File name field. Click Open.

- Enter it in the Load URL field (Figure 13-2). Press Enter. (If the field isn't displayed, choose View > Toolbars > Hyperlink Bar.)

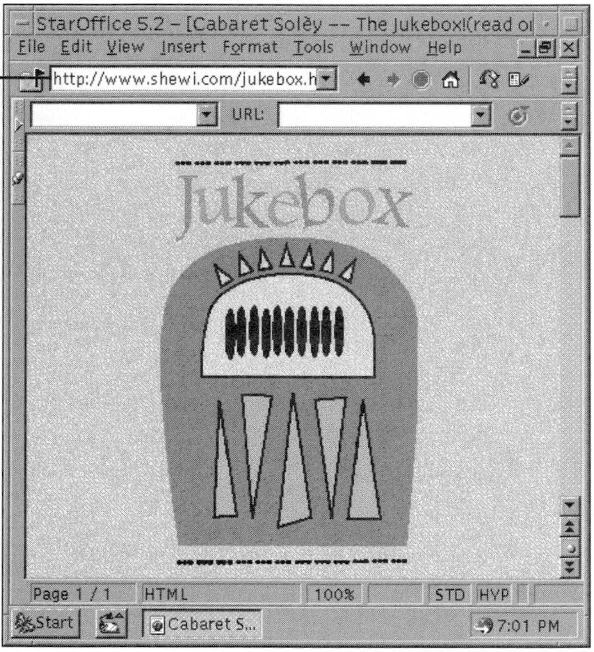

Type the URL in the Load
URL field and press Enter.

Figure 13-2   Entering an Internet URL to browse

Note – If you access a page by entering a URL in the Load URL field, the site you go to will replace the file you're currently working with. If there are unsaved changes, you'll be prompted to save them; if there aren't any, the file will be closed without any warning. See *Making Files Open in Their Own Separate Windows* on page 401 for how to prevent this.

If graphics aren't displayed, choose Tools > Options > HTML Document > Contents and under the Display caption, select the Graphics and object option. You also can right-click in the page and choose Load Graphics.

Using Web's Search Engine Connections

Complete the setup for searches first. See *Search Options* on page 375.

You can search the Internet using the capabilities of the search engines provided with StarOffice or that you've set up.

1   Enter the item you want to search for in the URL Name field, in the hyperlink bar.

2   Click the Find icon in the hyperlink bar and select the search engine you want to use.

3   The search engine you selected will be loaded and displayed in StarOffice, with the matches to the search.

Finding Out When a Site Has Changed

StarOffice lets you subscribe to a site if you want to be notified when there are changes to it.

1   Open Explorer (choose View > Explorer) and click the Bookmarks slider.

2   Right-click in the work area of the Explorer and choose New > Subscriptions.

3   In the window that appears, enter a name such as subscriptions and click OK.

4   Select the new folder and right-click on it. Choose New > Bookmark subscription.

5   In the Properties of Bookmark subscription window, enter the name and URL of the site, and a name and password if the site requires one for access. The window is shown in Figure 13-3 on page 394.

6   Set additional options in the Notification, Contents, and Time Interval tabs.

7   Click OK.

8   To view information about the subscribed site, expand the subscription option, then double-click the link to the site.

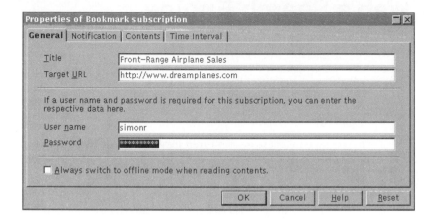

Figure 13-3   Setting up a site subscription

Working With Bookmarks

Note – If you have problems adding or importing bookmarks, you probably don't have rights to the bookmark directory. See your system administrator or move your bookmarks to a different directory (see *Changing Where Your Bookmarks Are Stored* on page 399).

Importing Bookmarks

StarOffice lets you import existing bookmarks, add new ones, and organize them.

Importing Netscape Bookmarks

There's an Import Netscape Bookmarks link under the StarOffice Bookmarks link in the Bookmarks slider in Explorer. However, this only works when the moon is full or the gremlins are happy. Here's the quick-and-dirty way to import Netscape bookmarks.

Note – Never edit your bookmarks file in StarOffice. If you've got the bookmarks organized in folders, editing removes that structure and you end up with one very long list of bookmarks.

If double-clicking the Import Netscape Bookmarks doesn't do anything:

1   Show Explorer (choose View > Explorer) and click the Bookmarks slider. See Figure 13-4 for an example of how it will look when you're done.

2   Open your bookmarks file by typing the path into the Load URL field in the function
bar and press Enter. For example, in Solaris the path could be
`/home/solveigh/.netscape/bookmarks.html`

3   Click on the Bookmarks icon next to the Load URL field and drag it into the
Bookmarks area. A link named "Link to Bookmarks for..." will appear.

When you want your bookmarks, just double-click that link, and an HTML page
displaying them will appear in the work area.

Enter the path to the
bookmarks file.

Drag the Bookmarks icon
to the work area below to
create a link to the
bookmarks file.

When you double-click
the bookmarks link, the
bookmark file appears in
the work area. Click a link
to go to a site.

The bookmark link
appears here; drag it to a
folder if you like.

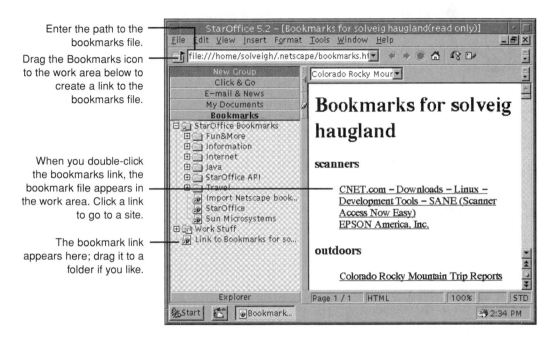

Figure 13-4   Quick-and-dirty Netscape bookmark import

If double-clicking the Import Netscape Bookmarks works:

1   In Explorer, click the Bookmarks slider.

2   Expand the StarOffice Bookmarks item.

3   Under Travel, double-click the Import Netscape
Bookmarks option.

4   In the window that opens, select your
`bookmarks.html` file.

If your bookmark is in a hidden folder, enter a path as
shown in step 2 in the previous procedure.

They will be imported into the Bookmarks slider, with their current folder organization.

Importing Internet Explorer Bookmarks

If IE was already installed when you installed StarOffice, a link to your Favorites from StarOffice Explorer was created automatically.

If you install IE after StarOffice, follow these steps to create the link:

1   In the StarOffice Explorer, open the Workplace item.

2   Locate the Favorites folder.

3   Drag the folder onto the New Group field in Explorer.

     A link is automatically created from Explorer to your Favorites folder.

Using Bookmarks

Bookmarks aren't complicated, but here are the basics:

Where Bookmarks Are Displayed

Bookmarks are accessed through Explorer. Choose View > Explorer, then click the slider labeled Bookmarks.

Opening a Bookmark

You can double-click on a bookmark, or right-click and choose Open With to select the application to open it with.

If you haven't set up the bookmark to open in a new window, rather than replacing the current document, hold down the Ctrl key while double-clicking. This will achieve the same effect.

Creating Bookmarks

You can add any local file, an executable (a program), a folder, an FTP site, or a Web page to your bookmark list.

You can do this in several ways; using the hyperlink bar is the quickest, but using the New Link feature lets you have the most control.

For information on inserting links in documents, rather than adding them to your bookmarks, see *Adding Hyperlinks to StarOffice Documents* on page 431.

Creating Bookmarks Using the Hyperlink Bar

If the hyperlink bar isn't displayed, choose View > Toolbars > Hyperlink Bar.

1   Enter the name of the site in the URL Name field.

2   Enter the site URL in the Internet URLs field (Figure 13-5).

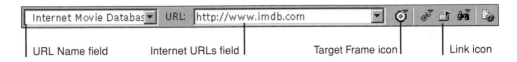

URL Name field   Internet URLs field   Target Frame icon   Link icon

Figure 13-5   Adding a bookmark using the function bar

3   Click the Link icon; the bookmark will appear in Explorer, with the name if you gave it one, in the Bookmark area.

4   To make sure the item you're linking to opens in its own window, select the bookmark, right-click it, and choose Properties. In the Frame field, select the target frame _blank. (See *Understanding Target Frames* on page 383 for more information.)

5   Drag the bookmark to a folder, if you want.

Creating Bookmarks Using the URL Field in the Function Bar

If the function bar isn't displayed, choose View > Toolbars > Function Bar.

1   Enter the full URL in the Load URL field (Figure 13-6).

Load URL field
Bookmark icon

Figure 13-6   Adding a bookmark using the function bar

2   Press Enter to go to the site.

3   Once the site is displayed, click and hold down the mouse on the Bookmark icon next to the URL field.

4   Drag the mouse into the Bookmarks area.

5   To make sure the item you're linking to opens in its own window, select the bookmark, right-click it, and choose Properties. In the Frame field, select the target frame _blank. (See *Understanding Target Frames* on page 383 for more information.)

6   Drag the bookmark to a folder, if you want.

Creating Bookmarks Using the New Link Feature

Note – Setting up a link to a folder adds a folder with the directory name to your bookmarks, plus links to all the files and folders within it.

1   In Explorer, click the Bookmarks slider. In the Bookmarks area, right-click and choose New > Link.

2   In the Properties of Link window, enter the appropriate information as shown in Figure 13-7.

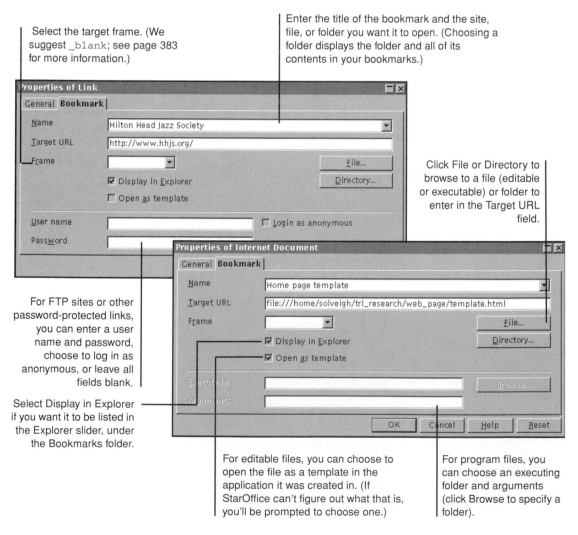

Select the target frame. (We suggest _blank; see page 383 for more information.)

Enter the title of the bookmark and the site, file, or folder you want it to open. (Choosing a folder displays the folder and all of its contents in your bookmarks.)

Click File or Directory to browse to a file (editable or executable) or folder to enter in the Target URL field.

For FTP sites or other password-protected links, you can enter a user name and password, choose to log in as anonymous, or leave all fields blank.

Select Display in Explorer if you want it to be listed in the Explorer slider, under the Bookmarks folder.

For editable files, you can choose to open the file as a template in the application it was created in. (If StarOffice can't figure out what that is, you'll be prompted to choose one.)

For program files, you can choose an executing folder and arguments (click Browse to specify a folder).

Figure 13-7   Entering link properties

Organizing Bookmarks

You can create folders, change the location of all your bookmarks, and set various options for the Bookmark slider area.

Creating a New Folder

1   In Explorer, click the Bookmarks slider. In the Bookmarks area, right-click and choose New > Folder.

2   Enter the folder name and click OK.

3   Drag links into the folder.

Changing Where Your Bookmarks Are Stored

If you want to change the location of the folder where your bookmark links are stored, you can do so through the Paths options window.

1   If you want to, import bookmarks from your current browser (see *Importing Bookmarks* on page 394).

2   Create a new folder for the bookmarks; the contents of the entire folder are displayed in the Bookmarks area, so any existing files in a current folder will be shown, as well.

3   Choose Tools > Options > General > Paths.

4   Locate the Bookmarks item and note the current location of your bookmarks.

5   Click Edit. Select the folder you created in step 2 and click Select.

6   Copy the contents of your old bookmarks folder to the new one.

Bookmark Area Properties

When you right-click anywhere in the Bookmark area, you can choose Properties to open the properties window. See *About the StarOffice Desktop* on page 93 for more information about the desktop and Explorer.

Downloading Web Pages

To download just one graphic or only the text in a page, you can use any of the following methods.

Downloading Pages

Use any of the following to download any document posted on the Internet or on an intranet. (To download graphics, see the next procedure.)

Save the File to Your Computer

Downloading the text portion of a page is the same as in other browsers: choose File > Save as. Then choose File > Open and open the page in StarOffice.

Change to Edit Mode

Click the Edit File icon in the function bar; the StarOffice Web toolbar will appear and you can edit the file on the spot. Choose File > Save as to save the file on your computer.

Copy the HTML Source

You also can copy the HTML source and paste it into a text document.

1   Right-click in the page and choose View Source.

2   Choose Edit > Select All.

3   Choose Edit > Copy.

4   Open a new Writer or other text document and paste. (If pasting into Writer doesn't work, just use Text Editor, Notepad, or another application.)

5   Save the file with an .html extension.

Downloading a Graphic

To download a graphic, right-click on it and choose Save Graphics.

To copy a graphic, right-click on it and choose Copy Graphics, then paste it into the appropriate location.

Making Files Open in Their Own Separate Windows

The default behavior throughout StarOffice, whether you're clicking a hyperlink in a Writer file or opening one of your documents from your work folder use Beamer, is to replace the current document with the one you're opening.

This can be annoying and unexpected, but there are a couple ways around it.

* For hyperlinks in StarOffice documents, the main desktop work area, Beamer, and Explorer, just hold down the Ctrl key when you click or double-click the file or hyperlink.

* Choosing File > Open also opens the file in a new window instead of replacing the current one.

* Set up hyperlinks and bookmarks to open in a new blank window automatically (see *Adding Hyperlinks to StarOffice Documents* on page 431 and *Creating Bookmarks* on page 396).

Using FTP: File Transfer Protocol

One of the most unexpected and useful features of StarOffice is that it lets you set up your system to transfer files via FTP from your computer to another one. This, of course, is particularly useful if you want to put files on a Web server. (We used it, ourselves, to send files to our editor, and it was simple and easy to set up and use.)

Note – You can't use the FTP account if you're behind a *firewall* (Internet security software). If you're using your work computer and you work for a company with a good Internet security setup, for instance, you probably won't be able to use this feature.

Setting Up an FTP Account

1   In order to set up and use an FTP account, you need to obtain the following:

* The name or IP address (such as 255.01.998.001) of the FTP server computer

* The name of the FTP account, if this is required

* The user name and password to access the FTP account

* The start directory on the server (the part of the path after the site, like `biology/ deptinfo` for `ftp.montanastate.edu/biology/deptinfo`)

2   Create a folder where you'll store the account.

3   Select the folder in Explorer and right-click it, then choose New > FTP Account.

4   In the Properties of FTP window, click the General tab and enter an account name.

If you don't enter a name, StarOffice will use the name of the FTP server.

5   Click the Server tab and enter your information. Click OK when you're finished. The example in Figure 13-8 sets up an account for the anonymous site `ftp://ftp.highlander.org/pub/highlander/`

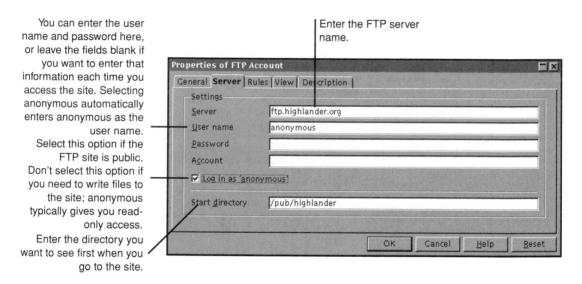

You can enter the user name and password here, or leave the fields blank if you want to enter that information each time you access the site. Selecting anonymous automatically enters anonymous as the user name. Select this option if the FTP site is public. Don't select this option if you need to write files to the site; anonymous typically gives you read-only access.

Enter the directory you want to see first when you go to the site.

Enter the FTP server name.

Figure 13-8   Setting up an FTP account

Viewing the Site Using StarOffice

1   Double-click the FTP item that was created in the folder.

2   The account will be displayed in StarOffice.

The Internet URL field (Figure 13-9) displays the site and the user name, or anonymous, used to access the site.

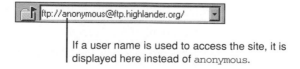

If a user name is used to access the site, it is displayed here instead of anonymous.

Figure 13-9   How FTP site and access method are displayed in StarOffice

The contents of the FTP path you specified (the server plus the folder, if any) are shown in the work area (Figure 13-10). The folder you're in isn't displayed anywhere.

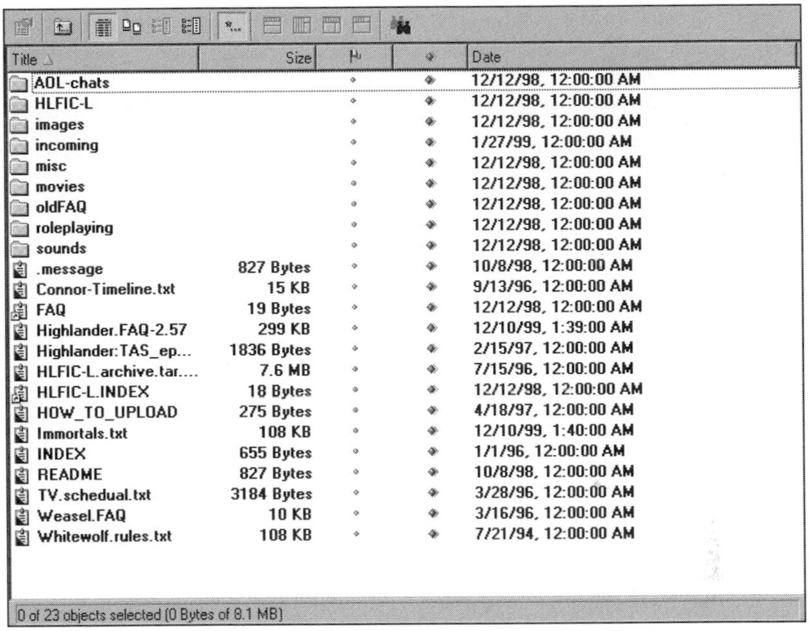

Figure 13-10   How the contents of the FTP site are displayed in StarOffice

Downloading Files From a Server Using Your FTP Account

1   Be sure you're connected to the Internet; click the Internet Online/Offline icon if necessary.

1   In Explorer, double-click the FTP item that was created in the folder. Enter a password if prompted.

2   StarOffice connects to the account and opens it in the workspace, displaying the current contents.

3   Select the files you want to download and drag them to the appropriate folder in Explorer.

Uploading Files to a Server Using Your FTP Account

1   Open Explorer in hierarchical view (right-click the Explorer slider and choose Hierarchical).

2   In Explorer, double-click the FTP item that was created in the folder.

3   StarOffice connects to the account and opens it, displaying the current contents.

4   Navigate to the folder on the server where you want to put files.

5   In Explorer, expand the Workplace item and navigate to the files you want to upload.

6   Drag the files to the folder on the FTP server.

    • To move individual files, open Beamer, then select the files and drag them to the FTP server folder.

    • To move a folder and its subfolders, if any, select the folder and drag it to the FTP server folder.

Creating Web Pages

Creating New HTML Files

StarOffice has extensive setup options that let you pick default values for any new HTML files you create or open. Before you begin, see *HTML Document Options* on page 369 and *URL Options* on page 379.

Note – If you want your documents to be read by a browser other than StarOffice Web, be sure to test your HTML documents in that browser before you distribute them. StarOffice Web text formatting, especially multiple levels of bulleting, doesn't always translate well. In addition, if you edit the document with another HTML editor, the odds increase that the formatting you originally applied will be changed when you view the file again, in Web or another browser.

Creating a New Blank HTML Document

Choose File > New > HTML Document. This creates a blank document with the following styles:

- Heading
- Heading 1 through Heading 6
- Horizontal line
- Sender
- Standard
- Text body (12-point Times)
- Table contents
- Table heading
- List Contents (sometimes, depending on what mood the gremlins are in)

It also has, by default, a header containing the full path to the file, date, time, and document title. To change either, see *Using Headers and Footers* on page 428.

Creating a New HTML Document Based on a Template

StarOffice provides two distinct sets of templates you can use for HTML documents:

- One in the `/share/template/`*`language`*`/` folder (this is on the server, in a multi-user system), which you've probably seen before.
- A different set that you can access only through AutoPilot

The `template` folder doesn't have many templates suitable for Web pages; you'll probably be able to find what you want more easily by using AutoPilot.

To create templates, see *Creating and Modifying Styles and Templates* on page 411.

Using AutoPilot

1   Choose File > AutoPilot > Web Page.

2   In the AutoPilot Web Page: Template window (Figure 14-1), select the template you want. It will be displayed behind the window in the work area.

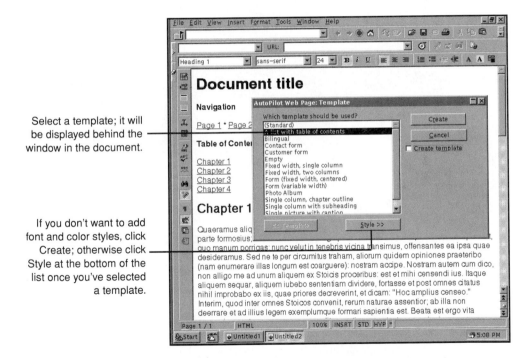

Select a template; it will be displayed behind the window in the document.

If you don't want to add font and color styles, click Create; otherwise click Style at the bottom of the list once you've selected a template.

Figure 14-1   Selecting a template on which to base a Web page

3   If you want to embellish the page with font and color styles, click Styles. (Otherwise, just click Create now.)

4   In the AutoPilot Web Page: Style window (Figure 14-1), select the style you want. Then click Create.

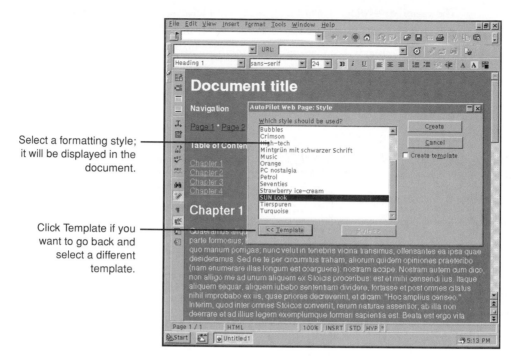

Select a formatting style; it will be displayed in the document.

Click Template if you want to go back and select a different template.

Figure 14-2   Selecting a style

Using the File > New > From Template Feature

This lets you base a document on one of the predefined Writer templates, or any template you've created.

1   Choose File > New > From Template.

2   In the New window, select the category and template.

New window, select the category and template.

None of the categories scream "Web," but you can use anything you see listed (Figure 14-3) that was created for Writer.

To see the template before you click OK, click More, then select the Preview option.

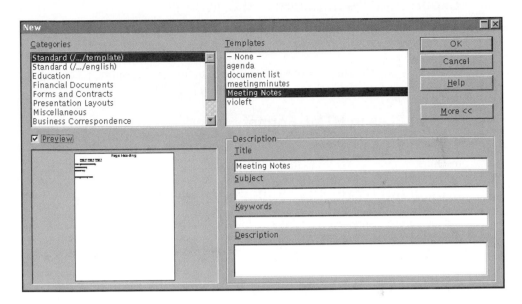

Figure 14-3   Creating a new file from a template

Checking What Template Your Document Is Based On

If your document is acting weird and you want to make sure you created it based on the right template, choose File > Properties and click the General tab. The template used by the document is displayed at the bottom of the window.

Changing Defaults for New Documents

You can change the default font (not the font size) for Standard, Heading, List, Caption, and Index styles. Choose Tools > Options > Text Document > Default Font. Select the defaults you want. Don't select the Current heading only option if you want this to apply to all subsequent documents.

To change the attributes of styles that appear in each new document you create, or to add styles, see *Styles* on page 413.

Extensive file and template information is also included in Writer, since Writer and Web have very similar functions. See *Creating and Modifying Styles and Templates* on page 411, and *Styles* on page 413.

Changing Existing Documents to HTML for Web Publication

You can get virtually anything you create or import into StarOffice onto the Web.

Exporting Presentations and Drawings

You can easily convert Impress and Draw documents to HTML. See *Creating an HTML Version of Your Presentation* on page 710 for more information.

Choose Tools > Options > Browser > HTML to define basic import and export options. See *Inserting Spreadsheets and Other Objects* on page 441.

Saving Files in HTML Format

You also can choose File > Save As to save in an HTML format. StarOffice Calc, for instance, has the HTML(StarOffice Calc) format.

Publishing HTML Files With Embedded Documents

You can insert a spreadsheet, Writer document, or other StarOffice file in an HTML document, and post the HTML document on the Web. See *Inserting Spreadsheets and Other Objects* on page 441.

Opening any Text File in HTML

Select the file in Beamer and choose Open With, then select HTML or HTML (StarOffice Writer).

StarOffice will give you an error message sometimes, though not consistently, when you do this. If it happens, just sigh and open the file, then use Save As to pick the format you want.

Saving a Writer File in HTML

You can easily convert Writer files, or any file you can open in Writer, to HTML. (If you need to get a document into Writer, the best way is to save it in .RTF format, then choose File > Open in StarOffice.)

1   Open the Writer document.

2   Choose File > Save As.

3   Select the HTML (StarOffice Writer) format and enter a new name if you want. Click Save.

Note – The document icon in the task bar will change to the HTML icon, but you won't see the HTML-specific toolbars and menu commands until you close the file and reopen it. It doesn't work to choose File and then select the name of the file, to reopen it—you have to close it, then choose File > Open to open it as a true HTML file.

Opening an HTML Document

Before you start opening files, it's a good idea to set options for opening Web pages created using other browsers. See *HTML Options: Font Size, Import, and Export* on page 363.

Choose File > Open to open another HTML file.

Keeping a File in Edit Mode

If you click the Reload icon, use the forward or backward arrows, or go to a Web page and then return to the document, you might find the toolbar gone and the file uneditable. This is just StarOffice's default behavior; click the Edit File icon again and you'll be back to edit mode.

Creating and Modifying Styles and Templates

Templates are predesigned files with styles, sometimes text, and other elements that reduce the amount of work you need to do every time you create a new document. Styles are pre-set groups of formatting characteristics that you can apply to text or graphics. Styles and templates go hand-in-hand for a number of reasons:

- They're both really good ways to cut down on the time it takes to do your work
- Templates are the primary way your styles are organized and stored

Since Writer and Web are so similar, you can learn how to use styles and templates in Web by just going to the sections of the Writer documentation where it's covered:

- *Power Formatting With Styles* on page 201
- *Using Templates* on page 220

This section covers a few things that are specific to Web, or are so common that we didn't want to send you chasing cross-country across the book for them.

Templates

Writer contains extensive information on templates, most of which is applicable to HTML as well as Writer files.

Using AutoPilot to Create an HTML Template

There are two ways to create a new document based on a template: AutoPilot (see page 406), or just choosing File > New > From Template. Using the steps in the following procedure makes a template that's available for either approach.

1   Choose File > AutoPilot > Web Page.

2   In the AutoPilot Web Page: Template window, select the template you want to base the new template on.

3   Select the Create template option and click Create.

4   In the Document Templates window (Figure 14-4), make entries and click OK.

Enter the name of the new template here. ⟶

Use the Organizer to rearrange templates, or click Edit (the dimmed button) to edit the template now.

Select a template category.

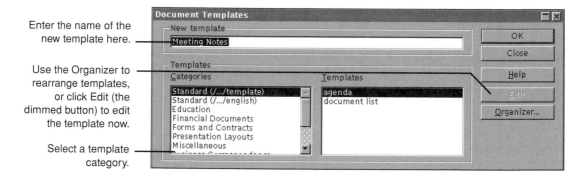

Figure 14-4   Creating a new template using AutoPilot and Document Templates windows

5   To add keywords, a document title, or other information, see Figure 14-20 on page 430. To modify the template, see *Modifying Any HTML Template*.

Creating a Standard HTML Template

You can base a document on this type of template only by choosing File > New > From Template; they don't show up in the list of templates in AutoPilot.

1   Create an HTML document with the fonts, graphics, and other formatting that you want to base other documents on.

> **Note –** It doesn't work to create the styles in a Writer document, or find a document containing those styles and open it in Writer, and then save as HTML. The styles disappear. You need to create the styles in the actual HTML document.

2   Choose File > Save As.

3   In the Save As window, select StarWriter/Web Template as the file type. Select the automatic file name extension option or type `.vor` as the extension.

4   Save the file in the appropriate subfolder of `share/template/`*`language`* (in a multi-user environment, these files are on the server computer), or in your `user/template` folder.

5   To add keywords, a document title, or other information, see Figure 14-20 on page 430.

Modifying Any HTML Template

1   Open the template you want to modify, in `share/template/`*`language`* (in a multi-user environment, these files are on the server computer), or in your `user/template` folder.

2   Make the changes.

3   Save the file, making sure that the file format remains StarWriter/Web Template.

Styles

This section covers a couple tips on Web and styles. For full coverage of the ins and outs of styles in StarOffice, see *Power Formatting With Styles* on page 201.

To get styles from one document to another, follow the instructions the Writer documentation for *Loading All Styles* on page 221 and *Loading Individual Styles* on page 222.

You can also just create a new template that has the styles you want, and use that template as the basis for all new documents. Create an HTML file, create the styles, then save as an HTML/Writer template. For more information, see *Creating a New HTML Document Based on a Template* on page 406.

Note – When you're looking for the style in Stylist, select All Styles in the dropdown list at the bottom.

Using Frames

You can use **sections** and **frames** to partition off parts of an HTML page to be treated differently from others.

Sections are also a way to partition text off for separate treatment: a different background, number of columns, protected from editing, etc. They're the same in Web as Writer; see *Modifying and Deleting Sections* on page 339.

The example in Figure 14-5 shows a typical example of frame use: one for the task bar on the left, one for the area at the top, and one for main content, below the banner.

Frames let you arrange two or more documents within the same page of your browser. A *frameset* is the HTML file that defines how many documents are grouped together and what documents and characteristics belong to each.

To use frames, first create a frameset, then specify its HTML documents.

This frame contains an HTML file displaying navigation icons. If the author added 5 or 6 more icons, the frame would scroll independently of the other frames.

The file home.html is the frameset that organizes the displayed files and sets properties for the individual frames.

This frame contains a file displaying the home page icon shown, so that the icon is still displayed regardless of how much text fills up the other two frames.

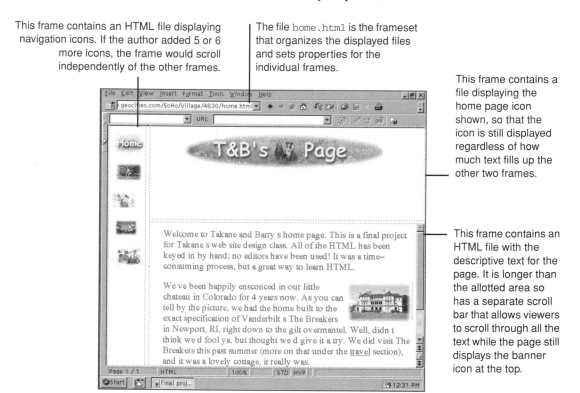

This frame contains an HTML file with the descriptive text for the page. It is longer than the allotted area so has a separate scroll bar that allows viewers to scroll through all the text while the page still displays the banner icon at the top.

Figure 14-5   Example of frame use (dotted lines added to show frame boundaries)

Creating Frames

1   Choose File > New > Frameset.

2   The new frameset and the frameset object bar will appear (Figure 14-6) at the top of the StarOffice work area, and a blank gray document will appear in the main work window.

Click the Edit
Frameset icon to edit
frameset attributes.

Split selected frame or the
entire frameset
horizontally or vertically.

Shows the frameset
HTML source.

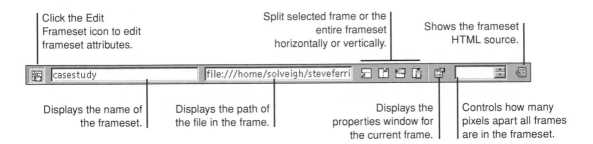

Displays the name of
the frameset.

Displays the path of
the file in the frame.

Displays the
properties window for
the current frame.

Controls how many
pixels apart all frames
are in the frameset.

Figure 14-6   Frameset object bar

Note – The Split Frameset Horizontally and Vertically icons have the same function as the
Insert Horizontal and Insert Vertical commands that are available when you right-click in
the frameset. Likewise, the Split Frame icons have the same function as the Insert commands.

---

3   Use the split icons in the object bar to divide the frameset or a frame (Figure 14-7), or
right-click on the frameset and choose the appropriate command.

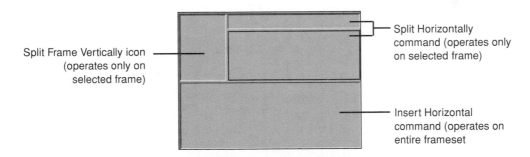

Split Frame Vertically icon
(operates only on
selected frame)

Split Horizontally
command (operates only
on selected frame)

Insert Horizontal
command (operates on
entire frameset

Figure 14-7   Dividing frameset into frames

4   Drag the borders, if necessary, to change the size.

5   Enter more specific information about the frame name, file, and dimensions in the
Floating Frame window (Figure 14-8). Right-click and choose Properties to open it.

Enter the name, using only numbers and letters, without spaces. Don't use an underscore to begin the name.

Enter the URL of the file to display. The file can be any type that can be displayed in a browser, and locally or on the Internet.

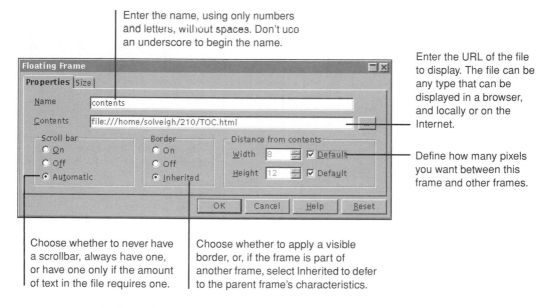

Define how many pixels you want between this frame and other frames.

Choose whether to never have a scrollbar, always have one, or have one only if the amount of text in the file requires one.

Choose whether to apply a visible border, or, if the frame is part of another frame, select Inherited to defer to the parent frame's characteristics.

Figure 14-8   Entering frame display options

6   Click the Size tab (Figure 14-9) to enter frame size properties.

Enter information for the frame height.

Enter the frame width measurement, then specify whether it is in pixels, percentage of the total frameset width, or relative.

Both Resizeable options must be marked for this or any other frame in the frameset to be resized by others (when the document isn't in edit mode).

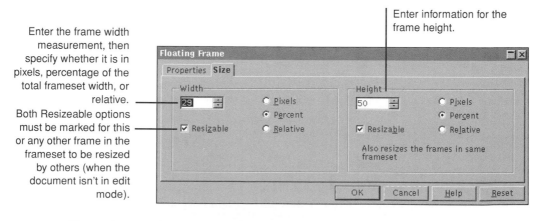

Figure 14-9   Entering frame size options

Note – The resize options work a little differently than you might expect. It's all or nothing: you can't specify that one frame is resizeable and the others aren't. In addition, both need to be marked in order for the frameset frames to be resizeable; if only one is marked, none of the frames are resizeable.

7   Click OK; the frame will have the information you entered and display the file you specified.

8   If there are hyperlinks within any of the documents in any of the frames, modify the links so that they open in the same frame, a new frame, and so on.

- Select the link.
- Click the Hyperlink Dialog icon.
- In the Hyperlink window, select the appropriate target frame.

The following table gives more explicit information about all four options.

Table 14-1   Target frame options

Option	Result
_top	Opens the linked document in the highest StarOffice task bar frame of the hierarchy; if none exists, it will be loaded in the same frame. (It generally behaves a lot like _parent.)
_parent	The frameset is closed and the document that the link connects to will open instead (the frame on the task bar that was occupied by the frameset will now be occupied by the newly opened document).
_blank	Always opens the linked document in a new empty frame. The frameset will stay open and the document that the link connects to will open instead in its own separate frame (a new icon on the task bar).
_self	Always opens the linked document in the same frame. The frameset stays open and the current document is replaced by the new document, within that part of the frame.
Other	If the current document itself is a frameset, all its frames will be listed. You can select one of them as the frame that the linked document will open in, replacing what was in that frame.

9   Choose File > Save Frameset. Be sure to select the Frameset (HTML) file type.

Modifying Frames

To edit the frameset properties again, press Ctrl, then click the Edit File icon on the function bar. Otherwise, you'll only see the HTML editing object bars and toolbar.

To edit an HTML file within a frame, click in the frame, then click the Edit File icon.

Creating Tables

Before you begin, complete table setup options first. See *Table Options* on page 371.

The table feature in Web is similar to Writer's, though not identical. When you select or insert a table (choose Insert > Table), the table object bar appears (Figure 14-10).

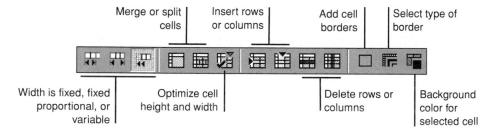

Figure 14-10   Table object bar

Note – If you don't see the table object bar, choose View > Toolbars and mark Object Bar. If it still doesn't appear, click the arrow at the far right of the object bar. See Figure 14-13 on page 420.

For extensive formatting information, see *Formatting Documents* on page 177.

StarOffice enables you to set up numbering for a variety of elements; see *Using Basic Numbering, Bullets, and Outlining* on page 194, as well as *Inserting Captions* on page 259.

Inserting a New Table

To insert a new blank or preformatted table, follow these steps.

1   Choose Insert > Table.

2   If you want to make a relatively basic table, make the appropriate entries in this window (Figure 14-11) and click OK.

The table name is
displayed only in
Navigator, not in HTML
source or in the Web page.

Select Header to include a
row that prints the table
title, and select Repeat
header to print it at the top
of every page.

Choose whether there
should be a border
around each cell in the
table.

Select this option if you
don't want the table to be
split over two pages when
printed.

Click AutoFormat to
choose from predefined
table formats.

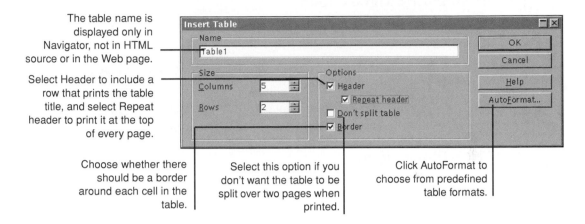

Figure 14-11   Creating a table

3   To take advantage of StarOffice's predefined formats, click AutoFormat and select
one of the formats in the AutoFormat window (Figure 14-12), then click OK.

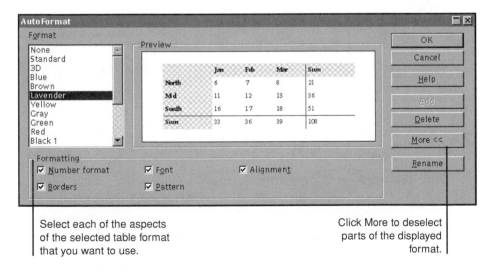

Select each of the aspects
of the selected table format
that you want to use.

Click More to deselect
parts of the displayed
format.

Figure 14-12   Selecting or creating a predefined format for the table

Modifying Table Dimensions

Once you've got the table, here's how to tweak it using menus and the table object bar. (If
you don't see the table object bar, see Figure 14-13 on page 420.)

Column/Row Dimensions

Select the cell, column, or row you want, and right-click. Choose Row, Column, or Cell to get options for modifying the width, etc.

You also can click anywhere in the table and see the vertical bars marking each column. Drag them to change column width.

The table generally wants to keep its full width and won't let you modify it via changing column width. You'll need to change the overall table dimensions.

Table Dimensions

1   To change overall table width, right-click and choose Table.

2   In the Table window's Table tab, select any alignment except Automatic.

Note – This is important; in order to make the table width relative to the page, for example, the Relative option in the Table tab needs to be enabled. It's grayed out, however, when Automatic alignment is selected, and Automatic is the default when StarOffice creates a table.

---

3   To enter an absolute width, enter a measurement in the Width field; to make the width a proportion of the displayed page, select Relative and enter a percentage.

Using the Text Formatting Icons in a Table

When you insert a table, the text object bar disappears and the table object bar replaces it. To get at the text formatting object bar when you're in a table, use the arrow at the far right side of the object bar. (If you can't see it, enlarge the StarOffice window or click the small down arrow at the right side of the object bar.)

Figure 14-13   Switching between the text object bar and table object bar

Just click the arrow circled in Figure 14-13 to switch from one object bar to the other.

Once in a while, you'll click in a table and the table object bar won't appear. Again, just click the arrow to get the table object bar.

Inserting Notes

Notes are a way to insert comments in an HTML document, using a flag that shows that a note is there, but without showing the text itself. Note indicators are shown in HTML editors when you're in edit mode, but not when the page is being viewed. The icon at the right shows both the Netscape and the StarOffice note indicators.

The insert note feature in StarOffice is essentially a way to add the following HTML text:

```
<!--notetext-->
```

or

```
<!--notetext

----author_and_date_information-->
```

StarOffice provides you with a window for inserting, and one for editing, which makes it a little simpler.

StarOffice notes can be read by other browsers, and vice versa.

Showing and Hiding Note Indicators

To show or hide note indicators in StarOffice, choose Tools > Options > HTML Document > Contents and select or deselect the Notes option. This applies to the indicator for scripts, as well. (See See *Adding Applets and Plugins* on page 449.)

Inserting Notes

1   Choose Insert > Note.

2   In the Insert Note window (Figure 14-14, enter the appropriate information.

The information currently entered in the Initials field of the User Data window (Tools > Options > General > User Data) are displayed here and printed above the note.

Enter the note in the Text field.

Click Author to add the contents of the Initials field and the time the note was written. You can edit the author text after it's added.

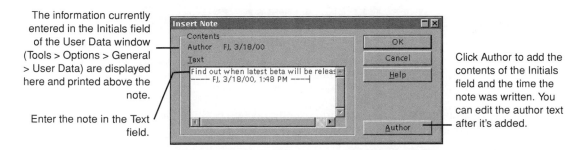

Figure 14-14   Inserting a note

3   Click OK. The note will be indicated with a yellow rectangle at the point in the text where you

> We expect to see the next version April 1.

inserted the note. This yellow note flag is visible only when you're in edit mode, as with most Web page editors.

Note – The indicator is visible only if you selected the Display notes option in the Tools > Options > HTML Document > Contents window.

Editing Notes

1   Double-click the yellow note indicator, just barely visible under the W in the illustration at right.

2   The Edit Note window is like the Insert Note window, except that you can browse from note to note using the arrows.

3   You can change the note, or add your own comments below the current note. If you're adding to a current note, your initials from the general user options window will replace the ones currently identifying the note.

Printing Notes

The Print Options window lets you choose whether to print notes, and where. See page 465 for more information, and an illustration of how notes are printed.

Note – Printing isn't all that it could be; the notes are printed only after each page, or at the end of the entire document. You can't print them right where they appear in the document, and the yellow note indicator isn't printed, either. However, the printed note does cite the line and page where the note appears.

Viewing and Editing HTML Source

Before you begin, complete the HTML Document setup, particularly in the window on page 372, which lets you determine the colors for different types of tags in the HTML source.

If you want to have precise control over the document you're developing, you can edit the HTML source code in your document.

To see the HTML, just choose View > HTML Source.

You can edit the HTML source directly in StarOffice Web; you don't need to open the HTML file in a text editor. Just choose View > HTML source, click the Edit File icon in the function bar, and make your changes. Then deselect the HTML source in the View menu and save changes.

To get the HTML source into a separate file, you can copy and paste, or choose File > Export source.

The file must be saved in order to view the source; if nothing shows up, check to be sure you've saved the file at least once already.

Adding and Formatting Text

Most of the text-formatting capabilities in StarOffice Web are the same as in Writer. See *Formatting Documents* on page 177 for more information. This section describes the few features specific to HTML documents.

Before you begin, make sure you're in edit mode (click the Edit File icon).

Note – The text formatting icons should be displayed on the object bar whenever you're inserting or formatting text. If table-related icons or other non-text icons are displayed instead, click the arrow at the far right of the object bar. See Figure 14-13 on page 420. (If the object bar itself isn't displayed, choose View > Toolbars > Object Bar.)

Figure 14-15 points out the primary HTML text formatting capabilities.

You can promote and demote headings to quickly reorganize your document, using Navigator. (Press F5 to display it.) See *Paragraph Formatting* on page 184 for more information.

If you want your documents to be read by a browser other than StarOffice Web, be sure to test your HTML documents in that browser before you distribute them. StarOffice Web text formatting, especially multiple levels of bulleting, doesn't always translate well. In addition, if you edit the document with another HTML editor, the odds increase that the formatting you originally applied will be changed when you view the file again, in Web or another browser.

The text object bar lets you apply standard Writer formatting like font size and justification.

Standard HTML styles are available by default; you can modify and create them using the same features as in Writer.

Heading 2 style, centered using the Centered icon on the text object bar.

Horizontal line (choose Insert > Horizontal Line).

Text body style.

Text body style, with bullets added using the text object bar, and spacing below first and second lines modified using the Paragraph window (choose Format > Paragraph).

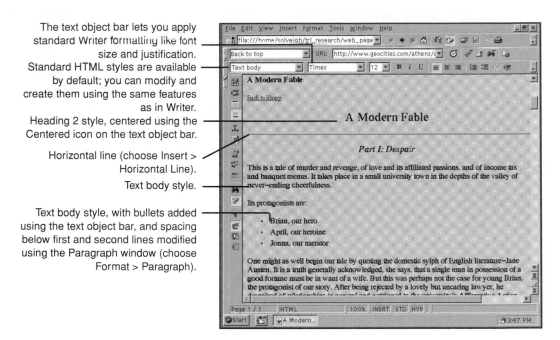

Figure 14-15   Basic HTML-specific text formatting features

Adding and Formatting Graphics

Adding graphics can enliven your Web pages, and slow them to a crawl when people try to view them on the Internet. How you use them is up to you; when creating pages, do refer to information sources on design and on how to maximize visual interest while minimizing load time.

Graphics are pretty much the same throughout StarOffice; they're already covered in the StarWriter documentation in *Graphics and Drawings* on page 228. This section covers graphics information specific to Web, or that's common enough to put here, too.

Note – For information on animated GIFs and image maps, see *Using Animated Text and Graphics* on page 445 and *Creating Image Maps* on page 448. To use numbered captions on graphics and tables, refer to *Inserting Captions* on page 259.

Adding a Graphic

You can add graphics three ways:

- Insert one using Insert > Graphic.

- Insert one by inserting a text-based file containing graphics: choose Insert > File.

- Paste in a graphic from another document like Draw, using standard operating-system commands.

Inserting

Choose Insert > Graphics and navigate to the graphic you want. The resulting HTML source will look something like this:

```
<IMG SRC="file:///home/solveigh/graphics/lorenzo.gif"
NAME="Graphic2">
```

Note – You can click the Properties button in the Insert Graphics window if you want to set properties like wrapping, the graphic name, etc. Information about using the Graphics window and the graphics object bar is included in *Graphics and Drawings* on page 228. To use the Hyperlink and Macro tabs of the Graphics window, see *Adding Hyperlinks to Graphics* on page 439 and *Linking Macros and Scripts to Graphics* on page 454.

Pasting and Inserting via Another File

Choose Insert > File and select the file, containing graphics, to insert.

All graphics in the inserted file will be saved with the document. The HTML source will look something like this:

```
<IMG SRC="sv302303.jpg" NAME="Graphic1" >
```

The name of the graphic is generated automatically, and the file is saved as a JPG.

Note – Each time you save the document, the graphic will be saved again under a different automatically generated name. If you save five times. for example, you'll have five JPG graphics in the folder with your HTML document, with various automatically generated names. This can add up, so use pasting or insertion via another document judiciously.

Changing Links to Graphics or Other Documents in a Document

If you moved one or more graphics or OLE objects (such as spreadsheets or drawings) to a different location, you can update the links in your document using the Edit Links window.

1   Choose Edit > Links; all non-text links in the document will be displayed in the Edit Links window (Figure 14-16).

2   Select any link or links to change and click Modify.

   •   If you selected only one link, the Link graphics window will appear; select the correct path to the graphic.

   •   If you selected two or more links, the Select Directory window will open. Select the folder where you want the selected links to point.

3   The new location or locations for the selected link is displayed in the Edit Links window. Click Close when you're done.

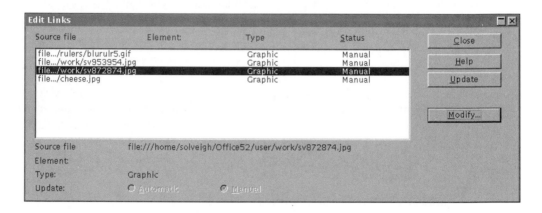

Figure 14-16   Viewing and editing links in a document

Setting Graphics Properties

Once you've added the graphic, you can use the StarOffice graphics properties tools to edit it as necessary. Properties are illustrated in Figure 14-17 on page 427.

Information about using the Graphics window (right-click the object and choose Graphics) and the graphics object bar is included in *Graphics and Drawings* on page 228.

To use the Hyperlink and Macro tabs of the Graphics window, see *Adding Hyperlinks to Graphics* on page 439 and *Linking Macros and Scripts to Graphics* on page 454.

Graphics positioning and
formatting object bar
appears when you select
an object.

Graphic is anchored to, or
associated with, the page,
a paragraph, or a
character. You also can
anchor it as a character.

Text wraps around
graphics based on your
settings in the Graphics
window (right-click the
graphic and choose
Graphics).

You can resize objects
using the same window,
and set borders using the
object bar.

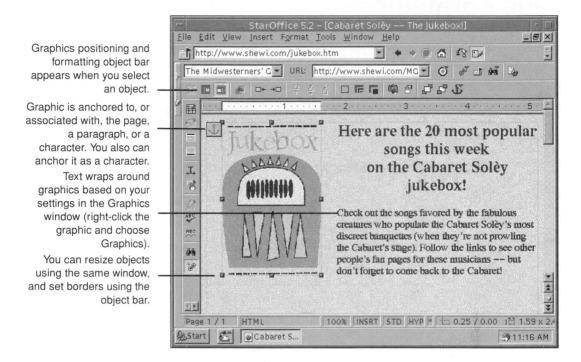

Figure 14-17   Inserting and formatting graphics

Inserting a Horizontal Line

You can use the Horizontal line style for a simple line, or choose Insert > Horizontal Line
to select a graphical line (Figure 14-18).

Select Single for the basic
line that's used with the
Horizontal line style, or
select one from the list.

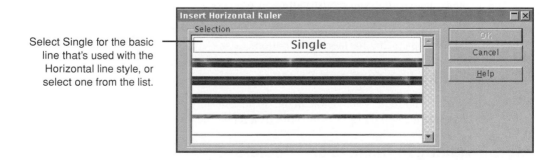

Figure 14-18   Inserting a graphical horizontal line

You can resize the inserted graphical line, but not reposition it.

Page Formatting

StarOffice provides a number of document-wide properties and setup options.

Page Setup

Choose Format > Page to view page setup windows for HTML documents; use the Page, Header, and Footer tabs. The windows are the as in Writer; see *Page Styles* on page 211.

Seeing How the Document Will Look When Printed

Generally, an HTML document displayed in StarOffice just fills up all the available space and wraps when it needs to, regardless of the settings you've entered in the Page tab of the Page styles window (choose Format > Page).

To see how the document will look when printed, with the page and margin settings you've applied, click the Print Layout On/Off icon on the toolbar.

For information on using Page Preview, which lets you print multiple pages on one sheet of paper and other options, see *Printing More Than One Page on a Sheet of Paper* on page 464.

Using Headers and Footers

You can use the Insert menu or the Insert Header and Insert Footer icons to reserve an area to print information on each page, such as page numbers, file name, and so on. This can be particularly useful with Web pages because they aren't divided into pages online, and it can be difficult to keep track of page order, the document name, and so on if you're distributing printed copies.

Headers and footers function similarly in Writer and Web. See *Headers, Footers, and Fields* on page 267 for more information.

Seeing Headers and Footers

Headers and footers are visible in the document only when Print Layout is activated using the Print Layout On/Off icon on the toolbar.

Adding to Headers and Footers

Use the header and footer in combination with the Insert Fields icon, which lets you insert fields containing page numbers, dates, etc.

Removing and Modifying Headers and Footers

To edit the information in the headers and footers, be sure you're in Print Layout view (see previous section); the headers and footers will be displayed. To remove a row in the header or footer, just delete it as you would a table row (select it, then click the Delete Row icon in the object bar).

You also can delete the header or footer through the Page Format window. Just choose Format > Page and click the Header and Footer tabs. Deselect the Header on and Footer on options.

Setting and Viewing Document Properties

Document properties include the name that's displayed in your browser title bar and the task bar at the bottom of StarOffice, as well as statistics like the number of links and lines in the document, and how the page is opened in a browser.

1   Choose File > Properties.

2   For the General, Description, Internet, and Statistics tabs, enter or view the appropriate information, as shown in Figure 14-19 through Figure 14-22.

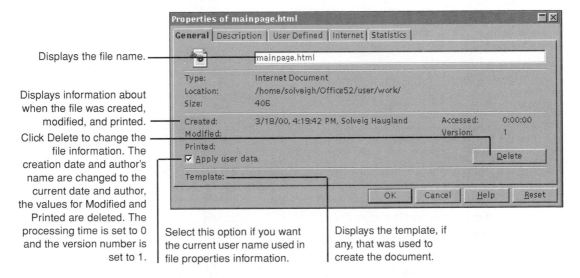

Figure 14-19   Setting and viewing file creation and modification

Enter the name you want displayed in browser title bars and in the StarOffice task bar.

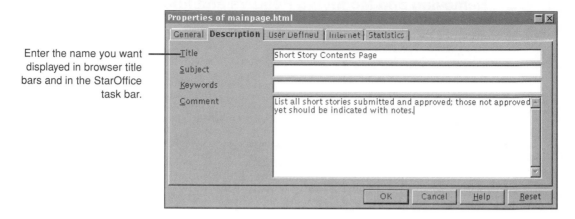

Figure 14-20   Entering the file display name and descriptive information

Enter any additional information about the file here and in the next tab, User Defined. If the file is a template, this will be displayed when you choose File > New > From Template > More.

You can force the page to be reloaded after a certain time interval.

Enter the document URL.

This field controls the default behavior for all hyperlinks in the document. See page 383 for a description of each option.

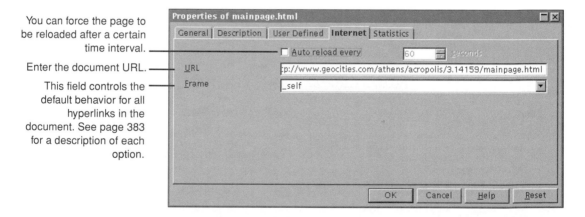

Figure 14-21   Setting reload, URL, and hyperlink frame information

The Statistics tab lets you view information about objects in the file such as the number of words. This window is available for HTML documents, but not for frameset documents.

Separators Enter a separator if it's important to you that the number of words in a document be counted accurately. Normally, words that are connected by a non-alphabetic character, such as Prentice-Hall, are considered as one word. Richter&Lemke is also counted as one word, rather than two. If you want words connected with characters like these to be counted as separate words, enter the characters used to connect them in the Separator field. You can enter all existing characters. Enter special characters and nonprintable characters hexadecimally. Special characters such as \n (line feed) and \t (tab) are also supported.

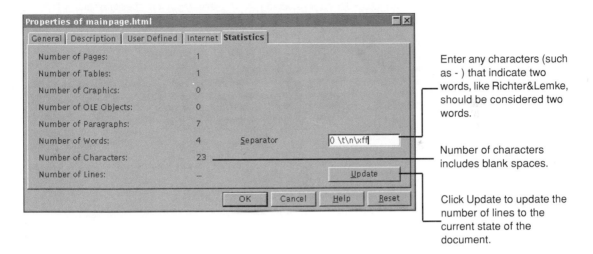

Figure 14-22   Viewing file statistics

Adding Hyperlinks to StarOffice Documents

One of the most powerful features of StarOffice is the ability to insert a link to any file or site, into any StarOffice document. With the document open in edit mode, or in other modes such as delivering a presentation, you can click the link to go to the file or site.

You can insert links not only in HTML documents but in Writer, Calc, Impress, and any other StarOffice documents where the hyperlink bar is available.

To **unlink** items, see *Unlinking* on page 440.

Overview of the Hyperlink Toolbar

The three different URL fields, and all sorts of Link and Hyperlink icons, make it a little hard to figure out what kinds of links you can do with each of the parts of the work area. Figure 14-23 points out the key differences among the link-related features, for inserting hyperlinked text and buttons (inserting graphics that you can hyperlink is covered later in this section).

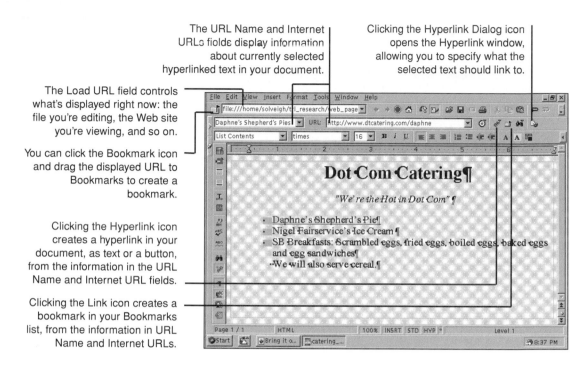

Figure 14-23   Getting to know the link tools

Setting URL Save Options

The Save options window contains two fields that control how URLs are saved: relative to the file system or Internet, or absolute. See *URL Options* on page 379 to specify how you want URLs saved.

Note – Tool tips always display the absolute path, even if only the relative path is saved. In HTML files, you can choose View > HTML Source to see what's really in the link.

Linking to a Web Page

If you've found a Web page while browsing that you want to add to one of your documents, follow these steps.

1   Go to the Web page containing the link.

2   Open the file you want to add the link to.

3   Hold down the Shift or Ctrl key, then click and hold down the mouse on the link.

4   Drag it into the Internet URL field on the hyperlink bar.

5   Name the link (add text that you want to appear in the document).

6   Click the Hyperlink icon to add it to the document.

Linking to a File or Site Using the Hyperlink Toolbar

1   Open any document.

2   Enter the name of the link—the text you want in the document—in the URL Name field. Enter the file or site to link to in the Internet URL field (Figure 14-24).

Figure 14-24   Adding a link to a document using the hyperlink bar

3   Click the Link icon.

4   Select the linked text, then click on and hold down the Target Frame icon.

5   The selections control whether the document or site you link to will close the current file and open the link in its place (select _self) or open in a new window (select _blank).

Linking to a File, Site, or Event

The Hyperlink window lets you create links not only to Web sites and files, but to items such as new email or news documents and scripts. It also lets you set up names for the links, so you can reference those links in scripts. This procedure provides an overview; more advanced features such as linking to a macro are covered in other sections in this and other StarOffice Web chapters.

An *event* is a StarOffice function such as clicking, passing the mouse over an object, and so on.

1   Open any document.

2   Position the cursor in the document where you want the link to appear.

3   Click the Hyperlink Dialog icon.

Note that this is the **Hyperlink Dialog** icon, not the **Hyperlink** icon to the left of it.

4   On the left side of the window (see Figure 14-25), leave Internet selected, or select Document.

Enter as many links as you want, then click Close.

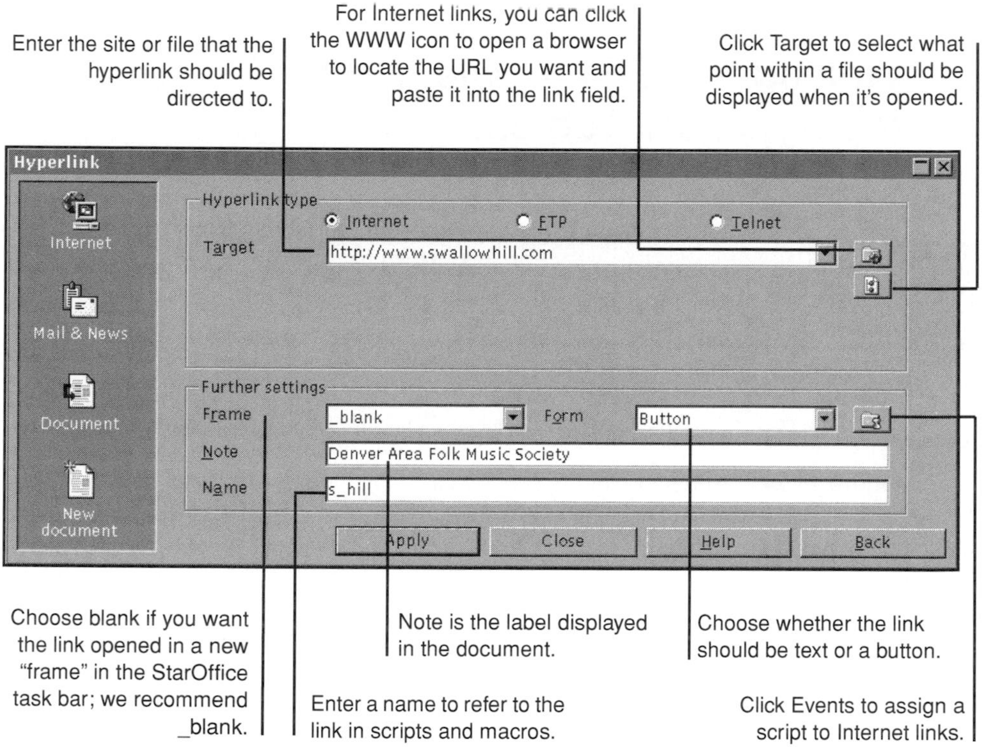
For Internet links, you can click the WWW icon to open a browser to locate the URL you want and paste it into the link field.
Enter the site or file that the hyperlink should be directed to.
Click Target to select what point within a file should be displayed when it's opened.
Hyperlink
Internet
Mail & News
Document
New document
Hyperlink type
Internet
FTP
Telnet
Target
http://www.swallowhill.com
Further settings
Frame
_blank
Form
Button
Note
Denver Area Folk Music Society
Name
s_hill
Apply
Close
Help
Back
Choose blank if you want the link opened in a new "frame" in the StarOffice task bar; we recommend _blank.
Note is the label displayed in the document.
Choose whether the link should be text or a button.
Enter a name to refer to the link in scripts and macros.
Click Events to assign a script to Internet links.

Figure 14-25 Adding an Internet or file link to a document: Internet Selection

---

Note – To change the link later, you can't select it and click the Hyperlink Dialog icon again. You need to select it and choose Edit > Hyperlink.

Linking to Targets

Targets are points within your document that you can specifically link to; for example, you might want to set up a short table of contents at the beginning of the document, and link each line to a particular heading within the document. You can also link to specific objects (these vary depending on the application you're using). This is particularly useful for going to a specific paragraph within a long document.

Linking to a Heading or Object Within a Document

This works with Web, Writer, and Calc documents, but not Impress, Draw, or Image. In Calc you can link to other sheets, and to range names and database ranges.

> **Note** – The heading-linking feature is extremely inconsistent; if you find that clicking on your hyperlink takes you absolutely nowhere, you'll need to do it in the HTML. We've covered that in the next procedure, *Linking to Any Point Within a Document, Using HTML* on page 436.

1   Open the document.

2   If you're linking to a heading, be sure that one of the styles in heading1 through heading5 is applied. (Choose Format > Stylist.)

3   Select the text that you want hotlinked, so that users clicking on that text will go to a graphic, table, heading, or other element of a document.

4   Click the Hyperlink Dialog icon to display the Hyperlink window (Figure 14-26).

5   In the region on the left side of the window, select Document.

6   If the target item is in a different document, click the Open file icon next to the Path field and select the file.

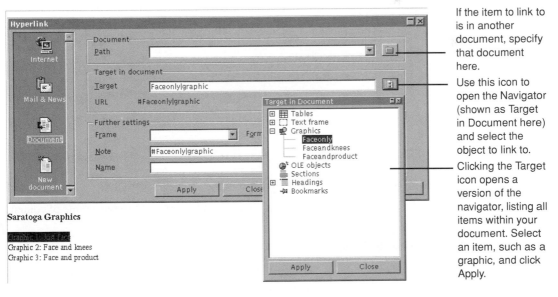

Figure 14-26   Linking to a graphic target or other object target

7   Click the Target in document icon by the Target field to open the navigator, then select the item you want to link to.

8   Click Apply, then Close. In the Hyperlink window, click Apply and Close also.

Note – To name graphics and tables so you can tell which one to select in Navigator, right-click and choose Graphics or Table. Enter a name in the Graphics or Table tab

---

Linking to Any Point Within a Document, Using HTML

The Hyperlink window doesn't let you link to any text that doesn't have a heading style in the range Heading 1 through Heading 5 applied to it. It also frequently falls flat when you try to link to headings. We've provided instructions on how to do it the old-fashioned way in HTML. (HTML novices, this is extremely easy.)

1   Open the document containing the items you want to be able to jump to, such as headings within a long document, graphics, or other elements.

2   Plan what you want name the targets: for example, if you have a series of ten headings named "The Oatmeal Saga," "The Oatmeal Crisis," "The Fall of the House of Oatmeal," and so on, you could name the targets `oatmeal1` through `oatmeal3`; `saga`, `crisis`, and `fall`; or another system. Just make sure they're all unique.

3   Click the Show HTML Source icon on the toolbar (the last tool) or choose View > HTML Source.

4   Locate the first heading and type the following in front of the heading text:

```
<A NAME="target_name"></A
```

For example, the line for the heading "The Oatmeal Saga" might look like this:

```
<H2><A NAME="saga"></A>The Oatmeal Saga</H2>
```

5   Repeat the previous step for all elements in the document that you want to be able to jump to.

6   Save the file first, then switch off the HTML source, returning to normal view.

7   If you want to link from a different document, open it.

8   Select the text you want to link from. For example, you might have a table of contents at the beginning of the document:

   •   The Oatmeal Saga

   •   The Oatmeal Crisis

   •   Fall of the House of Oatmeal

   You would select the text "The Oatmeal Saga."

9   Click in the Internet URLs field (labeled URL) and type a pound sign (#) followed by the name of the target to link to. If the target is in another document, enter the file name first, then the pound sign and target, like this: `oatmeal.html#saga`. Then press Return; the selected text will become hotlinked.

   An example is shown in Figure 14-27.

The selected text is
displayed here. ———

Enter the target here,
preceded by a pound sign
(#). If the target is in another
document, enter the file
name first, then the pound
sign and target. Then press
Return.

Select the text you want
hotlinked.

In the HTML for this ———
heading, "saga" has already
been set up as a target that
can be linked to.

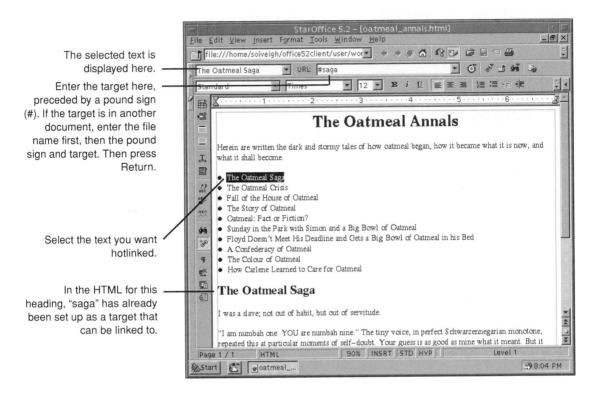

Figure 14-27   Linking to a text target

Linking to a New Email or News Document

The Hyperlink window lets you create links not only to Web sites and files, but to items
such as new email or news documents and scripts. It also lets you set up names for the
links, so you can reference those links in scripts.

Note – More advanced features such as linking to a macro are covered later.

---

1   Open any document.

2   Position the cursor in the document where you want the link to appear.

3   Click the Hyperlink Dialog icon.

4   In the region on the left, select Mail&News (see Figure 14-28).

Enter as many links as you want, then click Close.

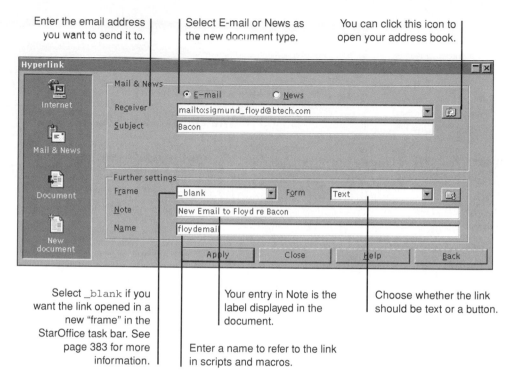

Figure 14-28   Linking to a new email document or news document

Linking to a New Empty File

This feature opens a new empty file of the type you specify when the hyperlink is clicked.

1   Open any document.

2   Position the cursor in the document where you want the link to appear.

3   Click the Hyperlink Dialog icon.

4   In the region on the left, select New Document (Figure 14-29).

Enter as many links as you want, then click Close.

The files are created based on the standard template for the application you select.

Enter the file name; it will be created in your work folder if you don't specify a path.

Select Edit now to open the document when you create it, or Edit later to only create it.

Select the type of document to create.

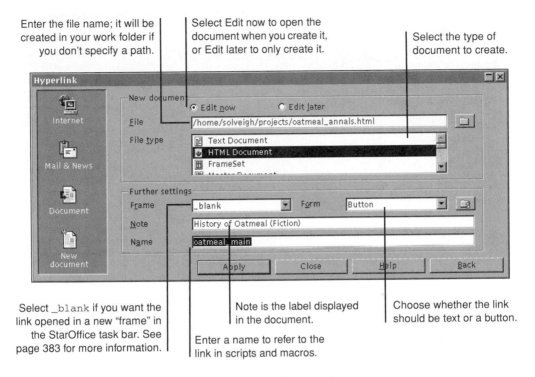

Select _blank if you want the link opened in a new "frame" in the StarOffice task bar. See page 383 for more information.

Enter a name to refer to the link in scripts and macros.

Note is the label displayed in the document.

Choose whether the link should be text or a button.

Figure 14-29   Adding a new document link to a document

Adding Hyperlinks to Graphics

This procedure describes how to add a hyperlink to a graphic you've **already** inserted. To insert a graphic, see *Adding and Formatting Graphics* on page 424.

Note – This works only with graphics added using Insert > Graphic, not pasted graphics.

1   Select the graphic, then right-click it and choose Graphics.

2   In the Graphics window, click the Hyperlink tab.

3   Enter the hyperlink information, as shown in Figure 14-30.

Enter the file or site you want to appear when the graphic is selected.

Enter the name to appear in the HTML source.

Choose whether the file or site in the URL field should open in a new browser window (_blank), or select another option. See page 383 for more information.

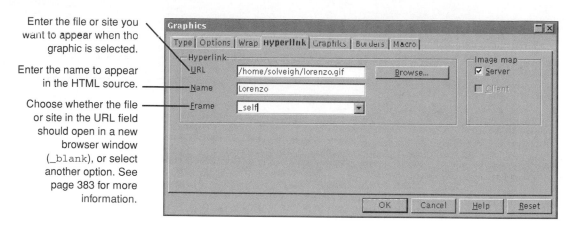

Figure 14-30   Hyperlinking a graphic

Unlinking

To unlink a graphic, just open the Graphics window again (right-click and choose Graphics), then click the Graphics tab, delete the URL and click OK.

To unlink a text or button hyperlink, deleting the URL doesn't work. To unlink any text, button, or graphic, select and choose Format > Default.

Viewing and Editing Links in a Document

To change existing links, or see exactly what the link is, you have several options. You can edit the HTML source code (see page 422), of course. The rest of the options are covered here.

Using the Hyperlink Window

Just select the item and open the Hyperlink window again (click the Hyperlink Dialog icon) to make changes.

Unlinking a Text Link

Select it and choose Format > Default.

Quickly Changing a Text or Button Link

Select a text or button link in the window, change the URL in the Internet URL field, then click the Hyperlink icon on the hyperlink toolbar or press Enter.

Editing an Individual Text Link

Select a link and choose Edit > Hyperlink.

Curiously, this works only for text links created using the Internet URLs or Hyperlink window, not for button links created using that window, or for any graphics links.

Inserting Spreadsheets and Other Objects

StarOffice lets you insert the following into an HTML document:

- Graphics: any existing raster (GIF, JPG, etc.) graphic. See *Adding and Formatting Graphics* on page 424.
- Files: any existing StarOffice or other document that can be converted to text, such as HTML or Writer. See *Inserting a Text-Based File* in this section.
- OLE objects: new or existing spreadsheet, drawing, chart, image, formula, or presentation. See *Inserting Files and Objects* in this section.

Note – OLE objects aren't dynamically updated. If you change the original, the inserted object doesn't change, and vice versa. The advantage of using OLE objects is that they retain their original properties, and you can edit them in the HTML document.

- Formulas and charts. See *Charts* on page 243 and *Mathematical Formulas* on page 251.

Inserting a Text-Based File

Note – The font size of the file might be a lot different when it's inserted.

---

1   Choose Insert > File and navigate to the file you want.

   Insert > File can convert only text-based files. To insert other files, use one of the other Insert menu options.

2   Select the closest filter to convert with, if you're prompted to (see Figure 14-31), and click OK.

   The contents of the file will be inserted, with their original formatting in an editable format.

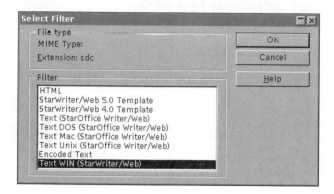

Figure 14-31   Selecting a filter for an inserted file

Inserting Files and Objects

A very useful feature in StarOffice is inserting OLE objects—it's just a techy way of inserting another file, like a drawing or a spreadsheet, into your document. OLE stands for object linking and embedding; it means you can edit the file using its native editing capabilities, even when it's inserted in a different document. OLE objects include new or existing spreadsheets, drawings, charts, images, formulas, and presentations.

You can't move OLE objects to other applications via the clipboard or drag and drop in or out of StarOffice.

Inserting an Existing Object

Editing OLE objects that exist as separate files varies, depending on which files are open.

- If you edit the inserted OLE object, the original never changes.

- If the original and the HTML file containing the inserted object are both open, changes you make in the original take effect only in the inserted object.

- If the HTML document is not open, the changes take place only in the original.

Once you've inserted the object, the next time you save the HTML document, the object will be saved and a `.gif` file, such as `sv335337.gif`, will be created in the same directory as the HTML file. A new `.gif` will be created each time you save the HTML file.

1   Choose Insert > Object > OLE Object.

2   In the Insert OLE Object, select Create from file and select the file you want.

3   The file will appear in the HTML document (see Figure 14-32).

The object toolbar is displayed; right-click and choose Edit to display the toolbar for the type of file you inserted.

The anchor for the object is displayed here.

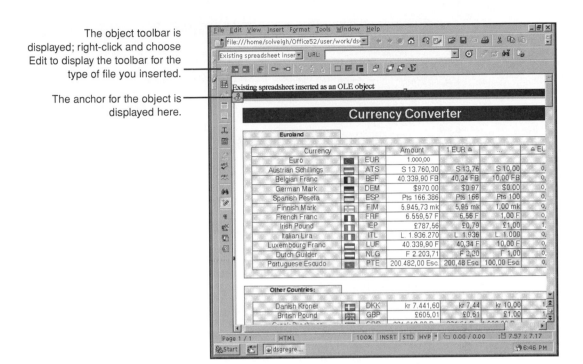

Figure 14-32   Inserted object

4   If Navigator is active, a form of the Navigator will appear, allowing you to manage the object.

5   To edit the object in your HTML document, right-click it and choose Edit. See the notes at the beginning of this procedure on how editing is affected by which files are open.

Inserting a New Object

1   Choose Insert > Object > OLE Object.

2   In the Insert OLE Object window (Figure 14-33), select Create New, then select the type of object to insert.

Figure 14-33 Inserting a new OLE object

3 Click OK; the new object will appear.

4 If Navigator is active, a form of the Navigator will appear, allowing you to manage the object.

Click in the object to access the file type's object bar. Right-click to access the standard options (Figure 14-34).

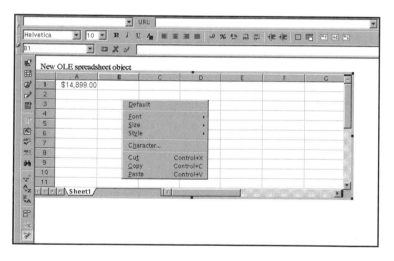

Figure 14-34 New OLE spreadsheet inserted into an HTML document

Using Animated Text and Graphics

Scrolling or blinking text marquees and animated GIFs can create startling effects in your pages and presentations; however, use them with caution. You've probably seen animated graphics in Web pages, where they can be attention-grabbing and effective if used properly, and annoying and distracting if not. In addition, note that marquees are supported only in the StarOffice browser and in Internet Explorer, not in Netscape Navigator.

Creating a Text Marquee

StarOffice provides its own way to insert a piece of text that scrolls across your Web page, such as "All Hipwaders 50% Off," or "Enter Our Haiku Contest".

1   Click the Text animation icon in the toolbar.

2   Draw the rectangle where you want the text. If you want the text to scroll, draw the rectangle across the entire scrolling area (Figure 14-35).

    Be sure to draw it in the correct place in the page; you can drag the borders later to resize it, but you can't move it.

Figure 14-35   Creating a text marquee text box

3   Immediately type the text in the rectangle. (This is important; if you click outside the rectangle, it will disappear and you won't be able to reselect it.)

4   Select the text. Use the Character window or the text object bar to format the text.

5   Be sure the text isn't selected, then right-click on the text frame and choose Text. Click the Text Animation tab (Figure 14-36) and enter the appropriate information.

6   Click outside the frame; the text will run.

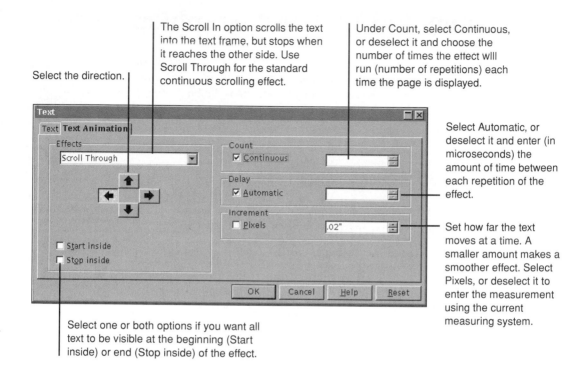

Select the direction.

The Scroll In option scrolls the text into the text frame, but stops when it reaches the other side. Use Scroll Through for the standard continuous scrolling effect.

Under Count, select Continuous, or deselect it and choose the number of times the effect will run (number of repetitions) each time the page is displayed.

Select Automatic, or deselect it and enter (in microseconds) the amount of time between each repetition of the effect.

Set how far the text moves at a time. A smaller amount makes a smoother effect. Select Pixels, or deselect it to enter the measurement using the current measuring system.

Select one or both options if you want all text to be visible at the beginning (Start inside) or end (Stop inside) of the effect.

Figure 14-36   Setting text marquee options

Creating an Animated GIF

Creating animated GIFs actually uses Impress and Draw, not HTML tools. However, animated GIFs are typically used most on Web pages, so we've included them in this chapter.

You can animate any graphic in a GIF format (a raster format that you can create in Image). A series of graphics is used to create the illusion of a moving image. For examples of animated graphics included with StarOffice, see the `gallery/www-anim` folder.

1   You first need to create the series of images, in Image, Draw, or using existing ones. If you already have the images, skip to the next step.

They don't need to be in GIF format right now; they'll be saved in a GIF file at the end of the process.

You can use a series of images of a cartoon character in different positions, text combined with a blank background to create a flashing effect, or anything else that produces the effect you want.

2 Paste or import the graphics into a blank slide in Impress. (Choose File > New > Presentation. If AutoPilot starts, close it and choose Tools > Options > Presentation > Other and deselect Start with AutoPilots.)

3 If each image is composed of more than one element, such as a sign with a circle and text inside it, be sure to group them. (Select all elements that go together, then right-click and choose Group.)

4 Arrange the images in the order you want them to appear, from *right to left*.

5 Select all images that will be part of the animated GIF.

6 Choose Presentation > Animation.

7 In the Animation window, select the Bitmap object option.

8 Click the Apply Objects Individually button.

9 The last object (farthest right or down) will be displayed (Figure 14-37) with its corresponding number below it. Enter the appropriate settings for this object: how long it will be displayed and the number of times the series of GIFs will be displayed (make sure this is the same for all graphics).

10 Click the back arrow icon and repeat the previous step for all other graphics.

11 Click Create to create the animated GIF.

12 Copy the GIF into your Web page.

13 To save it, right-click and choose Save Graphics.

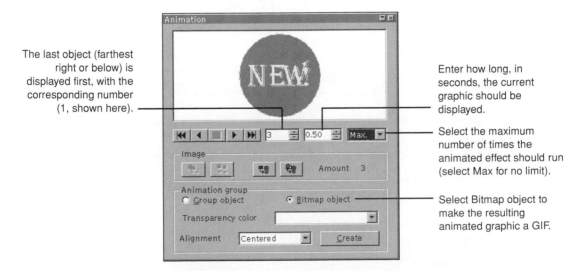

Figure 14-37   Creating an animated GIF

Creating Image Maps

You can make a useful, impressive-looking Web page with an image map, a graphic that has multiple hyperlinks to different locations.

The Web page in Figure 14-38 is a good candidate for an image map; the blueprint of the house provides information as well as a good way to navigate through the site.

An image map of this graphic could link to a different site for each room in the house.

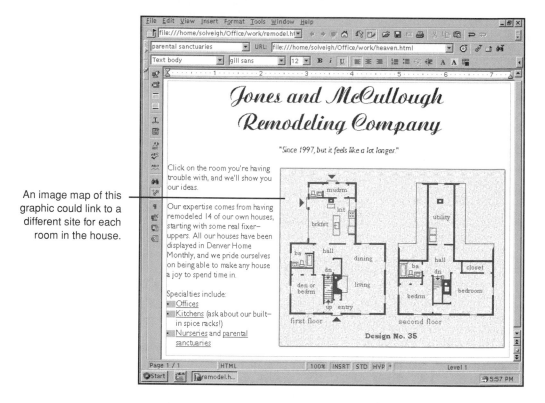

Figure 14-38   Web page with graphic that can be used as an image map

Image maps are remarkably straightforward to use. Follow these steps.

1. Add the graphic to your Web page. (See page 424 for more information.)

2. Select the graphic; the graphic object bar will appear.

3. Click the Image Map icon.

4. The Image Map Editor window will appear (Figure 14-39).

5. Click one of the four shape tools, such as Rectangle, and draw on the graphic the outline of the first area you want to link.

6   Enter link information for the area. Click the green Apply arrow to save changes after you draw and enter information for each area.

Use these tools to change the shape of the area you draw. See page 739 for more information.

The text you enter here will appear when the mouse passes over the area; if you don't enter anything, the address will be displayed.

Enter the site or file to link to. To link to a macro or script, click the Macro icon and refer to page 454.

Any area you've defined is shown dimmed, with green handles.

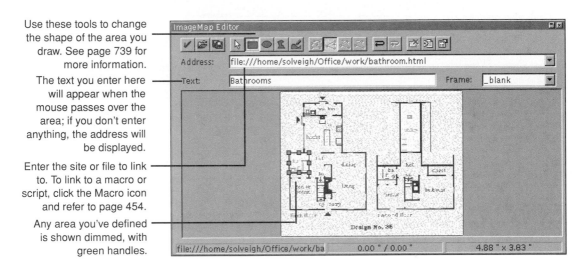

Figure 14-39   Drawing areas to link from in the image map

Adding Applets and Plugins

Applets are mini-programs, written in the Java programming language, that can run within a browser. Plugins add functionality such as the ability to play certain sound formats.

Applets

It's up to you to either locate or write the applet itself. Once you have the file, though, follow these steps to add it to any StarOffice document.

1   Use the Insert Applet feature on the toolbar's Insert tearoff menu, or choose Insert > Object > Applet.

2   The Insert Applet window will appear (Figure 14-40). Enter the applet information and click OK.

Note – If you enter parameters, be sure that you enter them exactly right, especially paths to files. StarOffice won't do any checking for you, and will continue to attempt to find the referenced file, slowing down your system. "Applet not initialized" will appear in the status bar.

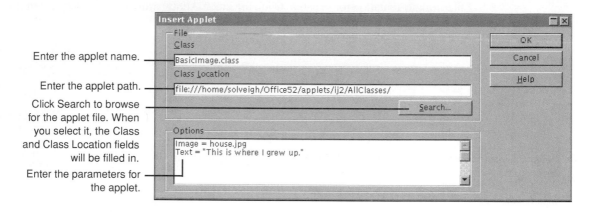

Enter the applet name.

Enter the applet path.

Click Search to browse for the applet file. When you select it, the Class and Class Location fields will be filled in.

Enter the parameters for the applet.

Figure 14-40   Inserting an applet

Plugins

Plugins are browser extensions that offer additional functions. If you need to add one to a StarOffice document, follow these steps.

1   Use the Insert Plugin feature on the toolbar's Insert tearoff menu, or choose Insert > Object > Plugin.

2   The Insert Plugin window will appear (Figure 14-41). Enter the plugin information and click OK.

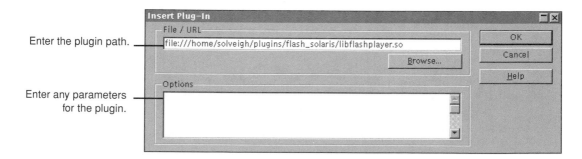

Enter the plugin path.

Enter any parameters for the plugin.

Figure 14-41   Inserting a plugin

Using Macros, Scripts, and Events

This section covers how to add scripts to any StarOffice document, whether by inserting them in a document so that they're run when the document is loaded, or associating them with a graphic or text link.

You can also link StarOffice Basic macros and JavaScript to text or button hyperlink events.

Finally, you can create controls, like a push button, and attach them to macros or events. *Events* are actions like moving the mouse over the hyperlink, clicking the mouse on the hyperlink, and moving the mouse away from the hyperlink.

Inserting Scripts in Documents

You can insert JavaScript, JavaScript 1.1, Live Script or VBScript to documents. The inserted script is indicated by a small green square.

To attach JavaScript to a control, such as a button; see Figure 14-48 on page 460; to attach it to a hyperlink, see *Using Macros, Scripts, and Events* on page 451.

Showing and Hiding Script Indicators

To show or hide note indicators in StarOffice, choose Tools > Options > HTML Document > Contents and select or deselect the Notes option. This applies to the indicator for notes, as well. (See *Inserting Notes* on page 421.)

Inserting a Script

1   Choose Insert > Script.

2   The Insert Script window will appear (Figure 14-42). Enter the plugin information and click OK.

Enter the type of script:
JavaScript, JavaScript
1.1, Live Script or
VBScript
Select the source for the
script, then enter the URL
or the script text.

Figure 14-42   Inserting a script

Note – If you use the <SCRIPT> tag to enter or edit the HTML source yourself, the SRC option in HTML is only evaluated if the LANGUAGE is defined as "JavaScript", "JavaScript1.1" or "LiveScript". The content of the script text will then be ignored.

```
<SCRIPT LANGUAGE="JavaScript" SRC="url">
/* ignore all text here */
</SCRIPT>
```

The MIME type of the loaded script should be "text/javascript", though this is not automatically verified.

Editing Scripts

1   Double-click the green script indicator.

2   The Edit Script window is like the Insert Script window, except that you can browse from script to script using the arrows.

Printing Scripts

The Print Options window lets you choose whether to print document scripts and notes, and where. See page 465 for more information.

Inserting Hyperlinks to Macros and Scripts

You've already learned how to make text and graphics hyperlinks that will take you to a file or Web page. You can also make them run scripts, using the procedures in this section.

For information on recording and editing macros, see *Using Macros to Automate Tasks* on page 1037.

To set up standard hyperlinks, see *Adding Hyperlinks to StarOffice Documents* on page 431.

Linking Macros and Scripts to Text or a Button

1   Open any document.

2   Position the cursor in the document where you want the link to appear.

3   Choose Insert > Hyperlink or click the Hyperlink Dialog icon.

4   On the left side of the Hyperlink window, select any of the options: Internet, New Document, etc.

5   Set up the link for the appropriate type of link (see page 433 through page 438).

6   Click the Events icon.

7   In the Assign Macro window (Figure 14-43), select one of the events.

8   Select StarBasic to assign your own or StarOffice macros to the event; or select JavaScript to type your own script and assign it to the event.

Note – If you add an existing StarOffice macro, be sure the macro's library (the category it's listed within) is activated. Choose Tools > Macros, click the Organizer button, then click the Libraries tab and be sure the checkbox next to the library is checked.

Enter the appropriate information, then click OK.

Select the event that you want to associate a macro or script with.

Click Assign to assign a macro or script to the selected event. To remove it later, click Remove.

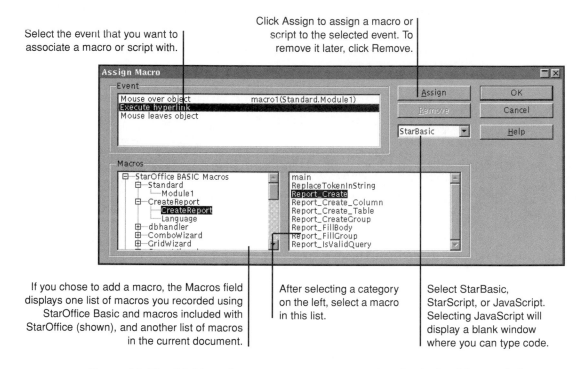

If you chose to add a macro, the Macros field displays one list of macros you recorded using StarOffice Basic and macros included with StarOffice (shown), and another list of macros in the current document.

After selecting a category on the left, select a macro in this list.

Select StarBasic, StarScript, or JavaScript. Selecting JavaScript will display a blank window where you can type code.

Figure 14-43   Linking a button or text to a macro using the Assign Macro window

Linking Macros and Scripts to Graphics

If you've added a graphic to a document, you can use the Graphics window to make it trigger an action.

1   Right-click the graphic and choose Graphics.

2   In the Graphics window, click the Macro tab (Figure 14-44).

3   Select an event that will trigger the macro or JavaScript.

4   Select StarBasic to assign your own or StarOffice macros to the event, or select JavaScript to type your own script and assign it to the event.

Note – If you add an existing StarOffice macro, be sure the macro's library (the category it's listed within) is activated. Choose Tools > Macros, click the Organizer button, then click the Libraries tab and be sure the checkbox next to the library is checked.

Enter the appropriate information, then click OK.

Select the event that you want to associate a macro or script with.

Click Assign to assign a macro or script to the selected event. To remove it later, click Remove.

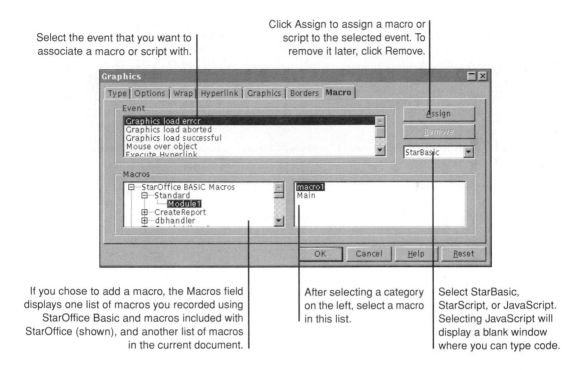

If you chose to add a macro, the Macros field displays one list of macros you recorded using StarOffice Basic and macros included with StarOffice (shown), and another list of macros in the current document.

After selecting a category on the left, select a macro in this list.

Select StarBasic, StarScript, or JavaScript. Selecting JavaScript will display a blank window where you can type code.

Figure 14-44   Linking a graphic to a macro or JavaScript using the Graphics window

---

Note – Most of the macro-insertion features in StarOffice let you insert a macro from the Standard and other libraries, and from the document you're currently in, but not any other documents you've created. If you're having trouble finding the macro you want, it's probably in a separate document. You'll need to cut and paste it into a module in the Standard library, a new library, or create a module for it in your current document.

Attaching Actions to Form Controls

The Form Functions tearoff menu (Figure 14-45), available from the toolbar, lets you add controls such as buttons, radio buttons, check boxes, and so on to your Web pages. These controls can be attached to macros or events, such as clicking them or moving the mouse over them. The form controls are available in text documents, HTML documents, presentations, or drawings in StarOffice.

Note – The coverage of StarOffice Calc describes what to do once you've got the controls in a document and want to distribute it. See *Using the Controls* on page 564.

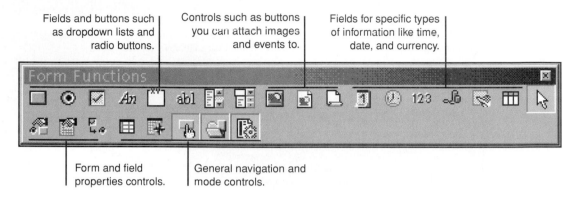

Fields and buttons such as dropdown lists and radio buttons.

Controls such as buttons you can attach images and events to.

Fields for specific types of information like time, date, and currency.

Form and field properties controls.

General navigation and mode controls.

Figure 14-45   Forms and form components

Note – In HTML documents, all possibilities for preparing a form are available; however, only the form characteristics that are supported in the selected HTML version can be exported. You can select the HTML version for the export by choosing Tools > Options > Browser > HTML Export.

What's a Form?

There isn't any Form icon on the toolbar since form isn't an actual thing that you draw; it's just a term for a document containing interactive elements. As such, it is most useful if you've got it connected to something that takes in data, and possibly sends other data back out again. To use fields and forms with StarOffice databases, see *Creating and Modifying Databases* on page 987.

This section pretty much ignores forms; we cover how to create and hyperlink controls on the Form Functions menu. Creating forms involves setting up submission encoding, inserts and deletes permissions, and other technical topics that fall outside the scope of this book. The advanced part of the StarOffice User's Guide in the online help has information about creating forms that users enter over the Internet and similar topics; refer to the help if you're interested in that type of functionality.

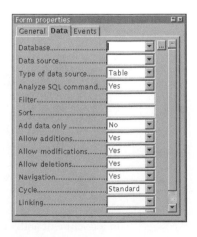

Creating a Control

1   Click and hold down the mouse on the Form icon on the toolbar, and tear off the Form Functions menu.

2   Click the icon for the type of control you want: button, field label, dropdown list, etc.

3   Draw the control where you want it in the document.

Applying URL and Display Properties

1   Right-click the control and choose Control.

2   In the Properties window, click the General tab and enter the appropriate information, then close the window (Figure 14-46).

Changes are saved as you make them.

Depending on the type of control, the options vary. For information about a specific field not addressed here, including more detailed information on events, refer to the help.

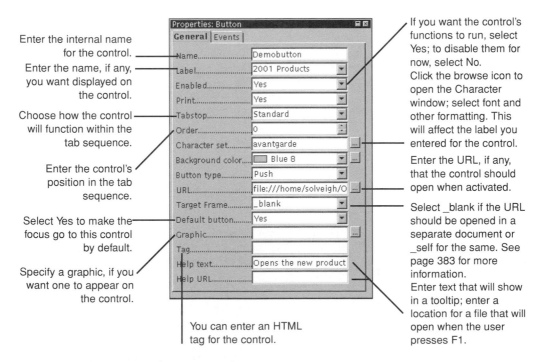

Enter the internal name for the control.

Enter the name, if any, you want displayed on the control.

Choose how the control will function within the tab sequence.

Enter the control's position in the tab sequence.

Select Yes to make the focus go to this control by default.

Specify a graphic, if you want one to appear on the control.

You can enter an HTML tag for the control.

If you want the control's functions to run, select Yes; to disable them for now, select No.

Click the browse icon to open the Character window; select font and other formatting. This will affect the label you entered for the control.

Enter the URL, if any, that the control should open when activated.

Select _blank if the URL should be opened in a separate document or _self for the same. See page 383 for more information.

Enter text that will show in a tooltip; enter a location for a file that will open when the user presses F1.

Figure 14-46   Entering URL and display properties for a control

Specifying Actions for the Control

In addition to just specifying a URL for the control, you can specify StarOffice macros, either existing ones or macros you've recorded, or enter JavaScript, to be executed when certain *events* happen. Events are actions like clicking the mouse, releasing the mouse, moving the focus (pressing Tab), and typing.

Table 14-2 lists the events and what each means. All events are not available for each control

Table 14-2   Control events

Event	Description
Before update	This event takes place before the content of the control field is updated from a linked data base.
After update	This event takes place, after the content of a control field was updated from attached data.
Item status changed	This event takes place if the status of the control field is changed.This event takes place if you select a new entry in a list or a combo box or with a check box or option field if the condition of the control field changes.
Text modified	This event takes place if you enter or modify text in an input field.
Before commencing (also called Action started)	This event takes place if an action is executed by clicking the control field. Initiating an action is not the same as executing an action. If you click a Submit button, it initiates the "send" action but the send process will start when the "Action performed" event occurs. With "Action started" you have the possibility to choose. If the linked method sends back FALSE, "Action performed" will not be executed.
When initiating (also called Action performed)	This event takes place if an action actually starts executing. If, for example, you have a Submit button type in your form, the send process executes the action. The "When executing" event corresponds to the start of the send process. This field is only available if you have inserted normal buttons. It isn't available with graphic buttons.
Focus gained	This event takes place if a control field receives the focus (if it is selected or gets the focus because a user tabs to it). The focus is the thin dotted line visible around the selected item in a window.
Focus lost	This event takes place if a control field loses the focus (if you tab to another field, for example).
Key typed	This event takes place if the user presses any key. For example, this event can be related with a macro input verification.
Key released	This event takes place when the user releases the pressed key.
Mouse inside	This event takes place if the user presses any key. For example, this event can be related with a macro input verification.

Table 14-2   Control events

Event	Description
Mouse dragged while key pressed	This event takes place if the mouse is dragged while a key is pressed.
Mouse moved	This event takes place if the mouse is moved.
Mouse pressed	This event takes place if any mouse button is pressed.
Mouse released	This event takes place if a pressed mouse button is released.
Mouse outside	This event takes place when the mouse is outside the control field.
Reset	This event takes place if the status of the control field is reset to its default value using the Reset type button.

Follow these steps to assign macros or scripts to events.

1   Right-click the control and choose Control.

2   Click the Events tab (Figure 14-47 or Figure 14-48).

3   Select an event to assign a macro or script to.

4   Select StarBasic to assign your own or StarOffice macros to the event, or select JavaScript to type your own script and assign it to the event.

> **Note –** If you add an existing StarOffice macro, be sure the macro's library (the category it's listed within) is activated. Choose Tools > Macros, click the Organizer button, then click the Libraries tab and be sure the checkbox next to the library is checked.

5   Enter the appropriate information, then close the window.

Note – Most of the macro-insertion features in StarOffice let you insert a macro from the Standard and other libraries, and from the document you're currently in, but not any other documents you've created. If you're having trouble finding the macro you want, it's probably in a separate document. You'll need to cut and paste it into a module in the Standard library, a new library, or create a module for it in your current document.

Click the browse icon next to the event you want to associate with a macro or JavaScript.

Click Assign to assign a macro or script to the selected event. To remove it later, click Remove.

When you click Assign, the macro or script you assigned is displayed next to the event it's assigned to (the events are the same ones listed in the Properties window).

Select StarBasic, StarScript, or JavaScript. Selecting JavaScript will display a blank window where you can type code.

The Macros field displays a list of macros you recorded using StarOffice Basic and macros included with StarOffice. The current document and any macros in it are included at the bottom of the list.

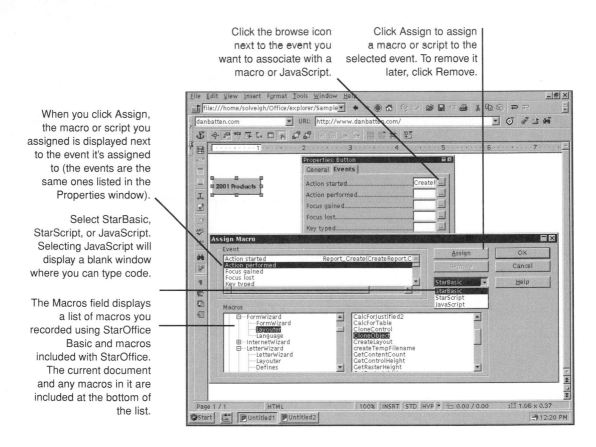

Figure 14-47   Assigning a StarOffice macro to a control's events

Enter the JavaScript here.

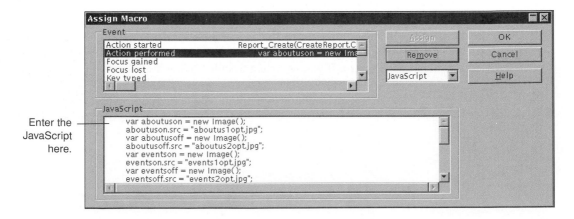

Figure 14-48   Assigning JavaScript to a control's events

Editing or Using a Control

You can toggle between two modes: one in which you can edit the control (design mode), and one in which the control performs whatever actions you've assigned to it. The controls function only when design mode is off; you can edit the control only in design mode.

To switch, use the Design Mode On/Off icon on the Form Functions tearoff menu or on the form functions object bar.

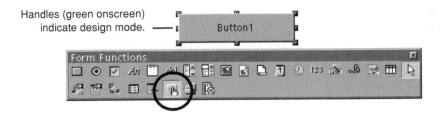

Figure 14-49   Design mode on/off icon

If you distribute the file for use, keep in mind that others will open the file in design mode, by default. To use the controls, they'll need to switch off design mode with the icon in Figure 14-49, or switch off editing for the entire document using the Edit File icon in the function bar, shown at the right.

Printing in StarOffice Web

Printer and Document Setup

Set any of the following options before you begin printing.

Note – The printing information here is specific to this application; see *Printing in StarOffice* on page 61 of Getting Started for more information.

Printer Setup

For information about setting up printers and printing to files, refer to *Printer Setup* on page 62 and *Printing to a PostScript or PDF File* on page 77.

Printing More Than One Page on a Sheet of Paper

Use the Page Preview window to specify the number of pages to be printed on one page. Activate Print Layout by clicking the Print Layout On/Off icon, then choose File > Page Preview (see Figure 15-1). Click the Print options page view icon in the object bar and use the Print Options window to specify the number of pages across and down, and orientation.

For a list of other ways you can control the number of pages, refer to *Fitting Multiple Pages Onto One Sheet* on page 83.

Note – The settings entered in the Print Options window that you access from the Page Preview window will be used for printing only if you print the document using the Print Page Preview button.

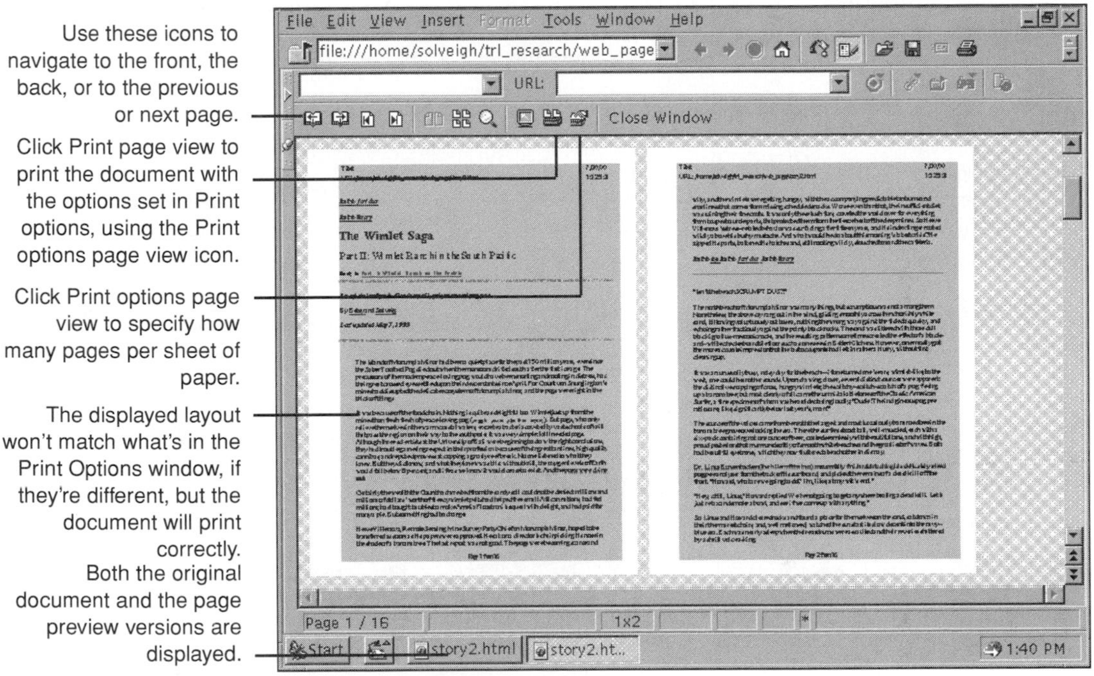

Use these icons to navigate to the front, the back, or to the previous or next page.

Click Print page view to print the document with the options set in Print options, using the Print options page view icon.

Click Print options page view to specify how many pages per sheet of paper.

The displayed layout won't match what's in the Print Options window, if they're different, but the document will print correctly.
Both the original document and the page preview versions are displayed.

Figure 15-1   Page Preview

Specifying Landscape or Portrait Orientation

To specify whether the presentation should be portrait or landscape, choose Format > Page and select the Page tab.

You *can* also set orientation in the Printer Options window. (Choose File > Printer Setup, click Properties and select the Paper tab.) However, all testing indicates that the setting in the Printer Setup window is completely irrelevant; sometimes it changes to reflect what you've set in the Page Setup window, but if you make any changes there, it doesn't affect printing.

See also *Specifying Portrait or Landscape Orientation* on page 82 for more information on the ways you can set orientation throughout StarOffice.

Printing Options

1   Choose Tools > Options > HTML Document > Print, or choose File > Print and click the Options button.

2   Select what you want to print.

It's a good idea to select the Create single print jobs option. If you don't select it, the first page of the second copy might be printed on the back of the last page of the first copy.

If you select a printer in the Print window and a fax here, the printer will be used.

The Print Options window is shown in Figure 15-2.

Select the elements you want to print. Select Print black if you want all text printed black, regardless of its onscreen color.

Choose to print in reversed order, or to print as a brochure (see page 85).

Choose how to print notes (see information on page 466).

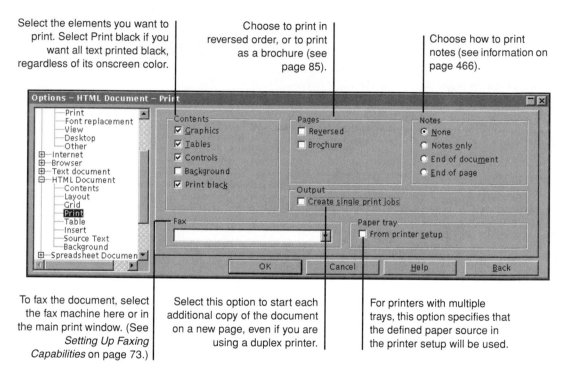

To fax the document, select the fax machine here or in the main print window. (See *Setting Up Faxing Capabilities* on page 73.)

Select this option to start each additional copy of the document on a new page, even if you are using a duplex printer.

For printers with multiple trays, this option specifies that the defined paper source in the printer setup will be used.

Figure 15-2   Selecting printing options

Brochures The Brochure feature is implemented in an extremely clumsy way. If you'd like to read more about it, however, see *Printing Brochures* on page 85.

Printing notes The Print Options window lets you choose whether to print notes in the page. (To add notes to your documents, see *Inserting Notes* on page 421.)

You can choose one of the following note printing options:

*   None – Notes aren't printed.

*   Notes only – Only the notes are printed, not the page content.

*   End of document – The notes are printed on one or more separate sheets of paper, at the end of the document.

*   End of page – The notes for each page are printed on one or more separate sheets of paper, after each page on which there are notes.

The yellow note flag is never printed; you'll need to locate where the note was originally positioned using the line/page info in the printed note. Notes are printed as shown in Figure 15-3:

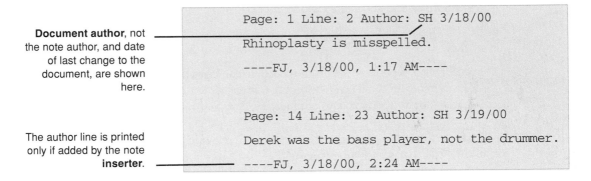

Document author, not the note author, and date of last change to the document, are shown here.

```
Page: 1 Line: 2 Author: SH 3/18/00

Rhinoplasty is misspelled.

----FJ, 3/18/00, 1:17 AM----


Page: 14 Line: 23 Author: SH 3/19/00

Derek was the bass player, not the drummer.

----FJ, 3/18/00, 2:24 AM----
```

The author line is printed only if added by the note **inserter**.

Figure 15-3   How notes are printed

Printing an HTML Document or Web Page

Once you've set the options that determine how pages will be printed, you're ready for a hard copy.

Using Page Preview

Click the Print Layout On/Off icon on the toolbar, then choose File > Page Preview. Follow the instructions specified earlier in *Printing More Than One Page on a Sheet of Paper* on page 464.

Printing Brochures

See *Printing Brochures* on page 350.

Printing

You can print the whole document, selected slides, or selected objects within a slide to a printer or file. For more information about printing to files, refer to *Printing to a PostScript or PDF File* on page 77.

Follow these steps if you want to specify particular options, or use the Print File Directly icon on the StarOffice toolbar, which uses the options and printer last selected.

1   To print selected objects within a drawing, select them now.

2   Choose File > Print.

3   Select a printer, or select the Print to file option and enter a file name. To print to a PostScript file, enter a name with a .ps extension.

4   Click Options and select the appropriate print options (see Figure 15-2), then click OK.

5   Select what to print: All (the entire document), Pages (a range of pages), or Selection (the currently selected text or objects). Use dashes to form ranges, and use commas or semicolons to separate pages or ranges (1, 3, 4, 6-10).

Note – StarOffice often defaults to Selection, rather than All, as the range of pages to print. Check this each time you print.

---

6   Enter the number of copies and, if it's two or more, choose whether to collate.

7   Click Print.

StarOffice Calc

Part 4

Getting Started With Calc

Quick Start

This section contains the following information to help you get started quickly:

- A checklist that points you to common tasks for quick reference
- Feature overview
- Multiple ways of starting Calc
- An overview of the Calc work area
- A five-minute tutorial

See 3, *Taming the StarOffice Environment*, on page 91 for general tips that can make working with StarOffice a lot easier.

Quick Start Checklist

If you need to create a spreadsheet quickly, the following sections should be particularly helpful:

- Starting a document based on a template – *Creating a Calc Document From a Template* on page 485
- Adding and renaming sheets – *Maintaining Sheets* on page 488
- Formatting cells – *Formatting Cells* on page 507
- Adding charts – *Inserting Charts* on page 552 and *Modifying Charts* on page 554
- Adding headers and footers – *Setting Up Headers and Footers* on page 602
- Controlling printing, including repeating headings – *Determining What Gets Printed* on page 598

StarOffice Calc Features

Calc is every bit as powerful as any spreadsheet application on the market, and in many ways it's superior. Following are some of the features that set Calc apart:

Document Filters Calc has a huge number of filters for opening documents created in other formats. Its filter for Microsoft Excel is particularly good.

Graphics Support You can insert graphics of just about every conceivable format, including Adobe Photoshop PSD.

Conversion from Microsoft The AutoPilot (wizard) lets you convert Microsoft Office documents (even entire directories of them) with a few clicks.

Version Control You can store versions of a Calc document as it moves through a lifecycle, letting you revert back to an earlier version if necessary. Calc also offers a full set of editing aids that display changes made to a document.

Sort Lists You can define lists of items, such as months, that sort in a particular order rather than alphabetically or numerically.

Conditional Formatting You can set cells to dynamically change formats based on the values in cells.

Seamless Compatibility With Databases You can drag a database table and drop it into Calc to open it in a spreadsheet, and you can turn a spreadsheet into a database by dragging it onto a database table in the Explorer window. Calc also lets you save spreadsheets as dBase database tables.

Cell Protection You can lock cells so the data can't be changed manually.

Controlling Valid Entries Calc lets you allow only specific values or ranges of values to be entered in a cell.

Scenarios You can store many sets of data within the same block of cells, letting you select from a list of scenarios you set up. For example, you can store interest rate information for many banks in the same cell, and switch between the banks from a drop-down list. If the cell is used in a formula, the results of the formula change when you select a different bank.

Goal Seek If you know the total you want a cell to contain, but you don't know one of the values needed in a formula to reach that total, this feature calculates the missing value.

Starting Calc

You can launch Calc in a number of ways:

- Start > Spreadsheet
- File > New > Spreadsheet
- From the Click & Go slider in the Explorer window (clicking the Spreadsheet shortcut)
- With a task bar shortcut. (See *Adding Shortcuts to the Task Bar* on page 123.)

The Calc Work Area

Use tooltips to get to know Calc. There are tooltips for almost all StarOffice fields and icons. Just position your mouse over anything you want to know the name of. You can turn tooltips on and off by choosing Help > Tips.

Clicking the Help button in a window or pressing F1 is the quickest way to get help for that window. If only general help appears, click in a field in the window.

Figure 16-1 shows the major components of the Calc environment.

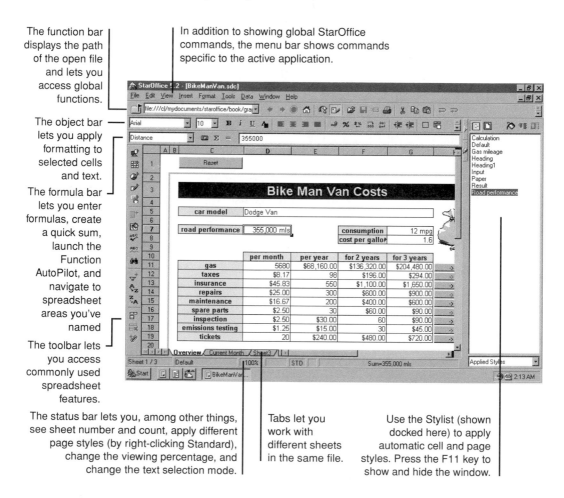

The function bar displays the path of the open file and lets you access global functions.

In addition to showing global StarOffice commands, the menu bar shows commands specific to the active application.

The object bar lets you apply formatting to selected cells and text.

The formula bar lets you enter formulas, create a quick sum, launch the Function AutoPilot, and navigate to spreadsheet areas you've named

The toolbar lets you access commonly used spreadsheet features.

The status bar lets you, among other things, see sheet number and count, apply different page styles (by right-clicking Standard), change the viewing percentage, and change the text selection mode.

Tabs let you work with different sheets in the same file.

Use the Stylist (shown docked here) to apply automatic cell and page styles. Press the F11 key to show and hide the window.

Figure 16-1   The Calc work area

Guided Tour

Use this tutorial to give you a brief introduction to the Calc environment.

1   Launch Calc.

2   Click cell **A1**, type Credit Card Calculator, and press Enter. Cell A2 becomes selected.

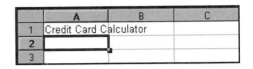

3   Click cell **A1** again, and in the object bar, change the font size to 24.

You can also right-click the cell, choose Format Cells, and in the Cell Attributes window select the Font tab to change the font size.

4   Click the number 1 in the gray box of row 1. The entire row is selected.

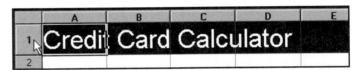

5   In the object bar, click the Background Color icon, and select a light background color for row 1.

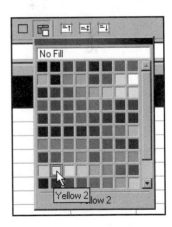

6   In this step you'll enter some row headings. Enter the following text in the corresponding cells, pressing Enter after each entry. (Click each cell to enter the text):

- **A4** – `APR

(Don't forget the single quote at the beginning. It allows you to use the acronym APR [annual percentage rate] in all capital letters so that Calc doesn't read it as the month April.)

- **B4** – Monthly Interest
- **C4** – Starting Balance
- **D4** – Monthly Payment

Notice that not all the text shows in the cells now, as shown in Figure 16-2. Normally you can resize the column widths, have the text wrap in the cells, or both. In this tutorial we'll have you wrap the text.

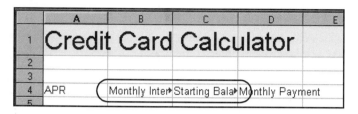

Figure 16-2   Text that is too wide for cells

7   Click and hold down the mouse button in cell A4, and drag across the row so that rows **A4 through D4** are selected.

8   Choose Format > Cells.

9   In the Cell Attributes window, click the Alignment tab.

10 Select the Line break option and click OK. The text in those cells wraps to show all the text, as shown in Figure 16-3.

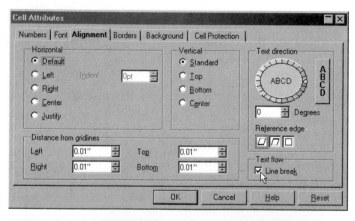

Figure 16-3   Wrapping text in cells

11 Select cells **A4 through D4** again.

12 In the object bar, click the Bold icon to make the text bold, and click the centered text alignment icon to center the text in the cells.

13 With the cells still highlighted, in the object bar click and hold down the Borders icon, and select the border that shows a line beneath a cell.

14 Select cell **A5** and click the % icon on the object bar. This tells the cell to display a percentage (even though there's no confirmation when you click the icon). Enter the number .18 (don't forget the decimal point). Press the Tab key.

15 In cell **B5**, click the % icon on the object bar. Now enter the following small formula in the cell, pressing the Tab key afterwards:

```
=A5/12
```

This formula means divide the contents of cell A5 by 12. What you're doing is figuring a monthly interest rate percentage by dividing the annual percentage rate by 12 months.

16 In cell **C5**, click the Currency icon. This tells the cell to display a dollar amount. Enter 7000. This beginning balance is the amount you have charged to your credit card (ouch!). Press the Tab key.

17 In cell **D5**, click the Currency icon and enter the number 250. This is the amount you're going to pay each month. Press Enter.

Figure 16-4 shows how your spreadsheet should look so far:

	A	B	C	D
1	Credit Card Calculator			
2				
3				
4	APR	Monthly Interest	Starting Balance	Monthly Payment
5	18.00%	1.50%	$7,000.00	$250.00
6				

Figure 16-4   This is how your spreadsheet should look at this point

18 In cells **A8 through D8**, enter the following text, then make the text bold and centered with a line under the cells (as you did starting in step 11), as shown in Figure 16-5.

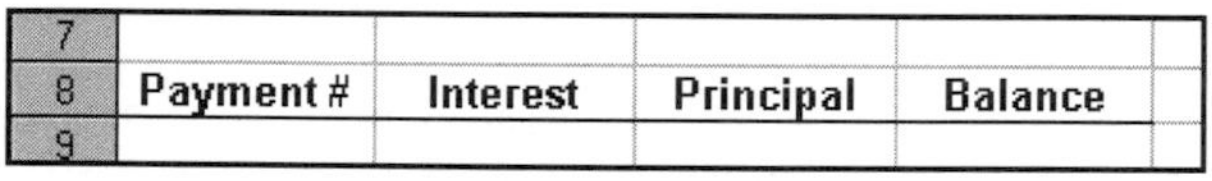

7				
8	Payment #	Interest	Principal	Balance
9				

Figure 16-5   Formatting heading cells

19 In cell **A9**, under Payment #, type 1.

20 In cell **B9**, under Interest, click the currency icon on the object bar and enter the following formula, then press the Tab key:

`=$B$5*$C$5`

This formula multiplies the contents of cell B5 by the contents of cell C5 (multiplying the monthly interest rate by the credit card balance). The dollar signs ($) are absolute cell references, which we go into detail about on page 530.

21 In cell **C9**, under Principal, click the Currency icon and enter the following formula, then press the Tab key:

`=$D$5-B9`

This formula subtracts the amount of interest you're paying that month from your monthly payment, which gives you the amount of principal subtracted from your overall credit card balance.

22 In cell **D9**, under Balance, enter the following formula, then press the Tab key:

`=$C$5-C9`

This subtracts the Principal of the monthly payment from the Starting Balance credit card balance. Your spreadsheet should now look like Figure 16-6.

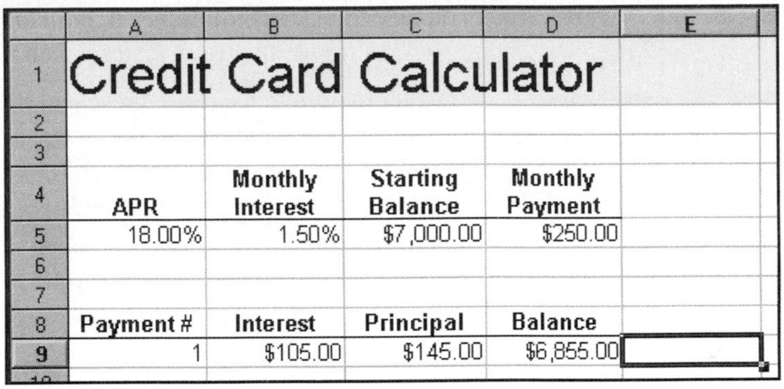

	A	B	C	D	E
1	Credit Card Calculator				
2					
3					
4	APR	Monthly Interest	Starting Balance	Monthly Payment	
5	18.00%	1.50%	$7,000.00	$250.00	
6					
7					
8	Payment #	Interest	Principal	Balance	
9	1	$105.00	$145.00	$6,855.00	

Figure 16-6   This is how your spreadsheet should look at this point

The next steps may seem a little redundant, but they set the stage for the really cool part of the tutorial.

23 In cell **A10**, the Payment # column, type the number 2.

24 Select cells **B10 through D10** and click the Currency icon.

25 In cell **B10**, in the Interest column, enter the following formula, followed by the Tab key:

=D9*$B$5

26 In cell **C10**, in the Principal column, enter the following formula followed by the Tab key:

=$D$5-B10

27 In cell **D10**, in the Balance column, enter the following formula followed by the Tab key:

=D9-C10

Your spreadsheet should now look like Figure 16-7.

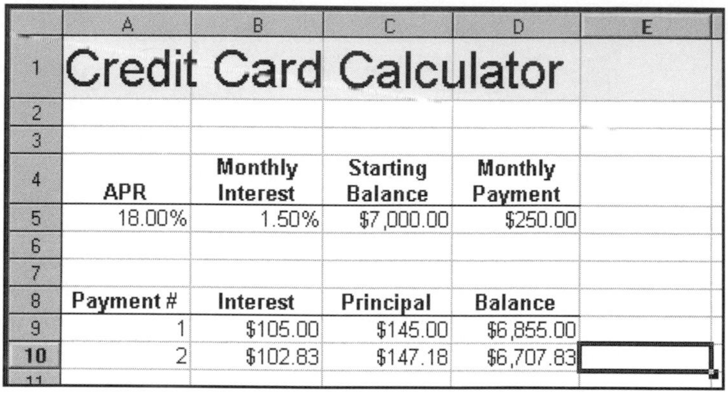

Figure 16-7   This is how your spreadsheet should look at this point

Now comes the fun part. You're going to fill in data about successive payments automatically by clicking and dragging.

28 Select cells **A10 through D10**.

29 On the lower right corner of the selected area, there's a little black square (called the automatic fill handle). Move the mouse pointer on top of that little square. The pointer changes to cross hairs. Click and hold down the mouse button, drag down to row 19, and release the mouse button. The entire selected area fills in with data.

Figure 16-8 illustrates this.

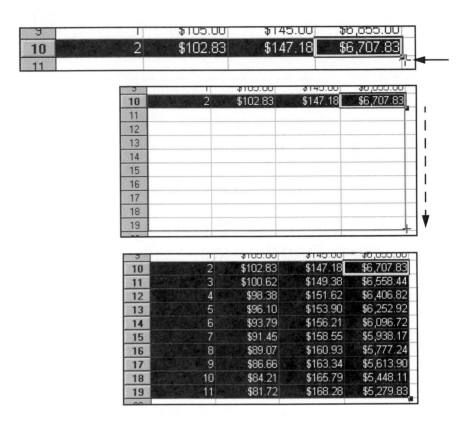

Figure 16-8   Dragging to fill down

If the new information is all exactly the same, press the F9 key to recalculate the spreadsheet.

If you hadn't used absolute and relative cell references in your formulas (discussed on page 530), you would have gotten some crazy results that didn't make sense financially when you filled down.

You can fill down even further the same way by selecting cells A19 through D19 and dragging down. You can drag down to where you can see how many payments it's going to take to pay off the credit card.

Now let's do something depressing and calculate the total amount of interest you're going to pay based on the number of payments you've filled in.

30   In cell **E8**, create a column heading called Total Interest Paid, formatted the same way as the other column headings.

31   In cell **E9**, click the Currency icon and enter the following formula, followed by the Tab key:

```
=SUM(B9:B500)
```

This formula simply adds up all the amounts in the Interest column, from cells B9 to B500 (in case you ever fill down that far), as shown in Figure 16-9.

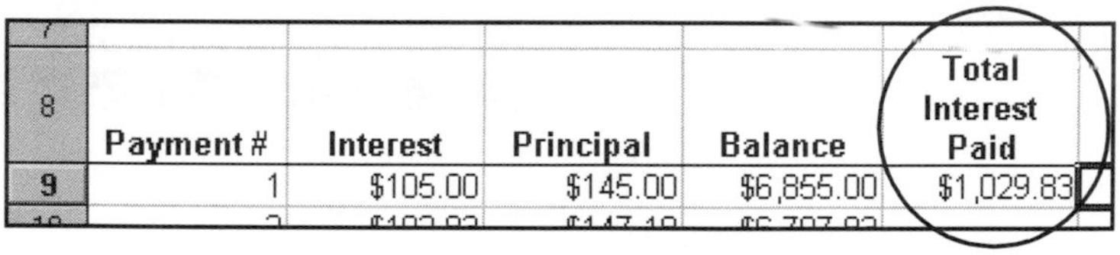

	Payment #	Interest	Principal	Balance	Total Interest Paid
9	1	$105.00	$145.00	$6,855.00	$1,029.83

Figure 16-9   Calculating the total interest paid

32   Get out your scissors and cut up your credit card!

Post-Tutorial Tips

The beauty of spreadsheets is that, if they're set up somewhat correctly (that is, if you set cells up to calculate based on values in other cells, as you did in this exercise), you can change a value in one or two cells to update the values in the entire spreadsheet.

For example, if you change the APR percentage in the tutorial spreadsheet (don't forget to start with a decimal point), your entire spreadsheet updates to show what your payment information would be at a different annual interest rate. You can also see different payment scenarios by entering a different monthly payment amount.

Make sure you don't try to change spreadsheet information by typing inside cells that have formulas in them. That messes up the whole automated nature of the spreadsheet and can throw off lots of other cell amounts. You can tell if a cell has a formula in it by selecting the cell and looking in the formula bar.

Note – You can protect yourself *from* yourself by protecting certain cells you don't want changed, making it so you can't type anything in them. See *Protecting Cells From Modification* on page 572.

Calc Setup Options

StarOffice lets you control hundreds of options—probably more than you will ever need to control. Choose Tools > Options > Spreadsheet to view the Calc options.

We don't go through each window of options one by one, for the following reasons:

• The important settings are covered in procedures throughout the book.

• Many are self-explanatory.

- The default settings for these options are generally well chosen.

However, the options aren't in an obvious place in any of the menu bars or object bars—you need to choose Tools > Options > Spreadsheet—so we've pointed them out here to make sure you're aware of them (see Figure 16-10). It's also helpful to know what types of functions these options do control, so if you want to know that before you start using this program, open the options now to get an idea of their scope before continuing.

The options are default values used for each new Calc spreadsheet.

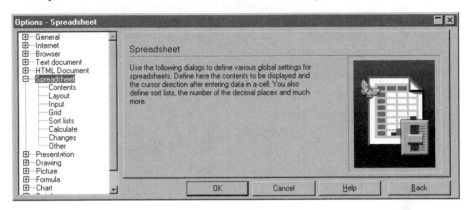

Figure 16-10   Location of Calc setup options

Keyboard Shortcuts

Table 16-1 lists some of the more useful keyboard shortcuts that can save you time while working with Calc spreadsheets.

Table 16-1   The more useful Calc keyboard shortcuts

Pressing this...	Does this
Backspace	Deletes the contents of a cell without bringing up the Delete Contents window.
F5	Opens/Closes Navigator window (whether it's docked or undocked).
F11	Opens/Closes the Stylist window (whether it's docked or undocked).
F9	Recalculates the spreadsheet if it's not set to recalculate automatically (Tools > Cell Contents > AutoCalculate).

Table 16-1   The more useful Calc keyboard shortcuts

Pressing this...	Does this
Home	Moves to the first cell in a row.
End	Moves to the last cell in a row, corresponding to the last column in the spreadsheet that contains data.
Shift+F4	Lets you apply absolute and relative cell references to selected cell address text. For example, if you have the text C4 highlighted in a formula, press Shift+F4 to toggle among different absolute/relative combinations, such as $C$4, C$4, and $C4. See *Relative and Absolute Cell References* on page 530.
Shift+F5	Trace dependents. Arrows point to the cells that depend on the selected cell (refer to it). This is a great spreadsheet troubleshooting tool.
Shift+F6	Trace precedents. Arrows point to the cells that the current cell refers to. This is a great spreadsheet troubleshooting tool.
Ctrl+Page Up	Move to previous sheet.
Ctrl+Page Down	Move to next sheet.
Ctrl+b	Applies/Removes bold formatting in selected text.
Ctrl+i	Applies/Removes italic formatting in selected text.
Ctrl+u	Applies/Removes underlining in selected text.
Ctrl+z	Undo. Reverses the last action made.
Ctrl+a	Selects all of the document.

Creating a New Document

You can create a new Calc document in a number of ways:

- From scratch
- Using a template
- Using an existing Calc document (by using File > Save As)

Creating a Document From Scratch

You can create a new, empty Calc document in a number of ways:

- Start > Spreadsheet
- File > New > Spreadsheet

- From the Click & Go slider in the Explorer window (clicking the Spreadsheet shortcut)

- With a task bar shortcut (see *Adding Shortcuts to the Task Bar* on page 123)

Creating a Calc Document From a Template

You can create new documents from templates. For more information on templates, see *Using Templates* on page 220.

1   Choose File > New > From Template (see Figure 16-11).

2   In the New window, select a template category from the Categories list.

3   Select the spreadsheet template you want from the Templates list.

If you want to preview the template and see a description of it, click the More button and select the Preview option.

4   Click OK. A new Calc document opens with the template formatting and styles.

When you save the document, it saves as a Calc document (not as a template) by default.

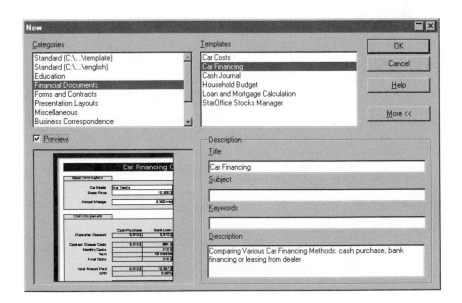

Figure 16-11   Creating a new document from a template

If your template is located in a folder other than one of the StarOffice template folders (Office52\share\template*language**template_folder* or Office52\user\template*template_folder*), you won't be able to select the template in the New window. Either move the template to one of the template folders so you can select it in the New window, or choose File > Open to open the template and create a new document.

Calc Tips

The following sections give valuable tips to help you get the most out of Calc.

Deleting Cell Contents

When you select a cell and press the **Delete** key, Calc brings up the Delete Contents window to let you select specific cell elements, such as text, numbers, formulas, and formatting. This is a tremendously useful feature if you want to delete some elements in a cell but not others.

However, if all you want to do is delete the contents without being prompted, select a cell and press the Backspace key.

Setting Up Sort Lists

Calc makes filling in cell information easy and automatic by using the automatic fill feature (see *Filling to Increment Data* on page 503). The idea is to type one piece of information in a cell, select the cell, and drag the little square in the lower right corner of the cell in any direction to fill in a consecutive list of items.

For example, say you want to track sales in your organization's five biggest cities, and you either want to list those cities in regional order (or you don't want to have to type each one in manually in every spreadsheet you create). Set up a sort list for those cities so that when you enter one city name, you can use automatic fill to enter the names of the remaining cities, as shown in Figure 16-12.

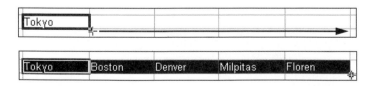

Figure 16-12   A sort list of cities

Adding a Sort List

1   Choose Tools > Options > Spreadsheet > Sort lists.

2   Click the New button.

3   In the Entries area, type the list of items in the order you want them, as shown in Figure 16-13.

Press Enter after each entry. You can also separate entries with a comma. If you use a comma to separate items, don't add a space after each comma.

4   When you're finished entering the list, click the Add button and click OK.

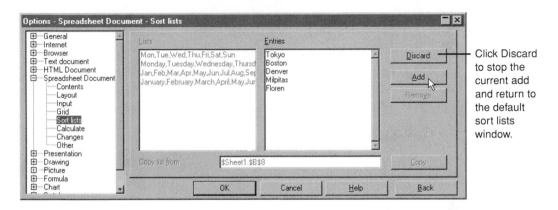

Figure 16-13   Adding a sort list

When you do an automatic fill for the sort list, dragging to the left or up fills in cells with the values that precede the one you entered.

Note – You can also enter a new sort list by selecting a range of cells in Calc, opening the Sort List options window, clicking the Copy button, and clicking OK (see Figure 16-14).

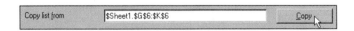

Figure 16-14   Copying a sort list from the spreadsheet

You don't have to set up sort lists for numbering or dates. Calc knows how to handle those already.

Modifying a Sort List

1   Choose Tools > Options > Spreadsheet > Sort lists.

2   In the Lists box, select the list you want to edit. Its contents display in the entries box, as shown in Figure 16-15.

3   Edit the list by changing the text in the Entries list and pressing Enter after each item

4   Click the Modify button.

5   Click OK.

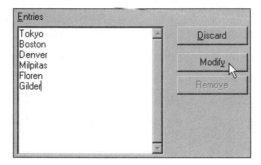

Figure 16-15   Modifying a sort list

Deleting a Sort List

1   Choose Tools > Options > Spreadsheet > Sort lists.

2   In the Lists box, select the list you want to remove.

3   Click the Remove button, click Yes in the confirmation window, and click OK.

Maintaining Sheets

A Calc file can contain multiple spreadsheets (called sheets), each of which has a tab at the bottom of the Calc window. This helps you keep different financial information separate in a single file. For example, you can set up a sheet for income information, a second sheet for expense information, and a third sheet that contains combined information about the first two sheets along with a chart. You switch between sheets by clicking their tabs.

When you start a new spreadsheet document, the file comes with three sheets by default, called Sheet1, Sheet2, and Sheet3. These are just a starting point to get you going.

This section shows you how to add, rename, reorder, and delete sheets, and resize the viewing area of the sheet tabs.

Adding Sheets

1   Select the sheet tab you want to add sheets before or after.

2   Right-click the sheet tab, and choose Insert.

3   In the Insert Sheet window, set the insertion options. Use Figure 16-16 for guidance.

4   Click OK.

If you select only one sheet to insert, you can Name the tab for the new sheet. If you select more than one sheet to insert, Calc creates generic sheet names.

You can insert sheets from an existing Calc file. Select From file, click Browse, and select the file.

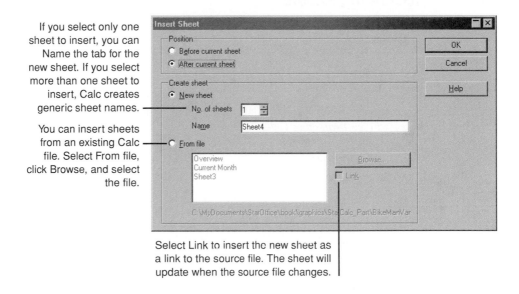

Select Link to insert the new sheet as a link to the source file. The sheet will update when the source file changes.

Figure 16-16   Adding a sheet

Updating Linked Sheets

If you add a sheet in Calc that is a link to a sheet in another spreadsheet file (see previous procedure), you can update the added sheet when the source file containing that sheet is modified. When you open the file containing the link, StarOffice by default prompts you to update links. (You can change this default in Tools > Options > Spreadsheet Document > Other.)

You can also update the link as you're working by choosing Edit > Links, selecting the linked sheet in the Edit Links window, and clicking the Update button. Changes you make to the source file must be saved before changes are reflected in the linked sheet.

Note – If you don't see the Links item in the Edit menu, or if you don't see the linked sheet listed in the Edit Links window, the sheet was inserted as a copy rather than a link. Delete the sheet and re-insert it as a link. (See *Adding Sheets* on page 488.)

Renaming Sheets

1   Select the sheet you want to rename.

2   Right-click the tab, and choose Rename.

3   Type the new name in the Rename Sheet window and click OK.

Reordering Sheets

1   Select the sheet you want to move.

2   Drag the tab to the new location in the row of tabs.

Deleting Sheets

Deleting a sheet deletes all the data on the sheet. You can't delete sheets that have been protected (see *Protecting Cells From Modification* on page 572).

1   Select the sheet you want to delete.

2   Right-click the tab, and choose Delete.

3   Click Yes in the confirmation window.

Resizing and Navigating in the Tab Area

As you add sheets and change sheet names, you may not be able to see all tabs at once. Use the tips in Figure 16-17 to navigate in the tab area of a spreadsheet document.

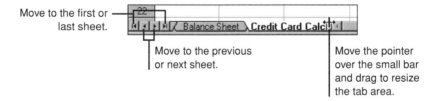

Move to the first or last sheet.

Move to the previous or next sheet.

Move the pointer over the small bar and drag to resize the tab area.

Figure 16-17   Navigating the tab area

Creating Non-Scrolling Regions

If you have long rows or columns of data that extend well beyond the viewable area of the spreadsheet window, scrolling to the areas you want to see means you no longer see the column or row labels associated with the data you're viewing. For example, if you have a spreadsheet that has columns for different types of dollar amounts (interest paid, payment, and balance), and you scroll down to see data beyond the bottom border of the work area, you may not remember which column corresponds to which type of dollar amount because your column headings have scrolled up.

To fix this problem, you can make column or rows non-scrolling (see Figure 16-18).

This entire area is non-scrolling, letting you see Payment #, Interest, Principal, and Balance column headings as you scroll through the remaining data.

This area can scroll.

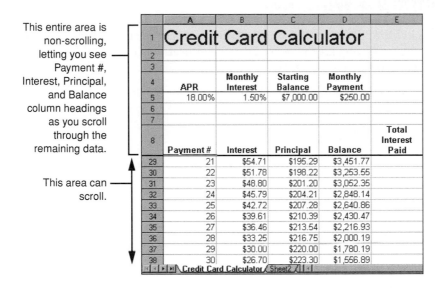

	A	B	C	D	E
1	Credit Card Calculator				
2					
3					
4	APR	Monthly Interest	Starting Balance	Monthly Payment	
5	18.00%	1.50%	$7,000.00	$250.00	
6					
7					
8	Payment #	Interest	Principal	Balance	Total Interest Paid
29	21	$54.71	$195.29	$3,451.77	
30	22	$51.78	$198.22	$3,253.55	
31	23	$48.80	$201.20	$3,052.35	
32	24	$45.79	$204.21	$2,848.14	
33	25	$42.72	$207.28	$2,640.86	
34	26	$39.61	$210.39	$2,430.47	
35	27	$36.46	$213.54	$2,216.93	
36	28	$33.25	$216.75	$2,000.19	
37	29	$30.00	$220.00	$1,780.19	
38	30	$26.70	$223.30	$1,556.89	

Credit Card Calculator / Sheet2

Figure 16-18   Non-scrolling region

Horizontal Non-Scrolling Region

1   Select the row below the row you want to be in the non-scrolling region. All rows above the selection will be non-scrolling.

2   Choose Window > Freeze.

Vertical Non-Scrolling Region

1   Select the column to the right of the column you want to be in the non-scrolling region. All columns to the left of the selection will be non-scrolling.

2   Choose Window > Freeze.

Horizontal and Vertical Non-Scrolling Regions

1   Click the cell that is below the row and to the right of the column you want to make non-scrolling; for example, cell B2.

2   Choose Window > Freeze.

Turning Off Non-Scrolling Regions

Choose Window > Freeze.

Splitting a Window

If your spreadsheet is larger than the boundaries of your screen, and you're constantly scrolling to work with different parts of the spreadsheet, consider splitting it. Splitting lets you view and work with different sections of a spreadsheet simultaneously.

You can split the spreadsheet vertically, horizontally, or into fourths, depending on which cell is selected.

The split command won't work if cell A1 is selected.

Splitting Vertically Select any cell in row 1 (except cell A1) and choose Window > Split.

Splitting Horizontally Select any cell in column A (except cell A1) and choose Window > Split.

Splitting Into Fourths Select any cell in the middle of the spreadsheet and choose Window > Split.

If you want to work with more than one spreadsheet or any combination of documents simultaneously, see *Working With Documents Side by Side* on page 134.

Resizing the Split You can resize the split areas by moving the cursor over the split line until it changes shape, then clicking and dragging the line to the new position.

See Figure 16-19 on page 493.

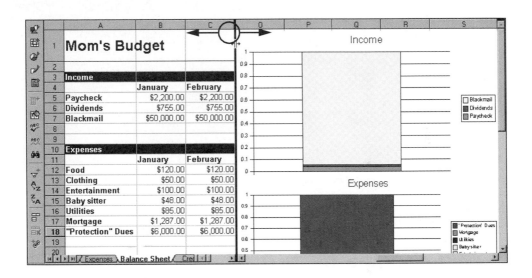

Figure 16-19   Resizing a split area

To unsplit the window, choose Window > Split.

Changing Grid Lines

You can hide or change the color of the spreadsheet's grid lines (cell boundaries). The change you make applies to all spreadsheets you open or create.

1   Choose Tools > Options > Spreadsheet > Layout.

2   Set the grid line options you want, as shown in Figure 16-20.

3   Click OK.

Deselect the
Grid Lines
option to hide
the grid lines,
or change the
grid lines
Color.

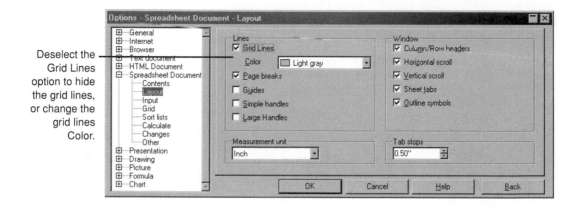

Figure 16-20   Changing grid lines

Changing 1/2 to .5

The StarOffice AutoCorrect feature automatically corrects common typos as you're typing and converts character combinations into special characters.

When you're working with Calc, you may not want certain items replaced as you're typing. For example, if you type .5, StarOffice changes it to the fraction 1/2 by default, which isn't good for spreadsheet entry. To change the way StarOffice handles AutoCorrect:

1   Choose Tools > AutoCorrect.

2   Modify the AutoCorrect options in one of two ways:

•   Select the Replace tab to modify or delete AutoCorrect entries.

•   Select the Options tab to deselect the text replacement settings you don't want to use.

Using Navigator

Navigator is a tool used throughout StarOffice. In Calc, Navigator serves two main purposes:

- Navigator lets you locate and jump to different parts of your document quickly
- Navigator lets you drag and drop hyperlinked references from one part of a document into another part, or from one document to another.

Launching Navigator

Press the F5 key to open and close the Navigator window, or choose Edit > Navigator.

The Navigator window can be floating or docked. (See *Making Windows Anchored or Floating* on page 120.) In this section, Navigator is shown floating.

Navigating and Inserting

The Navigator window displays all the parts of your document: sheets, named areas, inserted objects, and so on. These different parts are displayed in a hierarchical tree view that lets you expand and contract groups of things. You can also customize the way Navigator displays its contents.

Navigator also offers a variety of ways you can jump to different parts of your document.

See Figure 16-21 for guidance.

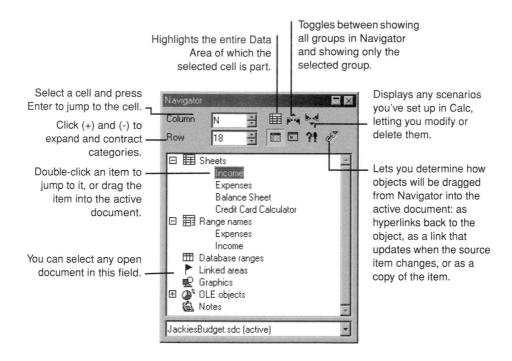

Figure 16-21   Navigator

Working With Non-Calc Spreadsheets

One of StarOffice's greatest strengths is its ability to open documents that were created in other spreadsheet applications—in fact, in a multitude of other applications. In particular, StarOffice is good at opening and converting documents that were created in Microsoft Office. See also *Converting Microsoft Office Documents* on page 148.

Opening and Saving to Other Document Formats

Calc can open spreadsheets that were created in many types of applications. If you want to view the file types StarOffice can convert, choose File > Open. In the Open window, click the File type field and scroll through the list of formats.

To see which kinds of document formats Calc can save to, make sure Calc is active and choose File > Save As. Click the File type field and scroll through the list of formats.

Converting to HTML

You can convert a Calc document to an HTML (Hypertext Markup Language) document for Web delivery. StarOffice tries to simulate in HTML the layout of the original document.

With the Calc document open, choose File > Save As. In the File type field, select HTML (Calc). Name the file and click Save.

Sending a Document as Email

Instead of launching Mail, creating a new mail message, and attaching a Calc file to it, you can send an open Calc file as an Email attachment or as the contents of an Email message.

1   With the document you want to mail open, choose File > Send > Document as Email.

2   In the Send Mail window (see Figure 16-22), select whether you want the file sent as an attachment or as the contents of the Email and click OK.

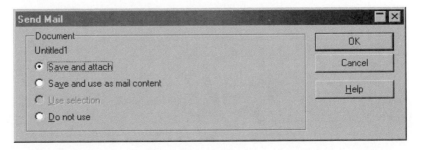

Figure 16-22   Sending a spreadsheet as an Email

If the document is unsaved, StarOffice displays the Save As window. Save the file.

Mail launches with the document either as an attachment or as the contents of the Email message, depending on which option you selected.

chapter

17

chapter

Data Entry and Formatting

Entering Text and Numbers

You may see the title of this section and say, "Duh." Yes, you just use the keyboard for basic text and number entry in a spreadsheet. But there are a few issues and considerations to take into account while entering stuff into cells. Those issues and considerations are presented in the following sections.

Text That Is Wider Than Cells

By default, text you enter into a cell that is too wide for the cell just runs through the next cell(s)—unless you enter data into a cell that the text runs through, as shown in Figure 17-1.

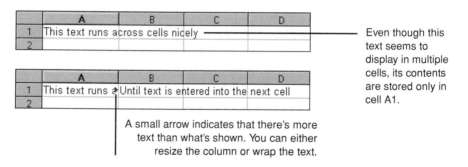

Even though this text seems to display in multiple cells, its contents are stored only in cell A1.

A small arrow indicates that there's more text than what's shown. You can either resize the column or wrap the text.

Figure 17-1   Default behavior of text that is wider than a cell

You can fix text that gets cut off by either resizing the column (see page 506) or by wrapping text inside the cell (next).

Wrapping Text in Cells

1   Select the cell(s) in which you want text to wrap.

2   Right-click the cell and choose Format Cells.

3   In the Cell Attributes window, select the Alignment tab.

4   In the lower right section of the window, select the Line break option.

5   Click OK.

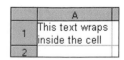

Use the object bar to control the alignment of wrapped text.

Numbers That Are Wider Than Cells

If you enter a number that is longer than the width of the cell (see Figure 17-2), pound characters (###) are displayed instead of the number when you press Enter. This can also happen when decimal places and symbols are added to a number automatically, as in a currency amount, or when you increase font size or apply bold formatting. To fix this, resize the column. (See *Resizing Rows and Columns* on page 506.) If you don't want to resize the column, you can try reducing the font size of the number.

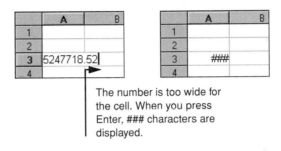

The number is too wide for the cell. When you press Enter, ### characters are displayed.

Figure 17-2   Numbers that are wider than cells

Keeping Text Exactly as You Typed It

Sometimes Calc will change the format of the text or number you enter in a cell. In particular, Calc removes the zeros you enter in front of numbers to the left of a decimal point, and it turns certain words you may enter in all capital letters to lowercase letters. For example, if you

With single quote	Without single quote
APR	Apr
01	1
JUNE	June

type 01 into a cell, Calc turns changes it to be just 1; or if you type in APR (for annual percentage rate), Calc thinks you mean the month April and changes it to Apr.

To make Calc display exactly what you type, begin the entry with a single quote mark, such as '01 or 'APR.

Entering Percentages

When you set cells to display numbers as percentages (by selecting the cells and clicking the % icon in the object bar, Calc multiplies numbers you enter in those cells by 100. So when you enter numbers you want to display as percentages, be sure to start with a decimal point.

For example, if you want a cell to display 9%, enter the number as .09.

By default, Calc adds two decimal places to percentages. So when you enter `.15`, Calc turns the number into `15.00%`. To remove decimal places, select the cells, right-click them, choose Format Cells, and make the change on the Numbers tab. For more information on this and other cell formats, see *Formatting Cells* on page 507.

Editing Cell Contents

You can edit the contents of a cell in a number of ways:

*   Select a cell and edit its content in the formula bar.

*   Double-click a cell and edit its content directly in the cell.

    This is particularly useful when you're pasting text from a text document into a cell, because the paragraphs won't be put into separate cells.

*   Select a cell and press Enter to edit its contents directly in the cell. To set this up, choose Tools > Options > Spreadsheet > Input, select the option next to Press Enter to switch to edit mode, and click OK.

Filling

You can enter data into cells automatically by using Calc's fill feature. There are two different ways to fill, depending on whether you want to fill the exact same data or increment data.

You can fill data in any direction: down, up, left, or right.

Filling the Exact Same Data

Use this procedure to duplicate the contents of a cell down a column or across a row.

1   Click and hold down the left mouse button on the cell whose contents you want to fill.

2   Drag in the desired direction to highlight the cells you want to contain the data.

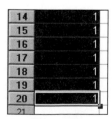

3   Choose Edit > Fill > *direction*, where *direction* is the direction you dragged to select the cells.

You can also fill the exact same data by holding down the Ctrl key and filling with the automatic fill handle (next procedure).

Filling to Increment Data

Use this procedure to automatically increment data as you fill down a column or across a row.

Automatic fill only increments data that Calc recognizes, for example, numbers, dates, and cell references. If Calc doesn't recognize data, automatic fill simply duplicates the data exactly. You can create sort lists that contain lists that Calc will recognize and automatically increment. See *Setting Up Sort Lists* on page 486.

1   Select the cell(s) whose contents you want to fill.

2   Move the mouse pointer on top of the automatic fill handle in the lower right of the selected cell. The mouse pointer changes shape.

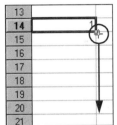 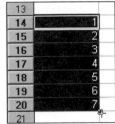

3   Click and hold down the left mouse button on the automatic fill handle, and drag in the desired direction of the fill, selecting all the cells you want to contain data.

When you use automatic fill on cells that contain cell references, you can get strange results if you don't use the correct combination of absolute and relative cell references. For information on this, see *Relative and Absolute Cell References* on page 530.

If you hold down the Ctrl key while you drag the automatic fill handle, the data will stay the same rather than increment.

AutoInputting Text

You can have Calc automatically fill in text as you're entering it. Using the AutoInput feature (Tools > Cell Contents > AutoInput), Calc matches the text you type in a cell against text entered in the same column. For example, if the name *Derek Smalls* is entered in a column, and you type the letter *D* in another cell in that column, Calc automatically fills in the rest of the word for you. So all you'd have to do is type *D* and press Enter to put another *Derek Smalls* in a cell.

However, if the name *Derek Smalls* is in a cell and the name *David St. Hubbins* is in another cell in that column (both start with *D*), Calc waits for the next unique letter before it tries to AutoInput the text.

Using Selection Lists

If you do a lot of repetitive text entry in spreadsheets, and you don't want to use AutoInput (previous section), you can use selection lists to select text you've entered previously.

1   Select the cell in which you want to enter text.

2   Right-click the cell, and choose Selection List.

    A list of all text entered in the column is displayed.

3   Choose the text you want to enter in the cell.

If you don't get a selection list, the column may contain data that's too varied.

Changing Enter Key Direction

By default, when a cell is highlighted and you press Enter in Calc, the cell selection jumps down. You can change the direction from jumping down to jumping right, left, or up.

1   Choose Tools > Options > Spreadsheet > Input.

2   Make sure the Press Enter to move selection option is selected, and change the direction in the drop-down list to the right.

3   Make sure the Press Enter to switch to edit mode option in the same window is deselected.

4   Click OK.

Working With Columns and Rows

This section contains basic shortcuts for selecting cells, and for resizing, selecting, hiding, inserting, and deleting rows and columns.

Selecting Cells

Following are shortcuts for selecting entire rows and columns, an entire spreadsheet, and nonadjacent cells.

Selecting Entire Rows, Columns, and Spreadsheets

You can select entire rows and columns, or the entire spreadsheet (see Figure 17-3) to format, cut, copy, paste, or delete the contents of cells.

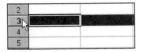

To select an entire row, click the gray box containing the row number.

To select an entire column, click the gray box containing the column letter.

To select the entire spreadsheet, click the empty gray box in the upper left of the spreadsheet.

Figure 17-3   Selecting an entire row, column, and spreadsheet

You can also press Ctrl+A to select all cells in a spreadsheet.

Selecting Non-Adjacent Cells

Calc lets you select cells that aren't right next to each other for formatting or deleting the contents of cells (see Figure 17-4). You can't copy, cut, or paste selected non-adjacent cells.

1   Shift+click the first cells you want to select.

2   Release the Shift key, hold down the Ctrl key, and click the cells you want to select.

   While you're holding down the Ctrl key, you can also hold down the Shift key to select a range of cells.

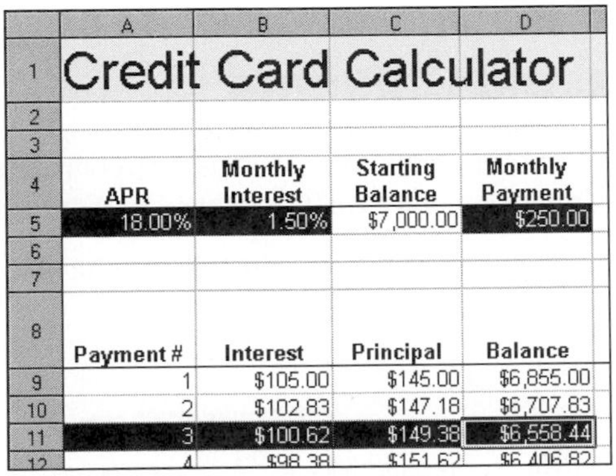

	A	B	C	D
1	Credit Card Calculator			
2				
3				
4	APR	Monthly Interest	Starting Balance	Monthly Payment
5	18.00%	1.50%	$7,000.00	$250.00
6				
7				
8	Payment #	Interest	Principal	Balance
9	1	$105.00	$145.00	$6,855.00
10	2	$102.83	$147.18	$6,707.83
11	3	$100.62	$149.38	$6,558.44
12	4	$98.38	$151.62	$6,406.82

Figure 17-4   Selecting non-adjacent cells

Resizing Rows and Columns

Resizing Rows

1   Move the mouse pointer over the bottom border of the gray box containing the row number. The pointer changes shape.

2   Drag to the new size, or double-click the line below the row to set the row height to fit the row height to the tallest piece of data.

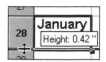

Drag or double-click.

If you drag to a new height, keep an eye on the tooltip while you're dragging. It displays the height of the row.

You can also control the height of rows more precisely by selecting the row(s), right-clicking, choosing Height, and entering an exact width.

Resizing Columns

1   Move the mouse pointer over the right border of the gray box containing the column letter. The pointer changes shape.

2   Drag to the new size, or double-click the line to the right of the column to set the column to fit the widest piece of data.

Drag or double-click.

If you drag to a new width, keep an eye on the tooltip while you're dragging. It displays the width of the column.

You can control the widths of columns more precisely by selecting the column(s), right-clicking, choosing Column Width, and entering an exact width. You can also resize multiple columns at the same time.

Hiding Rows and Columns

One of the main reasons to hide rows or columns is if they contain information that is used to aid in calculations, but that you don't want to display in the spreadsheet.

As an alternative to hiding rows and columns, consider putting different types of data on separate sheets. See *Break It Up* on page 549.

Hidden columns and rows don't print.

1   Select the entire row or column you want to hide. (See *Selecting Entire Rows, Columns, and Spreadsheets* on page 505.)

2   Right-click the gray box of the selected row or column and choose Hide.

Showing Hidden Rows and Columns

1   Select the entire rows or columns on both sides of the hidden row(s) or column(s).

2   Right-click the gray box of the selected row or column and choose Show.

Inserting and Deleting Rows and Columns

Inserting Rows and Columns

When you insert columns or rows, Calc automatically adjusts all cell references in the spreadsheet so that your calculations don't get goofed up.

1   Select an entire row or column. (See *Selecting Entire Rows, Columns, and Spreadsheets* on page 505.)

    Rows are inserted above the selected row; columns are inserted to the left of the selected column.

2   Right-click the gray box of the selected row or column and choose Insert Rows or Insert Columns, depending on which is selected.

You can insert multiple rows or columns. The number of rows or columns inserted is exactly the number you selected.

Deleting Rows and Columns

When you delete columns or rows, Calc automatically adjusts all cell references in the spreadsheet so that your calculations don't get goofed up. However, any information contained in the deleted rows or columns is also deleted.

1   Select the entire rows or columns you want to delete. (See *Selecting Entire Rows, Columns, and Spreadsheets* on page 505.)

2   Right-click the gray box of the selected row(s) or column(s) and choose Delete Rows or Delete Columns, depending on which are selected.

Formatting Cells

This section provides information for basic cell formatting techniques in Calc you perform manually by selecting cells and applying different attributes to them. Cell formats apply to cells and to the data contained within them.

If you work with spreadsheets a lot, and you reuse a lot of common elements and formatting such as headings, totals, borders, colors, and so on, we highly recommend using styles. See *Power Formatting With Styles and Templates* on page 515.

For simple, quick-and-dirty cell formatting such as changing font and font size, applying bold, italic, and underline, applying vertical and horizontal text alignment, applying background colors and borders to cells, and making cells display currency or percentage formats, use the object bar. For more advanced character formatting options, see *Using the Cell Attributes Window* on page 511.

Protected cells cannot be formatted. Format menu options are not available for cells that are protected. For more information, see *Protecting Cells From Modification* on page 572.

Conditional Formatting

Because conditional formatting is closely related to cell contents that change as a result of formulas, it is covered in the next chapter. See *Conditional Formatting* on page 538.

Quick Cell Formatting

Using the object bar for cell formatting is fairly straightforward. Following are a few quick cell formatting tricks you might not be aware of.

Quick Number Formats

You can apply basic currency and percentage formats to cells by selecting the cells and clicking either the Currency or Percent icons on the object bar. You can also remove currency or percent formatting by selecting the cells you want and clicking the Standard icon in the object bar.

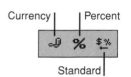

Quick Decimal Control

You can add decimals places to and remove them from selected cells by clicking the Add Decimal Place or Delete Decimal Place icons on the object bar.

Removing decimal places means that calculated or manually entered amounts that have decimals are rounded to the nearest decimal place. For example, if a cell is set to show a currency amount with no decimal places, and you enter the number 15.75, Calc displays $16.

Changing the Default Number of Decimal Places

By default, Calc includes two decimal places in number formats. You can change the default number of decimal places. Removing decimal places means that calculated or manually entered amounts that have decimals are rounded to the nearest decimal place. For example, if a cell is set to show a currency amount with no decimal places, and you enter the number 15.75, Calc displays $16.

1   Choose Tools > Options > Spreadsheet > Calculate.

2   Change the number in the Decimal places field and click OK.

Quick Font and Cell Background Color

You can change font and background colors from the object bar for selected cells.

1   Select the cells whose font or background color you want to change.

2   Click the Font Color or Background Color icons on the object bar, shown in Figure 17-5.

3   Select the color you want.

The colors are from the standard StarOffice color palette.

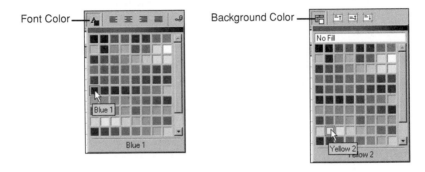

Figure 17-5   Setting font and cell background colors

Quick Cell Borders

Select the cells you want to apply a border to, click the Borders icon on the object bar, and select the type of border you want to apply.

For different types of lines, use the Borders tab in the Cell Attributes window. See *Using the Cell Attributes Window* on page 511.

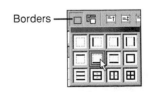

Quick Vertical Alignment

If row heights are larger than the height of the data inside the row cells, you can change the vertical alignment of the cell data, as shown in Figure 17-6. Select the cells you want to vertically align and click one of the Align icons on the object bar.

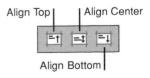

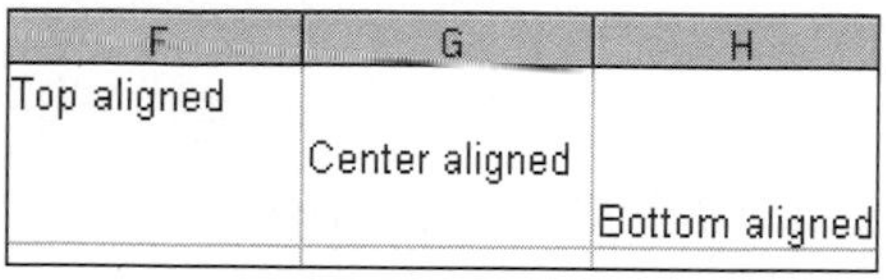

Figure 17-6 Different vertical alignments

Hiding Zero Values

You can show only relevant spreadsheet data by hiding cell values that are zero.

1   Choose Tools > Options > Spreadsheet > Contents.

2   Deselect the Zero Values option and click OK.

Merging Cells

You can select multiple cells and make them, in appearance, as one cell. This is particularly useful, for example, when you want to apply background formatting to text that spans multiple cells. When the multiple cells are merged, you only have to set the background color for one cell. If you don't merge the cells, you'd have to set the background color for each cell the text spans.

1   Select the cells you want to merge.

2   Choose Format > Merge Cells > Define.

If more than one of the cells contains data, a dialog box asks you how you want to handle the data, as shown in Figure 17-7.

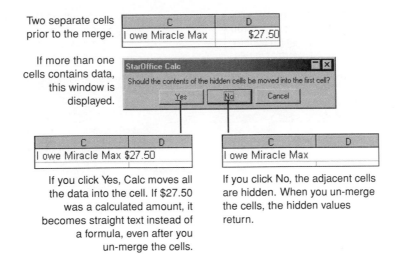

Figure 17-7   Merging cells

To un-merge cells, select the merged cell and choose Format > Merge Cells > Remove.

Instead of merging cells that contain text and numbers, which removes any formulas that generated the numbers (as shown in Figure 17-7), you can combine those cells in a different part of the spreadsheet through concatenation. Concatenation leaves the original data, including formulas, intact. See *Concatenating Cells* on page 541.

Using the Cell Attributes Window

This section describes the more advanced cell formatting options of the Cell Attributes window. To access the Cell Attributes window, select the cells you want to format, right-click a selected cell, and choose Format Cells. You can also choose Format > Cells in the menu bar.

Figure 17-8 through Figure 17-13 describe paragraph formatting options on each of the tabs in the Paragraph window.

When you select the
Currency category, you can
choose which country
currency format to use.

Set values for numbers that
can use decimals, leading
zeros, negative values, or
thousands separators,

When you select
a data type, you
can choose
different Format
options.

You can change
the language for
category types
that use text
such as month
names.

You can create
your own number
formats by
entering a
Format code,
clicking the
Comment icon to
name it, and
clicking the
check mark icon
to add it. See
online help for
more
information.

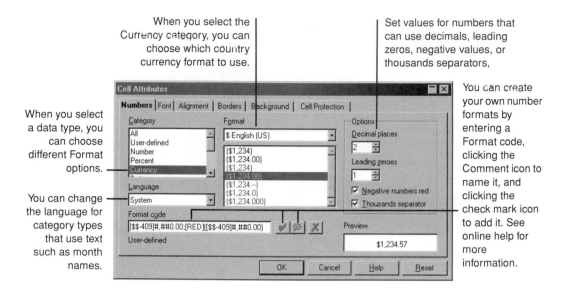

Figure 17-8   Cell Attributes window, Numbers tab

Setting the font
format is
straightforward.
To view fonts in
the font list as
they really look,
choose Tools >
Options >
General > View,
and select the
Preview in font
lists option.

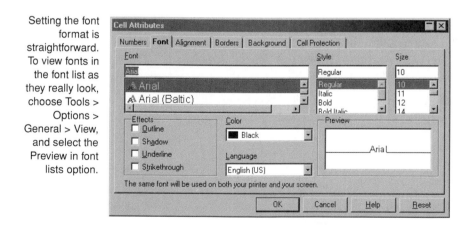

Figure 17-9   Cell Attributes window, Font tab

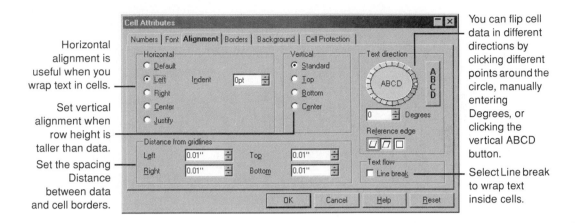

Horizontal alignment is useful when you wrap text in cells.

Set vertical alignment when row height is taller than data.

Set the spacing Distance between data and cell borders.

You can flip cell data in different directions by clicking different points around the circle, manually entering Degrees, or clicking the vertical ABCD button.

Select Line break to wrap text inside cells.

Figure 17-10   Cell Attributes window, Alignment tab

Click one of the Presets boxes to apply that border style. Click the empty first box to clear all line (not shadow) settings.

Select a Line Style for the border.

Click a Shadow style Position box to apply that shadow angle to the line. Click the first box to clear shadow settings.

The gray boxes in the Frame area represent the selected cells. You can add or remove borders relative to the cells by clicking above, below, or to either side of the gray boxes.

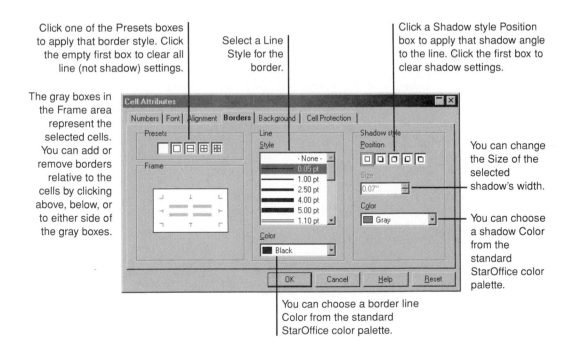

You can change the Size of the selected shadow's width.

You can choose a shadow Color from the standard StarOffice color palette.

You can choose a border line Color from the standard StarOffice color palette.

Figure 17-11   Cell Attributes window, Borders tab

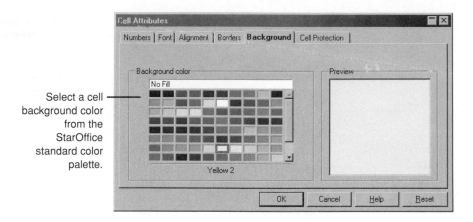

Select a cell background color from the StarOffice standard color palette.

Figure 17-12   Cell Attributes window, Background tab

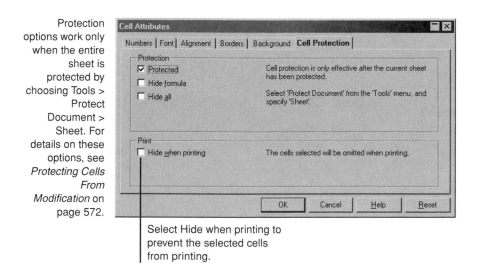

Protection options work only when the entire sheet is protected by choosing Tools > Protect Document > Sheet. For details on these options, see *Protecting Cells From Modification* on page 572.

Select Hide when printing to prevent the selected cells from printing.

Figure 17-13   Cell Attributes window, Cell Protection tab

Power Formatting With Styles and Templates

In the previous sections we talked about formatting cells manually, which is how most people format: selecting cells and either clicking quick-formatting tools on the object bar and ruler or choosing Format > Cells to set specific formatting options.

There are legitimate reasons to use only manual formatting (such as quick formatting of a short spreadsheet whose styles you don't plan to reuse). However, to get the most out of Calc and to work more quickly with more consistency, use styles and templates.

There are two types of styles in Calc: Cell Styles, which affect cells and their contents, and Page Styles, which affect pagination and print output.

Why You Should Use Styles

Using styles in Calc is a no-brainer, especially if you work with spreadsheets a lot.

Following are the reasons why you should use styles. Any one of these reasons alone justifies using them.

Instant Formatting With a double-click you can transform a plain cell into one with a different font, font size, font color, indentation, spacing, alignment, and background color. All cells that are given that style are identical.

Automation When you modify a style, all cells with that style are updated automatically. Automation is good! It doesn't mean "cookie-cutter"; it means you work more quickly, efficiently, and consistently.

Maintaining Consistency Using styles ensures your spreadsheets will maintain a consistent style.

Conditional Formatting You can set a cell to take on specific cell formats automatically when the contents of the cell reach a certain state, or condition (see *Conditional Formatting* on page 538).

Using the Stylist

If you use styles in Calc, the Stylist should be your closest companion. To show it (and hide it), press the F11 key. By default it is displayed as a floating window, but we recommend docking it to an edge of the Calc work area (see *Making Windows Anchored or Floating* on page 120). When you dock it, it stays docked when you press the F11 key to show it.

Styles apply only to the spreadsheet in which you create them. To make styles in one document available to other documents, see *Loading Individual Styles* on page 222.

The Stylist, shown in Figure 17-14, is the control center for viewing, applying, adding, modifying, and deleting styles. The following picture and table describes the elements of the Stylist.

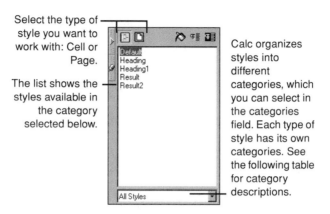

Select the type of style you want to work with: Cell or Page.

The list shows the styles available in the category selected below.

Calc organizes styles into different categories, which you can select in the categories field. Each type of style has its own categories. See the following table for category descriptions.

Figure 17-14   The Stylist

Table 17-1 describes style categories found in the drop-down list at the bottom of the Stylist.

Table 17-1   Calc Stylist categories

Category	Description
All	Shows all defined styles for each style type.
Applied Styles	Shows all the styles you've used in your spreadsheet so far.
Custom Styles	Shows the styles you've created beyond the default styles provided by Calc. The styles you create remain in this category even if you assign them to a different category.
Hierarchical	Displays styles in a hierarchical tree view. If a style has a plus sign next to it (+), click the plus sign to view the styles that were created based on that style.

The Style Catalog You can also create, modify, and delete styles using the Style Catalog (Format > Style Catalog).

Tips for Using Styles

With the Stylist docked, make sure you have tooltips turned on (Help > Tips) to help you select the style type you want. When the mouse pointer hovers over a style type icon, its name is displayed. (If the Stylist is a floating window, the name of the selected style category is displayed in the window's title bar.)

You don't have to have all your styles perfect before you start using them. You'll want to make adjustments to them as you work. The great thing about styles is that you can change them when you want, and all of the cells and pages that use them are updated automatically.

Cell Styles

Cell styles control all elements included in cell formatting.

This section describes how to create cell styles. For information on applying styles, see page 518; for modifying styles, see page 518; for deleting styles, see page 518.

Creating a Cell Style

Creating a cell style is fairly easy. In fact, if you know how to format text manually (see *Formatting Cells* on page 507), you know 90 percent of creating a text style.

1   In the Stylist, click the Cell Styles icon.

2   Select the category in which you want to put the new style.

3   Right-click in the Stylist and select New. The Cell Style window is displayed.

    If you want to create a new style based on an existing style, select the style you want to base it on before you right-click.

4   Set the options you want for the cell style.

5   Click OK.

Page Styles

Page styles control such elements as margins, borders, background, headers, footers, and spreadsheet printing options.

Creating a Page Style

This procedure shows you how to create a page style. Because page styles in Calc affect printing, the Calc Page Style options are described in different procedures throughout 22, *Printing in StarOffice Calc*, on page 597.

1   In the Stylist, click the Page Styles icon.

2   Select the category in which you want to put the new style.

3   Right-click in the Stylist and select New. The Page Style window is displayed.

4   Set the options you want for the page, and click OK.

If you need help setting Page, Borders, and Background options, see the Page Styles section in Writer on page 211.

Applying Styles

1   Select the cell(s) or page to which you want to apply a style.

2   In the Stylist, select the type of style you want to apply (cell or page), select a category, and double-click the name of the style you want to use.

To return to a generic style, double-click the Default style.

Modifying Styles

1   In the Stylist, select the style type containing the style want to modify.

2   Select the category the style belongs to.

3   Right-click the style and select Modify.

4   Change settings for the style.

5   Click OK.

6   If a style doesn't update automatically in the document, select the name of the style in the Stylist and click the Update Style icon at the top of the Stylist.

Deleting Styles

You can't delete default StarOffice styles. You can delete only custom, user-defined styles.

Before you delete a style, select it in the Stylist, right-click it, select Modify, and select the Organizer tab. Look at style selected in the Based on field (if applicable). When you delete the style, if it was used in the spreadsheet, the parts of the spreadsheet with that style become the style shown in the Based on field.

1   In the Stylist, select the style you want to delete.

2   Right-click it, and select Delete.

3   Click Yes in the confirmation window.

Templates

Calc uses the same template principles as other StarOffice applications. For a full description of templates and procedures for previewing, creating, maintaining, and applying templates to documents, see the Writer section, *Using Templates* on page 220.

The only sub-section that doesn't apply to Calc is *Loading All Styles* on page 221.

Themes

Calc also comes with a predefined set of themes you can apply to your spreadsheets. Themes are like templates that contain only predefined styles.

You can't add themes to Calc, and you can't modify them. You can, however, modify their styles after you apply them to your spreadsheets.

1   Click the Choose Themes icon on the toolbar.

2   In the Theme Selection window, select the theme you want to apply to the spreadsheet.

3   Click OK.

To remove the effects of a theme, click the Choose Themes icon in the toolbar and select the Standard theme.

Calculating and Manipulating Data

About Spreadsheet Calculations

Spreadsheet cells seem simple enough. You just type stuff in a little box, format it, and maybe even enter small formulas that add up numbers in a column. But when you understand what's possible inside of a single cell, a blank spreadsheet looks less like a blank white space with a bunch of lines and more like complex organism waiting to take shape.

A single cell, which can contain a large formula for making a complex calculation, can also be referenced by other cells, letting you nest formulas within formulas. Spreadsheets can get tricky, but they can also be fun to use. If you understand the basics of how to perform calculations in Calc, you can go a long way in creating and troubleshooting spreadsheets.

Formula Basics

This section describes the basic elements used in formulas and the rules Calc uses to calculate formulas.

Basic Operators

Table 18-1 shows the operators (symbols that enable calculations and other operations) you'll use frequently in formulas.

=   The equals sign is the most important symbol in formulas. All formulas must begin with it. Without it, a formula is not a formula, but a text string.

Table 18-1   Basic operators you'll use in formulas

Operator	Description	Example
=	Equals sign. All formulas must begin with this.	=2+2
^	Exponent. Raises the number to the left of the operator to the power of the number on the right.	=10^2 (same as 10^2)
*	Multiply	=5*5
/	Divide	=24/6
+	Add	=B5+12
-	Subtract	=C1-E17
<	Less than	=If(A4<45;"Buy more Sun stock";"Sell")
>	Greater than	=If(A5>45;"Sell";"Buy more Sun stock")

Table 18-1   Basic operators you'll use in formulas

Operator	Description	Example
<=	Less than or equal to	=If(F2<=.05;"Refinance";"Don't refinance")
>=	Greater than or equal to	=If(F3>=.24;"Call to lower interest rate";"Grin and bear it")
<>	Not equal to	=If(D3<>D4;"Debits do not equal credits";"Your books balance")
:	Range of cells. Includes all cells from the cell to the left of the colon to the cell to the right of the colon.	=sum(A1:A25) (Adds up all cells from A1 to A25)
;	Non-consecutive cells and separating formula parts. Let's you include non-consecutive cells in a calculation.	=sum(A1;A7;A25) (Adds up cells A1, A7, and A25) See also the IF() formulas above. Semi-colons are used where commas are used in other spreadsheet applications.
!	Intersection	=sum(A1:B3!B2:C7) (Calculates the sum of all cells in the intersection. In this example, the result is the sum of cells B2 and B3)

Algebra 'R' Us

What's the answer to the following math problem?

=5+10*2-14/2+4

If you start the problem left-to-right, the answer is 12. Calc also calculates left-to-right, but it also follows algebraic ordering rules for the order it calculates: it multiplies and divides first, then adds and subtracts. With that in mind, let's simplify the problem by solving the multiplication and division parts first:

=5+20-7+4

Then handle the addition and subtraction, working left-to-right, and the answer is 22.

Exponents If you include exponents in your formulas (for example, 10^2, which is written as 10^2 in Calc), those are calculated before multiplication and division.

Using Parentheses to Control Calculation Order

You can exercise more control over the calculation order by using parentheses. This is also an algebra thing. Calc solves formulas within parentheses first (using algebraic ordering within the parentheses) before it solves the rest of the formula.

Using the previous formula as an example, Table 18-2 shows how using parentheses in different ways can produce different solutions.

Table 18-2   Using parentheses to control calculation order

Formula	Solution
=(5+10)*2-(14/2+4)	19
=5+(10*2-14)/2+4	12
=(5+10*2)-14/(2+4)	22.67
=5+10*(2-14/2)+4	-41

Inevitably as you use parentheses, you'll need to control calculation order further by nesting parentheses within parentheses. For example:

=(9*(10-7))/((8*3)-(7*3))+10^2

Calc solves formulas the inner parentheses first. The solution to this formula is 109 (10^2 is the same as 10^2, or 100).

Since most of your formulas will contain cell references (rather, *should* contain cell references), creating a calculation order with parentheses can get tricky, because you're constantly trying to see which cell references represent which numbers. For example, =(A7*(SUM(B5:B7)))/D2. There are a couple of tricks you can use to help visually map cell references to the numbers they reference:

- Even if you're not finished with your formula, press Enter to save the formula in its current state. Most likely you will get an error message in the cell, which is okay. Double-click the cell. Calc color codes the cell references in the formula and highlights the referenced cells in with corresponding colors. This helps you edit the formula.

- Use the trace precedents and dependents feature to have arrows point back and forth from the cell containing the formula to all the referenced cells. See *Tracing Precedents, Dependents, and Errors* on page 550.

Entering Formulas

The previous section, Formula Basics, provides the basic information necessary for entering formulas. This section expands on that by highlighting tools that help automate formula entry, going into more detail on using cell references, and showing a couple of power user formula procedures.

Functions

Calc makes the formula entry process easier and more powerful by providing a library of functions. Functions are keywords like SUM, SQRT, and IF that let you perform specific tasks.

For example, the SUM function lets you add an entire range of cells. Without the SUM function you'd have to enter =B1+B2+B3+B4+B5 to add up the contents of those cells. With the SUM function, you can write the same formula as =SUM(B1:B5). Because functions are so useful, powerful, and essential in creating spreadsheets, Calc comes with a veritable boatload of them; functions that do everything from figuring sums and square roots, to letting you set up conditions within a cell that can make the cell display different values depending on whether the condition is true or false. (That's the IF function). There's even a function to help you figure out monthly payments on a loan (the PMT function).

The following sections highlight useful functions and tools.

Quick Sum

Calc lets you add up rows or columns with a mouse click.

1   Click the cell that you want to contain the sum of the row or column.

2   Click the Sum icon on the function bar.

   Calc automatically enters the sum function and the appropriate range of cells in the row or column, as shown in Figure 18-1.

3   Make sure the range of cells is correct, change the range if necessary, and press Enter.

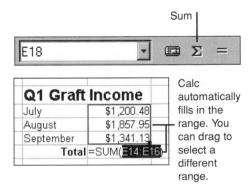

Figure 18-1   Doing a quick sum

Changing the Range Selection   You don't have to be directly in the row or column you want to add up. You can click any cell, click the Sum icon, and change the range of cells simply by dragging through the range of cells you want to include. You can also select non-adjacent cells and cell ranges by holding down the Ctrl key while you select.

Inserting Subtotals Automatically

If you have a column of numbers you plan on adding up, Calc has a tool to let you insert automatic subtotals after selected rows to generate a running balance. Figure 18-2 shows what subtotals look like.

This feature inserts rows for the generated subtotals. So if you have links set up to cells prior to inserting subtotals, references to those cells could be thrown off after you insert subtotals. For example, if a formula points to cell $A$5, the data in that cell could get bumped to a different cell address by the insertion of subtotals, making the formula point to the wrong cell. (See *Using Cell References* on page 529 for information that can help you avoid this problem.)

The moral of the story is that if you want to insert subtotals, be aware of the potential impacts of inserting extra rows.

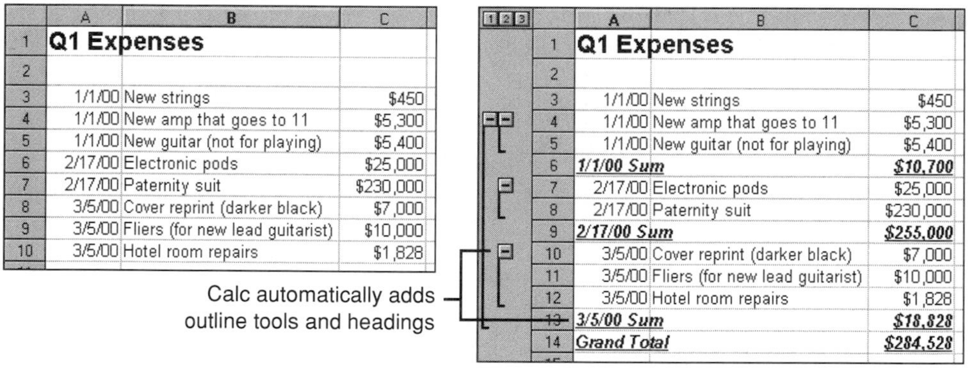

Calc automatically adds
outline tools and headings

Figure 18-2   Before and after subtotals are inserted

1   Select the area of data for which you want to create subtotals.

2   Choose Data > Subtotals.

3   In the Subtotals window, set the options you want. Use Figure 18-3 for guidance.

In the Subtotals window, you can add more layers to the data groupings (creating groups within groups) by entering the appropriate settings in the 2nd Group and 3rd Group tabs, as well. In the example in Figure 18-2, the data is grouped by date and the dollar amounts are subtotaled, as the settings in Figure 18-3 indicate.

4   Click OK.

Setting up subtotal options is a logical process. For example, you wouldn't want to subtotal a column containing names. The Subtotals tool will let you set any options you want. Just be aware that if the results look strange, you may have to go back and think through the setup process.

When you create subtotals, Calc also adds outline functionality, letting you expand and contract groups, as shown in Figure 18-2.

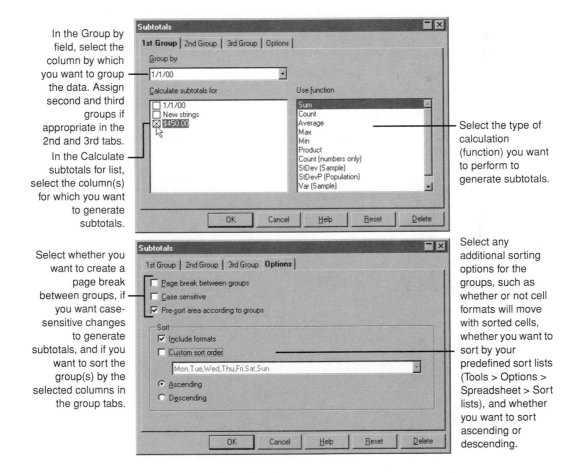

In the Group by field, select the column by which you want to group the data. Assign second and third groups if appropriate in the 2nd and 3rd tabs.

In the Calculate subtotals for list, select the column(s) for which you want to generate subtotals.

Select the type of calculation (function) you want to perform to generate subtotals.

Select whether you want to create a page break between groups, if you want case-sensitive changes to generate subtotals, and if you want to sort the group(s) by the selected columns in the group tabs.

Select any additional sorting options for the groups, such as whether or not cell formats will move with sorted cells, whether you want to sort by your predefined sort lists (Tools > Options > Spreadsheet > Sort lists), and whether you want to sort ascending or descending.

Figure 18-3   Setting subtotal options

Function AutoPilot

Calc has a wizard called the Function AutoPilot that helps you build formulas. To use the Function AutoPilot:

1   Click the cell that you want to contain the function.

Function AutoPilot

2   Click the Function AutoPilot icon on the function bar.

3   In the Function AutoPilot window, select the function you want, and click the Next button.

4   In the second Function AutoPilot window, build the formula. Use Figure 18-5 for guidance.

5   When you're finished building the formula, click OK.

You can view all available functions or view them by category.

Select the function you want to build. A description of the selected function is displayed in the open area to the right of the list.

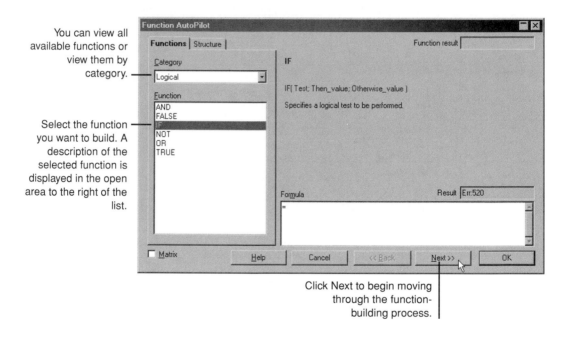

Click Next to begin moving through the function-building process.

Figure 18-4   Using the Function AutoPilot to select functions

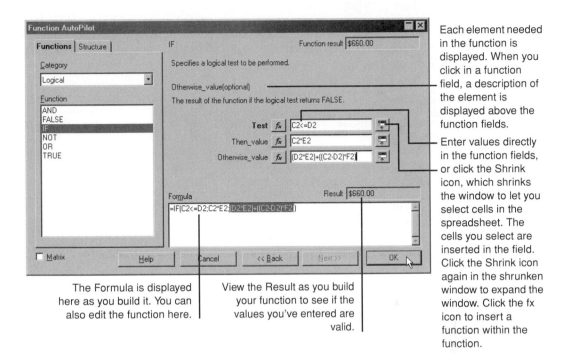

Each element needed in the function is displayed. When you click in a function field, a description of the element is displayed above the function fields.

Enter values directly in the function fields, or click the Shrink icon, which shrinks the window to let you select cells in the spreadsheet. The cells you select are inserted in the field. Click the Shrink icon again in the shrunken window to expand the window. Click the fx icon to insert a function within the function.

The Formula is displayed here as you build it. You can also edit the function here.

View the Result as you build your function to see if the values you've entered are valid.

Figure 18-5   Using the Function AutoPilot to build functions

Using Cell References

Cell references are cell addresses, such as A1, B4, and C5, entered into formulas. Cell references are what make spreadsheets so flexible, because as the values within cells change, the cell references stay the same: cell B4 is cell B4, whether the value inside it is 2 or $(5*(4^3))/7$.

When you build formulas with cell references, the formulas not only stay smaller and more manageable, but they also stay the same even when the contents of cells change.

Following are tips for using cell references.

Click, Don't Type

You don't have to type cell references manually into a formula. As you're building a formula, you can click cells and cell ranges in a spreadsheet to enter those cells and ranges as cell references, as shown in Figure 18-6.

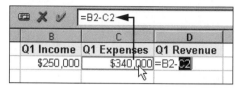

As you build the formula in cell D2, you can click cells B2 and C2 to enter those cell references in the formula. You can also drag through a range of cells. For example, if you dragged through cells B2 and C2, the cell reference entry would be B2:C2.

Figure 18-6   Clicking cells to include them as cell references in a formula

Relative and Absolute Cell References

Figure 18-7 shows a quick look at the physical makeup of relative and absolute cell references before we begin the discussion of them.

A1	$A$1	$A1
Relative reference	Absolute reference to the column and row	Absolute reference to the column and relative reference to the row.

Figure 18-7   Relative and absolute cell references

Relative Cell References   When you select and cut or copy a group of cells that have a calculated value, then paste the cells into a new location, Calc changes the cell references in the formulas so that the calculated values remain intact.

This is possible because the cell references in the formulas are **relative** to the rest of the cells. No matter where the group of cells moves, they keep the same relation to the other cells, as Figure 18-8 illustrates.

To see how relative cell references differ in looks from absolute cell references, see the section on absolute cell references, next.

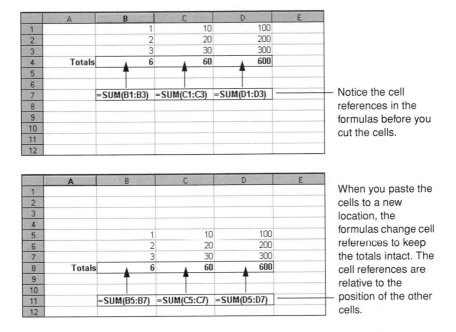

Notice the cell references in the formulas before you cut the cells.

When you paste the cells to a new location, the formulas change cell references to keep the totals intact. The cell references are relative to the position of the other cells.

Figure 18-8   Relative cell references

Absolute Cell References   There may be times when using relative cell references doesn't work well; for example, when you're referencing cells whose locations will never change. These cells have an **absolute** position.

Absolute cell references come mainly into play when you're using Calc's automatic fill feature (see *Filling to Increment Data* on page 503), which increments values and cell references as you fill.

Sometimes you may not want cell references to increment. Using the Credit Card Calculator in the *Guided Tour* on page 475, there is a row of cells containing values that need to be referenced at all times, whose locations will never change, as shown in Figure 18-9.

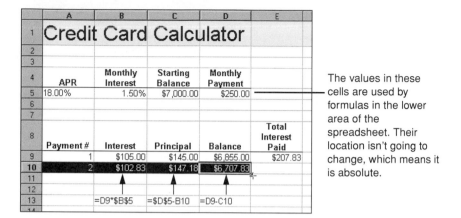

The values in these cells are used by formulas in the lower area of the spreadsheet. Their location isn't going to change, which means it is absolute.

Figure 18-9   Using absolute cell references

To set up references to cells that aren't going to change locations, put a dollar sign in front of the column letter and row number. For example:

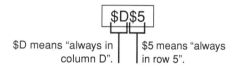

$D means "always in column D". $5 means "always in row 5".

In Figure 18-9, if you didn't use absolute cell references in the formulas in row 10, and you tried to do an automatic fill, the references to the cells in row 5 would increment from, for example, D5 to D6, from D6 to D7, and so on, throwing off your calculations. When you enter the absolute cell reference to $D$5, the cell reference stays pointed at cell D5 even when you use automatic fill.

You don't have to put a dollar sign in from of the column *and* the row. You can use different combinations of absolute/relative cell references, depending on how you're going to use automatic fill. As a general rule:

- If you're going use automatic fill to fill across rows (left and right), put a dollar sign before column letters.

- If you're going to use automatic fill up and down in columns, put the dollar sign in front of row numbers.

- If you're referencing cells that will never change location, put a dollar sign in front of the column letter and row number.

Note – Calc has a keyboard shortcut for setting absolute cell references. In a formula, when you highlight a cell reference, press Shift+F4 repeatedly to set the absolute cell reference combination you want, as shown in Figure 18-10.

The absolute cell reference combination
changes each time you press Shift+F4.

Figure 18-10   Using Shift+F4 to set absolute cell references

Updating Calculations

As you change values and formulas in your spreadsheet, you want the contents of the entire spreadsheet to update accordingly. You can set up Calc to update the spreadsheet automatically as you make each change, or you can update the spreadsheet manually.

One reason you might want to update a spreadsheet manually is if it's large and has a lot of linked elements, like charts and linked content from other spreadsheets. If it takes a second or two for the linked elements to update each time you make a change in the spreadsheet, that can get frustrating. Manually updating the spreadsheet lets you make all your changes and then update all at once.

Updating Automatically

1   Update links to data in other sheets or Calc files (if applicable). See *Updating Linked Sheets* on page 489.

2   Choose Tools > Cell Contents.

3   If AutoCalculate doesn't have a check mark next to it, choose AutoCalculate. (A check mark means it's activated.)

Updating Manually (F9)

1   Update links to data in other sheets or Calc files (if applicable). See *Updating Linked Sheets* on page 489.

2   Choose Tools > Cell Contents.

3   If AutoCalculate has a check mark next to it, choose AutoCalculate to remove the check mark.

4   When you want to update the spreadsheet, press the F9 key.

Manipulating Data

Following are some of the more useful techniques for manipulating spreadsheet data.

Sorting

You can change the order of data in a spreadsheet by sorting it; for example, to arrange a list of items and its corresponding data in alphabetical order.

1   Select *all* of the cells you want to sort, as shown in Figure 18-11.

2   Choose Data > Sort.

3   In the Sort window, set the sort options you want. Use Figure 18-12 for guidance.

4   Click OK.

Be sure to select *all* the cells you want included in the sort. Any cells that aren't selected aren't included in the sort, which could throw your data off quite a bit.

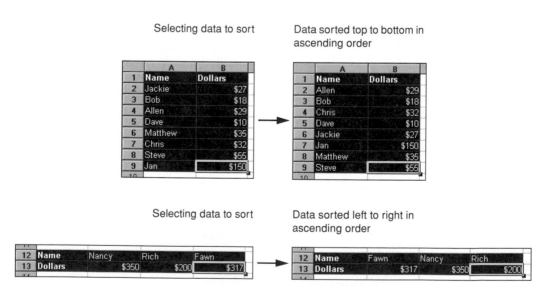

Figure 18-11   Examples of sorted data

Select the columns or rows for which you want to set specific sort options. If no header name was selected in the spreadsheet, "Column" or "Row" is displayed in the field, depending on the sort Direction you select on the Options tab (below). You don't have to set options for each column or row you selected. Calc sorts them automatically.

Select whether you want the sort order to be Ascending (for example, a-z), or Descending (z-a). If you want to keep corresponding data in sync (for example, keeping names with their corresponding dollar amounts), select the same sort order for all columns or rows you set.

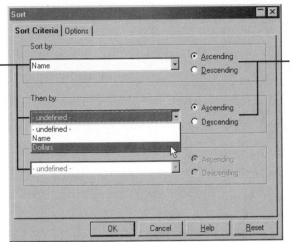

If you selected column or row headers in the spreadsheet and you don't select the Area contains option, the headers are sorted.

Select Include formats to keep data with its corresponding cell format.

If you want to sort the data vertically, select Top to bottom. If you want to sort horizontally, select Left to right.

Select the Copy sort results to option to copy the sort results to either a named area in the spreadsheet (see page 582) or to a designated cell or range on the current sheet or on another sheet. Select a named area in the drop-down field, or enter a spreadsheet address in the field to the right of the drop-down list; for example, enter *Shee1.A5* to send the results to Sheet1 beginning at cell A5.

If the selected cells are defined as a sort list (see page 486), you can select the Custom sort order option and select the custom order in which to sort the data.

Figure 18-12   Sorting data

Note – You can also use sort buttons on the toolbar for quick sorting in ascending or descending order.

Filtering

While sorting rearranges spreadsheet data, Calc also lets you filter spreadsheet data to display only the data you want to see.

There are different complexity levels of filtering you can perform, represented in the following subsections. Advanced filtering isn't covered, because it involves working with spreadsheets as databases, which also isn't covered.

AutoFilter

AutoFilter is the quickest and easiest way to filter in Calc. It inserts a drop-down list button on one or more data columns that lets you select from a list of data that appears in the column(s). For example, if you have a spreadsheet that lists projects, deliverables, owners, due dates, and comments, you could set up an AutoFilter to let you select and view only the entries for one project, as illustrated in Figure 18-13.

The spreadsheet has three projects in the Project column: PDQ, XYZ, and IOU.

	A	B	C	D	E
1	Project	Deliverable	Owner	Date Due	Lame Excuses for Late Delivery
2	PDQ	Sabotage SadisTech's Web site	Darlene	1/17/00	Marketing set the deadline
3	XYZ	Put Broomfield campus on top of Flatirons for April Fool's joke	McNealy	4/1/00	My boss is a tyrant and hates me
4	IOU	Rewrite OO-666	Surupa	1/27/00	Ran out of Advil
5	IOU	Convert OO-666 to Kanji	Elizabeth	3/4/00	I thought you wanted it by MY due date
6	XYZ	Show up for work	Floyd	6/21/99	Too many beer lunches
7	PDQ	Convert War and Peace to XML	Solveig	12/25/99	The t-shirts weren't made, so I didn't think it was an official project yet
8	XYZ	Convert Broomfield campus to digital for move to top of Flatirons	Simon	3/30/00	Used the vi editor I developed myself
9	PDQ	Write "StarOffice Guide for Ultimate Frisbee Players"	Bryan	3/30/00	The restricted space of my cubicle stifles my creativity
10	IOU	Install rear view mirrors in all cubes	Jeannie	2/29/00	Had to clean poop off the carpet from when I brought my dog in
11	PDQ	Commission cubist portrait for next all-hands meeting	Hambly	5/7/00	The company's insulated coffee mugs leak, and I've spent a lot of time—and money—at the cleaners

When you set up an AutoFilter for the Project column, you can click the drop-down arrow to select a project name to display only those project items.

	A	B	C	D	E
1	Project	Deliverable	Owner	Date Due	Lame Excuses for Late Delivery
2	PDQ	Sabotage SadisTech's Web site	Darlene	1/17/00	Marketing set the deadline
7	PDQ	Convert War and Peace to XML	Solveig	12/25/99	The t-shirts weren't made, so I didn't think it was an official project yet
9	PDQ	Write "StarOffice Guide for Ultimate Frisbee Players"	Bryan	3/30/00	The restricted space of my cubicle stifles my creativity
11	PDQ	Commission cubist portrait for next all-hands meeting	Hambly	5/7/00	The company's insulated coffee mugs leak, and I've spent a lot of time—and money—at the cleaners

Figure 18-13   Using an AutoFilter

To use AutoFilter:

1   In your spreadsheet, select the columns you want to use AutoFilter on. (Select a column by clicking the column letter.)

If you want to use AutoFilter on all columns, don't select any columns. Just perform the next step.

2   On the toolbar, click the AutoFilter icon.

Run the filter by clicking the drop-down arrow in the column heading and choosing an item.

To view the entire spreadsheet after you select an AutoFilter item, click the drop-down arrow and choose All. If you choose Standard, the Standard Filter window is displayed to let you set up a standard filter. Choose Top 10 to display the highest 10 values only.

If AutoFilter is set up for more than one column, you can select one item with AutoFilter, then narrow the list further by selecting a second AutoFilter item. An AutoFilter drop-down arrow turns blue when you've selected an item in its column.

After you filter using AutoFilter, you can run the standard filtering tool to further pinpoint the data you want to see.

To stop using AutoFilter, click the AutoFilter icon on the toolbar. If for some reason your row numbers and column letters stop at the end of your spreadsheet data after you turn AutoFilter off, click the AutoFilter icon twice to turn to turn AutoFilter on and off again.

Standard Filtering

Calc's Standard filtering tool let you refine your filtering options further than you can with AutoFilter, letting you more pinpoint the exact data you want to view.

A main physical difference between AutoFilter and standard filtering is that AutoFilter provides a drop-down list of items to select from. Standard filtering simply applies the filtering options you've set and displays the relevant data.

1   Choose Data > Filter > Standard Filter.

2   In the Standard Filter window, set the filtering options you want. Use Figure 18-14 for guidance.

3   Click OK.

The spreadsheet displays only the items that meet the filtering criteria.

To turn filtering off and return to the original spreadsheet, choose Data > Filter > Remove Filter.

The standard filter lets you select up to three filtering criteria. Select a column heading (Field name), a comparison operator (Condition), and the Value the Condition will measure against. Selecting AND means that condition must *also* be met.

If the spreadsheet uses column headings, select this option so you can select the heading names in the Field name list.

If you want to copy the filter results to another area or sheet instead of displaying the results in the active sheet, select the Copy option and either select the named area or click the Shrink icon to select the sheet/area you want to copy to.

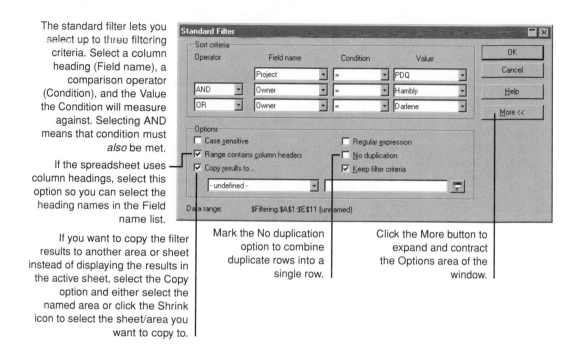

Mark the No duplication option to combine duplicate rows into a single row.

Click the More button to expand and contract the Options area of the window.

Figure 18-14   Setting standard filtering options

Conditional Formatting

You can set cells up to take on specific formatting characteristics automatically when certain conditions are met. For example, when the calculated value in a cell meets or exceeds a specific number, a plain cell with plain text can become a cell with large text, a colored background, and a thick border.

In order for this to work, you have to create the cell styles you want to use in conditional formatting. See *Cell Styles* on page 517.

1   Select the cell(s) to which you want to apply conditional formatting.

2   Choose Format > Conditional Formatting.

3   In the Conditional Formatting window, set up conditions and assign styles to them. Use Figure 18-15 for guidance.

4   Click OK.

Select the condition you want to apply.
If you select "between", you can specify
two values or cell references

Enter the value or cell reference that will trigger the
condition. Click the Shrink icon to shrink the
window so you can click cells.

You can set
conditions on cell
values or cell
formulas.

Select the Condition
option to add
another condition.

Select the cell format
that will be applied
when the condition is
met.

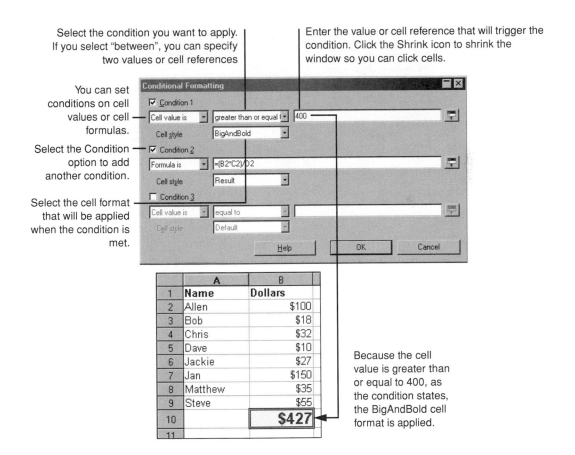

Because the cell
value is greater than
or equal to 400, as
the condition states,
the BigAndBold cell
format is applied.

Figure 18-15   Setting conditional formatting

Using Conditional Formatting for Text Entries   Conditional formatting can also work for
text you enter in cells. For example, if you're building a data sheet for a software product
that lists different features by operating system (Solaris, Linux, and Monopoly), you can
apply different cell background and font color automatically for of each operating system
name you enter. Use Figure 18-16 for guidance.

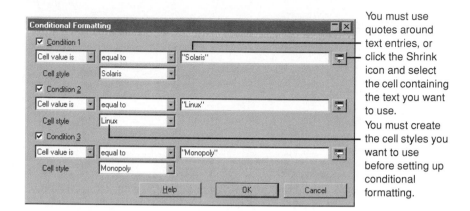

You must use quotes around text entries, or click the Shrink icon and select the cell containing the text you want to use.

You must create the cell styles you want to use before setting up conditional formatting.

Figure 18-16   Conditional formatting on text entries

Paste Special

Calc's Paste Special feature gives you a lot of flexibility with how you paste cell contents from your system's clipboard.

With a normal copy (or cut) and paste, the cells you copy and paste elsewhere in a spreadsheet simply replace the values in the target cells. With Paste Special, you can copy a group of cells that contain, for example, the number 2; and when you paste onto a group of target cells, Paste Special lets you add, subtract, multiply, or divide by the values you're pasting (in this case, the number 2).

Paste Special works just as well when you're pasting values generated by a formula. However, when you paste formula-generated values onto target cells, the target cell values don't update when the formulas that were pasted on them change.

1   Copy or cut the values you want to paste.

2   Select the target cells you want to manipulate.

3   Choose Edit > Paste Special.

4   In the Paste Special window, set the paste options. Use Figure 18-17 for guidance.

5   Click OK.

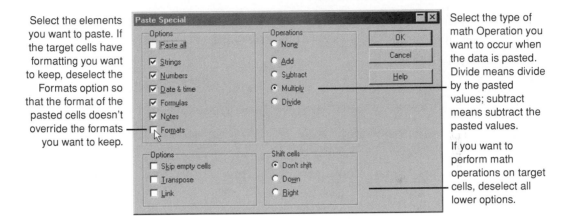

Select the elements you want to paste. If the target cells have formatting you want to keep, deselect the Formats option so that the format of the pasted cells doesn't override the formats you want to keep.

Select the type of math Operation you want to occur when the data is pasted. Divide means divide by the pasted values; subtract means subtract the pasted values.

If you want to perform math operations on target cells, deselect all lower options.

Figure 18-17   Using Paste Special to manipulate data

Concatenating Cells

There may be times when you need to concatenate, or combine, text and calculated numbers in a single cell. You may also need to combine the contents of multiple text cells or multiple calculated amount cells into a single cell.

Figure 18-18 shows two concatenation examples.

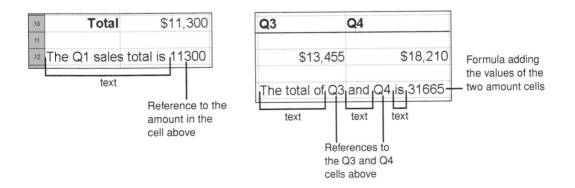

text

Reference to the amount in the cell above

Formula adding the values of the two amount cells

text   text   text

References to the Q3 and Q4 cells above

Figure 18-18   Concatenation examples

There are two ways to concatenate cells: a simple way that lets you combine text with a single cell reference or formula (used in the first example in Figure 18-18), and a more advanced way that lets you combine multiple text strings and cell references (used in the second example in Figure 18-18).

Simple Concatenation

When you want to combine text with a single cell reference or a formula (that can include multiple cell references), use the following syntax in a cell:

```
="The text you want to type "&C5
```

or

```
="The text you want to type "&sum(C2:C4)
```

After you type the ampersand (&) in the formula, you can click cells in the spreadsheet rather than typing them manually to insert them in the formula.

Notice this is written as a formula, which begins with the equals sign (=). Notice the space between the last letter of text and the quotation marks. You need to add that space if you want a space between the text and the amount.

Here is how the first example in Figure 18-18 is written:

```
="The Q1 sales total is "&B10
```

Advanced Concatenation

When you want to combine multiple amounts and text strings in a cell, use the following syntax in a cell. This involves using Calc's CONCATENATE function.

```
=CONCATENATE(cell/text/formula;cell/text/formula;...)
```

In this syntax example, cell/text/formula means you can use a cell reference, text, or a formula. Each item is separated by a semicolon (;). You can use as many items as you want.

Here's how the second example in Figure 18-18 is written:

```
=CONCATENATE("The total of";D4;" and ";E4;" is ";SUM(D6:E6))
```

Notice the spaces in the " and " and " is " items. These are necessary to separate the text from the amounts.

This syntax of using a semicolon (;) to separate items is an important difference between Excel and Calc. In Excel, you separate items with a comma (,).

In this example, there are five semicolons that separate six items. You could instead write the formula differently to combine text and numbers, reducing the number of items you need to separate from six to three:

```
=CONCATENATE("The total of "&D4;" and "&E4;" is "&SUM(D6:E6))
```

This technique is accomplished by putting an ampersand in front of a cell reference or formula when it's directly combined with text, as illustrated in the previous Simple Concatenation procedure.

Advanced Techniques

Spreadsheets are versatile creatures. Oftentimes your spreadsheet use is limited only by your imagination. Use the following procedures as a mental primer to help expand your understanding of what's possible with Calc.

Because these procedures add power to your spreadsheets, they also add complexity and increase the potential for fairly intense troubleshooting.

If you're new to these types of techniques, start simple at first until you get a solid understanding of all the pieces and issues involved. For example, start building simple IF functions to get comfortable with their logic and syntax before you dive in and add complexity. (The IF function example in Figure 18-22 borders on the complex.)

Combining Data From Many Sheets Into One Sheet

It's good practice to use multiple sheets to organize spreadsheets (see *Break It Up* on page 549).

The main idea behind this procedure is to build separate pieces of information on different sheets, then include bits of data from each of the separate sheets onto another sheet (which we'll call a master sheet in this procedure). A good example of this is a profit and loss (P&L) report, which combines data from separate income and expense sheets to create a report on a third sheet, as shown in Figure 18-19. The data from the income and expense sheets is pasted into the P&L sheet as links, so that when the data on those sheets changes, the data on the P&L sheet updates automatically.

1   In one of the sheets, select the cell(s) you want to reference.

     You can select an individual cell or a range of cells that are adjacent. You can't copy a group of non-adjacent cells.

2   Choose Edit > Copy.

3   Switch to the master sheet, and click the cell(s) or inside of the formula you want to insert the reference into.

4   Choose Edit > Paste Special.

5   In the Paste Special window, select the Link option at the bottom of the window, and click OK.

     The data is inserted as a reference to the sheet it was copied from.

6   Repeat these steps for all data in other sheets you want to reference.

As an alternative to using the Paste Special command, you can enter the reference manually using the following syntax:

=$SheetName.$A$1

(SheetName is the exact name that appears on the sheet's tab at the bottom of the Calc window.) Use that exact syntax (without the equals sign) when using that cell reference inside formulas.

Strictly speaking, this isn't a link by normal StarOffice standards that is updated like a link (by choosing Edit > Links and clicking Update). It's a reference that is automatically or manually calculated (see *Updating Calculations* on page 533).

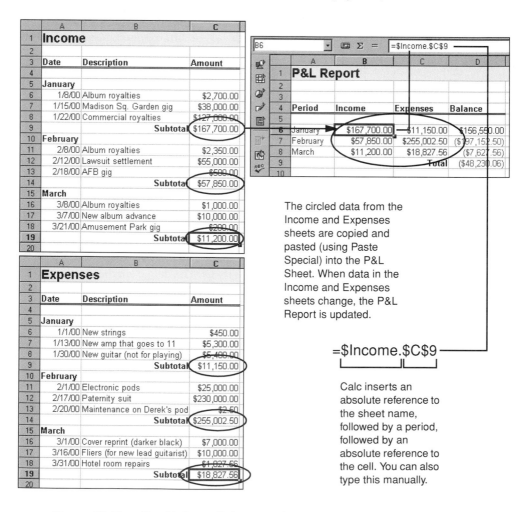

Figure 18-19   Combining cells in many sheets on a master sheet

---

Note – Notice the use of the $ in the cell references. This signifies an absolute reference. For more information, see *Relative and Absolute Cell References* on page 530.

You can also insert entire sheets from other Calc files into a spreadsheet, by copy or by link. See *Adding Sheets* on page 488.

About the Calc Consolidation Feature Calc also has a feature called Consolidation (Data > Consolidate) that lets you combine and perform calculations on separate groups of data. The effect of creating links to data is identical to the more manual copy and paste special process in the previous procedure. However, Consolidate isn't an extremely intuitive tool, and you're likely to get more predictable results by using the previous copy/ paste special procedure for combining separate pieces of data in one sheet or area and setting up calculations manually.

Linking to Data in Other Calc Files

This procedure is the same in concept to the previous procedure, Combining Data From Many Sheets Into One Sheet, except that you link to cells in other Calc files.

1 Open the file(s) containing the cells you want to reference in the current spreadsheet.

2 Select the cell(s) in the other spreadsheet file you want to reference.

You can select an individual cell or a range of cells that are adjacent. You can't copy a group of non-adjacent cells.

3 Choose Edit > Copy.

4 Switch to the working spreadsheet file, and click the cell(s) or inside of the formula you want to insert the reference into.

5 Choose Edit > Paste Special.

6 In the Paste Special window, select the Link option at the bottom of the window, and click OK.

Calc inserts the reference as a DDE link to the source file.

7 Repeat these steps for all the data in other spreadsheets you want to reference.

As an alternative to having other spreadsheet files open, you can enter the reference manually using the following syntax:

On Linux and Solaris

=DDE("soffice";"/home/docs/Filename.sdc";"'SheetName'.A1")

On Windows

=DDE("soffice";"C:\My Documents\Filename.sdc";"'SheetName'.A1")

The Windows example shows a path to a hard drive rather than to a network location.

/home/docs and C:\My Documents are the paths to the file. The filename is the exact filename. SheetName is the exact name on the sheet tab containing the data. A1 is the cell being referenced. The SheetName is enclosed in single quotes, and the SheetName and cell reference are enclosed together in double quotes.

Use that exact syntax (without the equals sign) when using that cell reference nested within formulas.

Double-Checking Totals

Because calculations can get tricky, especially if you're using cell references in other sheets and other Calc files, it's good practice to double-check results.

Double-checking a total is simply a matter of calculating the total a different way, as Figure 18-20 illustrates.

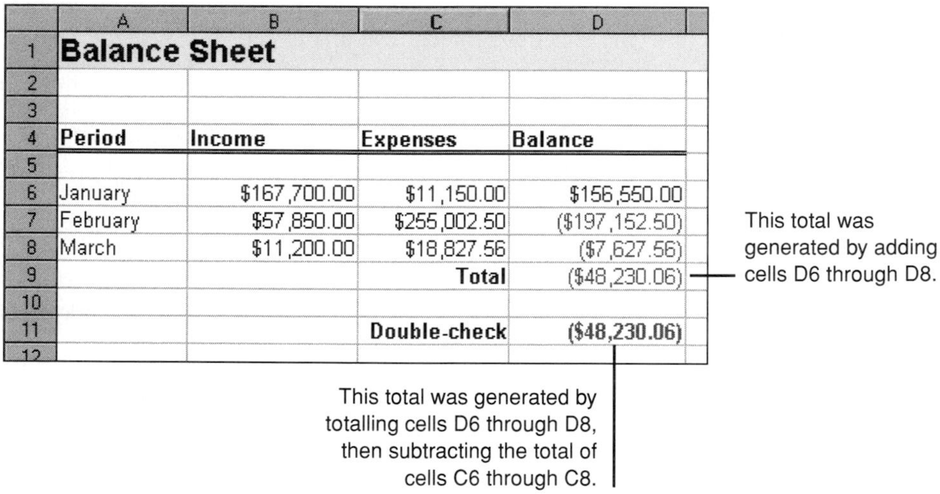

	A	B	C	D	
1	**Balance Sheet**				
2					
3					
4	Period	Income	Expenses	Balance	
5					
6	January	$167,700.00	$11,150.00	$156,550.00	
7	February	$57,850.00	$255,002.50	($197,152.50)	This total was
8	March	$11,200.00	$18,827.56	($7,627.56)	generated by adding
9			Total	($48,230.06)	cells D6 through D8.
10					
11			Double-check	($48,230.06)	
12					

This total was generated by totalling cells D6 through D8, then subtracting the total of cells C6 through C8.

Figure 18-20   Double-checking totals

You can also double-check totals in conjunction with conditional formatting to visually set off totals that don't match (see *Conditional Formatting* on page 538). You can also use the IF function (next) to generate text if your totals don't match. For example, "Your totals don't match. You're in big trouble. Call your attorney."

IF Function

The IF ("if") function is one of the most useful functions. It's described here to not only help you use it, but to illustrate the possibilities that functions present.

The logic that Calc uses in the IF function is the same logic you use in language all the time. For example: "If you put that wagon wheel coffee table in the living room, I'm leaving; otherwise, I'll stay." In other words, if something is true, something specific will happen. Otherwise, something else will happen.

Here's how you would give Calc your wagon wheel coffee table (WWCT) ultimatum:

=IF(WWCT in living room;"I'll go";"Otherwise I'll stay")

(You really don't need to tell Calc this. Calc is not notorious for putting wagon wheel coffee tables in people's living rooms, unlike other spreadsheet programs.)

So let's get real. In your spreadsheets, you'll use the IF function when the value of a specific cell will fluctuate. For example, if you're keeping track of a budget, and you want a visual cue to tell you when the total amount you've actually spent is over your budget, you can have a cell display certain text to indicate when you're still within your budget and display different text when you're over budget, as shown in Figure 18-21.

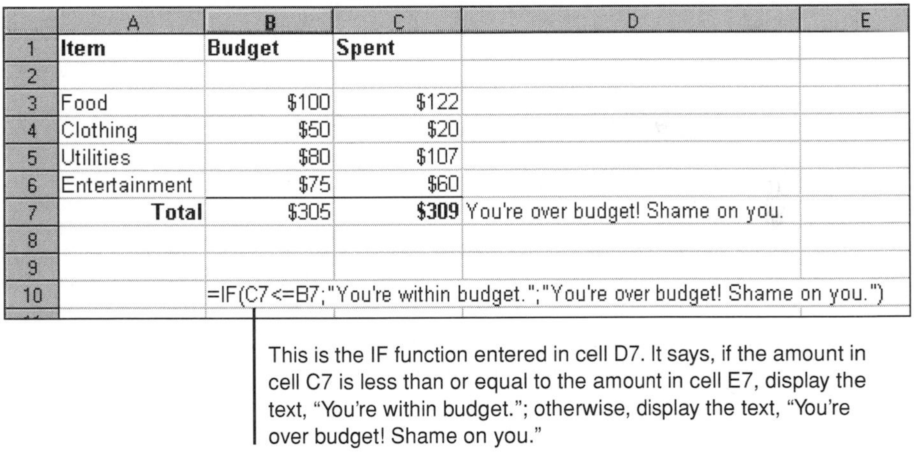

	A	B	C	D	E
1	Item	Budget	Spent		
2					
3	Food	$100	$122		
4	Clothing	$50	$20		
5	Utilities	$80	$107		
6	Entertainment	$75	$60		
7	Total	$305	$309	You're over budget! Shame on you.	
8					
9					
10		=IF(C7<=B7;"You're within budget.";"You're over budget! Shame on you.")			

This is the IF function entered in cell D7. It says, if the amount in cell C7 is less than or equal to the amount in cell E7, display the text, "You're within budget."; otherwise, display the text, "You're over budget! Shame on you."

Figure 18-21   Using IF to berate oneself for going over budget

Notice that each section inside the IF function is separated by a semi-colon. This differs from Excel, which uses commas. Put text within double quotes.

A more complex use of the IF function involves using cell references as conditions, as the following example illustrates.

Let's say a salesperson makes 5 percent commission on sales up to $10,000, and 8 percent on the amount of sales over $10,000.

You could set up an IF function that calculates the total amount of commission, taking into account a higher percentage on sales over $10,000, as shown in Figure 18-22. The math in this kind of formula can get really tricky, so be sure you check your work.

Here's a logical representation of the formula.

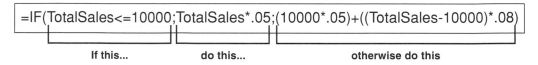

=IF(TotalSales<=10000;TotalSales*.05;(10000*.05)+((TotalSales-10000)*.08))

| **If this...** | **do this...** | **otherwise do this** |

Here's how the formula would actually look in Calc using cell references.

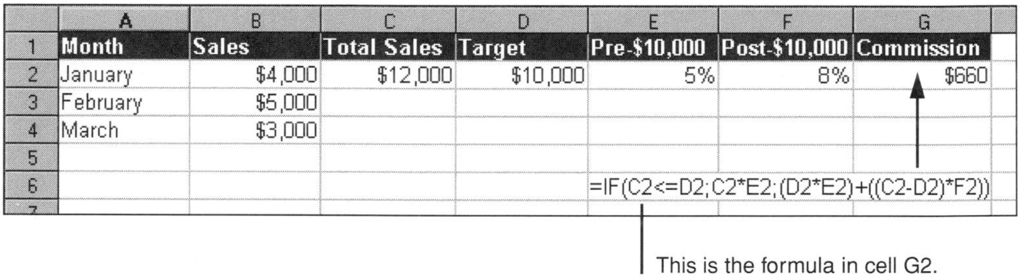

	A	B	C	D	E	F	G
1	Month	Sales	Total Sales	Target	Pre-$10,000	Post-$10,000	Commission
2	January	$4,000	$12,000	$10,000	5%	8%	$660
3	February	$5,000					
4	March	$3,000					
5							
6					=IF(C2<=D2;C2*E2;(D2*E2)+((C2-D2)*F2))		
7							

This is the formula in cell G2.

Figure 18-22   IF function used for calculating total commission earned

The spreadsheet in Figure 18-22 is set up to allow flexibility. Instead of entering the numbers $10,000, 5%, and 8% directly into the formula, they are entered into cells. The formula then references those cells, which means you can change the values in the cells without changing the formula. For example, if the Target amount changed from $10,000 to $8,000, or if the commission percentages changed, you can change those values in the cells, and the commission amount is adjusted automatically.

You can also use the IF formula in conjunction with conditional formatting to have the cell contents display in different styles when conditions change. See *Conditional Formatting* on page 538.

Using Form Controls to Enter Values

You can enter values in cells by creating drop-down lists to select different values. For more information, see *Drop-Down Lists, Buttons, and Other Controls* on page 560.

Using Spreadsheets Wisely

Using spreadsheets wisely has a lot to do with making spreadsheets as automated as possible, which ultimately makes it easier for you to maintain them. The following considerations explain this further.

Put Every Piece in a Separate Cell

Put every piece of data in a separate cell as much possible. For example, if you want to divide a dollar amount by 12 to get a monthly dollar amount, consider putting 12 in a separate cell; so that instead of 30000/12, you get 30000/B5. That way, you can change 12 to 4 to show a quarterly amount, or to 6 to show a semi-annual amount.

When you put everything in cells, all your formulas can contain cell references, making them more dynamic (they update automatically when cell contents change). Automation also means you spend less time tinkering with numbers that are manually entered in formulas.

Break It Up

In the same way that it's good practice to put values in cells and reference them in formulas (rather than entering values in the formulas themselves), it's also good practice to divide your spreadsheets into logical parts, with each part on a separate sheet. For example, if you're maintaining income and expense information to create a balance sheet, a single sheet containing all that data could get pretty crowded. A better way would be to track income on one sheet, expenses on another sheet, and build the balance sheet report on a third sheet.

Putting different types of information on different sheets is essential to managing complexity and minimizes the amount of tinkering you have to do, such as hiding rows and columns.

For example, separate sheets are good for reusing data that you need on many sheets, such as interest rates, budget limits, dates, recurring dollar amounts (like mortgage payments), and so on. You can set up such information on a single sheet and reference it on all your other sheets.

At the very least, even if you're going to keep all your data on a single sheet, keep common data in a separate area for easy reference.

Troubleshooting Spreadsheets

Following are useful ways to troubleshoot and fix problems with spreadsheets.

Calculated Amounts Are Incorrect

There could be a few causes for calculated amounts that are incorrect.

- If your spreadsheet contains numbers that don't show decimal places, Calc rounds numbers to the nearest dollar, throwing off calculated amounts in the spreadsheet Simply add decimal places to cells. See *Quick Decimal Control* on page 508.

- If your spreadsheet contains links to data in other sheets or other Calc files, make sure you update the links to that data so that the most current data is shown. See *Updating Linked Sheets* on page 489.

- If you used automatic fill to enter spreadsheet data automatically, make sure your relative and absolute cell references are set correctly. See *Relative and Absolute Cell References* on page 530.

Showing Formulas in Cells

You can switch from displaying calculated amounts to displaying the actual formulas used to generate values. This helps you better see relationships among cells.

Choose Tools > Options > Spreadsheet > Contents, select the Formulas option, and click OK.

Tracing Precedents, Dependents, and Errors

You can have Calc display arrows to and from a selected cell, pointing to the other cells that the current cell references, called *precedents*, or the cells that reference the current cell, called *dependents*. Tracing precedents, dependents, and errors help troubleshoot calculated amounts by showing you exactly which cells are used in a calculation.

If a cell contains an error, Calc's error tracing can point to the cell(s) causing the error.

For more information, see *Pointing to Cell References and Errors* on page 586.

Value Highlighting

Use Calc's value highlighting feature to visually set off different types of elements in a spreadsheet to help you differentiate between calculated amounts, values entered manually, and text.

Choose View > Value Highlighting to turn value highlighting on and off. See *Value Highlighting* on page 587 for more information.

Value highlighting is a great troubleshooting tool to help you better see different spreadsheet elements, which you can use in conjunction with other troubleshooting tools like tracing precedents and dependents.

Adding Objects to Spreadsheets

Charts

StarOffice has a wizard that guides you through creating graphical charts that represent your spreadsheet data.

While you can create charts for data in non-adjacent cells, you'll get the best chart results if you use data in adjacent cells.

Inserting Charts

1   Select the cells you want to include in the chart.

2   In the toolbar, click and hold down the Insert Object icon, and click the Insert Chart icon.

    As you move the mouse pointer into the spreadsheet, the pointer changes to cross hairs.

3   In the spreadsheet, click and drag to create the area that the chart will fill.

    The AutoFormat Chart wizard launches. While the wizard is mostly self-explanatory and guides you through the chart creation process, Figure 19-1 and Figure 19-2 provide some specific guidance.

You can create the chart at any point in the wizard by clicking the Create button. If you click Create in the first window, StarChart inserts a default chart.

In this data example, the selected cells include the column headings (months) and row headings (income categories).

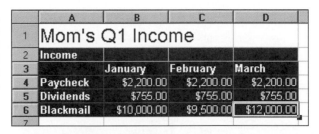

You can create data captions for the table by designating all selected cells in the first row as labels, all cells in the first column as labels, or both. If you use both, one set of labels is used for the chart's legend.

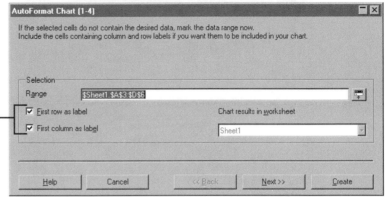

Select the type of chart you want to use. Some types of charts may not be appropriate for the table information you've selected.

Select the Show text elements in preview option to see how each chart type you select displays your table data.

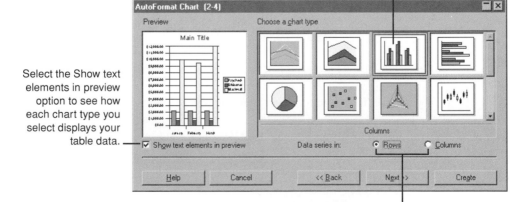

The Data series option you select determines which information is displayed in the axes and which is displayed in the legend.

Figure 19-1   Selected data and the first two AutoFormat Chart windows

The third window lets you select a specific style of chart of the type you've selected. You can also add and remove grid lines in this window.

In the last window, you can enter a chart title and any axis titles.

If you choose not to display a legend, you may be removing a piece of information that's critical to the chart. In this chart, the legend will show income categories.

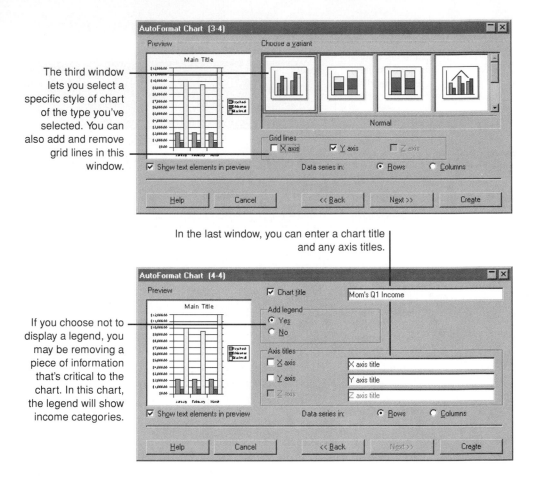

Figure 19-2 The second and third AutoFormat Chart windows

If you have trouble getting your chart the way you want it, try different combinations of the First row as label and First column as label options in the first window, and the Data series in (Rows and Columns) in the last three windows.

Modifying Charts

Once you've created a chart, you can change it in lots of ways. A chart is composed of many different parts, each of which you can modify. Figure 19-3 shows these parts as they appear in a 2D bar chart.

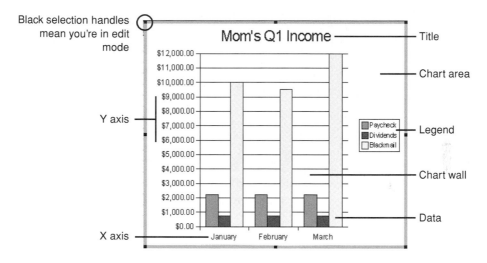

Figure 19-3   Parts of a bar chart

About Selection Handles After you insert a chart, it is automatically selected for editing. A chart selected for editing has black border handles, as shown in Figure 19-3. If you click out of the chart in the spreadsheet, the handles disappear. If you click the chart again, green selection handles appear. These green handles mean the chart is selected for moving, copying, cutting, and modifying position and size, rather than for editing. To begin editing a chart, double-click it to get the black selection handles back.

Selecting and Modifying Parts When a chart is selected for editing, you can select different parts of the chart for modification. Sometimes you have to click in succession multiple times to select the object you want. For example, if you want to select a data series in a bar chart (all the data for a certain category), you have to first click the chart to select the chart wall, then click one of the bars of the data area you want. Click again to select an individual bar. Figure 19-4 illustrates this concept.

Once you select the part you want to modify, right-click and choose Object Properties to make modifications. Each part of the chart has its own modification window. Table 19-1 describes the different tabs that appear in these windows. Use it as a reference for modifying parts of the chart.

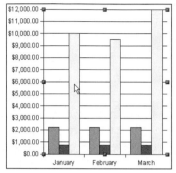
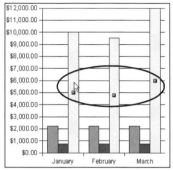
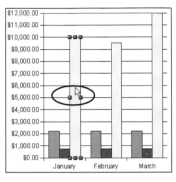

The first click selects the chart wall.

The second click selects the whole data series.

The third click selects one bar in the data series.

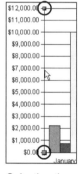

Selecting the Y axis

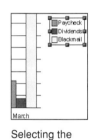

Selecting the legend

Figure 19-4   Selecting parts of the chart for modification

Chart Modification Options Table 19-1 describes the tabs you'll encounter in the different chart modification windows. Use these descriptions as a reference for the procedures that follow.

Table 19-1   Tabs in chart modification windows

Tab	Description
Lines/Borders	Lets you select a line or border style, color, width, and transparency for the selected chart object.
Area	Lets you select a color, gradient style, hatching pattern, or bitmap for the area of the selected object. You can also set more specific options for the selection you make.

Table 19-1   Tabs in chart modification windows

Tab	Description
Transparency	Lets you set transparency (color intensity) options for the option you selected in the Area tab. The higher the transparency, the lighter the color, hatching, or bitmap will be. You can also choose to set gradient transparency options that let you fade the color or bitmap from darker to lighter in different ways.
Characters	Lets you change font characteristics of the selected element.
Data Labels	Lets you add the value (as a number or percentage) and the heading label to the selected data.
Statistics	2D charts only. Lets you view statistical information in the chart, such as mean, variance, standard deviation, and margin of error.
Options	Lets you view a secondary Y axis and set the spacing between data in the chart.
Position	Legend only. Lets you position the legend in relation to the chart.
Alignment	Title only. Lets you set the angle of the title text.
Scale	Axes only. Lets you change aspects of the axis scaling, such as minimum and maximum axis values, intervals, axis marks, and tick marks.
Numbers	Axes only. Lets you change the numbering format or type for the axis.
Label	Axes only. Lets you set the angle and text flow of the axis text. Also lets you stagger axis text.

Adding and Changing Chart Details

After you generate a chart you can go back and change specific details about the chart, such as the title, axes labels, grid lines, and whether the data series is in rows or columns.

1   Make sure the chart is selected with black selection handles.

2   Right-click the chart, and choose AutoFormat.

3   The AutoFormat Chart wizard launches to let you modify the elements you want.

4   When you're finished, click Create.

Changing a Chart's Background

When a chart is selected for editing, you can change the background of the chart area and chart wall.

1   Make sure the chart is selected with black selection handles.

2   Right-click the chart, and choose Chart Area (or Chart Wall).

3   Modify the options for Line, Area, and Transparency. See Figure 19-1 on page 556 for more information.

If the chart is 3D, you can also change the chart floor (the base of the X axis).

Changing the Type of Chart

After you generate a chart, you can change the chart type. For example, if you generate a bar chart, you can change it to a pie chart.

1   Make sure the chart is selected with black selection handles.

2   Right-click the chart, and choose Chart Type.

3   At the top of the Chart Type window, select whether you want the chart to be 2D or 3D.

4   Select the type of chart you want, and select a variant of that chart at the bottom of the window.

5   Click OK.

Rotating 3D Charts

If you generate a 3D chart, you can rotate the chart to a different 3D angle.

Figure 19-5 shows how to rotate 3D charts.

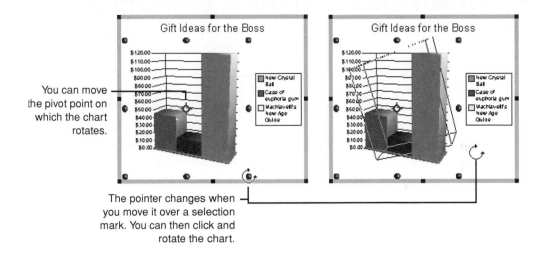

You can move the pivot point on which the chart rotates.

The pointer changes when you move it over a selection mark. You can then click and rotate the chart.

Figure 19-5   Rotating 3D charts

Updating Charts

Charts in Calc follow the same update rules as the spreadsheet. See *Updating Calculations* on page 533.

Changing Default Chart Colors

StarOffice uses a standard set of colors for data when it generates a chart. You can change the default colors used.

1   Choose Tools > Options > Chart > Default colors.

2   Select the color of the data series you want to change, and click a new color in the color palette.

Repeat for each color you want to change.

3   Click OK.

Drop-Down Lists, Buttons, and Other Controls

You can add controls to your spreadsheets, such as drop-down lists and buttons, that are attached to macros that were recorded or written in StarBasic or JavaScript. You're only limited by your imagination in how you can use controls in your spreadsheets.

This sections describes two possibilities for using controls in spreadsheets: adding a drop-down list that lets you select from a predefined list of values to populate a cell; and adding buttons that let you sort spreadsheet columns in ascending or descending order by clicking them.

Even though these sections give you the specific procedures for implementing these controls, the principles and mechanics are the same for setting up controls using other scenarios.

Adding a Drop-Down List Box

This procedure will show you how to insert a drop-down list in a spreadsheet and insert the selected value in a cell.

1   Start a new spreadsheet and save it with the name *Dropdown*.

2   With the spreadsheet open, choose Tools > Macro.

3   In the Macro window, scroll to the bottom of the Macro from list and select Standard (under the name Dropdown.sdc).

4   Click the New button.

5   In the New Module window, click OK to accept the new name of Module1.

6   In the macro writing window, enter the following lines of code to make them look exactly as what's shown in Figure 19-6. Enter them under the `Sub Main` and `End Sub` lines that are already listed.

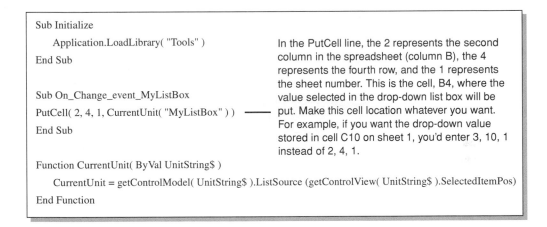

```
Sub Initialize
    Application.LoadLibrary( "Tools" )
End Sub


Sub On_Change_event_MyListBox
PutCell( 2, 4, 1, CurrentUnit( "MyListBox" ) )
End Sub

Function CurrentUnit( ByVal UnitString$ )
    CurrentUnit = getControlModel( UnitString$ ).ListSource (getControlView( UnitString$ ).SelectedItemPos)
End Function
```

In the PutCell line, the 2 represents the second column in the spreadsheet (column B), the 4 represents the fourth row, and the 1 represents the sheet number. This is the cell, B4, where the value selected in the drop-down list box will be put. Make this cell location whatever you want. For example, if you want the drop-down value stored in cell C10 on sheet 1, you'd enter 3, 10, 1 instead of 2, 4, 1.

Figure 19-6   Creating the drop-down list box macro

7   Choose File > Save.

8   Close the macro editing window.

9   Choose Tools > Macro to bring up the Macro window.

10   In the Macro from list, scroll down to the bottom and select Module1 under Dropdown.sdc > Standard.

11   Click the Organizer button.

12   In the Macro Organizer window, select the Libraries tab and click the box next to the Tools library, as shown in Figure 19-7.

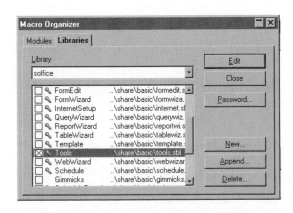

Figure 19-7   Adding the Tools library

13 Click Close.

14 Close the Macro window.

15 Click and hold down the Form icon on the toolbar and select the List Box icon, as shown in Figure 19-8.

Figure 19-8   Selecting the List Box control

16 In the spreadsheet, click and drag to draw the drop-down box the size you want it.

When you release the mouse button, the control is displayed with green selection handles.

17 Right-click the control and choose Control.

18 In the Properties window, click General tab. Enter the following information in the following fields:

- Name: `MyListBox`

- List entries: `100, 200, 300`

  As you begin to type the 100, the field becomes a drop-down list. After you enter 100, press Shift+Enter to drop to the next line, and enter 200. Do the same to enter 300. After you type 300, press Enter.

- Dropdown: `Yes`

19 Select the Data tab, and enter 100, 200, and 300 in the List content field the same way you entered them in the List entries field on the General tab.

20 Select the Events tab, and click the ellipses button next to the Item status changed field.

21 In the Assign Macro window, in the Macros area, select Module1 under Dropdown.sdc BASIC Macros > Standard.

22 Select the "On_Change_event_MyListBox" item in the right pane.

23 Click the Assign button.

24 Click OK.

25 Close the Properties window.

To use your new list box in the spreadsheet, see *Using the Controls* on page 564.

The drop-down list box control sits on top of the spreadsheet, even though it may look like it replaces a cell in the spreadsheet. That's why you have to specify a cell for the selected value to be put in the spreadsheet, as shown in Figure 19-6 on page 561.

Adding Buttons

This procedure shows you how to add buttons to a spreadsheet that, when clicked, will sort each of your columns by ascending and descending order. This procedure requires that you already have a spreadsheet set up with columns containing data that can be sorted.

1 Select the first column, and record and name two separate macros: one that sorts the columns first by descending order, and the other that sorts ascending.

Give each macro a unique name, such as `ColumnAdescending`.

Repeat this step for each column you want to be able to sort.

If you need help recording and naming macros, see 36, *Using Macros to Automate Tasks*, on page 1037.

2 Click and hold down the Form icon on the toolbar and select the Push Button icon.

3 In the spreadsheet, click and drag to draw the push button the size you want it somewhere in the first column heading.

When you release the mouse button, the button is displayed with green selection handles.

4 Right-click the control and choose Control.

5 In the Properties window, click General tab. Enter the following information in the following fields:

- Name: `SortDescending`
- Graphic: Click the ellipses button, locate the Office52/share/gallery/www-graf folder, and double-click the bludown.gif file. The face of the button in the spreadsheet becomes the graphic. (For the buttons you will use for the ascending sort, use the bluup.gif file.)

6 Select the Events tab, and click the ellipses button next to the Mouse pressed field.

7 In the Assign Macro window, in the Macros area, select the Module1 category.

8 Select the "ColumnAdescending" macro in the right pane.

9 Click the Assign button.

10 Click OK.

11 Close the Properties window.

12 Create new buttons for each of the remaining sort macros you created by repeating this procedure.

To use your buttons in the spreadsheet, see *Using the Controls* on page 564.

Using the Controls

When you set up controls in Calc and assign macros to them, you have to turn design mode off to actually use the controls. Whenever you open the document, the document opens with design mode on by default. That means if someone tries to use one of the controls you worked so hard to create, they'll click it and get only green selection handles. To get past this problem, you have to record a macro that turns design mode off, then assign that macro to the document every time the document opens. That way, when the document opens, the controls will work right away.

1 Choose Tools > Macro.

2 In the Macro window, scroll to the *bottom* of the Macro from field, and select the item "Standard" under the name of the document containing the control(s).

3 In the Macro name field, enter a name for the macro, such as "DesignModeOff".

4 Click the Record button. The Macro window disappears.

5 On the toolbar, click and hold down the Form icon, then click the Design Mode icon.

Note – The Design Mode icon is active only if you have a control in the spreadsheet. If the Design Mode icon was the *only* active icon when you clicked it, that means design mode was already off, and you just turned it back on. In that case, repeat the previous step to turn design mode off again.

---

6 In the upper left corner of the StarOffice window, click the floating icon with the red dot to stop recording the macro.

7 With the spreadsheet open containing the new macro, choose Tools > Configure.

8 In the Events tab of the Configuration window, select the Open Document event.

9 Select the Document option to the right of the Event list.

10 In the Macros list, expand the item that shows the document name, and select "Module1" under "Standard". In the right pane of the Macros area, select the "DesignModeOff" macro you recorded.

11 Click the Assign button, click OK, and save the document.

Every time that document is opened, the controls will be active.

Graphics and Drawings

The procedures for adding graphics and drawings to spreadsheets are similar to those used in Writer. See *Graphics and Drawings* on page 228.

Mathematical Formulas

The procedures for adding formula objects to spreadsheets are similar to those used in Writer. See *Mathematical Formulas* on page 251.

Floating Frames

The procedures for adding floating frames to spreadsheets is similar to those used in Writer. See *Inserting a Floating Frame* on page 250.

Updating Links

Whenever you add an object to a spreadsheet as a link, such as a graphic file you want to update in the spreadsheet when the file changes, you can determine how the link is updated.

Automatically Updating Links

To have Calc automatically update links to files in a spreadsheet:

1   Choose Tools > Options > Spreadsheet > Other.

2   Select the Always option.

If you select On request, Calc prompts you to update the links whenever you open the document. If you select Never, Calc opens the document without updating the links, and you need to update them manually.

Manually Updating Links

If you don't have Calc set up to update links automatically, here's how to update them manually:

1   Choose Edit > Links.

This menu option is available only if you've inserted an object in the spreadsheet by link.

2   In the Edit Links window, select the link you want to update, and click the Update button.

Useful Spreadsheet Tools

Importing and Exporting Text Data

In terms of getting database-type data from other applications into StarOffice, whether it's a regular database table or something like an Email address book, Calc is the application to use.

Calc, however, doesn't automatically translate data from other applications. Instead, it opens text data that has been created through other applications. For example, if you want to convert a Microsoft Outlook address database to StarOffice, you must use Outlook to create a text file of its data, then open the text data in Calc. Once in Calc, you can save the file as a dBase file for use in StarOffice.

Likewise, you can use Calc to export data from StarOffice for use in other applications that can't read StarOffice files. For example, if you wanted to send Calc spreadsheet data to someone using Lotus 1-2-3, you'd export the Calc data to a text file that Lotus 1-2-3 could open into a spreadsheet. (You don't have to go through that process for conversion to Excel, because you can save a Calc file as an Excel file.)

Importing a Text File

Make sure the text file you want to import is set up with delimiters. A delimiter is some kind of character, such as a semicolon, that marks the stopping and starting points of data that will be separated into different spreadsheet cells.

For example, the semicolons in the text line in Figure 20-1 allow Calc to import the data into separate cells in a spreadsheet row:

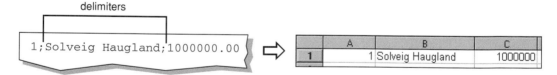

Figure 20-1   Text delimiter

Delimiters can be any character that your system supports. You can even use tab character or a space as your delimiter.

Text files can also be fixed width. That means your text file doesn't necessarily use delimiters, but each "column" in your text file is a specific width that Calc can translate into a spreadsheet column.

If you're creating a text file from data in another application, such as a payroll or address database, the export procedure for that application should automatically create the delimiters or fixed widths you want to use.

1   Choose File > Open.

2   In the File type list, select Text - txt -csv (StarOffice Calc).

   If you select only Text, this procedure won't work. The text file will open in Writer rather than Calc.

3   Select the text file you want to open, and click Open.

4   In the Import Text window, set the options for the import. Use Figure 20-2 for guidance.

5   Click OK.

The text file uses semicolons as delimiters.

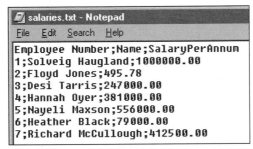

Select the row number of the text file you want the import to begin with.

Select the type of delimiter your text file uses. If your delimiter isn't one of the default options, mark Other and type the delimiter used.

If you select Compressed display, any empty fields in the text file that are empty in all rows of the text file will be excluded from the import.

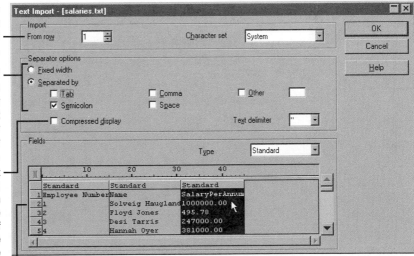

The Fields area displays how the text file data will be brought into the spreadsheet. You can select a column and apply a certain data Type (format) to it, such as a date format, or you can select Hide to keep the column from being imported. If you selected Fixed width as your separator, you can click the ruler in the Fields area and drag columns to the desired widths.

Figure 20-2   Setting text import options

Figure 20-3 displays the result of the import set up in Figure 20-2.

	A	B	C
1	Employee Number	Name	SalaryPerAnnum
2	1	Solveig Haugland	1000000
3	2	Floyd Jones	495.78
4	3	Desi Tarris	247000
5	4	Hannah Oyer	381000
6	5	Nayeli Maxson	556000
7	6	Heather Black	79000
8	7	Richard McCullough	412500

Calc imports the text file into rows and columns.

Figure 20-3   Result of the import

Saving to a Text File

You can save a Calc spreadsheet or a StarOffice database as a delimited text file for import into a non-StarOffice application. If you want to save a database as a text file, follow the steps in *Getting a StarOffice Database into Calc* on page 571 before performing the next procedure.

Saving a Calc Spreadsheet as a Text File

When you save a Calc spreadsheet as a delimited text file, only the active sheet in the spreadsheet is saved. To save more than one sheet as a text file, you must repeat this procedure for each sheet.

1   With the spreadsheet open, select the sheet containing the data you want to save as a text file.

2   Choose File > Save As.

3   In the File type list, select Text - txt -csv (StarOffice Calc).

4   Type a File name.

   If you mark the Automatic file name extension option, StarOffice will automatically add a .txt extension.

5   Set the path to the folder in which you want to save the file.

6   Click Save.

7   Set the options you want in the Export of text files window. Use Figure 20-4 for guidance.

8   Click OK.

9   If you get a subsequent warning saying that only the active sheet was saved, click OK.

Select the delimiter character that will separate each field, or piece of data —

Select the text character set you want to use —

Select double or single quote marks to surround text data. Some import programs differentiate between text and numbers in this way.

Figure 20-4   Setting options for exporting to a text file

If you want to open the text file, first close the spreadsheet file you used to create the text file. Otherwise the text file will open in read-only mode.

Getting a StarOffice Database into Calc

Opening a StarOffice database table or query in Calc is just a matter of dragging the table or query from the Explorer window into a Calc spreadsheet.

1   Start a new Calc spreadsheet.

2   In the Explorer window, click on the [+] next to the database containing the table or query you want to open in a spreadsheet.

3   Click the [+] to expand the Query or Table group.

4   Click and drag the query or table you want into the open spreadsheet document, as shown in Figure 20-5.

The cell that you drag into is the cell that will contain the beginning data in the table or query.

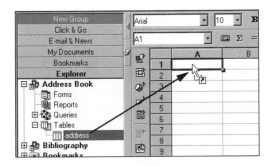

Figure 20-5   Dragging a database table into a Calc spreadsheet

Protecting Cells From Modification

You can protect any and all cells in a spreadsheet from being modified in any way. When someone clicks a protected cell, StarOffice displays a message saying that the cell can't be modified.

Cell protection is useful when you want to protect calculated amounts, protect cells containing formulas you painstakingly created, or to help guide data entry. In short, cell protection helps make your spreadsheets dummy-proof.

There are two aspects to the cell protection process, as illustrated in Figure 20-6. First, each cell has a "Protected" option you can select or deselect. Second, you must turn cell protection on from the Calc menu, which protects all cells that have their Protected option selected.

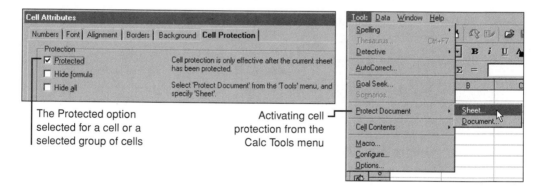

Figure 20-6   The two aspects of cell protection

By default, all cells in a spreadsheet have the Protected option selected. Because you may want to protect only a handful of cells, you may find it easier to turn cell protection off for all cells, then go back and select only the cells you want to protect. This procedure guides you through this process.

The procedure assumes that the cells you want to protect already contain the data you want in them and are formatted the way you want them.

1   Click the gray box above row 1 and left of column A to highlight the entire spreadsheet.

2   Right-click in the spreadsheet and choose Format Cells.

3   In the Cell Attributes window (Figure 20-6), select the Cell Protection tab and deselect the Protected option.

4   Click OK.

5   In the spreadsheet, select the cells you want to protect.

See *Selecting Non-Adjacent Cells* on page 505.

6 Right-click one of the selected cells and choose Format Cells.

7 In the Cell Protection tab, select the Protected option.

8 Click OK.

9 Choose Tools > Protect Document > Sheet to protect the sheet.

If you've set up cells for protection on multiple sheets, choose Tools > Protect Document > Document to protect all sheets.

10 In the Protect Sheet (or Protect Document) window that appears, you can set a password that applies to unprotecting the cells.

If you don't want to require a password for unprotecting the cells, don't enter a password in this window. Just click OK.

If you forget your password for unprotecting sheets, you're out of luck. You have to live with the cell protection. You can't even delete a protected sheet. You can, however, copy a protected cell to and paste it into an unprotected cell, where it will become unprotected.

Protected cells can still change format with conditional formatting if the conditional formatting was applied before the cells were protected.

Controlling Valid Entries

You can help guide yourself and others through data entry in Calc by restricting cells to receive specific values and ranges of whole numbers, decimal values, dates, and times. You can also specify specific text lengths allowed in cells.

For example, you can have a cell reject decimal or negative entries by setting it up to receive only whole numbers. Or you can set up a cell to reject any text entries longer than 20 characters.

When you set up validity rules for cells, you can also create help text that will pop up when any of the cells is selected, telling the user what's allowed in the cell. You can also provide warnings when invalid entries are made, and allow invalid entries to be either accepted or rejected.

1 Select the cell(s) for which you want to set up validity rules.

See *Selecting Non-Adjacent Cells* on page 505.

2 Choose Data > Validity.

3 Set the validity rules, help text, and error messages. Use Figure 20-7 through Figure 20-9 for guidance.

4 Click OK.

The results of setting up validity rules are shown in Figure 20-7 through Figure 20-9.

Select the type of data allowed in the cell(s). Select the Allow blanks option if you want to allow empty spaces in the cell(s).

Select the operator that will let you set the allowable values.

Enter the appropriate values and limits for the data type and operator you selected. Use appropriate formats. For text limits, enter numeric values.

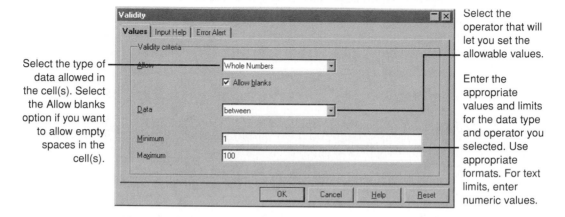

Figure 20-7 Setting the values for valid entries

Mark the Show input help option to display a popup help explanation when the cell is selected in the spreadsheet. Type the popup help Title and text. In the text, consider giving format hints, such as "MM/DD/YY" for a date entry.

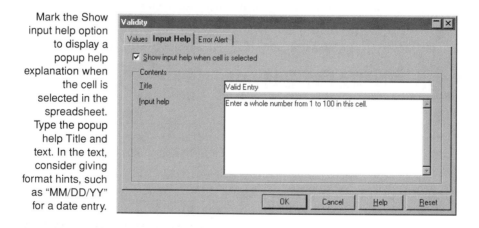

Figure 20-8 Entering pop-up text to help users with entry

Mark the Show error message option to display an error message on an invalid entry. Enter the error message Title and text. (We recommend creating error messages that are kinder and gentler than the one in this example.)

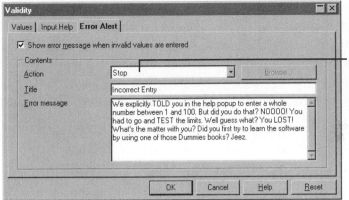

Select the type of message that will be displayed. Stop is the only option that rejects an invalid entry and restores the previous value. The others allow invalid entries. Use a macro, for example, to play a sound file when an invalid entry is made.

Figure 20-9   Typing the text that will appear on an invalid entry

For more information on macros, see 36, *Using Macros to Automate Tasks*, on page 1037.

Figure 20-10 shows the results of the settings in Figure 20-7 through Figure 20-9.

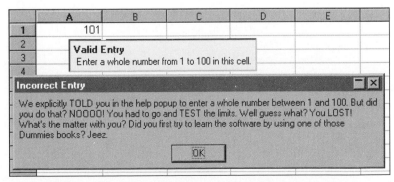

The help title and text are displayed when the cell is selected.

When an invalid entry is made in the cell, the title and text of this extremely encouraging error message are displayed.

Figure 20-10   The valid entries feature in action

Using Scenarios

Calc's scenarios tool is one of the coolest features any spreadsheet application could provide. In its simplest form, it lets you create a drop-down list of values to select from for a given cell. In its fullest form, it lets you enclose a set group of cells whose contents change when you select a different item from the drop-down list.

For example, you could set up a scenarios list that lets you choose among different percentage rates for a cell. That cell, in turn, is used in formulas elsewhere in the spreadsheet; so when you select a different percentage rate from the drop-down list, the values in the spreadsheet adjust automatically.

In a more involved example, you could set up a scenarios list that lets you choose among names of different home equity lenders. As you select a different lender, you get different values for things like annual percentage rate, the percentage of equity you can borrow against, and the number of loan years. The cells containing these values, in turn, can be referenced in formulas elsewhere in your spreadsheet to calculate things like the total amount of money you can borrow from that lender, the total amount of interest you'll end up paying, and how much of your credit card debt you'll be able to pay off with the loan amount.

In the latter example, each home equity lender you set up would be a single scenario. A single drop-down list contains multiple scenarios.

Figure 20-11 shows three examples of scenarios.

One Variable

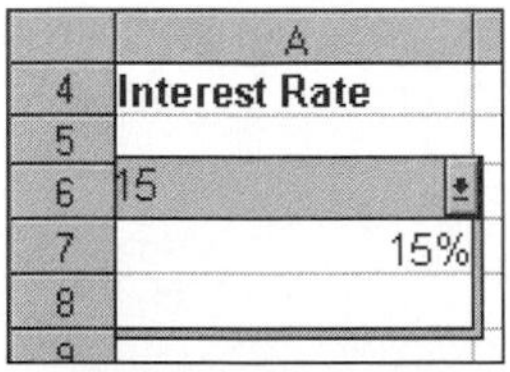

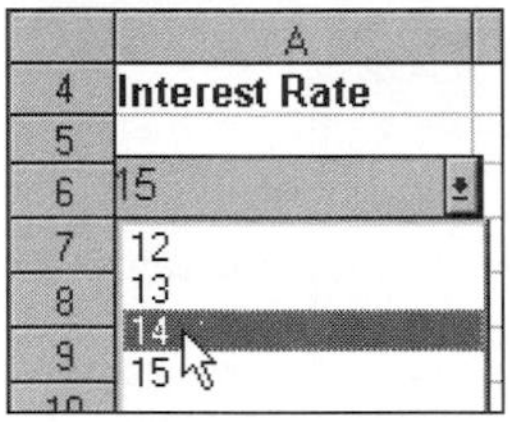

	A
4	**Interest Rate**
5	
6	15
7	15%
8	

	A
4	**Interest Rate**
5	
6	15
7	12
8	13
9	14
	15

In this simple set of scenarios, you can select from a list of percentage rates. The drop-down list is how you select different scenarios.

Two Variables

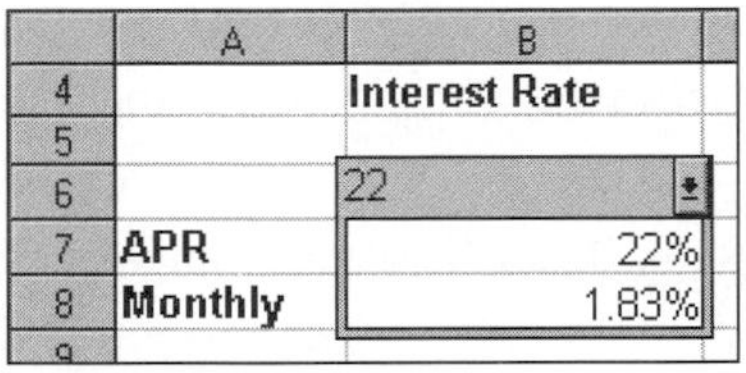

	A	B
4		**Interest Rate**
5		
6		22
7	**APR**	22%
8	**Monthly**	1.83%

This set of scenarios includes predefined interest rates and an automatic monthly interest rate calculation. Cell B8 is a formula based on the value in cell B7. As you create new scenarios, you only need to change the percentage value and the formula stays the same (=$B$7/12).

Six Variables

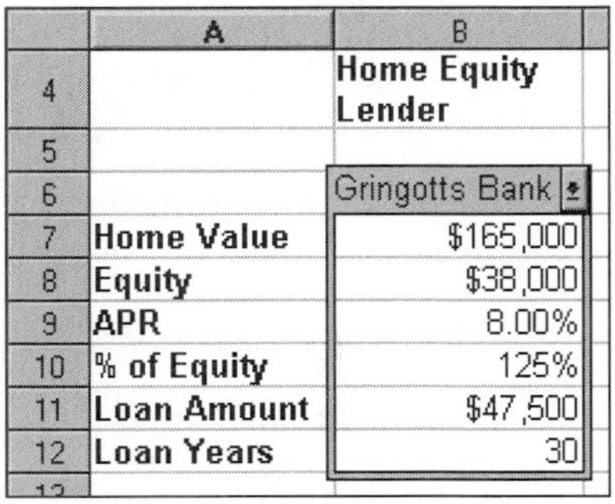

	A	B
4		**Home Equity Lender**
5		
6		Gringotts Bank
7	**Home Value**	$165,000
8	**Equity**	$38,000
9	**APR**	8.00%
10	**% of Equity**	125%
11	**Loan Amount**	$47,500
12	**Loan Years**	30

This set of scenarios lets you select from a list of home equity lenders, each with its own set of information, such as annual percentage rate, percentage of equity you can borrow against, and loan years. Cell B11 is calculated by multiplying cells B8 and B10.

Figure 20-11   Examples of scenarios

Creating Scenarios

Before you jump in and start creating scenarios, set up your spreadsheet, and try to group your scenario variables in a single area of the spreadsheet. In particular, set up row or column labels next to the values that will be used in the scenarios.

1   Select the cells you want to include in your scenarios.

   You must select at least two cells to create a scenario. If you only have one cell you want to create a drop-down list for, just leave the second cell blank.

   You can select cells vertically and horizontally. All selected cells will be included in your scenarios. You can also select non-adjacent cells. Each non-adjacent cell will have its own drop-down list, but you can switch among scenarios from any of the non-adjacent drop-down lists to change all non-adjacent cell values.

2   Choose Tools > Scenarios.

3   In the Create Scenarios window, type a name for the scenario, add comments about the scenario, and mark the settings you want.

4   Click OK.

5   To add another scenario to the drop-down list, select all the cells in the scenarios area, choose Tools > Scenarios, create the new scenario, and click OK.

The name of the new scenario is displayed in the scenarios list title bar. Change all appropriate cell values in the scenario area of the spreadsheet to reflect the scenario you just added.

6   Rinse and repeat. (Sorry. Just a little clean humor.)

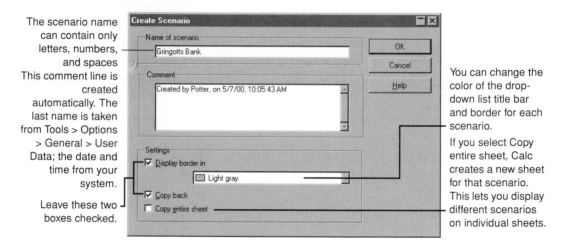

The scenario name can contain only letters, numbers, and spaces

This comment line is created automatically. The last name is taken from Tools > Options > General > User Data; the date and time from your system.

Leave these two boxes checked.

You can change the color of the drop-down list title bar and border for each scenario.

If you select Copy entire sheet, Calc creates a new sheet for that scenario. This lets you display different scenarios on individual sheets.

Figure 20-12   Creating a scenario

Scenarios are stored in individual sheets, not for the entire document. So you can have duplicate scenario names from sheet to sheet.

You can also apply conditional formatting to scenario cells to display different scenario values using different cell formats.

You cannot switch between scenarios if cell protection is turned on.

Modifying Scenarios

There are two different aspects of modifying scenarios: by modifying the values in each scenario, or by modifying the properties of each scenario (name, comments, or border color).

Changing Scenario Values

1   Select the sheet containing the scenario(s) you want to modify.

2   In the scenarios drop-down list, select the scenario containing the values you want to modify.

3 Change the scenario's values directly in the spreadsheet.

You might be tempted to apply cell protection to scenarios so they can't be easily changed. Resist that temptation, because with cell protection turned on you can't switch among scenarios.

Changing Scenario Properties

After you've created scenarios, you can rename them, modify their comments, and change the border colors of the scenarios area.

1 Select the sheet containing the scenario(s) you want to modify.

2 Press the F5 key to display Navigator.

3 In the Navigator window, click the Scenarios button to display the list of scenarios.

4 Right-click the name of the scenario you want to modify, and choose Properties.

5 In the Edit Scenarios window (Figure 20-12 on page 578), change the properties for the scenario.

6 Click OK.

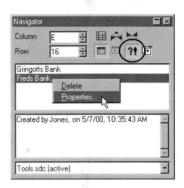

Deleting Scenarios

When you delete a scenario, you also delete the spreadsheet values associated with it—unless the scenario you're deleting is the currently selected scenario in the spreadsheet. In that case, the values remain in the spreadsheet, but the scenario title bar says "(empty)". When you switch to another scenario, the data in the (empty) scenario is replaced by data for the newly selected scenario.

1 Select the sheet containing the scenario(s) you want to modify.

2 Press the F5 key to display Navigator.

3 In the Navigator window, click the Scenarios button to display the list of scenarios.

4 Right-click the name of the scenario you want to delete, and choose Delete.

5 Click Yes in the confirmation window.

Using Goal Seek

Sometimes you'll know the desired result of a problem before you know a crucial piece needed to reach that result. For example, say you hold 200 shares of stock that you bought at $52 a share. You've told yourself you're going to hold onto the stock until your earnings on it reach $100,000. You know what the end result should be ($100,000), but you don't know what price the stock needs to reach to make your earnings equal $100,000. One of the variables, in this case the desired stock price, is unknown.

Calc's goal seek feature is perfect for this type of unknown variable math problem.

The key to using goal seek is to set up all the variables in the spreadsheet (except for the unknown variable you're trying to solve), and enter the necessary formula in the cell that contains your desired goal. Figure 20-13 provides an example of how you'd set up a spreadsheet for using goal seek.

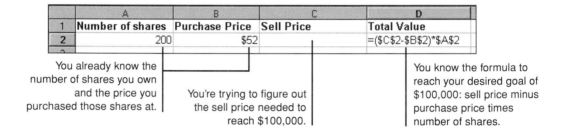

Figure 20-13   Preparing your spreadsheet for using goal seek

Goal seek works by looking at the formula that will be used to reach the desired goal, taking the desired goal value you enter to know what the result of the formula should be, and performing the behind-the-scenes math necessary to produce the unknown variable.

Following is the procedure for using goal seek once your spreadsheet is prepared.

1   Select the cell containing the formula that will result in your desired goal.

2   Choose Tools > Goal Seek.

3   Enter the necessary information in the Goal Seek window. Use Figure 20-14 for guidance.

4   Click OK.

5   If your formula is set up correctly and the necessary variables are set up in the spreadsheet to support the formula, goal seek tells you it was successful.

6   Click OK in the confirmation window.

Calc fills in the missing variable to make the formula cell equal the desired goal.

If you selected the cell containing the formula before you launched goal seek, that cell reference is displayed automatically.

Enter your target value, or goal. This value is what the formula will result in.

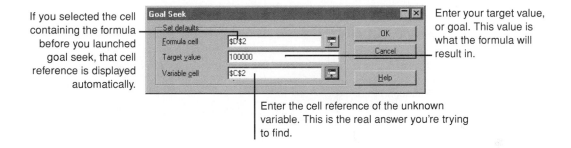

Enter the cell reference of the unknown variable. This is the real answer you're trying to find.

Figure 20-14   Entering values in the Goal Seek window

If goal seek wasn't successful, the confirmation window tells you it was unsuccessful and asks if you want to insert the suggested value displayed. It doesn't matter if you accept this value or not, since you'll probably need to double-check your formula and the cells it references to make sure everything is set up correctly, then run goal seek again to insert the correct value for the variable.

Outlining

Calc's outline feature is simply a way to let you select the rows and columns you want to expand and contract. This feature is particularly useful when you've got a large spreadsheet that has multiple parts. For example, if a single sheet contains detailed income *and* expense information, you can group rows by month so you can expand and contract those rows. In addition, you could group the entire income area, making it easy to contract so you can get to the expense section more quickly.

1   Select the rows or columns you want to group.

2   Choose Data > Outline > Group.

If you grouped rows, the outline pane is displayed to the left of the spreadsheet, letting you expand and contract the groups.

If you grouped columns, the outline pane is displayed above the spreadsheet.

3   Create additional groups or subgroups.

Figure 20-15 illustrates how to expand and contract outline groups.

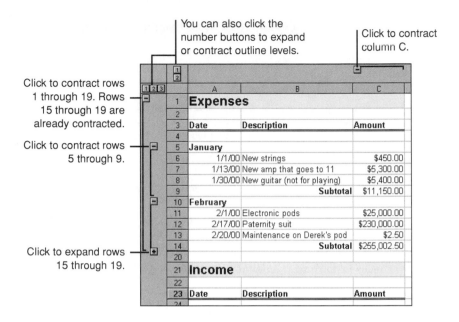

Figure 20-15   Using outline to expand and contract spreadsheet areas

To ungroup an area, select its rows or columns and choose Data > Outline > Ungroup.

You can't switch between showing a sheet in outline view and hiding outline view. If you no longer want to use outlining for a sheet, or if you want to recreate outlining from scratch, choose Data > Outline > Remove.

Naming Spreadsheet Areas

Calc lets you name sections of your spreadsheet to make those areas more meaningful. For example, you can select a column of first quarter sales numbers and name that area "Q1Sales".

This is a useful feature for a couple of reasons. When you name areas in Calc, you can jump to those areas quickly in the spreadsheet, either from the Navigator window or from the drop-down list in the formula bar, as shown in Figure 20-16. You can also include names in formulas rather than cell ranges, making formulas more meaningful. The following example illustrates this:

`=SUM(B6:B9)` can be written as `=SUM(Q1Sales)`

You can jump to named areas of a spreadsheet by selecting a name in the formula bar drop-down list (above), or by double-clicking the named area in the Navigator window (right).

Figure 20-16   Jumping to named areas of a spreadsheet

You can name ranges individually, or select multiple rows and columns and create multiple named areas automatically with one procedure.

Naming a Single Region

1   Select the region you want to name.

2   Choose Insert > Names > Define.

3   In the Define Names window, type the name of the named area in the top box, as shown in Figure 20-17.

4   Click OK.

If you want to name more than one region, you can keep the Define Names window open by clicking Add instead of OK in step 4. You can then enter another name, click the Shrink button to select a new region in the spreadsheet, click the Shrink button again, and click Add.

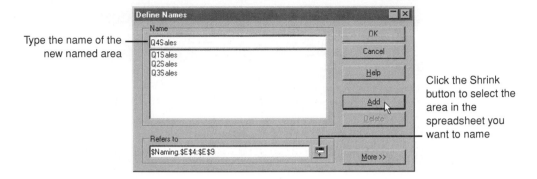

Type the name of the new named area

Click the Shrink button to select the area in the spreadsheet you want to name

Figure 20-17   Defining a named region

Naming Multiple Regions Automatically

You can select a big area of a spreadsheet that contains multiple regions you'd like to name, then use this procedure to create multiple named areas out of the big area.

When you use this procedure, Calc creates names for regions based on column and/or row headings in the selected area.

1   Select the area containing all the regions you want to name.

2   Choose Insert > Names > Create.

3   In the Create Names window, select the naming options you want. Use Figure 20-18 for guidance.

4   Click OK.

In the selected area, there are many possibilities for named regions. The descriptions in the Create Names window below show the different possible named areas that will be created when each option is selected.

Will create 4 column areas called "Region", "Q1", Q2", "Q3", and "Q4"

Will create 5 row areas called "Region", "East", Central", "Mountain", and "West"

Same effect as the Header option if the column labels are at the bottom of the area

Same effect as the Left Column option If the row labels are on the right

You can also select multiple options to create more areas. In this example, if you selected Header and Left Column, 9 areas would be created.

Figure 20-18   Creating multiple named regions with one procedure

Deleting Area Names

You can delete the name assignments you've given to areas. Deleting names doesn't affect the data areas they were assigned to. However, if you delete the names of areas you've used in formulas (such as =sum(Q1)), the formulas will no longer work. Also, if you delete a name that was used to create a hyperlink to the area by dragging from Navigator, the hyperlink will no longer work.

1   Choose Insert > Names > Define.

2   In the Define Names window, select a name you want to delete, and click the Delete button.

3   Click Yes in the confirmation window.

4   Click OK.

Pointing to Cell References and Errors

Cells can sometimes contain references to a lot of other cells, especially when you use more complex formulas and functions. Also, a single cell can be referenced in a lot of other cells. Calc has a couple of great tools that draw arrows to or from a selected cell, pointing to the other cells that the current cell references, called *precedents*, or the cells that reference the current cell, called *dependents*.

Tracing precedents and dependents are great for troubleshooting, because they show you exactly which cells are used in a calculation, making it easier to spot incorrect cell references.

Calc also includes an error tracing tool, which points to the cells causing an error in a particular cell.

1   Select the cell you want to trace.

2   Choose Tools > Detective > (Trace Precedents, Trace Dependents, or Trace Error).

Arrows appear, pointing to the relevant references, as illustrated in Figure 20-19.

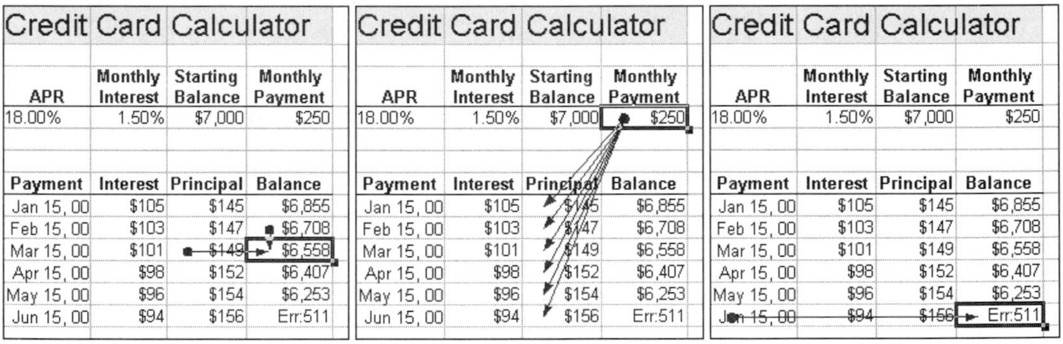

Tracing precedents   Tracing dependents   Tracing an error

Figure 20-19   Tracing precedents, dependents, and errors

You can remove the arrows by choosing Tools > Detective, and selecting the relevant remove item. If you're going to use traces on a regular basis, consider assigning a shortcut key removing traces. See *Assigning Shortcut Keys* on page 100. Select the Options category, then select the Remove All Traces command.

Value Highlighting

Use Calc's value highlighting feature to visually set off different types of elements in a spreadsheet. Value highlighting assigns the following colors to different spreadsheet elements, which override all font colors while value highlighting is activated:

- **Black** – Text displays in black.
- **Blue** – Numbers entered manually and dates display in blue.
- **Green** – Calculated amounts, formulas, and other information display in green.

To use value highlighting, choose View > Value Highlighting. To use globally for all spreadsheet documents, choose Tools > Options > Spreadsheet > Contents, mark the Value Highlighting checkbox, and click OK.

Value highlighting is a great troubleshooting tool to help you better see different spreadsheet elements.

Version Control and Editing Tools

Maintaining Incremental Versions of a Document

StarOffice lets you save different versions of a single document as the document goes through incremental changes.

The process of saving document versions is exactly as it is for saving versions of Writer documents. See *Maintaining Incremental Versions of a Document* on page 334.

Recording and Showing Spreadsheet Changes

You can have Calc keep track of changes made to a spreadsheet and insert colored cell borders and row/column lines at the areas where additions, modifications, or deletions were made.

Calc also tracks changes by the users making them. Calc identifies users by the settings in the Tools > Options > General > User Data window.

Calc does more than just mark changes. It also lets you accept or reject the changes made to the spreadsheet.

Setting Change Options

Before you begin recording and showing changes to a spreadsheet, set the color options Calc will use to mark changes.

1   Choose Tools > Options > Spreadsheet > Changes.

2   In the Changes window, set the color options you want for each type of modification. Use Figure 21-1 for guidance.

3   Click OK.

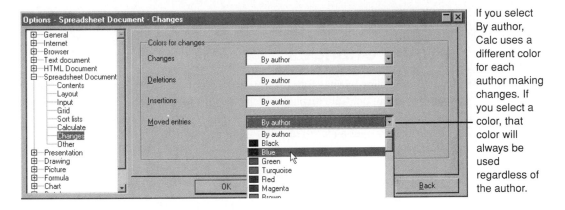

Figure 21-1   Setting color options for spreadsheet changes

Recording Changes

Once your color options are set for spreadsheet changes (previous procedure), use this procedure to begin recording changes.

Recording and showing changes are two different things. You can record changes without actually showing them in the spreadsheet, and you can switch back and forth between showing and hiding the changes being recorded.

1   Choose Edit > Changes > Record.

A check mark next to the Record item means Calc is recording changes.

2   Set the options for showing the changes (page 592).

Calc keeps track of deleted rows and columns, drawing a colored line across or down the borders at the points where the rows or columns were deleted.

To stop recording changes, choose Edit > Changes > Record to remove the check mark next to the Record item.

Adding Comments to Changes

When you change a spreadsheet cell, you can also add a comment to that change. This helps people understand why you made the change. This feature works only when changes are being recorded, as described in the previous procedure.

1   Choose Edit > Changes > Comments.

2   In the Comments window, enter your comment and click OK.

Change notes are displayed in the popup message of a changed cell (Figure 21-2).

You can also review all the comments attached to changes by clicking the arrow buttons in the Comments window.

Showing Changes

Calc gives you many options for viewing recorded spreadsheet changes. By default, when you turn recording on, Calc displays all changes made to cells by putting colored borders around modified cells and providing a popup note of the change when you select or move the mouse pointer over a modified cell. Figure 21-2 illustrates this.

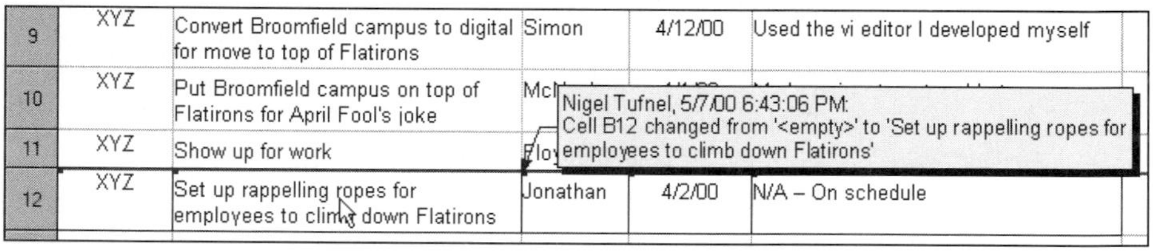

9	XYZ	Convert Broomfield campus to digital for move to top of Flatirons	Simon	4/12/00	Used the vi editor I developed myself
10	XYZ	Put Broomfield campus on top of Flatirons for April Fool's joke	McIr		
11	XYZ	Show up for work	Flo		
12	XYZ	Set up rappelling ropes for employees to climb down Flatirons	Jonathan	4/2/00	N/A – On schedule

Nigel Tufnel, 5/7/00 6:43:06 PM:
Cell B12 changed from '<empty>' to 'Set up rappelling ropes for employees to climb down Flatirons'

Figure 21-2   Calc's default mode for showing changes

Calc lets you be more selective in which changed cells are shown, letting you view changes by a specific author, between specific dates and times, within a specific range of cells, with certain words in the comments, and by changes that have been accepted or rejected.

1   Choose Edit > Changes > Show.

2   In the Show window, set the show options you want. Use Figure 21-3 for guidance.

3   Click OK.

The Show changes option must be selected to set the remaining options.

Select the Date option and set the criteria if you want to narrow the changes shown according to date and time. Click the clock icon to insert the present time.

Select the Author option to display changes made by a specific author.

Select Range and click the ellipses button to select the range of cells that will show changes.

Select Comment and enter any words a change comment must contain in order to show a changed cell.

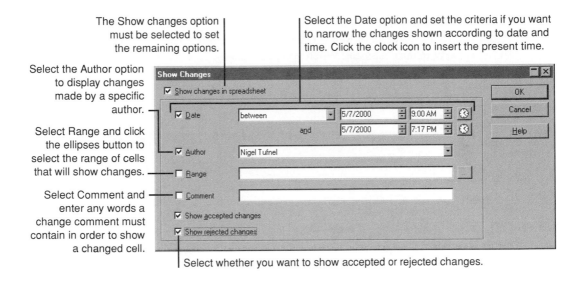

Select whether you want to show accepted or rejected changes.

Figure 21-3   Setting options for narrowing which changed cells are displayed

Calc's change indicators don't print.

If you want to continue recording changes but hide all the change indicators in the spreadsheet, deselect the Show changes in spreadsheet option.

Accepting or Rejecting Changes

Calc gives you the opportunity to accept or reject changes made to a spreadsheet. When you accept a change, the content becomes a normal part of the spreadsheet without change indicators. When you reject a change, the change returns to its previous state in the spreadsheet as items with change indicators.

In order to accept or reject changes, Calc needs to know that changes have occurred, which means that the Record feature needs to be activated while you work with spreadsheets (Edit > Changes > Record).

To accept or reject changes:

1   Choose Edit > Changes > Accept or Discard.

2   In the Accept or Reject window (Figure 21-4), you can select one or more items in the list to accept or reject.

You can modify the list of changes by clicking the Filter tab and setting the criteria for which changes will be shown in the List tab. These criteria are the same as those shown in Figure 21-3.

3   Click the appropriate button at the bottom of the window.

Whether you accept or reject changes, the items you accept or reject are removed from the Accept or Reject Changes window. When you accept changes, the change is kept in the document. When you reject changes, the change is reversed to its prior state.

4   Close the window when you're finished.

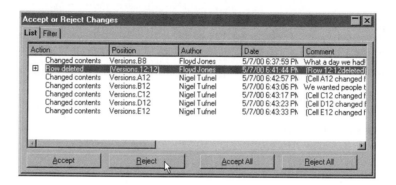

Figure 21-4   Accepting and rejecting changes

Using Notes

Calc lets you attach notes to individual cells. Notes are a great tool for elaborating on cell contents without putting all that extra information in cells, especially when the cell contains a formula. Notes are also good for suggesting that changes be made to cells.

1   Select the cell you want to attach a note to.

2   Choose Insert > Note.

A small popup box with a yellow background appears.

3   Type the text of the note in the popup box.

You can press Enter to break to a new line in the note box.

4   When you're finished, click outside the note box to insert the note.

A tiny red nonprinting square is displayed in the upper right corner of the cell to indicate that a note is attached to the cell.

To view the note, select or move the mouse pointer onto the cell. The note displays in a popup window, as shown in Figure 21-5.

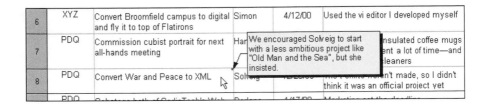

Figure 21-5   Viewing a note

To modify a note, select the cell, right-click, choose Show Note, and change the note contents. To delete the note, simply delete the entire contents of the note.

Printing in StarOffice Calc

Things that Control Spreadsheet Printing

There are many factors that determine what gets printed in a spreadsheet document and how it looks when it's printed. It's helpful to know some of these factors up front to give you a general idea of how to set up a spreadsheet for printing and where to look if you're having trouble controlling printing.

- The Page Style window – You get to this window by choosing Format > Page with the spreadsheet open that you want to print. You can also get to this window from the Stylist, by right-clicking the page style used for the sheet and choosing Modify.

  The Page tab determines margins, paper size, orientation (portrait or landscape), page layout, page numbering style, and placement of the cells relative to the page (horizontally and vertically).

  The Sheet tab determines which spreadsheet elements are printed, direction that sheets are printed (top to bottom or left to right), the first number used for page numbering, scaling of the printed pages, and the maximum number of pages that will print.

  The Page Style window also lets you set page borders, background colors, and page headers and footers.

- The Cell Attributes window, Cell Protection tab – You get to this window by selecting the cells you want, right-clicking, and choosing Format Cells. You can also get to it by choosing Format > Cells.

  In the Cell Protection tab of this window, there's an option to let you hide selected cells when printing. If this option is selected for cells, their contents will not print.

- Print Ranges – If you define a specific range of cells to print by choosing Format > Print Ranges > (Define, Add, or Edit), only those cells will print. If you select the Edit item, you can also determine which row or column headings will repeat on each printed page.

- Your printer's properties – Most printers let you set properties such as orientation (portrait or landscape), print scaling, and the range of pages to print. Make sure these settings aren't conflicting with the print results you want.

Determining What Gets Printed

There are many ways to determine which parts of a spreadsheet are printed, as the following procedures illustrate.

Selecting Spreadsheet Elements to Print

The first place to determine what gets printed in a spreadsheet is in the Page Style window on the Sheet tab, where you can include or exclude such fundamental elements as charts, graphics, and drawings.

1   With the spreadsheet open that you want to print, choose Format > Page.

You can also get to this window from the Stylist (F11) by clicking the Page Styles icon, right-clicking the page style used for the sheet, and choosing Modify.

2   In the Sheet tab (Figure 22-1), select the elements you want to print, and deselect the elements you don't want to print.

3   Click OK.

Column and row headers are the column letters (A, B, C) and row numbers (1, 2, 3). Grid represents the spreadsheet gridlines that mark the cell boundaries. Notes are the notes attached to cells (using Insert > Note). The remaining elements are self-explanatory.

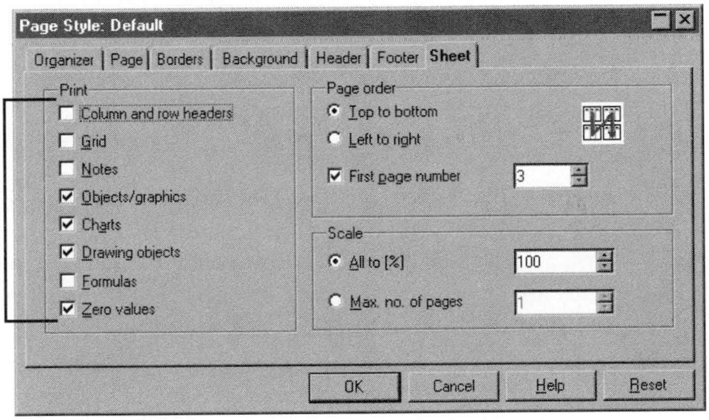

Figure 22-1   Selecting spreadsheet elements to print

Keeping Specific Cells From Printing

Calc lets you prevent the contents of certain cells from printing. This feature is useful if you want to print spreadsheets for general distribution, but you want to suppress sensitive information such as payroll or personnel information.

1   Select the cells containing the values you don't want to print.

2   Right-click one of the selected cells and choose Format Cells.

3   In the Cell Attributes window, select Cell Protection tab.

4   Select the Hide when printing option.

5   Click OK.

You can also keep entire rows and columns from printing by hiding them. See *Hiding Rows and Columns* on page 506.

Setting a Print Range

By default, Calc prints all sheets containing data in a spreadsheet document. You can designate a specific group of cells as the only cells in the spreadsheet that will print. This feature is useful when you want to print an individual sheet or select parts of a spreadsheet rather than the whole document.

1   Select the cells you want to include in the print range.

2   Choose Format > Print Ranges > Define.

To add cells to the already defined print range, select the new cells and choose Format > Print Ranges > Add. You can also add cells to the print range by choosing Format > Print Ranges > Edit, and entering the cell references in the Print Area field.

To remove a print range so that the entire spreadsheet is available for printing, choose Format > Print Ranges > Remove.

Repeating Spreadsheet Headings

If you have a single heading row or column for a particularly large amount of data, you can set up the heading to repeat on each new printed page.

1   Choose Format > Print Ranges > Edit.

2   In the Edit Print Areas window (Figure 22-2), enter the row or column references containing the headers you want to repeat.

3   Click OK.

You can designate more than one row or column as repeatable, as shown in Figure 22-2.

In the Rows to repeat and Columns to repeat, notice the cell references are just row numbers or column letters, such as $1 and $A. In this example, rows 1 and 2 will be repeated ($1:$2). You can also fill in the cell references by clicking the Shrink icon and select cells in the row(s) or column(s) you want to repeat.

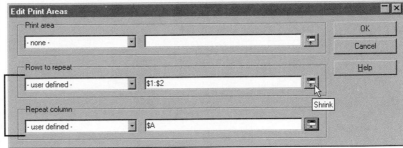

Figure 22-2   Setting up spreadsheet headers to repeat on printed pages

Controlling Pagination and Formatting

You can control the look of the spreadsheet printout in a number of ways, as illustrated in the following procedures.

Setting Page and Sheet Printing Options

Calc page styles control many aspects of how a printed spreadsheet looks. They also control other printing aspects such as the paper size used, page numbering style, and the direction Calc uses to create the flow of pages (top to bottom or left to right).

You'll set the majority of these options on the Page and Sheet tabs of the Page Styles window.

1   With the spreadsheet document open containing the sheets you want to set options for, choose Format > Page to display the Page Styles window.

    You can also get to this window from the Stylist (F11) by clicking the Page Styles icon, right-clicking the page style used for the sheet, and choosing Modify.

2   Set the appropriate options in the Page and Sheet tabs. Use Figure 22-3 for guidance.

3   Click OK.

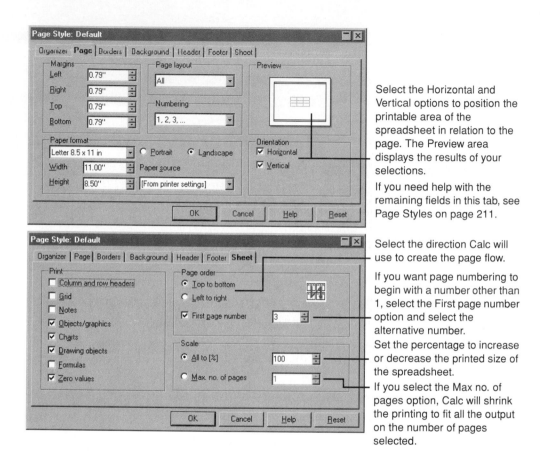

Select the Horizontal and Vertical options to position the printable area of the spreadsheet in relation to the page. The Preview area displays the results of your selections.

If you need help with the remaining fields in this tab, see Page Styles on page 211.

Select the direction Calc will use to create the page flow.

If you want page numbering to begin with a number other than 1, select the First page number option and select the alternative number.

Set the percentage to increase or decrease the printed size of the spreadsheet.

If you select the Max no. of pages option, Calc will shrink the printing to fit all the output on the number of pages selected.

Figure 22-3   Setting Page and Sheet printing options

Setting Border and Background options for page styles are the same in Calc as they are in Writer. See the *Page Styles* on page 211 if you need guidance.

Keep in mind that each sheet can be assigned to a different page style, so you may need to set options for multiple page styles.

Setting Up Headers and Footers

You can print spreadsheets with header and footer information that includes any text you type, the name of the spreadsheet file, the name of the sheet, page numbers, total page count, date, and time. You can also format the header and footer font.

Each page style has its own header and footer information.

1   With the spreadsheet document open containing the sheets you want to set header and footer information for, choose Format > Page to display the Page Styles window.

You can also get to this window from the Stylist (F11) by clicking the Page Styles icon, right-clicking the page style used for the sheet, and choosing Modify.

2   Set the appropriate options in the Header and Footer tabs. Use Figure 22-4 for guidance.

3   Click OK.

Select Header on (or Footer on) to print headers and footers.
Manually set the spacing between the header or footer and the spreadsheet and the height of the header or footer area, or select AutoFit to make those settings automatically.

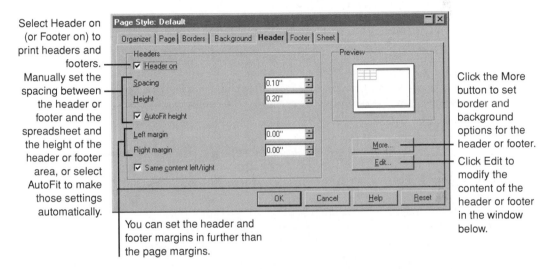

Click the More button to set border and background options for the header or footer.

Click Edit to modify the content of the header or footer in the window below.

You can set the header and footer margins in further than the page margins.

The Left, Center, and Right areas correspond to the left, center, and right areas of the page area within the margins. Click in a box and type the text you want, or click one of the icons to insert its variable.

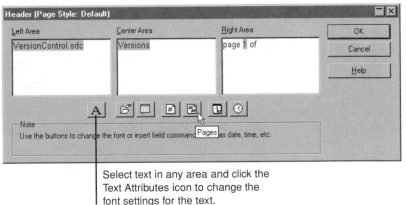

Select text in any area and click the Text Attributes icon to change the font settings for the text.

Figure 22-4   Setting up headers and footers

You can also edit headers and footers for the active page style by choosing Edit > Headers & Footers.

If Calc won't let you insert page numbers in a header or footer, make sure you have a numbering style selected in the Page Style window on the Page tab. If numbering is set to None, you can't insert a page number in a header or footer.

Previewing Page Breaks

To give you an idea of how pages are going to break when you print your spreadsheet, and to show you the page flow direction Calc is going to create, turn on Calc's Page Break Preview feature by choosing View > Page Break Preview.

Calc reduces the viewing percentage of the spreadsheet, displays large nonprinting page number watermarks behind each page, and inserts nonprinting page break lines (see Figure 22-5).

With Page Break Preview activated, you can still work in the spreadsheet, and you can increase the viewing percentage by right-clicking the viewing percentage box in the status bar and choosing the viewing percentage you want.

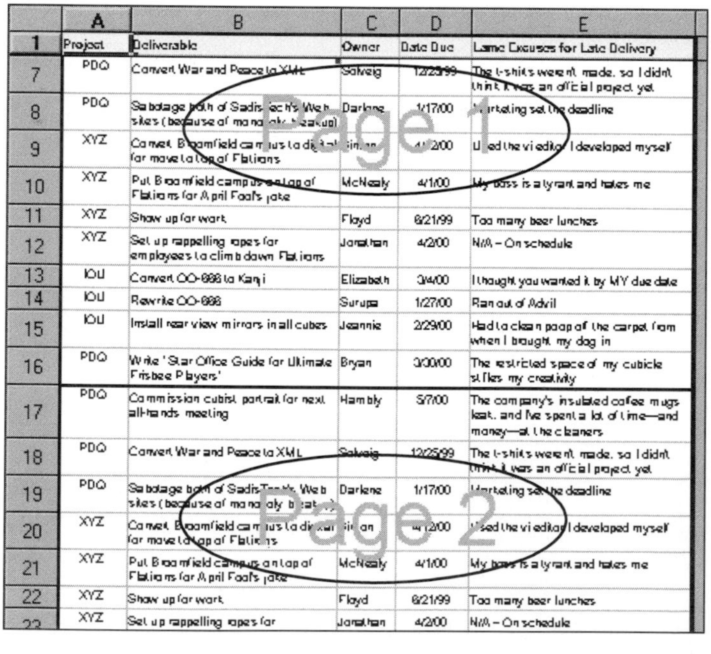

Figure 22-5   Using Page Break Preview

To increase the amount of spreadsheet that fits on a page, choose Format > Page, and in the Page Style window, select the Pages tab and decrease the margin settings. If after that you still need to fit more on a page, try resizing the columns. You can also go to the Page

Style window, select the Sheet tab, and adjust the Scale settings. See Figure 22-3 on page 602 for details

Inserting Manual Row and Column Breaks

If while in Page Break Preview (previous procedure) or by using the print preview (File > Page Preview) you see the need to create manual page breaks to better control the print output of your spreadsheet, select the row or column you want to break on and choose Insert > Manual Break > (Row Break or Column Break).

To remove manual breaks, choose Edit > Remove Manual Break > (Row Break or Column Break).

Manual breaks may not always be the answer, however. Sometimes creating good page breaks may just be a matter of resizing rows or columns.

Jazzing Up Spreadsheets With AutoFormat

StarOffice comes with a set of predefined table formats that can help jazz up a spreadsheet for printing. To apply one of these AutoFormats to a spreadsheet:

1   Select the area to which you want to apply an AutoFormat.

2   Choose Format > AutoFormat.

3   In the AutoFormat window, select the format and options you want.

4   Click OK.

See Figure 22-6 on page 606 for guidance.

Select the AutoFormat you want to use.
Click the More button to display the Formatting overrides that will be applied to your spreadsheet. If you want to keep any of the settings in your spreadsheet, such as row height and column width, deselect those options.

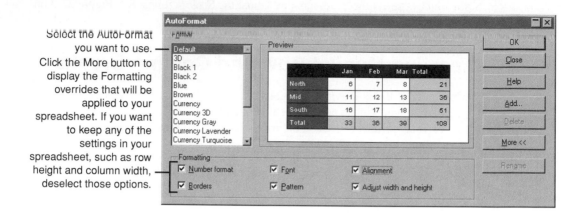

Figure 22-6   Applying an AutoFormat to a spreadsheet

If you don't like the results of the AutoFormat, click the Undo icon in the function bar until your spreadsheet is back to where it was before you applied the AutoFormat. If you don't have enough undos to get back to your starting format, reformat the spreadsheet manually.

A more automated way to get back to a previous format is if you add the previous format as an AutoFormat that you can select in the AutoFormat list (next procedure).

Adding an AutoFormat

You can add your own spreadsheet formats to the list of StarOffice's AutoFormats.

1   Format the spreadsheet the way you want it.

Your don't have to include data in the spreadsheet; just column, row, and cell formatting.

2   Select the formatted area, and choose Format > AutoFormat.

3   In the AutoFormat window, click the Add button.

4   In the Add AutoFormat window, type a name for the new format, and click OK.

Your format is added to the list.

5   Click OK in the AutoFormat window.

You can delete or rename AutoFormats by selecting them in the AutoFormat window and clicking the Delete or Rename buttons.

Printing to PostScript and PDF

The procedures for printing Calc files to PostScript and PDF files are identical to those used in Writer. See *Printing to PostScript and PDF* on page 352.

StarOffice Impress

Creating Presentations

Quick Start

This section contains the following information to help you get started quickly:

- A checklist for quickly making a presentation
- Feature overview
- A tutorial

See *Taming the StarOffice Environment* on page 91 for general tips that can make working with StarOffice a lot easier.

Note – Many features are available throughout StarOffice, but we don't cover them in every program's section. Check the index, or refer to *Taming the StarOffice Environment* on page 91 or *StarOffice Writer* on page 151 if you can't find the information you need in the chapters for StarOffice Impress.

Quick Start Checklist

If you've got a presentation to deliver tomorrow at 8:00 AM and it's 10:00 PM now, here's what to do:

- Create the presentation – *Using AutoPilot to Create a Presentation* on page 620
- Add content and insert objects – *Adding Text* on page 664 and *Adding Files and Objects* on page 679
- Run it to preview it – *Delivering a Presentation* on page 706
- Print it – *Printing a Presentation* on page 727

StarOffice Impress Features

StarOffice Impress lets you create professional-looking presentations, or slide shows, for delivery at business meetings, sales conferences, and other events. StarOffice Impress includes StarOffice Draw's vector graphics features, as well as the usual StarOffice capabilities of inserting charts, OLE objects, and other items.

Note – To see examples of StarOffice Impress's capabilities, open some of the sample files in `samples/`*`language`*`/presentations`.

StarOffice Impress features include, but aren't limited to:

Powerful file-creation features The Impress AutoPilot lets you quickly and easily pick attributes like introduction page, formatting, and background from templates and samples.

File formats Supports an array of file types for opening and saving as, including PowerPoint.

HTML/WebCast export You can export Draw and Impress slides to HTML, with or without frames. The exported presentations also can be run automatically for use in kiosk-type environments, or created for use in a webcast.

Special effects Animated objects and text, sound, and slide transitions.

Text formatting Full Writer text entry and formatting, as well as FontWork, a program for advanced text formatting and manipulation effects.

Customized presentations You can save several different versions of a presentation within the same file, without deleting or rearranging slides. In addition, you can attach speaker's notes to each slide, and create handouts by printing several condensed slides on one page.

Insert other documents as OLE objects, insert graphics You can insert other StarOffice documents such as spreadsheets and graphs as OLE objects, which means you can still edit them once they're inserted. You can include any graphics by inserting graphics or using Draw's graphics tools, all of which are available in Impress.

Forms and fields You can add a variety of buttons, dropdown lists, and so on, linking them to a site or to a database.

Enhanced delivery StarOffice has a standalone Impress program you can install on your laptop or delivery computer. A compress feature lets you save the presentation in multiple files that can be stored on diskettes, so you can easily take your files with you.

The Impress Work Area

StarOffice Impress has five different master views; we've chosen the Drawing view, shown in Figure 23-1, because that's where you'll typically do most of your work. (For more information, see *Using Master Views* on page 636.)

The **text object bar** is
similar to the one in Writer.

Use the **master view navigation
bar** to select a view, or (bottom) to
run a presentation.

The **toolbar** contains
the same tools as
Draw, with a few
differences.

The **Presentation
menu** lets you
navigate through and
modify slides. Choose
View > Toolbars >
Presentation.

These toolbar icons
provide effects like 3D
and predefined events
you can apply to
objects.

The navigation bar lets
you change **views**,
and select a tab of the
layer or slide to work
with.

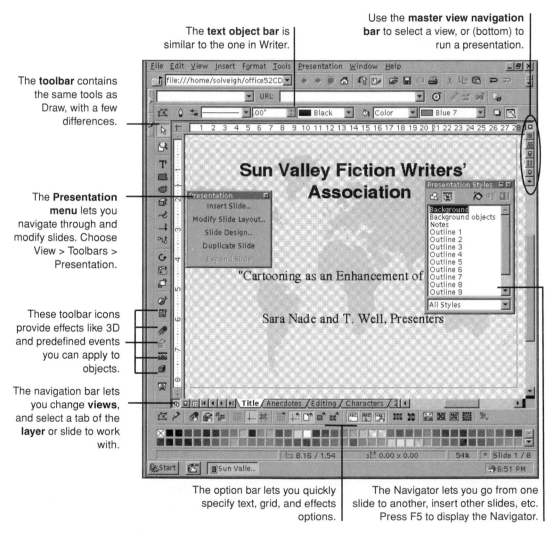

The option bar lets you quickly
specify text, grid, and effects
options.

The Navigator lets you go from one
slide to another, insert other slides, etc.
Press F5 to display the Navigator.

Figure 23-1   StarOffice Impress work area

Guided Tour

Completing all three sections will give you an idea of how the program works.

Creating a Presentation

1   Choose File > AutoPilot > Presentation.

2   Select the From template option. (It might take a while to be available.) Select the Introducing a New Product template from the list.

3   Be sure the Preview option is selected.

4   Click Next.

5   Make a selection in the Page style list. These are the backgrounds for the presentation.

6   Click Next.

7   In the Effect list, select Cross-Fade from Left.

8   In the Presentation type selection area, select Automatic and enter 5 seconds as the duration of each page.

9   Click Next.

10   Enter company and presentation information:

- Name of your company: Six-Fingered Man Home Construction
- Presentation subject: Fireswamp Summer Homes
- Further ideas to be presented: Flame-spurt barbecues with each home

11   Click Next.

12   Select the Customer Wishes slide. Click the green arrow to deselect it and remove it from the presentation.

13   Select the Create summary option.

14   Click Create.

15   The presentation will be displayed. In the navigation bar immediately below the work area, click the far left arrow, circled at right.

16   Click the tab for the first slide (Title).

17   Choose File > Save to save the presentation.

18   In the Save window, be sure the Automatic filename extension option is selected. Then enter a name without an extension (no period and nothing after it).

19   For the format, select StarOffice Impress 5.0 presentation. Note the other formats that are listed, including MS PowerPoint presentation and template. Click Save.

Modifying the Presentation

20　Press F5 and use the Navigator to locate the Future Steps slide. Close the Navigator if it gets in your way.

21　Enter the following text:

- `Stabilize quicksand sauerkraut storage`

- `Domesticate remaining ROUSes`

- `Flavor flame-spurt barbecues with mesquite`

22　Select the second and third bulleted items and indent them. (Click the Demote icon on the object bar above the work area.)

23　Change the bullet style of all three bulleted items (choose Format > Numbering/Bullets).

24　Change the font of bulleted items in the slide (use the Font and Size lists in the object bar, or choose Format > Character).

25　Change the font of all slide titles throughout the presentation. (Choose View > Background > Drawing.) Make the titles red and a little smaller. Switch back to regular view (choose View > Slide).

26　Click through a few of the slides to verify that the slide format was changed everywhere.

27　Right-click on any slide tab and choose Insert Slide. Name the slide and select the Title, Clipart, Text layout, then click OK.

28　In the new slide, double-click the clipart placeholder and select a piece of art from the Insert Graphics window.

29　Go to another slide and choose Insert > Spreadsheet. Make a few entries in the resulting spreadsheet.

30　Delete that spreadsheet, then choose Insert > Object > OLE object.

31　In the Insert OLE Object window, select the Create from file option and click the Search button.

32　In the resulting Open window, go to the following folder. (If you're in a multi-user environment, this will be located on the StarOffice folder on the server.)

`/office52/share/samples/language/spreadsheets`

33　Select the `CurrencyConverter.sdc` file. Click Open, then click OK in the Insert OLE Object window.

34　Change the layout of the Strengths and Advantages slide from one column to two (choose Format > Modify Layout).

35　Change the background for this slide.

- Choose View > Toolbars > Presentation.

- In the Presentation Menu, click Slide Design.

- Click Load.

- In the Categories list, select Presentation Layouts.

- Select the World background from the Templates list.

- Click More.

- Select the Preview option.

- Click OK.

- Be sure the new background is selected in the Slide Design window, then select the Exchange background page option and click OK. (The new background will be used for the entire presentation, replacing the current background.)

36 Choose View > Background > Drawing again (or click the Background view icon).

37 Delete the blue world background. (The background is a graphic, so just click on the blue rectangle and when green handles appear on all sides, press Delete.)

38 Choose View > Slide, or click the Slide view icon to move back to the foreground of the slide. Note that the background is now plain white.

39 Select the Title slide. Choose Format > Page and click the Background tab. Select Color, then select a pale yellow from the scrolling list and click OK.

40 The message "Background setting for all pages?" will appear. Click No.

41 Click in the title of the slide, then click the Interaction icon in the toolbar at the left side of the work area.

42 Set up an interaction so that clicking on the title takes you to Next Steps of Action slide.

43 Choose View > Preview to display the Preview window.

44 Click in the main area of the slide, where the subpoints are. Click the Effects icon (above the Interaction icon in the illustration at right).

45 In the Effects window, click the Text Effects icon and select a category and effect. Click the green arrow to apply the effect.

46 In the master view navigation bar at the right side of the work area, click the Slide view icon. Drag one of the slides to a different position in the presentation.

47 Use the object bar at the top of the work area to switch the slide's transition to automatic and set it to be displayed for 20 seconds (0:00:20).

48 Hide the slide (right-click the slide and choose Show/Hide Slide).

49 Click the Notes view icon. Add speaker's notes about the slide. Change the font size to something more suitable for notes, such as 12-point.

50 Click the Handouts view icon.

51 Choose View > Toolbars > Presentation if the Presentation menu isn't showing, then click Modify Slide Layout.) Select the layout that prints two slides per page, then click OK to close the Modify Slide window.

52 Drag the slides to reposition one above the other, rather than side by side.

53 Choose Insert > Fields > Page Numbers and position it in the lower right corner. (If you have trouble getting a dragging pointer, rather than a text cursor, click in the text until the text frame appears and drag that, or draw a rectangle around it to select it and hold down Shift while using the arrows to position it.)

54 Use the drawing tools to add a blue horizontal line between the first and second rows.

55 Choose Format > Page and click the Page tab; the orientation is shown as landscape. Select Portrait and click OK, then observe the changes on the presentation. Repeat the previous steps to change the orientation back to landscape.

56 Save your changes.

Producing the Presentation

57 Start the presentation. Click the Start Slide Show icon in the toolbar at the right side of the work area.

58 Let the presentation run, to see how it looks and how the slide transitional effects work that you selected.

59 Press Esc to stop the presentation.

60 Export the presentation to HTML.

- Choose File > Export.

- In the Export window, enter any name and select HTML as the type. Click Save.

- Complete the export process, entering the information you're prompted for.

- For the publication type, select Standard HTML with frames.

- When you're done, locate the folder you exported to. To start the presentation in StarOffice Web, choose File > Open and open the `siframes.htm` file in the folder where you exported the presentation.

Creating a New Presentation

You can create a new presentation in a number of different ways:

*   Using AutoPilot, the Impress wizard (simplest, if you're just starting out)
*   Using a template, without AutoPilot
*   Using a Writer document
*   From scratch

Note – To open a PowerPoint presentation in StarOffice Impress, see *Opening Existing Presentations* on page 632.

A Little AutoPilot Setup

Completing these procedures will make life simpler when you start using Impress.

Turning Off Automatic AutoPilot

AutoPilot is a powerful "wizard" tool that lets you define many of the features of a new presentation. However, it appears with somewhat annoying and surprising frequency (under File > New, primarily). You can always get to AutoPilot by choosing File > AutoPilot, so you'll probably find it more convenient to keep it from coming up when you choose File > New.

1   Choose Tools > Options > Presentation > Other.

2   Deselect the Start with AutoPilot option.

Adding Places for StarOffice to Look for Impress Files

AutoPilot has a window that lists the templates and presentations you can base your new presentation on. However, it's pretty exclusive—it only looks in `share/template/language/`, in the `educate`, `layout`, and `presnt` folders. The same applies to windows you'll use to create any presentation from a template using File > New > From Template.

Note – If you're in a multi-user system, the template folders are typically on the server, not among your own local files.

If you're on a multi-user system and have created your own templates in a different folder, for instance, you won't be able to see them in AutoPilot. Follow these steps to add the locations where you store Impress templates, presentation backgrounds, and presentations.

1 Choose Tools > Options > General > Paths.

2 In the list of paths, select Document Templates.

3 Click Edit.

4 In the Select Paths window, click Add.

5 Navigate to a folder where you store Impress templates, such as your StarOffice work folder (office52/user/work) and click Select. Add any other folders.

6 Click OK in the Select Paths and Paths windows.

The folders you added will show up in AutoPilot with the name Templates.

Using AutoPilot to Create a Presentation

You can use AutoPilot to base a presentation on a template, a presentation layout (predefined background and other elements) or an existing presentation. For all, you can then modify the background, transition type, individual pages you want to use, summary information, and other elements.

Use this method if you don't have an existing template that is defined as you need it to be. If you just want to base a presentation on an existing template or presentation and not make many changes, it's much quicker to choose File > New > From Template. Refer to *Basing a Presentation on a Template or Background (Without Using AutoPilot)* on page 624.

1 Choose File > AutoPilot > Presentation.

2 In the first window (Figure 23-2), select the Empty presentation or From template option. (Select From template to use either a template or a presentation.) It takes a few seconds for all options to be available.

Note – If the From template option never becomes available and you're in a multi-user StarOffice environment, you don't have the right permissions to access the templates folder on server. Contact your system administrator.

Select Empty presentation to design your own, or From template. (The third option just lets you open an existing presentation and doesn't offer any additional design capabilities.)

If you selected From template, select a category, then a name.

Select Preview throughout AutoPilot to see an example of your selections.

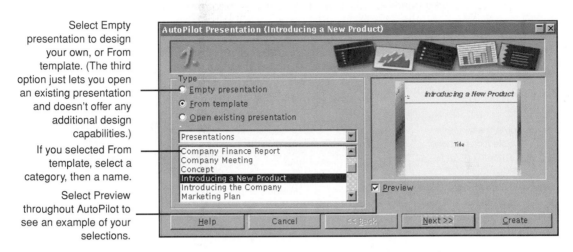

Figure 23-2   AutoPilot window 1: Selecting basis of presentation

3   If you selected From template, select a template category and template or presentation. Select Preview to see an example.

4   In the second window (Figure 23-3), select a design for the background of your presentation. You can select from Presentations, Presentation Layouts, or Education sources.

Select a style for the background of your presentation. Select Original to use the template's layout.

Indicate how you'll be delivering the presentation. If you'll be presenting it on a computer, select Screen. "Original" appears only if you're basing it on a template and means "whatever the template's set to now."

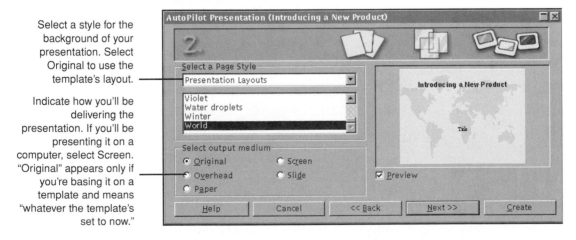

Figure 23-3   AutoPilot window 2: Selecting the background and presentation style

Your selection here is displayed in the background of all slides in your presentation, though you can make slide-specific changes later. It also affects other issues, including font style and color.

Backgrounds are discussed further in *Presentation Backgrounds* on page 683.

5   Select the appropriate option in the Presentation medium selection area.

6   The options in the third window (Figure 23-4) relate only to presentations you'll run onscreen, not to presentations you'll just be printing on acetate. Select the transition type you want.

Experiment with these selections; each combination is demonstrated in the preview window, if Preview is selected.

Switch slides manually, or automatically at timed intervals. Enter the time to display each slide, and the time to pause after each time the presentation is run, in hours:minutes:seconds format.

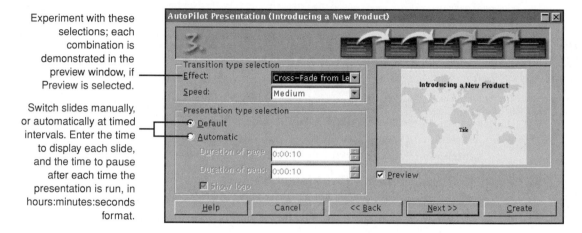

Figure 23-4   AutoPilot window 3: Selecting transition effects

Be sure Preview is selected, if you want to see an example. Each time you change your selections in the Transit or type selection area, the transition will be demonstrated in the preview window.

7   In the Presentation type selection area of the same window, choose whether the presenter will manually change from one slide to another, or if the slide will automatically be shown for a set time.

To prevent the StarOffice logo from being displayed, select Automatic. Deselect the Show logo option. Then if you want to switch back to manual transitions, select the Default option.

8   If you didn't select a template in the first window, skip to step 11.

9   In the fourth window (Figure 23-5), enter descriptive information about the presentation. AutoPilot uses this information in the title page (shown in Figure 23-6).

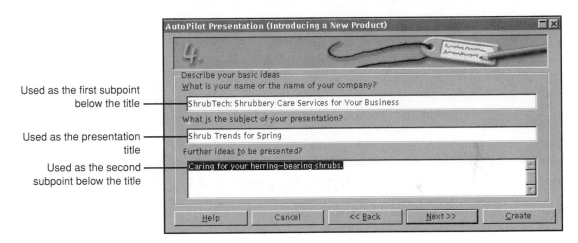

Used as the first subpoint
below the title

Used as the presentation
title

Used as the second
subpoint below the title

Figure 23-5   AutoPilot window 4: Entering title page information

10 Each template comes with defined slides (referred to in this window as pages). The
window in Figure 23-6 lets you select the ones you want to use.

You can add or delete slides later, as well: they can be from any template or
presentation, or blank.

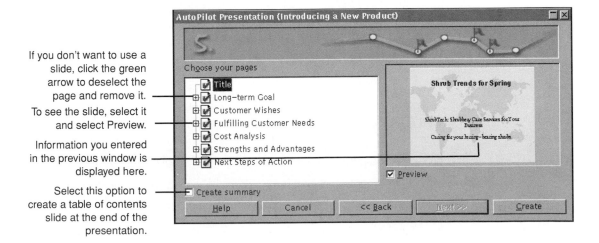

If you don't want to use a
slide, click the green
arrow to deselect the
page and remove it.

To see the slide, select it
and select Preview.

Information you entered
in the previous window is
displayed here.

Select this option to
create a table of contents
slide at the end of the
presentation.

Figure 23-6   AutoPilot window 5: Deleting unwanted slides

11 Click Create to create the presentation.

12 If you didn't select a template or a background, you'll be prompted to choose a slide design in the Modify Layout window. Select a design (select one with bullets shown, if you'll be using bulleted text) and choose OK.

13 Choose File > Save to save the presentation.

In the Save window, save it as a file rather than leaving it as a template. Select StarImpress 5.0 or another presentation format. (If you want to use it as a template in the future, see *Creating and Modifying Templates* on page 632.)

Basing a Presentation on a Template or Background (Without Using AutoPilot)

A template typically has multiple slides with "canned text" you can add to; a presentation layout only has background design.

To bring consistency and clarity to StarOffice's inconsistent terminology, keep in mind that the items labeled in StarOffice as presentation layouts are really just backgrounds. (A *slide layout* is something else; see *Using the Right Slide Layout* on page 670.)

Use this procedure if you have a template or background that has most of the features you need. Use *Using AutoPilot to Create a Presentation* on page 620 if you want to make considerable changes to the template for your presentation.

1 Choose File > New > From Template.

2 In the New window, select from one of the following categories: **layout** (backgrounds), **presnt** (presentation templates), or **Standard** (/.../template), which lists all the templates you've created yourself and saved in your user/template folder.

Note – Additional categories will appear if you've added paths using the instructions in *Adding Places for StarOffice to Look for Impress Files* on page 619.

---

3 After selecting a category, select a template from the Templates list (Figure 23-7).

Click More if you want to see more information about each. Select the Preview option to see an example of each selection.

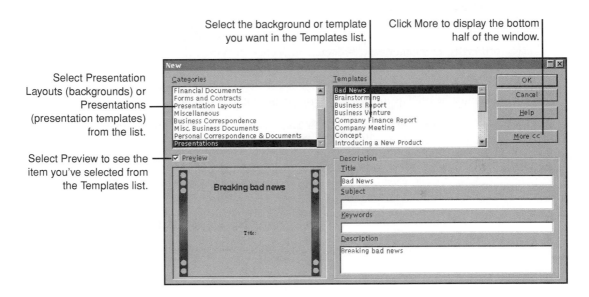

Select the background or template you want in the Templates list.

Click More to display the bottom half of the window.

Select Presentation Layouts (backgrounds) or Presentations (presentation templates) from the list.

Select Preview to see the item you've selected from the Templates list.

Figure 23-7   Creating a new presentation from a template or presentation layout (a background)

4   Click OK. The selection will be displayed in Impress.

5   Choose File > Save to save the presentation.

In the Save window, be sure to select StarImpress 5.0 or another presentation format as the file type, instead of the default StarOffice Template format.

Basing a Presentation on a StarOffice Writer Document

You can generate an outline, or all the content of a presentation, by using a Writer document as the source. This can be useful if you've already written a report or training manual, for instance, and want to give a presentation of similar material, especially if it's a long document. This creates an extremely simple presentation with no background.

There are two ways to generate the presentation from a Writer document: sending an outline to a presentation, and sending an autoabstract to a presentation. They sound complicated, but essentially they just take a Writer document and use behind-the-scenes processing and a little setup information from you to generate slides based on the text in the Writer document.

Both approaches get the job done, but using the Send Outline feature is simpler. Review the Before You Begin information, next, then use either of the subsequent procedures to generate the presentation.

Before You Begin

The document you base the presentation outline on **must** be a Writer document, either originally, or another type of document opened in Writer. It also must use the Writer heading styles: Heading 1, Heading 2, and so on. It's all right if you've modified the style attributes, or created new ones with those names, but the styles must have those names, and must be used as the heading styles in the source document.

Don't use bullets in a document you base a presentation on. They end up in the presentation as shown in Figure 23-8.

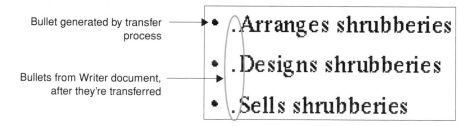

Figure 23-8 Effect of transfer on Writer bullets

Creating a Presentation Using the Send Outline to Presentation Feature

Figure 23-9 shows an example of a Writer document, with styles applied appropriately for transfer via this method, and the styles and formatting the document is converted to in Impress.

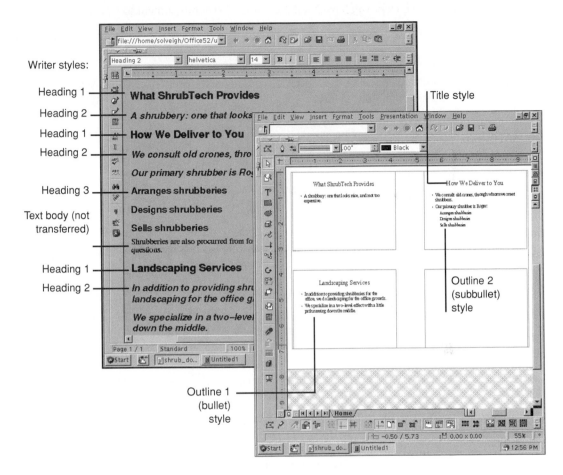

Figure 23-9   Transferring via Send Outline to Presentation

Table 23-1 shows which Writer styles are read by the conversion process and which styles they are converted to in Impress.

Table 23-1   Writer-to-Impress style conversion: Send Outline to Presentation

Writer	Impress
Heading 1	Title (slide title) Each slide title has its own slide.
Heading 2	Outline 1 (first bullet)
Heading 3	Outline 2 (indented bullet)
Heading 4	Outline 3 (indented bullet)
Others	Not converted

Follow these steps to prepare and convert the Writer document to a presentation.

1   If the source document isn't in Writer, import it or paste it into a Writer document.

2   Apply styles in Writer.

If all three heading styles aren't listed in the styles dropdown list, select the text you want to apply one of the missing headings to. Choose Format > Stylist and double-click the style you need.

3   Choose File > Send > Outline to Presentation.

4   The presentation will appear in StarOffice in outline view.

Creating a Presentation Using the Send AutoAbstract to Presentation Feature

This feature is a little more complicated and non-intuitive than sending an outline to a presentation. Figure 23-10 on page 629 shows an example of the same original Writer document, with styles applied appropriately for transfer via this method, and the styles and formatting the document is converted to in Impress. Table 23-2 expands on the details.

Table 23-2   Writer-to-Impress style conversion: Send AutoAbstract to Presentation

Writer	Impress	Comments
Any Heading style: Heading 1, 2, etc.	Title (slide title) Each slide title has its own slide.	You can limit the levels of headings that are converted; for the Outline levels to convert option (see Figure 23-11 on page 630), enter 2 if you don't want any Heading 3s to have their own slide. However, any text assigned a heading style that you exclude will not be converted at all. For example, if you specify outline levels to convert as 2, no Heading 3 text will be converted at all, to a title *or* an outline. You can convert down to Heading 5; Heading 6 and below can't be converted to a slide title.
Any non-heading style, but not any heading style that you didn't choose to convert with the Outline levels to convert option. (If you converted only down to Heading 3, then Heading 4 and below will be ignored.)	Outline1 (first bullet) Each paragraph becomes a bullet.	Up to five paragraphs below each heading that's converted to Title style can be converted. You can convert fewer if you want. Here's the tricky, non-intuitive part. Assume that the following list is part of your Writer document. You specify only one outline level to convert, so that only Heading 1s are converted to slide titles. You also choose to convert five subpoints in the conversion window. Therefore, you'd assume that the text body text below will be converted: Heading 1 text Heading 2 text text body text However, in reality you'll end up with only one slide, with the Heading 1 text as the title. Not only is the Heading 2 text ignored, but any text following a non-converted heading style is ignored.

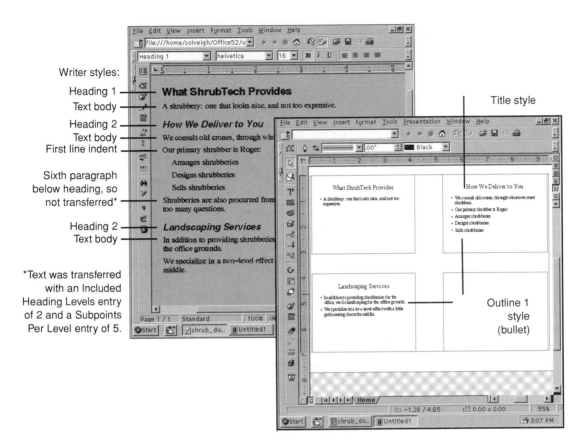

Figure 23-10   Transferring via Send AutoAbstract to Presentation

Follow these steps to prepare and convert the Writer document to a presentation.

1   If the source document isn't in Writer, import it or paste it into a Writer document.

2   Apply styles. Any text having any Heading style will have the Title style in the presentation and have its own slide.

   If Heading styles aren't available in the style dropdown list, select the text you want to apply one of the missing headings to. Choose Format > Stylist and double-click the style you need.

3   Choose File > Send > AutoAbstract to Presentation.

4   In the dialog box (Figure 23-11), enter the transfer options.

Enter the number of heading levels to make into slide headings. If you want all text that has the style Heading 1 or Heading 2 made into slide headings, for instance, enter 2.

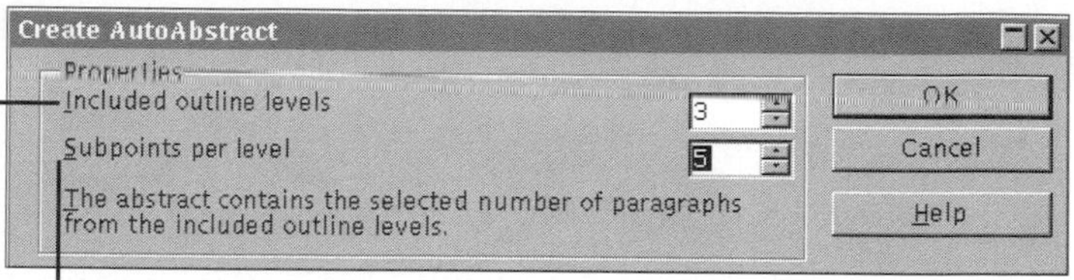

Enter the maximum number of paragraphs below each heading to make into bulleted items in the presentation. (5 is the maximum for this and the outline levels option.)

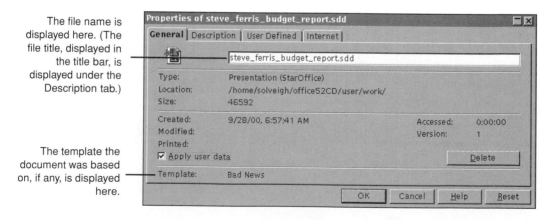

Figure 23-11   Conversion options for Send AutoAbstract to Presentation

Note – Any text in heading styles below the number in the Included outline levels field will be completely ignored by the conversion, and prevent any non-heading text below them from being converted. We recommend that you always convert 5 levels of heading styles.

5   The presentation will appear in StarOffice in outline view.

Checking What Template Your Document Is Based On

If your document is acting weird and you want to make sure you created it based on the right template, choose File > Properties and click the General tab. The template used by the document is displayed at the bottom of the window, as shown in Figure 23-12.

The file name is displayed here. (The file title, displayed in the title bar, is displayed under the Description tab.)

The template the document was based on, if any, is displayed here.

Figure 23-12   Viewing the template a document was based on

Creating a New Empty Presentation

If you really want to, you can do all the work of formatting and organizing the presentation yourself. This will create an empty presentation with one slide.

1 Choose File > New > Presentation.

If AutoPilot starts, selecting the Do not show this dialog again option, and clicking Cancel, won't make it go away. Refer to *Turning Off Automatic AutoPilot* on page 619.

2 Choose Format > Modify Layout and select the type of slide structure you want. (For more information, see *Selecting a Slide Layout for a New or Existing Slide* on page 657.)

Entering a Presentation Title

Your presentation is probably still named "Untitled," or the name of the document you based on it. Impress displays this name in the Impress title bar, in the navigation bar at the bottom of the StarOffice work area, and in template and presentation layout (background) selection windows.

To change the name:

1 Choose File > Properties.

2 Click the Description tab (Figure 23-13) and enter a different title.

File name is displayed at the top of the properties window and in the General tab. The document title, displayed in the StarOffice title bar and task bar, is displayed here.

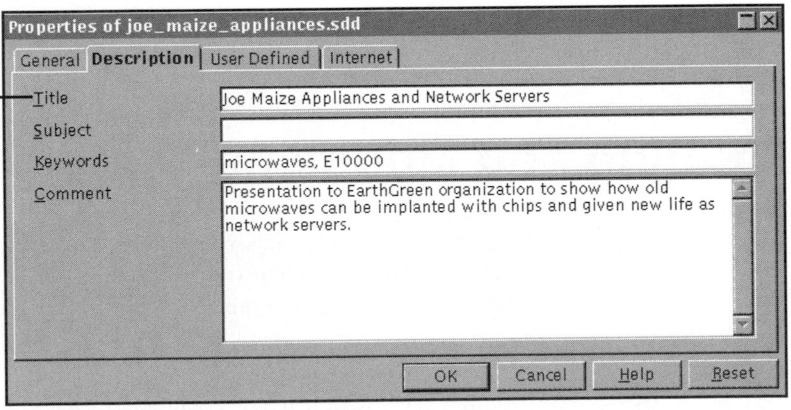

Properties of joe_maize_appliances.sdd

| General | **Description** | User Defined | Internet |

Title Joe Maize Appliances and Network Servers

Subject

Keywords microwaves, E10000

Comment Presentation to EarthGreen organization to show how old microwaves can be implanted with chips and given new life as network servers.

OK Cancel Help Reset

Figure 23-13 Changing the presentation title

Opening Existing Presentations

You can open Impress files as well as those in formats by other vendors, such as PowerPoint.

Not only can you open a Powerpoint file in Impress, but you can save it again as a PowerPoint file. However, both opening and saving take much longer than if you convert the file to Impress.

If you're prompted to select a Filter when opening files, select the type of file. If the file doesn't open correctly, try selecting StarOffice Draw instead of Impress.

Opening a Presentation File

Choose File > Open and navigate to the file you want, then click Open. If you don't see it, be sure All is selected in the File type list.

Note – If you're opening a file that wasn't created in StarOffice, such as a PowerPoint presentation, save it in StarImpress 5.0 first. A lot of the features in StarOffice won't be available until you do.

Opening a Draw File as a Presentation

Choose File > Open and navigate to the file you want. In the File type list, select Impress and click Open.

You also can select the file in Beamer and choose Open With, then select StarImpress.

Creating and Modifying Templates

Having the templates and backgrounds you need makes creating presentations much quicker and more efficient. If you find yourself making the same changes repeatedly to your presentations, it's a good idea to create templates with the elements you need already in them.

Note – By default, when you base a new document on a template, StarOffice lets you pick templates from only a couple different folders, including the `presnt` folder in `share/template/language/`. If you've added folders using the instructions in *Adding Places for StarOffice to Look for Impress Files* on page 619, you'll be able to pick from those, as well. However, to be on the safe side, the procedures in this section tell you to put your templates in only those folders where StarOffice looks by default.

Presentation Templates

Follow the appropriate procedure to create, modify, or name a template.

Creating a Presentation Template

If you want to create your own template to base other presentations on, follow these steps.

1   Select or create the presentation to base the template on.

2   Make any necessary changes; remove any text you don't want in the template.

> **Note –** You can't delete slide layout elements, such as the text frame for the header. The message "This function cannot be completed with the selected objects" will be displayed, or only the text will be deleted. Refer to *Selecting a Slide Layout for a New or Existing Slide* on page 657 to remove elements by applying a blank slide layout, or changing it to one that meets your needs more closely.

3   Choose File > Save as. Save it as an Impress template to the `share/template/` *language*`/presnt` folder, or in your `user/template` folder.

The template will be listed with the other Impress templates in AutoPilot and other template-related windows.

Modifying a Presentation Template

If you want to change one of the templates provided by Impress, or that you've created yourself, follow these steps. (If you're changing the template, it's a good idea to save the template under a new name, because you won't be able to get the original back except by reinstalling.)

1   Open a template file, typically in the `share/template/`*language*`/presnt` folder, or in your `user/template` folder.

2   Make the changes you want to the slides, background, transitions, and other elements.

3   Choose Save as to save it under a new name in the `presnt` folder. Be sure that StarImpress 5.0 Template is the file type.

Naming a Presentation Template

You can give it a name like the other templates ("Annual Report" and so on) the same way you name presentations.

1   Choose File > Properties and click the Description tab.

2   Enter a name and click OK.

If the template doesn't have a name, the file name will appear in template lists instead.

Background Templates

Follow the appropriate procedure to manage templates for use as backgrounds in your presentations. These templates contain only the background elements; no individual slides are included.

Note – Remember that backgrounds are referred to inconsistently by a variety of names in StarOffice, including *presentation layouts*.

Creating a Background Template

If you want to create your own background to base other presentations on, follow these steps.

1   Choose File > New > Presentation to open a new, blank presentation.

2   Switch to Background view (see *Using Foreground/Background Views* on page 640).

3   Create the background.

4   Choose File > Save as. Save it as an Impress template to the `share/template/` `language/layout` folder, or in your `user/template` folder.

It will be listed with the other Impress backgrounds in AutoPilot and other windows.

Modifying a Background Template

If you want to change one of the backgrounds provided by Impress, or that you've created yourself, follow these steps. (It's a good idea to save the background under a new name, because you won't be able to get the original back except by reinstalling.)

1   Open a background file from the `share/template/`*`language`*`/layout` folder, or in your `user/template` folder.

2   Switch to Background view.

3   Make the changes you want.

4   Choose Save as to save it under a new name. Be sure that StarImpress Template is the file type.

Naming a Background Template

You can give it a name like the other backgrounds ("Blue Border," "Sun," and so on) the same way you name presentations and templates.

1   Choose File > Properties and click the Description tab.

2   Enter a name and click OK.

If the background template doesn't have a name, the file name will appear in background lists instead.

Master Views, Foreground/ Background Views, and Layers

Review this overview section before you continue to the next chapter, so that you know how to get to the part of your presentation that you need, and view it the way you want to.

You can think of Impress as three-dimensional in its display and editing capabilities. It has three different systems to show different aspects of your presentation: master views, foreground/background views, and layers. It's a good idea to get to know them now, because it can make finding your way through a presentation and getting to the parts you need to edit a lot less frustrating.

Master views Show different parts of your presentation, such as only the handouts, or only the slide, as well as different displays: one slide at a time or all at once. The Master views are Drawing, Outline, Slide, Notes, and Handout.

Foreground/background views These let you work with the main content of your presentation (content such as charts and text, in Slide view) or the background (page design, in Background view) of your presentation.

You also can choose Layer view, which lets you divide the objects in Slide view and in Background view into layers. Most views are not available in all master views.

Layers When you're in Layer view, you can separate a slide into layers. Layers are similar to the illustrations in anatomy books, with each layer belonging to a different system: the skeletal system, the digestive system, and so on. Layers let you separate items in one slide into separate groups.

Figure 23-14 shows aspects of master views, foreground/background views, and layers.

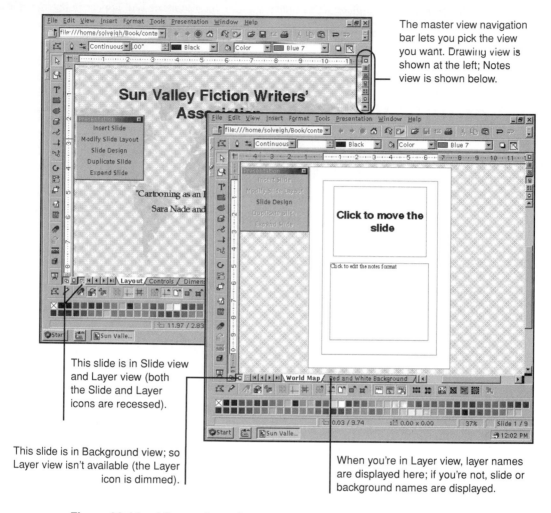

The master view navigation bar lets you pick the view you want. Drawing view is shown at the left; Notes view is shown below.

This slide is in Slide view and Layer view (both the Slide and Layer icons are recessed).

This slide is in Background view; so Layer view isn't available (the Layer icon is dimmed).

When you're in Layer view, layer names are displayed here; if you're not, slide or background names are displayed.

Figure 23-14   Master views, foreground/background views, and layers

Using Master Views

Displaying all the elements of a presentation—slides, notes, structure, and so on—would be visually dizzying and logistically difficult. Impress has divided the ways you can look at your presentation into five **master views**: Drawing, Outline, Slide, Notes, and Handout.

Changing From One View to Another

To get to a particular view, use the view bar at the right side of the work area.

Note that the bottom icon, Start slide show, doesn't take you to a different view. It's easy to click this icon by accident. It starts the presentation, giving you a blank screen at first that is somewhat alarming if you don't expect it. To stop the presentation, just press Esc.

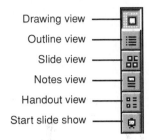

Drawing view

Outline view

Slide view

Notes view

Handout view

Start slide show

Drawing View

You'll spend most of your time in the Drawing view, adding text and graphics. You have the same capabilities here as in Draw, with additional text and effects features.

See Figure 23-14 on page 636 and Figure 23-1 on page 614 for examples of the Drawing view.

Outline View

This view shows the outline of your presentation (Figure 23-15). You can expand and contract heading levels to view only top-level headings, all text, and everything in between, and reorganize the presentation.

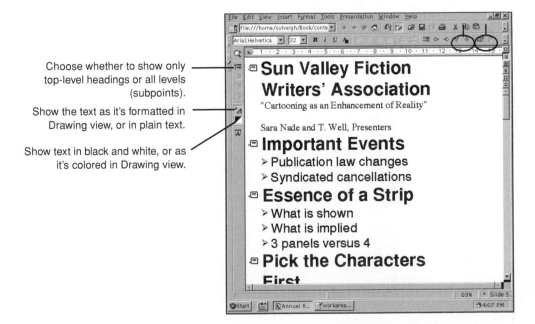

Choose whether to show only top-level headings or all levels (subpoints).

Show the text as it's formatted in Drawing view, or in plain text.

Show text in black and white, or as it's colored in Drawing view.

Figure 23-15   Outline view

Slide View

Use the Slide view (Figure 23-16) to get a bird's eye view of your presentation, to rearrange, add, and delete slides, and to specify how each slide changes to the next.

The features on the toolbar are probably still unfamiliar to you at this point; the terms are presented here so that you can start getting oriented, and get to know the work area. All features, such as rehearsing timings and setting up transition types, are covered throughout the Impress chapters.

Note – Choose View > Toolbar > Presentation to display the Presentation menu, which shows the selected effects.

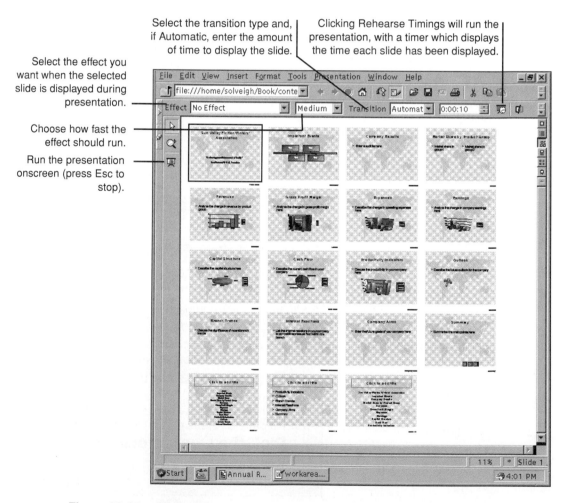

Figure 23-16   Slide view

Notes View

Add speaker notes in this view (Figure 23-17), below the slide area. When you print, you can choose to print with or without the notes. (See *Setting Printing Options* on page 726.) You can use Draw tools to edit in this view.

Check the font size for your notes before you begin; the default may be larger than you want.

You can use the icons in the toolbar in the slide and the notes area, in Slide or in Background view (slide only).

Move from slide to slide the same way you do in Drawing view.

Slide and Background view are available in Notes view.

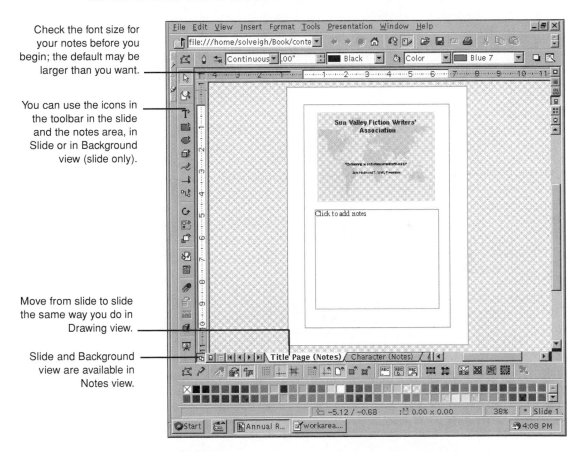

Figure 23-17   Notes view

Handout View

Create audience materials out of the slides using this view (Figure 23-18), which lets you specify the number of slides per page. What you see in the work area is what will be on each page of handouts given to people attending the presentation. You have access to Draw tools here, as well.

You can drag and resize the slides manually. To set the number of slides per handout page, choose Format > Modify Layout. (The maximum per page is six.)

You can use the icons in the toolbar to add to the handouts, but not to edit the slides.

You can use only Background view in Handout view, so any change you make appears on all pages of the handouts.

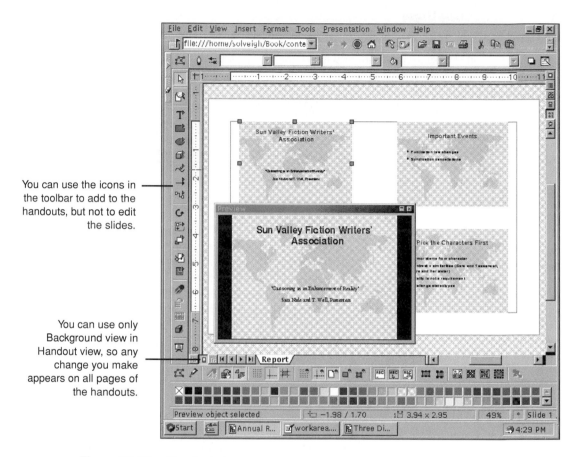

Figure 23-18   Handout view

Using Foreground/Background Views

Impress has three additional views that let you see the foreground or background of a slide, as well as layers within each: Slide view, Background view, and Layer view.

- Slide view displays the normal content of a slide.

- Background view displays the elements that are in the background of every slide in the presentation. Use this view to make changes to show up in all slides.

- Layer view lets you see the different layers within a slide foreground, or within a background.

They're available in only two of the master views.

- In Drawing view, you can access all three.

- In Notes view, you can access Slide and Background.

Slide View

In Slide view, you have all the Draw tools and can do the standard editing for developing the presentation. You'll spend much of your time in Drawing view and Slide view.

The changes you make apply only to the current slide, even if you're changing items that belong to a design component used throughout the presentation.

Background View

This view lets you make changes to the background and related items. The page style (the background design) that you selected in AutoPilot or added yourself is shown in this view.

Layer View

You can divide the contents of the slide foreground or background into an unlimited number of *layers*. Layer view is an enhancement to the other two views; when you are in Layer view, you're also in either Slide view or Background view.

Changing From One View to Another

Choose View from the menu bar, then choose Slide, Background (Drawing, Title, Notes, or Handout), or Layer.

When you're in Drawing, Notes, or Handouts view, you also can use the icons in the navigation bar at the bottom of the work area (Figure 23-19).

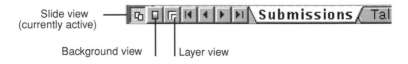

Figure 23-19   Navigating between foreground (slide) and background, and layers for each

Using Layers

When you're in Layer view, you can use layers to separate parts of a slide so that each group can be edited and viewed by itself.

Impress comes with default layers:

- Slide view: Layout (the default), Controls, and Dimension lines
- Background view: Background objects

For example, layers let you draw a car engine diagram with a different subsystem in each layer, or draw a new interdepartmental process with the parts for each department in a different layer. Figure 23-20 shows how layers look alone and together.

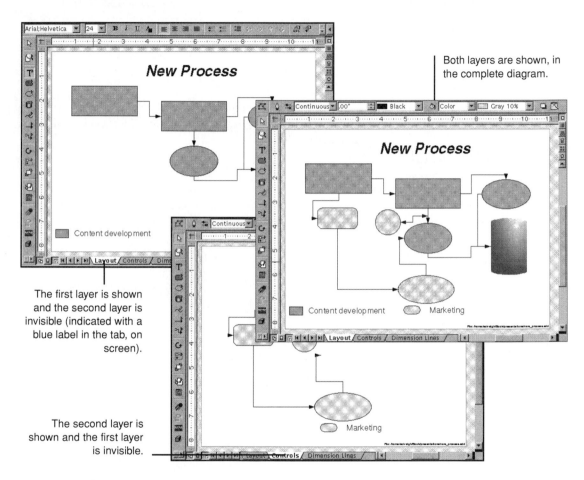

Figure 23-20   Layered diagram

Layer Quick Facts

You can't delete or rename the default layers, but you can hide them or prevent them from being printed (see *Controlling Whether a Layer Is Printable or Editable (Locked)* on page 644). The default layers are provided with all slides; however any layer you add is specific to the slide you're in when you add it.

You can use layers only when you're in the Drawing master view. Every layer is included in all slides in the presentation; there are no slide-specific layers.

Layers are displayed from left to right and front to back: that is, the layer whose tab is displayed on the left side of the navigation bar is the top layer, and so on. Objects in the top layer will block the view of objects in the same position in subsequent layers.

Changing Layers

Be sure you're in Layer view. (See *Using Foreground/Background Views* on page 640.) Then click the tab for the layer you want, in the navigation bar at the bottom of the work area (Figure 23-21).

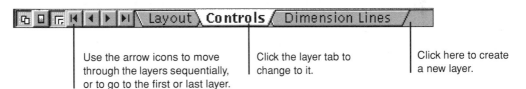

Use the arrow icons to move   Click the layer tab to   Click here to create
through the layers sequentially,   change to it.   a new layer.
or to go to the first or last layer.

Figure 23-21   Working with layers

Creating a Layer

This will add a layer to the right of the Dimension Lines layer—*not* to the right of the layer tab you select. You can't control where they are created. If you create two new layers, Layer4 and Layer5, Figure 23-22 is the result.

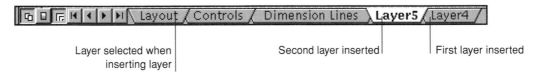

Layer selected when   Second layer inserted   First layer inserted
inserting layer

Figure 23-22   Order in which layers are inserted

1   Be sure you're in Drawing or Notes view, and Layer view.

2   Click the blank area to the right of the last layer, or right-click a layer tab and choose Insert.

3   Enter the name and other options in the Insert Layer window (Figure 23-23).

Deselect Visible if you
ever want to hide the
elements of this slide.

Deselect Printable if you
don't want this layer's
elements to be printed.

Select Locked to prevent
the draw elements on the
layer from being edited.

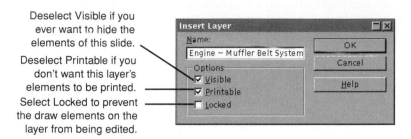

Figure 23-23   Creating a new layer

4   The layer will be created for all slides in the presentation.

Controlling Which Layer Is on Top

There isn't a way to explicitly reorder the layers; however, there are a few workarounds:

- Make a layer invisible (see *Hiding One or More Layers*)

- Move objects from one layer to another (see *Moving Objects Among Layers*)

- Delete and re-create layers

The default layer Controls is always on top. As for the other layers, the order in which you draw the objects controls what's on top: the first is on the bottom and last on the top, regardless of the layer.

Changing the arrangements of the objects using the Arrange > Send to back and similar features doesn't change the relationship of objects in different layers, though it does change object relationships within a layer.

Controlling Whether a Layer Is Printable or Editable (Locked)

To protect elements of a layer from being changed, or to keep them from being printed, you can lock the layer.

1   Enter layer view by clicking the Layer icon in the lower left corner.

2   In the navigation bar, right-click the tab of the layer you want to lock.

3   Choose Modify.

4   In the Modify Layer window (it has the same options as the Insert Layer window in Figure 23-23), select Printable, Locked, or both.

5   You'll need to select Printable again when you're ready to print it; selecting the Hidden pages option in the print options window doesn't make it print (see Figure 25-23 on page 726).

Hiding One or More Layers

The layer view in StarOffice is a little unintuitive. If you have three layers and you click the tab of any of them, you still see all the objects in all layers. You can even edit one layer's objects when you've clicked the tab of another layer. To show only the objects of one layer, or of two, you have to hide the layers that you don't want to see.

1   Right-click the layer tab in the navigation bar.

2   Choose Modify.

3   Deselect Visible.

Note – Invisible layers' names always appear in blue.

Renaming a Layer

1   Right-click the layer tab and choose Rename.

2   Type the new name on the tab.

Deleting a Layer and All Objects in It

This deletes the layer and all objects in it, so move objects out of the layer before beginning if you want to preserve them. Also, remember that the layer will be deleted from all slides in the presentation.

1   Right-click the layer tab.

2   Choose Delete.

3   Click Yes when prompted.

Moving Objects Among Layers

Surprisingly, you can't just cut and paste to move objects from one layer to another; you'll need to drag them instead. You'll need to make sure the tabs of both layers can be displayed simultaneously, so widen the main StarOffice window if necessary, or follow the directions in step 3 when you get to it.

1   Navigate to the slide containing the object you want to move.

    To copy instead of just moving the object, you need to copy the object in the current slide, then move the copy to the new layer.

2   Switch to Drawing master view, to the view (Slide or Background) that the object is in, and then choose View > Layer.

3   Select the layer that the object is in.

If you can't display the tabs of the current and target layers at once, click on the narrow vertical blank area between the rightmost layer tab and the left scrolling arrow in the navigation bar (Figure 23-24).

Figure 23-24   Increasing display space for layer tabs

The cursor will change to a two-ended arrow. Drag the blank area to the right until there's enough space to display all layer tabs.

4   Be sure that the tab of the layer you want to move the object **to** is showing in the navigation bar.

5   Click on the object, click it again and hold down the mouse, then drag the object a bit. A gray rectangle will appear at the base of the cursor. (Keep holding the mouse button down.)

6   Drag the object to the tab of the layer you want it to be in; the tab will be highlighted when you've succeeded.

7   The object will appear in the same location within the work area in the new layer.

Controlling Workspace Display

You can control several aspects of how your presentations look while you're working with them. Factors such as how large they seem, whether you're using black-and-white or color, can make it easier to develop your work and make it match your needs more closely.

Selecting a Measurement System

To display the top and left rulers, choose Tools > Options > Presentation > Layout and select the Rulers visible option.

1   Right-click on the ruler at the top or right of the workspace. (If it isn't displayed, choose View > Rulers.)

2   Select a measurement system.

Increasing or Decreasing Display Size (Zooming)

StarOffice lets you control the size at which your drawing is displayed. If you need to have particularly precise control over how you move objects in the workspace, or want to see an object close-up, you might want to use a high zoom, such as 400%, to view the objects as very large. If you want to see how the object might seem to an audience seeing it from a distance, you can reduce the view to smaller than 100%.

Selecting a Preset Zoom

1   Right-click the zoom field in the status bar below the work area.

2   Select one of the displayed percentages.

Selecting a New Zoom

1   Double-click in the zoom field.

2   Select an existing zoom or enter your own in the Variable field at the bottom of the Zoom window.

3   Click OK.

Using the Zoom Icon

1   Click and hold down the mouse on the Zoom icon in the toolbar, to display the Zoom tearoff menu.

2   Select the type of zoom you want in the Zoom menu.

You can quickly zoom in, out, to 100%, to the previous zoom, and several other options (displayed in tool tips). Each time you click to zoom in or out, the zoom changes by 50% of the current display.

Showing Object Outlines

StarOffice lets you show object outlines when you move them. The default behavior is that, if you have selected several objects to drag across the work area, only a rectangle outlining the group as a whole will be shown. If you want to see the outlines of every object, use this procedure.

1   Choose Tools > Options > Drawing > Layout.

2   Select the Contour of each individual object option, then click OK.

You can make your files appear faster if you reduce what the program needs to draw; you can turn off display of pictures and objects (this includes graphics-based backgrounds) and text.

1   Choose Tools > Options > Drawing > Contents.

2   Select the options you want (Figure 23-25).

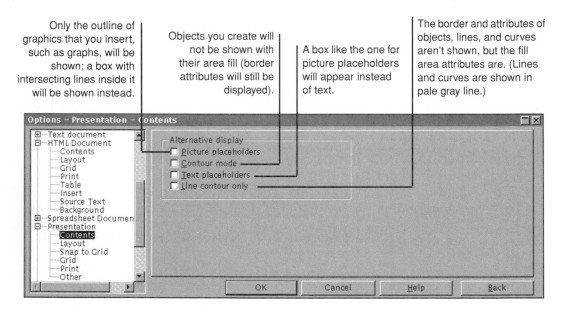

Only the outline of graphics that you insert, such as graphs, will be shown; a box with intersecting lines inside it will be shown instead.

Objects you create will not be shown with their area fill (border attributes will still be displayed).

A box like the one for picture placeholders will appear instead of text.

The border and attributes of objects, lines, and curves aren't shown, but the fill area attributes are. (Lines and curves are shown in pale gray line.)

Figure 23-25   Choosing which items to hide

Note – This doesn't affect printing—if you turn on picture placeholders here, none of your objects or backgrounds will be displayed, but they'll still print normally.

Showing Extended Object Lines When Moving Objects

You can display objects with lines coming out of both axes when you move them, to show more clearly where the object will be (Figure 23-26).

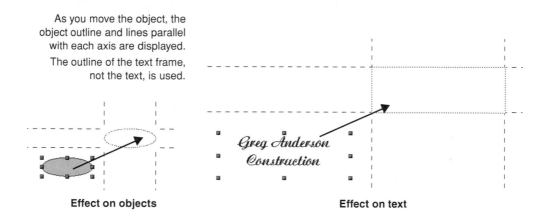

As you move the object, the object outline and lines parallel with each axis are displayed.

The outline of the text frame, not the text, is used.

Effect on objects   **Effect on text**

Figure 23-26   Displaying extended object lines

To use this feature, choose Tools > Options > Presentation > Layout, then select the Guides when moving option.

Using the Grid to Draw and Position Objects

This is covered in the Draw chapter; see *Using the Grid* on page 785. Using the grid lets you "snap" objects you draw and move to the grid lines, so that lines are straight and objects are aligned.

Use the icons on the option bar to control the grid functions (to display it, choose View > Toolbars > Option Bar). Click the Show Grid icon to activate it (Figure 23-27).

Show Grid   Use Grid (snap objects to grid

Figure 23-27   Grid option icons

Viewing in Grayscale, Color, or Black and White

You can reduce the RAM required to display images by switching to grayscale or black and white, or preview how something will look when printed, if you print in grayscale or black and white.

Note – The settings covered in this procedure don't affect printing, but the effects you see are the same you'd get if you printed in grayscale or black and white. To print in grayscale or black and white, see *Printing Without Dark Backgrounds* on page 724.

---

1   Choose View > Display Quality.

2   Select Color, Grayscale, or Black and White.

Figure 23-28 illustrates the effects. The original slide has a light blue center with bars at the side that fade from light to dark blue. The heading is dark blue and the text is black.

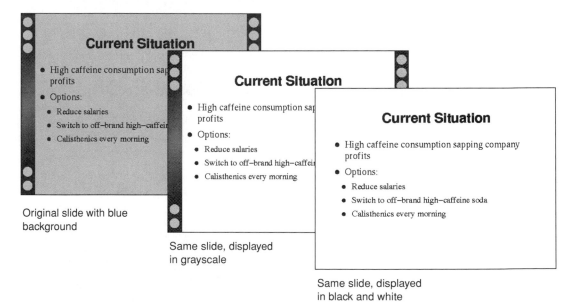

Original slide with blue background

Same slide, displayed in grayscale

Same slide, displayed in black and white

Figure 23-28   Displaying in grayscale or black and white

Developing
Presentations

Using the Navigator to Move Among Slides

You can use the Navigator, a cross-StarOffice feature, to easily move from one slide to another, among all your open presentations. It's especially useful for editing long documents, for going directly to a certain slide in an extensive presentation, or quickly switch between open documents. The Navigator is a dockable window.

You also can move slides around within and between presentations; see *Inserting Slides Using the Navigator* on page 658 for more information.

1   If you're editing, rather than running the presentation, move to Drawing view.

2   Choose File > Edit > Navigator.

3   To move to a specific slide in the same document, double-click it.

     To move forward or backward in the displayed list of slides, use the arrow icons at the top.

4   To see a list of slides in other presentations or drawings, select it from the list at the bottom of the Navigator (Figure 24-1).

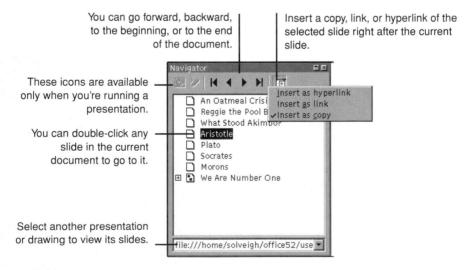

Figure 24-1   Using the Navigator

Organizing Presentations

We assume at this point that you've created a presentation file using the information starting on page 619, and now want to modify the slide order, and insert new ones.

To get your slides and headings in the right order, Impress provides you with several tools. Each one has a different set of capabilities, though there are some overlaps.

- Right-clicking the slide tab in Drawing view
- The Presentation menu, shown in Figure 24-2 (choose View > Toolbars > Presentation, or click the Presentation Box On/Off icon on the right of the object bar)

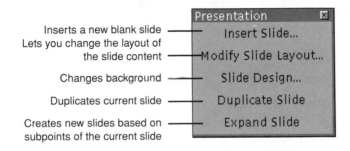

Figure 24-2   Presentation menu

- Outline master view
- Slide master view
- Navigator
- Insert menu (lets you insert a presentation in your current one)

You can also use the summary slide generator to document the slide order once you're done (see *Creating a Summary Slide* on page 663).

Renaming a Slide

In Drawing view, use either method:

- Right-click the slide tab, choose Rename Slide, then type the new name.
- In the Presentation menu, click Modify Slide Layout, then enter a new name in the Modify Slide window.

Deleting a Slide

Use either of the following methods:

- In Drawing view, right-click the slide tab and choose Delete Slide.
- In Slide view, right-click the slide tab and choose Delete Slide.

Rearranging Slides

When you rearrange the order of slides in a presentation you'll be presenting on a computer, you'll need to reassign the transition effects between slides. Refer to *Applying Slide Transition Effects* on page 697 for more information.

Slide View

In Slide view, you can quickly rearrange slide order. If you want to move subpoints from one slide to another, refer to the following section, which describes the process in Outline view. However, moving slides in Slide view is simpler and less error-prone.

Refer to *Using Master Views* on page 636 if you want more information about Slide view.

1   Switch to Slide view.

2   Select the slide you want to move.

3   Drag the slide to where you want the slide to be; a thick black bar will appear where the slide will be positioned when you release the mouse. Figure 24-3 illustrates this.

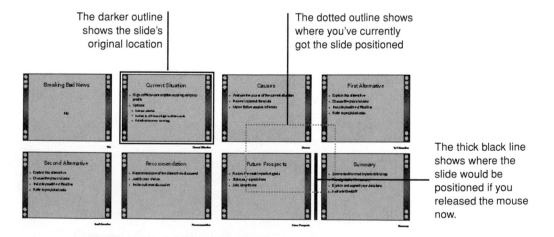

Figure 24-3   Moving a slide in Slide view

Outline View

You can move a part of your presentation to a new location by **dragging** its heading to a different place in the outline, or by using the Move Up and Move Down icons in the **object bar**.

The advantage of using Outline view is, among other factors, that you can view just the text of each heading, as well as viewing or hiding subpoints (the text within each slide).

See *Using Master Views* on page 636 if you want more information about Outline view.

If you're repositioning a slide heading, its subpoints will be moved, as well. (It's possible to insert a heading in the middle of a slide, though, separating heading and bullets— though this might not be what you want.) Graphics remain with the original slide heading.

Dragging

1   Switch to Outline view.

2   Choose to show all text within the presentation, or only level 1 (slide headings), using the icons on the toolbar.

3   Select the slide icon for the a slide heading, or select a subpoint.

The pointer won't change to a positioning pointer; it will still look like an insertion pointer, like one you'd use to type text.

4   Drag the item to its new location.

A thin gray line indicates where the item will be repositioned when you release the mouse (below the line it will appear after).

Note – If you're showing all levels of the presentation, be careful not to accidentally reposition a slide heading in the middle of another slide. You'll get illogical, if amusing, topic mixes.

Using the Object Bar

1   Switch to Outline view.

2   Choose to show all text within the presentation, or only level 1 (slide headings), using the icons on the toolbar.

3   Select the slide heading or subpoint you want to move.

4   Click Move Up or Move Down until the item is in the desired location.

Inserting a New Empty Slide

You can add a slide at a specific spot in your presentation in several ways; we'll cover two here.

When you add a slide, it is added with a specific *layout*. The layout is the structure of the slide: this can include features such as default area for a heading and text, a blank chart with text bullets above it, etc. Depending on how you add the slide, a default will be used, or you can select the one you want.

Note – Impress uses the term "layout" frequently and inconsistently. A layout, or slide layout, is the structure of one slide. A presentation layout (see *Presentation Backgrounds* on page 683) is the background for an entire presentation.

Quickly Adding a Slide

1   Select the slide that you want the new slide to appear immediately after.

2   Click the blank area to the right of the last slide.

The new slide will be added after the selected slide, and will have the same slide layout and background.

Adding a Slide and Selecting the Layout

1   Move to Drawing view.

2   Select the slide that you want the new slide to appear immediately after.

3   Do one of the following:

   •   Click the Insert Slide option in the Presentation menu.

   •   Right-click the tab of the current slide and choose Insert.

   •   Click the Insert icon on the toolbar and display the Insert tearoff menu, then click the Insert Slide icon.

4   Enter the slide name and select the slide layout you want, and click OK (Figure 24-4 on page 657). The slide will have the same background as the slide right before it.

Note – We strongly recommend that you select the layout in Figure 24-4 that most closely matches the content you're going to add. A lot of default formatting, which makes it easier to add text, comes with the preset layouts. Unless you're just going to import an object and have no text, there isn't much reason to use the completely unformatted layout in the upper left corner.

For instance, if you're a PowerPoint user, you're used to being able to press the Tab key to indent a bulleted item to the next line. This won't happen unless you choose a layout that contains bulleted items.

This name will appear on the slide's tab in the navigation bar.

It's a good idea not to select the unformatted layout if you want text in the slide.

Select the slide layout you want.

Choose whether to include the background (attributes like page color) or background objects (objects like logos).

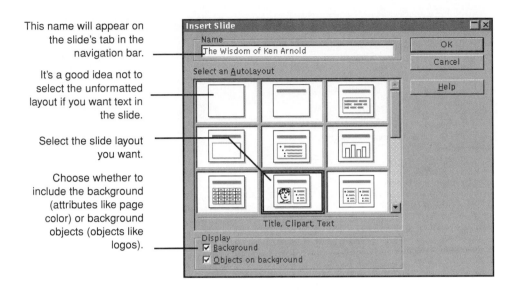

Figure 24-4   Setting new slide attributes

Selecting a Slide Layout for a New or Existing Slide

This is very similar to adding a new slide. Review the precautions at the beginning of *Inserting a New Empty Slide*, then follow these steps.

1   Move to Drawing view.

2   Select the tab of the slide whose layout you want to change.

3   Click the Modify Slide Layout option in the Presentation menu.

4   Select the slide layout you want, then click OK.

Specifying Slide Orientation and Margins

Selecting the slide layout takes care of most of the slide options. However, you can use the Page Setup window to specify other aspects, including slide orientation (portrait or landscape). The options you set here are not slide-specific; they affect the entire file.

For more information on page setup, see Figure 5-32 on page 212.

1   Choose Format > Page.

2   Set page margins and orientation as shown in Figure 24-5, then click OK.

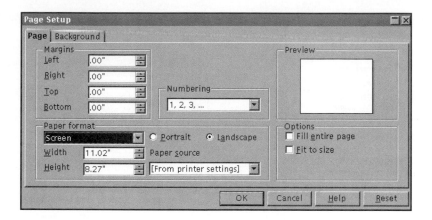

Figure 24-5   Setting slide margins and orientation

3   Slide layouts are designed for portrait orientation, so if necessary, switch to Background view and adjust the text frames of the heading and body to fit the new dimensions.

Inserting Existing Slides From Impress or Draw

Draw and Impress are both based on slides as the basic component of the file, so adding a slide from another presentation or a graphic in an existing Draw file creates a new slide in your presentation. The slides will keep the background and styles from the documents where they are now; they won't get the background and styles of the presentation you insert them in.

Inserting Slides Using the Navigator

You can insert a Draw graphic or a Impress slide from any open presentation or drawing document.

1   Move to Drawing view.

2   Be sure the document you want to copy from (source) and the one you want to copy to (target) are open.

3   Choose Edit > Navigator (Figure 24-6).

You can go forward, backward, to the beginning, or to the end of the document.

Use this icon to insert a copy, link, or hyperlink of the selected slide immediately after the current slide.

These icons are available only when you're running a presentation.

You can double-click any slide in the current document to go to it.

Select another presentation or drawing to view its slides.

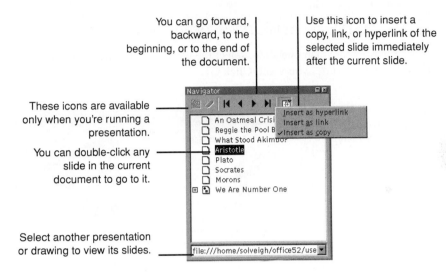

Figure 24-6   Inserting a slide using the Navigator

4   The slides in the current presentation are displayed. Double-click to move to the one you want in front of the slide you'll insert.

5   If you want to copy from another document, select it from the list at the bottom of the Navigator.

6   Select the slide you want to insert.

7   Click the Drag Mode icon and be sure the Insert as copy option is selected.

8   Drag the selected slide to the work area of the current slide.

9   Enter a new name if you're prompted to.

Inserting Slides Using the Insert File Feature

You can insert Draw and Impress files, which will be created as separate slides to the right of the current slide.

For information on inserting HTML and text files into a selected slide, see *Adding Files and Objects* on page 679.

HTML and text files will be inserted into the current slide, as noneditable text. However, we found that doing so was extremely aggravating—performance in StarOffice and other open applications slowed down considerably. Therefore, we recommend that you paste in the contents, rather than inserting the file.

1   Click the Insert icon on the toolbar at the left of the work area, and display the Insert tearoff menu. Click the Insert File icon.

2   Select the file you want.

3   The file will be listed in the Insert Slides/Objects window (Figure 24-7).

   If the file has more than one slide, select the whole file, or click the + icon and select only the slide or slides you want. Click OK.

Click the + icon if the file has
more than one slide and you
don't want all of them.

Select one slide, or Shift + click
to select more than one.

Select this option to insert the
slide or slides as links. The slides
will be updated when the source
file is changed.

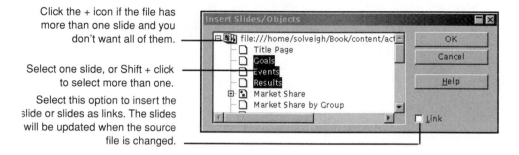

Figure 24-7   Inserting slides from Draw or Impress files

Inserting All the Slides in Another Presentation

1   Move to Drawing view.

2   Move to the slide that's right before where you want the presentation to be inserted.

3   Choose Insert > File.

4   Select the presentation you want, then click OK.

Copying and Duplicating Slides

The goals achieved by copying and duplicating are, of course, the same. Impress provides several ways to do this.

Copying a Slide From Any Presentation in Slide View

You can copy a slide from the current presentation or another one, and paste it into the location you select.

1   Move to Slide view.

2   Select the slide you want to copy.

3   Choose Edit > Copy.

4   Move to the location where you want to paste it.

   The slide will be inserted to the right of the selected slide.

5   Choose Edit > Paste.

Duplicating a Slide in the Same Presentation in Drawing View

The new slide will be added immediately after the duplicated slide, and named "Slide *n*+1." (if you select the fifth slide and duplicate it, the duplicated one will be named "Slide 6").

1   Move to Drawing view.

2   Select the tab of the slide to duplicate.

3   Display the Presentation menu.

4   Click Duplicate Slide.

Promoting and Demoting Subpoints

Promoting subpoints (the bulleted items in each slide) is similar to the expand function on the Presentation menu, which lets you automatically create a new slide for each subpoint in a slide. Refer to *Expanding: Creating a Slide for Each Subpoint* on page 661 if you'd rather use that feature.

Demoting a slide heading to a subpoint will delete all the items in the slide and any objects. Promote subpoints before you demote the slide heading they're under. Also, note that corresponding graphics are not preserved or moved when you delete a slide.

1   Switch to Outline view.

2   Choose to show all text within the presentation, or only level 1 (slide headings), using the icons on the toolbar.

3   Select the slide heading or subpoint you want to change.

4   Click the Promote or Demote icon until the item is at the desired level.

    If you're demoting a slide heading to a subpoint, click Yes to delete the slide and its contents.

Expanding: Creating a Slide for Each Subpoint

You can generate new slides based on the topics, or *subpoints*, in an existing one. This is useful if you find you're trying to cover too much in one slide. For instance, you might have a slide titled "Tourist Destinations of North Dakota" with five bulleted subpoints, then realize that this is far too big a topic to cover in one slide. Expanding the Tourist Destinations slide would delete it and create five new slides, one for each subpoint.

When you expand a slide, the expanded slide is deleted, and one new slide is created for every paragraph you've applied Outline 1 style to. Outline 1 is a presentation style, listed in the Stylist (Format > Stylist) and defined in the Style Catalog (Format > Styles >

Catalog). The slides must contain two or more Outline 1 elements to activate the Expand option.

If you want to keep the main slide and expand it into multiple slides, duplicate it first. Also, note that graphics in the expanded slide are not preserved or moved with the subpoints.

1   Move to Drawing view, Outline view, or Slide view.

2   Select the slide to expand.

3   Duplicate it, if you don't want to delete it.

4   Click Expand Slide.

5   Click Yes to delete the expanded slide, when prompted.

The new slides will appear after (to the right of) where the expanded slide was.

Showing and Hiding Slides

You can temporarily hide a slide, without deleting it.

Note – If you often need to hide and show slides to customize presentations for different audiences, refer to *Creating Custom Presentations* on page 705.

1   Move to Slide view.

2   Right-click the slide and choose Show/Hide Slide.

You also can click the Show/Hide icon on the object bar.

3   A hidden slide is indicated by a shadow behind its name (Figure 24-8).

Figure 24-8   Hidden slide

Showing and Hiding Subpoints

You can hide all bulleted items, or subpoints, at or below a particular level, using outline view. The subpoints will always be printed; there's no way to control printing hidden subpoints.

1   Click the Outline icon to go to outline view, or choose View > Master View > Outline View. Outline view is shown in Figure 24-9.

2   To hide all subpoints, click the First Level icon on the left side of the window.

3   To hide specified levels of subpoints, put your cursor at the lowest hierarchical level you want **displayed**. Click the Hide Subpoints icon. There must be bullet points below the selected level, or the Hide Subpoints icon won't be active.

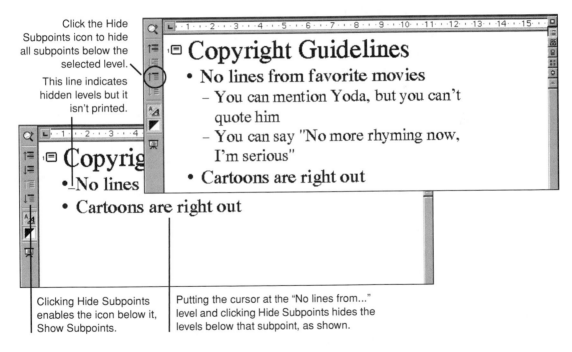

Click the Hide Subpoints icon to hide all subpoints below the selected level.

This line indicates hidden levels but it isn't printed.

Clicking Hide Subpoints enables the icon below it, Show Subpoints.

Putting the cursor at the "No lines from..." level and clicking Hide Subpoints hides the levels below that subpoint, as shown.

Figure 24-9   Hiding subpoints

Creating a Summary Slide

A summary slide functions as a table of contents of your slide titles. It's inserted at the end of your presentation.

You can't update a summary slide if you rearrange slides; you can only delete the existing one and create a new one.

1   Move to Drawing view.

2   Select the tab of the first slide in your presentation that you want included in the summary slide.

3   Choose Insert > Summary Slide.

Adding Text

Be sure you're in Drawing view, in the correct view (Slide or Background), and the correct layer, if you're using layers. (You can use text in Handout and Notes views, as well, but not to add to the slide contents.)

You'll need to set text editing options, then add a text frame if necessary, and finally the text itself.

Text Editing Options

To know how the text tools will work, you need to set your text editing options first. Use the text icons in the object bar below the work area to set text options. An option is on when it's dimmed and looks indented.

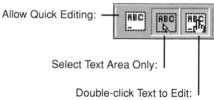

In our experience working with Impress and Draw, we concluded that it's most convenient to choose only the Double-click Text to Edit option.

Allow Quick Editing   Choose this option if you want to be able to just click in text once and start adding to it or editing it. This option can be a little annoying—it makes it difficult to click on text in order to select the text frame. We recommend that you choose Double-click Text to Edit instead.

Select Text Area Only   This option means that you can't click on the text in order to select the whole text frame, and move it, delete it or perform other actions. In order to select the text frame, you need to get into text edit mode first by clicking or double-clicking text. We recommend that you not use it, unless you don't think you'll be frequently selecting text frames.

Double-click Text to Edit   This option lets you quickly, but not accidentally, get into text edit mode for any text you double-click. We recommend using this option.

Adding a Standard Preset Text Frame to Your Slide

To add an Impress preset text frame to a blank slide, see *Selecting a Slide Layout for a New or Existing Slide* on page 657. This is the best way to create the structure within which you'll add text.

Using the Text Icons to Create Text Frames

You can create two types of text frames—the area defining where and how text is positioned in your presentation, as well as callout text frames, which include a line extending from the text box to an object.

Use the tools available from the Text icon in the toolbar at the left side of the work area to create text.

You also can double-click any object, such as a rectangle you've drawn, and type inside it.

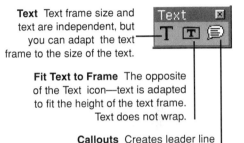

Text Text frame size and text are independent, but you can adapt the text frame to the size of the text.

Fit Text to Frame The opposite of the Text icon—text is adapted to fit the height of the text frame. Text does not wrap.

Callouts Creates leader line and box for callout text

Making Your Own Text Frames for Presentation Content: Not a Good Idea

We strongly recommend that, for the main text of your presentations, you choose a slide layout that has a text frame in it already instead of using a blank slide layout and adding your own text frames using the text tool. Using a slide layout with text frames in it is the fastest, easiest, least frustrating way to make a professional-looking presentation, for the following reasons:

- The slide layouts provide a lot of preset formatting that takes a lot of time to re-create on your own.

- Formatting, especially involving tabs, that you add in your own text frames sometimes just up and disappears.

- You can see the text frames of the preset slide layouts when they're not selected and when there's no text in them, which is not possible with the text frames you make with the text icons.

- You can't use the Presentation styles to apply style formatting with text in text-tool frames. You can only use the Character and other formatting windows, which takes longer because you can only apply a few characteristics at a time.

If you don't like the formatting for text in the preset slide layouts, you can change it much more easily than you can the text in your own text frames. See *Creating and Modifying Styles* on page 678.

Text Icon: Drawing a Text Frame With a Specific Size

This tool is best if you want to control how the text wraps: if you want to write a paragraph that is exactly four inches wide, for instance. Use this tool for most of the text in your presentation.

1   Click the icon.

2   Draw the text frame in the work area.

Note – This is important: if you don't define a width for the text by drawing the text frame and you just start typing, the text won't wrap.

---

3   Type the text you want.

4   Click the Arrow icon when you're done, or you'll keep accidentally creating more text frames each time you click in the work area.

To set text frame options, see *Setting Text and Text Frame Options* on page 667.

Fit Text to Size Icon: Sizing the Text to the Frame

This tool is best for short pieces of text, or if you want to quickly but roughly set the size of the text in the frame. The text will be approximately the same height as the frame you draw. (That's **approximately**; the font shrinks somewhat when you deselect the text frame.) In addition, the text won't wrap; it will begin in the center of the text frame and, as you type, extend to the right and left, potentially completely out of the work area. (We generally found this frame annoying.)

1   Click the icon.

2   If you just click in the work area and start typing, the text will have the default font attributes shown in the object bar.

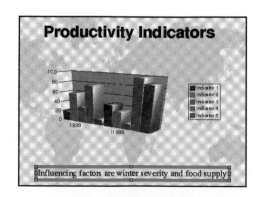

If you draw a text frame, the text will be as large as necessary to fit the text from top to bottom. If you resize the text frame later, the text will be adjusted to fit the new size.

To set text frame options, see *Setting Text and Text Frame Options* on page 667.

Callouts Icon

This tool draws a line and text frame.

1   Click the icon.

2   Click the mouse where you want the callout line to begin, and drag it to where you want the text to be.

3   Resize the text frame.

4   To enter text, double-click in the frame and start typing.

    By default, the text frame will grow as you type; the text won't wrap. To make the text wrap, right-click the text frame and choose Text, then deselect the Fit width to text option in the Text window.

5   Apply line and fill attributes to the callout line and box.

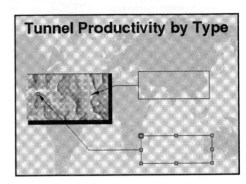

To set additional text frame options, see *Setting Text and Text Frame Options*.

Setting Text and Text Frame Options

Use these options for text in any text frame, including the ones provided in slide layouts, and the text frames. The options also apply to objects you've typed text in by double-clicking in the object.

1   Switch to Drawing view.

2   Select a text frame or object.

3   Choose Format > Text to display the Text window (Figure 24-10).

    If Text is dimmed, right-click the frame and choose Text.

4   Make the appropriate changes to the text frame or object.

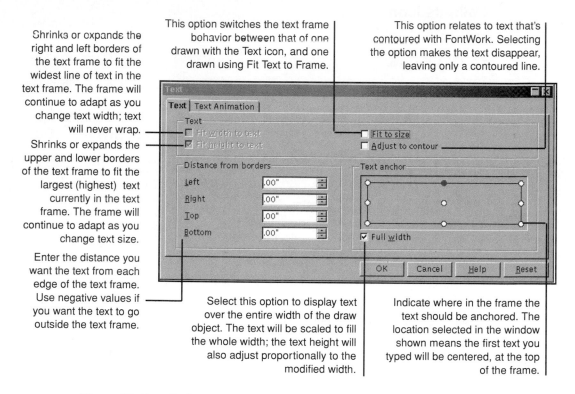

Shrinks or expands the right and left borders of the text frame to fit the widest line of text in the text frame. The frame will continue to adapt as you change text width; text will never wrap.

Shrinks or expands the upper and lower borders of the text frame to fit the largest (highest) text currently in the text frame. The frame will continue to adapt as you change text size.

Enter the distance you want the text from each edge of the text frame. Use negative values if you want the text to go outside the text frame.

This option switches the text frame behavior between that of one drawn with the Text icon, and one drawn using Fit Text to Frame.

This option relates to text that's contoured with FontWork. Selecting the option makes the text disappear, leaving only a contoured line.

Select this option to display text over the entire width of the draw object. The text will be scaled to fill the whole width; the text height will also adjust proportionally to the modified width.

Indicate where in the frame the text should be anchored. The location selected in the window shown means the first text you typed will be centered, at the top of the frame.

Figure 24-10   Options controlling text in objects and in text frames

Adding Your Text

The most important part, of course, is getting what you want to say into the slide. Again, StarOffice offers a variety of ways to do this.

Typing

Click or double-click in the text frame, depending on the setup options you chose, and add your presentation's contents.

Inserting a File

See *Inserting Text and HTML Files* on page 680.

Pasting

Don't overlook simply pasting in text from other documents. Unless it's from another presentation file, pasting in generally works better than importing or inserting a file.

Position the cursor in the text frame before pasting. If you don't position the cursor in a text frame before pasting, a new Text icon type text frame is created for the pasted text.

Writing Text Inside an Object

You also can double-click an object to type text inside it. This is useful in drawings such as flow charts, maps, and diagrams.

Getting Into Text Editing Mode

Even with the correct options selected, getting into text editing mode in Impress can be a little tricky. We've found a couple tricks that help:

*   Be sure your text editing options are set up correctly (see page 664).

*   Click in another text frame, such as the title frame, then click back in the subpoint frame.

*   Be sure to click in an area of the text frame where there's text.

*   Just keep clicking in it—you'll get in eventually (not a clever workaround, but one we found did work consistently, if slowly).

To format your text, refer to *Formatting Text* on page 669. That section contains a few key tips that will keep your frustration level down.

Formatting Text

You have the combined capabilities of Draw, Writer, and a few extras that are only in Impress.

Note – Some features, like the features in *Applying Standard Text Formatting* on page 673, need to be applied to the text itself; others, like the formatting covered in *Setting Text and Text Frame Options* on page 667, need to be applied to the text frame. Be sure to select the appropriate item before you start formatting.

It's a good idea to have the Preview window (choose View > Preview; see Figure 24-11) displayed when you're doing any slide editing. It's particularly useful for seeing effects and animation, which you can't see in a static slide.

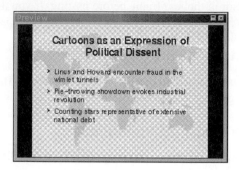

Figure 24-11   Preview window

Using the Right Slide Layout

While you can choose a completely unformatted layout for a slide, then use the Text tool to create a text frame for it, that's the hard way. A lot of automatic formatting that will make your life easier is included in the preset layouts (see *Selecting a Slide Layout for a New or Existing Slide* on page 657). If you don't like how the Outline 1 and other styles look, you can change them using procedures in this section.

Using Columns

You can divide your slide into two or more columns using the Modify Layout window described in *Selecting a Slide Layout for a New or Existing Slide*, or by simply manually resizing and copying the text frames.

1   Select the text frame and shrink it to slightly less than half the width of the text area. (For more columns, make the text frame smaller.)

2   Apply any formatting to it; styles, character formats, etc.

3   Copy it and paste it.

4   Position it to the right of the original.

5   Align the text frames using the Alignment tearoff menu, or select the text frames, right-click them, and choose an alignment option. (See *Aligning Objects* on page 779.)

Using the Object Bar for General Formatting

The object bar for text (choose View > Toolbars > Object Bar; see Figure 24-12) lets you quickly apply features like bullets, alignment, and basic text formatting. Tool tips describe each function; most are also available in the other text-related window.

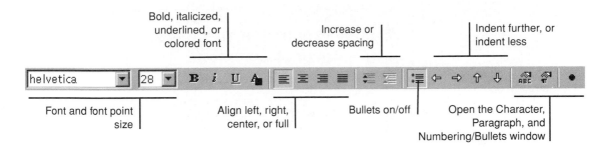

Figure 24-12   Quick formatting using the object bar for text

The default text values for any text that you enter is shown in the object bar. To change these values, first be sure no text is selected in the work area. Then choose Format > Character and make the appropriate selections.

Working With Spacing and Indents

Impress has good automatic-indenting features; you can use several approaches, including just pressing Tab or using the indent/promote icons.

Text Frame Adjustments

Resize or move the text frame so the farthest-left text starts where you want it.

Indenting Text to Make Subbullets

You can press the Tab key to indent text, or use the Promote and Demote icons on the object bar. These are the most convenient methods for quickly indenting or "outdenting" any text. When you press Tab or use the Promote and Demote icons, the styles are automatically changed (one demotion changes Outline1 to Outline2, and so on). See Figure 24-13.

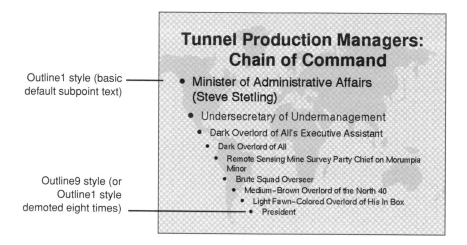

Outline1 style (basic default subpoint text)

Outline9 style (or Outline1 style demoted eight times)

Figure 24-13   Indenting subpoints

Justifying Text

Use the alignment icons to left-justify, center, right-justify, or fully justify your text.

The Paragraph Window

This window (choose Format > Paragraph; see Figure 24-14) lets you set up spacing, indents, and tabs. Use this window in Drawing, Handout, or Notes view. See *Paragraph Formatting* on page 184 for more information.

Figure 24-14   Options controlling indent, alignment and tabs

Applying Standard Text Formatting

The Character window (choose Format > Character; see Figure 24-15) lets you apply standard text formatting attributes like font and point size. Use this window in Drawing, Handout, or Notes view. See *Character Formatting* on page 178 for more information.

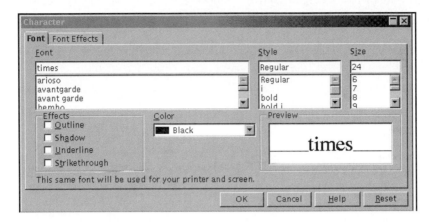

Figure 24-15   Options controlling text formatting

Using Numbering and Bullets

You can quickly control these features on the object bar, or use the numbering and bullets formatting window.

Note – If you've got a dark background, be sure that your bullets are light-colored, or they'll be difficult or impossible to see. Choose Format > Number/Bullets and click the Customize tab to select light-colored bullet graphics from the gallery, or from a file you've created yourself.

Turning Numbering and Bullets On and Off

You can turn this feature on or off for the text that's currently selected using the Bullets on/off icon in the object bar.

If that doesn't work, you'll need to change the slide design to one that contains bullets, to add them, or doesn't contain bullets, to turn them off. Choose Format > Modify Layout and select a layout with the right contents. (For more information, see *Selecting a Slide Layout for a New or Existing Slide* on page 657.)

Full Formatting Capabilities

The Numbering/Bullets window lets you choose what symbols or numbers appear next to paragraphs, and where they're positioned. Bullets and numbering are paragraph-specific; that is, each line in a list can have a different bullet or number style.

Use this window (Figure 24-16) in Drawing, Handout, Outline, or Notes view. Refer to *Using Basic Numbering, Bullets, and Outlining* on page 194 for more information.

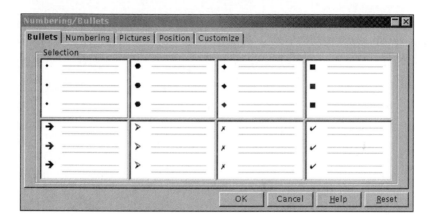

Figure 24-16   Options controlling bullet and numbering type and spacing

Using Styles

Most of your presentations will contain formatting that's already automatically applied through the slide layout or AutoPilot features, and each piece of text has a specific style assigned to it.

Impress is very rigid about what styles it wants in a slide. You can't create new text-formatting styles, or add new styles through the Stylist. The only way you can make other styles available to a slide is to change the slide layout, or to modify existing styles.

To create new graphics styles, or to modify either type of style, see *Creating Sets of Attributes Using Styles* on page 773 in *StarOffice Draw: Creating Vector Graphics*.

Text Effects

As in Draw, you can play with the text to create interesting effects.

Converting Text to 3D

You can convert text to 3D easily by following these steps.

1 Click in the text.

2 Click on the text frame that appears. The lines marking the text frame should disappear and only the green handles will appear.

Note – Getting the right right-click menu is tricky; you won't get the Convert menu unless you follow these steps.

---

3 Right-click the **text frame** (not the text itself) and choose Convert > Convert to 3D (see Figure 24-17).

Don't choose 3D Rotation; that will make the text look cool, but completely illegible.

Figure 24-17   Text before and after 3D conversion

Distorting Text

To skew or curve text, refer to *Distorting and Curving Objects* on page 788.

FontWork

StarOffice includes FontWork, a program that allows you to create exceptional font effects. Choose Format > FontWork, or right-click on a text frame and choose FontWork (Figure 24-18). (Follow the directions in steps 1 through 3 in the previous procedure if you have problems getting the right right-click menu.)

It's beyond the scope of this book to describe all the features of the FontWork program; however, we encourage you to explore it, because not only is it a powerful tool, but it's a lot of fun to use.

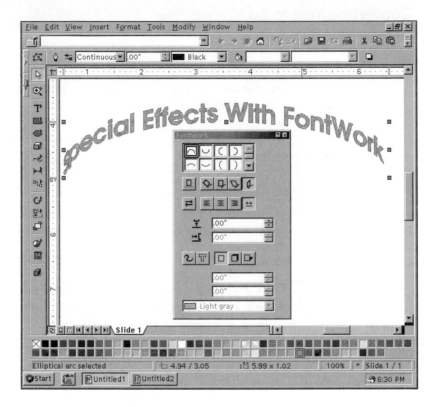

Figure 24-18   FontWork window and effects

Modifying Presentation Default Fonts

You can use Background view to easily change text elements that appear throughout your presentation, like the font and font size of the heading in each slide, in Drawing and Notes master views. (You also can use styles to modify defaults; see *Using Text and Object Styles* on page 677.)

Any change you make using this procedure will be effective in every slide in the presentation, regardless of the slide layout used.

1   Choose View > Background, then select Drawing, Notes, or Handout (or switch to Drawing, Notes, or Handout master view, then click the Background view icon). See Figure 24-19

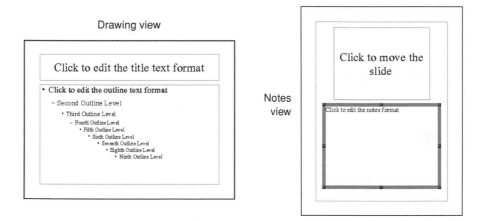

Figure 24-19   Changing default fonts for Drawing and Notes master views

2   Placeholder text for the styles used in the presentation will appear. Make the changes you want: change the font, font size, style, and so on.

Switch out of Background view to add content to your presentation.

Using Text and Object Styles

Styles let you save a particular set of attributes, such as font, spacing, and bullets; and, for drawing objects, area fill, color, line ends (round, arrow), and so on. It's a good idea to use styles if you need to use an object frequently that's formatted in a particular way, such as a line with an arrow that you've defined yourself, or text formatting for headings.

There are two types of styles in Impress: presentation styles, for text, and graphics styles, for objects.

For an extended explanation of how to import styles, and the ways you can save time using styles, refer to *Power Formatting With Styles* on page 201.

Modifying the default formats for headings and other elements is covered in *Modifying Presentation Default Fonts* on page 676.

Available Styles

The styles available for use, and to be modified, depend upon the slide layout. This is determined by one of the following:

- The layout you selected in the Modify Slide window (choose Format > Modify Layout)
- The template or background you based the presentation on

Applying Styles

Select the object or text, then use either of the following methods to apply the style.

- Display the Stylist (choose Format > Stylist), select the style category you want, and double-click the style.
- Choose Formats > Style > Catalog, select the style category you want, and double-click the style.

Creating and Modifying Styles

Impress doesn't allow you to create new presentation styles. To create new graphics styles, or to modify either type of style, see *Creating Sets of Attributes Using Styles* on page 773 in *StarOffice Draw: Creating Vector Graphics*.

Making Styles Reusable in Other Documents

Unless you jump through a couple hoops, any styles you create or modify will be available only in the document where you made them. To make them available in other documents:

- Create the styles in a document that you then save as a StarImpress template.
- Then base new documents on that template by choosing File > New > From template.

You can also import styles from other documents following the instructions in *Loading Individual Styles* on page 222.

Changing the Font Styles for All New Presentations

You can change the styles for a particular presentation, but if you want all new presentations to have a particular set of styles, you need to create a template. (See *Creating and Modifying Templates* on page 632.) Then base new presentations on that template. (See *Basing a Presentation on a Template or Background (Without Using AutoPilot)* on page 624 and *Using AutoPilot to Create a Presentation* on page 620). To affect other StarImpress documents, you need to modify the template.

Adding Files and Objects

The Insert icon lets you access a variety of features. There isn't much that you can't include in a slide. Most of these capabilities are documented in other parts of this book; references are included on this page.

Figure 24-20 shows the Insert tearoff menu, where many of the insert functions are located.

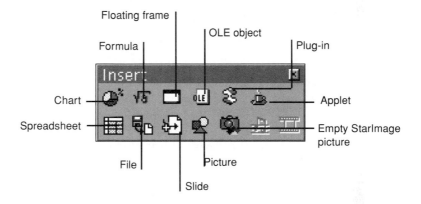

Figure 24-20   Items you can add to presentations

Inserting Other Objects and Files

These features are covered in *Adding Objects to Documents* on page 227.

You can insert pretty much any kind of file, whether StarOffice or other types, in any StarOffice document.

The most flexible way to insert files is to use the OLE object icon in Figure 24-20 or to choose Insert > Object > OLE Object. ("OLE object" is an unnecessarily techy way of putting it—OLE is the technology that lets you edit the file once you've inserted it in another file. For example, you can insert an "OLE object," a Draw file, in a Writer file, and edit the drawing right in Writer.

Inserting Applets and Plug-ins

These features are covered in *Adding Applets and Plugins* on page 449.

Inserting Text and HTML Files

You can insert HTML and text (ASCII, not Writer) files into the current slide. The contents are inserted in a Text icon text frame; if your slide layout contains a preset text frame, it will be ignored and a Text icon text frame will appear over it, with the contents of the imported file.

Formatting for HTML files is retained as are URLs, which remain functional. Importing an HTML file containing URLs can be a very useful technique in some presentations. When you click a link while you're editing a presentation, the Impress file closes and StarOffice Web opens the file the URL linked to.

For text files, you might want to paste the contents into a preset Impress text frame, instead of importing.

1   Click the Insert icon on the toolbar at the left of the work area, and display the Insert tearoff menu. Click the Insert File icon on that menu.

2   Select the file you want.

3   The file will be listed in the Insert Text window (Figure 24-21). Select Link if appropriate, then click OK.

Select Link if you want to insert only a link to the file, which is automatically updated if changes are made to the original file. It also helps reduce presentation file size. (Changing the location of the inserted file will break the link.)

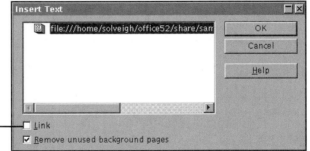

Figure 24-21   Inserting an ASCII or HTML text file

Note – If you select Link and the file is on a Web page or other location you don't own, you could be left hanging during a presentation if the Web server goes down, or the file becomes otherwise unavailable.

Inserting Pictures (Images and Drawings)

You can add empty graphics frames or existing graphics files.

Inserting an Existing Graphics File

You can insert any raster file, such as a GIF or JPG, into the current slide.

1   Click the Insert icon on the toolbar and display the Insert tearoff menu, then click the Picture icon.

You also can choose Insert > Picture > From File.

2   Select the file you want (Figure 24-22), then click Open.

Select Preview if you want to see it first; select Link if you want to be connected to the original file. Your presentation will be updated when the file is updated. It also helps keep your presentation file size down. However, note that changing the location of the inserted file will break the link.

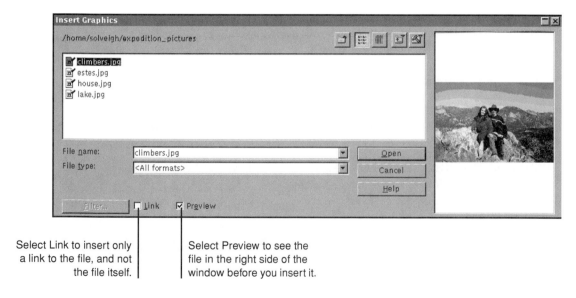

Select Link to insert only a link to the file, and not the file itself.

Select Preview to see the file in the right side of the window before you insert it.

Figure 24-22   Inserting a raster image file in the current slide

Inserting an Empty Image

You can insert what is in essence an empty picture frame—a framed area that lets you use Image tools within your presentation.

1   Click the Insert icon on the toolbar and display the Insert tearoff menu, then click the Insert From Image Editor icon.

You also can choose Insert > Graphics > From Image Editor.

2   Enter the attributes you want in the New Image window. (See *Creating a New Image* on page 807 for more information.)

3 Click Create. The image will appear in the work area.

4 The object bar and toolbar will change to show StarImage tools. Draw the image.

Click elsewhere in the slide to return to Impress tools. To edit the image later, double-click the image.

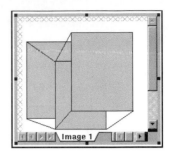

5 You can right-click the Image 1 tab and choose Insert Image if you want to add another within the same image frame. Right-click again and choose Remove Image to remove it.

Inserting a Drawing Into the Current Slide

To add a new drawing or existing drawing to the slide, use the Insert OLE object feature.

Note – To insert a drawing as a new separate slide, see *Inserting Existing Slides From Impress or Draw* on page 658.

---

1 Move to Drawing view.

2 Choose Insert > Object > OLE object.

3 In the Insert OLE Object window, select Create new or Create from file (Figure 24-23).

   • If you select Create new, select a file type and click OK. A new empty Draw frame will appear in the slide.

   • If you select Create from file, click Search and select the file, then click OK.

The contents of this file will be inserted in the current slide. (If you insert a draw file with multiple slides, only the first slide will be inserted.)

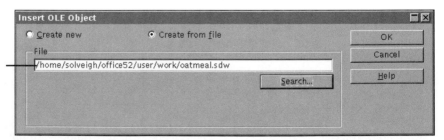

Figure 24-23 Inserting a Draw graphic in the current slide

Inserting Files and Objects on page 442 illustrates inserting an OLE spreadsheet.

Inserting Page, Date, Time, and Filename Fields

Choose Insert > Field to add a page, date, time, or filename field. Add the field in Slide view if you want it on only one slide, or in Background view if you want it on all slides.

If you're going to be creating handouts with several slides on each page, you can add page numbers to each handout page. See *Creating Slide Handouts* on page 703.

Inserting Buttons, and Other Controls

Figure 24-24 shows form options.

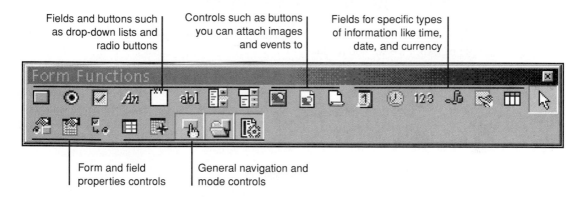

Fields and buttons such as drop-down lists and radio buttons

Controls such as buttons you can attach images and events to

Fields for specific types of information like time, date, and currency

Form and field properties controls

General navigation and mode controls

Figure 24-24   Forms and form components

The Form Functions bar lets you insert buttons, drop-down lists, etc., and attach them to data or events. For example, you could create a button that would open a particular file whenever you clicked on it.

It's beyond the scope of this book to cover them in detail, but some aspects of these features are covered in *Attaching Actions to Form Controls* on page 455. To learn how to use the form functions with databases, see *Modifying and Enhancing a Form* on page 1013.

Presentation Backgrounds

This section covers how to create and modify what's behind the content of your presentation: the colors, logos, or other elements that are repeated on each page.

Before you begin working with backgrounds, be sure that none of the placeholder options in the Presentation Options window are selected. (Choose Tools > Options > Presentation > Contents.)

Creating your own background templates is covered in *Creating and Modifying Templates* on page 632.

Modifying the default formats for headings and other elements is covered in *Modifying Presentation Default Fonts* on page 676.

Note – Graphics in backgrounds generally don't work well when transferred to HTML. Even light-colored ones are sometimes converted to a much darker color. If you need to have an HTML version of the presentation created using the Export to HTML feature, don't use a background with any graphics.

Understanding Backgrounds

Backgrounds are relatively simple, but some of the terminology and the interface raised a couple of issues we wanted to clarify.

Terminology

StarOffice refers to the background elements of your presentation using many terms: the page layout, presentation layout, slide design, slide layout, and so on. We use *background* for consistency and clarity.

Number of Backgrounds Allowed

When you create a new presentation using AutoPilot, the "page layout," which is the background that you selected, applies to the entire presentation. When you make changes to the presentation in Background view, those changes apply to the whole presentation, as well. However, the Slide Design option in the Presentation menu lets you change backgrounds on a slide-by-slide basis.

Backgrounds and Orientation

Before you begin, be sure the current orientation of your slides is appropriate for the background graphic (if there is a graphic in the background you'll be using). The graphic will be automatically reproportioned to fit the slide orientation, so if you're using portrait orientation and load a landscape-oriented background like World, the world map that appears in the background will be "squished" and lengthened to fit the portrait orientation. You can go into background view and reshape the graphic, but it's still kind of a pain. Likewise, make sure any backgrounds you create are proportioned correctly for portrait orientation, since that's the most common for slide presentations.

Background Images and File Size

If you use raster images as backgrounds (.GIF files and so on, like those you can create in Image), the file sizes of any PostScript files you create will be much larger than if you use vector graphics (like those you can create in Draw).

Backgrounds and Printing Issues

In general, it's a good idea not to use gradient fills, gradient text or complex backgrounds in Star Office presentations as this drastically affects disk space, printing, or download time. You can do a colored background easily that doesn't take much disk space by choosing Format > Page and in the Page tab, selecting a color.

Changing or Adding Backgrounds for a Slide or Presentation

This option lets you select a background from Impress's predefined list, and from any backgrounds you may have created. You can apply the background to one slide, or to the entire presentation.

1   Move to Drawing view or Notes view.

2   Display the Presentation menu. (Choose View > Toolbars > Presentation, or click the Presentation Box On/Off icon on the right side of the object bar.)

3   Select the slide you want to change the background for.

4   Click Slide Design to display the Slide Design window.

5   If the design you want isn't displayed in the Slide Design window, click Load to display the Load Slide Design window (Figure 24-25).

6   Select any category that contains a presentation, presentation layout, or presentation template. Presentation Layouts contains backgrounds only.

7   Select a layout and click OK.

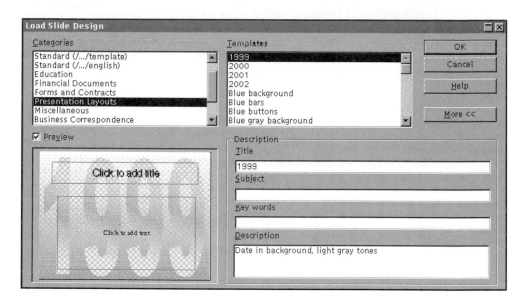

Figure 24-25   Selecting a new background design

8   Select the new background you just loaded.

> **Note –** If you don't select the new background, it won't be saved in the Slide Design window. Impress doesn't allow you to load a new background without applying it to at least one slide.

9   Select the appropriate options in the Slide Design window (Figure 24-26); click OK.

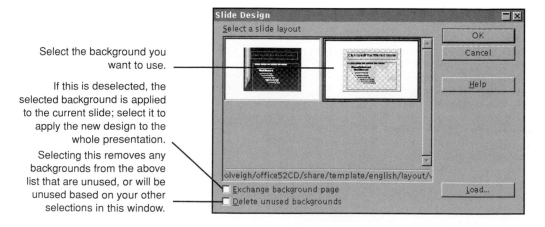

Select the background you want to use.

If this is deselected, the selected background is applied to the current slide; select it to apply the new design to the whole presentation.

Selecting this removes any backgrounds from the above list that are unused, or will be unused based on your other selections in this window.

Figure 24-26   Selecting background exchange options

Note – If you select both options, all backgrounds but the selected one will be removed from this window and from your presentation.

Saving Disk Space by Deleting Unused Backgrounds

The graphics in a presentation can add up to really large file sizes. You can reduce the file size by deleting all the backgrounds you're not using. See Figure 24-26; be sure to select the Remove unused master pages when you add backgrounds.

To compress a presentation, see *Using the Pack Feature to Reduce Presentation File Size* on page 720.

Adding a Color, Bitmap, Hatch, or Gradient to a Background

Before you begin, be sure that none of the placeholder options in the Presentation Options window are selected. (Choose Tools > Options > Presentation > Contents.)

If you've already got a background Any changes you make using this method are incorporated into the current background. You can rearrange the current elements of the background so that they're in front of or behind what you've added. (Right-click the element and choose Arrange and the option you want.)

Replacing the current background with another background All changes you make using these steps become part of the background you make them in. If you choose another background according to *Changing or Adding Backgrounds for a Slide or Presentation* on page 685, all your changes will be overridden. They won't be incorporated into the new background.

Caution Backgrounds are all made differently, some with actual graphics and some using the very gradient, color, hatch, and bitmap features you're modifying. If you're not careful to note how the background is made, you may get results you don't want, and will be unable to change it back. Luckily, the changes are applied only to the presentation and not to the background template itself. If you get results you don't want, you can reload the background. Apply a different background to the affected slides, then reapply the original background you were modifying. (See *Changing or Adding Backgrounds for a Slide or Presentation* on page 685.)

In addition, crosshatches and gradients can reduce readability. Plain colors (choose Format > Page and click the Page tab, then select a color) and simple graphics with **small** storage sizes are the best backgrounds.

Follow these steps to add to the background.

1   Switch to Drawing view.

2   Either switch to Background view and select the background you want to modify, or in Slide view, select a slide with the background you want to modify.

3   Save the presentation. The Undo function works inconsistently with page formatting.

4   If you're using more than one background, click the tab of the background you want to modify.

5   Choose Format > Page.

6   Click the Background tab (Figure 24-27).

7   Select options you want.

For more information on bitmaps, hatches, and gradients, refer to *Applying Attributes Using the Area Window* on page 753, and *Creating and Modifying Gradients, Hatches, and Bitmaps* on page 761.

Select Color, Bitmap, Hatch, or Gradient.

Select the background.

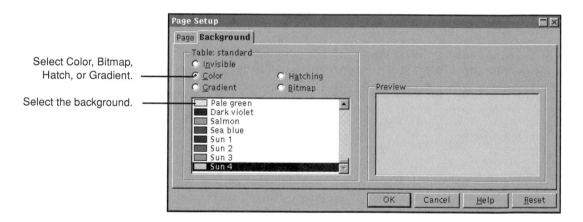

Figure 24-27   Selecting options for a background

Adding Objects and Text

If you want to draw, type, or paste things into the background, just switch to Background view and add the elements you want.

Any changes you make using this method are incorporated into the current background, if you have one.

Arranging Objects in a Background

Some objects may appear in front of objects you want seen, or vice versa. Switch to Background view (choose View > Background > Drawing). Right-click on an object and choose Arrange and the option you want. This option is available for all objects, in backgrounds or slide foregrounds. See *Arranging Objects in Layers* on page 782.

Creating and Modifying Background Templates

See *Background Templates* on page 634.

Applying a Blank Background

You can make the background blank two different ways: by simply deleting all elements of the background, or by applying a white color to the page.

You can print a dark background as white (and light text in black) by selecting the Black and White option or Grayscale in the Print window (Figure 25-22 on page 725).

You can also create a blank background to apply when you need it. See *Creating a Background Template* on page 634.

You can always apply the background again, by clicking the Slide Design option in the Presentation menu.

To delete background elements:

1   Switch to Background view.

2   If there are two or more backgrounds, select the tab of the one to delete.

3   Delete all components of the background.

4   If color is still displayed, choose Format > Page and click the Background tab. Select the Invisible option.

To temporarily remove a background (this works for most backgrounds, though not all):

1   You can be in either Background or Slide view.

2   Choose Format > Page and click the Background tab.

3   Select Color and select White or another neutral color.

4   If background elements still show, switch to Background view. Select them all and move them to the back. (Right-click and choose Arrange > Send to Back.)

Headers and Footers

Headers and footers, where you can put information like date, time, title, and so on, aren't included in any of the preset slide designs. However, you can add them relatively easily.

Adding a Header or Footer to a Current Document

1   Go to Background view, by clicking the Background icon or choosing View > Background > Drawing. See Figure 24-28.

2   Use the Text icon to draw a text box below the slide.

3   Choose Insert > Fields and select the type of information you want to insert, or type additional information.

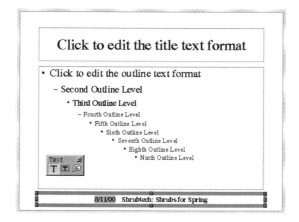

Figure 24-28   Adding a header or footer to a presentation

4   Format the text appropriately.

5   Switch back to Slide view. Choose Format > Page and click the Page tab. Make sure that any margins you've set don't cut off the header or footer text.

Adding a Header or Footer to a Template

You can include a header or footer by default by repeating the previous procedure on a template, then using that template for future presentations.

Adding a Header or Footer to Handouts

Follow the instructions in *Adding Notes and Creating Handouts* on page 702 to use Impress's Handouts master view. You can add headers and footers there using a text box, as well.

Applying Special Effects to Slide Contents

While the charts and graphs in your presentation will impress the audience, the special effects add interest and splash. You can also use effects to emphasize certain points during your presentation.

Note – You can create impressive effects by combining Draw's 3D graphics and Impress's special effects. See *Working With Three-Dimensional Objects* on page 767.

To allow effects to run while you're editing a presentation (not running the presentation), use the Allow Effects icon on the Option bar below the work area.

Using Movement, Color, and Sound Effects

Impress has a wide variety of object and text effects you can apply to individual elements of your presentation. This include standard effects, such as moving each line of text in from the left when the slide is shown, and unusual effects such as moving an object along a specific line. The effects are run starting when the slide is displayed.

Note – You can use the Effects window to make an object move along the path of a Bezier curve. Just draw the appropriate path using the Line tool, and edit it if necessary using the Bezier editing tools. Then draw or paste in the object that you want to move along that path. Select the line and object. In the Effects icon's set of selections, select the Other category and Along a Curve effect.

To apply special slide transition effects, see *Applying Slide Transition Effects* on page 697.

1   Switch to Drawing view and click the Effects icon on the toolbar. (If you can't find the Effects icon, your StarOffice window is too small. Lengthen it, or look for the tiny black right-pointing arrow at the bottom of the toolbar and click it; the rest of the toolbar will be displayed.)

2   Choose View > Preview; the Preview window demonstrates each effect you'll select.

3   In the slide, select the object or text in the slide you want to apply the effects to. (If you don't select an object, some icons won't be enabled.)

• Effects and objects – If you select two or more objects, the effect will be applied to each object, but sequentially, not simultaneously. Group the objects to apply the effects to two or more objects simultaneously (select them and right-click, then choose Group).

• Effects and text – Text effects are applied to all text in the text frame, paragraph by paragraph. For instance, if you click somewhere in the **second** subpoint in a text frame that has three subpoints and apply an effect, the effect will be sequentially applied to all three subpoints, to the **first** subpoint first (see Figure 24-29).

4   In the Effects window, click the Effects icon (object and text effects) or Text Effects icon.

5   Make the appropriate object or text effect selections.

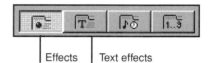

Effects | Text effects

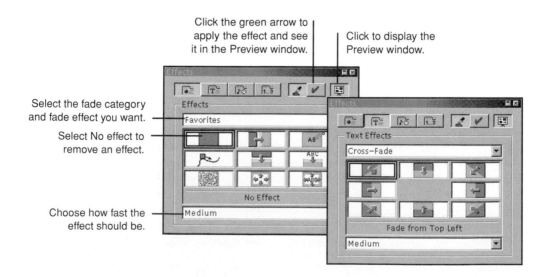

Figure 24-29   Object and text effects

6   Click the green arrow in the upper right corner to apply the effect; it will be run in the Preview window. Make any necessary changes.

Note – By default, a sound accompanies each effect. Be sure to have the Preview window showing so you're aware of the sounds. If your computer doesn't have sound, that doesn't mean the computer where you do the presentation won't, so be sure to test before you present. To remove a sound, click the Extras icon at the top of the Effects window, then click the Sound icon to deactivate the displayed sound.

---

7   Click the Extras icon and make the appropriate selections (Figure 24-30). These will be applied to the currently selected effect.

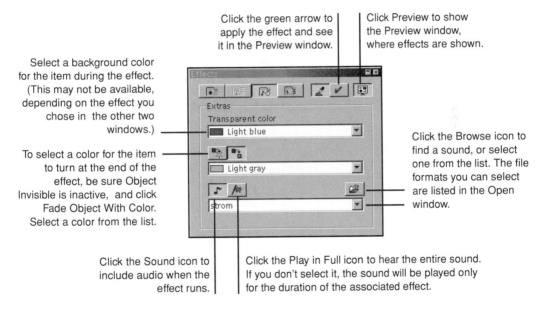

Figure 24-30   Additional options for a text or object effect

8   Click the green arrow in the upper right corner to apply the sound.

If the arrow isn't enabled or sound doesn't run, be sure you've got an object selected, that the Sound icon is selected as shown in Figure 24-30, that the Preview window is displayed, and that your computer's sound volume is turned up high enough.

9   Click the Order icon (Figure 24-31). All effects are listed in the order in which they'll be run. If you want to rearrange them, drag them to a new position in the list.

Figure 24-31   Viewing and changing effects order

10 Click the Presentation icon, if you want to run the presentation. Click the mouse or press the space bar to move from one slide to another; press Escape to end it.

Adding Actions Using Interaction Effects

Impress lets you apply a variety of abilities to any object in a presentation. When you click on the drawing, chart, or other item, you can go to the next or previous slide, a specific slide in another presentation, a Web page, and so on. You can apply the capabilities to any object in the document—a rectangle you've drawn or a graphic you've imported—but not to text. (StarOffice will let you apply the feature, but nothing will happen when you try it out.)

These are similar to the capabilities that you could also add by just using the hyperlink capabilities described in *Adding Hyperlinks to StarOffice Documents* on page 431. However, the features in *Linking to Any Point Within a Document, Using HTML* on page 436 don't work for Impress or Draw documents.

This is a powerful feature with several possible applications, including the following:

*   You can add buttons that help you navigate the presentation, such as first, last, and next, and add sounds to them.

*   If your presentation discusses applications, you can create an object (button, rectangle, etc) that you can click on to start each application.

The features while you're editing the presentation; you don't need to run the presentation to see them work. The mouse pointer changes to a pointing hand when ready. However, you need to specify that you're allowing
interactivity to run. Use the Allow Interaction icon on the Option bar below the work area.

1 Switch to Drawing view.

2   Move to the slide you want to add the interactive object to.

3   Select or add the object; it can be a drawing object, a chart, or any other object, including the controls in the Form tearoff menu.

4   Right-click the object and choose Interaction, or click the Interaction icon in the toolbar.

5   The Interaction window will be displayed (Figure 24-32). Select what you want to happen when the control is clicked.

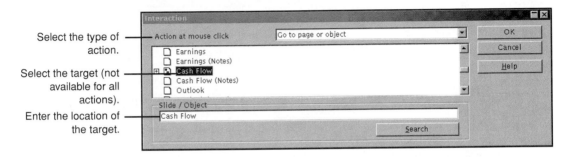

Figure 24-32   Setting target of an interactive control

Background pages are listed as targets when you select the Go to page or object option. However, choosing to go to one of the background pages takes you to the first slide in the presentation, so it's not a good idea to select a background page.

The Action at mouse click list contains the following options:

- No action – Use this to remove an existing target.

- Go to previous slide

- Go to next slide

- Go to first slide

- Go to last slide

- Go to page or object – Go to one of the pages or objects in the current presentation, in Drawing or Notes view.

- Go to document – Closes the presentation and opens the document. You can select any document, including Writer documents and graphics.

- Make object invisible

- Play sound – Plays a sound you select using the Browse button. You can use several sound formats, including files with the extensions .au, .snd, .wav, .voc, .aiff, and .iff.

- Start object action – With this selection, you can edit or open the object you're applying this capability to. (Open isn't available for all objects.) For example, if you're applying this capability to an imported Image graphic and select Edit, the image will change to edit mode when clicked, and you'll see the Image toolbar at the left. If you select Open, the object will open in a separate window within the Impress work area.
- Fade object – Fades the object, based on the options you select, in Figure 24-33.

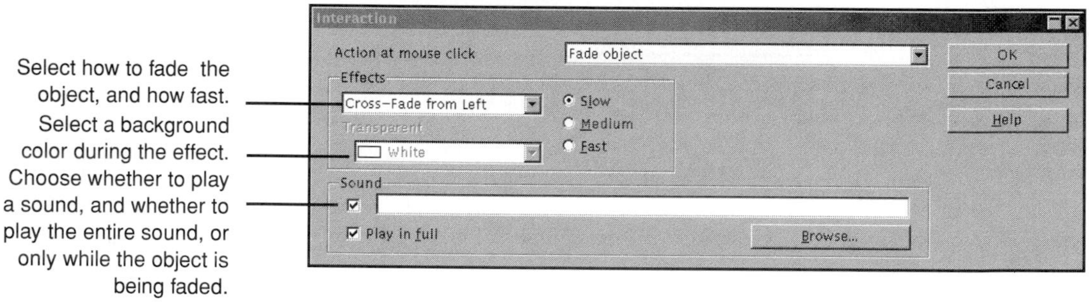
Select how to fade the object, and how fast.
Select a background color during the effect.
Choose whether to play a sound, and whether to play the entire sound, or only while the object is being faded.
Interaction
Action at mouse click
Fade object
OK
Cancel
Help
Effects
Cross-Fade from Left
Slow
Medium
Fast
Transparent
White
Sound
Play in full
Browse...

Figure 24-33 Fade object options

- Execute program.
- Run macro – Runs a StarOffice Basic macro. See *Linking Macros and Scripts to Graphics* on page 454 for more information.

Note – If you add an existing StarOffice macro, be sure the macro's library (the category it's listed within) is activated. Choose Tools > Macros, click the Organizer button, then click the Libraries tab and be sure the checkbox next to the library is checked.

- Quit presentation – Stops running the presentation (doesn't close the file).

Animated GIFs

If you've surfed the Web much, you've seen animated icons flashing information like "New!" or "Brad Pitt Married Today; Millions Mourn!" with text, graphics, or both. You can add these to your presentations, following the instructions in *Creating an Animated GIF* on page 446.

You can add scrolling text marquees to HTML files that run in StarOffice and in Internet Explorer; keep this in mind if you create an HTML version of your presentation. See *Creating a Text Marquee* on page 445.

Applying Slide Transition Effects

Impress lets you transition from one slide to another with a variety of effects: having the slide appear from the top of bottom, appear Cheshire-cat-like from the middle of the screen, and so on. You also can change from one slide to another manually (by clicking the Space bar or clicking the mouse) or automatically, after a set period of time. These effects, of course, are only available when you run the presentation on a computer.

These effects are in addition to the effects in *Using Movement, Color, and Sound Effects* on page 691; those are applied to individual slide components, whereas these are applied to the entire slide. They take place before the individual effects are run.

1   Switch to Slide view.

2   Select a slide.

3   Open the Preview window (choose View > Preview).

    The Preview window demonstrates each transition effect you select.

4   Choose Presentation > Slide Transition.

5   Using the options corresponding to the Effects and Extras icons, select the transition you want, for when you change **to** the selected slide (Figure 24-34 on page 698). Click the green arrow after you apply each effect.

    Transition type There are three transition types: automatic, semiautomatic, and manual.

    •   Automatic – The slide is displayed without any input (like clicking the mouse) and any object or text effects are run as soon as the slide is displayed. The slide is displayed for the specified amount of time.

        You can set the time to display each slide using the Rehearse Timings feature; see *Timing Automatic Presentations* on page 699.

    •   Semiautomatic – The slide is displayed only when you click the mouse or press the space bar (when the previous slide is displayed), but any object and text effects are run automatically as soon as the slide is displayed.

    •   Manual – You must click the mouse or press the space bar to show the slide, then click or press the bar again to run any object or text effects.

Note – The text effects are run one paragraph at a time—even though you only had to select one line of text when selecting the effect to apply the effect to all text within the text frame, the effects are run only one at a time, for the Manual slide transition.

You can set some options in the object bar, as well as the Slide Transition window.

Click Effects or Extra, then select an effect category below.

Select this for no effect, or make another selection.

Choose how fast the transition should go.

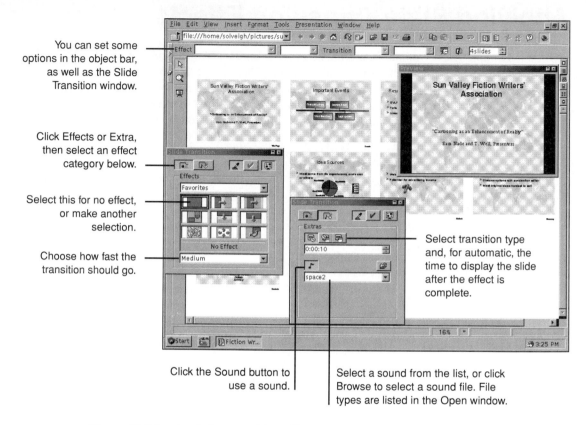

Select transition type and, for automatic, the time to display the slide after the effect is complete.

Click the Sound button to use a sound.

Select a sound from the list, or click Browse to select a sound file. File types are listed in the Open window.

Figure 24-34 Applying transition effects to a slide

6 Click the green arrow to apply the effect.

A small arrow icon appears below the lower left corner of each slide that has an effect assigned to it. You can click it to run the transition (in the work area, not the Preview window).

7 You can click the Presentation icon at the left side of the work area to run it. Press Esc at any time to end the presentation.

Timing Automatic Presentations

If you want to switch automatically from one slide to another, you can set a specific time for each slide to be displayed. To make it easier for you to figure out how much time each slide should spend onscreen, Impress has a Rehearse Timings feature that displays a counter, and automatically records the time you spend displaying each slide. This lets you rehearse the presentation ahead of time and fine-tune the timing.

You can make adjustments later is necessary, following the instructions in *Applying Slide Transition Effects* on page 697.

1   Apply effects, if you want, to individual elements of the slides. See *Using Movement, Color, and Sound Effects* on page 691.

2   Set slide transition effects.

    The type of timing—manual, etc.—can be anything; it will be overridden with Automatic and the time set by this process.

3   Prepare to deliver your presentation; assemble any notes you'll need, etc.

4   Switch to Slide view.

5   Click the Rehearse Timings icon in the object bar.

6   Deliver the information you'll be talking about during this slide, then note the time displayed when you're done.

    The presentation will start running, with the a timer showing how many seconds the slide has been displayed, in the lower left corner of the screen. Note the time when you're done speaking. The time recorded for each slide begins, **not** when the slide is displayed, but when all effects are complete, so take that into account when you note the time.

7   Click the timer to move to the next slide. Repeat the process for each slide.

8   Use the Slide Transition window to adjust the time for each slide, if necessary. (For slides with extensive individual object or text effects, during which you'll be talking, you may want to decrease the time slightly.)

Note – In general, it's a good idea to err on the generous side when setting timing; you can manually switch to the next slide before the timing is over but you can't delay the transition.

---

9   Click the Rehearse Presentations icon again, and run the presentation and your delivery again to be sure the timing is correct.

Delivering Presentations

Adding Notes and Creating Handouts

Once your slides are in good shape, add the speaker's or audience notes, as well as handouts that contain reduced versions of the slides.

Adding Notes

You can use Notes view to add speaker's notes, or to add expanded information based on the slides. You can create training manuals, for instance, by printing student manuals in Notes view with the slides and notes, and giving the instructor the slides to display and discuss during class.

1   Switch to Notes view.

2   Move to the first slide you want to add notes to (Figure 25-1 on page 703).

3   Switch to Background view (choose View > Background > Notes). Click in the notes area and set the correct point size, using the object bar or by choosing Format > Character.

4   Switch back to Slide view.

5   Right-click the zoom field in the status bar below the work area, to zoom in enough to see what you'll be typing.

6   Enter the notes for the speaker. You can use the usual set of editing tools in the toolbar and in the object bar.

7   If you find that you need more room than is available in the notes area, you have a few options:

   • Decrease the font size slightly.

   • Drag the corners of the notes area to resize it.

     Note that the page size is displayed; don't go outside this area. The page size is set using the Page tab of the Page Setup window. If you need to reset margins, choose Format > Page.

   • Split the slide into two or more slides. To add a slide for each subpoint, see *Expanding: Creating a Slide for Each Subpoint* on page 661.

Note – When you print (see *Printing a Presentation* on page 727), be sure to select the Notes option in the Print Options window.

Check the font size for your notes before you begin; the default may be larger than you want.

You can use the icons in the toolbar in the slide and the notes area, in Slide or in Background view (slide area only).

Margins, set using the Page tab of the Page Setup window, are shown; any text outside this area won't be printed.

Move from slide to slide the same way you do in Drawing view.

Slide and Background view are available in Notes view.

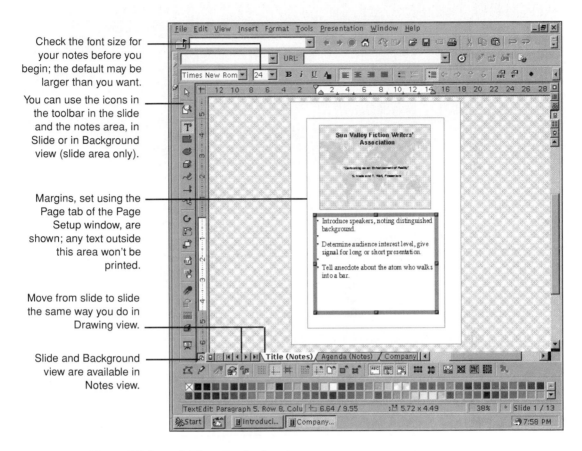

Figure 25-1   Adding speaker's notes

Creating Slide Handouts

If you want to save paper when printing presentations, or provide the audience with reduced-size versions of all your slides, use Handout view.

1   Switch to Handout view, shown in Figure 25-2, by clicking the Handout View icon in the master view navigation bar, or choosing View > Background > Handout.

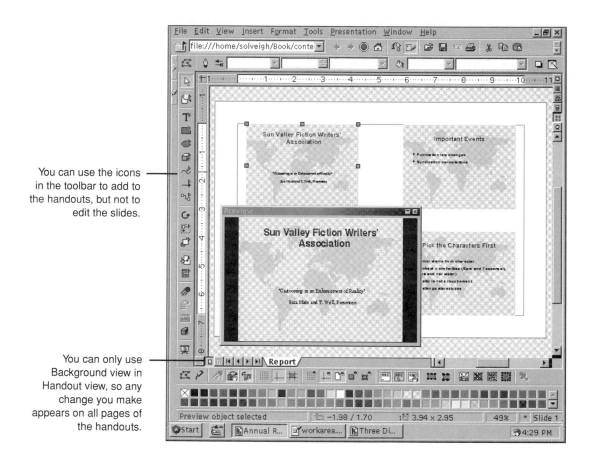

You can use the icons in the toolbar to add to the handouts, but not to edit the slides.

You can only use Background view in Handout view, so any change you make appears on all pages of the handouts.

Figure 25-2   Page setup for handouts

2   To set the number of slides per handout page, choose Format > Modify Layout and make a selection in the Modify Slide window.

Note – You'll be able to see only the first page of grouped slides. This is normal; the rest of the slides have been arranged correctly and will be printed. Be careful about the changes you make, since all changes will appear on all pages of the handouts.

3   The default layout is Landscape (paper is wider than it is high). If you want to print in Portrait view, choose Format > Page and click the Page tab. Select the Portrait option.

4   Manually resize or rearrange the slides, if necessary.

5   Add a title, date fields, or graphics, if you want. You're automatically in Background view when in Handout view, so everything you add will appear on every page as a header, footer, background graphic, or whatever you choose.

- Title and other text – Use the Text tools to add a title at the top of the page, the name of the presenter, or other information.

- Fields – Choose Insert > Field to add a page, date, time, or filename field.

- Graphics – Use the drawing tools to add a logo or other graphic.

Note – When you print (see *Printing a Presentation* on page 727), be sure to select the Handouts option in the Print Options window.

Creating Custom Presentations

Impress lets you create several different preset customizations of the same presentation. For instance, if you're presenting a new technology, you may want to give similar information to engineers and their managers, but each audience needs a different depth of technical information.

Note – For information about saving several versions of the same document, see *Version Control and Editing Tools* on page 333.

Creating a Custom Presentation

1   Open the presentation and move to Drawing view.

2   Choose Presentation > Custom Slide Show.

3   In the Custom Slide Shows window, click New.

4   In the Define Custom Slide Show window (Figure 25-3), enter the appropriate information.

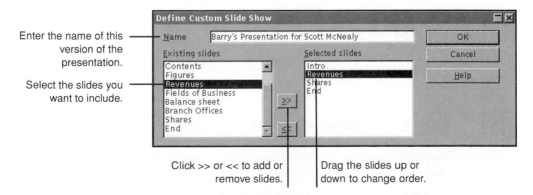

Figure 25-3   Defining a custom presentation

Editing or Copying a Custom Presentation

1   Open the presentation.

2   Choose Presentation > Custom Slide Show.

3   Select a customized version and choose Edit or Copy.

Running a Custom Presentation

1   Choose Presentation > Custom Slide Show; the Custom Slide Shows window is displayed in Figure 25-4.

2   Select the slide show to run.

3   Select the Use Custom Slide Show option. If you don't, the entire original presentation will be run.

4   Click Start.

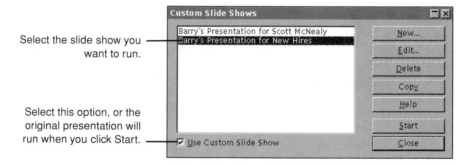

Figure 25-4   Running a custom presentation

Delivering a Presentation

Now that everything's entered and formatted, it's a relatively simple process to do what you need to present it.

Setting Presentation Preferences

This lets you control how your presentation is run, including how you switch from one slide to another in Manual mode.

1   Choose Presentation > Presentation Settings.

2   Enter the appropriate information in the Slide Show window (Figure 25-5).

If you have interactive elements in your presentation, be sure to select the Mouse pointer visible option.

The Mouse pointer as pen option lets you use the mouse to circle areas onscreen during the presentation. The pointer will change to a pen icon during the presentation, and lets you draw a light green freehand line.

The Change slides manually option overrides, but doesn't delete, automatic settings that you've entered in the Slide object bar or the Slide Transition window.

Choose to show the whole presentation, or from a specific slide to the end.
You can show a custom version of the presentation, if you've created one.

Run the presentation normally (full screen), within the current window, or in a repeating loop (Auto).

Set the timing for an Auto presentation using this field, or the Rehearse Timings feature.

Select this option to show the Created with StarOffice logo between loops.

Select the transition and display options you want.

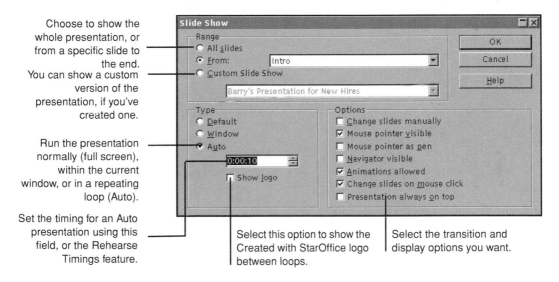

Figure 25-5   Entering presentation information

Starting and Ending Presentations

Click the Presentation icon, displayed in the navigation bar or toolbar of most views, to start a presentation. Press Esc at any time to quit.

You also can press Ctrl+F2, or right-click and choose Slide Show.

Switching From One Slide to Another

Automatic   If your slide show is automatic, just wait for the slide show to run according to its preset times. You can click the mouse or press the spacebar to switch to the next slide at any time. (Be sure the Change slides manually option is deselected in the Slide Show window.)

Manual To run a manual presentation, switch slides according to the options you chose in the Slide Show window. You can click the mouse or press the spacebar, Enter key, page down key, or right arrow key to move forward. To move back, right-click the mouse or use the page up or left arrow key.

Press the Home key to go back to the first slide; press End to go to the last slide.

Using the Navigator to Run Presentations

For particularly lengthy presentations, it's convenient to have the Navigator, which lets you go directly to the slide you want, rather than simply going from one to the next sequentially.

Choose Presentation > Presentation Settings and select the Navigator visible option. Use the navigation arrows to get to the slide you want, or double-click a slide.

Note – If you don't start the presentation with the Navigator, you can open it by pressing F5.

You can resize the Navigator if it gets in your way but is still useful enough to you to keep open.

The selections you make in the Navigator don't override automatic settings, which can interfere with using the Navigator. Be sure to select the Change slides manually option in the Slide Show window. Also, slide transitions cause the Navigator to disappear and reappear; you may not want to use the Navigator with slide transitions.

You also can activate the Mouse pointer as pen option with the Navigator; just click the Pointer icon at the top of the Navigator, if it's not already active.

Running and Editing a Presentation Simultaneously

Impress's Live mode lets you run and edit at the same time. For example, if you're teaching the latest StarOffice course to a group of instructors and they keep interrupting you to ask for changes, this is a good solution.

Note – Select the Change slides manually option in the Slide Show window when using Live mode, to make sure you have enough time to make the changes in each slide.

To enter Live mode, run the presentation with the Navigator. When it's displayed, click the Live Mode icon.

Changing Presentation File Format

You can save the presentation in one of a number of other text or presentation formats, and export any slide to HTML or a raster graphics format.

Saving the Presentation in Another Presentation Format

These formats are all variations on PowePoint, Impress, Draw, and templates for Impress and Draw.

1   Choose File > Save as.

2   The file formats you can use are listed in the Save as window. Select a format and enter a name.

3   Click Save.

Note – You can open a number of other presentations in StarOffice, including PowerPoint presentations, by simply choosing File > Open.

Converting a Slide to a Raster Graphic

You can export any slide to create a raster graphics version of it (GIF, JPG, EPS, TIF etc.). The TIF and EPS formats are especially useful if you need to make professional-quality graphics.

1   Move to Drawing view.

2   Move to the slide to export.

3   Choose File > Export.

4   Enter a name and choose the file you want.

5   Click Save.

6   Enter options, if prompted to. (For more information, see *Saving Images and Changing Image Format* on page 832.)

Creating an HTML Version of Your Presentation

You can change your presentation to a Web-enabled HTML format using the StarOffice Export feature.

Before you begin, check the current settings for export to HTML. See *HTML Options: Font Size, Import, and Export* on page 363.

For information about adding Web features, see *Creating Web Pages* on page 405.

You have two types of output formats:

*   Standard HTML pages, with frames or without
*   Automatic or Webcast (for use in kiosk-type environments, or for WebCasting)

The options are sufficiently different that we've created a different procedure for each category.

Before You Begin

Backgrounds We suggest that before you start conversion, you save the presentation under a different name and change the background to a plain, light color without graphics. When setting the background, you may want to just select the Invisible option or select White in the Page Setup window, because the conversion process doesn't usually do a good job of matching the color. Refer to *Presentation Backgrounds* on page 683 for more information.

Slide transitions and sound The Automatic and Webcast formats have options that allow you to either retain the slide-transition effects in the original presentation, or specify them in the export wizard. If you have slide transitions or sound and export to HTML or HTML with Frames, you might be prompted to download a plugin, to get the same functionality. (This varies depending on your operating system, browser, and what plugins you have now.)

Exporting to Standard HTML

Follow these steps to convert a presentation to HTML.

1   Create a folder to hold the HTML and graphics files for the exported presentation.

2   Open the presentation.

3   Choose File > Export.

4   Enter the file name and, in the File type list, select HTML (see Figure 25-6).

Note – In a multi-user StarOffice environment, the default location in the Export window is a location on the server. Be sure to change the location if this isn't where you want the exported presentation.

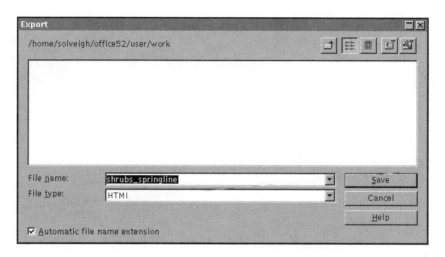

Figure 25-6   Entering the exported presentation name

5   In the first HTML Export window (Figure 25-7), select New design or select an existing one.

If you select an
existing design (one
you created when
exporting previously),
you can modify it as
much as you want,
and save or discard
the changes later.

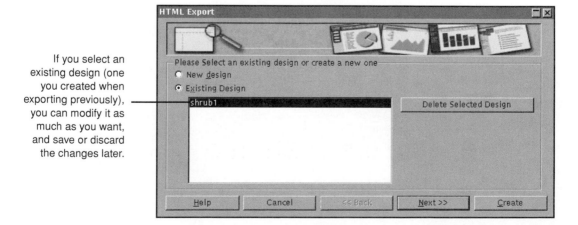

Figure 25-7   Selecting a design or starting a new one

Even if you select an existing design, you can see the following windows where you can modify any of the settings in a current design. If you don't want to make any modifications, click Create now.

6   In the second window (Figure 25-8), select the type of presentation: HTML with or without frames.

Using frames lets you show a collapsed or expanded navigation frame at the left of the presentation.

Selecting this option will create a separate page preceding the presentation.

Selecting this option will reserve a space for notes even if the presentation doesn't have any.

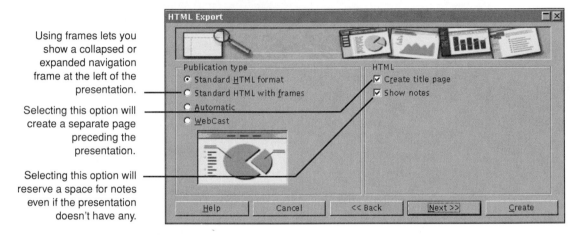

Figure 25-8   Entering design and image options

If you select the Browser frames, you can still browse a non-frames, text-only version (text instead of navigation buttons) by clicking the text-only button or navigation option at the top of each HTML page.

7   The next window (Figure 25-9) lets you select the graphics type and resolution, and decide whether to export any sound files associated with effects in the presentation.

Select the type of graphics you want to use, and for JPGs, how much each should be compressed.

Any sound effects you defined for slide transitions will be exported. This isn't available for WebCast presentations.

Select the screen resolution of the monitor you'll be showing the presentation on.

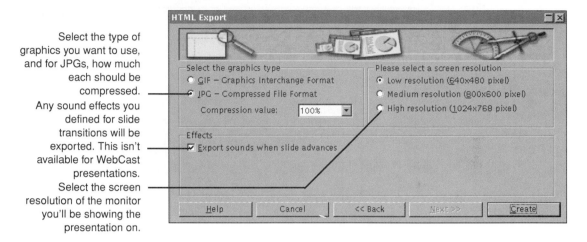

Figure 25-9   Selecting graphics, screen resolution, and sound-export options

8   In the next window (Figure 25-10), enter information about the presentation.

This information will be added to the title page, if you chose to create one previously.

A link is created on the contents page and a copy of the presentation in .sdd format is created in the export folder with the name specified in the Export window.

Adds the text "Best viewed with" and the logo "Created with StarOffice" to the contents page.

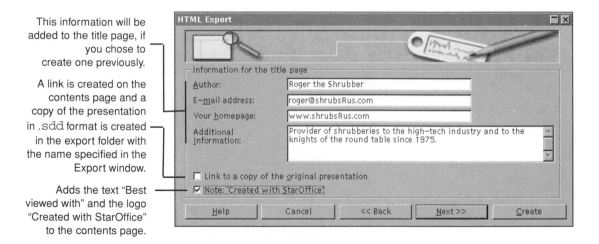

Figure 25-10   Entering author information

Don't select the Link to a copy of the original presentation option unless you want it for informational purposes. Clicking the link just displays garbage characters.

9   In the next window (Figure 25-11), select the type of buttons to use for navigation, or choose text only (the hot-linked words Forward and so on will be used). They will be added at the top of the presentation.

Select the Text only option if you don't want to use the displayed buttons for navigation.

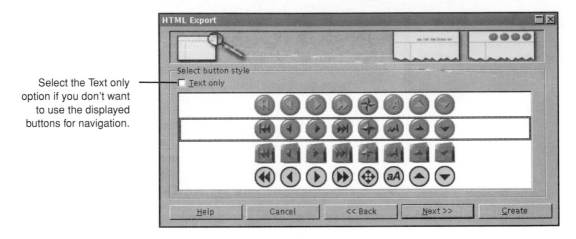

Figure 25-11   Selecting navigation method

10   In the next window, select color options.

Note that the background you choose in Figure 25-12 is used in the background of the HTML pages, behind and in addition to any background or backgrounds used in the presentation you're converting. See Figure 25-13 for an example.

Clicking any of these buttons will open the Color window. Color translation is inexact, at best.

This will not replace the background of your presentation—it serves only as the background in the HTML page.

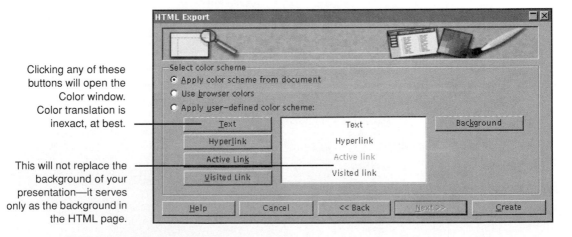

Figure 25-12   Selecting a color scheme

When you click any of the buttons, the Color window will appear. Refer to *Working With Color* on page 757 if you want more information about using it.

The color that you get when you look at the HTML version may be only loosely related to the color you choose here. Light green here might end up as light yellow in HTML. Be prepared to tinker a little with the color, or to just choose white.

11   Click Create; to save the design, enter a name and choose Save.

12   To run the HTML version, double-click the appropriate file.

- If you created a content page, double-click the *x*.htm file, where *x* is the name you entered in the Export window.

- If you didn't create a content page:

  For a frames version, double-click the `siframes.htm` file.

  If you didn't convert to frames, double-click the `text0.htm` file.

A converted presentation is shown in Figure 25-13.

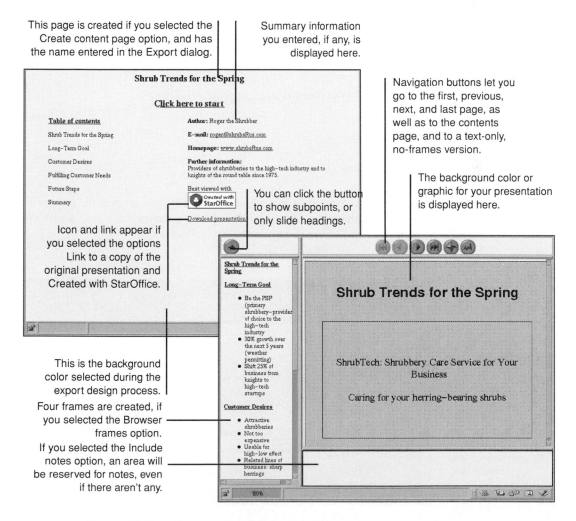

Figure 25-13   Converted HTML presentation

Exporting to an Automatic or WebCast Presentation

An automatic presentation runs in a continuous loop; it's convenient in kiosk-type environments. In a WebCast Export, automatic scripts are generated with Perl or ASP support. This enables the speaker (for example, a speaker in a telephone conference using a slide show in the Internet) to switch to other slides using the audience's Web browser.

Note – The WebCast needs an HTTP server offering Perl or ASP for scripting, such as Microsoft Internet Information Server, or Apache. Therefore, the exporting option depends on the server used. In addition, you need solid knowledge of the server and ASP or Perl so that you can keep on working with the WebCast exported files. The online help included with StarOffice provides additional information about using the exported Web-Cast presentation.

1   Create a folder to hold the files for your exported presentation.

2   Open the presentation.

3   Choose File > Export.

4   Enter the file name and, in the File type list, select HTML (see Figure 25-14).

Note – In a multi-user StarOffice environment, the default location in the Export window is a location on the server. Be sure to change the location if this isn't where you want the exported presentation.

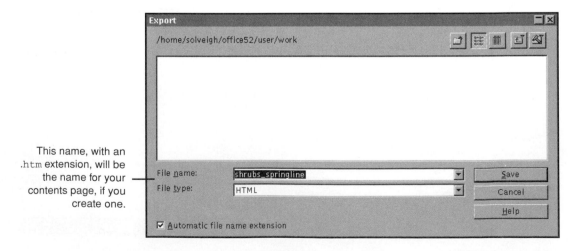

This name, with an .htm extension, will be the name for your contents page, if you create one.

Figure 25-14   Entering the exported presentation name

5   In the first HTML Export window (Figure 25-15), select New design or select an existing one.

If you select an existing design, you can modify it as much as you want, and save or discard the changes.

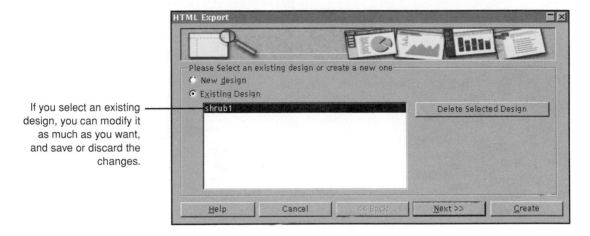

Figure 25-15   Selecting a design or starting a new one

Even if you select an existing design, you can see the following windows where you can modify any of the settings in a current design. If you don't want to make any modifications, click Create now.

6   In the second window, select the type of presentation, Automatic or WebCast. Enter the corresponding options, in the window shown in Figure 25-16 or Figure 25-17, then click Next.

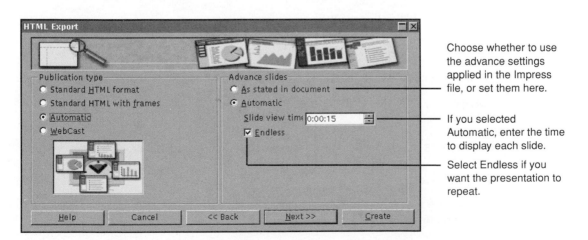

Choose whether to use the advance settings applied in the Impress file, or set them here.

If you selected Automatic, enter the time to display each slide.

Select Endless if you want the presentation to repeat.

Figure 25-16   Entering Automatic options

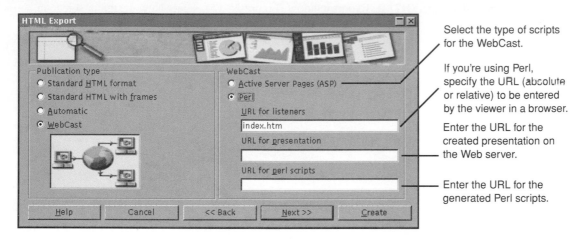

Select the type of scripts for the WebCast.

If you're using Perl, specify the URL (absolute or relative) to be entered by the viewer in a browser.

Enter the URL for the created presentation on the Web server.

Enter the URL for the generated Perl scripts.

Figure 25-17   Entering WebCast options

7   The next window (Figure 25-9) lets you select the graphics type and resolution, and decide whether to export any sound files associated with effects in the presentation.

Select the type of graphics you want to use, and for JPGs, how much each should be compressed.

Any sound effects you defined for slide transitions will be exported. This isn't available for WebCast presentations.

Select the screen resolution of the monitor you'll be showing the presentation on.

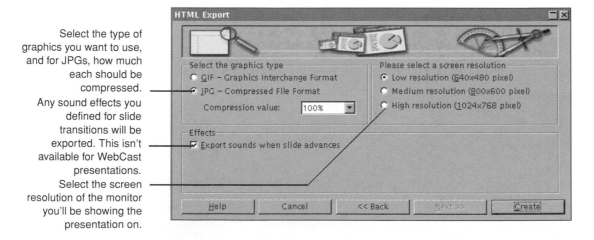

Figure 25-18   Selecting graphics, screen resolution, and sound-export options

8   Click Create.

9   To open the presentation, locate the *filename*.htm file in the folder you exported the presentation to.

Taking It With You

Two new features in Impress make it easier to go on the road with your presentation.

- Standalone StarOffice Player program
- Packing (compressing and/or dividing a presentation into multiple files)

Using the Standalone Presentation Program

To run an onscreen presentation, you just need StarOffice and your presentation, or the standalone version of Impress that lets you just run presentations. You can run presentations, drawing files, and packed presentations (see *Using the Pack Feature to Reduce Presentation File Size* on page 720).

Installation

To install the standalone version, see *Installing StarOffice Player for Impress Presentations* on page 53.

Using the Standalone Player

1   Once the player is installed, go to the `soplayer` folder and either double-click the `soplayer` file or run the command `./soplayer`.

2   The window in Figure 25-19 will appear.

Figure 25-19   StarOffice Player window

3   Click Options to set playing options in the window in Figure 25-20.

4   Open the file you want to run by selecting it and clicking Run.

> **Note** – You can open .sdw (Draw), .sdp (packed Impress), and .sdw (Impress) files. Don't open one of the additional .sxy files generated for a packed presentation; it'll open as gibberish in a text editor.

See *Delivering a Presentation* on page 706 for more information on running presentations.

Select this option to run the transitions as set originally in StarOffice.
Select Manual to control all objects and transitions yourself.
Select Semiautomatic to run object transitions automatically and the slide transition manually.
Select Automatic to run all transitions manually, and select a duration for transitions.

In addition to the above, you can choose to show the presentation repeatedly; instead of ending it will go to the first slide (first pausing for the amount of time you specify).

Choose whether the pointer should be visible, and usable as a pen.

Choose whether to show the presentation full-screen.

You can prevent animations from running with this option.

Choose whether to change slides this way, and whether the presentation should run in the foreground.

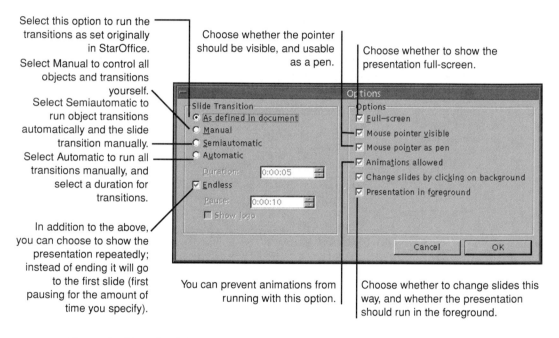

Figure 25-20   StarOffice Player options window

Using the Pack Feature to Reduce Presentation File Size

The pack feature in StarOffice Impress allows you to transport presentations more easily with two effects: it compresses the presentation and, if necessary for the file size options you choose, divides it into two or more files. StarOffice and the Player can run the packed file or files. The files take a little longer to display when packed, but are a pretty good solution to the problem of transferring a 5 MB file to your laptop, if they aren't connected via a network.

The packed files are about half the size of the original. For example:

- Original 72-page StarImpress .sdd file: 9.5 MB
- Packed version, StarImpress .sdp: 5 MB

The pack process creates one or more packed files, depending on what you specify for the file size. You can select three different options:

- **1.44 MB or 720 KB diskette**s – Compresses the presentation and saves it onto one or more files that don't exceed the specified diskette size. If you need to insert another diskette, you'll be prompted to do so.

- **Variable (free space on medium)** – Simply compresses the presentation without dividing it into separate files.

- **User-defined file sizes** – Compresses the presentation and divides it into one or more files, not exceeding the size that you specify. You can enter a maximum size of 20 KB or 2000 KB, whatever suits your needs.

Note – StarImpress.sdp files can be opened **only** with StarOffice or Player version 5.2; they aren't recognized in earlier versions of the product.

If you're using links to objects, rather than including the objects in the file, you can use the Compress feature to save the objects in the file, as well.

Both features save the file under a different name, so the original file is unchanged.

1   Open the presentation file.

2   You can't save changes to the packed version without making it a regular presentation again. If space is extremely limited on the medium where you'll be running the presentation, be sure you've made all the changes you need to.

3   Choose File > Pack and set options in the Pack window (Figure 25-21).

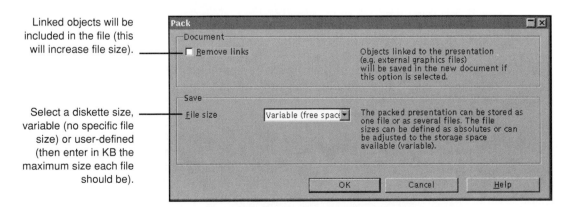

Linked objects will be included in the file (this will increase file size).

Select a diskette size, variable (no specific file size) or user-defined (then enter in KB the maximum size each file should be).

Figure 25-21   Compressing and including linked objects

4   Click OK; enter a name for the new file.

The first packed file will have an .sdp extension; any additional files will have the extension .sxy, where x and y are symbol and number variables, respectively.

5   If you chose to pack the file to diskettes, insert additional diskettes if prompted.

6   Copy the packed files to the laptop or other computer you'll be using to give the presentation. You can use StarOffice Impress Player or StarOffice to open the packed files.

Playing and Editing Packed Files

When you open a packed file in StarOffice or the Player, open the *filename*.sdp file, not any of the additional *filename*.sxy files—they'll just be gibberish in a text file.

If you open a packed .sdp file and want to make changes, you'll need to save it as a regular presentation, not a packed one. Repack it if you want it back in packed format.

Printing in StarOffice Impress

Printing presentations is a little more complex than printing other documents, because there might be notes, handouts, and other components that you might not want printed every time. If you just choose File > Print > OK, you'll get *everything*, including an outline. See *Setting Printing Options* and *Printing a Presentation* to make sure you're printing what you want.

Note – The printing information here is specific to this application; see *Printing in StarOffice* on page 61 of *Getting Started* for more information.

Printer Setup

For information about setting up printers and printing to files, refer to *Printer Setup* on page 62 and *Printing to a PostScript or PDF File* on page 77.

Note – The paper size you select is important; if you're having printing problems, check the paper size. If you're in the United States, for example, make sure you select Letter or Legal in the Printer Properties window. (Choose File > Print, select a printer, and click Properties. In the Paper tab, select the right paper size from the Paper size list.)

Setting Up Colors for Commercial Printing

If you'll be printing high-quality color copies of the presentation, you should probably switch color models from RGB (red-green-blue, the model used by your monitor) to CMYK (cyan-magenta-yellow-black, the model used by commercial printers).

Both palettes are included in StarOffice, though RGB is the default. Follow these steps to switch to CMYK.

1   Choose Format > Area.

2   In the Area window, click the Colors tab.

3   Click Open.

4   Select CMYK from the Color sample list.

5   Click the Load Color List icon.

6   In the `config` folder, select the `cmyk.soc` file and click Open.

7   Assign CMYK colors to the presentation.

Printing Brochures

See *Printing Brochures* on page 350.

Printing More Than One Slide on a Page

Use the Handouts feature (see page 703). (The Tile option in the Print Options window (see page 726) works inconsistently or not at all.)

In addition, refer to *Fitting Multiple Pages Onto One Sheet* on page 83 for information on printing multiple images per page across StarOffice.

Cramming a Slide Onto a Page

Sometimes you just need to squish or expand a drawing to get the printed output right. If the slide is too big, you'll generally be notified when you print, and you can choose the Fit to Size option at that point. To be prepared ahead of time, however, you can mark the Fit to Size option using either of the following navigations:

Page Format Window

1   Choose Format > Page and click the Page tab.

2   Select Fit to size and click OK.

Note – If you want to print an image in landscape that's too long to fit the short way onto the landscape page, choose Format > Page. In the Page tab, select Landscape and select Fit to size, then click OK. If Fit to size isn't selected when you mark Landscape, it won't work to apply it after the fact.

Print Options Window

1   Choose File > Print and click the Options button.

2   Select the Fit to page option and click OK.

3   Click OK to print.

You also can refer to *Fitting Multiple Pages Onto One Sheet* on page 83 to see how it's done across StarOffice.

Stretching a Small Slide to Fill a Page

There's a Fill entire page option in the Page Format window, but it doesn't have any effect. You can use the Scale field in the Paper tab of the Printer Properties window (File > Printer Setup, or File > Print > Properties.) (This works intermittently, but with enough consistency to be worth trying.)

Your best bet is to just manually enlarge the elements of the slide; increase font size, etc. Group the graphical elements of the slide, if there are more than one. Then see *Resizing Objects* on page 782.

Printing Without Dark Backgrounds

If you have a presentation with a heavy dark background that you want to print without bringing your toner cartridge to its knees, you have a couple options:

•   The simplest approach is to select either Grayscale or Black-and-White in the print options window (Figure 25-23 on page 726).

•   Remove the background (see *Applying a Blank Background* on page 689).

Figure 25-22 illustrates the effects of printing in grayscale or black and white. The original slide has a light blue center with bars at the side that fade from light to dark blue. The heading is dark blue and the text is black.

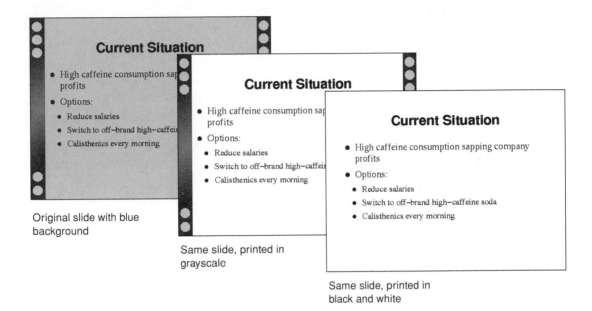

Original slide with blue
background

Same slide, printed in
grayscale

Same slide, printed in
black and white

Figure 25-22   Printing in grayscale or black and white

Backgrounds and File Size Issues

If you find that printing the presentation takes longer than it would to transcribe it onto
paper by hand, check what's in the background. (See *Presentation Backgrounds* on
page 683.) In general, it's a good idea not to use gradient fills, gradient text, or complex
backgrounds in Star Office presentations because this drastically affects disk space,
printing, or download time. You can do a colored background easily that doesn't take
much disk space by choosing Format > Page and in the Page tab, selecting a color.

Specifying Landscape or Portrait Orientation

To specify whether the presentation should be portrait or landscape, choose Format > Page
and select the Page tab. (This affects all slides in the document, if there is more than one.)

You *can* also set orientation in the Printer Options window. (Choose File > Printer Setup,
click Properties and select the Paper tab.) However, all testing indicates that the setting in
the Printer Setup window is completely irrelevant; sometimes it changes to reflect what
you've set in the Page Setup window, but if you make any changes there, it doesn't affect
printing.

See also *Specifying Portrait or Landscape Orientation* on page 82 for more information
on the ways you can set orientation throughout StarOffice.

Setting Printing Options

1   Choose Tools > Options > Presentation > Print (Figure 25-23). (You can also choose File > Print and click the Options button.)

Using the first approach applies the options you select to all subsequent documents; using the second approach applies the options only to the document you print next.

2   Select what you want to print.

Be sure that you select only what you want to print, in the Contents area. If you want to print handouts for your audience, select only Handouts, not Drawing, as well.

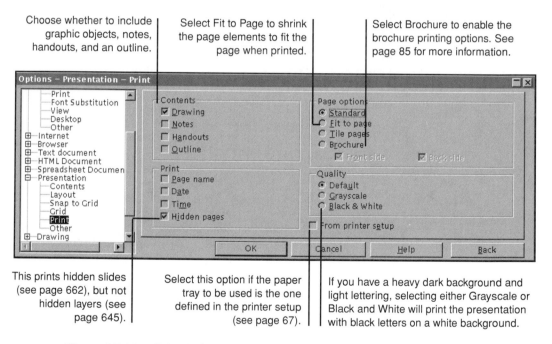

Choose whether to include graphic objects, notes, handouts, and an outline.

Select Fit to Page to shrink the page elements to fit the page when printed.

Select Brochure to enable the brochure printing options. See page 85 for more information.

This prints hidden slides (see page 662), but not hidden layers (see page 645).

Select this option if the paper tray to be used is the one defined in the printer setup (see page 67).

If you have a heavy dark background and light lettering, selecting either Grayscale or Black and White will print the presentation with black letters on a white background.

Figure 25-23   Selecting printing options

Note – The Tile option seems to be "unimplemented features," working inconsistently and rarely at best. To print two or more slides on a page, use the handouts feature (see *Creating Slide Handouts* on page 703) and select only Handouts in the Contents section of this window.

Selecting an Option in the Print Warning Window

If you set up the notification described in *Managing Print Warnings* on page 80, or if a slide won't fit the page setup options you've specified, the window in Figure 25-24 will appear when necessary:

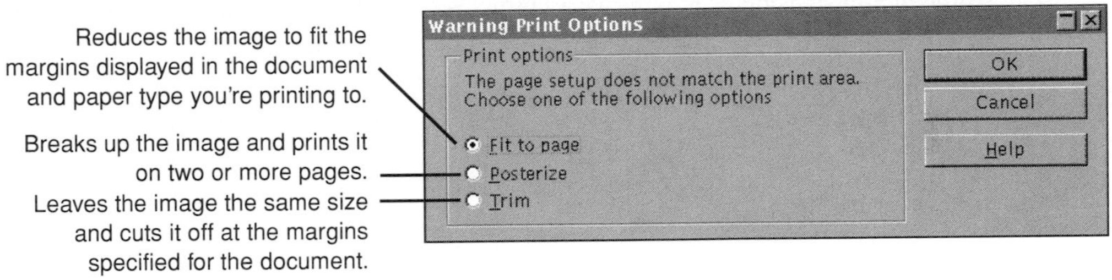

Reduces the image to fit the margins displayed in the document and paper type you're printing to.

Breaks up the image and prints it on two or more pages.
Leaves the image the same size and cuts it off at the margins specified for the document.

Figure 25-24   Print Options warning window

Note – If you select Fit to page, the warning won't appear again for this document.

Printing a Presentation

Note – To print to a file, refer to *Printing to a PostScript or PDF File* on page 77.

You can click the Print File Directly icon on the function bar, or follow these steps:

1   Check printing options to choose what parts of the presentation to print (see *Setting Printing Options*).

In particular, be sure to select only Drawing if you just want a regular printout; only Handouts if you want handouts but not the regular presentation, etc.

2   Choose File > Print.

3   Select a printer, or select the Print to file option and enter a file name. To print to a PostScript file, enter a name with a .ps extension.

4   Select what to print: All (the entire document), Pages (a range of pages), or Selection (the currently selected text or objects). Use dashes to form ranges, and use commas or semicolons to separate pages or ranges (1, 3, 4, 6-10).

The page range refers to slides, not pages. If you're printing handouts, keep in mind that entering a range of 1-4 will print only 4 slides, which is only one or two pages.

Note – StarOffice often defaults to Selection, rather than All, as the range of pages to print. Check this each time you print.

5   Enter the number of copies and, if it's two or more, choose whether to collate.

6   Click OK.

Note – If all slides or layers aren't printing, check whether the layers are printable (see page 645) and whether the slides are hidden (page 662). You can choose whether to print hidden slides, using print options (Figure 25-23 on page 726) but you need to go back to the layer tab in the presentation to switch it back to being printable.

URL:

StarOffice
Draw and
Image

Part 6

StarOffice Draw: Creating Vector Graphics

Quick Start

This section contains the following information to help you get started quickly:

- A checklist for quickly making StarOffice Draw graphics
- Feature overview
- How to create a new Draw file
- A tutorial

See *Taming the StarOffice Environment* on page 91 for general tips that can make working with StarOffice a lot easier.

Note – Many features are available throughout StarOffice, but we don't cover them in every program's section. Check the index, or refer to *Taming the StarOffice Environment* on page 91 or *StarOffice Writer* on page 151 if you can't find the information you need in the chapters for StarOffice Draw.

Quick Start Checklist

If it's 2:45 and you need a drawing for a meeting at 3:00, try these sections:

- Creating or opening a new file – *Creating and Opening Draw Files* on page 737
- Adding shapes – *Creating Basic Objects* on page 739
- Adding and formatting text – *Working With Text* on page 775
- Printing the graphic – *Printing in StarOffice Draw* on page 799

StarOffice Draw Features

Draw and Image allow you to create and edit both types of images: those based on lines and shapes, or *vector images*, and those based on individual pixels, or *raster images*. Draw is based on lines and shapes and is similar to products such as CorelDraw; Image is based on raster images and is similar to products such as Adobe Photoshop.

Note – If you're not familiar with the terms *vector* and *raster*, make a note of them at this point; they'll be used in this chapter and the next to differentiate the types of images you can create with each program.

Draw manages graphics that are composed of objects that you can manipulate and edit on an object basis. For instance, when you draw a square in Draw, you can move it around, apply different colors, duplicate it several times, and so on.

Draw's features include, but aren't limited to, the following.

Extensive object creation and formatting Includes 2D and 3D images, lines, text, and formatting features for each.

Multi-application availability Draw's features are available when you use StarOffice Writer, Calc, and Impress.

Full Writer text formatting Most of Writer's text features are available in Draw. You can use the existing styles (preset groups of attributes) with objects, lines, and text, or create and modify styles.

FontWork The FontWork program is included, which lets you apply an extraordinary array of font effects, including distorting and curving.

Insert files, OLE objects, graphics You can insert a variety of other files, as well as insert OLE objects such as spreadsheets and graphs.

File formats In addition to supporting an array of files for opening and saving as, you can export Draw and Impress slides to HTML.

Trouble-Shooting Note

If you did the minimal installation, you're going to run into problems with Draw and Image. The minimal installation leaves out Image entirely, and some of the filters that let you read multiple image formats. To get the necessary programs installed so you can read all Draw and Image files, run the installation again (run the installed `setup` or `setup.exe` file) and choose to add components in the first window. Select anything that's dimmed and select it to make the icon colored, rather than dimmed or white. See *Installation* on page 3.

Creating a Drawing

To create a new file, choose File > New > Drawing.

The Draw Work Area

The Draw work area is shown in Figure 26-1.

The toolbar down the loft side of the work area lets you create 2D and 3D shapes, lines, and insert objects like charts. It also includes tools like arranging and skewing objects.

Click the Line and Arrow Style icons to control how lines appear.

Use the icons on the toolbar to create objects, align and arrange them, insert objects, and so on.

To see all the options for an icon, click it, then click the submenu that appears to "tear" it off, as shown.

The option bar offers you precision text, line and object positioning.

The color bar lets you select the color for an object; the same colors are available in the object bar.

To change the measurement system right-click the ruler and select one.

The object bar controls item attributes.

When you use the Text tool, the object bar displays text formatting icons.

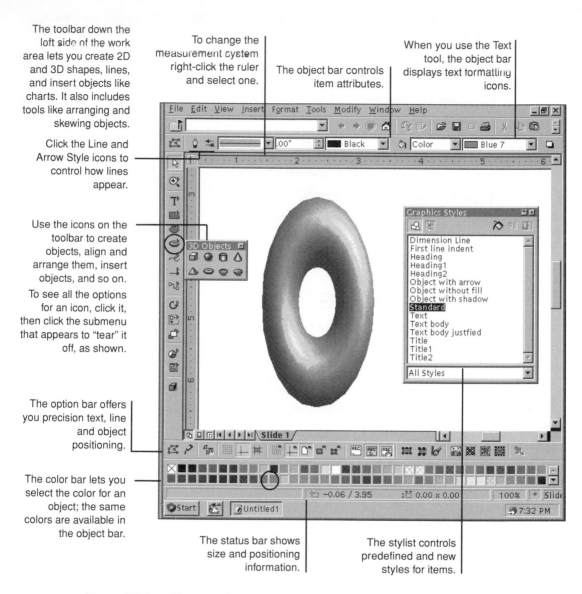

The status bar shows size and positioning information.

The stylist controls predefined and new styles for items.

Figure 26-1   Draw work area

Guided Tour

This should take you around ten minutes to complete, and will quickly give you an idea of how the program works.

1   Choose File > New > Drawing.

2   In the option bar below the work area (choose View > Toolbars > Option Bar if it's not displayed), double-click the zoom field that displays a percentage, like 48%. In the Zoom window, select Variable and enter 95%.

3   Click the Rectangle icon on the toolbar at the left side of the work area. Hold down the mouse until the Rectangles tearoff menu appears. Release the mouse, then click again on the top of the menu to "tear it off" (display the menu separately). Move the menu to the right an inch or two.

4   Click the filled square icon in the tearoff menu and draw a square.

5   Change the color of the border using the fields in the object bar above the ruler (the toolbar showing selections like colors and measurements). Hint: The border must have width. If the object bar isn't displayed, choose View > Toolbars > Object Bar.

6   Fill the area with a gradient, also using the object bar. (Select Gradient from the list that displays the word Color, shown at right.)

7   Right-click on the ruler and change the measurement system to centimeters.

8   Select the square and choose Edit > Duplicate. Make one copy of the square, five centimeters to the *left*.

9   Right-click one of the squares and choose Position and Size. Increase the size, and rotate the square 47 degrees around the lower left corner.

10   Choose Format > Stylist.

11   Select one of the squares and apply the Object without fill style. (Hint: double-click the style.)

12   Click the Connector icon in the toolbar.

13   Connect the left side of the left square with the right side of the right square.

14   Convert one of the squares to a 3D rotation object (right-click and choose Convert).

15   Click the Text icon and in the work area, type What is the airspeed of a laden swallow? Click outside the text.

16   Note that the text frame around the text keeps enlarging to accommodate the text. To make the text wrap at a certain point, click in the text again, right-click on the

text frame, then choose Format > Text. In the Text tab, deselect the Fit width to text option.

17   Double-click the text again, move the cursor to the end of the line and type the following line: `African or European Swallow?` Note that the text now wraps.

18   Click the Text icon again. Draw a text frame approximately two inches wide by one inch high. In it, type `It's not a question of where he grips it! It's a simple question of weight ratios!` When you draw a text frame, the text frame stays at the original horizontal measurement, but lengthens to accommodate additional lines.

19   Select the text you just typed, right-click on it, and choose Format > Character. Make the text 12-point blue Conga.

20   Use the fields on the object bar (above the ruler) to change the text to 23-point red Bembo. (Hint: Select "Conga" and type "Bembo" over it, then press Return.)

21   Right-click the text frame (the rectangle around it—not the text itself) and choose FontWork. Curve the text using any of the icons, then close the window.

22   Double-click in the square that you didn't convert and type `Explain again how sheeps' bladders may be employed to prevent earthquakes.`

23   If the text isn't readable due to the rotation of the object, right-click it and choose Position and Size again, and rotate it so that the text is legible.

24   Right-click the square and choose Text. In the Text tab, select the Fit to Size option.

25   The text is a little too small to read now. Right-click the square again and unmark Fit to size. Select Adjust to contour instead.

26   Move the 3D square so that it overlaps part of the other square. If it's behind the other square, right-click and choose Arrange > Bring to front.

27   Click the Curve icon to display the Curves tearoff menu.

28   Draw a filled polygon. (Double-click to stop drawing.)

29   Click the Edit Points icon on the left side of the object bar and select one of the object handles; drag the handle to skew the polygon.

30   Click the Edit Points icon again and select an object handle; see what happens now when you drag a handle.

31   Create a new drawing and draw a rounded rectangle that touches all four margins on the page.

32   Choose Format > Page and click the Page tab. Select Landscape rather than Portrait and click OK.

33   The drawing shows the new margins, within which the image will be printed.

34   Choose Format > Page again and in the Page tab select Fit to size. Click OK. Note that the rectangle still doesn't fit within the margins.

35   Create another new drawing with a rounded rectangle that touches all four margins. This time, choose Format > Page and in the Page tab, select Landscape and Fit to size at the same time. Click OK.

36   Note that this time the shape fits within the margins of the landscape page setup.

37   Choose File > Print and print the drawing to a printer.

38   Choose File > Export and save the drawing as a GIF file. Leave both options marked in the GIF Options window and click OK.

Creating and Opening Draw Files

Creating a new file is simple; you can open only certain file formats in Draw.

Creating a New Draw File

Choose File > New > Drawing to open a new blank file.

Note – Periodically, StarOffice gives you bad default margins for a new file. For example, you might end up with the top margin 25 inches below the top of the page (which doesn't leave much room for your drawing). You can't tell just by looking at the work area, so choose Format > Page and in the Page tab, set the orientation and margins correctly.

In addition, check the paper size and select the appropriate size—this depends on the country where you're located, of course. It's a good idea to stay away from User, however, and United States users should typically select Letter.

Make a selection here appropriate for the country where you're located (User format can cause problems; select a different format for best results.)

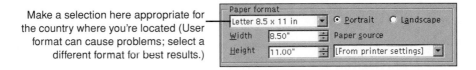

Figure 26-2   Selecting the right paper format

To base a drawing on a template, choose File > New > From template and select the appropriate StarDraw Template file.

Opening a File

You can open vector-based art files, Draw files, or Impress files as a Draw document.

Draw uses only vector graphics. If you open a file saved in any of the following raster formats, it will be opened in Image: BMP, GIF, JPG, PCX, PNG, TIF, PCT, PSD, PBM, PGM, PPM, RAS, TGA, and XPM.

To get a raster image from Image into Draw, use the arrow tool in Image to select a region, then copy and paste the selected area into Draw.

Opening a Draw or Vector Art File

To open an existing Draw file, choose File > Open and select the file, then click Open.

Opening an Impress File as a Draw File

Choose File > Open and select the file. In the File type list, select StarDraw and click Open.

You also can select the file in Beamer and choose Open With, then select StarDraw.

Creating a Template

To use a drawing as the basis of subsequent drawings, just choose File > Save as and select the StarDraw template file format. Save it in your office52/user/template folder, or in one of the folders within share/template/*language*/. Only files in these locations are available when you choose File > New > From Template, unless you've added locations according to *Adding Places for StarOffice to Look for Impress Files* on page 619.

The section on Writer contains comprehensive information on styles and templates; see *Using Templates* on page 220.

Checking What Template Your Document Is Based On

If your document is acting weird and you want to make sure you created it based on the right template, choose File > Properties and click the General tab. The template used by the document is displayed at the bottom of the window.

Page Setup

Note – You can create the effect of a multi-page document in Draw using multiple slides; you also can have multiple layers within the same slide. See *Inserting a New Empty Slide* on page 655 and *Using Layers* on page 641 for more information.

You can control the background color and orientation of each slide.

- To control the background of a StarDraw document, choose Format > Page, then click the Background tab.

- To specify whether a document is portrait or landscape orientation, choose Format > Page, then click the Page tab. (This affects all slides in the document, if there is more than one.)

  When you change orientation, the margins often get kerflummoxed and the top margin ends up, for example, 25 inches down from the top. Be sure to check the margins before you click OK (you'll get a warning anyway if the margins are out of range). In addition, check to make sure the paper format is correct; stay away from User, since it can cause a variety of problems.

See Figure 5-32 on page 212 and *Specifying Portrait or Landscape Orientation* on page 82 for more information on these Page Setup options.

Creating Basic Objects

Creating a basic object, such as a square or ellipse, is easy. Use the rectangle or ellipse icon in the toolbar on the left side of the work area.

Toolbar navigation note The green arrows on each icon in the toolbar indicate that you can click on the icon, then click on the menu that appears, and "tear it off"—the menu will remain in the work area. For example, the Rectangle icon has a tearoff menu containing eight shapes.

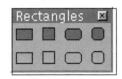

The icons on the toolbar won't always look the same, however. The last shape that you chose is the shape displayed in the toolbar. The first time you open Draw, the icon looks

like this: But if you then draw an empty rounded-corner square, the next time you

look for the rectangle icon on the toolbar, the icon will look like this:

Note – You can click an icon and use the tool once (for instance, to draw one rectangle) and then you need to click an icon again. Or you can double-click an icon and use the tool as many times as you want. Just double-click again in the work area when you're done using the tool.

Drawing a Square, Rectangle, Circle, or Ellipse

1   Click the Rectangle or Ellipse icon on the toolbar and choose the shape you want to draw.

2   From the tearoff menu, select the object you want.

3   Draw the object in the work area.

Rounding the Corners of an Existing Rectangle or Square

1   Select the object in the work area.

2   Click the Edit Points icon on the left end of the option bar.

3   The drawing handles will change, and one corner's handles will increase in size.

Move the mouse pointer over the larger handle; when the mouse icon changes to a hand, drag the handle to round the corner; all corners will be rounded identically.

Drawing an Arc or Filled Segment

You can draw an arc or a filled segment using the ellipse icon.

1   Click the Ellipse icon on the toolbar and choose the shape you want to draw.

2   Draw a circle or ellipse.

3   The radius of the shape will appear, and the mouse icon will change to a crosshairs. Click at the point where you want the pie-shaped cutout of the circle to begin.

4   The line will be set, and another moveable radius will appear. Click where you want the other side of the pie-shaped cutout.

The object will appear. You can use the large handles to change the size of the empty area.

Working With Lines

Draw provides you with several types of lines: simple lines, connectors that you can use in diagrams and flowcharts, dimension indicator lines, and Bezier curves. You also can apply a variety of attributes, including types of ends, color, width, and so on.

Drawing a Basic Line or Arrow

1   Click the Lines and Arrows icon in the toolbar and in the tearoff menu, select the type of line or arrow you want.

2   Draw the line. Use the handles to adjust the line if necessary.

Note – The crosshairs icon allows you to draw a line that is exactly horizontal, perpendicular, or at a 45-degree angle. To use the dimension line icon, see *Using Dimension Lines and Connectors* on page 745.

Occasionally you'll draw a line that looks fine onscreen but prints with a slight crook in it. You can correct it either of the following ways:

- Select the line, click and hold down the mouse on the end you want to adjust, then press Shift and adjust it. This snaps the line to a vertical or horizontal orientation.

- Zoom in to 400% or higher and adjust it (see *Increasing or Decreasing Display Size (Zooming)* on page 647).

- Snap to the grid or snap points (see *Snapping Objects to a Grid* on page 786).

Quickly Changing Line Attributes

Use the object bar at the top of the work area, shown in Figure 26-3.

Figure 26-3   Line attribute fields

1   Select a Line end type for each end of the line.

2 Select the Line type: Invisible, Continuous, or one of the listed patterns.

3 Select a Line width. The measurement is calibrated in the current measuring system.

4 Select a Line color.

Changing Attributes Using the Line Window

Once you've drawn a line, you can apply a variety of characteristics to it like color, arrows, width, and pattern.

It also lets you set and modify line styles and line style lists, a way of categorizing those styles. See also *Creating and Modifying Styles* on page 773.

1 Open the Line window using either method:

- Right-click and choose Line.

- Click the Line icon on the left side of the object bar.

2 The Line window will be displayed (Figure 26-4).

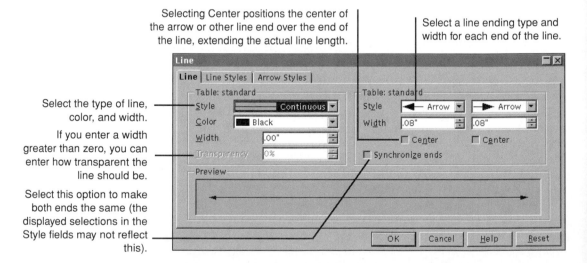

Figure 26-4   Applying line attributes

3 Modify any of the displayed options.

4 Click Reset to change the settings back to the originals, click Cancel to close the window without applying changes, or click OK to apply the changes you've made.

Creating and Modifying Line and Arrow Styles

You can modify the preset types of lines and arrows, such as Ultrafine Dashed and Rounded Short Arrow, that are displayed in the Line tab of the Line window, and elsewhere in StarOffice. You also can create your own.

1 Choose Format > Line, or right-click a line object and choose Line.

2 Click the Line Styles or Arrow Styles tab.

3 If you're modifying an existing style, select it.

Note – If the style you want to modify isn't displayed in the Line window, click the Load Styles icon and select the list where it is stored. See *Working With Style Lists* on page 744 for more information.

---

4 Define the style appropriately, as shown in Figure 26-5.

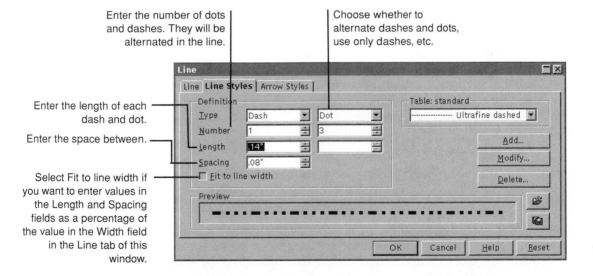

Figure 26-5   Creating new lines and arrows

5 Click Add for a new style or Modify for an existing style; enter a name and click OK.

6 Click OK to close the window and save changes.

Creating Your Own Arrows and Line Endings

To draw your own endpoints for a line, such as unusual arrows, pictures, or other shapes, follow these steps.

Note – This works only with vector objects, not with raster images such as scanned photos, even if you convert them to polygons or contours. For curves, draw them and convert them to polygons.

---

1   Draw or paste into a document the shape you want on the end of the line.

2   Select it, then open the Line window. Select the Arrow Styles tab.

3   Click Add and enter a new style name.

4   The new style will appear in the Preview area, as shown in Figure 26-6. (It might appear somewhat different from the original.)

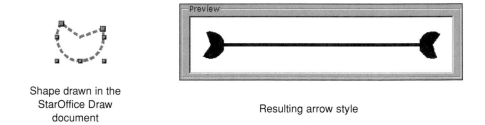

Shape drawn in the
StarOffice Draw
document

Resulting arrow style

Figure 26-6   Hand-drawn arrow style

Working With Style Lists

You can group the sets of line styles and arrow styles in StarOffice into *style lists*. Many of the attributes in StarOffice, including lines, colors, and gradients, are stored in these groups, and only one is displayed in the workspace and in the Line window at a time (Figure 26-7). This is convenient if you have several different styles of attributes for different projects and want to keep them separate, so that you don't need to scroll through a long list, looking for the one you need.

Line and arrow lists are stored in the config folder with the file extension .sod and .soe, respectively.

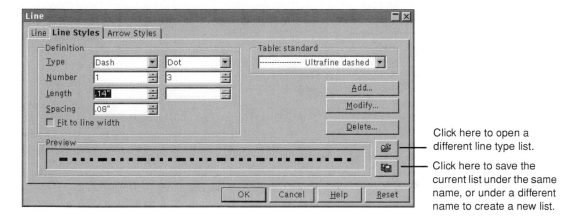

Figure 26-7   Style list management icons

Selecting a Different List

In the Styles tab, click the Load Styles icon and select the `.sod` or `.soe` file you want.

Saving Changes to a List

If you've added or modified a style, click the Save Styles icon to save it in the current list.

Using Dimension Lines and Connectors

Draw provides two useful tools for flowcharts, architectural drawings, and other drawings that are very technical or precise. The tools are the dimension line and the connector.

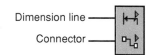

Drawing a Dimension Line

1   Click the Lines and Arrows icon and select the dimension tool.

2   Draw the dimension line next to the object whose measurement you want to display (Figure 26-8).

The actual length or width of the object will be displayed, using the measuring system currently selected for the ruler. Modify the drawn line with the handles; you can change the angle or length.

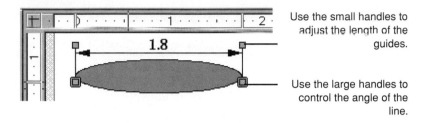

Use the small handles to adjust the length of the guides.

Use the large handles to control the angle of the line.

Figure 26-8   Adjusting a dimension line

Applying Attributes to a Dimension Line

The Dimensioning window allows you precise control over the position, distance, and text position of the line.

To draw the dimension line perfectly straight or to "snap" them to grid lines, be sure the grid is on. See *Setting Up the Grid* on page 784.

1   Open the Dimensioning window (Figure 26-9) by right-clicking a dimension line and choosing Dimensions, or choose Format > Dimensions.

2   Make the appropriate changes and click OK.

Line distance controls the distance from the point in the workspace where you drew the line to the point where it is displayed. (Original location is selected by the two large handles.)

Guide overhang controls where the guides begin, relative to the line, and is indicated by small handles. (Up/left is positive; down/right is negative.)

Guide distance controls where the guides end, relative to the line, and are not selected by handles.

Select the Automatic options to automatically determine the optimum horizontal and vertical dimensions.

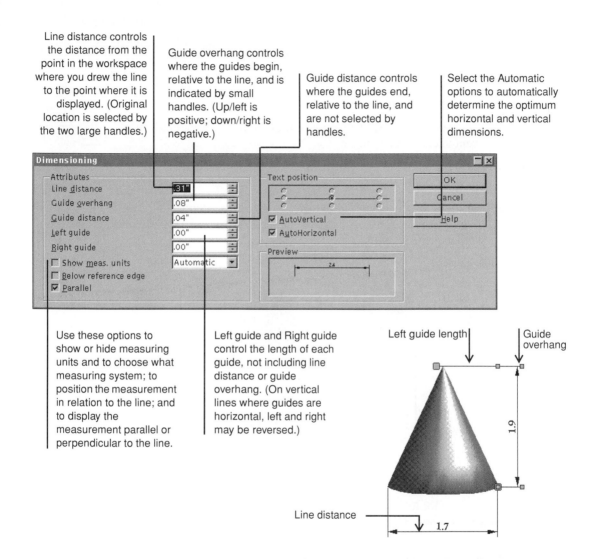

Use these options to show or hide measuring units and to choose what measuring system; to position the measurement in relation to the line; and to display the measurement parallel or perpendicular to the line.

Left guide and Right guide control the length of each guide, not including line distance or guide overhang. (On vertical lines where guides are horizontal, left and right may be reversed.)

Figure 26-9   Changing dimension line attributes

Drawing a Connector

Connectors are excellent tools for creating precise diagrams. The connectors automatically attach precisely to the edge of the object you specify, which saves time you would otherwise spend at an 800% zoom, for example, trying to position an ordinary line correctly.

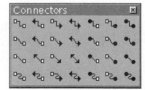

1   Determine the two objects you want to connect.

2   Click the Connector icon and select the type of connector you want to draw.

Tools in the second and third rows with diagonal lines always take the shortest path from one object to another, and only connect the closest connector points.

3   Move the mouse pointer over the first object; its connection points will appear.

4   Click and hold down the mouse on the connection point that you want to connect the line to.

5   Drag the mouse to the second object; its connection points will appear.

6   Position the connector line endpoint on the correct connection point and release the mouse (Figure 26-10). If you move or resize either object, the connector will move with the object.

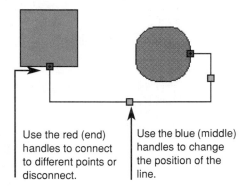

Figure 26-10   Adjusting or connecting connector lines

Only connector tools in the first and fourth rows of the tearoff menu draw lines that, as shown, have multiple directions.

Applying Connector Attributes

The Connector window allows you precise control over the position, distance, and text position of the line.

1   Open the Connector window (Figure 26-11) by right-clicking a connector and choosing Connector, or choose Format > Connector.

2   Make the appropriate changes; applying changes to a multi-directional connector line is shown.

Controls the offset from the original location (left/up is negative, right/down is positive) for each line segment.

Controls the type of connector, also displayed in the Connector menu.

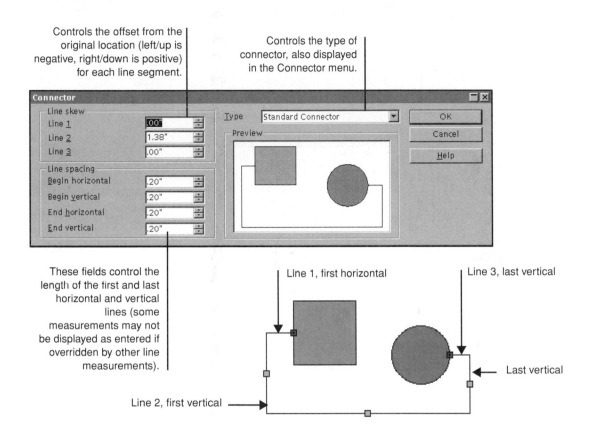

These fields control the length of the first and last horizontal and vertical lines (some measurements may not be displayed as entered if overridden by other line measurements).

Line 1, first horizontal

Line 3, last vertical

Last vertical

Line 2, first vertical

Figure 26-11   Changing connector attributes

Working With Bezier Curves

Bezier curves, lines defined by a series of points, allow you a great deal of control over the shapes you create. Draw provides curved, polygon, and freeform tools.

Creating a Bezier Curve

1   Click the Line icon and select the kind of line you want to draw.

2   Draw the line in the workspace.

Click and drag the mouse to the first point where you want to change directions. From then on just move the mouse to the next point where you change directions, and double-click to stop drawing.

Editing a Bezier Curve

Use the object bar (Figure 26-12) to edit a Bezier curve.

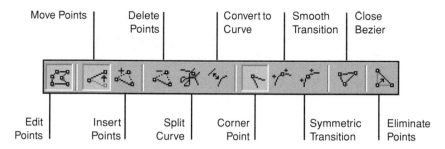

Figure 26-12   Edit Points icons on the object bar

Note – If you want all of the points on a curve to be selected if you only select one, you can set that up in Draw options. Choose Tools > Options > Drawing > Layout. Select the All handles in Bezier editor option, then click OK.

---

1   Select the object.

2   Be sure that the Edit Points icon is clicked, that the Bezier icons are active in the object bar, and that blue handles, rather than green handles, are displayed when you select the object.

Some icons are available only when you select a point.

Click the Edit Points icon if the handles are green. Green handles let you move the object and resize the object proportionately, the same way you would resize a polygon.

3   A number of handles are shown on the curve, one for each point. Select a point to apply changes to; it will turn dark green.

4   Make the appropriate edits, using the editing icons. An example of possible edits is shown in Figure 26-13.

Edit Points Lets you edit a curve.

Move Points Must be active to let you drag a point to a different location.

Insert Points Adds points to the curve. Note: This lets you add points until you click it again to turn it off.

Note – Be sure the Eliminate Points icon is inactive while you're inserting points, or you'll be adding a point and eliminating it a microsecond later.

Delete Points Removes the selected point. The shape will change, connecting the two points on either side.

Split Curve Disconnects the curve at the selected point; incomplete curves can't have fill, so the fill will be removed.

Convert To Curve Changes straight points to curved points, and back. Set Corner Point, Smooth, and Symmetric are applicable only to curved points (when To Curve is active).

Corner Point Lets a point have two separate control handles rather than the usual one.

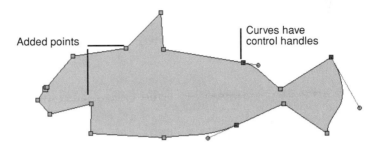

Figure 26-13   Editing Bezier curves

Smooth Transition Reshapes a curve so that both handles of the corner point are aligned parallel, and can only be moved simultaneously. The curves on either side of the point can be different.

Symmetric Transition Converts a corner point or smooth point to a symmetrical point. Both handles of the corner point are aligned parallel and also have the same length. These can only be moved simultaneously. The degree of curvature is in both directions the same.

Close Bezier Closes an open curve. The two points connected are not necessarily the end ones. A line is closed always by combining the last point with the first point (indicated by an enlarged square).

Eliminate Points Deletes the selected (dark green) point.

Applying Basic Object Attributes

This section describes how to use the attributes that can be applied to all types of objects, including 3D objects: colors, patterns, gradients, and other attributes. You'll also learn how to create predefined styles to easily apply the same set of attributes to multiple objects.

You can quickly apply attributes using the work area, or you can use the Area window to have greater control over precisely which attributes you apply.

Note – Unfortunately, there is no "flood fill" tool, in StarOffice Draw or Image. The closest thing is the Eyedropper; see *Changing All Occurrences of a Color* on page 820 and *Making a Multicolored Image One Color* on page 821.

Quickly Applying Object Attributes

Note – To select attributes that will be applied to *successive* objects instead of a *current* object, first be sure no objects are selected, then follow the steps in this procedure.

---

1   Select the object you're working with.

2   Select border options, apply color to the area or border, or select a fill type such as a hatch or bitmap, using the options illustrated in Figure 26-14.

If the object bar doesn't appear when you select a curve, click the Edit Points icon; green object handles will be displayed instead of blue.

Choose whether to have a border in the line type list. If you choose Continuous or a pattern, width and color options appear in the two lists to the right.

Select color, hatch, gradient, or bitmap from the area fill type list. Selecting a different option overrides the previous option.

When Color is selected in the area fill type list, the colors from the color bar are listed in the area fill list with their names.

Turn shadowing on or off.

Choose Format > Stylist or click the Stylist On/Off icon on the function bar to apply graphics styles.

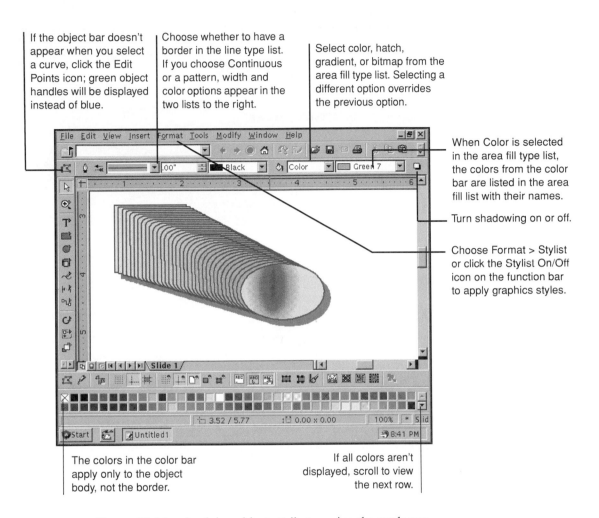

The colors in the color bar apply only to the object body, not the border.

If all colors aren't displayed, scroll to view the next row.

Figure 26-14   Applying object attributes using the work area

Applying Attributes Using the Area Window

1   To open the Area window, choose Format > Area or click the area icon in the object bar

2   Using each tab, select options shown in the following illustrations (Figure 26-15 through Figure 26-22), then click OK.

The object will have no fill, and will be see-through so that an object in back of it will be visible. ——

Select the color to apply to —— the object.

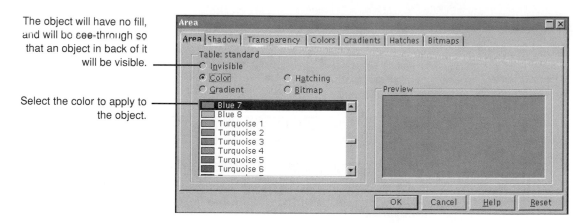

Figure 26-15   Selecting a color

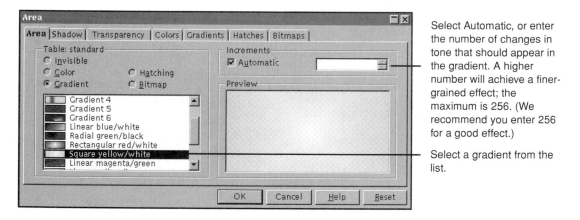

Select Automatic, or enter the number of changes in tone that should appear in the gradient. A higher number will achieve a finer-grained effect; the maximum is 256. (We recommend you enter 256 for a good effect.)

Select a gradient from the list.

Figure 26-16   Selecting a gradient

Note – Your computer or printer might not be able to handle gradients. If your system grinds to a halt and never actually prints anything, or if you end up with only 1 or 2 color changes instead of the number you entered in the Automatic field, gradients have proved too much for your system. Try a plain color or a bitmap instead.

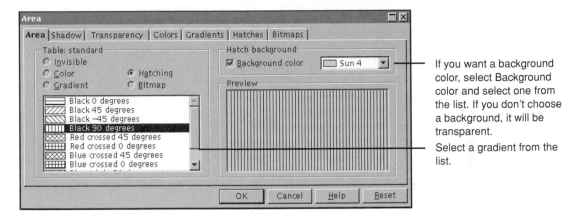

Figure 26-17   Selecting a hatch

If you want a background color, select Background color and select one from the list. If you don't choose a background, it will be transparent.

Select a gradient from the list.

Select Tile to repeat the bitmap throughout the object area and make the rest of the window options available, or select Autofit to display the bitmap just once, adjusting it to the size of the object.

Under Size:
Select Original to show the bitmap at its original size. Deselect Original and enter measurements for the bitmap in the Width and Height fields.
Or select Relative and enter percentages of the bitmap's size in the Width and Height fields.

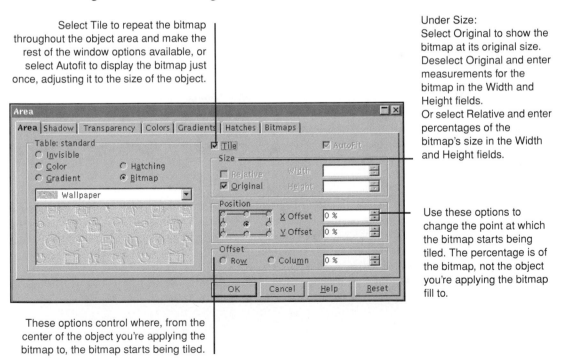

Use these options to change the point at which the bitmap starts being tiled. The percentage is of the bitmap, not the object you're applying the bitmap fill to.

These options control where, from the center of the object you're applying the bitmap to, the bitmap starts being tiled.

Figure 26-18   Selecting a bitmap and bitmap options

Note – Unmark both Tile and AutoFit to see the bitmap as it is stored on your system, without any effects.

Figure 26-19 illustrates the effects of offset.

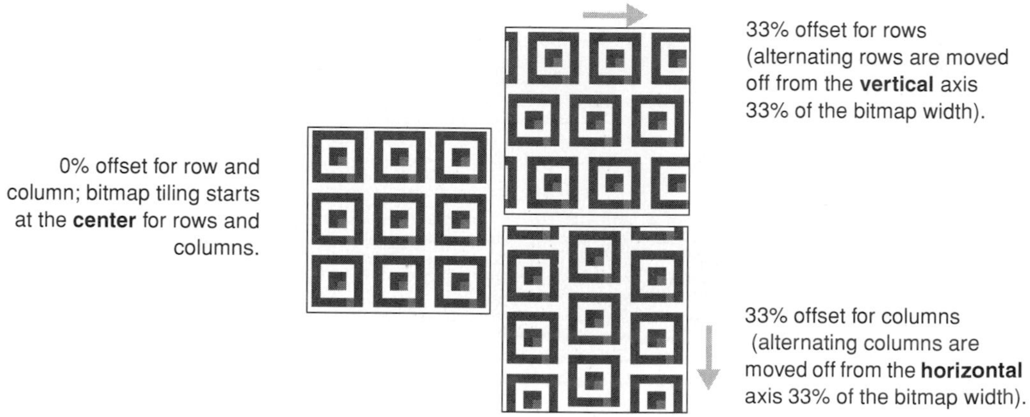

33% offset for rows (alternating rows are moved off from the **vertical** axis 33% of the bitmap width).
0% offset for row and column; bitmap tiling starts at the **center** for rows and columns.
33% offset for columns (alternating columns are moved off from the **horizontal** axis 33% of the bitmap width).

Figure 26-19 Offset for columns and rows

If you use graphics from the Gallery, or other pictures, as bitmaps, Autofit is probably a better choice than Tile. Figure 26-20 illustrates how they contrast.

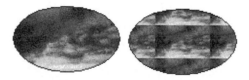

`clouds.jpg`, Autofit
`clouds.jpg`, Tile

Figure 26-20 Tiling and autofitting a bitmap

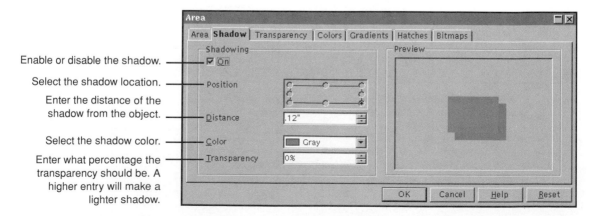

Enable or disable the shadow.
Select the shadow location.
Enter the distance of the shadow from the object.
Select the shadow color.
Enter what percentage the transparency should be. A higher entry will make a lighter shadow.
Area
Area
Shadow
Transparency
Colors
Gradients
Hatches
Bitmaps
Shadowing
On
Position
Distance
.12"
Color
Gray
Transparency
0%
Preview
OK
Cancel
Help
Reset

Figure 26-21 Selecting a shadow

Select the transparency you want. Linear transparency
lets you control the transparency degree through the
percentage in the Linear transparency field;
Transparency gradient is controlled through the fields in
the Transparency gradient area.

Select the type of
transparency gradient.

For some types, enter the
center coordinates for how
much the center of the color
gradient is to be moved on
each axis. The usable scale
is from 0% to 100%; less
than 50% moves to the left
and above, and more than
50% moves to the right and
below.

To set the angle for the
color gradient, enter a value
between 0° and 360°.

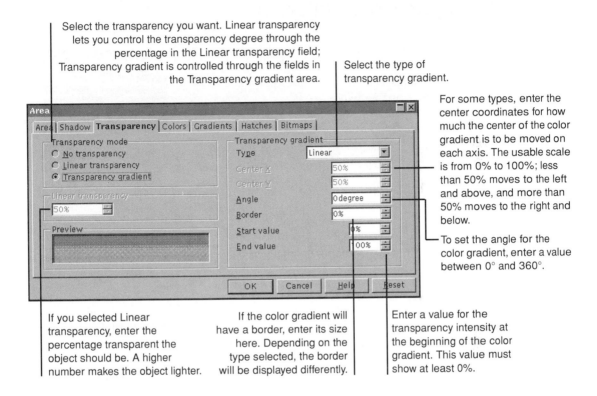

If you selected Linear
transparency, enter the
percentage transparent the
object should be. A higher
number makes the object lighter.

If the color gradient will
have a border, enter its size
here. Depending on the
type selected, the border
will be displayed differently.

Enter a value for the
transparency intensity at
the beginning of the color
gradient. This value must
show at least 0%.

Figure 26-22   Selecting a transparency

Working With Color

You can change any of the colors that are displayed in the color bar, or in any of the color
lists in StarOffice. This section covers how to create or modify an *individual color* or a
color palette.

Note – StarOffice doesn't provide a revert feature to change back modified colors, so we
suggest that you create new ones when possible, rather than modifying.

StarOffice includes both color models in Draw: RGB and CMYK.

Changing Color Palettes

A color palette is a collection of colors displayed in the color bar, or listed in a color list. The file name for the standard color palette is standard.soc, and stored in the StarOffice user/config folder.

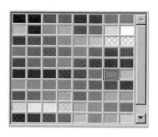

StarOffice provides five palettes: standard.soc, web.soc, html.soc, cmyk.soc, and palette.soc. To change to a different color palette:

1   Choose Format > Area and click the Color tab.

2   Click the Load Color List icon and select any file with a .soc extension.

Changes and additions to individual colors are palette-specific; changing in one palette doesn't change the same color in another palette.

Changing Color Models

The color model is what the available colors in the color bar, color lists, and color definition windows are based on. There are two standards: RGB (red-green-blue, the model used by your monitor) and CYMK (cyan-magenta-yellow-black, the model used by commercial printers). RGB is the default. CMYK looks distinctly different, with more pastel colors.

If you'll be printing high-quality color copies of the presentation, you should probably switch color models from RGB to CYMK.

Note – CMYK is available in Draw, but not Image.

To change the color model before you begin applying colors:

1   Open the Area window, use either of the following methods:

    •   Click the Area icon in the object bar.

    •   Right-click an object and choose Area.

2   In the Area window, click the Colors tab.

3   Click Open.

4   Select CMYK or RGB from the Color sample list. This changes the fields below it that you can use to adjust a particular color.

5   To select a different color list and change the colors that appear in the Table area, click the Load Color List icon. In the user/config folder, select a file such as cmyk.soc file.

Adding or Modifying an Individual Color

1   Open the Area window, use other of the following methods:

* Click the Area icon in the object bar.
* Right-click an object and choose Area.

2   Click the Color tab.

3   Click the Load Color List icon in the color window to switch palettes, if necessary. That is how you can switch to another palette, such as CMYK; selecting CMYK or RGB from the Color sample list will change only the fields that you can use to adjust an individual color.

4   To change or create a color by changing only the RGB or CMYK values, use the following steps, in the Area window only (Figure 26-23):

* Select a color in the Table area.
* Change the CMYK or RGB values in the fields below the color sample list.
* To add the changes as a new color, click Add and enter a new name. To change the color, just click Modify.

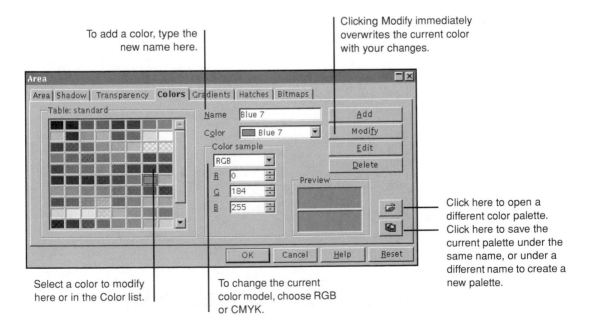

Figure 26-23   Color tab of Area window

5   To change or create a color and modify the hue, saturation, and brightness as well as the RGB or CMYK values, use these steps and the Color window (Figure 26-24):

- To create a new color, click Add and enter a new name, then click Edit.
- To modify a color, click Edit.

Color and other setting fields display the colors for the color selected in the Area window, or the color selected in the right color area.

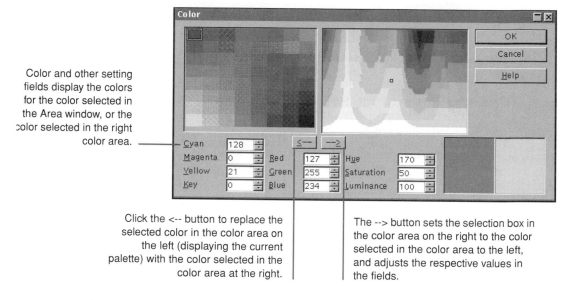

Click the <-- button to replace the selected color in the color area on the left (displaying the current palette) with the color selected in the color area at the right.

The --> button sets the selection box in the color area on the right to the color selected in the color area to the left, and adjusts the respective values in the fields.

Figure 26-24   Modifying a color in the Color window

Adding or Modifying a Color Palette

1   Open the Area window (choose Format > Area or click the Area icon).

2   Change the palette, if necessary, by clicking the Load Color List icon.

3   Make changes to colors in the palette.

4   Click the Save Color List icon.

5   Add or modify the palette:

- To modify, save the color palette with the current name.
- To add a palette, save it with a different name.

Changing Colors Using the Eyedropper

If you're working with bitmaps or metafiles, including any image pasted in from Image, you can use the eyedropper tool to *sample*: specify up to four colors in an image that will be changed to colors you select. For more information, refer to *Changing All Occurrences of a Color* on page 820, in the Image chapter.

Creating and Modifying Gradients, Hatches, and Bitmaps

You can change or add to what StarOffice provides for object area fills.

As with colors and lines, you can add or modify *individual fills*, and you can add or modify *lists of fills*. These lists also are stored in the StarOffice config folder, with the file extension names .sog, .soh, and .soe for gradients, hatches, and bitmaps, respectively.

Gradients

1 Open the Area window by choosing Format > Area.

2 Click the Gradient tab (Figure 26-25).

3 Use the Load Gradients List icon to load the appropriate gradient set, if necessary.

4 Create a new gradient or modify an existing one:

- To create a new gradient, click the Add button and enter a new name; click OK.

- To modify a gradient, select a gradient and click the Modify button, leave the existing name in the field, and click OK.

If you want to save your changes in a different list, click the Save Gradients List icon and save the list under a new name.

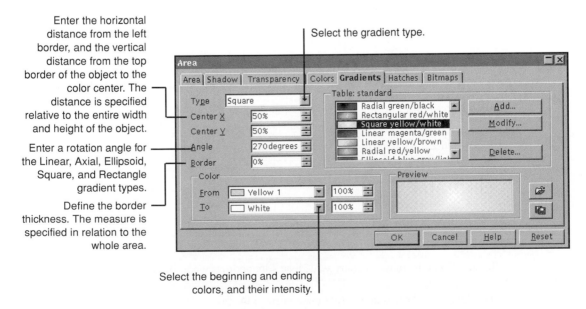

Enter the horizontal distance from the left border, and the vertical distance from the top border of the object to the color center. The distance is specified relative to the entire width and height of the object.

Select the gradient type.

Enter a rotation angle for the Linear, Axial, Ellipsoid, Square, and Rectangle gradient types.

Define the border thickness. The measure is specified in relation to the whole area.

Select the beginning and ending colors, and their intensity.

Figure 26-25   Creating and modifying gradients

Hatches

1   Open the Area window (choose Format > Area).

2   Click the Hatches tab (Figure 26-26).

3   Use the Load Hatches List icon to load the appropriate hatch list, if necessary.

4   Create a new hatch or modify an existing one:

  •   To create a new hatch, click the Add button and enter a new name, then click OK.

  •   To modify a hatch, select a hatch and click the Modify button, leave the existing name in the field, and click OK.

Keep in mind that when the hatch is applied, you can choose a background color for it, or leave the background blank. See Figure 26-17 on page 755.

If you want to save your changes in a different list, click the Save Hatch List icon and save the list under a new name.

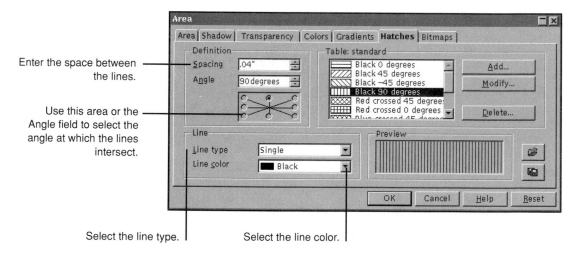

Figure 26-26   Creating and modifying hatches

Bitmaps

You can fill an area with a graphical design of your choosing. You can create one in the Bitmaps tab, import one, modify one, or use existing ones provided with StarOffice.

Note – Some formats, such as .WMF, lose some colors when imported.

1   Open the Area window (choose Format > Area).

2   Click the Bitmaps tab (Figure 26-27).

3   Use the Load Bitmaps List icon to load the appropriate bitmaps list, if necessary.

4   Select the source of the bitmap.

- To **draw a new bitmap**, first select Blank at the top of the Table:Standard list to enable the Add and Modify buttons. Then click the Add button and enter a new name; click OK.

- To **import a new bitmap**, click Import and select any graphics file, then enter a name and click OK.

- To **modify a bitmap** that you created using the pixel editor, select the appropriate bitmap, click the Modify button, leave the existing name in the field, and click OK.

If you want to save your changes in a different list, click the Save Bitmap List icon and save the list under a new name.

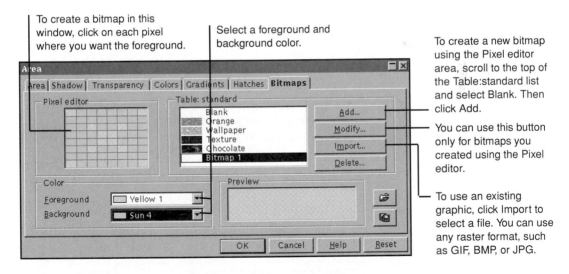

Figure 26-27   Creating and modifying bitmaps

Note – The bitmaps you create with the pixel editor are going to be a little rough, as shown in Figure 26-28. You'll generally get better results by using Image or Draw to create a raster file, then importing it by clicking Import.

Figure 26-28   Bitmap shown in Figure 26-27, used in the background of a slide

Editing Raster Objects

When you have a raster object (a bitmap-based graphic like a scanned photo) in the Draw work area, by pasting it in or by conversion, you can edit it as you would in Image.

To convert a Draw object to a raster, see *Converting a Draw Object to a Raster* on page 796. (In order to edit the resulting raster using the methods described in this section, you need to convert it to a bitmap, not a metafile.)

The *graphics object bar* (Figure 26-29) is only available when you select a raster object. It allows you to change color saturation, etc. If it isn't displayed, choose View > Toolbars > Object Bar.

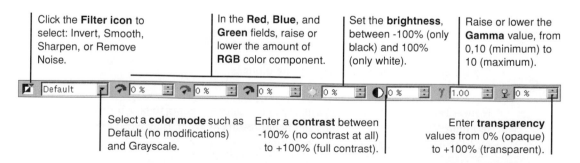

Click the **Filter icon** to select: Invert, Smooth, Sharpen, or Remove Noise.

In the **Red**, **Blue**, and **Green** fields, raise or lower the amount of **RGB** color component.

Set the **brightness**, between -100% (only black) and 100% (only white).

Raise or lower the **Gamma** value, from 0,10 (minimum) to 10 (maximum).

Select a **color mode** such as Default (no modifications) and Grayscale.

Enter a **contrast** between -100% (no contrast at all) to +100% (full contrast).

Enter **transparency** values from 0% (opaque) to +100% (transparent).

Figure 26-29   Graphics object bar – available when raster object is selected

Note – The gamma value is a measurement unit used for contrasting gray tones.

Applying Filters

1   Select a bitmap; filters can't be used with metafiles.

Anything you bring in from a graphics editing program is going to work fine; this just means that if you've followed the instructions in *Converting a Draw Object to a Raster* on page 796, you need to have converted it to a bitmap.

2   Click the Filter icon in the graphics object bar (see Figure 26-29) and display the Filter tearoff menu. Select the filter you want.

Figure 26-30 shows examples of the filters.

Figure 26-30   Graphics object bar filters (bitmaps only)

Note – Other filters are available from the Effects tearoff menu when you're in edit mode. To switch to edit mode, see *Editing a Raster Using the Image Toolbar* on page 766; for more about filters, see *Applying Filters* on page 826.

Applying Color Modes

Color modes also let you apply effects: black-and-white, grayscale, and watermark.

1   Select a bitmap or metafile.

2   Use the Color Mode list in the graphics object bar if you want to convert to grayscale, black and white, or watermark effects. Figure 26-31 shows examples of each.

Grayscale

Watermark

Black and white

Figure 26-31   Graphics object bar color modes

Applying Color Effects

Color effects include features such as varying the RGB percentages, contrast, etc.

1   Select the bitmap or raster.

2   Adjust the color as necessary; see Figure 26-29 on page 764 for information on each item on the object bar.

Editing a Raster Using the Image Toolbar

If you've pasted an image from StarOffice Image into the Draw work area, you can edit it using the same toolbar available in Image. This isn't available with Draw objects you've converted to metafiles or bitmaps.

1   To see the full Image toolbar, right-click the image and choose Image > Edit.

2   The Image toolbar will appear, and the standard object bar will appear in place of the graphics object bar (Figure 26-32).

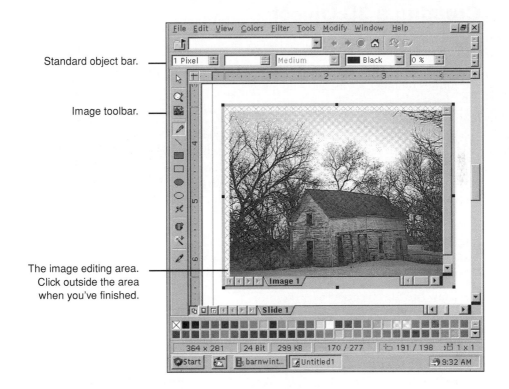

Figure 26-32   Editing a raster image in Draw

The graphics object bar (Figure 26-29) isn't available in edit mode. However, you can still adjust color values by clicking the Color Bar icon on the toolbar and using the Color tearoff menu.

Working With Three-Dimensional Objects

Draw lets you create impressive three-dimensional, *3D*, effects. You can create a new 3D object or convert a 2D object to 3D, as well as control the appearance of shading and other effects. Use the 3D icon in the toolbar on the left side of the workspace.

Note – You can get particularly interesting-looking 3D objects by converting 2D polygons, using the Effects icon. See *Converting Any Object to 3D Using the Effects Menu* on page 794 for more information.

Creating a 3D Object

1 Click on the 3D Objects icon and select an object to draw.

The possible objects are cube, sphere, cylinders, cones, pyramids, toruses (donuts), shells, and half-spheres.

2 Draw the object in the work area.

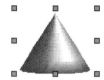

You can show the contour lines in a 3D object by selecting Continuous in the Lines list in the object bar. Selecting Invisible shows the object without contour lines. Borders don't apply to 3D objects. Objects in this section are shown both with (in the next procedure) and without contour lines (in the previous step).

Merging 3D Objects

You can create the effect of one object intersecting with another using the merging feature.

1 Draw two 3D objects.

2 Select the object you want to appear in front and press Ctrl+X to "cut" the object.

3 Select the object you want to appear in back and press F3.

4 Press Ctrl+V; this pastes the front object onto the back object. Move either object around to position it (the pasted object might not appear at first; move the back object around and it will appear).

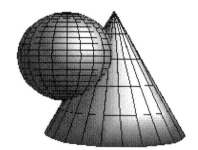

Any 3D effects you apply are applied to both objects. Any standard effects, like color, are applied only to the back object.

5 When you have finished modifying it, right-click the object and choose Exit Group.

Note – Any additional 3D objects you create will be added to the group. To edit the group later, right-click it and choose Edit Group.

Applying 3D Attributes to 3D Objects

Draw provides an almost bewildering array of attributes that you can apply to 3D objects, shown in Figure 26-33.

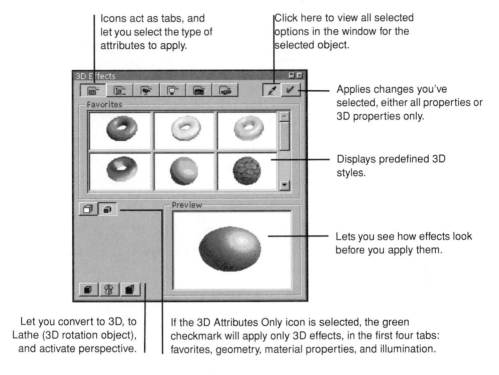

Icons act as tabs, and let you select the type of attributes to apply.

Click here to view all selected options in the window for the selected object.

Applies changes you've selected, either all properties or 3D properties only.

Displays predefined 3D styles.

Lets you see how effects look before you apply them.

Let you convert to 3D, to Lathe (3D rotation object), and activate perspective.

If the 3D Attributes Only icon is selected, the green checkmark will apply only 3D effects, in the first four tabs: favorites, geometry, material properties, and illumination.

Figure 26-33   Applying 3D effects

This includes lighting and shading features, rounded or straight edges, colors, and many other features. You can apply these features to 2D objects if you convert them to 3D first; this includes Bezier curves and text.

It's beyond the scope of this book to tell you how to create the best 3D objects. You'll need to experiment with each of the features to see which ones achieve the specific effects you need for your projects. However, the following procedures do tell you how to apply each type of feature, and show some examples.

1   Draw or select a 3D object.

2   Choose Format > 3D Effects, or click the 3D Controller icon in the toolbar, to open the 3D Effects window.

3   Select any of the effects, then specify which effects you want to apply by clicking the 3D Attributes Only icon (left) or the Assign

All Attributes icon to apply only 3D effects: favorites, geometry, material properties, and illumination.

4 Click the green checkmark in the upper right corner to apply changes.

Favorites – Applying a Predefined 3D Style The Favorites icon and corresponding options is selected by default when you open the 3D Effects window. Twelve predefined combinations of effects, or favorites, are available, combining selections from all categories in the 3D Effects window. Select any one to view in the Preview window how it would affect your object.

Geometry – Modifying Angle, Depth and Other Features These allow you to change a variety of features, including the number of segments. The horizontal and vertical are typically the same; the following illustration shows a normal cone, then the same cone with the settings of 2 horizontal and 14 vertical.

Standard   2H, 14V

Material Properties – Controlling Shading and Focal Properties This section lets you control shade mode, as well as shadow, camera distance, and focal length. The following illustration shows the different modes.

Gouraud (default)   Phong   Flat

Illumination The Illumination section lets you set options for the light source. You can select a color for the light source, as well as a color for the ambient light.

Light source: Light gray

Ambient light: Ambient light:
Yellow 1   Yellow 8

You can modify the colors for each light source and ambient light setting by clicking the tricolored icon by each list to open the Colors window, which allows you to set color values, hue, saturation, and brightness. However, the changes are permanent and cannot be reset to the originals. You may want to leave the defaults as they are and create new settings.

Ambient light: Light gray

Light source: Light source:
Magenta 1   Magenta 8

As you can see in the illustration, the differences are sometimes slight.

To change or add a color listed in any color list, refer to *Working With Color* on page 757.

Textures You can use the options available through the Textures tab **only** if the object has a gradient, hatch, or bitmap applied to it, using the Areas window. (Select the object and right-click, then choose Areas.) You can modify a number of attributes, including changing an object to black-and-white and back, without losing the color.

Material – Choosing a Finish and Color This tab lets you specify color for a set of finish favorites such as gold or plastic: object color, illumination color, specular color, and specular intensity. As in the Illumination tab, you can modify the colors, hue, saturation, and brightness for each selection in each list, using the tricolored icon.

Adding Files and Objects

You can insert nearly anything into a StarOffice file. Most of these capabilities are part of other parts of StarOffice, however. This section lists the features you have available, and where to find the information.

The Insert icon lets you access the Insert tearoff menu (Figure 26-34), where many of the insert functions are located.

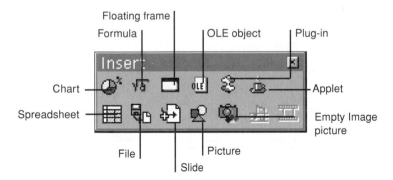

Figure 26-34 Items you can add to drawings

Inserting Other Objects and Files

These features are covered in *Adding Objects to Documents* on page 227.

You can insert pretty much any kind of file, whether StarOffice or other types, in any StarOffice document.

The most flexible way to insert files is to use the OLE object icon in Figure 26-34 or to choose Insert > Object > OLE Object. ("OLE object" is an unnecessarily techy way of putting it—OLE is the technology that lets you edit the file once you've inserted it in another file. For example, you can insert an "OLE object," a Draw file, in a Writer file, and edit the drawing right in Writer.

Inserting Applets and Plug-ins

These features are covered in *Adding Applets and Plugins* on page 449.

Inserting Text and HTML Files

You can insert HTML, and text (ASCII, not Writer) files into a drawing. See *Inserting Text and HTML Files* on page 680 in *Developing Presentations*.

Inserting Pictures

You can add empty graphics frames or existing graphics files. See *Inserting Pictures (Images and Drawings)* on page 680 in *Developing Presentations*.

Inserting Forms, Buttons, and Other Controls

Figure 26-35 shows form options.

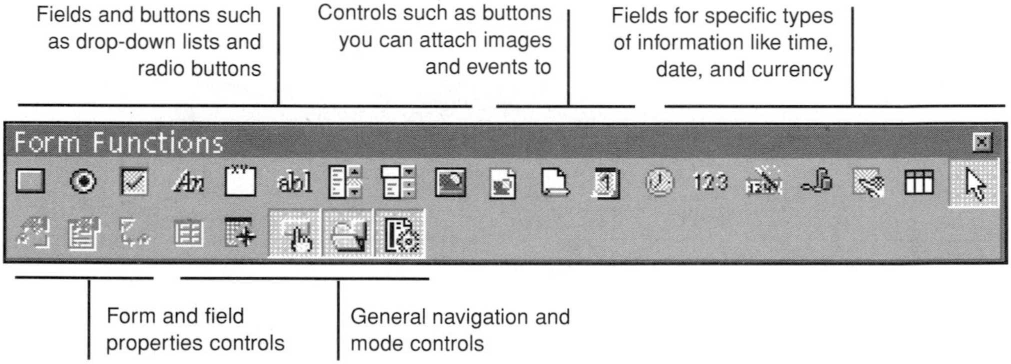

Figure 26-35   Forms and form components

Aspects of these features are covered in *Attaching Actions to Form Controls* on page 455. To learn how to use the form functions with databases, see *Modifying and Enhancing a Form* on page 1013.

Inserting Page, Date, Time, and Filename Fields

Choose Insert > Field to add a page, date, time, or filename field. Add the field in Slide mode if you want it on only one slide, or in background mode if you want it on all slides. See also header and footer information in *Creating Slide Handouts* on page 703.

Creating Sets of Attributes Using Styles

Styles let you save a particular set of attributes, such as font, color, line ends (round, arrow), for text and for objects. It's a good idea to use styles if you need to use an object frequently that's formatted in a particular way, such as a line with an arrow that you've defined yourself, or text formatting for headings.

For an extended explanation of the ways you can save time using styles, refer to *Power Formatting With Styles* on page 201.

Applying Styles

Select the object, then use either of the following methods to apply the style.

- Display the Stylist (choose Format > Stylist), and double-click the style.
- Choose Formats > Styles > Catalog, and double-click the style.

Creating and Modifying Styles

Once you modify an existing style, you cannot reset it back to the original settings, though you can modify it again if you remember the original values. You may want to create new styles, rather than changing existing ones.

1   Choose Format > Styles > Catalog to display the Style Catalog (Figure 26-36).

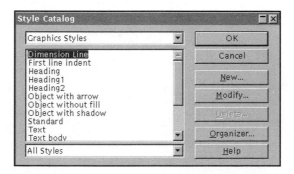

Figure 26-36   Style list

2   Select Graphics Styles; you'll use Presentation Styles in StarImpress.

3   Select a style that you'll base a new style on, or that you want to modify.

4   Create a new style by clicking Create, or modify an existing one by selecting a style and clicking Modify.

5   The Graphics Styles window appears (Figure 26-37). Make the appropriate entries in each tab, then click OK. Information on the entries for the tabs are covered throughout this chapter.

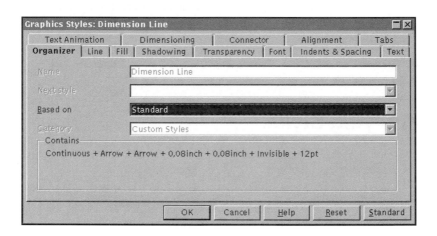

Figure 26-37   Defining new object styles

Making Styles Reusable in Other Documents

Unless you jump through a couple hoops, any styles you create or modify will be available only in the document where you made them. To make them available in other documents:

- Create the styles in a document that you then save as a StarDraw template

- Then base new documents on that template by choosing File > New > From template.

You can also import styles from other documents following the instructions in *Loading Individual Styles* on page 222.

Working With Text

Draw has extensive text formatting capabilities; you have the same character formatting options as in StarOffice Impress and StarOffice Writer, plus the ability to enter text in objects, and manipulate text with special effects.

Text Tools

Use the tools available from the Text icon in the toolbar at the left side of the work area to create text.

Text entry and text formatting features are the same in Impress; refer to *Adding Text* on page 664 and *Formatting Text* on page 669 for more information.

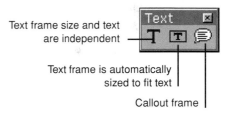

Text frame size and text are independent

Text frame is automatically sized to fit text

Callout frame

Typing Inside an Object

Double-click any polygon object, such as a rectangle, and start typing when you see the cursor appear inside the object.

Fill out checklist

Formatting Text Using the Object Bar

When you type or select text, the object bar icons (Figure 26-38) change to tools you can use with text. Tooltips describe the function of each icon.

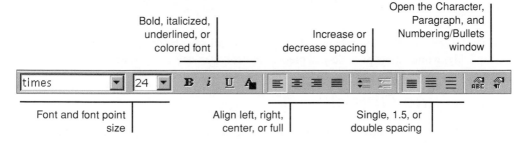

Bold, italicized, underlined, or colored font

Increase or decrease spacing

Open the Character, Paragraph, and Numbering/Bullets window

Font and font point size

Align left, right, center, or full

Single, 1.5, or double spacing

Figure 26-38   Quick formatting using the object bar for text

The default text values for any text that you enter is shown in the object bar. To change these values, first be sure no text is selected in the work area. Then choose Format > Character and make the appropriate selections.

Text Effects

Text effects can make any drawing or presentation you're doing much more attention-getting.

Converting Text to 3D

You can convert text to 3D (Figure 26-39) by right-clicking the **text frame** (not the text itself) and choosing Convert > Convert to 3D.

Figure 26-39   Text before and after 3D conversion

Choosing 3D Rotation Object will result in a cool effect, but it won't be legible. Be sure to select 3D.

Distorting Text

To skew or curve text, refer to *Distorting and Curving Objects* on page 788.

FontWork

StarOffice includes FontWork, a program that allows you to create exceptional font effects. Refer to *FontWork* on page 675 for more information.

Copying and Duplicating Objects

StarOffice provides multiple tools to copy and duplicate objects; some allow you to do so quickly, while others provide you precise control over size and positioning.

Copying Objects

1   Select an object using the arrow-shaped Select icon (active by default) and choose Edit > Copy.

2   Move to the drawing where you want the copy, if necessary, and choose Edit > Paste.

Note – The object may appear on top of the original; if so, move it to the side.

Duplicating Objects

You can duplicate quickly, or with more options.

Quickly Making One Copy

1   Select the object.

2   Choose Edit > Duplicate.

3   In the Duplicate window, choose OK.

Advanced Duplicating

You can control the number of copies, the location to which they are moved, rotation, size change, and color change. For example, the original on the left in Figure 26-40 was rotated, enlarged, and changed in color through five copies.

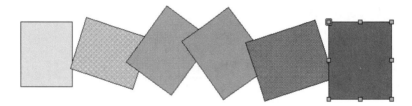

Figure 26-40   Advanced duplicating capabilities

1   Select the object.

2   Choose Edit > Duplicate to open the Duplicate window.

3   Make the appropriate changes (Figure 26-41), then click OK to duplicate.

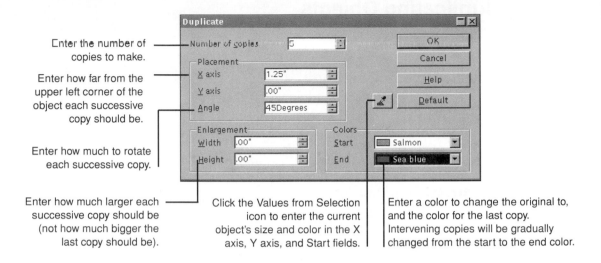

Enter the number of copies to make.

Enter how far from the upper left corner of the object each successive copy should be.

Enter how much to rotate each successive copy.

Enter how much larger each successive copy should be (not how much bigger the last copy should be).

Click the Values from Selection icon to enter the current object's size and color in the X axis, Y axis, and Start fields.

Enter a color to change the original to, and the color for the last copy. Intervening copies will be gradually changed from the start to the end color.

Figure 26-41   Advanced duplicating

Controlling Object Position and Size

StarOffice provides a variety of tools that let you position, align, resize, and group objects with precision.

General features:

- Alignment
- Distribution
- Manual or measurement-based positioning
- Arranging objects in layers
- Resizing
- Grouping

Snap/grid features (illustrated in Figure 26-42):

- Grid you can display and/or snap objects to
- Snap points and lines
- Snapping to page margins, and object borders and points.

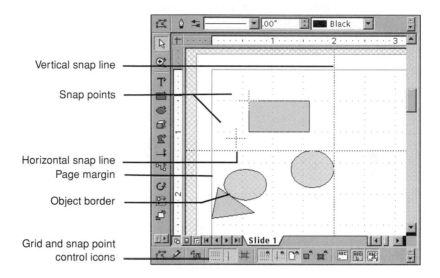

Vertical snap line

Snap points

Horizontal snap line
Page margin

Object border

Grid and snap point
control icons

Figure 26-42   Snap/grid object positioning features

Aligning Objects

You can align all objects to uniform lines using the grid or snap points, or align one group at a time.

1   Select the objects.

2   Do either of the following:

 • Right-click the objects and choose Alignment.

 • Click the Alignment icon on the toolbar to display the Alignment tearoff menu.

3   Select the type of alignment you want.

Distributing Objects

You can position objects evenly, horizontally or vertically, using the Distribute window. The selected objects will be distributed so that the object's borders (or their center) maintain the same distance from each other.

The objects that are located on the outsides (the first and fifth of five objects, for example), vertical or horizontal, will be considered as borders. That means that they won't be moved when the distribution takes place. The inner objects will be moved to evenly space the objects.

1 Select **three or more objects** to distribute.

2 Right-click on them and choose Distribution. (If Distribution doesn't appear as an option, you haven't selected three or more objects.)

3 Select the option you want in the Distribution window (Figure 26-43) and click OK. (If you're distributing copies of the same object, it doesn't matter which option you select as long as it's within the correct category, Horizontal or Vertical.)

The horizontal distance between the objects' left edges, center, left and right edges, or right edges, will be the same.

The vertical distance between the objects' top, center, top and bottom, or bottom, will be the same.

Figure 26-43 Distributing objects evenly within a drawing

Figure 26-44 shows how each of the four Horizontal options works when you're distributing objects with different shapes. The grid is shown so you can see the contrast in positioning more easily.

The original set of three objects, not distributed evenly

Distributed using the Left option

Distributed using the Center option

Distributed using the Spacing option

Distributed using the Right option

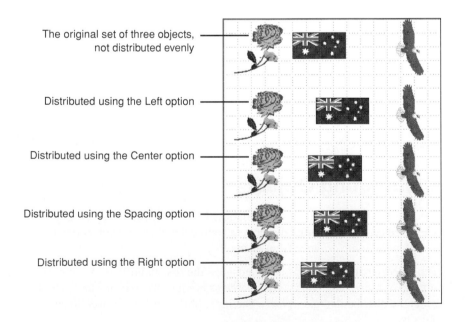

Figure 26-44 Effects of the four Horizontal distribution options

Positioning Objects

Use the arrow keys, or the Position and Size window. The following procedures include more detail on both approaches.

Moving Objects a Small Amount

To move an object a very small distance in one direction, select the object, then hold down the Shift key. Press the up, down, left, or right arrow key on your keyboard to move the object.

Positioning Objects Using the Position and Size Window

1   Select an object or objects.

2   Choose Format > Position and Size, or right-click the object and choose Position and Size.

3   Choose the Position tab.

4   Enter the new X and Y axes for the object.

5   Select the base point from which the change will be based.

    If you've selected two or more objects, the base point will be for the collective size, not the size of one of the objects.

6   Select Protect if you don't want to be able to reposition the object with the mouse.

7   Click OK to position the object.

Showing Extended Object Lines When Moving Objects

You can display objects with lines coming out of both axes when you move them, to show more clearly where the object will be (see Figure 26-45).

As you move the object, the object outline and lines parallel with each axis are displayed.

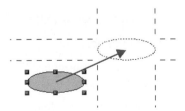

Figure 26-45   Displaying extended object lines

To use this feature, choose Tools > Options > Drawing > Layout, then select the Guides when moving option.

Arranging Objects in Layers

To determine what objects appear in front of others in your work, you can use StarOffice's arranging features. The features let you put an object on top or bottom, as well as move it up or down one layer at a time.

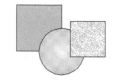

1   Select an object

2   Right-click the object and choose Arrange, or use the Arrange icon in the toolbar at the left side of the work area.

3   Select the appropriate option.

Bring to Front Puts the object on the top layer.

Bring Forward Brings the object one layer forward; it will still be behind an object that you've brought to the front, unless it was only one layer behind, previously.

Send Backward Sends the object one layer back.

Send to Back Puts the object on the bottom layer.

In Front of Object Puts the object immediately in front of the object you select next.

Behind Object Puts the object immediately behind the object you select next.

Resizing Objects

You can do most resizing quickly with your mouse; for more precise resizing, use the Position and Size window.

Using the Mouse

You can resize Bezier curves as well as other shapes, using the mouse.

1   Select an object or objects.

2   Be sure that the green object handles are displayed; if blue object handles are displayed, click the Edit Points icon on the left side of the object bar.

3   To resize proportionately, hold down the Shift key and drag a handle on the object.

    To resize disproportionately, don't hold down the Shift key.

Using the Position and Size Window

1 Select an object or objects.

2 Choose Format > Position and Size, or right-click the object and choose Position and Size.

3 Choose the Size tab.

4 Enter the new height and width of the object. To be sure the object is redrawn proportionately, select the Match option.

   If you've selected two or more objects, the new size will be for the collective size.

5 Select the base point from which the change will be based.

   If you've selected two or more objects, the base point will be for the collective size.

6 Select Protect if you don't want to be able to resize the object with the mouse.

7 Click OK to resize.

Grouping Objects

To more easily move objects that belong together, you can group them. Once grouped, you can manipulate the objects as one so that they are easier to move and apply attributes to. If you group three objects of different colors, for instance, you can simply select the group and apply one color to all of them in one step.

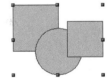

1 Select two or more objects.

2 Choose Format > Group, or right-click the objects and choose Group.

3 To ungroup them, make the same selections but choose Ungroup.

Editing Object Groups

1 Right-click the group and choose Edit Group.

2 Make your changes.

When you're done, choose Exit Group.

Setting Up the Grid

You can use the grid to help you visually position objects, or "snap" objects to the grid to automatically position objects.

Note – The Snap Grid is referred to periodically in StarOffice; however, we've concluded that this in an unimplemented feature.

Setting up the Grid

1   Choose Tools > Options > Drawing > Grid.

2   Enter the grid dimensions and whether the standard and snap grids should be synchronized (Figure 26-46). Note that Snap to grid and Visible grid are also controllable using the icons on the option bar in the work area.

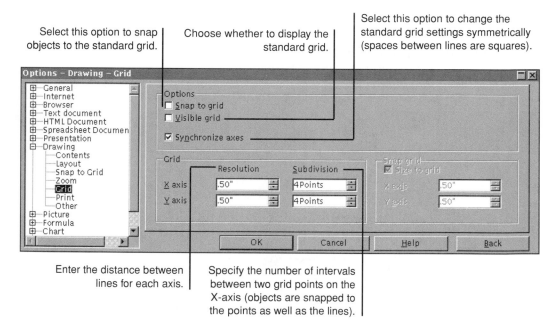

Select this option to snap objects to the standard grid.

Choose whether to display the standard grid.

Select this option to change the standard grid settings symmetrically (spaces between lines are squares).

Enter the distance between lines for each axis.

Specify the number of intervals between two grid points on the X-axis (objects are snapped to the points as well as the lines).

Figure 26-46   Setting grid dimensions

3   In the left side of the window, select Snap to Grid. Enter the appropriate options in the window displayed in Figure 26-47, then click OK. (The options on the left side of the window are controllable through the options bar in the work area, so are not covered here.)

Rectangles and ellipses are snapped based on a square or a circle, created according to their measurements. Mark this option to create the square or circle based on the long side of the shape; leave it unmarked to use the short side.

Select this option to restrict object motion to only three directions: up/down, left/right, and 45 degrees.

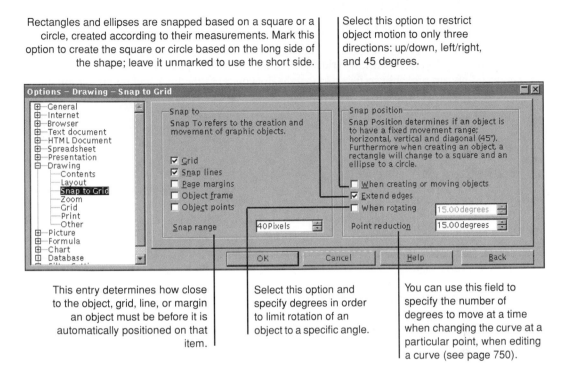

This entry determines how close to the object, grid, line, or margin an object must be before it is automatically positioned on that item.

Select this option and specify degrees in order to limit rotation of an object to a specific angle.

You can use this field to specify the number of degrees to move at a time when changing the curve at a particular point, when editing a curve (see page 750).

Figure 26-47 Setting additional grid options

Using the Grid

Once you've specified the dimensions and other options for the grid, you can show it and snap to it.

Use the icons on the option bar, to control the grid functions shown in Figure 26-48. To display it, choose View > Toolbars > Option Bar.

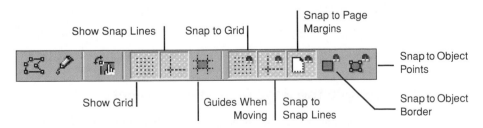

Figure 26-48 Grid option icons

Displaying the Standard Grid

Click the Show Grid icon in the option bar (see Figure 26-48).

Note – If you click Show Grid and nothing seems to appear, have a closer look. The grid points are probably so far apart that the dots marking the lines and points are too light and intermittent to notice at first.

Snapping Objects to a Grid

You can make sure all objects you move or create are automatically aligned on the grid. This also helps you draw straight lines more easily. Just click the Use Grid icon in the option bar of the work area to activate that option.

Note – If you're set up to snap to the grid or other items but don't want to snap a particular object, hold down the Ctrl key while you create or move the object.

Creating and Using Snap Points and Lines

In addition to the snap capabilities of the grid, you can set up specific snap points and lines in the work area to use as guidelines for creating and moving objects. How close you need to move an object to the point or line before it snaps is determined in the snap grid setup window (Figure 26-46).

1   Choose Insert > Insert Snap Point/Line.

2   Select an X and Y axis position.

3   Select the type: the point of intersection of two lines, a horizontal line, or a vertical line.

4   Click OK to close the window and save changes; the point should appear.

5   If the point doesn't appear, click the Show Snap Lines icon in the option bar.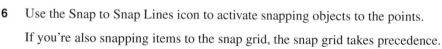

6   Use the Snap to Snap Lines icon to activate snapping objects to the points.

    If you're also snapping items to the snap grid, the snap grid takes precedence.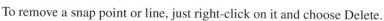

To remove a snap point or line, just right-click on it and choose Delete.

Snapping to the Page Margin and Objects

You can align objects to the page margin and to object borders or *points*. Page margins and object borders are relatively straight-forward; objects you draw or move are snapped to the nearest object's borders, or to the page margin, if you move the object close enough. When you snap to object points, you won't be able to draw or select anything that isn't an object point; your mouse will be drawn to the nearest point of the nearest object. This might be useful in some circumstances; however, we primarily found it annoying.

To snap to any of the three options, just click the appropriate icon (see Figure 26-48 on page 785).

Manipulating Objects

Draw provides you with a great deal of control over changing the orientation and shapes of objects. You also can create interesting effects by "cross-fading" one object gradually into another.

For information on manipulating text (curving, etc.), refer to *Working With Text* on page 775.

Flipping Objects

If you're drawing an image that is the same (a mirror image) on the right and left, you can cut your work in half by creating and copying one side, then flipping the copy. A drawing of a face, some computers, or the front view of a ship could all be done this way.

1   Select an object or objects.

2   Click the Effects icon in the toolbar on the left side of the work area, and select the Flip icon.

3   The flip axis will appear; move it to the right or left, or rotate it to make it horizontal.

4   Right-click and choose Flip > Vertical or Flip > Horizontal.

Rotating Objects

To rotate and duplicate at the same time, see *Advanced Duplicating* on page 777.

Rotating Objects Manually

1   Select an object or objects.

2   Click the Effects icon in the toolbar on the left side of the work area, and select the Rotate icon.

3   The rotate icon will appear in the center of the object; reposition it if you want to rotate around a different point.

4   Click one of the corner handles and rotate the object.

Rotating Objects Using the Position and Size Window

1   Select an object or objects.

2   Choose Format > Position and Size, or right-click the object and choose Position and Size.

3   Choose the Rotation tab.

4   Select a rotation point.

5   Enter a rotation angle.

6   Click OK to rotate the object.

Distorting and Curving Objects

You can use the Set in circle, Set to circle, and Distort icons on the Effects tearoff menu to achieve extremely interesting effects with objects or text. Figure 26-49 illustrates possible effects on text and objects.

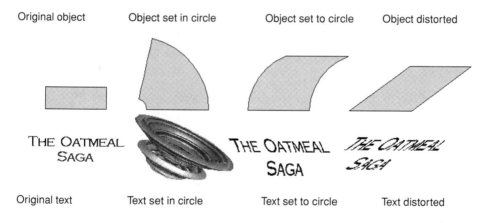

Original object   Object set in circle   Object set to circle   Object distorted

Original text   Text set in circle   Text set to circle   Text distorted

Figure 26-49   Distorted and curved text

Note – This requires a lot of RAM, so expect it to go slowly. Save frequently; this is the kind of thing that can bring StarOffice to its knees.

1   Select an object or objects.

2   Click the Effects icon in the toolbar on the left side of the work area, and click either of the Set in Circle icons, or the Distort icon.

3   Choose Yes when prompted to change the object to a curve.

4   If you selected a Set in circle or Set to circle icon, position the mouse over a corner; the pointer will change to a crown shape. If a line appears at the left of the item (typically text), drag either end to the right or left, and just see what happens.

Cross-Fading One Object Into Another

Cross-fading incrementally changes one shape into another, as shown in Figure 26-50.

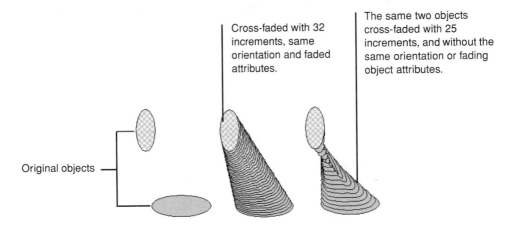

Figure 26-50   Cross-faded objects

1   Select two objects. (The one created second will appear in full in the resultant cross-fade. In Figure 26-50, the top objects were created second.)

2   Choose Edit > Cross-fading.

3   Make the appropriate changes and click OK (Figure 26-51).

Enter the number of increments between the beginning and ending image; enter a higher number for a finer-grained effect. ——

Select Fade object attributes to fade from the beginning object to the ending object gradually. If this option is deselected, the first copy made will have the attributes of the ending object.

Select the Same orientation option to keep rotation going the same way.

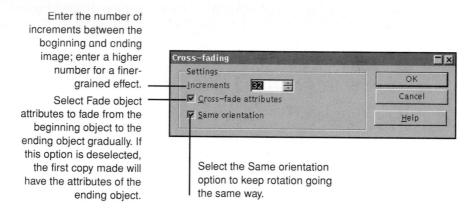

Figure 26-51   Cross-fading objects

Controlling Workspace Display

You can control several aspects of how your drawings look while you're working with them. Factors such as how large they seem, scale, and whether you're using black-and-white or color can make it easier to develop your work, and make it match your needs more closely.

The options are the same as in StarImpress, except for setting drawing scale. See *Controlling Workspace Display* on page 646.

Note – You can set many of the options controlling workplace display by choosing Tools > Options > Drawing.

Setting Drawing Scale

You can set the *scale* of drawings. This is particularly useful for architectural drawings. In a 1 to 10 scale in centimeters, for instance, every centimeter you draw on-screen will print as 10 centimeters. You can set the scale, anywhere from 1:1 to 1:100, and 2:1 to 100:1.

1   Choose Tools > Options > Drawing > Layout and be sure the correct measurement system is selected in the Meas. units field.

2   In the options navigation tree on the left, select Zoom.

3   From the Scale list, select the scale you want.

4   Click OK.

Converting Files and File Types

There's not much you can't do in Draw to convert from one type of object to another. You can make polygons into bitmaps, 3D objects into metafiles, and connect objects in a variety of ways. Some objects can be manipulated in different ways than others, so you may find it useful if you want to tweak an object in a way that its type doesn't allow.

There are several main categories:

- Conversion – Converting from a Draw object to another Draw object, or a bitmap or metafile
- Connection – Turning two or more objects into connected unfilled lines, which you can manipulate as you would Bezier curves
- Combining – Two or more objects are turned into lines, preserving the fill color of one, which you can manipulate as you would Bezier curves
- Shapes features – Merge, Subtract, and Intersect
- Exporting Draw files – Available formats include Sun Raster, JPG, and so on
- Cutting and pasting between Draw and Image

Figure 26-52 shows a few examples.

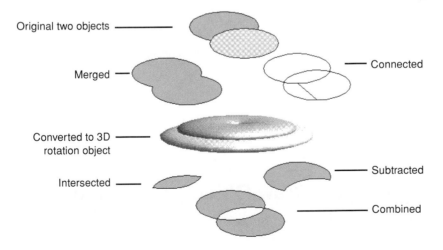

Figure 26-52   Conversion examples

Conversion Options

Right-click on any graphic in Draw, choose Convert, and you'll see what you can convert it to. Table 26-1 summarizes those options.

Metafile is a format specific to Microsoft Windows. Unless you've got a good reason, choose bitmap instead, since some of the features for editing rasters in Draw don't work with bitmaps.

Table 26-1   File format conversion

Image to convert	Conversion option	Comments
Polygon (square, oval, etc.)	Curve, contour, 3D, 3D rotation object, bitmap, metafile	
Curve	Polygon, contour, 3D, 3D rotation object, bitmap, metafile	
Contour	Curve, 3D, 3D rotation object, bitmap, metafile	A contour is a group of polygons that make up the object.
Line	Curve, contour, 3D, 3D rotation object, bitmap, metafile	
Bitmap	Polygon, contour, 3D, 3D rotation object, metafile	See *Converting a Raster Object (Image) to a Draw Polygon Object* on page 795.
Metafile	Polygon, contour, 3D, 3D rotation object, bitmap	Conversion to 3D or 3D rotation object loses all color. Only black and white are used in the result.
3D object	Bitmap, metafile	
3D rotation object	Bitmap, metafile	

Converting a Draw Object to Another Draw (Vector) Type

1   Select a curve, line, polygon, or metafile (such as a GIF image you've pasted in from Image).

Some types can't be converted; for instance, 3D object or 3D rotation objects can't be converted to any other shape. In addition, curves drawn with the Polygon curve tools are already considered polygons for this purpose, so they can't be converted to polygons.

2   Right-click it and select Convert.

3   Select one of the listed object types.

You can now edit the
object based on its new
type; if you converted a

polygon to a curve, for instance, you can edit points using the curve icons on the object
bar.

Notes on the different types of conversions follow.

Lines to curves   Converting a line to a curve lets you bend it and offers all standard
Bezier curve editing features, such as the control handle (shown in Figure 26-53).

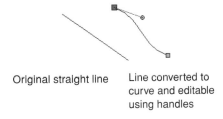

Original straight line   Line converted to
curve and editable
using handles

Figure 26-53   Converting a line to a curve

Polygons to 3D   You can convert any object to a 3D object or 3D rotation object;
polygons and curves result in the most interesting effects (see Figure 26-54).

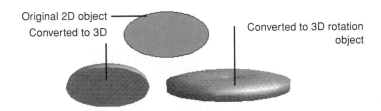

Original 2D object
Converted to 3D

Converted to 3D rotation
object

Figure 26-54   Converting a polygon to 3D

Curves to 3D Rotation   You can achieve surprising effects by converting Bezier curves to
3D rotation objects (see Figure 26-55).

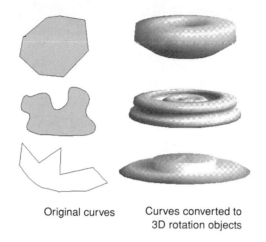

Original curves   Curves converted to
                       3D rotation objects

Figure 26-55   Converting a curve to a 3D rotation object

Curves to polygons Converting a curve to a polygon is possible, but doesn't result in many useful changes. Many more points are added, dragging a point results in a pointed shape rather than a curve, and the control handle is no longer available. Figure 26-53 shows two curves converted to polygons.

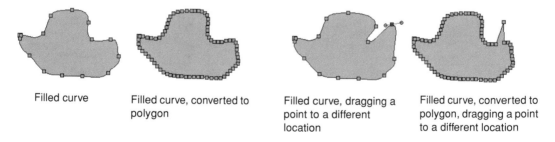

Filled curve   Filled curve, converted to   Filled curve, dragging a   Filled curve, converted to
                    polygon   point to a different   polygon, dragging a point
                                                    location   to a different location

Figure 26-56   Converting a curve to a polygon

Converting Any Object to 3D Using the Effects Menu

The previous procedure tells you how to convert an object to 3D with relatively interesting results. However, the 3D conversion icon on the Effects tearoff menu gives you much more flexibility. Figure 26-27 shows the contrast.

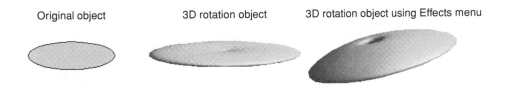

Original object   3D rotation object   3D rotation object using Effects menu

Figure 26-57   Converting to 3D using the Effects tearoff menu

1   Select an object that is a polygon, or convert a raster to a polygon. (You can get some pretty interesting effects applying this to a scanned photo.)

2   Click the Effects icon to display the Effects tearoff menu, then click the In 3D Rotation Object icon.

3   A line will appear to the left of the object. Drag the end to the left or right (in Figure 26-27, the top end of the line was dragged to the left a few degrees).

4   Click in the empty shape to the left of the object; the conversion will take place.

Converting a Raster Object (Image) to a Draw Polygon Object

You can convert raster objects to Draw objects such as polygons and 3D objects.

For all formats but polygons, simply right-click on the object and choose Convert and the type of object you want.

If you're converting a bitmap (not a raster) to a polygon, the window in Figure 26-58 will appear. Choose the appropriate options and click OK.

Note – If you convert a curved bitmap, such as the oval shown in Figure 26-58, then apply a different fill such as another color or pattern, the shape will change to a square or rectangle and you'll lose the original shape.

All polygons are generated using 0 pixels. If you enter a number, polygons for which the rectangle surrounding them contains fewer pixels than that number will not be generated.

Color layers might not be superimposed over each other precisely. This option enables you to generate a background fill. This fill consists of individual rectangles; specify the size using the Tile size field.

The current object is shown on the left; click Preview to see the image on the right side as it would look with the changes you've selected.

Enter the maximum number of colors here. Be sure to take into account the numbers in the bitmap.

Adjust the size of the rectangles for background fill for the Fill holes option.

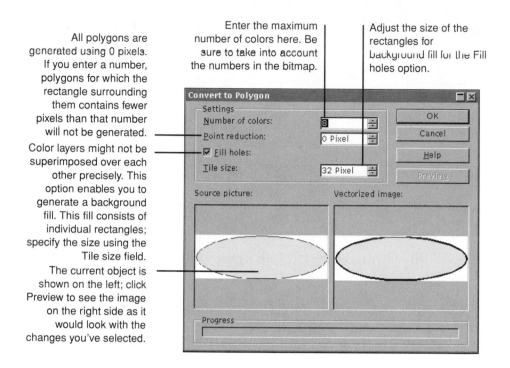

Figure 26-58   Converting a raster image to a polygon

Converting a Draw Object to a Raster

You can convert a Draw object (a vector graphic) to a raster type (Image object), so that it's composed of pixels rather than lines. This is useful if you want to sample (refer to *Changing Colors Using the Eyedropper* on page 760) or do other editing not allowed in Draw.

To edit raster objects in Draw, see *Editing Raster Objects* on page 764.

Note – Don't save any file as a GIF if you want to be able to print it from another application that's not in the StarOffice suite. Across platforms and applications, GIFs print illegibly as a series of vertical lines. This applies to when you insert the image into another application, such as FrameMaker, and print it.

Converting by Right-Clicking

As noted in *Conversion Options* on page 792, you can convert most Draw objects to a bitmap or metafile. Simply right-click on an object or objects and choose Convert > Metafile.

Pasting from Draw to Image

Any object you paste into Image automatically becomes a raster object.

1   Copy the graphic.

2   Choose File > New > Image and select any resolution, or open an Image file.

3   In the new image file, paste the graphic.

Using the Modify Menu

1   Select an object.

2   Choose Modify > Convert, then select the object type. See *Saving Images and Changing Image Format* on page 832 for information about each type.

Converting Polygons to Bezier Curves Using the Connect and Combine Features

The combine and convert features offer you a great deal of control over how to treat two or more objects as one.

Connecting Objects as a Bezier Curve

1   Select two or more objects.

2   Right-click and choose Connect.

3   The objects will be turned into unfilled lines (Figure 26-59), which you can manipulate as you would Bezier curves.

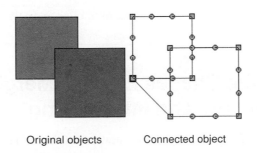

Original objects   Connected object

Figure 26-59   Connecting objects

4   Click the Edit Points icon to stop editing; it will become a normal object.

5 Right-click the object and choose Break if you want to turn the object into a set of individual lines.

Note – To return the objects to normal, right-click and select Split, then click the Edit Points icon.

Combining Objects as a Bezier Curve

1 Select two or more objects.

2 Right-click and choose Combine.

3 The objects will be turned into lines, preserving the fill (Figure 26-60), which you can manipulate as you would Bezier curves.

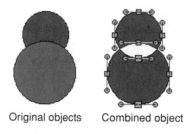

Original objects   Combined object

Figure 26-60   Combining objects

4 Click the Edit Points icon to stop editing; it will become a normal object.

5 Right-click the object and choose Break if you want to turn the object into a set of individual lines.

Note – To return the objects to normal, right-click and select Split, then click the Edit Points icon.

Using the Shapes Effects: Merging, Subtracting, and Intersecting

See Figure 26-52 on page 791 for illustrations of these effects.

1 Select two or more objects.

2 Right-click and choose Shape, then Merge, Subtract, or Intersect.

Exporting a Draw File to Another File Type

You can use the export feature to convert a Draw slide to a variety of other file types, including GIF, metafile, and Sun raster file. Exporting lets you do only one slide at a time. The File > Save As feature only allows you to save in Draw or StarImpress formats, but lets you convert the entire file at once.

1   Open a file.

2   Choose File > Export.

3   Select one of the file types listed, and enter a name, then click Save. Enter additional type-specific information if prompted (see See *Saving Images and Changing Image Format* on page 832).

The HTML export option starts the HTML export feature described in *Creating an HTML Version of Your Presentation* on page 710.

Printing in StarOffice Draw

Use the information in this section to print your graphic, including controlling its size and how many images are printed on a page.

Note – The printing information here is specific to this application; see *Basic Printing and Faxing for StarOffice Documents* on page 75 of Getting Started for more information.

Printer Setup

For information about setting up printers, refer to *Printer Setup* on page 62.

Printing Brochures

See *Printing Brochures* on page 350 if you want to print the drawing as a brochure.

Printing More Than One Slide on a Page

For printing purposes, each slide you add to the drawing is considered a page. There is a tile feature that theoretically prints four slides on a sheet of paper; however, it works inconsistently or not at all. For precise control over the number of slides per page, save your drawing file as a presentation and use the handouts feature in StarOffice Impress.

See also *Fitting Multiple Pages Onto One Sheet* on page 83 for information on documents throughout StarOffice.

Cramming a Slide Onto a Page

Sometimes you just need to squish a drawing to get the printed output right. If the slide is too big, you'll generally be notified when you print, and you can choose the Fit to Size option at that point. To be prepared ahead of time, however, you can mark the Fit to Size option using either of the following navigations:

Page Format Window

1   Choose Format > Page and click the Page tab.

2   Select Fit to size and click OK.

Note – If you want to print an image in landscape that's too long to fit the short way onto the landscape page, choose Format > Page. In the Page tab, select Landscape and select Fit to size, then click OK. If Fit to size isn't selected when you mark Landscape, it won't work to apply it after the fact.

Print Options Window

1   Choose File > Print and click the Options button.

2   Select the Fit to page option and click OK.

3   Click OK to print.

You also can refer to *Fitting Multiple Pages Onto One Sheet* on page 83 to see how it's done across StarOffice.

Stretching a Small Drawing to Fill a Page

There's a Fill entire page option in the Page Format window, but it doesn't have any effect. Use the Scale field in the Paper tab of the Printer Properties window (File > Printer Setup, or File > Print > Properties). This works intermittently, but with enough consistency to be worth trying.

Your best bet is to just manually enlarge the drawing, if you want it to fill more of a page than it is now. Group the elements of the drawing, if there are more than one. Then see *Resizing Objects* on page 782.

Specifying Landscape or Portrait Orientation

To specify whether the document should be portrait or landscape, choose Format > Page and select the Page tab. (This affects all slides in the document, if there is more than one.)

You *can* also set orientation in the Printer Options window. (Choose File > Printer Setup, click Properties and select the Paper tab.) However, all testing indicates that the setting in the Printer Setup window is completely irrelevant; sometimes it changes to reflect what you've set in the Page Setup window, but if you make any changes there, it doesn't affect printing.

See also *Specifying Portrait or Landscape Orientation* on page 82 for more information on the ways you can set orientation throughout StarOffice.

Printing Options Setup

Use the Draw printing setup window (choose Tools > Options > Drawing > Print) to set up printing options. See Figure 26-61. You can also choose File > Print, then click the Options button.

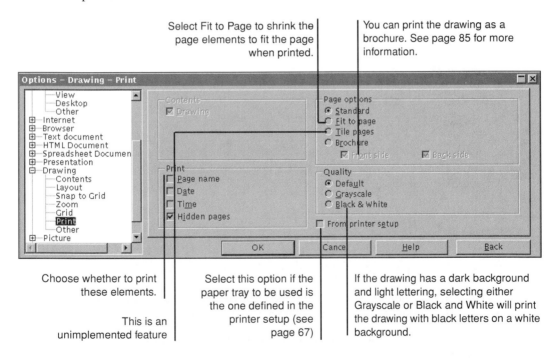

Select Fit to Page to shrink the page elements to fit the page when printed.

You can print the drawing as a brochure. See page 85 for more information.

Choose whether to print these elements.

This is an unimplemented feature

Select this option if the paper tray to be used is the one defined in the printer setup (see page 67)

If the drawing has a dark background and light lettering, selecting either Grayscale or Black and White will print the drawing with black letters on a white background.

Figure 26-61   Printing options

Note – The Tile option is an "unimplemented feature," working inconsistently at best. To print several drawings on a page, you might want to create your drawing as a presentation and use the handouts feature in Impress (see *Creating Slide Handouts* on page 703), which is more dependable.

Selecting an Option in the Print Warning Window

If you set up the notification described in *Managing Print Warnings* on page 80, or if a slide won't fit the page setup options you've specified, the window in Figure 26-62 will appear when necessary:

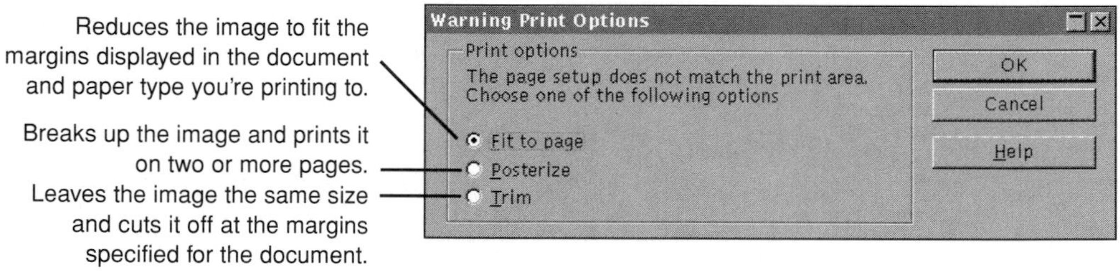

Reduces the image to fit the margins displayed in the document and paper type you're printing to.

Breaks up the image and prints it on two or more pages.

Leaves the image the same size and cuts it off at the margins specified for the document.

Figure 26-62   Print Options warning window

Note – If you select Fit to page, the warning window won't appear again for this document.

Printing a Drawing

You can print the whole document, selected slides, or selected objects within a slide to a printer or file. For more information about printing to files, refer to *Printing to a PostScript or PDF File* on page 77.

Follow these steps if you want to specify particular options, or use the Print File Directly icon on the StarOffice toolbar, which uses the options and printer last selected.

1   To print selected objects within a document, select them now.

2   Choose File > Print.

3   Select a printer, or select the Print to file option and enter a file name. To print to a PostScript file, enter a name with a .ps extension.

4   Click Options and select the appropriate print options (see Figure 26-61), then click OK.

5   Select what to print: All (the entire document), Range (a range of slides), or Selection (the currently selected text or graphics). Use dashes to form ranges, and use commas or semicolons to separate pages or ranges (1, 3, 4, 6-10).

Note – StarOffice often defaults to Selection, rather than All, as the range of pages to print. Check this each time you print.

---

6 Enter the number of copies and, if it's two or more, choose whether to collate.

7 Click Print.

Note – If you have problems printing, check to be sure the margins and orientation are set correctly. (Choose Format > Page and select the Page tab; see Figure 26-63.) You might be printing within margins that aren't actually on the page. In addition, make sure you've selected the right paper format, such as Letter. Sometimes it helps to just close StarOffice and restart.

Make a selection here appropriate for the country where you're located (User format can cause problems; select a different format for best results.)

Figure 26-63 Setting paper size

StarOffice Image: Creating Raster Graphics

Quick Start

This section contains the following information to help you get started quickly:

- A checklist for quickly making StarOffice Image graphics
- Feature overview
- How to create a new Image file
- A tutorial

See *Taming the StarOffice Environment* on page 91 for general tips that can make working with StarOffice a lot easier.

Note – Many features are available throughout StarOffice, but we don't cover them in every program's section. Check the index, or refer to *Taming the StarOffice Environment* on page 91 or *StarOffice Writer* on page 151 if you can't find the information you need in the chapters for StarOffice Image.

Quick Start Checklist

If your boss needs an image scanned and edited before the golf game (15 minutes from now), try these sections:

- Creating or opening a new file – *Creating and Opening Image Files* on page 812
- Scanning – *Scanning an Image* on page 816
- Creating or editing images – *Using the Object Tools* on page 814 and *Changing Selected Colors in Images* on page 819
- Printing the image – *Printing in StarOffice Image* on page 836

StarOffice Image Features

Image is based on *raster images* and is similar to products such as Adobe Photoshop. Image doesn't treat objects in a graphic, such as a square, as a distinct object; the object is only a collection of pixels.

Note – If you're not familiar with the terms *vector* and *raster*, make a note of them at this point; they'll be used in this chapter and the next to differentiate the types of images you can create with each program.

Draw has more powerful capabilities for creating complicated graphics with special effects such as 3D, and maintains better quality when shrunk or enlarged. Image is much less powerful. However, if you want to edit an existing graphic like a scanned photograph that's stored as a GIF, JPG, or other raster format, you must use Image.

A few of Image's top features include:

File formats You can open almost any graphics format with Image, and you can save to a wide variety, as well.

Basic object creation Includes standard polygon shapes, and lets you specify color and fill.

Special effects You can apply image effects such as charcoal sketch, mosaic, and pop art.

Color You can control color aspects such as saturation and brightness, as well as converting to grayscale and black-and-white. You also can *sample* (change specific colors in an image) use the Eyedropper tool.

Creating a New Image

To create a new file, choose File > New > Image. Enter dimension (in pixels) and color information.

The Image Work Area

Image has fewer features than Draw, but it still lets you make a wide variety of modifications to images. The Image work area is shown in Figure 27-1.

The object bar controls item attributes like color and border width.

The toolbar allows you to crop, zoom, draw objects and lines, adjust color, apply effects, and flip and resize objects.

Toolbar icons with small green arrows have tearoff menus, as shown. Click a toolbar icon and hold down the mouse to view the menu; select the top border to display it separately.

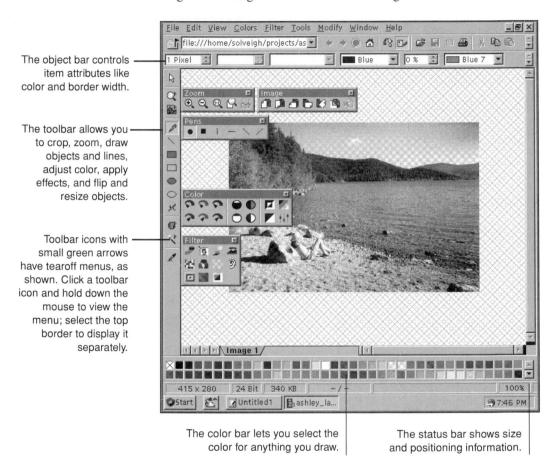

The color bar lets you select the color for anything you draw.

The status bar shows size and positioning information.

Figure 27-1   Image work area

Guided Tour

Each of these should take you five or ten minutes to complete, and will quickly give you an idea of how each program works.

The first walks you through the main Image capabilities; the second shows you how to get around some of Image's limitations by combining it with Draw.

Using Image by Itself

1 If you completed the Draw guided tour, choose File > Open to open the file you created in that. Note that it automatically is opened in Image, because it's a GIF and therefore a raster file.

2 Choose File > Open and open the `apples.jpg` file in StarOffice's `share/ gallery/photos` folder.

Note – If you're in a multi-user system, the `share` folder is on the server, not among your own local files.

---

3 Choose File > Save As and save it as a TIFF (`.tif`).

4 Choose Colors > Modify Color Depth > 16 Colors. Note the change.

5 Click the Arrow tool and draw a rectangle around the apple in the center of the photo.

6 Copy the apple (choose Edit > Copy), then paste it (Edit > Paste). Note that the apple has replaced the original image, rather than adding to it.

7 Click the Image Toolbar icon on the toolbar and display the Image tearoff menu.

8 Click the Free Rotation icon, circled above. Note that the icon doesn't let you choose a number of degrees.

9 Choose Tools > Options > Picture > Colors.

10 In the Angle field, enter 7 degrees, and select the To the right option.

11 Click the Free Rotation icon again.

12 Click the Color Bar icon and display the Colors tearoff menu.

13 Increase the red, and decrease the brightness. Note that a square surrounding the apple gets darker, too. This is part of the image.

14   Choose Filter > Aging to simulate the picture as an old photo.

15   On top of the apple, draw a 5-pixel-wide red straight line. (Use the fields in the object bar above the work area.)

16   Below the straight line, draw a 5-pixel-wide red curved line. (Click the Pen icon and display the Pens tearoff menu, then click the round or square icon.) Hint: The Pen tool uses foreground color; the Line tool uses background color.

17   Draw a yellow filled square with rounded corners and a thick blue border.

18   Using the Color tearoff menu, convert the image to grayscale.

19   Choose File > Print. Select a printer and click OK to print the image. (To print to a file, select Print to file and enter a file name ending in .ps.)

20   Choose File > Print again. Select a printer and click Properties. In the Printer Properties window, click the Paper tab. In the Orientation list, select Landscape. Click OK, then click OK again to print the image.

21   Choose File > Page Setup.

22   In the Page Layout window, from the Resolution list, select User. Deselect Scale. Enter a 2-inch square printing area for the image and move the image to the upper left corner of the page. Click OK and print the image again.

Combining Image and Draw

When you paste anything into an Image file, the image changes into whatever you've pasted. For example, if you've got a scanned picture from your birthday party and want to paste in some clipart of a birthday cake, you can't. Image also has no text tool, which you might find limiting.

This tutorial shows you how to get around these two limitations.

1   Choose File > Open and open the ocean.jpg file in the share/gallery/photos folder.

2   Open the castle.jpg in the same folder.

3   The files might be read-only if they're on a server. If the title bar says "read only," save them both to your local StarOffice folder.

4   Your goal is to paste part of the castle onto the ocean scene, and put a label below. Go to the castle.jpg file and select part of the castle (draw a rectangle around a couple turrets). Choose Edit> Copy to copy the selection.

5   Go to the ocean.jpg file. Choose Edit > Paste. You'll see that the ocean disappears and you're left with part of a castle. This is not what you want. Choose Edit > Undo to get the ocean back.

6 In the ocean image, use the arrow tool (the tooltip says Select) on the toolbar to select the entire image (draw a rectangle around the image at its borders).

7 Choose Edit > Copy.

8 Choose File > New > Drawing and paste the image into the new file.

9 Go to the `castle.jpg` file. Select part of the castle (draw a rectangle around a couple turrets).

10 Copy the selected part of the image and paste it into the new Draw file, as well.

11 Position the castle so that it looks like it's an island in the middle of the ocean.

12 Select the castle and choose Tools > Eyedropper.

13 In the Eyedropper window, select the first checkbox at the left in the Source color list, then click on the blue in the castle. Select a 50% tolerance and Transparent as the replacement. Click Replace.

14 Click the Text tool. Draw a text box below the images and type the words `Castle Aaagh`. Format the text if you want.

15 Choose File > Export and export the file to a GIF. (Enter the filename `castleaagh`, select GIF format, and select the Automatic file extension option.)

Castle A aagh

16 Choose File > Open and open the `castleaaagh.gif` file.

17 Crop the image to include only the picture and text. To do so, use the arrow tool again to draw a rectangle around them, excluding excess white space. Then click the Image Toolbar icon and display the tearoff menu. Click the Crop icon.

18 Choose File > Save to save the file.

Creating and Opening Image Files

> **Note –** Don't save any file as a GIF if you want to be able to print it from another application that's not in the StarOffice suite. Across platforms and applications, GIFs print illegibly as a series of vertical lines. This applies when you insert the image into another application, such as FrameMaker, and print it.

Creating a New Image File

1   Start a new file:

  •   From the File menu, choose File > New > Image.

  •   From the StarOffice Start button, choose Start > Image.

2   Enter dimension and color information (Figure 27-2).

Enter the dimensions of the drawing area you want. 256 pixels is approximately 3 inches.

Choose how many colors to use. More colors will give you greater flexibility, but also larger file size.

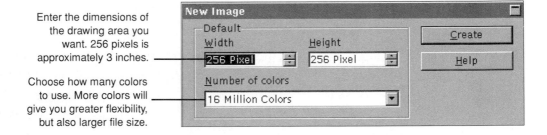

Figure 27-2   Entering information for a new image

Image is somewhat restrictive in what it lets you do with the work area. For instance, it doesn't let you enlarge the drawing area, just the image within it. This means that if you fill up the drawing area, you can't add more space around the image.

You can change the height and width of the image, and the number of colors, later, using Modify > Modify Size and Colors > Modify Depth. For more information, refer to *Controlling Image Size* on page 822 and *Working With Color* on page 817.

You can set image properties for printing in *Page Setup* on page 836.

Opening an Image File

Use any of the following methods:

- From the File menu, choose File > Open.
- In the StarOffice toolbar, click the Open File icon.

Note – If you open a file that has a raster type, such as JPG, it will automatically be opened as an Image file. You can't open it in Draw. However, in Image all images will be converted to raster and opened in Image, even if they were originally vector images.

Using Multiple Images in the Same Document

As with Draw and Impress, you can have multiple images within the same document, using the Image tabs at the bottom of the work area. These are similar to the multiple-slide capabilities in Impress and Draw. All are saved in the same file format, though they can have different page setup options. Each is treated as a different page when you print.

Note – To combine different images in the same tab—copying an apple from one file and a pear from another file and combining them in the same Image file—you'll need to use Draw. Do your combining and arranging in a Draw file, then export the Draw file to a raster format. See *Combining Image and Draw* on page 810 for a tutorial on doing this.

Adding an Image Tab

1   Right-click the Image1 tab and choose Insert Image, or click the gray blank area to the right of the last Image tab.

2   Enter image properties (see *Creating a New Image File* on page 812).

Deleting an Image Tab

Right-click the corresponding tab and choose Delete Image.

Using the Object Tools

Drawing objects is very simple in Image—select the color, width, and so on that you want the object to have, then draw it.

Drawing With the Rectangle and Ellipse Tools

As in Draw, you can create squares, rectangles, circles, and ellipses, or *polygons*, with or without a fill area.

Note – Unlike Draw, Image doesn't allow you to select an object and apply new attributes using the color bar or object bar.

---

1   Click an icon on the toolbar, at the left of the drawing area (Figure 27-3 on page 815).

2   Select the attributes you want for the object from the object bar at the top of the work area.

    You can select border width, border color, and background (fill) color.

3   For squares and rectangles, you can choose how rounded the corners are in the Corner Radius field.

4   Draw the shape.

    To draw a perfect square or circle, hold down the Shift key, then draw the shape.

Note – Unfortunately, Image has no Cut, Delete, or eraser features. To remove something you've drawn, choose Edit > Undo. You also can draw a white (or background-colored) shape covering the area you want to remove, following the steps in *Changing One Pixel at a Time* on page 819, or crop the image (see *Cropping an Image* on page 823).

Enter the corner curvature for squares and rectangles.

Select the color for borders.

Enter the transparency for borders.

Select the fill color for filled shapes, and the line color for the line tool.

Enter the border or line width.

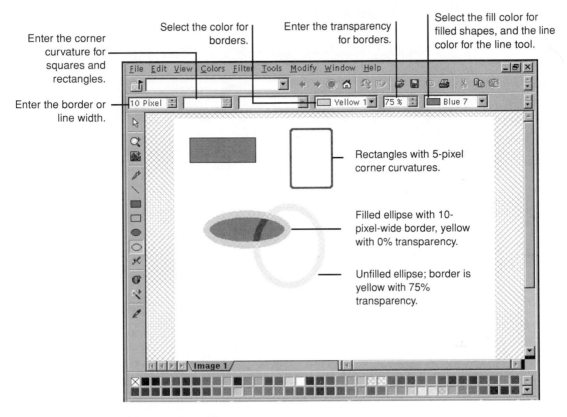

Rectangles with 5-pixel corner curvatures.

Filled ellipse with 10-pixel-wide border, yellow with 0% transparency.

Unfilled ellipse; border is yellow with 75% transparency.

Figure 27-3   Drawing polygons

Drawing With the Line, Pen, and Airbrush Tools

The line tool draws straight lines, the pen tool is for freehand lines, and the airbrush tool lets you draw lines of varying transparency (depending on how long you hold the mouse in one spot).

1   Select the object icon on the toolbar, to the left of the drawing area.

Airbrush tool

If you use the Pen tool, select the shape and orientation: vertical, horizontal, or angled.

Pen tool

Line tool

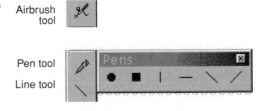

2   Select the attributes you want for the line from the object bar at the top of the work area.

3   Choose the line width and color, and draw the line (Figure 27-4).

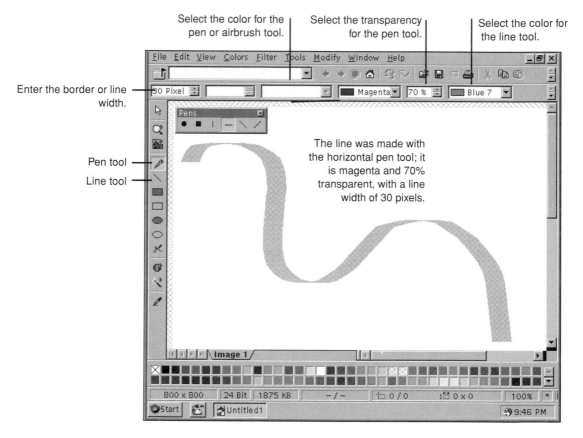

Figure 27-4   Drawing lines

Combining Text With Images

Image has no text tool; to add text to your image, paste it into Draw or StarImpress, or insert it in a Writer document. See *Combining Image and Draw* on page 810 for a tutorial on using Image and Draw together.

Scanning an Image

If you have a scanner, you can use it with Image to import the images and modify them.

1   Make sure your scanner and scanner software are properly installed and configured, and that the scanner is turned on and plugged into the computer.

2   Choose File > Scan > Request.

3   Your scanner software will launch; refer to the instructions for that program to scan the image.

Note – To scan directly into a Writer file, see *Scanning Images Into Writer* on page 255.

Working With Color

You can modify general color aspects such as brightness and RGB (red-green-blue) values, as well as changing specific colors in an image.

Note – Unfortunately, there is no "flood fill" tool, in StarOffice Draw or Image. The closest thing is the Eyedropper; see *Changing All Occurrences of a Color* on page 820 and *Making a Multicolored Image One Color* on page 821.

CMYK (the cyan-magenta-yellow-black color mode) is available in Draw, but not Image.

Entering Default Settings for the Color Tearoff Menu Functions

The color options setup window controls how the color modification icons in the Colors tearoff menu behave.

1   Choose Tools > Options > Picture > Color (Figure 27-5).

2   Enter the appropriate options in each field.

Enter the amount by which red, green, and blue are increased or decreased when you use the Add and Reduce icons in the Colors tearoff menu.

Enter the amount by which brightness and contrast are increased or decreased when you use the corresponding icons.

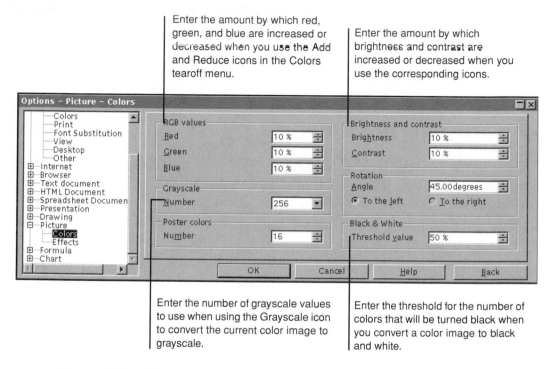

Enter the number of grayscale values to use when using the Grayscale icon to convert the current color image to grayscale.

Enter the threshold for the number of colors that will be turned black when you convert a color image to black and white.

Figure 27-5 Entering default color settings

Entering Color Settings

You can enter values for the following:

- RGB settings – Values from 0 to 100 for red, green, and blue.
- Contrast – Values between -100% (no contrast at all) to +100% (full contrast).
- Gamma – Values from .01 (minimum) to 10 (maximum).
- Brightness – Values between -100% (only black) and 100% (only white).

Adjusting Image Color Settings Incrementally

Gamma correction isn't available on the Color tearoff menu.

1 Select the part of the image to apply changes to, if you don't want to affect the entire image.

2 Click the Color icon in the toolbar to display the Color tearoff menu.

3   Click the appropriate icon, or choose the appropriate item from the menu, for the change you want. The values will be adjusted by the amounts you set up in Tools > Options > Picture > Color.

Entering Specific Color Values for an Image

1   Select the part of the image to apply changes to, if you don't want to affect the entire image.

2   From the Colors menu, choose the option you want to change.

To enter specific RGB values, you can also click the Set Colors icon on the Colors tearoff menu.

3   A window for the option you've chosen will appear. Click the negative or positive arrows, or enter an absolute value for each.

Changing Color Depth

Color depth refers to the number of colors supported for the image. Reduce color depth to lower the file size, or if you want the effect of fewer colors.

1   Select the part of the image to apply changes to, if you don't want to affect the entire image.

2   Choose Colors > Modify Color Depth.

3   Select the color depth you want.

Changing Selected Colors in Images

Image provides you with a great deal of control over every color in your image. You can change colors pixel by pixel, or change all occurrences of one color to a different color.

Changing One Pixel at a Time

You can change the colors in an image manually one pixel at a time: to remove a small object from an image, correct red eyes in a picture, and so on. To do so manually, use the square pen tool, set it to a 1-pixel width at a large zoom, such as 400%.

1   Double-click the zoom field in the status bar.

2   In the Zoom window, select the Variable option and enter a zoom of at least 400%; 800% may be preferable.

3   Click OK.

4   Click the pen tool icon and choose the square pen tool.

5   Enter a line width of 1 pixel, or wider if you prefer.

6   Select a color from the foreground color list and a transparency, if necessary, from the transparency list.

7   Click on each pixel you want to change.

Changing All Occurrences of a Color

One of the most powerful features of Image is the eyedropper. You can use the eyedropper tool to *sample*—change a color to a different color everywhere it appears in your image.

You may get unexpected results; one of the colors you select to be changed might show up in your graphic where you don't expect it. Carefully check the results you get, and be prepared to use the Undo feature.

1   Click the Eyedropper icon in the toolbar at the left side of the work area, or choose Modify > Eyedropper, to display the Eyedropper window (Figure 27-6).

If you want to simply replace a transparent value with a color, select the Transparency option and select a color. You can replace colors or transparency, but not both.

2   In the Eyedropper window, click the eyedropper icon in the upper left corner.

3   Move the mouse to the first color in the drawing area that you want to replace. You can see the color you're over in the color field in the Eyedropper window. When you see the color you want in that field, click the mouse.

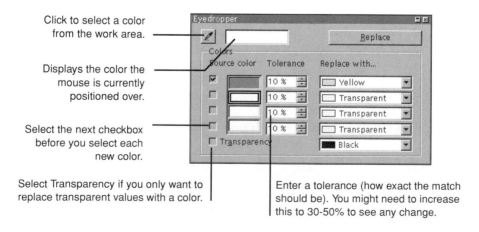

Figure 27-6   Using the Eyedropper

Note – If the mouse pointer turns to the "Ghostbusters" symbol, just click in the Eyedropper window and it'll return to normal.

---

4   Enter the tolerance—how exact the color match should be. Start with the default, 10%, but you'll probably need to increase it to 30% or 50%.

5   In the Replace with list, select the color to change to.

6   To select other colors to change, select the checkbox next to the second of the four color fields. Repeat steps 2–5.

7   Click Replace. If nothing happens, increase the tolerance and click Replace again.

Making a Multicolored Image One Color

To change all the colors in an image to one color, just follow the steps in *Changing All Occurrences of a Color* and enter a tolerance of 99%. Repeat a couple times with the colors that are left after each replace; this will turn everything one color fairly quickly.

Copying Images

Image doesn't let you to copy an area of an image and add it to the current file by pasting, as you can in most applications. Each time you paste in an Image document, the contents of the clipboard completely override what was there before. For instance, you can't copy part of the sky in a picture and paste it over other portions of the picture to hide clouds; once you paste, the image will contain only the sky portion that you copied.

To get around this, use Draw and Image together, and copy and past in Draw.

1   Open a file in each application.

2   Copy the whole image from Image into Draw (choose Edit > Copy).

3   Use the arrow tool to select the part of the Image graphic that you want to copy.

4   Paste it into the Image file.

5   Once you're done editing the image, you can:

- Copy the edited result back into a Draw file
- Export it to a raster file and open it in Image
- Just leave it in Image

Note – When you paste an Image graphic into Draw, you can right-click the pasted image and choose Image > Edit. The Image editing toolbar will appear.

Controlling Image Size

In Image, you can't just select an image or part of an image and resize it using handles, as in Draw. However, you can resize the entire image, and crop (remove the outside area of) an image.

Resizing an Image

Image lets you resize the entire drawing area; you can't just resize one part of the image. If you shrink the image, the entire drawing area will shrink.

You also can resize an image when you save it as a bitmap (see *Saving Images and Changing Image Format* on page 832) and when you print (see *Printing in StarOffice Image* on page 836).

Note – Enlarging the object will make it more "bitmapped" and jagged-looking.

---

1   Choose Modify > Modify Size.

2   In the Modify Size window (Figure 27-7), enter the new dimensions and other information, then click OK.

Enter the new width and height in pixels, in the current measuring system, or in percentages.

To resize proportionately, select Scale, then change either width or height.

If you're enlarging the image, select Interpolation to smooth the "bitmapped" effects of increased size.

Displays the size of the image with the new dimensions you entered.

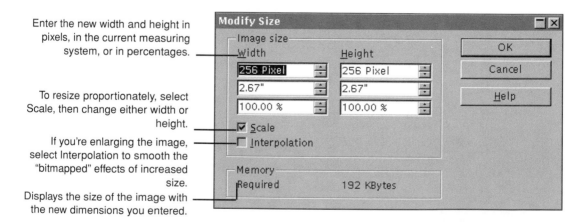

Figure 27-7   Resizing an image

It's a good idea to select the Interpolation option when enlarging; see Figure 27-8.

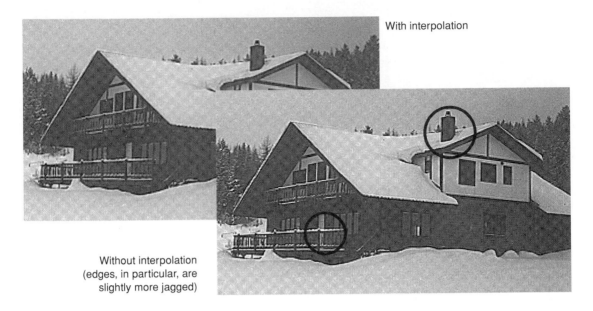

With interpolation

Without interpolation
(edges, in particular, are
slightly more jagged)

Figure 27-8   Enlarging with and without selecting the Interpolation option

Note – You also can paste an image into Draw and resize it using its handles, or the Position and Size window. For more information, refer to *Resizing Objects* on page 782.

Cropping an Image

To remove extraneous material around the outside of an image, you can crop it by selecting it and using the Crop icon.

1   Click the Arrow icon.

2   Draw a rectangle around the part of the image you want to keep (Figure 27-9).

Figure 27-9   Cropping an image

3   Click the Image Toolbar icon to display the Image tearoff menu, then click the Crop icon. The image will shrink to the size you defined in step 2.

Flipping and Rotating Images

One of Image's best effects is the ability to flip images and rotate them; it is one of the few features that lets you change the image after it's drawn or opened.

Flipping Images

1   Choose Modify > Flip, or click the Image icon in the toolbar and click the appropriate Flip icon.

2   Choose to flip the image horizontally or vertically; a horizontally flipped image is shown in Figure 27-10.

 Original

Horizontally flipped image

Figure 27-10   Flipping an image

Rotating Images

1   Choose Modify > Rotate, or click the Image Toolbar icon in the toolbar and click a Rotate icon on the Image tearoff menu.

2   Rotate the image with a pre-selected option, or use free rotation (Figure 27-11).

The amount that the Free rotation icon rotates the object when you click the icon is set in the StarOffice options. To change or view it, choose Tools > Options > Picture > Colors. In the Rotation area at the right side of the window, enter the number of degrees in the Angle field, and select To the right or To the left.

Original

Rotated 43 degrees

This area becomes part of the image

Figure 27-11   Rotated image

Using Filter Effects

The Effects icon on the toolbar and the corresponding Filter menu let you change how the image appears, using filters such as charcoal sketch and mosaic, and helps you improve the appearance of an image through defining, smoothing, and cleaning up the image.

Note – StarOffice uses the terms *effects* and *filters* inconsistently; for the rest of this section, we use filter.

Examples of each are shown in *Applying Filters* on page 826. You can also find the Relief filter at the beginning of some of the parts of this book.

Setting Default Values for Filters

These settings control the default values that appear when you use the Effects tearoff menu.

1   Choose Tools > Options > Picture > Effects.

2   In the effects settings window (Figure 27-12), make the appropriate changes.

Enter the degree of contrast between mosaics.

Enter the default number of pixels in each mosaic unit.

Enter the default tile size for the Tile effect.

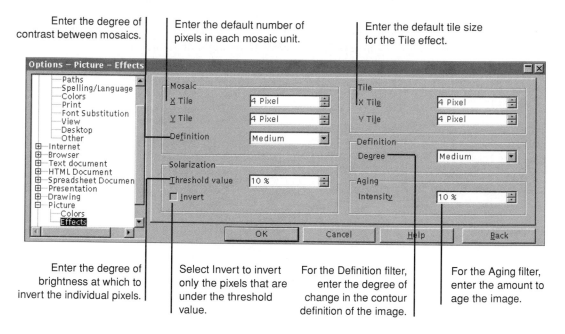

Enter the degree of brightness at which to invert the individual pixels.

Select Invert to invert only the pixels that are under the threshold value.

For the Definition filter, enter the degree of change in the contour definition of the image.

For the Aging filter, enter the amount to age the image.

Figure 27-12   Setting default effects values

3   To set the default number of pixels to use for the Poster effect, choose Tools > Options > Picture > Color and enter a value in the Poster Colors field.

Applying Filters

1   Click the Effects icon on the toolbar to open the Filter tearoff menu.

2   Select part of the image, if you don't want to apply the filter to the whole thing. (You can achieve some interesting effects with this approach.)

3   Select a filter from the examples shown in Figure 27-13 through Figure 27-23. If filters aren't available, you didn't install them.

Note – Two other filters, Invert and Sharpen, are available when you edit the image in Draw. See *Applying Filters* on page 765.

Charcoal sketch Outlines images in black and hides all other colors.

Figure 27-13   Charcoal filter

Mosaic Groups pixels into rectangles of the same color. In the Mosaic window, enter the width and height of the pixel, and the definition (contrast between adjacent pixels).

Figure 27-14   Mosaic filter

Relief Converts image to a relief, which has an effect like a carving or embossed paper. In the Relief window, enter the location of the light source the effect is based on.

Figure 27-15   Relief filter

Poster Reduces the number of colors. In the Posterize window, enter the number of colors to use.

Figure 27-16   Poster filter

Popart Reduces and changes colors.

Figure 27-17   Popart filter

Aging   Changes colors partially to grays and brown, to achieve the effect of an old photograph. In the Aging window, enter the percentage to age.

Figure 27-18   Aging filter

Solarization   Achieves the effect of a negative. In the Solarization window, enter the percentage controlling how much of the image will be effected. A low percentage will affect most of the image; a high percentage will affect very little of it. Select Invert to invert the pixel color, as well.

50% solarization, inverted

50% solarization

Figure 27-19 Solarization filter, with and without inversion

Tile Like Mosaic, groups pixels to produce a choppier, more "bitmapped" effect. In the Tile window, enter the size of the pixel group to use.

Figure 27-20 Tile filter

Definition Increases the contrast between pixels. In the definition window, select Low, Medium, or High.

High definition

Low definition

Figure 27-21   Definition filter

Smooth Decreases the contrast between pixels.

Figure 27-22   Smooth filter

Remove noise Removes extraneous pixels.

Figure 27-23   Remove noise filter

Note – You might not like the results you get by removing noise, depending on the pixels Image considers to be extraneous.

Saving Images and Changing Image Format

When you save the image, specifying a file format, you'll be able to specify several attributes of the image, such as color depth (number of colors used). These options depend on the format you save the image as.

Draw has a wider variety of possible formats than does Image (see *Conversion Options* on page 792). You also can convert Draw objects to a variety of formats using the Export feature (see *Exporting a Draw File to Another File Type* on page 799). To take advantage of those formats, put your Image graphic into Draw simply by cutting and pasting.

Note – Don't save any file as a GIF if you want to be able to print it from another application that's not in the StarOffice suite. Across platforms and applications, GIFs print illegibly as a series of vertical lines. This applies when you insert the image into another application, such as FrameMaker, and print it.

1   Choose File > Save, or File > Save As if you want to change the file format or file name.

2   Navigate to the correct folder and enter a file name; select the Automatic file name extension option if you want Image to fill it in automatically.

3 Select a file format, and enter options when prompted to do so.

Image doesn't have a native format, such as `.sda` for Draw. The options are listed in the Save and Save As dialog boxes, and are listed in Table 27-1.

Table 27-1   File formats for Image

Format	Options	Comments
BMP	**Color resolution** Select the color depth. Some depths allow you to use RLE Encoding, a lossless compression scheme for bitmaps. **Mode** Select Original to leave the size unchanged; select Resolution to change the dots per inch of the image; select Size to change the size of the image.	Bitmap. Bitmaps usually have very large file sizes.
GIF	See note on previous page. **Mode** Select Interlaced if you want the image to be displayed in a series of passes by browsers. **Drawing objects** Select Save transparent to make the background transparent. Only the objects will then be visible in the GIF image. Use the Eyedropper if you want to later set a color for the transparent value.	Graphics interchange format. Supports 256 colors; better for high-contrast images. Recommended for Web use. Supports image maps for the Web. (For more information, refer to *Creating Image Maps* on page 448.) If you have problems printing transparent graphics, enter the following line in the `.sofficerc` (UNIX) or `sversion.ini` (Windows) file under the section `[Common]`: `transparencyprint=1` After restarting StarOffice, the problems (depending on printer driver) may be resolved. If you make changes to the file, make a backup first. For more information on these files, see *Secret Install Files* on page 60.
JPG	**Quality** Enter a number below 100 if you want to reduce the file size; doing so also reduces some of the detail in the image **Color resolution** Select Grayscale or True Colors.	Joint photographic experiments group. Best choice for photographs and other scanned images; supports up to 16.7 million colors. Use this format if low file size is important; it may sacrifice image quality. Supports image maps for the Web. (For more information, refer to *StarOffice Web* on page 355.) Recommended for Web use.
PBM	**File format** Select Binary or Text format. Text results in a file size approximately 8 times bigger than binary.	Portable bitmap, originally developed to use with e-mail.

Table 27-1   File formats for Image (continued)

Format	Options	Comments
PNG	**Mode** Enter the compression. 9 is the highest quality. Numbers below 9 may result in loss of quality. **Interlaced** Select Interlaced if you want the image to be displayed in a series of passes by browsers.	Portable network graphic. Handles 24-bit color and better. Recommended for Web use (not supported by all browsers). Lets you save up to 16 million colors without compression.
PGM	**File format** Select Binary or Text format. Text results in a file size approximately 4 times bigger than binary.	Portable grayscale map, originally developed to use with e-mail.
PPM	**File format** Select Binary or Text format. Text results in a file size approximately 4 times bigger than binary.	Portable pixel map, originally developed to use with e-mail.
RAS	No save options.	Sun raster file.
TIF	No save options.	Tagged image file format. Most widely supported format between Macintosh and PCs.
XPM	No save options.	Supports up to 256 colors, and can be used in C programs.

Controlling Workspace Display

You can control several aspects of how your drawings look while you're working with them. Factors such as how large they seem, scale, and whether you're using black-and-white or color can make it easier to develop your work, and make it match your needs more closely.

Note – To set orientation, see *Specifying Landscape or Portrait Orientation* on page 836.

Selecting a Measurement System

1   Right-click on the ruler at the top or right of the workspace. (If it isn't displayed, choose View > Rulers.)

2   Select a measurement system.

Increasing or Decreasing Display Size (Zooming)

Draw lets you control the size at which your drawing is displayed. If you need to have particularly precise control over how you move objects in the workspace, or want to see an object close-up, you might want to use a high zoom, such as 400%, to view the objects as very large. If you want to see how the object might seem to an audience seeing it from a distance, you can reduce the view to smaller than 100%.

Selecting a Preset Zoom

1   Right-click the zoom field in the status bar below the work area.

2   Select one of the displayed percentages.

Selecting a New Zoom

1   Double-click in the zoom field.

2   Select Variable and enter a zoom value in the Variable field (Figure 27-24).

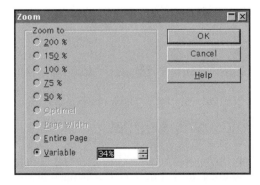

Figure 27-24   Entering your own zoom value

3   Click OK.

Printing in StarOffice Image

Use the information in this section to do any necessary setup, then print the image.

Note – The printing information here is specific to this application; see *Printing in StarOffice* on page 61 of Getting Started for more information.

Printer Setup

For information about setting up printers and printing to files, refer to *Basic Printing and Faxing for StarOffice Documents* on page 75 and *Printing to a PostScript or PDF File* on page 77.

See also *Fitting Multiple Pages Onto One Sheet* on page 83.

Enlarging or Reducing Printed Output

See *Page Setup* on page 836 and *Resizing an Image* on page 822. You also can refer to *Fitting Multiple Pages Onto One Sheet* on page 83, which addresses all types of StarOffice documents.

You also can use the Scale field in the Paper tab of the Printer Properties window (File > Printer Setup, or File > Print > Properties). This works intermittently, but with enough consistency to be worth trying.

Specifying Landscape or Portrait Orientation

To specify whether the document should be portrait or landscape, use the orientation setting in printer setup. Choose File > Printer Setup, click Properties and select the Paper tab. (You also can click the Properties button in the Print window.)

Page Setup

You can choose where in the page to print the image, as well as its dimensions and DPI.

1   The options are image specific. If you're using multiple images within the file (see *Adding an Image Tab* on page 813), click the tab for the appropriate image before you set options for each.

2   Choose File > Page Setup.

3   In the Page Layout window (Figure 27-25), enter the appropriate options.

Select a higher resolution for a better quality end result (not all printers support the DPIs listed).
To print the image in proportion to the page size, select Page.
To print the image as a specific size, select User.

If you selected User in the Resolution list, you can enter the exact width and height for the printed image.

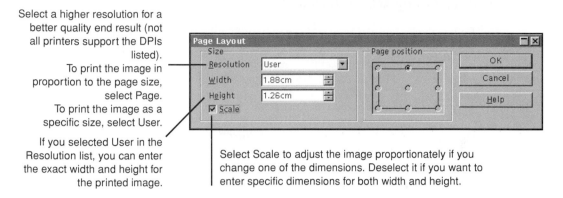

Select Scale to adjust the image proportionately if you change one of the dimensions. Deselect it if you want to enter specific dimensions for both width and height.

Figure 27-25   Page setup

Selecting an Option in the Print Warning Window

If you set up the notification described in *Managing Print Warnings* on page 80, or if an image won't fit the page setup options you've specified, the window in Figure 27-26 will appear when necessary.

Reduces the image to fit the margins displayed in the document and paper type you're printing to.

Breaks up the image and prints it on two or more pages.
Leaves the image the same size and cuts it off at the margins specified for the document.

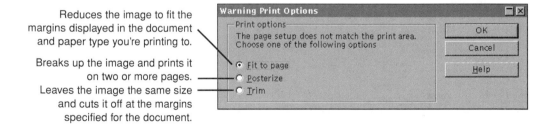

Figure 27-26   Print Options warning window

Note – If you select Fit to page, the warning window won't appear again for this document.

Printing an Image

Follow these steps if you want to specify particular options, or use the Print File Directly icon on the StarOffice toolbar, which uses the options and printer last selected. For more information about printing to files, refer to *Printing to a PostScript or PDF File* on page 77.

1   Choose File > Print.

2   Select a printer, or select the Print to file option and enter a file name. To print to a PostScript file, enter a name with a .ps extension.

3   Select what to print: All (the entire document) or Pages (a range of images). Use dashes to form ranges, and use commas or semicolons to separate pages or ranges (1, 3, 4, 6-10).

4   Enter the number of copies and, if it's two or more, choose whether to collate.

5   Click Print.

StarOffice
Schedule

StarOffice Schedule Setup

Getting Started With StarOffice Schedule

Setup for Schedule is pretty simple if you're just keeping your own schedule on your machine, in a single-user setup. If it's multi-user, it's a lot more complicated. In either case, follow the instructions in this chapter to get going.

Once you've done the necessary setup, see *Quick Start* on page 874.

Installation and Setup Checklist

You can set up StarOffice Schedule as a single-user or multi-user system, so the steps you follow in this chapter vary a bit, depending on what you choose.

Single-User Checklist

1   Complete the steps in *Reminder, Notification, and Email Setup* on page 860.

2   Complete the steps in *General Setup* on page 866.

Multi-User Checklist

1   If you haven't done so already, install the Schedule Server. See *Planning the Installation* on page 18 and *Installing Schedule Server* on page 33, in the *Installation* chapter.

2   Review *StarOffice Schedule Server Overview* on page 843.

3   Review *Schedule Server Administration and Configuration* on page 844.

4   Complete the steps in *Multi-User Setup Procedures* on page 849.

5   Complete the steps in *Reminder, Notification, and Email Setup* on page 860.

6   For each user, complete the steps in *General Setup* on page 866.

As a general reference, it's also a good idea to review the SCHEDULESERVER.PDF file included on the StarOffice CD-ROM.

StarOffice Schedule Server Overview

Use this section to find out about Schedule Server.

Schedule Server Features

StarOffice Schedule, along with the other standard packages in StarOffice, was probably installed when you installed StarOffice. Schedule is a standard standalone application for tracking one user's schedule. **StarOffice Schedule Server** lets you store all calendars in a central location. The Schedule Server lets users see each other's appointments and add appointments directly to others' calendars. (It also lets you set permissions to regulate this.) The StarOffice Schedule server communicates with the clients via TCP/IP.

Note that you can have a certain amount of connectivity through emailing appointments to other Schedule users, without installing Schedule Server. If you don't want to deal with the administrative work of installing, setting up, and maintaining the Schedule Server, you can still have some connectivity without it.

All users can use an event calendar on one or more StarOffice Schedule Servers as well as the normal calendar on their local computer that everyone using StarOffice has.

All users on the same server have read access to the "public" events that you enter on the server. The Access rights setting in the Details list box determines which details of an appointment or task other are viewed by other users. The levels of detail range from users being able to see all details of an event, to not seeing the event at all. Additional settings in the user setup process let you specify other users who can edit a user's schedule.

Participants in workgroups can log on to a StarOffice Schedule Server under a joint user name and work with the same event and task data. This makes it much easier to organize the availability of conference rooms.

System Requirements

Depending on the operating system the installation will need 20 up to 40 MB of free disk space in your Schedule Server installation directory. In addition, another 2 MB will be needed for every user who runs his or her schedule on that server.

For configuration information, see *Schedule Server Configuration Planning* on page 19.

Schedule Server Administration and Configuration

Administration is reasonably simple; Schedule's four services are started automatically after it is installed, and restarted if you restart the computer. Generally, no administration is necessary; however, if the server computer goes down or other problems occur, you can control the services through the windows described in this section.

You'll also need to stop the services when running backups; see *Backing Up and Archiving Schedules* on page 909.

Note – You'll do most of the setup and administration of Schedule Server, such as creating users and connections, through the StarOffice program. This section covers the "back-end," the services running to keep your clients connected to the server. It's most useful if you have more than one Schedule Server installed.

About the Services

The server starts automatically every time the operating system is booted. (In fact, if you kill the services, they start again.) There are three (four in Linux and Solaris) services, stored in the `SdlrSrv52/program/service` directory:

*   The service named **StarPortal Schedule Server** (`ssserver`) is the actual StarOffice Schedule Server. Make sure that (active) is shown in brackets after the name. Otherwise select the name and click Start.

*   The other two services, **StarPortal Admin Server** and **StarPortal HTTP Server**, belong together. If you activate both of them, you can start and stop StarOffice Schedule Server remotely. This additionally allows you to have up to 10 StarOffice Schedule Servers running on the same computer.

*   Under Linux and Solaris systems an additional service, **StarPortal Launcher Service**, is installed and it should be permanently active.

Running the Schedule Server

The server will run automatically every time you restart the computer where you installed it. The `sdadmin` program informs you about the services currently running.

You must continually run the StarPortal Schedule Server service, and either StarOffice or the Schedule standalone application, on the server computer. The standalone application and StarOffice will not restart automatically if you restart the server computer.

Accessing the Administration Windows

You can administrate either via a browser, or the Service Manager that gets installed on the server. Illustrations in this section show the browser administration.

Service Manager Administration

Use the Service Manager to start and stop, interrupt, and continue the various services.

- In Windows, the Windows > Start > Program Files folder now contains a new program group with entries for the StarOffice Schedule Server Setup program and the Service Manager.
- In Solaris and Linux, the service manager program sdadmin is located in the subdirectory of the folder containing the StarOffice Schedule Server installation.

Exit the service by clicking Stop and restart it with Start. Interrupt is used as a Pause key. The service stops using CPU time until you click Continue.

Browser Administration

You also can administer basic functions through a browser that is enabled for Java and JavaScript. If you are using Netscape Communicator you will need version 4.0.7 or higher.

Note – If you stop/pause the StarOffice Admin Server or the StarOffice HTTP Server, you won't be able to use the web-based administrator tools anymore.

---

1   Type into the URL field of your browser the complete name of your server:
    http://*server_name*

    If you chose a different HTTP port than 80 at the end of Schedule Server installation, add a colon followed by a colon and the port number at the end of *server_name*, such as http://fezzik:8080.

    You can start up to 10 schedule servers on the same computer.

2   The login window in Figure 28-1 will appear.

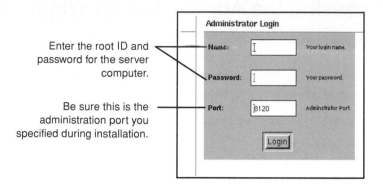

Enter the root ID and
password for the server
computer.

Be sure this is the
administration port you
specified during installation.

Figure 28-1   Logging into the server computer to access Schedule Server
administration windows

Note – If you're using Windows 9*x*, log in for the first time without a password. You can
set the password at a later stage. A password ensures that only the user knowing the password can maintain the StarOffice Schedule Server.

Maintaining the Schedule Server Processes

Once you've accessed the windows, a navigation bar appears on the left with the
administration options; see Figure 28-2.

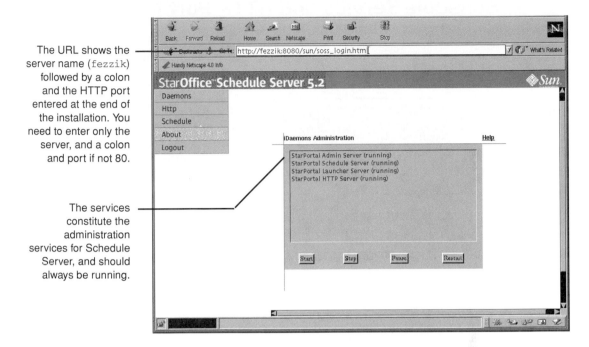

The URL shows the server name (fezzik) followed by a colon and the HTTP port entered at the end of the installation. You need to enter only the server, and a colon and port if not 80.

The services constitute the administration services for Schedule Server, and should always be running.

Figure 28-2   Viewing the Schedule Server Administration windows

Click the Daemons link on the navigation bar to view the Daemons Administration window, shown in Figure 28-3, allows you to start, stop, pause, and restart Schedule daemons. The actual state is displayed in brackets after the name of the daemon. Highlight a daemon and click the appropriate button to change state.

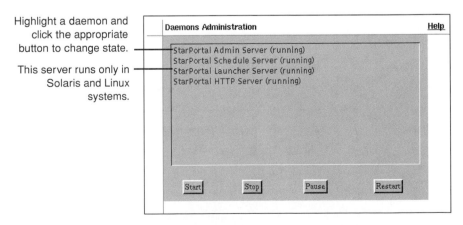

Highlight a daemon and click the appropriate button to change state.

This server runs only in Solaris and Linux systems.

Figure 28-3   Daemon administration for Schedule Server processes

Schedule Service and HTTP Port Maintenance

Click the HTTP on the navigation bar to view the HTTP Service Configuration window. Use this window, in Figure 28-4, to change the HTTP port for Schedule Server as well as changing the HTTP defaults.

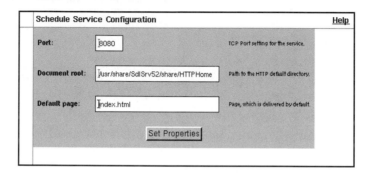

Figure 28-4   HTTP configuration for Schedule Server services

If the HTTP service is not started, you won't be able to display or change the configurations. In this case the error message "Error occurred while getting property..." is displayed. If you see that message, start the HTTP daemon with the Daemon Administration window shown in Figure 28-3.

3   Click Schedule in the navigation bar at the left. The Schedule Service Configuration window in Figure 28-5 will appear. (Not all fields are shown.)

Use this window to administrate each Schedule Server being run on the server computer. If you installed it only one time, only the top five fields are relevant.

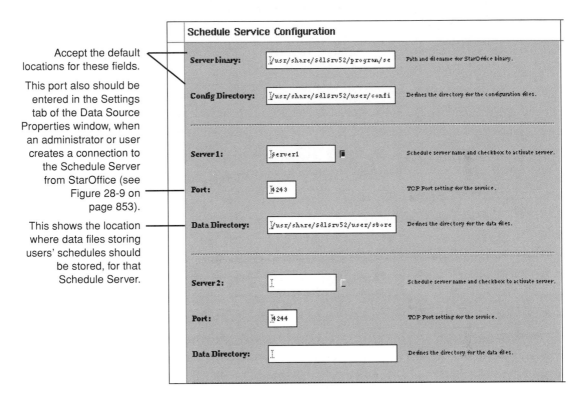

Accept the default locations for these fields.

This port also should be entered in the Settings tab of the Data Source Properties window, when an administrator or user creates a connection to the Schedule Server from StarOffice (see Figure 28-9 on page 853).

This shows the location where data files storing users' schedules should be stored, for that Schedule Server.

Figure 28-5   Schedule service configuration window

Multi-User Setup Procedures

The installation and setup process is a little convoluted; if you find your head reeling, that's normal. You have to keep track of the server software, server machine, a few different ports, and everything has to be set up through right-clicking on various links in the StarOffice Explorer. Sometimes it helps if you kill a chicken before you start. But this is the way we did it that finally worked; if you follow the instructions carefully, you should have a working multi-user Schedule system without excess agony.

Schedule Server Configuration Overview

Note – The instructions in this section assume you've got the StarOffice Explorer in hierarchical mode, as shown in Figure 28-6. If it isn't, right-click on the Explorer slider and choose Hierarchical.

Once you've got Schedule Server installed, you'll see the scheduling information in each client's Explorer, as shown in Figure 28-6.

You'll do nearly all Schedule setup by right-clicking on Tasks&Events, Data Source, connections in addition to My Computer, logins in addition to Default user, and (optional) on the Events and Tasks links.

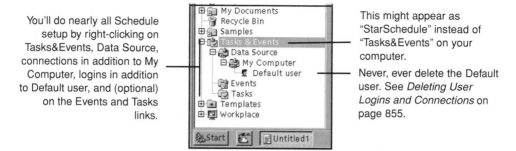

This might appear as "StarSchedule" instead of "Tasks&Events" on your computer.

Never, ever delete the Default user. See *Deleting User Logins and Connections* on page 855.

Figure 28-6   Schedule's navigation links, before setup

Note – The main link for navigation through Schedule's setup features in StarOffice 5.2 is either "Tasks&Events," as shown in Figure 28-6, or "StarSchedule." This is due to gremlin infestation. Both options are included in navigation instructions throughout the Schedule chapters.

In order to set up Schedule for multiple users, you'll first create a login for every user. (You might find it useful to set up additional IDs for meeting rooms, workgroups, etc., as well.) These user logins are stored on the server computer, so all users will be able to see the calendar of everyone who's set up to use Schedule. A calendar is stored on the server computer for every user login.

Each user will then create his or her own connection to the server, logging in with the ID and password you've set up for them. The connection information is stored on his or her own computer.

Once you're up and running, every user, unless otherwise specified, can see and edit his or her own calendar, and see the calendars of all other users you've set up.

Configuration Example

For example, Nigel and David are part of a band and each keeps his own schedule: haircuts, dates, going to hat shops, etc. David also keeps a general band schedule to track rehearsals, concerts, and publicity events. He's the owner of the band schedule, though Nigel can see it.

To set up Nigel and David's calendars, you'd create, on the server:

*   A user login for Nigel
*   A user login for David (with administrative rights)
*   A user login for the band

When Nigel and David start StarOffice at their computers, David creates a connection for himself, and Nigel creates one, as well.

David logs into his connection each day first as himself, then later, to update the band schedule, he logs in with the band ID and password. The login information that users enter in their connection determines the calendar that they then get editing privileges for.

The view from David's computer would look like Figure 28-7—he logged in using his own ID and password, so he can see and edit his own calendar. Right now, he can see Nigel's calendar and the band calendar, but can't edit either of them.

He's logged in now as David, but could log into the same connection later using the band ID and password in order to have editing rights to the band calendar.

This might appear as StarSchedule.

David can only see his own connection, not the one Nigel created for himself, or the administrative connection. David can see all user logins, set up on the Schedule Server computer.

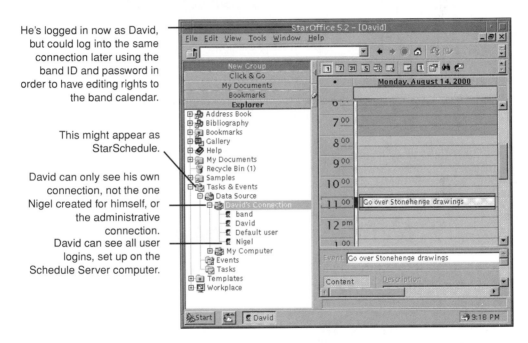

Figure 28-7   Example of a client's use of StarOffice Schedule, using Schedule Server

Administrator Setup Procedures

Complete the procedures in this section on the Schedule Server server computer.

Verifying Server Connectivity

See *Schedule Server Administration and Configuration* on page 844. Be sure that all services are running and available on the server computer.

Setting Up an Administrative Connection and User

Before you do anything else, set up an administrator connection and administrator user for Schedule. Administrative rights include the ability to see, add, and change delegates for users; create and delete users; change administrative status for other users; and change users' passwords and other setup information.

Figure 28-8 shows the difference between what an administrative user sees and what an ordinary user sees, when they look at the properties of the same user's setup window.

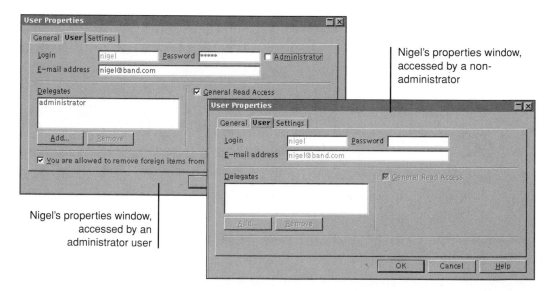

Figure 28-8   A user's properties, accessed by an administrator and a non-administrator

1   In Explorer, select Tasks&Events (or StarSchedule) and expand it so you can see Data Source.

2   Right-click Data Source and choose New connection.

3   In the New Connection window, enter a connection name like Administrator in the General field.

4   Click the Settings tab, shown in Figure 28-9. For now, just enter the name of the server computer where you installed Schedule Server, and enter the port for the Schedule Server you want to connect to. Click OK.

Note – The Port field defaults to the port for server1, shown in Figure 28-5 on page 849—if you've installed only one Schedule Server, leave the Port field as is.

Enter the port for the
Schedule Server you're
connecting to

Enter the name of the
server computer.

Leave these fields blank
for now.

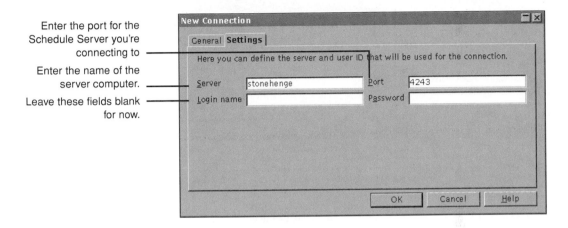

Figure 28-9   Creating a connection to Schedule Server

Note – If you run into problems connecting to the server computer, enter the IP address instead of the name. The IP address should be required only if the 'named' server is not available in the local NIS tables.

5   Right-click the connection you just created and choose New User.

6   In the New User window, click the General tab if it's not already displayed. Enter a name like Administrator.

7   Click the User tab in Figure 28-10 and make the appropriate entries; click OK.

8   Right-click on the administrator connection you created. In the Settings tab of the Data Source properties window, enter the administrator login. If you want to be prompted each time to enter the password, leave the Password field and click OK, then click Cancel in the warning window that appears next. However, only users on the Schedule Server computer will even see the Administrator connection, so if you want to enter the password as well, it's not a huge security risk.

In general, to log into StarOffice Schedule, you right-click on the connection that you use and enter the login and password in the Settings tab. To log out, delete them and click OK.

Creating User Logins

The next step is to set up user logins for every StarOffice Schedule user.

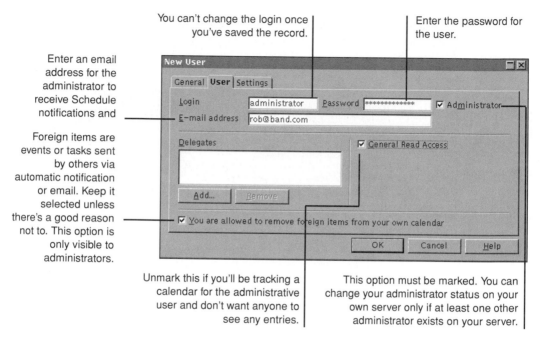

Figure 28-10   Adding users, General tab

On the Schedule Server server computer, complete this procedure to create a login for every Schedule user. It's similar to the procedure for creating your administrative user, but there are a few other considerations.

1   Right-click the administrative connection you just created and choose New User.

Note – Any users you create by right-clicking the My Computer connection will be displayed only on that computer.

---

2   In the New User window, click the General tab if it's not already displayed. Enter the full name of the user. This can be changed later; the login (in the User tab) can't be.

3   Click the User tab in Figure 28-11 and make the appropriate entries; click OK.

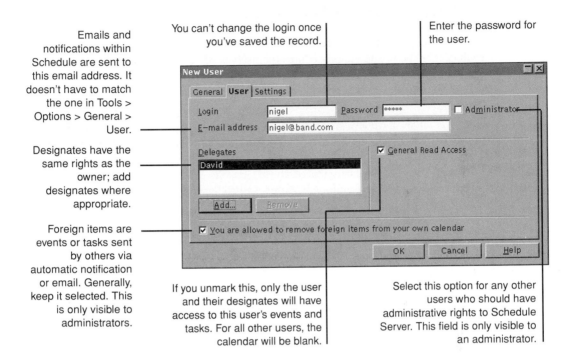

Emails and notifications within Schedule are sent to this email address. It doesn't have to match the one in Tools > Options > General > User.

You can't change the login once you've saved the record.

Enter the password for the user.

Designates have the same rights as the owner; add designates where appropriate.

Foreign items are events or tasks sent by others via automatic notification or email. Generally, keep it selected. This is only visible to administrators.

If you unmark this, only the user and their designates will have access to this user's events and tasks. For all other users, the calendar will be blank.

Select this option for any other users who should have administrative rights to Schedule Server. This field is only visible to an administrator.

Figure 28-11   Setting up user login data

Deleting User Logins and Connections

Deleting any existing or new user logins is, not surprisingly, fraught with peril. This section covers the issues we discovered.

Don't delete the Default user login It doesn't seem to be terribly useful in a multi-user environment; it just lets everyone keep a separate local calendar. However, if you delete it, your entire system will grind to a halt and no users will be able to use Schedule at all. If you do delete it, reinstalling the entire system will (probably) return everything to normal.

Stay away from the Delete key If you need to delete connections or users, don't use the Delete key: right-click on what you want to get rid of and choose Delete. StarOffice doesn't recognize this action and even though you might have deleted the user Nigel, for example, it will continue insisting that it wants his password when you attempt to create new users.

Be an administrator You need to be logged in as a user with administrative rights to delete users; the Delete option won't appear if you don't have administrative rights.

Client Setup Procedures

You can complete these procedures for each client, on his or her own computer, or have each of them complete the procedures themselves. If you have the users do it, provide them with their login data (user ID and password), the port to connect to, and the name of the server computer.

Note – If clients have any problems setting up connections on the client, check the file access permissions in the `SdlSrv52` directory on the Schedule Server computer. Clients need to be able to read and execute in all directories. They need to be able to write to the file where their schedules are stored, in `SdlSrv52/user/store/`*servername*, and where configuration information is stored, in `SdlSrv52/user/config`.

Creating a Connection to the Schedule Server

Create a connection to the server computer where your calendar will be stored.

1   In Explorer, select Tasks&Events (or StarSchedule) and expand it so you can see Data Source.

2   Right-click Data Source and choose New connection.

3   In the General tab of the New Connection window, enter a connection name that you'll recognize as yours. This will be stored on your computer, so you'll be the only one to see it.

4   Click the Settings tab, shown in Figure 28-12.

For now, just enter the name of the server computer where you installed Schedule Server, and enter the port for the Schedule Server you want to connect to. (The Port field defaults to the port for server1, shown in Figure 28-5 on page 849. If you've just installed one Schedule Server, leave the Port field as is.) Click OK.

Enter the port for the
Schedule Server you're
connecting to.
Enter the name of the
server computer.
Enter your user ID and
password.

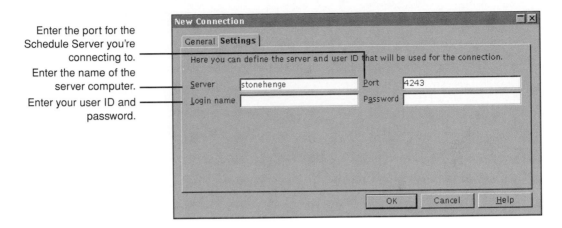

Figure 28-12   Creating your own connection to Schedule Server

Setting Up Your Events and Tasks Links

Within the scheduling tree in Explorer, the two items Events and Tasks are listed. Use this procedure to specify the connection and user login that should be used when you double-click these items. The advantage of using these links is that it's a little quicker; the functionality is the same.

1   In Explorer, select Tasks&Events (or StarSchedule), then select Events. Right-click it and choose Properties.

2   In the Events View Properties window, click the General tab. If you want to call Events something else, such as Nigel's Events, enter that in the field.

3   Click the Data tab (see Figure 28-13). Select your connection and user name. Click OK.

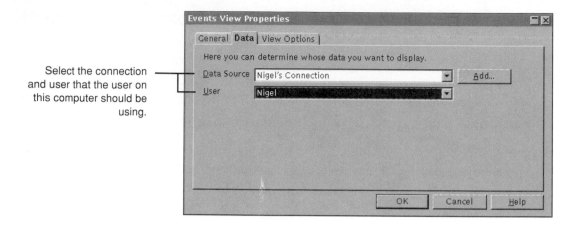

Select the connection and user that the user on this computer should be using.

Figure 28-13   Selecting the connection and ID for events

4   Repeat the previous steps for tasks.

Connection Properties

1   In Explorer, expand Tasks&Events (or StarSchedule) to see your connection.

2   Right-click the connection and choose Administrate. Click the Properties tab (Figure 28-14) if it's not already displayed. This tab lets you configure how many threads the server should use for the execution of requests. You typically don't need to change the setting.

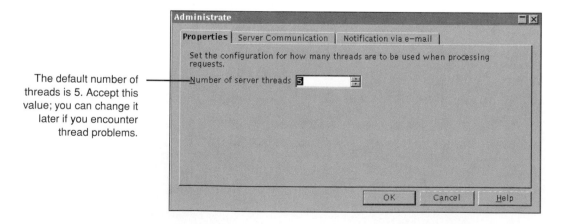

The default number of threads is 5. Accept this value; you can change it later if you encounter thread problems.

Figure 28-14   Setting thread information

3 Click the Server Communication tab (Figure 28-15). This tab lets you define how the server will communicate with other Schedule Servers in order to exchange tasks and events. Unless you only have one server or you want to separate the servers, leave both options selected.

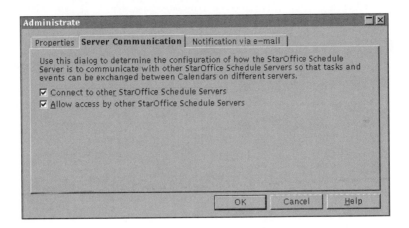

Figure 28-15   Setting server communication information

How to Log Into StarOffice Schedule

Follow these steps to access your calendar:

1 In Explorer, display your connection (StarSchedule > Data Source or Tasks&Events > Data Source).

2 If you've already specified your user and ID, just double-click your user name, under the connection.

   If you haven't specified your user and ID, right-click it and enter it in the Settings tab of the Data Source Properties window.

3 If the correct login information isn't entered, you'll be prompted with the window shown in Figure 28-16.

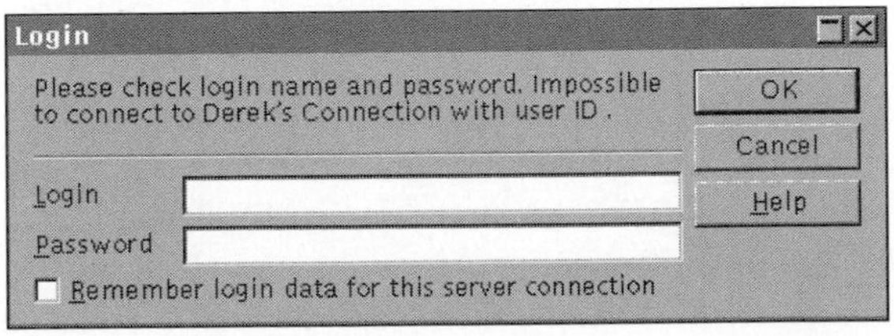

Figure 28-16   User being prompted to enter login and password

4   Enter your ID and password and click OK; you will be logged into your calendar in Schedule Server, via the selected connection, login, and password.

To see the calendar of another user, just double-click that user's name, under your own connection. Unless you're a designate, you won't be able to edit anyone else's calendar.

Reminder, Notification, and Email Setup

This section tells you what you need to do if you want to use any of the following features:

- Use **reminders** to remind yourself or others of events or tasks, using dialog boxes, sound files, or email (to use this feature, see page 887)

- Send events and tasks participants **automatic notifications**, which can be automatically added to their calendars (to use this feature, see page 889)

- **Email** selected events or tasks, which are automatically added to the recipients' calendars (to use this feature, see page 910)

Note – These options can be set up differently on every client, in a multi-user system.

Important Information to Know About These Features

Read this before you set up any options for these features.

All users must be set up to receive email through a StarOffice inbox, for any notifications to be received through StarOffice Scheduling features. See *Setting Up Mail and News* on page 940.

The First Question: Do These Features Really Work?

Unfortunately, the answer is "it depends." Emailing tasks and events works beautifully. Reminders and automatic notifications, however, are a little iffy; they work on Tuesdays and Fridays but less often the rest of the week. This book describes the way they're supposed to work—and it's entirely likely that you can get them to work that way. On the other hand, if you're having problems getting them set up right, don't beat your head against the wall too long. For connectivity, the simplest thing is just to let everyone edit everyone else's calendar (set designates as shown in Figure 28-11 on page 855), as long as there's a modicum of trust among them, and to email events and tasks (*Emailing Events and Tasks* on page 910).

Automatic Notifications and Emailed Tasks and Events

Of the three features listed above, the second two automatically import tasks and events into the recipients' calendars, either through the email or, if the recipients are on the same Schedule Server, directly into their calendars.

This also means, however, that those tasks and events are automatically added to the person's schedule. There is no way to selectively choose what events to add, though they can delete any events. (A setup option in Figure 28-17 on page 864 lets you choose whether to automatically add to recipients' calendars, but in that case they either aren't notified at all, or they receive an email and need to enter all the information themselves.)

If you choose automatic import of appointments, this is somewhat inconvenient for the people receiving the emails. Regardless of whether you send a serious event such as "Write to Judd about training issues," or "Sit on a zebra with arms akimbo, moistened espresso beans attached to each temple, and wait for the Mother Ship to arrive," it will automatically be added to the person's schedule.

How and Where Email Addresses Are Used in Schedule

As part of setting up StarOffice, you'll be entering your email address, which will show up in other people's inboxes when they receive your email. It also determines where returned mail (failed messages) are returned to.

Oddly enough, there are several places where you need to do this, and all the email addresses can be different. (None of them even have to be your real email address; that's defined in the properties of your inbox.) It's a good idea to keep every user's email the same everywhere, but it doesn't hurt to know how each address is used, as described in Table 28-1.

Table 28-1   Places in StarOffice Where You Can Enter a User Email Address

Window	Navigation	How the address is used
General user setup options	Tools > Options > General > User Data	Is used as a default when the outbox is created.
Schedule user properties	In Explorer or in the desktop, right-click Default user or your Schedule Server user login name, and choose Properties.	Any notifications or events must be sent to this email address in order to get into your calendar. Any reminders you send will (usually) show up in others' inboxes designated as being from this email address.

Table 28-1   Places in StarOffice Where You Can Enter a User Email Address (cont.)

Window	Navigation	How the address is used
Administrate window for a connection or My Computer	Right-click on a connection and choose Administrate, then click the Notification via email tab.	If you leave the placeholder as is, all reminders will be sent from "StarOffice Schedule Reminders" plus the sender's email address from his or her user properties window (see row above in this table) will show up in recipients' inboxes for reminders set up in the Reminders section of events setup. (This works inconsistently—sometimes the sender's email isn't inserted.) You can change it to a static value, including regular text and/or an email address; it will be used as the sender value, for all event reminders sent using that connection.
Outbox properties	In the Mail&News slider of Explorer, right-click the inbox and choose properties, then click the SMTP tab.	This is the displayed name in other people's inboxes when you send regular email, or any events or notifications. Gets its default value from the general user options email address, but you can change it to anything you want.

Note – If you make a mistake setting up the email address for the Outbox properties (or in the general user options, since that's where the default Outbox email comes from), your emails won't go anywhere. You won't get an error message and they'll show up in the Outbox, but no one will receive them. You'll be fine if you enter `solveigh@fun.com` instead of `solveigh@sun.com`, but StarOffice will balk at structural errors like "`sun..com`" (putting too many dots in dot-com).

The Automatic Notification Feature

Briefly: it's cool, but cranky, and especially if you're not set up on Schedule Server, it might be more trouble than it's worth. The window in which you use the feature is shown in Figure 29-13 on page 889.

Time of notifications The event or task notifications are sent as soon as you enter the event/task and participant information. Participant notification is unrelated to any Reminder information you set up.

Frequency of notifications This applies only when participants are receiving automatic email notifications (if they're **not** connected to you through Schedule Server), rather than having their calendar changed automatically. Use caution when choosing notification of participants. If you edit the entry, participants who are set up to receive notifications of changes will receive notifications each time, no matter how trivial the changes. Don't make any changes to the event that aren't necessary. If you change what kind of donuts will be served, all participants will be notified of the event or task again.

In addition, the notification options don't seem to work correctly. Our testing showed that all participants get notified every time you change the event, regardless of whether you just choose to notify them of the event, or to notify them every time something changes.

You might want to stay away from using the participant feature, and just send the event or task as an email (see *Emailing Events and Tasks* on page 910), or use the reminder feature (see page 887).

Warning for Schedule Server users If you change the notification option from "Automatically notify participant of changes" to "Automatically notify participant of the event," for a participant who previously received changes for this event, the event will be deleted from the his or her calendar.

Recommendations for use Especially if you're not set up to use Schedule Server, you'll do a little more work but have a lot less hassle if you just use the email reminder features (*Entering Event Reminder Information* on page 887) or email events (*Emailing Events and Tasks* on page 910) to make sure people show up at meetings.

Setting Up Email and Notification Options

These settings affect the features listed at the top of page 860, and in a multi-user system should be set up for each user, on each user's computer.

1   Show Explorer (choose View > Explorer).

2   Select Tasks&Events (or StarSchedule) and right-click it, then choose Properties.

3   Click the Settings tab in Figure 28-17 on page 864 and make the appropriate selections.

4   Click OK to close the window.

5   Still in Explorer, expand Tasks&Events (or StarSchedule) to see My Computer or the name of the user's connection.

6   Click the Notification via email tab (Figure 28-18 on page 864).

    About the Sender email address field If you leave the placeholder as is, all reminders will be sent from "StarOffice Schedule Reminders" plus the sender's email address will show up in recipients' inboxes for reminders set up in the Reminders section of events setup. You can change it to a static value, including regular text and/ or an email address; it will be used as the sender value, for all event reminders sent using that connection.

Select this option to add emailed tasks and events automatically to your calendar, and select the inboxes to check.

Select this option to check all incoming emails to see whether they contain appointments to be imported. Otherwise only emails with <!> in the header are checked. (This indicates an automatically generated email.)

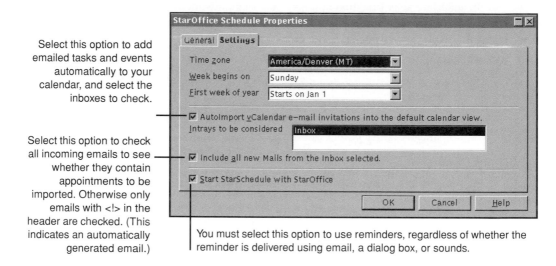

You must select this option to use reminders, regardless of whether the reminder is delivered using email, a dialog box, or sounds.

Figure 28-17   Activating reminders and automatic importing

Select this option if you want to be able to automatically send notification emails to participants in tasks and events. See *The Automatic Notification Feature* on page 862 and Figure 29-13 on page 889.

Select this option if you want to be able to send reminder emails. See Figure 29-11 on page 888 for information on this feature.

This is a placeholder that will be changed to the sender; you can leave it as is.

Enter the name of the mail server that will send the outgoing message on this computer. For single-user systems, it should be the same as the Outgoing mail field in Tools > Options > Internet > Mail/News.

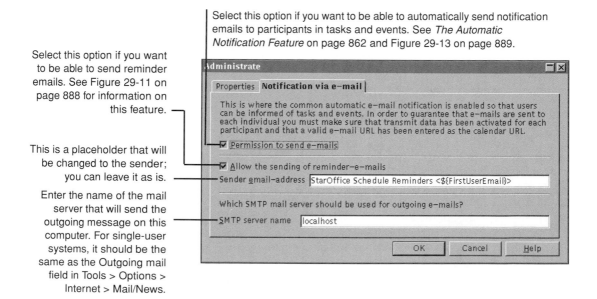

Figure 28-18   Entering server email settings

7   Click OK to close the window.

8   Expand My Computer or the connection name to see Default User, or a user ID.

9   Select it and right-click it; choose Properties.

10   Click the Settings tab (Figure 28-19).

The Send reminders option is automatically enabled for the default user's event calendar. If you create a new server connection, all event calendars on the server will have the Reminder function deactivated except your own.

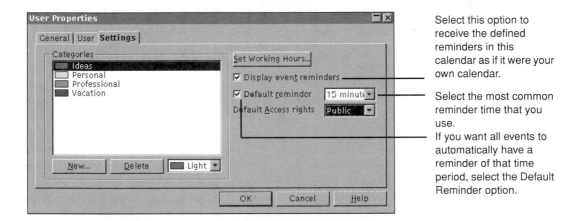

Select this option to receive the defined reminders in this calendar as if it were your own calendar.

Select the most common reminder time that you use.

If you want all events to automatically have a reminder of that time period, select the Default Reminder option.

Figure 28-19   Setting default reminder information

11   Click OK to close the window.

Setting Up StarOffice Inboxes and Outboxes

Of course, an inbox is necessary for receiving reminders, automatic notifications by email, and emailed events and tasks, and outboxes are necessary to send them. See *Setting Up Mail and News* on page 940 for more information.

General Setup

These options let you specify the time zone you use, your worktime, how you categorize tasks and events, and view options. Set these options on each user's computer, in a multi-user environment.

Note – These options can be set up differently on every client, in a multi-user system.

Time and Date Options

1   Show Explorer (choose View > Explorer).

2   Select Tasks&Events (or StarSchedule) and right-click it; choose Properties.

3   Click the Settings tab (Figure 28-20).

4   Select the time zone, first day of the week, and first week of the year.

The rest of the options in this window are explained in *Reminder, Notification, and Email Setup* on page 860.

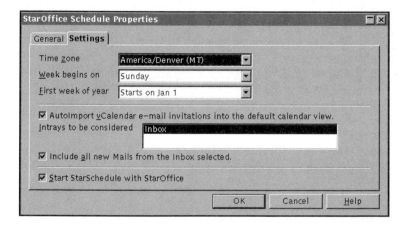

Figure 28-20   General time and date options

Setting Working Times

You can specify working hours, workweek, and holiday information.

Setting Work Hours

The default work hours are 8:00 AM to 5:00 PM. Your work hours affect items such as default event and task times, and the background color in views (see *Setting Calendar Sort and Display Options Using Task and Event Layouts* on page 899).

1   Open Explorer (click the arrow icon at the left side of the work area, or choose View > Explorer).

2   Under the Explorer group, locate Tasks&Events (or StarSchedule), then expand to see Default User or the appropriate user ID.

3   Right-click the user ID and choose Properties, then in the User Properties window, click the Settings tab.

4   Click the Set Working Hours button to display the window in Figure 28-21.

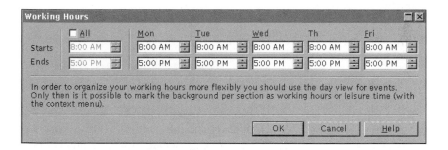

Figure 28-21   Setting working hours

5   In the Working Hours window, select the span of the workday for each day, then click OK.

Setting Work Days

The Workweek and Multiple Workweeks views are based on a work week of Monday through Friday. (For information on these views, see *Overview of the Schedule Views* on page 880.) If this isn't your standard work week, you can change it.

1   Choose View > Define Event Layout.

2   Click the Selection tab, if it's not already displayed.

3   Select the Default layout.

4   Click the Daily&Monthly View tab (see Figure 28-22).

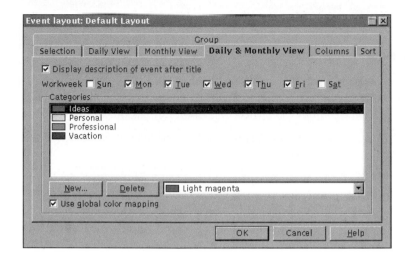

Figure 28-22   Setting workdays

5   Select or deselect the appropriate days.

6   Click OK.

Importing Holidays

Holidays are not included by default in Schedule. This feature lets you add holidays for a selected year, and for a country corresponding to the StarOffice language you've chosen. Holidays for the United States, for instance, include Thanksgiving, Labor Day, and so on. Do this procedure for each user who wants to import holidays.

The holidays are added as day-long events to your calendar and assigned to the Holiday category. To remove one after it's added, just right-click on it in any view and choose Delete.

1   Choose File > Import Holidays.

2   In the Add Holidays to Calendar window (Figure 28-23), select the year you want, then click Create.

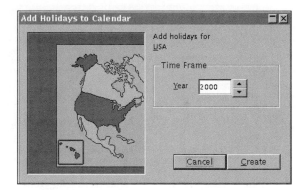

Figure 28-23   Importing holidays

Setting Up Event and Task Categories

Categories can be useful when you use layouts and filters (see page 897) to specify which events and tasks are displayed. In order to take full advantage of layouts and filters, it's a good idea to use categories. The default categories Private, Profession, Ideas, and Vacation are included. You can't rename these or any categories you create, but you can change their color, delete them, and create new ones.

These categories will be applied to the default layout, the one that's used whenever you start Schedule, unless you create a new layout first and apply the categories to that one, instead.

1   Open Explorer (click the arrow icon at the left side of the work area, or choose View > Explorer).

2   Under the Explorer group, display your user ID.

3   Right-click the user ID, then in the User Properties window click the Settings tab (Figure 28-24).

4   Delete categories, apply different colors to existing categories, and create new ones. You must click OK to save changes.

    When you delete a category, events and tasks in that category will retain that category. However, you won't be able to apply the category to any other items.

You can't modify the names of the default categories, but you can delete them and apply different colors.

Click New to create a new category; enter the name and select the color.

Change the color for an existing category here.

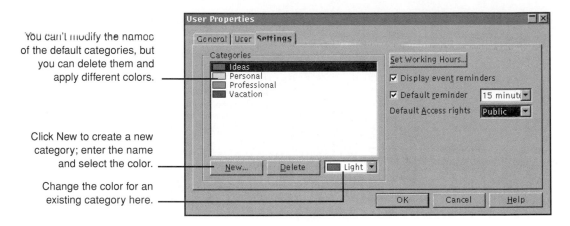

Figure 28-24 Creating and modifying categories

Default Settings for Event Views

You can specify whether, by default, a small calendar and a list of your tasks are also included in each event view (see Figure 28-25).

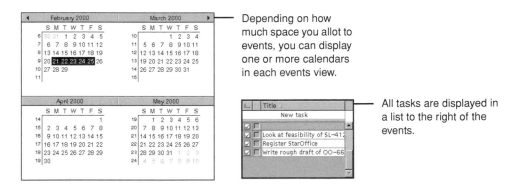

Depending on how much space you allot to events, you can display one or more calendars in each events view.

All tasks are displayed in a list to the right of the events.

Figure 28-25 Including calendars in the event view

You can change these options in all event views using the Calendar and Tasks icons in the Schedule object bar.

1   Select Events and right-click on it. Choose Properties.

2   Click the View Options tab (Figure 28-26) and make the appropriate selections, then click OK to close the window and save changes.

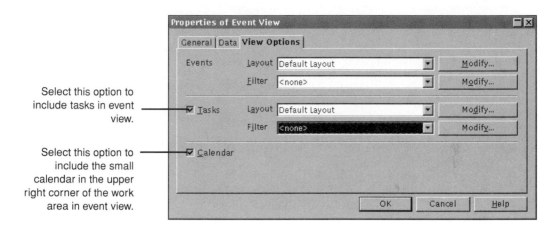

Figure 28-26   Selecting default event view information

3   In Explorer, select Tasks and right-click on it. Choose Properties.

Scheduling

Quick Start

This section contains the following information to help you get started quickly:

- A quick start checklist
- Feature overview
- How to start Schedule
- A tutorial

See *Taming the StarOffice Environment* on page 91 for general tips that can make working with StarOffice a lot easier.

Quick Start Checklist

To enter that important task or event right now (assuming you're already set up correctly), use these procedures:

- Importing another schedule – *Importing Calendar Files* on page 913 and *Synchronizing Schedule With a PalmPilot* on page 915
- Entering an event – *Entering a New Event* on page 885
- Entering a task – *Entering a New Task* on page 890

StarOffice Schedule Features

Review this section to get an idea of what you can do with StarOffice Schedule

Two types of appointments Schedule lets you enter two different types of appointments: events, which occur once or more at specific times, like meetings, and tasks, which are ongoing projects like writing a book or hiring new employees. Each has a fairly large set of options: recurrence, automatic notification, reminders via email, dialog boxes or sounds, attaching files, and so on.

Multi-user or single-user The Schedule Server lets you set up Schedule as a multi-user application, so that users can see each others' schedules, add to others' calendars (if permissions are set correctly), set varying levels of access for others to see their calendars, and so on. If you're in a multi-user environment, you can also enter appointments on your own computer in a separate schedule using My Computer and Default User.

Views with varying levels of detail Six different event views, from day through month, let you see as many or few as you want. You can display tasks and events at the same time.

Restricting and arranging appointments Layouts let you arrange your appointments in the order you want and add options like showing additional time zones. Filters and searches let you restrict what you see in each view.

Reminders and notification Three separate features let you email or otherwise notify yourself and others of appointments.

Multiple format compatibility You can import and export multiple calendar formats, including Microsoft Outlook, and synchronize with a PalmPilot.

Configurable printing You can use the included print templates as is, or create new or modified ones.

The Schedule Work Area

Schedule has six different views: day, week, month, workweek, workmonth (or multiple workweeks), and list. Week view is shown in Figure 29-1.

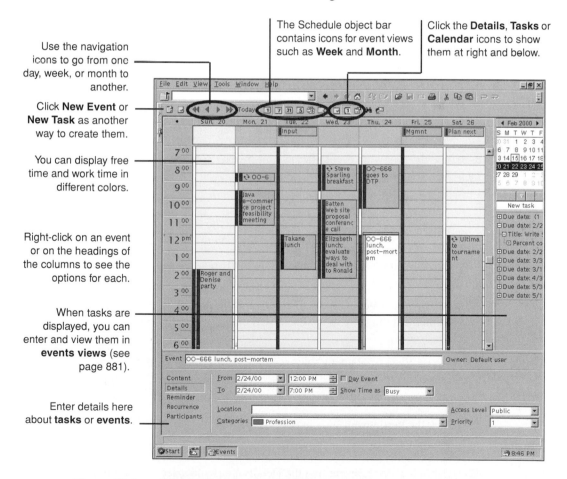

Figure 29-1   Schedule work area, Week view

Guided Tour

This should take about ten minutes, and will give you an idea of how the program works.

Note – Even if you're in multi-user mode, you can still use Default User, under My Computer, to do this tour.

---

1   Choose View > Explorer and expand Tasks&Events (or StarSchedule).

2   In the work area, expand Data Source, then My Computer, to display Default User.

3   Right-click on Default User and choose Properties, then click Settings.

4   Click New to create a new category, called Adventures, and apply your favorite color. Click OK to close the window.

5   Double-click Default user.

6   The events calendar will open. Click the Week View icon.

7   Double-click in the area for Wednesday at 10:00 a.m.

8   Type the following event title: Leave home and seek my fortune across the sea.

9   Press Enter.

10   A details area for event options will open at the bottom of the work area for this event. (If it doesn't, click the Details icon in the object bar.)

11   Select the Content item at the left side of the details area to display a Description and a Details area.

12   In Explorer, select a folder such as Samples/Texts/, then choose View > Beamer and drag any of the files listed to the Also refer to box in the Details area.

13   Choose View > Beamer to hide it again.

14   Click in the event again in the work area and drag the bottom border so that the event lasts from 10:00 a.m. until 12:00 p.m.

15   Click the Participants item in the Details area.

16   In the blank field at the top of the area, type buttercup@florin.net; press Enter.

17   Right-click on the event (not the Details area) and select Default mode, then choose Send as Email.

Note – If a message prompts you to set up an outbox first, see *Setting Up Mail and News* on page 940.

---

18 Choose the Default email format.

19 The email will appear (probably a little slowly). Note that it is already addressed to Buttercup. Add your own email address the same way you added Buttercup's, in the email field for this email to the right of the To dropdown list at the top of the window.

20 In the body of the email, change "invited" to "notified."

21 Click the Mail toolbar icon at the far right side of the object bar, then click the Send Message icon to send the email.

22 In events again, click the Month icon in the object bar.

23 Right-click in the Thursday header and choose Hide Day.

24 Click in the Tasks list on the right side of the work area.

25 Enter the following in the New task field at the top: Spend five years at sea as Dread Pirate Roberts.

Click in the blank area below the tasks to make the new task show up in the list.

26 Click the Details item in the Details section for the task and apply the category Adventures.

27 Enter three additional tasks:

- Study Bonetti's Defense
- Build up a tolerance to Iocane powder
- Train Arnaud as new cabin boy

In the Details section for each task, apply the Adventures category to the first two and the Personal category to the last one.

28 Right-click on the Title header above the tasks; choose Current Filter > Define Filter.

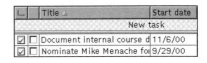

29 Click the Selection tab, then click the New button. Create a filter named Adventures.

30 Click the Settings tab and select the Adventures category.

31 Click OK to close the window and save the filter. Only the three tasks you specified as Adventures will be displayed. (The event you entered is still displayed.)

32 Right-click on the Title heading again and choose Current Filter > Filter Off.

33 Enter a few more events in the currently displayed month:

- `Storm the castle`

- `Find Buttercup`

- `Ride off on white horses`

34 Choose File > Print. (If Print doesn't appear, click in the events for your calendar.)

35 Click the Options button.

36 In the Print Form window, select Month Overview, and select a range of four or five days to print. Click Edit Form.

37 Click Next.

38 In the Header and Footer window, change the template title to `Westley's Events`.

39 Click Next two more times.

40 In the Page Settings window, select Landscape.

41 Click Create. Close all windows except the Print window, and print the document to a printer or to a file (select Print to file, then enter a filename ending in .ps).

Starting StarOffice Schedule

If you're in a multi-user environment, be sure your access to Schedule is set up correctly according to the instructions in *Multi-User Setup Procedures* on page 849.

Navigation Oddity

The main link for navigation through Schedule's setup features in StarOffice 5.2 is either "Tasks&Events", as shown at right, or "StarSchedule." There is no functionality-related reason for it; it's just a simple case of gremlin infestation. It won't affect how you use Schedule.

This might appear as "StarSchedule" instead of "Tasks&Events" on your computer.

Single-User

In Explorer, expand Tasks&Events (or StarSchedule). Double-click Events or Tasks.

You also can log in from the Task Bar Time Display. Double-click the time display on the task bar to start Schedule in Event view.

Multi-User

Follow these steps to access your calendar:

1   In Explorer, select and expand your connection under Tasks&Events > Data Source or StarSchedule > Data Source.

2   If you've already specified your user and ID, just double-click your user name, under the connection.

If you haven't specified your user and ID, right click it and enter it in the Settings tab of the Data Source Properties window.

3   If the correct login information isn't entered, you'll be prompted with a window (see Figure 29-2).

Figure 29-2   User being prompted to enter login and password

4   Enter your ID and password and click OK; you will be logged into your calendar in Schedule Server, via the selected connection, login, and password.

To see the calendar of another user, just double-click that user's name, under your own connection. Unless you're a designate, you won't be able to edit anyone else's calendar.

Note – You also can log in from the Task Bar Time Display. Double-click the time display on the task bar to start Schedule in Event view. Enter an ID and password if prompted. (In a multi-user system, you'll be logged into the connection and ID specified in *Setting Up Your Events and Tasks Links* on page 857.)

Overview of the Schedule Views

Note – If you want to get right into Schedule and start entering meetings and birthdays, skip this section. See *Starting StarOffice Schedule* on page 878 and *Entering and Managing Events and Tasks* on page 885. However, if you've got the time now, it's worth perusing; it provides a good, quick visual overview of Schedule.

The Task View

The Task view shows all your tasks, more extensively than in the side-view area where you can see them in Events view. Figure 29-3 shows the Task view. This view is the only one displayed one you double-click Tasks in the StarOffice desktop or in Explorer.

You can also see tasks in all event views if you click the Tasks button in the events object bar. This view lets you add tasks and see task details. See *The Event Views* for more information on showing tasks within events.

Click the Details icon to show the information at the bottom of the work area.

Click here to type the name of a new task.

Right-click any label at the top for a menu of options.

Click the green arrow icon to add a task you've just typed to the list below.

Drag the lines separating the columns to control width.

Click in the date fields to see a calendar; browse to different months by clicking the arrows beside the month name.

Add related files by dragging them from Explorer or Beamer.

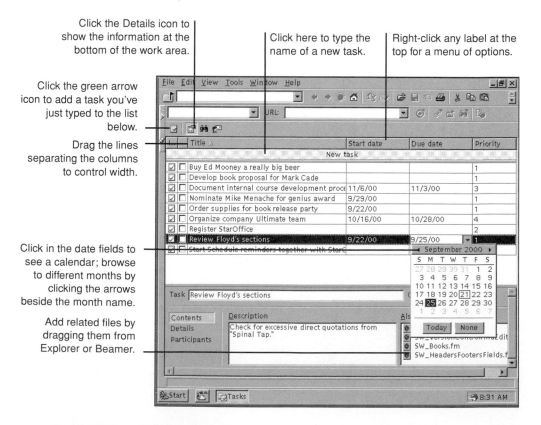

Figure 29-3   Schedule Task view

The Event Views

Schedule lets you view events in several different ways. There are six views: Day, Week, Month, Workweek, Multiple Workweeks (workweek-based month), and List. They contain similar information, but of course some will be more useful to you than others.

To set up whether calendars and tasks are displayed by default in each view, see *Default Settings for Event Views* on page 870.

You'll probably end up using two or more views, depending on what you want to see. Take a few minutes now to see each view, and the type of information displayed in it.

You can access each of the views using the object bar (Figure 29-4), above the work area. If it isn't displayed, choose View > Toolbars > Object Bar.

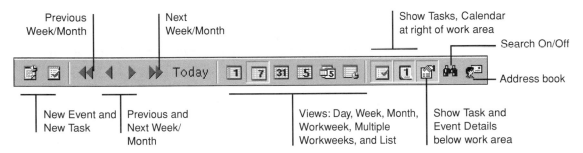

Figure 29-4   Schedule object bar

The following pages shown only Day, Week, and Month view; StarOffice goes into overkill a bit by providing the other three.

Figure 29-5 shows Day view.

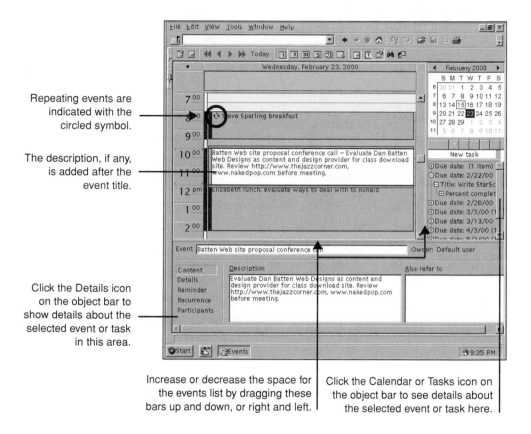

Repeating events are indicated with the circled symbol.

The description, if any, is added after the event title.

Click the Details icon on the object bar to show details about the selected event or task in this area.

Increase or decrease the space for the events list by dragging these bars up and down, or right and left.

Click the Calendar or Tasks icon on the object bar to see details about the selected event or task here.

Figure 29-5   Schedule Day view

Note – You can drag an event up or down to change its time, or change its size to change its duration. You also can use the Details section in the details area.

Figure 29-6 shows the Week view.

All seven days are displayed in Week view; the Workweek view shows only workdays.

All-day events are displayed at the top of the page.

The color of the event's category is shown here.

A small pink arrow appears if there are additional undisplayed events; an orange arrow indicates that the event continues.

Date, time, and other information are shown in the Details category.

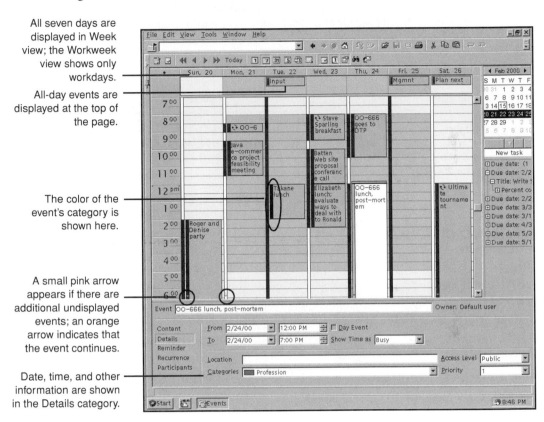

Figure 29-6   Schedule Week view

Figure 29-7 shows the Month view. The default is to show all seven days of the week; you can choose what days to display by right-clicking on a day heading at the top of the work area, or by modifying a layout. See *Setting Calendar Sort and Display Options Using Task and Event Layouts* on page 899.

The current, detailed calendar fills the work area if you don't choose to view the calendar or tasks.

All seven days are displayed in Month view; the Multiple Workweeks view shows only workdays.

You can show alternating months in different colors (see page 899).

The Reminder section lets you pick how and whether to be reminded of the event.

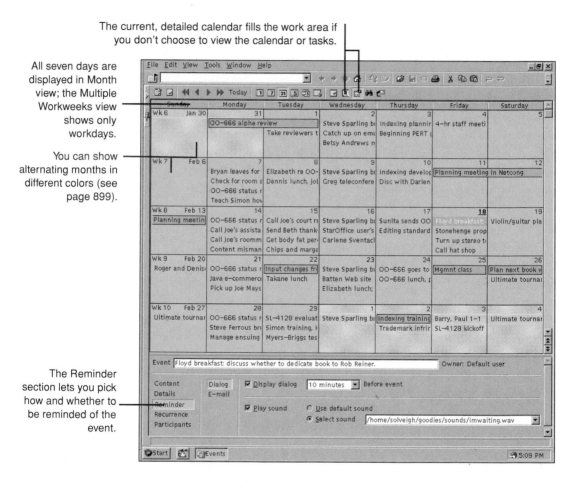

Figure 29-7   Schedule Month view

Entering and Managing Events and Tasks

There are two types of "things to do" in Schedule—*events* and *tasks*.

- Events are things that occur at a certain time, like meetings, picking up the kids after school, or training classes.

- Tasks are things you're working on over a period of time, like writing the first draft of a training manual, hiring new employees, or evaluating a new office suite software package.

Entering a New Event

Note – Events and tasks are saved as soon as you enter them.

The Quick Way

Assuming you've started events and are in the view you want (Day, Week, etc.), click in the view where you want the event. Enter the title. To adjust date, drag the event to the right place, or drag the bottom or top of the event box to make the event longer or shorter.

Use the procedures on the following pages to enter any additional details or activate features.

The Detailed Way

This procedure includes basic information such as time, date, and comments, as well as recurrence, participants, and notification.

1   Start events. (See *Starting StarOffice Schedule* on page 878.)

   To enter new events and tasks at the same time, start the events view.

2   Choose the view you want to use: day, week, and so on. (See *The Event Views* on page 881.)

3   Display the object bar, if it isn't showing. (Choose View > Toolbars > Object Bar.)

4   If the details area isn't displayed at the bottom of the work area, click the Details icon on the object bar.

5   Create a new event by doing one of the following.

- Double-click in the view on the line where you want the appointment to be.

- Click on the line where you want the appointment to be, then click the New Event icon in the object bar.

6   Enter the event title.

7   Use the procedures on the following pages to enter any additional details or activate features.

Entering Event Content Information

In the detail area below the calendar (Figure 29-8), click the Content label and make the appropriate entries.

Enter a description of the event. Descriptions can be printed and you can choose whether to display them in views.

Drag any related files to the Also refer to box from Beamer.

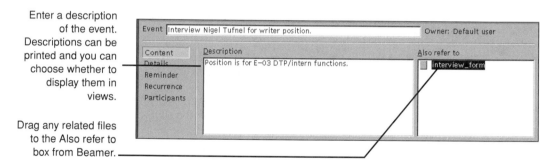

Figure 29-8   Entering event content information

Entering Event Detail Information

Click the Details label (Figure 29-9) and make the appropriate entries.

Two events can be simultaneous; they'll be displayed side by side in views.

If the event will take all day, select Day Event; it will be shown at the top of event views.

Choose how the time should be shown to other users, in Schedule Server. (See page 889).

Change the time and date, if necessary, by entering changes here, or by dragging the event into the view.

Enter a location and select a category (to set up new ones, see page 869).

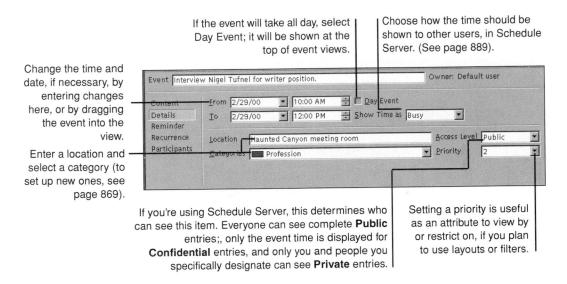

If you're using Schedule Server, this determines who can see this item. Everyone can see complete **Public** entries;, only the event time is displayed for **Confidential** entries, and only you and people you specifically designate can see **Private** entries.

Setting a priority is useful as an attribute to view by or restrict on, if you plan to use layouts or filters.

Figure 29-9   Entering event time and date information

Entering Event Reminder Information

1   Click the Reminder label (Figure 29-10) and make the appropriate entries.

For this feature to work, you must select the Start Schedule With StarOffice option in Figure 28-17 on page 864. Default values are set using Figure 28-19 on page 865.

You can choose reminder modes of email, or a dialog box and/or sound. Click Dialog first to see the following options. These options apply only to you; you can't set up an event to remind someone else with a dialog box or sound.

You can be reminded by a dialog box, which will be displayed before the event.

If you choose Dialog, you can also set up a sound, the default, or one of your own.

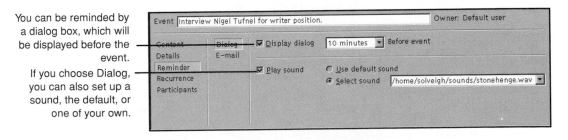

Figure 29-10   Entering event dialog/sound reminder information

2   Click the Email link if you want to send event reminders via email (see Figure 29-11).

An email reminder, unlike the notification feature in the Participants section (Figure 29-13 on page 889), doesn't send a calendar appointment. If you want to send emails to people to remind them of events, this is a less invasive way to do it. The email is sent only once, when you specify, and you have more control over the message text.

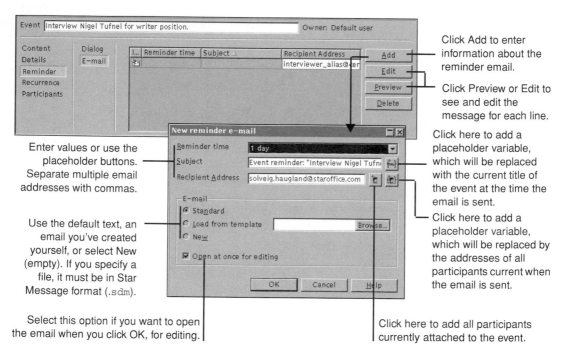

Figure 29-11   Entering event email reminder information

3   If you edit the file, or create a file to use instead of the Standard or a blank message, be sure it's in StarMessage format (.sdm) when you save it. If you edit the file, you don't need to do anything besides enter and save your changes; Schedule will keep track of it and use it for the corresponding reminder.

Entering Recurring Event Information

Click the Recurrence label (Figure 29-12) and make the appropriate entries.

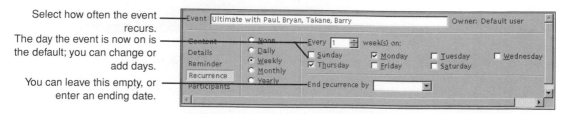

Figure 29-12   Entering event recurrence information

Note – You can't use the Send as Email feature with recurring events. See *Sending an Event or Task* on page 911.

Entering Event Participants and Notification Information

Click the Participants label. Read the *Important Information to Know About These Features* on page 860 before you do any setup, so that you understand the impact of using these features. Then make the appropriate entries, according to Figure 29-13.

For this feature to work, complete *Setting Up Email and Notification Options* on page 863.

Emails from your address book are listed here; you also can drag a name from the Schedule Server link in Explorer. To enter a new participant, enter information here and press Enter.

Users on the same server will have the event put in their calendar; others (with mailto:address as shown) will receive emails.

The participants you list here will be automatically added to the email if you send the event by email (see page 911), and if you choose email as the reminder method (see Figure 29-11 on page 888).

Choose whether to automatically notify the participant of any changes to the event, or to just send one notification.

Enter status for your own purposes; this also shows up in the automatically generated text for emailed events and reminders.

This is useful if you're using Schedule Server; it displays the times of the day when each participant already has events.

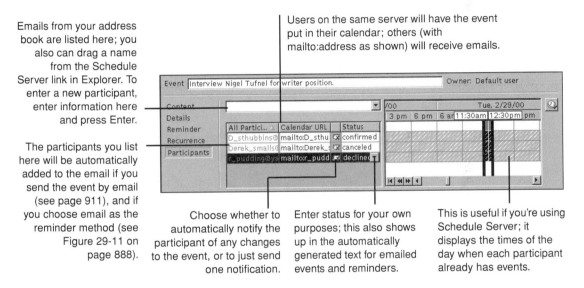

Figure 29-13   Entering event participants information

How the notification is delivered   The calendar URL is set automatically if there is one set up for the participant in the Other tab of the address book *and* if you dragged the name from the Schedule Server connection in Explorer or from the address book list. If an email URL is displayed instead (mailto:address), the notification is sent as an e-mail. Participants whose calendar is on the same server with you won't get an email; the event will be entered directly into their calendar.

Entering a New Task

Note – Events and tasks are saved as soon as you enter them.

The Quick Way

Assuming you've started tasks, click in the New Task line at the top of the task view.

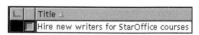

Enter the title, then click the New Task icon.

Use the procedures on the following pages to enter more detailed information.

The Detailed Way

This procedure includes basic information such as time and date and comments, as well as recurrence, participants, and notification.

1	Start tasks. (See *Starting StarOffice Schedule* on page 878.) To enter new events and tasks at the same time, start the events view.

2	Display the object bar, if it isn't showing. (Choose View > Toolbars > Object Bar.)

3	If the details area isn't displayed at the bottom of the work area, click the Details icon on the object bar.

4	Create a new task. Click in the New Task line at the top of the task view and type the title.

Then just click in a noneditable part of the work area, or click the New task icon in the object bar.

5	Use the procedures on the following pages to enter more details.

Entering Task Content Information

In the detail area below the calendar, click the Contents label (Figure 29-14).

Enter a description of the task. Descriptions can be printed, and you can choose whether to display them in views.

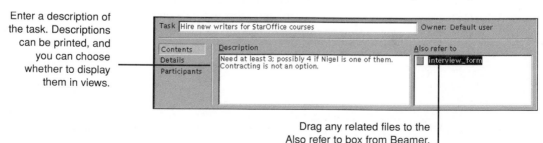

Drag any related files to the Also refer to box from Beamer.

Figure 29-14	Entering task content information

Entering Task Detail Information

Click the Details label (Figure 29-15).

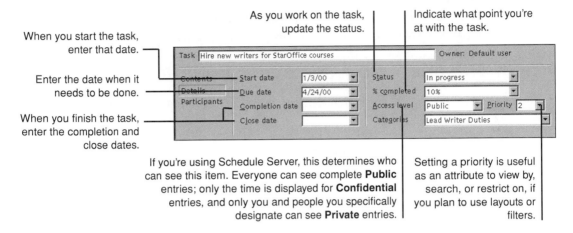

When you start the task, enter that date.

As you work on the task, update the status.

Indicate what point you're at with the task.

Enter the date when it needs to be done.

When you finish the task, enter the completion and close dates.

If you're using Schedule Server, this determines who can see this item. Everyone can see complete **Public** entries; only the time is displayed for **Confidential** entries, and only you and people you specifically designate can see **Private** entries.

Setting a priority is useful as an attribute to view by, search, or restrict on, if you plan to use layouts or filters.

Figure 29-15   Entering task time and date information

Entering Task Participants Information

Click the Participants label. Read the *Important Information to Know About These Features* on page 860 before you do any setup, so that you understand the impact of using these features. Then make the appropriate entries, according to Figure 29-16.

For this feature to work, complete *Setting Up Email and Notification Options* on page 863.

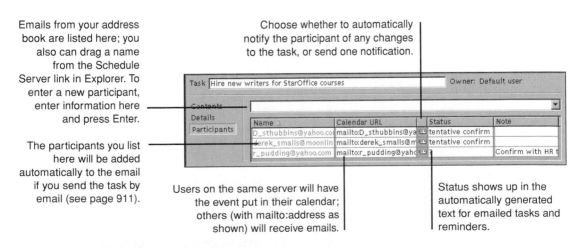

Emails from your address book are listed here; you also can drag a name from the Schedule Server link in Explorer. To enter a new participant, enter information here and press Enter.

Choose whether to automatically notify the participant of any changes to the task, or send one notification.

The participants you list here will be added automatically to the email if you send the task by email (see page 911).

Users on the same server will have the event put in their calendar; others (with mailto:address as shown) will receive emails.

Status shows up in the automatically generated text for emailed tasks and reminders.

Figure 29-16   Entering task participants information

How the notification is delivered The calendar URL is set automatically if there is one set up for the participant in the Other tab of the address book and if you dragged the name from the Schedule Server connection in Explorer or from the address book list. If an email URL is displayed instead (mailto:address), the notification is sent as an e-mail. Participants whose calendar is on the same server with you won't get an email; the event will be entered directly into their calendar.

Rescheduling Tasks and Events

When your entire project schedule changes, here's how you reflect those changes in your calendar.

Changing the Time or Date

You can use either of the following methods:

- Change the information in the Details section.

- Drag it to a different part of the calendar (this is best done in Month view). You can drag it within the work area, or click the Calendars icon in the object bar and drag it to a day in another month.

Copying

To copy an item, drag it to another location while holding down the Ctrl key.

Converting Tasks to Events, and Events to Tasks

Note – To *add* a new task that's the same as the event, or vice versa, instead of *converting* it to the other type, hold down the Ctrl key when dragging.

Converting Tasks to Events

1   Double-click the Tasks icon in the work area to get to Tasks view, or click Tasks in the Events view object bar.

2   Display an event view that contains the day on which you want the task to occur.

3   Click the checkmark icon to the left of the task (in the Image column) and drag the task to the appropriate day in the event view.

   The task is created as a day-long event by default.

4   Apply a category to the new event and enter Reminder and Recurrence information in the Details area, if appropriate. (Click Details in the object bar to display it.)

Converting Events to Tasks

Category, Reminder, and Recurrence information will be deleted when you convert an event to a task.

1   Click Tasks in the events view object bar to display tasks.

2   Select the event and drag it to the task area (shown in Figure 29-17).

> **Note –** You must drag it to a blank area of the task area, not to the list.

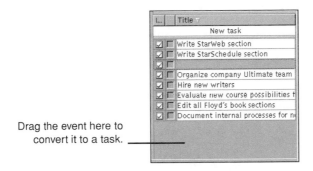

Drag the event here to convert it to a task.

Figure 29-17   Converting an event to a task

Deleting Events and Tasks

You can delete one at a time, or everything that's displayed.

One at a Time

Select it and press the Delete key. You can also right-click an item and choose Delete.

Deleting All Displayed Items

The Tools > Delete all visible events and Tools > Delete Tasks, despite their differing names, have the same function. They delete all displayed events or tasks, so if you're using a filter, only the events or tasks that the filter includes will be deleted.

1   Turn off the current filter, or select the filter you want, to show the items to delete.

2   Choose Tools > Delete all visible events or Tools > Delete Tasks.

3   Choose Yes in the window that asks if you're sure you want to delete.

4   A Confirm Deletion window will appear. Choose Delete to delete the named item, Don't Delete to skip to the next one, or Delete All.

Viewing Another User's Calendar

This is possible only if you're using Schedule Server. All users are listed under every connection; to see a user's calendar, just double-click that user's ID. You'll be able to view only events and tasks he or she has designated as public or confidential, unless you're a designate. (A designate has the same rights as the calendar owner.)

Display Options

Schedule has an array of features that let you have a lot of control over what shows up in each event and task view. These include everything from on-the-fly adding and removing of columns, to setting up event and task layouts and filters, to controlling what information is shown and how it's displayed.

Schedule's Quick Right-Click Display Options

In all of Schedule's views, you can choose what information about the appointment—title, time, owner, etc.—you want to display, simply by right-clicking on the day or title at the top of the view. Figure 29-18 illustrates this.

Right-click any of the labels at the top of any view for display and other options.

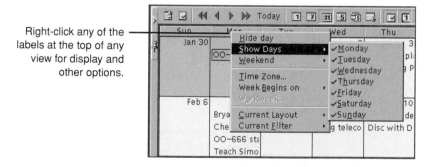

Figure 29-18   Right-click options in Month view

The options vary from one view to the next, and are listed in Table 29-1 and Table 29-2. Comments are provided only when necessary.

Table 29-1   Right-Click Options: Main Five Event Views

Option	View	Comments
Hide day	Month, Multiple Workweeks	
Show day > Previous, Next	Day, Week, Workweek	
Week begins on > Monday, Sunday	Day, Week, Month, Workweek, Multiple Workweeks	
Current Layout > [Selection list], Define Layout	All	See *Setting Calendar Sort and Display Options Using Task and Event Layouts* on page 899.
Current Filter > [Selection list], Define Layout, Filter Off	All	See *Restricting the Information Displayed Using Task and Event Filters* on page 897.
Show Days > [Monday through Sunday]	Month, Multiple Workweeks	
Weekend > Hide, Normal Display, Compress Horizontally	Month	Lets you hide the weekend completely, show both days the same width as each day of the workweek or show the days as half as wide.
Time Zone > [Window]	Month, Multiple Workweeks	
Workweek [Window]	Workweek, Multiple Workweeks	

Table 29-2 shows the options for the other two views.

Table 29-2   Right-Click Options: List Event View and Task View

Option	Comment
Hide Column	Modifies the current layout's definition.
Displayed Columns > [List of all columns]	Modifies the current layout's definition.
Column Selection > [Window]	Modifies the current layout's definition.
Sort	Modifies the current layout's definition. For more information, see *Restricting the Information Displayed Using Task and Event Filters* on page 897.
Group	Modifies the current layout's definition. For more information, see *Restricting the Information Displayed Using Task and Event Filters* on page 897.
Current Layout > [Selection list], Define Layout	See *Setting Calendar Sort and Display Options Using Task and Event Layouts* on page 899.
Current Filter > [Selection list], Define Layout, Filter Off	See *Restricting the Information Displayed Using Task and Event Filters* on page 897.

Selecting What Information Columns to Display

You can choose what columns—title, start time, end time, etc.—to display in the events List view and the Task view. All of these methods change the current layout (see *Setting Calendar Sort and Display Options Using Task and Event Layouts* on page 899).

The Quick Way

Right-click on a column and choose to hide it, or choose Displayed Columns, then select or deselect fields in the list.

Using the Displayed Columns Window

1   Right-click on a column and choose Column Selection, as shown in Figure 29-19.

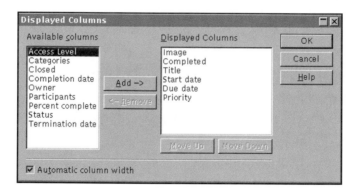

Figure 29-19   Selecting columns to display

2   Select columns you want to view and click Add; select columns you don't want and click remove.

3   Click OK.

Using a Layout

If you want to choose the layout that your changes apply to, choose View > Define Event Layout or View > Define Task Layout. Then follow the instructions on page 899.

Displaying Groups of Events and Tasks Using Filters and Layout

Schedule lets you set up **filters** and **layouts**, to control what's displayed, and in what order.

Understanding Layouts and Filters

Layouts let you view all of your events and tasks in a certain order: by participants, by category, and so on. For example, you could set up a layout that displays all your tasks in an order of priority, or by due date. Layouts also let you control things like the background color of appointments and displaying another time zone.

Filters let you restrict what events and tasks are displayed, in the default view or in a specific layout. You could set up a filter that shows only events for your book project, that contain "meeting" in the title, and that take place in the next month.

Restricting the Information Displayed Using Task and Event Filters

The processes of creating filters for tasks and events are the same, though the options for restrictions vary slightly.

Note – Illustrations of event filters are shown in this procedure, but this won't interfere with how you set things up.

---

1   Choose View > Define Event Filter, or View > Define Task Filter.

2   If it isn't in front, click the Selection tab to see existing filters and create new ones.

3   To modify a filter, select it from the list. (It's a good idea not to modify the default filter.)

To create a filter, click New, then select it from the list as shown in Figure 29-20.

Select this option and select a filter to make the new filter a copy of an existing one (you can then modify it as desired).

Figure 29-20   Creating a new filter

4   Choose whether to make the filter available only in the current view, or all the time (Figure 29-21).

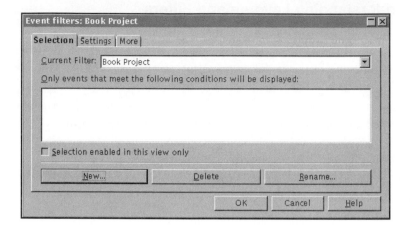

Figure 29-21   First filter tab

5   Click the Settings tab (Figure 29-22) to enter the first set of criteria for the filter.

It's a good idea not to enter too many restrictions at first, since it's easy to exclude relevant events by doing so.

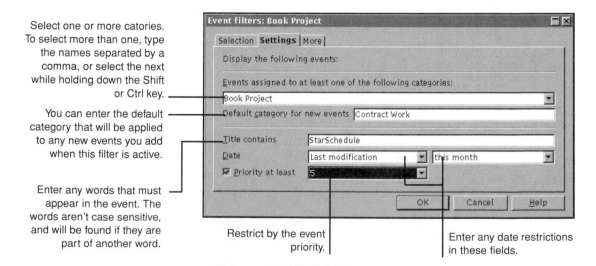

Select one or more catories. To select more than one, type the names separated by a comma, or select the next while holding down the Shift or Ctrl key.

You can enter the default category that will be applied to any new events you add when this filter is active.

Enter any words that must appear in the event. The words aren't case sensitive, and will be found if they are part of another word.

Restrict by the event priority.

Enter any date restrictions in these fields.

Figure 29-22   Entering restrictions for a filter

6   Click the More tab (Figure 29-23) to enter additional restrictions.

All restrictions you enter are displayed here. To be displayed in this filter, an event must meet all the criteria.

Use these fields to set up the restriction, then click Add.

The fields displayed here depend on your selections in the above fields.

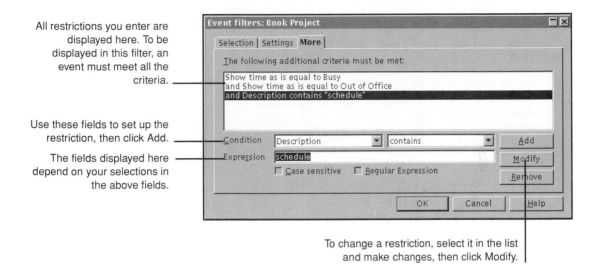

To change a restriction, select it in the list and make changes, then click Modify.

Figure 29-23   Entering additional restrictions for a filter

7   Click the Selection tab again; all restrictions will be listed below the filter name.

8   Click OK to save the filter.

Setting Calendar Sort and Display Options Using Task and Event Layouts

Creating an event or task layout is similar to setting up a report. You control the order in which information is presented, formatting options like colors, categories for organizing tasks and events, and many other options.

The options you select for an event layout are typically displayed in only some of the available views (Day, Week, Month, Workweek, and Multiple Workweeks).

Figure 29-24 shows a sample task layout; Figure 29-25 shows a sample event layout.

The information that is included in the layout (the column headings shown here) are controlled by the Columns tab in the Task Layout window.

The order in which the tasks appear is controlled by the Sort tab.

The fields that are displayed on the first, second, third, and fourth lines are controlled by the Group tab.

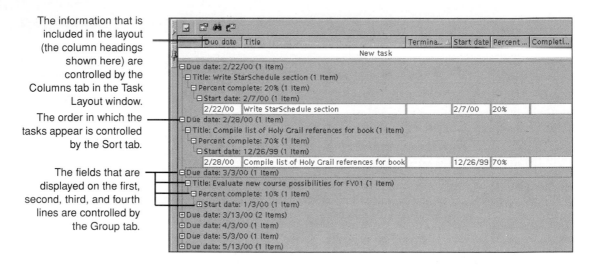

Figure 29-24 Sample task layout

Note – This layout was developed with four levels of information in the Group by tab; as you can see, you need to click four times to open the levels and see the task itself. It's a good idea to choose only one or two levels when you define how to group and sort the information.

The effects of event layouts vary considerably, based on the view (Day, Month, etc.) that you select. Another example, using Day view, is shown within the procedure on page 902.

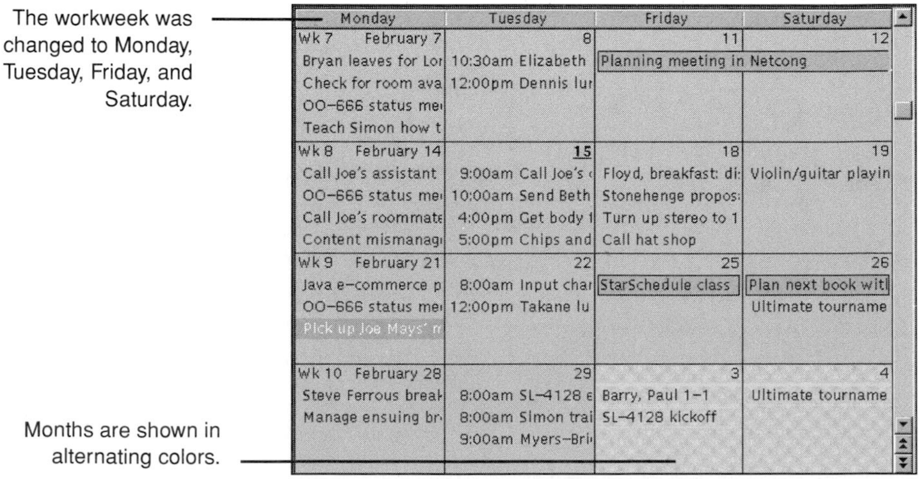

The workweek was changed to Monday, Tuesday, Friday, and Saturday.

Months are shown in alternating colors.

Figure 29-25 Sample event layout, Multiple Workweeks view

Note – Illustrations of task layouts are shown in this procedure for the steps that are applicable to events and tasks. The options are similar, and noted where different.

1   Choose View > Define Task Layout, or View > Define Event Layout.

2   Click the Selection tab, if it's not already displayed.

3   Choose whether to create a new layout, or modify an existing one (Figure 29-26).

Select this option and select a filter to make the new filter a copy of an existing one (you can then modify it as desired).

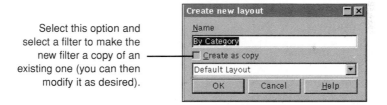

Figure 29-26   Creating a new layout

4   Choose whether to make the layout available only in the current view, or all the time (Figure 29-27).

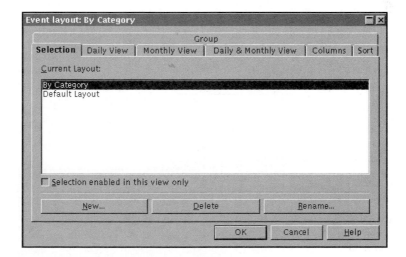

Figure 29-27   First layout tab

5   If you're creating a task layout, skip to step 9.

6   Click the Daily View tab (Figure 29-28) to set options for the Day, Week, and Workweek views.

(As with several other tab and field names throughout StarOffice, it's a good idea not to take the "Daily" in "Daily View" too seriously.)

Choose whether to display the time for another time zone beside your own time zone's hours.

Choose whether you want to be able to divide your time into one-hour increments, 10-minute increments, etc.

Select this option to automatically adapt the area for displaying the day events to the existing volume of text.

Choose the colors for the background of work time (see *Setting Work Hours* on page 867) and free time.

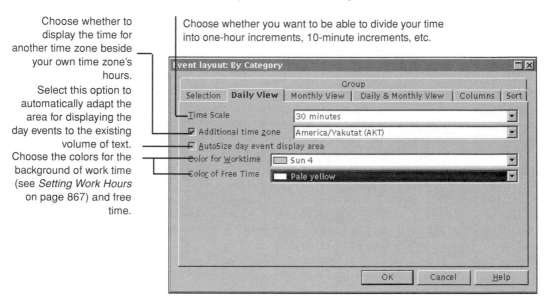

Figure 29-28   Selecting options for the Day, Week, and Workweek views

Figure 29-29 shows the effect of some of the options.

Free time color

Work time color

The Time Scale is 10 minutes.

The Autosize day event display area option was not selected (text wraps within allotted space).

An additional time zone is displayed here.

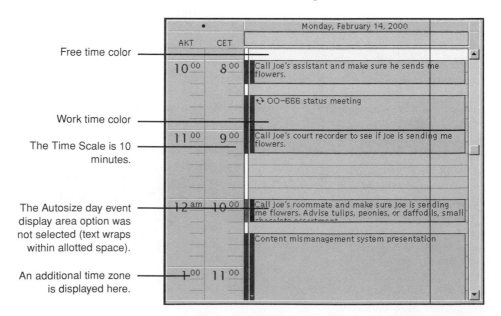

Figure 29-29   Daily view, effects of options in the Event Layout Daily View tab

7   Click the Monthly View tab (Figure 29-30)to set options for the Month and Multiple Workweek views.

Select the total area to be included by the right-hand scroll bar in Month View.

Select this option to halve the space allocated to any days not in the workweek.

Select this option to view the respective end times for your events.

Months are shown in these colors, alternating month by month.

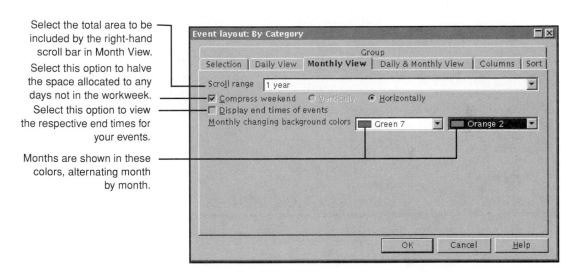

Figure 29-30   Selecting options for the Month and Multiple Workweek views

8   Click the Daily&Monthly View tab (Figure 29-31) to set additional options.

Select this option to display the entry in the Description in the Details area in your calendar.

Select or deselect any days you want considered part of your workweek.

Create new categories, or assign different colors to existing categories.

Select this to use the global color mapping defined by the user in StarOffice Schedule under *Data Source* > *User* > Properties.

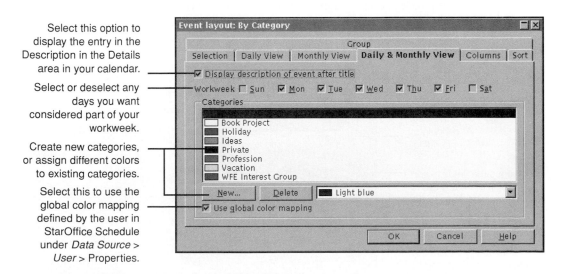

Figure 29-31   Selecting additional options

9   Click the Columns tab (Figure 29-32) to select the fields that will be displayed.

Use this column to select each field you want to display, and add it to the Displayed Columns list.

Select this option to display the columns as wide as the width of the window. If this field is not selected, you can scroll horizontally through the window. (You have more column and window width control if you don't select it.)

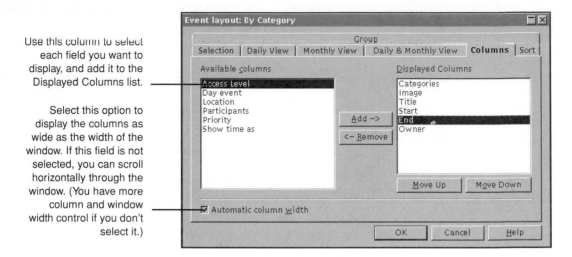

Figure 29-32   Selecting the columns for the layout

10   Click the Sort tab (Figure 29-33) to specify what order the tasks will be displayed in.

The features in the Sort and Group tabs affect events only in List view.

Note – The more options you choose in the Sort and Group tabs, the more times you'll have to double-click each item in the displayed layout to see all the detail. It's a good idea to only use one or two levels, then add more if necessary.

Select the main field to sort by, and select Ascending or Descending.

Choose the fields to sort by if there are two or more tasks with the same value for the first field.

All fields are included in each list; you can sort by fields you didn't include in the Columns tab.

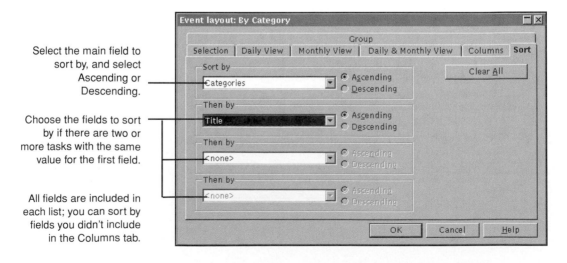

Figure 29-33   Selecting the task display order for the task layout

11   Click the Group tab (Figure 29-34) to specify what order the fields for each tasks will be displayed in (see Figure 29-24 on page 900 for an example of how the fields are grouped).

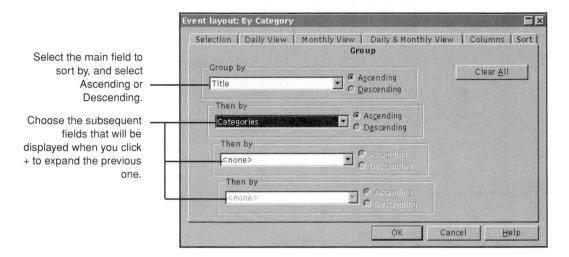

Select the main field to sort by, and select Ascending or Descending.

Choose the subsequent fields that will be displayed when you click + to expand the previous one.

Figure 29-34   Selecting the field display order for each task, for the task layout

12   Click OK to save the layout.

13   To see the effects, switch to Task view and choose View > Define Task Layout again, then select the layout and click OK.

Selecting a Filter or Layout

The quick way is to right-click in the bar at the top of any view. A menu will appear, showing a list of options such as hiding the selected field, showing or hiding a list of fields, selecting a filter or layout, and so on.

You also can open the appropriate window from the View menu, select it in the Selection tab, and click OK.

Setting Default Event and Task Filters and Layouts

1   In Explorer (choose View > Explorer), select Tasks&Events (or StarSchedule). Click the + icon to expand it.

2   Select Events and right-click on it. Choose Properties.

3   Click the View Options tab (Figure 29-35) and make the appropriate selections.

Select the default layout and filter to use for events in event view.

Select this option to include tasks in event view.

Select the default layout and filter to use for tasks in event view.

Select this option to include the small calendar in the upper right corner of the work area in event view.

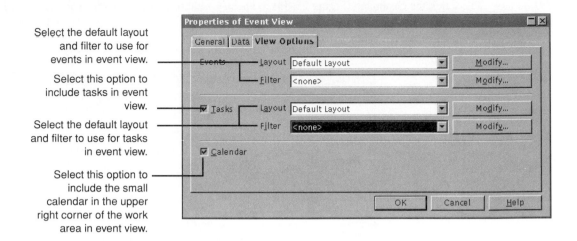

Figure 29-35   Selecting default event view information

4   Click OK to close the window and save changes.

5   In Explorer, select Tasks and right-click on it. Choose Properties.

6   Click the View Options tab (Figure 29-36) and make the appropriate selections.

Select the default layout and filter to use for tasks in task view.

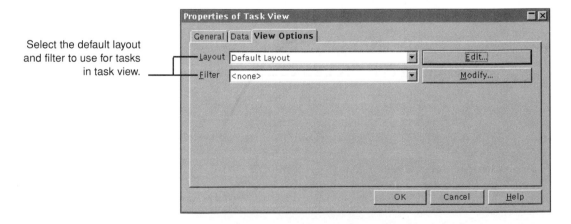

Figure 29-36   Selecting default task view information

7   Click OK to close the window and save changes.

Finding Events and Tasks

Schedule has two ways to search: the quick, simple way, and a powerful filter-like search.

Going to Today or a Specific Day

You can use these features only for events.

- Choose Tools > Go to Date and enter the date in the window that appears. Click OK.
- Choose Tools > Go to Today.

Specific Search

You can easily find a particular task or event using the Search feature. The information you can base the search on is very similar to the filter conditions. (See *Restricting the Information Displayed Using Task and Event Filters* on page 897.)

The search process will look at all appointments that are shown using the current filter. If you want to search all your events or appointments, be sure to turn off filters. (Right-click on an information column or date column and choose Current Filter > Filter Off.)

1   In any event or task view, choose Tools > Find. You also can click the Search On/Off icon on the Schedule object bar.

If nothing happens, or there's just a little bit of movement at the top of the work area, you need to adjust the display to add room for the find area. Drag the horizontal line below the object bar down (Figure 29-37); the find fields will be displayed.

Click here; when the pointer becomes a double-ended arrow, drag the line down.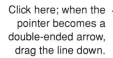

Figure 29-37   Adding room to the Find area

2   The Conditions window will be displayed (Figure 29-38). Make the appropriate selections.

The buttons at the top of the window for tasks and events are slightly different; the event buttons are shown separately in the following illustration.

Select the category that the item you want is in. To select more than one, type the names separated by a comma, or select the next while holding down the Shift or Ctrl key.

Click Update (for tasks) or Search backwards/Search forwards (for events) to be in the search.

Click Remove conditions to clear the window or Exit to close it.

Enter any words that must appear in the event. The words aren't case sensitive, and will be found if they are part of another word.

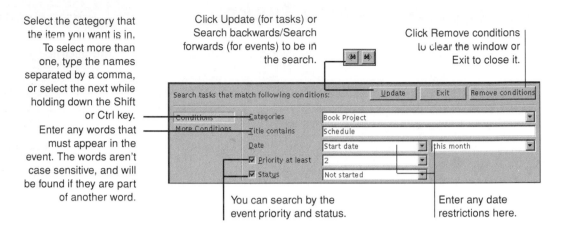

You can search by the event priority and status.

Enter any date restrictions here.

Figure 29-38   Entering restrictions for a search

3   Click the More Conditions link (Figure 29-39) to enter additional restrictions.

Click Update (for tasks) or Search backwards/Search forwards (for events) to be in the search.

Click Remove conditions to clear the window or Exit to close it.

All restrictions you enter are displayed here. To be displayed in this filter, an event must meet all the criteria.
Use these fields to set up the restriction, then click Add.

Any fields displayed here depend on your selections in the above fields.

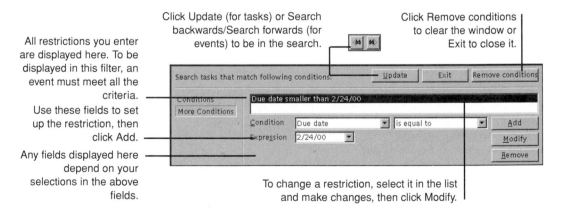

To change a restriction, select it in the list and make changes, then click Modify.

Figure 29-39   Entering additional restrictions for a search

4   Click Update (for tasks) or Search backwards/Search forwards to begin the search.

Backing Up and Archiving Schedules

It's a good idea to back up your scheduling information at least monthly.

Backing Up Schedules

You must first stop the Schedule Server process so that open files can be closed. See *Schedule Server Administration and Configuration* on page 844.

All Schedule information is stored in the following files on the server computer. Be sure to incorporate them into your regular backup processes.

Single-user installations:

*   `user/store/schedule.cal` – Saved events and tasks
*   `user/config/schedule.cfg` – Configuration information

Multi-user installations:

*   The files in `/user/store/` on the Server computer – Saved events and tasks
*   `user/config/schedule.cfg` on each client – Configuration information

Archiving

Archiving stores events or tasks in an .xcs file.

Note – It's not a backup equivalent—it *deletes* all tasks that have been completed or events that have taken place. It won't delete recurring events that are still recurring. You can restore archived events; see *Importing Calendar Files* on page 913.

---

1   Start Events or Tasks, then choose Tools > Archive (Figure 29-40). Make the appropriate selections, then click OK.

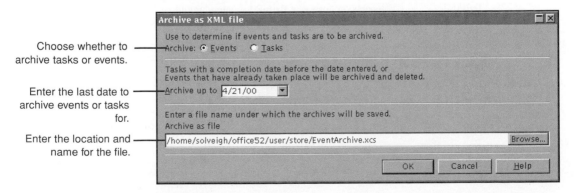

Figure 29-40   Archiving

Exchanging Data

As is the case throughout StarOffice, Schedule lets you import and export schedules in multiple formats. You also can email events and tasks to your associates, and synchronize Schedule with a PalmPilot. By and large, these features are pretty slick.

Data Exchange Overview

Table 29-3 summarizes the import/export and compatibility features provided by Schedule.

Table 29-3   Import, Export, and Email Formats

Function	Format, in addition to Schedule	How
Import	Microsoft Outlook (extension .csv)	Choose File > Import while in Events or Tasks view.
	XML-iCalendar (extension .xcs)	Importing and exporting are effective ways of importing an entire calendar.
	vCalendar (extension .vcs)	
	iCalendar (extension .ics)	
	Lotus Organizer to-do lists (extension .txt))	
Export	Netscape Calendar	Choose File > Export.
	Microsoft Outlook compatible	
Email	HTML	Right-click an event or task and choose Send as E-mail.
	ASCII	Emailing is a good way to distribute a single event or task.
	RTF	
	MS Outlook	
	Netscape	
PalmPilot	You can synchronize a PalmPilot calendar and address book with Schedule and Address if you're using a 3COM US Robotics PalmPilot II or later.	See procedure later in this section.

Emailing Events and Tasks

Before you begin, familiarize yourself with the mail tool, beginning on page 931.

About Emailing

Note – To make this feature to work, complete *Setting Up Email and Notification Options* on page 863.

Events and tasks that you email are automatically imported into the recipients' calendar; they don't need to do anything, except be set up correctly. This also means, however, that all appointments you send to anyone are automatically added to the person's schedule. There is no way to selectively choose what events to add, though any events can be deleted. (A setup option in Figure 28-17 on page 864 lets you choose whether to automatically add to recipients' calendars, but in that case when they receive an email, they need to enter all the task or event information in their calendar themselves.) We recommend that you to use the emailing feature judiciously.

Sending an Event or Task

You can email any event or task to one or more people, for them to add to their own Schedule calendars. If you have set up participants and their emails for an event, the message will be automatically addressed to them. (You can choose to add or delete addresses before sending.)

You don't need the Schedule server to do this, just email connectivity.

1   Right-click on the event or task you want to send, then choose Send as E-mail. You also can select an event or task and choose File > Send as E-mail. See Figure 29-41.

Right-clicking the event or task can be a little tricky for tasks, or the event List view. Follow these guidelines:

- Don't right-click on a task when you're in edit mode (when the cursor is a vertical line and is blinking in the field.) You'll only get the cut/copy/paste options.

- If you're using sorting or grouping in the event layout, you need to open the entire task; it won't work to right-click on a field that's not at the lowest level.

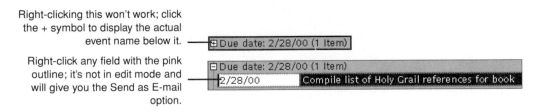

Right-clicking this won't work; click the + symbol to display the actual event name below it.

Right-click any field with the pink outline; it's not in edit mode and will give you the Send as E-mail option.

Figure 29-41   Right-clicking in Task or List view

2   A message will appear, prompting you to choose a calendar mode for the attachment.

3 A new email will appear in the workspace (Figure 29-42).

You can edit the text, add or remove email addresses, choose multiple email formats, and so on.

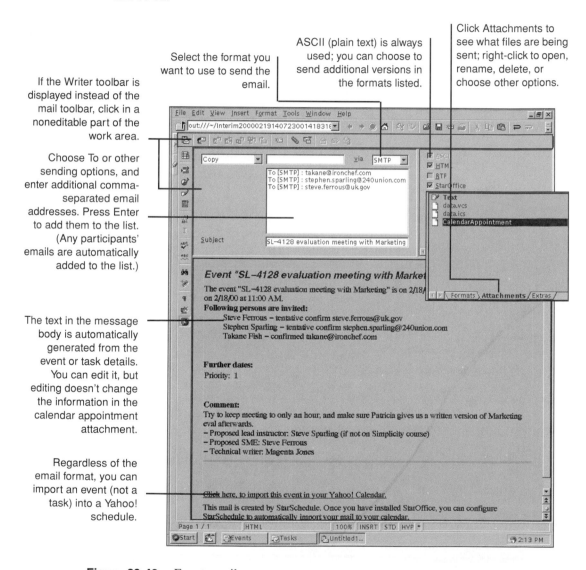

Click Attachments to see what files are being sent; right-click to open, rename, delete, or choose other options.

ASCII (plain text) is always used; you can choose to send additional versions in the formats listed.

Select the format you want to use to send the email.

If the Writer toolbar is displayed instead of the mail toolbar, click in a noneditable part of the work area.

Choose To or other sending options, and enter additional comma-separated email addresses. Press Enter to add them to the list. (Any participants' emails are automatically added to the list.)

The text in the message body is automatically generated from the event or task details. You can edit it, but editing doesn't change the information in the calendar appointment attachment.

Regardless of the email format, you can import an event (not a task) into a Yahoo! schedule.

Figure 29-42 Event email

4 Click the Send Message icon in the object bar.

If the object bar for email isn't displayed, click the Mail Toolbar/Text Object Toolbar icon at the far right end of the object bar. If it still doesn't show, simply close the message; a message will prompt you to send, cancel, or return to the message.

Receiving an Emailed Event or Task in StarOffice

The recipient of the task or event doesn't need to do anything, except be set up correctly. See *Reminder, Notification, and Email Setup* on page 860. Any appointments you send to anyone are automatically added to the person's schedule. There is no way to selectively choose what events to add.

If the task or event isn't imported automatically, you need to either enter all the information yourself in your calendar, or select the automatic import option in Figure 28-17 on page 864.

Note – In Solaris, you can receive a Schedule emailed task or event in your regular email program, and drag it to your Solaris calendar.

Note – Don't use the import feature to import the item; you'll end up with an empty calendar except for that event of task.

Receiving an Emailed Event or Task in Yahoo!

The link at the bottom of Figure 29-42 on page 912 is absolutely right; you can easily import events (not tasks) into a Yahoo! Calendar by clicking on the link at the bottom of the email.

In your Yahoo! email inbox, just click the link, and if you've got a Yahoo! calendar, the appointment will instantly be imported and displayed.

Importing Calendar Files

See Table 29-3 on page 910, or check the format list in the Import dialog box, for a list of importable formats.

Note – Importing a calendar file *overwrites* your entire calendar, even if it contains just one event or task. It does not synchronize by adding; it makes your calendar match the imported file. Any events or tasks in your current calendar that are not in the one you import will be wiped out.

We recommend that you make a backup before importing. See *Backing Up and Archiving Schedules* on page 909.

1   Choose File > Import.

2   Select the file you want to import.

3   Select the format, such as `.vcs` tasks or `.vcs` events. The correct format won't be selected for you by default, and you must select the right format for it to work.

Note – If you're currently using a filter that screens out any of the imported items, they will be imported but not displayed.

Exporting Your Schedule

See Table 29-3 on page 910, or check the format list in the Import dialog box, for formats.

Exporting exports all events or tasks (you choose which when exporting) in your current calendar, in all years. To create an importable file of just one event or task, use the email feature. (See *Emailing Events and Tasks* on page 910.)

1   Select a filter (right-click on any information heading and choose Current Filter) if you want to restrict the exported items. If you're currently using a filter but want to export all items, you can choose not to use the filter, in the Export window.

2   Choose File > Export.

3   In the Export window (Figure 29-43), make the appropriate selections.

In the Owner list, choose whether you want to remain the owner of the exported file (Always), let whoever imports the file be the owner (Never), or stay the owner for "internal" (StarOffice) schedules. It's simplest to just select Never.

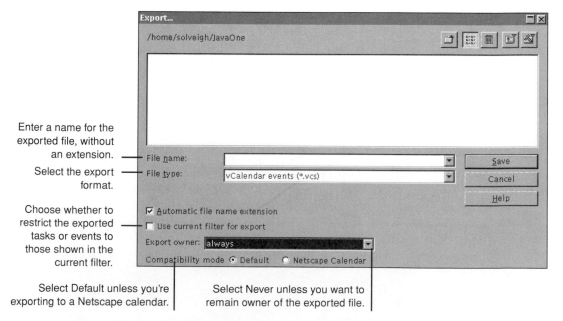

Figure 29-43   Exporting tasks and events

Synchronizing Schedule With a PalmPilot

If you use a 3COM US Robotics PalmPilot II or later, you can synchronize the calendar in your PalmPilot with Schedule, as well as your PalmPilot address book with the StarOffice address book. You can add appointments from PalmPilot to Schedule, vice versa, or both.

Follow these steps to do the necessary installation, setup, and synchronization.

Installing StarOffice PalmPilot Software on Your Computer

The necessary PalmPilot software is already installed on your computer if:

- If you currently use a PalmPilot and its configuration software is installed on your computer (the StarOffice installation recognized it and automatically installed the necessary software)

- If you used the custom installation to install the PalmPilot module

To check whether it's installed, first open an event or task, then check whether a PalmPilot selection is available under the Tools menu.

Otherwise, you'll need to install the StarOffice PalmPilot software manually.

If you haven't installed it already, run the StarOffice installation again. See *Installing Additional Components* on page 56. In addition to all other modules that you already have installed, select the **PalmPilot Integration** option in the **Program Modules** list, shown in Figure 29-44.

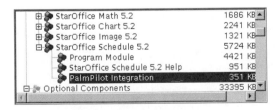

Figure 29-44   PalmPilot Integration install option

Installing StarOffice PalmPilot Software on Your PalmPilot

You need to load the `starsync.prc` module from the installed `Office52/share/palmpilot` folder to the PalmPilot (in a multi-user install, this folder was installed on the server computer). Your operating system contains several freeware tools to load .prc files to the PalmPilot, including Palm Install Tool.

Note – If you're running Windows, you can use the Windows software included with your PalmPilot. Choose Start > Programs > PalmPilot Desktop 2.0 > PalmPilot Installations-Tool. The Tool window will appear. Install the `starsync.prc` file.

Setting Up PalmPilot Synchronization

Once the necessary integration software is installed on your StarOffice computer and your PalmPilot, you need to do a little setup in StarOffice. These setup options will determine how the synchronization with Schedule works; you can set them up once and leave them, or modify them each time you run a Hotsync.

One of the options allows you to map corresponding Schedule and PalmPilot categories, such as Professional, Private, Vacation, and so on. (See Figure 29-48 on page 918.) If you want to modify Schedule categories before mapping them, refer to *Setting Up Event and Task Categories* on page 869.

1   Position your PalmPilot in its cradle and be sure it's connected to your computer.

2   Choose Tools > PalmPilot Hotsync Configuration.

The menu option will show up only if you've installed the synchronization software, **and** when you're displaying tasks or events.

3   In the StarOffice Sync Configuration window in Figure 29-45, enter the appropriate options. Refer to the documentation for your operating system to determine the right port. In Solaris, for example, it might be called `ttyS0`. Enter the same baud rate your PalmPilot uses.

Note – You can synchronize (see page 919) only if the Place port in synchronization readiness option is selected. However, the port won't be available to other programs or devices once it's selected. If you select the option, first close any application that, for example, expects a fax modem at the specified port. If you don't select it now, you need to do so each time you do a hotsync.

Enter the port that your
PalmPilot uses to connect to
your computer, and the baud
rate at which it connects.

This option must be marked for
a Hotsync to run.

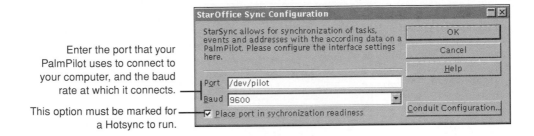

Figure 29-45   PalmPilot connectivity options

4   Click the Conduit Configuration button to open the StarOffice Sync Setup window in
    Figure 29-46. Click the General tab if it's not already displayed.

    In the Which data is to be matched by StarOffice Sync? list:

    • Synchronize Tasks synchronizes StarOffice and PalmPilot tasks.

    • Synchronize Events synchronizes StarOffice events with the PalmPilot calendar.

    • Synchronize Addresses synchronizes StarOffice and PalmPilot address books.

Select your schedule
server connection for a
multi-user environment, or
My Computer for single-
user.

Select your calendar
(Default User, or the login
assigned to you by the
Schedule administrator).

Select the items that you
want to be the same in
StarOffice and your
PalmPilot.

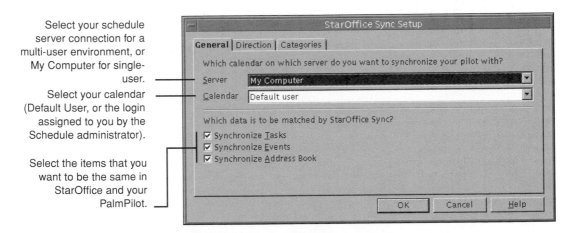

Figure 29-46   PalmPilot identity and information options

5   Click the Direction tab (Figure 29-47).

    If you select the first option in this tab, after synchronization all data on both systems
    will be identical. This means that the changes you make on one system are also
    applied to the other system. For example, if you deleted all events in StarOffice
    Schedule since the last time you synchronized and you re-synchronize the events after
    selecting this option, all events will be deleted in the PalmPilot as well.

The first option means any entry in either PalmPilot or Schedule will exist in both. The second option means Schedule will overwrite your PalmPilot schedule. The third option means the PalmPilot schedule will overwrite Schedule.

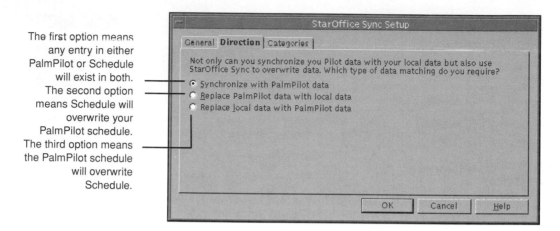

Figure 29-47   Synchronization-direction options

6   Click the Categories tab (Figure 29-48).

Here you can assign the categories of one system to those of another system. For example, you can correlate the "Ideas" category from StarOffice Schedule with your "Random Jottings" PalmPilot category.

Follow these directions if they apply.

Select a Schedule category (local) and the corresponding PalmPilot category.

Click Add to display the mappings here.

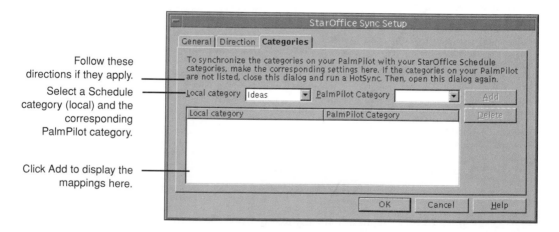

Figure 29-48   PalmPilot-Schedule category mapping options

Note – To detect identical address book records, a combination of first and last names is used. Therefore, if two records contain the same identical first and last names, the remaining content of this address will be synchronized. Multiple phone numbers of the same type in the PalmPilot will be converted to a comma-delimited list in StarOffice.

Synchronizing StarOffice With Your PalmPilot

Once the setup is complete, you can synchronize the systems.

1   Exercise normal caution by backing up your Palm Pilot and Schedule before
     beginning (see *Backing Up and Archiving Schedules* on page 909).

2   Start StarOffice.

3   Be sure the Place port in synchronization readiness option is selected (see Figure 29-
     45 on page 917).

4   Connect the PalmPilot to your computer.

5   Press the Sync button on the PalmPilot.

Printing in StarOffice Schedule

Printing Capabilities

Schedule allows you quite a bit of flexibility in printing. The options include:

- A set of predefined templates that determine what information is printed and how, for each of the event views and the task view
- Modifying the templates or creating new ones
- Printing a selected day, range of days, or a selected task or event
- Printing to a printer, a file, or generating a StarWriter document containing the appointments or tasks
- Adherence to filters—if you're screening out information using a filter, the screened information doesn't get printed

Note – The printing information here is specific to this application; see *Printing in StarOffice* on page 61 of *Getting Started* for more information.

Printing Setup

For information about setting up printers and printing to files, refer to *Printer Setup* on page 62 and *Printing to a PostScript or PDF File* on page 77.

Creating and Modifying Print Templates

Schedule comes with several default print templates, which determine how events and task information is laid out, what information is included, etc. You can modify these, or create new ones.

Figure 30-1 shows part of the Week Overview report.

Tuesday, 2/29/00	Wednesday, 3/1/00
10:00 AM Interview Nigel Tuffnel for writer position. (Haunted Canyon meeting room) 02:00 PM Compare interview results; make recommendations to Jaki	• Vacation
Thursday, 3/2/00	**Friday, 3/3/00**
09:30 AM SL-4128 meeting 02:30 PM Scott H meeting; get hiring paperwork signed	11:30 AM Review changes with Floyd and Greg 03:30 PM FAC (Haunted Canyon meeting room; bring guitar and Singletrack)

Figure 30-1   Week Overview default template

1   Choose File > Print. (If a Print menu option doesn't show up, click in the event or task view you want to print.)

2   Click the Options button to open the Print Form window (Figure 30-2). Create a new form or select one to modify.

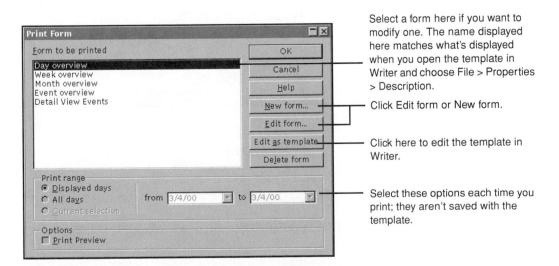

Select a form here if you want to modify one. The name displayed here matches what's displayed when you open the template in Writer and choose File > Properties > Description.

Click Edit form or New form.

Click here to edit the template in Writer.

Select these options each time you print; they aren't saved with the template.

Figure 30-2   Creating or modifying a form

About the Edit as Template feature You can modify and create templates using the rest of the windows in this wizard, or by clicking Edit as Template to edit a template in Writer. However, be forewarned that it's hit-and-miss to get the changes you make in Writer to show up when you print using the modified template. Our testing shows that changes you make using the Page Style window (choose Format > Page) are saved and used when you print, but anything you do just by adding text to the document is ignored when you print (even though it still shows up when you open the template).

Go ahead and use this feature if you like editing in Writer or you want to apply some features the wizard doesn't provide. But be prepared for a little aggravation, and make sure that when you save your changes, you save the template in the StarWriter template format, not the default format, which is regular StarWriter.

3 Choose general template options (Figure 30-3), then click Next.

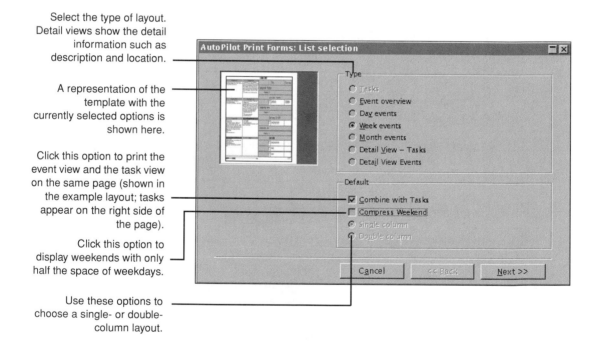

Select the type of layout. Detail views show the detail information such as description and location.

A representation of the template with the currently selected options is shown here.

Click this option to print the event view and the task view on the same page (shown in the example layout; tasks appear on the right side of the page).

Click this option to display weekends with only half the space of weekdays.

Use these options to choose a single- or double-column layout.

Figure 30-3   Selecting general template options

4 Choose header and footer options (Figure 30-4), then click Next.

This option is related to the Edit as Template feature; it's not necessary, because you can define the heading in the field below.

A representation of the template with the currently selected options is shown here.

Enter the title that you want to appear in the templates list in the Print Forms window.

Choose what information to include in the footer of the printed view.

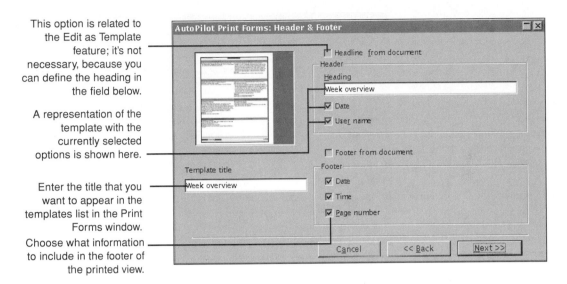

Figure 30-4   Selecting header and footer options

5   Choose additional general options as shown in Figure 30-5; these apply to the individual events. Click Next.

Select this option to show only starting dates (most events start and end on the same day).

You can only choose this option if your system is defined for a 12-hour day.

Select this option to print the location of an event, if one is given.

Choose whether to use fixed-height tables as shown in the preview box.

Select this option if you want to print days with no events (this means weekends are always printed).

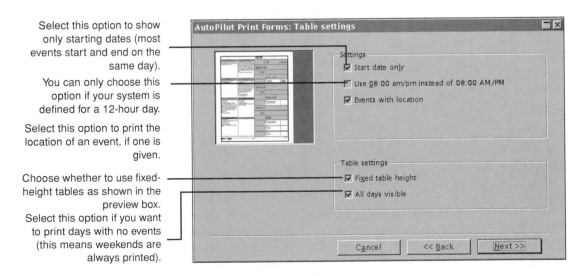

Figure 30-5   Selecting additional options

6   Choose the fields to include in the template, as shown in Figure 30-6. Click Next.

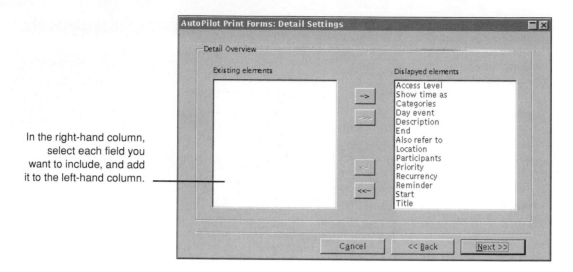

In the right-hand column,
select each field you
want to include, and add
it to the left-hand column.

Figure 30-6   Selecting the information to include

7   Choose margin and orientation settings (Figure 30-7), then click Next.

Aside from orientation, which you might want to change, you'll usually be fine if you just accept the default values in this window.

These options define the dimensions of the paper you'll be printing on. Select the paper format options before you make entries here.

These options control how far in from the edge of the paper printing will begin.

Select a paper format. If there isn't one that represents the paper you're using, enter a new name, enter options, then click Save.

Choose to print in portrait (as shown in the preview box) or landscape.

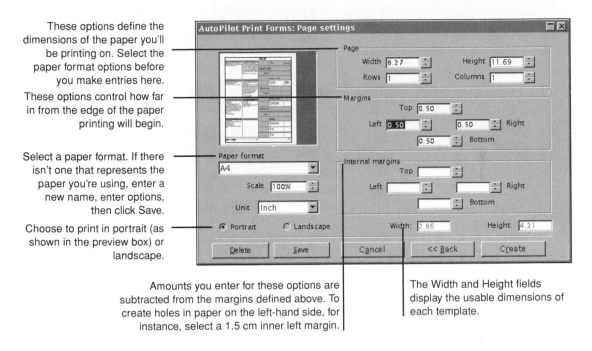

Amounts you enter for these options are subtracted from the margins defined above. To create holes in paper on the left-hand side, for instance, select a 1.5 cm inner left margin.

The Width and Height fields display the usable dimensions of each template.

Figure 30-7   Selecting margin and orientation options

If the dimensions of the paper you're using aren't covered by one of the selections in the Paper format list, enter a new name in that list, set all other options in this page, then click Save.

8   Click Create.

Printing Schedules

Printing in Schedule is similar to printing in other parts of StarOffice, except that you can choose a print template if you choose File > Print. (If you just click the Print File Directly icon on the StarOffice toolbar, the system default template for the current view is used.)

Follow these steps to print a view, choosing the layout and other options.

Note – For information about printing to files, refer to *Printing to a PostScript or PDF File* on page 77.

1   If you're not already there, move to the view—Day, Workweek, etc.—that you want to print.

2 If you're currently using a filter, it will affect what's printed. Turn on or off filters, according to what you want printed.

3 Choose File > Print; the window in Figure 30-8 will appear.

Select a printer if you want to print a hard copy.

Printing to a text file doesn't produce good results; a postscript file or Writer file works well. The extension you enter (.ps or .sdw) determines the file type. Automatic file extension doesn't work in this instance.

Click Options to print to a file.

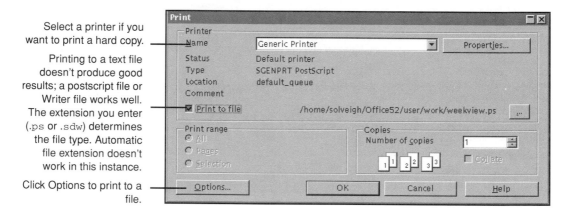

Figure 30-8 Choosing printing options

4 Select where to print the view: printer or a file, or click Options and select Print Preview if you want to generate a StarWriter document containing the information. Print Preview is the best way to get the event or task view into an editable file.

You can print to a file, or to Print Preview, but not both at the same time. If you choose both, only the Print Preview will be effective.

5 Click Options if you want to select a print template other than the default. Select options (Figure 30-9 on page 929), then click OK.

The selections you make in the Options window *aren't* saved until the next time you print.

6 Click OK to close the window.

7 Click OK to print.

Select the template you want to use.

Choose what events to print (you can print a range of days that is not currently displayed).

Select this only if you want to print a single selected event or task; if nothing is currently selected, nothing will be printed.

Select this option to print the view as a StarWriter file; it will be opened in StarOffice after you click OK in the print window.

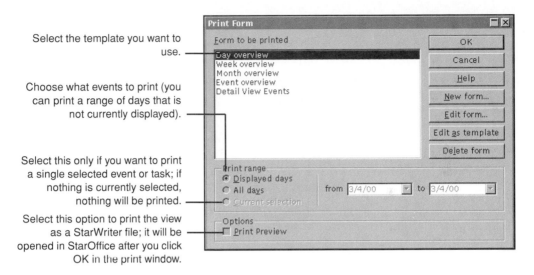

Figure 30-9   Choosing additional printing options

StarOffice
Mail and
Address Book

Setting Up Mail
and News

Quick Start

This section contains the following information to help you get started quickly:

- A checklist that points you to common tasks for quick reference
- Starting Mail and Address book
- The Email & News and Address Book work areas

See 3, *Taming the StarOffice Environment*, on page 91 for general tips that can make working with StarOffice a lot easier.

Quick Start Checklist

To get up and running quickly with Mail and Address book, the following sections should be particularly helpful:

- Connecting StarOffice Mail to your Email account(s) – *Creating an Outbox* on page 942 and *Setting Up Mail and News Accounts* on page 943
- Reading Email – *Viewing and Managing Incoming Mail* on page 952
- Creating Email – *Creating and Sending Email* on page 959
- Importing and adding Email addresses – *Importing Contacts* on page 973 and *Adding Contacts to Address Book* on page 978

Starting Email and News

The way you start Email & News depends on whether you want to read Email and newsgroup mail or create Email and newsgroup mail.

Reading Email and Newsgroup Mail

In order to read Email and newsgroup mail, you must connect StarOffice up to the Email and newsgroup servers. See *Setting Up Mail and News* on page 940. Once Mail is set up:

1   Log on to your internet service provider (ISP).

2   In the StarOffice Explorer window, select the slider (probably E-mail & News) containing your Email accounts.

3   Double-click the inbox for your Email or News account.

If your password isn't included with your account information, you'll be prompted to enter it. A list of your Email messages is displayed in the workspace.

Creating Email and Newsgroup Mail

You can start creating an Email or newsgroup message in a number of ways:

- Click the Start button and choose Mail.

- Choose File > New > Mail.

- In the Explorer window, right-click the inbox of your Email account and choose New > Message.

- With your inbox open in the workspace, click the New Mail icon in the object bar.

- From the Click & Go slider in the Explorer window (double-clicking the Mail shortcut).

- With a task bar shortcut. (See *Adding Shortcuts to the Task Bar* on page 123.)

Starting Address Book

There are a few ways to launch Address Book:

- Choose Edit > Address Book. Address Book opens in a graphical window.

- In the Explorer window, expand the Address Book database, expand the Tables item, and double-click the address table. The Address Book opens as a database in the workspace.

- If you're creating an Email, click the Show Address Book icon in the object bar.

The Mail and News Work Area

Use tooltips to get to know Mail and News. There are tooltips for almost all StarOffice fields and icons. Just position your mouse over anything you want to know the name of. You can turn tooltips on and off by choosing Help > Tips.

Clicking the Help button in a window or pressing F1 is the quickest way to get help for that window. If only general help appears, click in a field in the window.

Figure 31-1 and Figure 31-2 show the major components of the Mail/News environment.

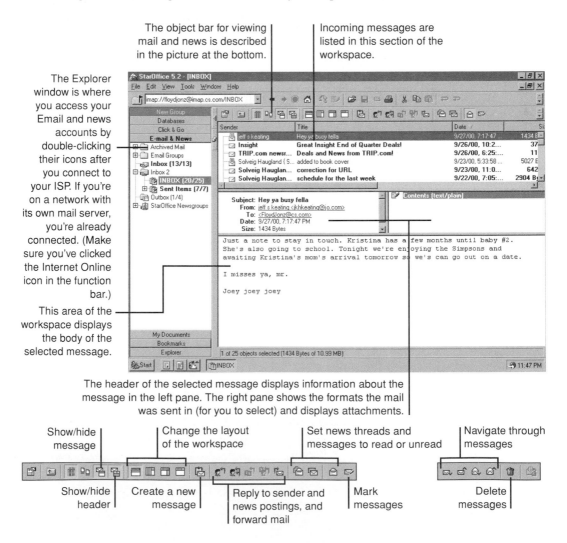

Figure 31-1   The environment for incoming mail and viewing newsgroups

The object bar lets you access the address book, send the message, add an attachment, and add an Email signature. When the cursor is in the body of the message, the object bar changes to show text formatting options.

When composing an Email, you can save, send, and print the message from the function bar.

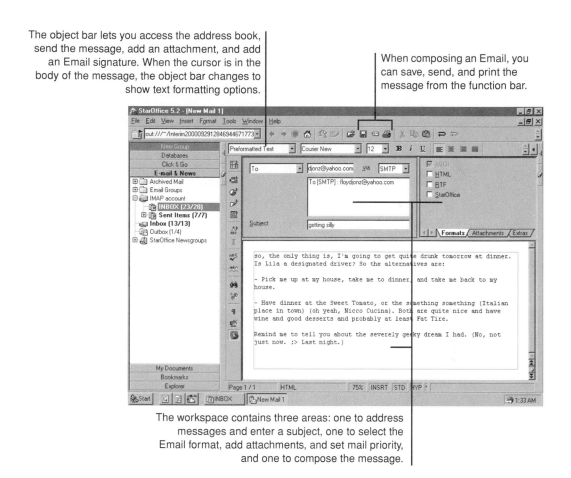

The workspace contains three areas: one to address messages and enter a subject, one to select the Email format, add attachments, and set mail priority, and one to compose the message.

Figure 31-2   The environment for composing an Email

The Address Book Work Area

You can work with the Address Book in a few different ways. Figure 31-3 shows Address Book in database view. If you view Address Book in the Beamer window, it is also displayed in database view. Figure 31-4 shows the Address Book in a more user-friendly window.

For an overview of Address Book, see *About Address Book* on page 972.

Clicking the Help button in a window or pressing F1 is the quickest way to get help for that window. If only general help appears, click in a field in the window.

The object bar lets you find, sort, and filter address information. When you double-click the address table, the Address Book opens as a database table, as shown here. You can create, modify, delete, search, sort, and filter data. The Explorer window must be set to hierarchical view for this to work (right-click the slider and choose Hierarchical).

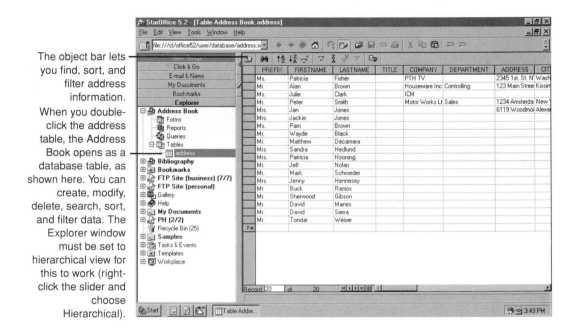

Figure 31-3   Address Book in database table view

The Address Book also lets you create, modify, delete, and search for data using the standard Address Book interface. You can also create Email and surf to a Web address for the selected contact. Choose Edit > Address Book.

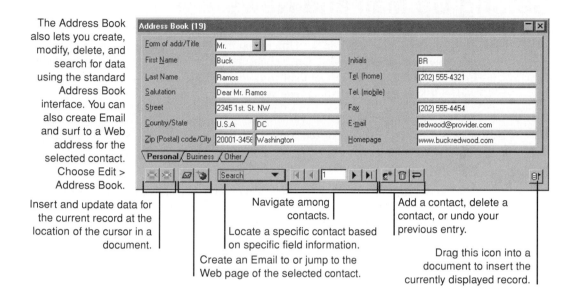

Insert and update data for the current record at the location of the cursor in a document.

Navigate among contacts.

Locate a specific contact based on specific field information.

Create an Email to or jump to the Web page of the selected contact.

Add a contact, delete a contact, or undo your previous entry.

Drag this icon into a document to insert the currently displayed record.

Figure 31-4   Address book as a more user-friendly window

How Mail and Address Book Work Together

Mail and Address Book are partners. Mail knows about the Email addresses stored in Address Book, and automatically enters an Email address when you start typing the last name or Email address of the recipient. Also, you can add the Email address of someone you received an Email from to the Address Book with a couple of clicks.

Address Book also lets you address an Email with multiple addresses using drag and drop, and you can set up an Email merge in Mail using Address Book.

Address Book is set up automatically when you install StarOffice. It's just up to you to enter the addresses you want. You can find the Address Book database in the Explorer window, under the Explorer beamer, or by choosing Edit > Address Book. For more information on using Address book, see 33, *Using Address Book*, on page 971.

While Address Book is set up automatically on installation, your Email accounts aren't. You have to set them up yourself in the Explorer window, and the most logical place to do that is under the E-mail & News slider. This chapter shows you how to set these Email accounts up. This chapter also shows you how to set up connections to the newsgroups you want to join.

Setting Up Mail and News

To send and receive Email in StarOffice, you must be connected to a network or to your ISP (Internet service provider). Once connected, your Email setup allows you to view your Email in StarOffice itself rather than with your network or ISP software. All you need to do is tell StarOffice where to retrieve your mail.

Another key to connecting with your network mail server or ISP is that you must be in online mode. Click the Internet Online icon on the function bar.

You can set up multiple Email and newsgroup accounts, each connected to a different internet service provider mail system. This is advantageous if you have multiple Email accounts but you don't want to have to log into each one individually to get your mail. You can access them all right from within StarOffice.

The Alphabet Soup of Protocols As you set up and modify Email and newsgroups, you'll run into a lot of acronyms for protocols that are used for sending and receiving. Following are brief explanations of each.

* POP3 (Post Office Protocol, version 3) – Email protocol used by your computer to get Email from the ISP mail server.

* SMTP (Simple Mail Transfer Protocol) – Email protocol used by your modem or ISDN (Integrated Services Digital Network) to communicate with the ISP to send and receive Email.

* IMAP (Internet Message Access Protocol) – Email protocol that was developed as an improvement to the POP3 protocol. IMAP, in essence, offers more functionality and lets you manage mail on the server rather than on your computer.

* VIM (Vendor-Independent Messaging) – A set of programming tools (an API, or Application Program Interface) that helps integrate Email functions. Use VIM if you use cc:Mail or Lotus Notes for Email.

* NNTP (Network News Transfer Protocol) – A protocol that is to using newsgroups what SMTP is to using Email.

ISPs That May Not Work in StarOffice A handful of other ISPs may either use their own mail protocols or not support the IMAP4 protocol used by StarOffice, which means you won't be able to set up POP/IMAP accounts for them in StarOffice.

These ISPs include AOL, AT&T Worldnet, Compuserve, Juno, Microsoft Network, Netcom, Prodigy, Sprint Mail, WebTV. If you do use one of these ISPs, double-check with them to be sure.

You may also not be able to access outside Email accounts if you're working inside a network firewall.

Hierarchical View When you work with Email and newsgroups, there can be a lot of subfolders involved. This means you should set the E-mail & News slider (or whichever slider you're going to use for Email and newsgroups) to hierarchical view. Do this by right-clicking the E-mail & News slider and choosing Hierarchical.

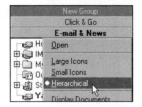

Setting Mail and News Options

The first thing you must do before setting up Email or newsgroup accounts is to tell StarOffice who you are and what your Email address is.

1 Choose Tools > Options > General > User Data.

2 Type a First Name/Last Name in this window (if you haven't already).

This is the name that will be used when you create your Outbox, which will be the name displayed in the mail recipients' inboxes for mail received from you.

3 Type your Email address in the lower right field of the window.

StarOffice requires that you enter an Email address if you are going to use StarOffice for mail.

4 In the Options window, choose Internet > Mail/News.

5 Set any default mail or news options in this window. Use Figure 31-5 for guidance.

These options aren't mandatory. They are used as default settings. For example, when you create a new Email or news account, any server, user name, and password you type in this window is used in the new account automatically.

6 Click OK.

If you want the Emails you send to be in a format
other than ASCII, select the format here. See
Creating Mail in Different Formats on page 963.

You can type
the default
servers you
want to use
and type a
default user
name and
password. For
more
information,
see *Setting
Up Mail and
News
Accounts* on
page 943.

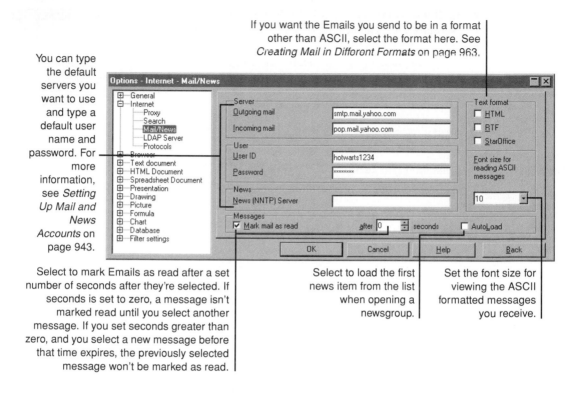

Select to mark Emails as read after a set
number of seconds after they're selected. If
seconds is set to zero, a message isn't
marked read until you select another
message. If you set seconds greater than
zero, and you select a new message before
that time expires, the previously selected
message won't be marked as read.

Select to load the first
news item from the list
when opening a
newsgroup.

Set the font size for
viewing the ASCII
formatted messages
you receive.

Figure 31-5   Setting default mail and news options

Creating an Outbox

The first thing you have to do before you set up your actual Email and News accounts is to
set up an Outbox. You can't use Email or News without one.

1   In the Explorer window, select the E-Mail & News slider.

2   In an empty area of the E-Mail & News group, right-click and choose New > Outbox.

3   In the Properties of Outbox window, type a name for the outbox in the General tab
(such as "Outbox").

4   In the SMTP tab, type the name of your email server, such as
`smtp.mail.yahoo.com`.

5   If you've already filled in your Email address in Tools > Options > General > User
Data, the Sender field in the Properties of Outbox window is filled in for you.

If the Sender field is empty, type your name, followed by a space, followed by your
email address in angled brackets. For example:

```
Floyd Jones <floydjonz@yahoo.com>
```

If you need to use the VIM protocol (cc:Mail or Lotus Notes), set the appropriate options in that tab.

6   **Optional** In the NNTP tab, type the name of your newsgroup server (such as `starnews.sun.com`), enter user name and password if your newsgroup requires them, and make sure the Sender field is filled in, as in the previous step.

7   Click OK.

The outbox is added to the Explorer window.

Changing Who You Are

If you want to change the name that is used for you on Emails you send, change that name in the properties of the Outbox (which you'll create in later procedures). To do this, right-click the Outbox in the Explorer window, choose Properties, and on the SMTP tab, change the Sender name (but leave the Email address alone).

You may also have to change the Sender name in your Inbox properties. Right-click the Inbox in the Explorer window, choose Properties, and select the Send tab. In the Private section of the window, if the As outbox settings option is selected, you don't have to change the Sender name. However, if the User-defined settings option is selected, click the User-defined Settings button and change the Sender name in the window that appears. See Figure 31-7 on page 947.

Keep in mind the ethical responsibilities involved with altering your name. Most companies will fire you on the spot for Emailing under a name that's not yours.

Setting Up Mail and News Accounts

Before you set up an Email account in StarOffice, you have to know a couple of things:

*   Your user name (your Email address before the @ symbol) and password

    For example, for the Email address floydjonz@yahoo.com, the user name is floydjonz.

*   The POP or IMAP servers for incoming mail (or VIM Post Office path for cc:Mail or Lotus Notes)

*   The SMTP server for outgoing mail

For example, the POP server name for Yahoo is `pop.mail.yahoo.com`, and the SMTP server is `smtp.mail.yahoo.com`.

Check with your ISP for its server names. You can often go to their Web sites and look in the support area for this information. See page 940 for a list of ISPs that may not work with StarOffice. If an ISP uses IMAP, it must support IMAP4 or IMAP4rev1.

Using AutoPilot to Set Up Email and News Accounts

The StarOffice AutoPilot has a tool that leads you through setting up POP and IMAP Email accounts and newsgroup accounts. If you have existing Email and newsgroup settings in Netscape, the AutoPilot can automatically use those when setting up an account. If you want to set up a VIM account (cc:Mail or Lotus Notes), see *Setting Up Email Accounts Manually* on page 945.

If this is your first time setting up an account, this process automatically creates an outbox, which StarOffice requires. See also *Creating an Outbox* on page 942.

1   Choose File > AutoPilot > Internet Setup.

2   In the first AutoPilot window, click Next.

   The settings in this window don't apply to this procedure.

3   In the next window, select the Apply single settings / manual selection option, and click Next.

4   In the next window, select the Do not apply browser settings, and click Next.

5   In the next window, you can select whether you want to import your Netscape Email settings (which include the Email server and user name).

   If you want to import your existing Netscape Email settings, select that option, select Netscape in the list, and click Next. Skip to step 7.

   If you're not importing existing Netscape settings, select the Manual e-mail settings option and click Next.

6   In the next window (Figure 31-6), select whether the Email account is a POP or IMAP account, type the name of the account (this will be displayed under the E-mail & News slider once you've completed the setup), type the server names for incoming and outgoing mail, and type your user name and password. Click Next.

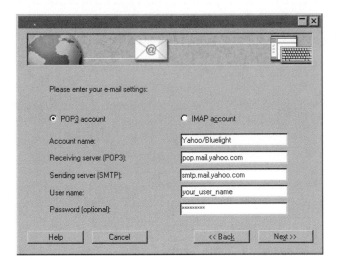

Figure 31-6   Setting up an Email account with AutoPilot

7   In the next window, you can select whether you want to import your Netscape newsgroup settings (which include the newsgroup server and user name).

In the next window, you can select whether you want to import your Netscape newsgroup settings (which include the newsgroup server and user name).

If you want to import your existing Netscape newsgroup settings, select that option, select Netscape in the list, and click Next. Skip to step 9.

If you're not importing existing Netscape settings, select the Manual news settings option and click Next.

8   In the next window, type an account name (this will be displayed under the E-mail & News slider), type in the news server name, and click Next.

For more information on identifying news server names, see *Setting Up Newsgroup Accounts Manually* on page 948.

9   In the next window, click Next to apply all your settings.

AutoPilot adds your new accounts to the Explorer window under the E-mail & News slider.

10   In the last window, click OK.

Setting Up Email Accounts Manually

If you don't want to use AutoPilot to set up Email accounts, or if you need to set up a VIM account (for cc:Mail or Lotus Notes), you can do so manually. In some ways, manually setting up accounts is easier than using AutoPilot, because you don't have to wade through Internet setup options.

1   In the Explorer window, select the E-mail & News slider.

2   Right-click in the explorer window, and choose New > (IMAP Account, POP3 Account, or VIM Account).

3   Enter the appropriate information in the Receive, Send, and General tabs. Use Figure 31-7 for guidance.

4   Click OK.

If you haven't already set up an outbox, StarOffice prompts you to set one up. See *Creating an Outbox* on page 942 for more information.

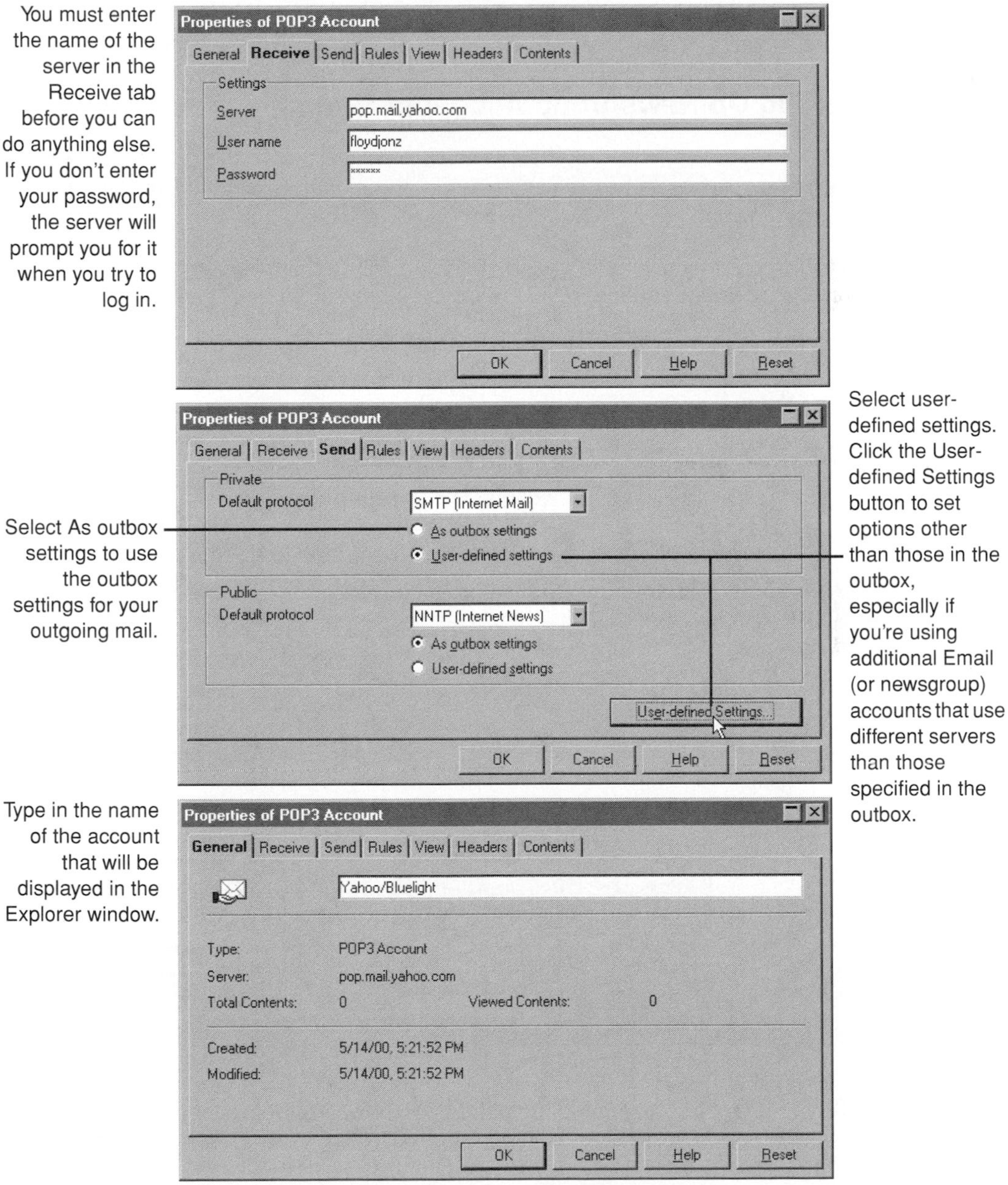

You must enter the name of the server in the Receive tab before you can do anything else. If you don't enter your password, the server will prompt you for it when you try to log in.

Properties of POP3 Account

General   **Receive** | Send | Rules | View | Headers | Contents |

Settings
Server   pop.mail.yahoo.com
User name   floydjonz
Password   ******

OK   Cancel   Help   Reset

Properties of POP3 Account

General | Receive | **Send** | Rules | View | Headers | Contents |

Private
Default protocol   SMTP (Internet Mail)
○ As outbox settings
● User-defined settings

Public
Default protocol   NNTP (Internet News)
● As outbox settings
○ User-defined settings

User-defined Settings...

OK   Cancel   Help   Reset

Select As outbox settings to use the outbox settings for your outgoing mail.

Select user-defined settings. Click the User-defined Settings button to set options other than those in the outbox, especially if you're using additional Email (or newsgroup) accounts that use different servers than those specified in the outbox.

Type in the name of the account that will be displayed in the Explorer window.

Properties of POP3 Account

General | Receive | Send | Rules | View | Headers | Contents |

Yahoo/Bluelight

Type: POP3 Account
Server: pop.mail.yahoo.com
Total Contents: 0   Viewed Contents: 0

Created: 5/14/00, 5:21:52 PM
Modified: 5/14/00, 5:21:52 PM

OK   Cancel   Help   Reset

Figure 31-7   Manually setting up an Email account

Set up only one outbox for all your Email accounts. When you add new Email accounts, be sure to set the server information specific to those accounts by using the User-defined option and button on the Send tab, as shown in Figure 31-7.

Setting Up Newsgroup Accounts Manually

If you don't want to use AutoPilot to set up newsgroup accounts, you can do so manually. In some ways, manually setting up newsgroup accounts is easier than using AutoPilot, because you don't have to wade through Internet setup options.

Before you set up a newsgroup, you need to know how to decode a newsgroup address to identify the server and the address of the newsgroup itself.

Oftentimes a newsgroup server will contain multiple newsgroups. For example, Sun Microsystems hosts a number of StarOffice newsgroups in a single location. Here are a few of them:

```
news://starnews.sun.com/staroffice.com.chat
```

```
news://starnews.sun.com/staroffice.com.feature
```

```
news://starnews.sun.com/staroffice.com.support.install.linux
```

Figure 31-8 shows how you'd use one of these addresses to set up a newsgroup in StarOffice.

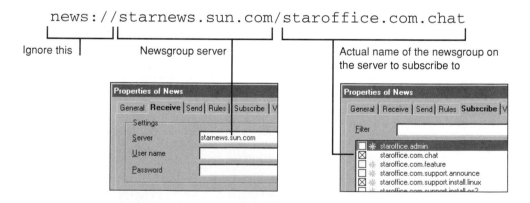

Figure 31-8   Deciphering a newsgroup address

1   In the Explorer window, select the E-mail & News slider.

2   Right-click in the explorer window, and choose New > News.

3   Set up the Send, Receive, and General tabs. Use Figure 31-7 for guidance.

4   Click OK. StarOffice adds the news account to the Explorer window.

5   Log on to your ISP.

6 Double-click the news account icon in the Explorer window. This logs you on to the newsgroup.

7 Right-click the news account icon, and choose Properties.

8 In the Subscribe tab, select the newsgroups you want to participate in. Use Figure 31-9 for guidance.

9 Click OK.

The newsgroups are displayed individually below the newsgroup account name.

To access a newsgroup, double-click it in the Explorer window.

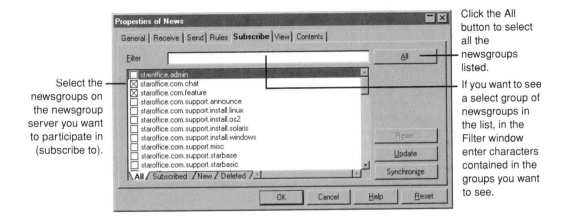

Figure 31-9 Subscribing to newsgroups

StarOffice Newsgroups Set up a newsgroup account and point it to the server `starnews.sun.com`. In the Subscribe tab (Figure 31-9) you'll see the list of all the newsgroups you can subscribe to.

Using Mail

Logging On

The previous chapter shows you how to create Email and news accounts so you can use StarOffice as your Email and newsgroup software. Once these accounts are set up, you're ready to log on.

1   Log on to your ISP.

If you're on a network that has its own mail server, you're already logged on. Just make sure you're in online mode by clicking the Internet Online icon in the function bar.

2   In the Explorer window, double-click the Email or newsgroup account icon.

You can also right-click the icon and choose Synchronize.

The contents of the account's inbox or newsgroup is displayed in the StarOffice workspace.

Viewing and Managing Incoming Mail

Once connected to your ISP (unless you're already connected on a network to your mail server), viewing mail is just a matter of double-clicking the mail account icon in the Explorer window and selecting the messages you want to read.

That said, there are many aspects to viewing and managing mail that are covered in this section:

- Checking for new mail automatically
- Determining whether you want to download incoming mail to your workstation for offline reading or if you want to view incoming mail directly on the mail server
- Setting up folders for storing Email.

This section covers these and other procedures.

Cruising Through Mail Quickly

If you want to get through your Email quickly, use the up and down arrow keys to move from message to message. To delete a message, press Delete and Enter in quick succession. This minimizes the annoyance of the Delete confirmation window popping up every time you want to delete a message.

To reply to Email messages quickly, select the message you want to reply to and press Ctrl+R.

Checking for New Mail

You can check for new mail or news to update your inbox manually or automatically.

Checking for New Mail Manually

To check for new mail or news manually, right-click the mail or news account icon in the Explorer window and choose Update.

Checking for New Mail Automatically

You can have StarOffice check for new mail automatically.

1   Right-click the mail or news account icon and choose Properties.

2   In the Contents tab of the Properties window, select the Include in Update function option.

3   Set the time interval for StarOffice to check for new mail.

4   Click OK.

When new mail arrives, the globe next to the clock in the task bar will blink.

If you're working offline and you keep getting error messages saying StarOffice can't connect to the Email account, it's because the Include in Update function option is selected. To prevent the error messages from appearing, deselect this option.

Replying to, Forwarding, and Deleting Email

Replying and forwarding Email is straightforward in Mail. Select the message and click the appropriate icon in the object bar (see Figure 31-1 on page 936). Then compose the message and click the Send icon on the object bar.

Deleting a message is also straightforward. Select the message(s) you want to delete, press the Delete key or click the Delete icon in the object bar, and respond to the confirmation window. What happens to a message after it's deleted isn't as straightforward, as the next procedure shows.

Deleting Email from the Mail Server

This procedure works only for POP3 mail accounts. IMAP accounts don't let you delete mail from the Email server.

When you delete Email from StarOffice, you may find that when you use your other Email application to view mail, the messages you thought you deleted are still showing up. StarOffice doesn't automatically delete the Email from the mail server. You have to specifically set StarOffice up to do this.

1   Right-click the Email account icon in the Explorer window, and choose Properties.

2   In the Contents tab of the Properties window, select the Remove messages from server option.

Note – Selecting this option automatically selects the Save document contents locally option in the same window. Be sure to deselect that option if you don't want to download your Email to your workstation.

---

3   Click OK.

Deleted messages are sent to the StarOffice Recycle Bin, unless you've set the Recycle Bin to not keep deleted items (in which case, the messages are deleted from your system). In order for the deleted messages to be deleted from the server, you must delete the messages from the Recycle Bin, then right-click the Email account icon and choose Update. See *Using the StarOffice Recycle Bin* on page 110.

Retrieving Deleted Mail

Deleted mail messages are sent to the StarOffice Recycle Bin (unless your Recycle Bin properties are set to not store deleted items). You can retrieve deleted messages by opening the Recycle Bin, right-clicking the message(s) you want back, and choosing Restore. The messages are sent back to the inbox.

Filing Email Messages

Very few people like, or can even handle, keeping all their mail in their inbox. Not only is it mentally healthful to save and organize your Email into different categories, but it can prevent you from losing messages, especially if your ISP automatically deletes read messages after a certain amount of time.

You can create folders and subfolders in the Explorer window to store and organize your Email. If you're using an IMAP account that has folders already set up, you can store Email in those folders.

To create your own folders in the Explorer window:

1   Right-click in the Explorer window (preferably in the E-mail & News slider), and choose New > Folder.

2   In the window that appears, type the name of the new folder and click OK.

Instead of creating a new set of folders, you can set up a link to an existing set of folders. To do this, right-click in the Explorer window, choose New > Link, and click the Directory button to select the directory you want to display in the E-mail & News area.

3   If you want to create a subfolder, select the folder you created, right-click, and repeat this procedure.

4   To move an Email message to a folder, drag it from the inbox into the appropriate folder.

Email moved to a folder this way is moved from the mail server to your workstation.

To read a saved Email, open the folder it's in and double-click the message.

Setting Mail Status

Depending on your Mark mail as read setting in Tools > Options > Internet > Mail/News (Figure 31-5 on page 942), StarOffice marks a mail or news message as read when you select it. The two most obvious ways you can tell if a mail message has been read are: if the icon to the left of the message shows a little envelope with a piece of paper sticking out of it, and a read message changes from bold to regular type.

Marking Messages Read or Unread

It's important to know if messages are read or unread, because ISPs often store messages you've read in an Old Mail folder, which is automatically emptied periodically by the ISP's mail server. By changing Emails from read to unread, you can prevent messages from being deleted by the mail server.

The best way to prevent Emails from being deleted is to file messages you want to keep. See *Filing Email Messages* on page 954.

To mark a read message as unread:

1   Select the read message(s) and click the Message Read/Unread icon on the object bar.

2   Right-click the Email account icon, and choose Update.

     Read messages that were marked as Old Mail on the server are restored to New Mail.

Marking Messages to Prevent Deletion

You can also literally mark a message by selecting it, right-clicking, and choosing Marked. This puts a little orange flag on the message icon. When you mark a message, it prevents it from being deleted from your StarOffice inbox if the message is deleted from the server outside of StarOffice.

Opening and Saving Attachments

When you receive an Email with file attachments, those attachments are displayed in the right pane of the header window when you select the Email message, as shown in Figure 32-1.

You can open an attachment (assuming it's in a file format that your system recognizes) by double-clicking it in the header window, or by dragging it onto an open area of the task bar. If you open it by double-clicking, the file replaces the Email message in the workspace. To return to the Email message, click another Email message, then click the original Email message again.

You can save an attachment by dragging it into a folder in the Explorer window, or by right-clicking and choosing Save As.

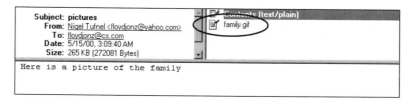

Figure 32-1   Email attachments

Changing What's Shown and Not Shown

You can modify how things are shown in the work area, and even whether or not they are shown. For example, you can sort Emails and rearrange columns, or you can add to or remove columns. You can also show specific fields in the header.

Sorting Messages

You can sort Email messages by the column information by clicking the appropriate column heading. Click again to switch between ascending and descending order for a column.

Showing Only Unread, Read, or Marked Messages

You don't have to see all messages in your inbox. You can show only messages that are unread, read, marked, or both marked and unread.

To do this, right-click the account icon and choose Show > (Unread, Read, Marked, or Marked or Unread). You can also right-click and choose Properties, and select an option on the View tab.

Rearranging Columns

You can rearrange Email columns in the workspace by clicking and dragging a column to a new location.

Adding and Removing Columns

You can add a column to the workspace by right-clicking a column and choosing Insert > (name of the column you want).

To delete a column, right-click it and choose Remove.

Showing Specific Header Information

You can determine the fields that are displayed in the Email header.

1   Right-click the account icon in the Explorer window, and choose Properties.

2   In the Headers tab of the Properties window, select the Selection tab below the list of headers to display all the possible header fields.

3   Select the header fields you want to be displayed in the header, and deselect the ones you don't want to be displayed, as shown in Figure 32-2.

4   Click OK.

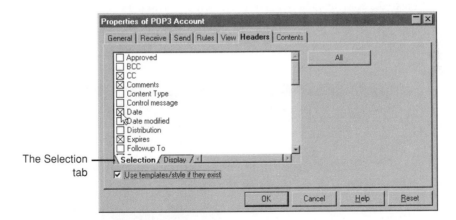

Figure 32-2   Selecting header fields to be displayed

Hiding the Header or Message

If you need to free up some screen space for viewing Emails, you can hide the entire header, the message window, or both by clicking the Message and Headers icons in the object bar (see Figure 31-1 on page 936).

Changing Fonts for Viewing Mail

StarOffice lets you change the default font size of the messages you receive in ASCII format. It also lets you customize the font used in the header window.

Changing the Font Size of Incoming ASCII Messages

1 Choose Tools > Options > Internet > Mail/News.

2 In the Font size for reading ASCII messages field, set the font size you want.

3 Click OK.

Customizing the Header Font

Though you can't do too much to change the look of your Email headers, you can change the font and make the contents bold.

1 Right-click the account icon in the Explorer window, and choose Properties.

2 In the Headers tab of the Properties window, select the Display tab below the list of headers.

3 Set the font properties.

Click the Default button to revert to the default font.

4 To make the contents of a field bold, right-click a field name and choose Highlight, as shown in Figure 32-3.

5 Click OK.

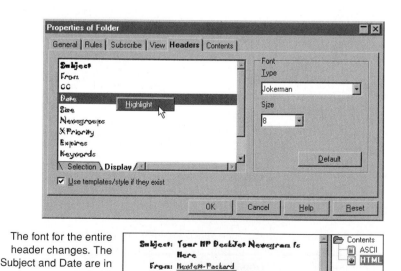

The font for the entire header changes. The Subject and Date are in bold.

Figure 32-3   Changing the font on header fields

Viewing Email Offline

If you don't want to stay logged on to your ISP to read your Email, you can set StarOffice to download your Email from the mail server to your hard drive or home directory, where you can read your Email offline.

Depending on the number and size of Emails you have, and your connection speed, the download process could take a while.

1   Right-click the account icon in the Explorer window, and choose Properties.

2   In the Contents tab of the properties window, select the Save document contents locally option.

3   Click OK.

Note – If you also select the Remove from server option on the Contents tab, the mail is deleted from the server when it moves to your hard drive or home directory.

Creating and Sending Email

Creating and sending an Email can be as simple or involved as you want. The basic mechanics are starting an Email authoring session, entering a recipient's address, typing a message, and clicking Send.

StarOffice lets you go beyond the basics by letting you set up a group containing multiple Email addresses, adding attachments, and creating Email in different formats.

Creating a New Email

You can create a new Email in a few ways:

*   Choose Start > Mail.

*   Choose File > New > Mail.

*   In the Explorer window, right-click the inbox of your Email account and choose New > Message.

*   With your inbox open in the workspace, click the New Mail icon in the object bar.

*   From the Click & Go slider in the Explorer window (double-clicking the Mail shortcut).

*   With a task bar shortcut. (See *Adding Shortcuts to the Task Bar* on page 123.)

Addressing Emails

After you create a new Email (see the previous procedure, Creating a New Email), StarOffice makes the simple task of addressing Emails even simpler with a few useful tools.

Figure 32-4 shows the fields you use to enter Email addresses.

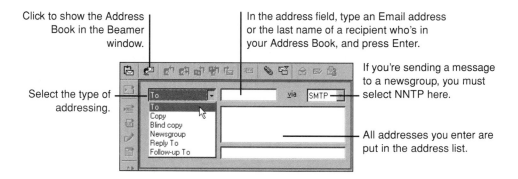

Click to show the Address Book in the Beamer window.

In the address field, type an Email address or the last name of a recipient who's in your Address Book, and press Enter.

Select the type of addressing.

If you're sending a message to a newsgroup, you must select NNTP here.

All addresses you enter are put in the address list.

Figure 32-4   The address fields for addressing an Email

Mail and Address Book work closely together (see *How Mail and Address Book Work Together* on page 939). As you type an Email address in the address field, and the Address Book finds a match, StarOffice fills in the rest of the address automatically. If there are similar addresses in address book, keep typing until the correct address is found.

You can also begin typing a last name of someone in the Address book. If there is a first name entered in Address Book as well, StarOffice detects the corresponding Email address and automatically fills it in.

After you enter an address, press Enter to move the address into the address list. As an alternative, you can enter multiple addresses in the address field, separated by a comma, to automatically put the addresses in the address list.

You can also click the Show Address Book icon in the object bar to display the Address Book in the Beamer window. From there you can select the contacts you want and drag them into the address list.

If you have an Email group set up, you can drag the name of the group from the Explorer window into the address list, and all the Email addresses for the group are inserted in the list.

If you're working on a network, you may notice that StarOffice recognizes Email addresses that aren't stored in your Address Book. This probably means StarOffice is reading user information on your organization's LDAP server. See *User Information Stored on a Network (LDAP Server)* on page 979 for more information. (However, this functionality seems to be hit and miss. So if you point to an LDAP server from StarOffice and you *don't* get Email address recognition, you may need to populate your Address Book to get it.)

Setting Up Email Groups and Aliases

An Email group is a single item in the Explorer window that contains multiple Email addresses. Email groups are an excellent way to both categorize Email addresses and enter multiple addresses for an Email with one step.

If you want to keep your Explorer window as clutter-free as possible, consider creating a folder to store multiple Email groups (by right-clicking in the Explorer window and choosing New > Folder). That way you can expand the folder to display all your groups, and you can collapse the folder so that only one item is displayed in Explorer.

To set up an Email group:

1   In the Explorer window, right-click the folder that will contain the Email group, and choose New > Link.

2   In the Properties of Link window, on the Bookmark tab, type the Name of the Email group.

3   In the Target URL field, type `mailto:` followed by all the Email addresses you want to include in the group, each separated by a comma, as shown in Figure 32-5.

Don't put spaces anywhere in this field.

4   Click OK.

The Email group appears in the Explorer window.

You can edit an Email group by right-clicking its icon in the Explorer window and choosing Properties.

If you double-click a group, a new mail window is launched with addresses of the group already entered. You can also drag a group's icon into the address box of the Email to add the addresses.

Addresses you add to a group are not automatically added to the Address Book.

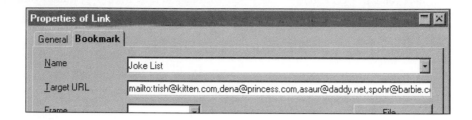

Figure 32-5   Setting up an Email group

Adding Attachments

Attachments are just files you send with your Emails—anything from the latest comic strip, to a music file, to an annual report. The only caveat to sending attachments is that your recipients must have the software to view or play the attachments installed on their systems.

You can add a file attachment to an Email message in a few ways. To add an attachment, the Attachments tab must be selected in the right pane of the header window (see Figure 32-6).

*   Drag a file from Beamer into the Attachments pane.

*   Right-click in the Attachments pane, choose Attach File, and select the file you want to attach.

*   Click anywhere in the address area, and click the Attach File icon in the object bar.

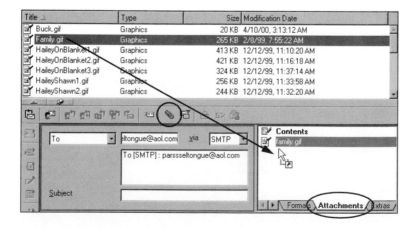

Figure 32-6   Adding an attachment to an Email

Creating Mail in Different Formats

StarOffice lets you create Email in up to four different formats: ASCII, HTML, RTF, and StarOffice. When you create a mail message, select the Formats tab in the area to the right of the address window, and select the formats you want to use for the Email.

Getting to Know the Formats

Following is a brief description of each format. But we advise you to not go crazy using different formats. See The Case for ASCII (Netiquette), next section.

- ASCII – Plain text. All messages are created in at least this format. ASCII text messages are small in terms of the amount of storage space they take up, and in many ways they're the best format to use.

- HTML – Web format. You can add anything to an HTML Email message that you can add to an HTML file for deployment on the Web, such as graphics and animated GIFs. Recipients' Email software must be able to view HTML files. While HTML itself is text-based and takes up relatively little storage space, any graphics you include in the message increases the amount of storage space needed for the Email.

- RTF – Rich Text Format. RTF is a standard format that most word processing software can read. It allows text formatting, but it takes up a relatively large amount of storage space.

- StarOffice – StarOffice Writer format. If your recipients have StarOffice (and only if they have StarOffice), you can create Email with all the formatting, graphics, tables, and other elements that you can in StarOffice Writer, as shown in Figure 32-7. But the more formatting and elements you include, the more storage space is used for the Email.

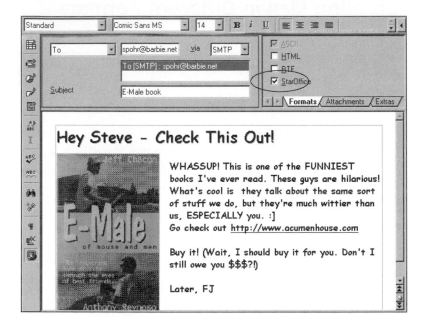

Figure 32-7   Creating an Email message in StarOffice format

You can create a single message in multiple formats, giving your Email recipients the choice of viewing the message however they like. But the more formats you select, the larger the Email is going to be, and the longer it's going to take to send and download.

If you create a formatted mail message but don't select any of the format options, the message will be sent in ASCII only, which will remove all the formatting you set up and turn the message into text only.

You can set the default formats that will be selected each time you start a new mail by choosing Tools > Options > Internet > Mail/News and selecting the formats you want.

The Case for ASCII (Netiquette)

People can get flooded with Email. A lot of people spend entire work days going through their inboxes. For most people, going through Email needs to be a quick process so they can work as efficiently as possible and avoid stress. This is particularly true for people who use newsgroups.

Using ASCII (simple, unformatted text) is the ideal Email format for a number of reasons:

* All Email software can view ASCII. It's a computer standard. If you format an Email with StarOffice formatting, but a recipient isn't using StarOffice, the message you send could be garbled on the recipient's system. At the very least, the recipient

wouldn't be able to see all your wonderful formatting and stellar use of graphics in the message.

• ASCII Emails are much smaller than Emails that contain formatting.

• People are used to reading ASCII text Email. If they see a bunch of inconsistently formatted Email, it takes more time for the brain to adjust to each Email. This works directly against the goal of reading through Emails quickly.

• Even though you can't insert graphics directly in an ASCII Email, you can attach graphics and other files to the message.

• People won't yell at you if you use ASCII, especially if you're in a newsgroup.

Adding a Signature

You can add a predefined signature to the end of your Emails containing whatever text and however number of lines you want. If you're creating Email in HTML or StarOffice formats, you can even include graphics in your signature—such as a scanned image of your real signature.

You're not limited to using just your name in a signature. You can define any amount or type of text. A lot of people also include a closing, such as "Regards", or a favorite quotation.

Your signature is defined as an AutoText entry. StarOffice has four predefined AutoText Email signatures that are used in Mail. You can modify any of these to suit your needs. To modify an AutoText Email signature, see *Creating and Inserting Predefined Text and Templates* on page 167.

This entire block of text is a signature.

1 Click anywhere in the address area of the Email you're creating.

   The object bar displays a row of icons.

2 Click and hold down the Insert Signature icon, and choose the AutoText signature you want to insert.

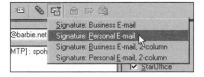

The signature is inserted at the end of the Email.

Sending, Replying to, and Forwarding Email

After you compose an Email, click the Send Message icon in the function bar to send it. If you click in the address area after you compose the message, you can also click the Send Message button in the object bar.

To reply to or forward a message (whether it's an Email message or a newsgroup message), click the appropriate icon on the object bar (see Figure 31-1 on page 936), compose the message, and click the Send Message icon.

Adding Email Addresses to Address Book

When you receive an Email and you want to add the sender's address, or any of the co-recipients' addresses, to the Address Book, right-click the address in the header, and choose Add to Address Book.

To add addresses to the Address Book manually, see *Adding Contacts to Address Book* on page 978.

Saving Emails to Send Later

If you want to stop writing an Email and come back to it later, you can save it.

1   Choose File > Save As.

2   In the Save As window, make sure StarMessage 5.0 is the selected file type.

3   Navigate to the folder in which you want to save the message, and click Save.

The message is saved as an `.sdm` file. You can open this file like you open any other file in StarOffice. When you open the file, StarOffice opens it in the Mail work area, where you can add to it and send it.

Note – When you send a saved Email message, the saved message still remains on your file system. It isn't deleted automatically.

Printing Emails

To print an Email to your default printer, select the message and click the printer icon on the function bar. If you want to select the printer you want to use, choose File > Print (or press Ctrl+P).

Redirecting Mail to the Recycle Bin, Automatic Forwarding, and Other Fun Rules

I once worked at a company who had a really obnoxious salesperson. Every time this person made a sale, even a small one, an Email would go out to the entire company. A lot of people got sick of these frequent Emails and we figured out a way through the Email software to redirect all of this person's mail out into the Great Cyber Void before it hit our inboxes.

Fortunately, this person used the exact same subject, "New Sale", on each Email. So we set a rule in our Email software to delete messages with the subject "New Sale". This worked great for a while, until the salesperson realized what we were doing and changed the subject of the Emails to "Another Sale". All we had to do then was set up another rule that deleted messages with that subject. The salesperson changed the subject of the messages yet again (I told you this person was obnoxious). At that point, instead of setting up another rule for the text in the subject line, we simply set up a rule to delete any messages sent by this person.

This ability to set Email rules is a beautiful thing, and StarOffice maintains this fine tradition of functionality.

There are lots of situations to set up rules in Mail, and there are lots of things you can do with Emails automatically. For example:

- You're working on five projects simultaneously (and who isn't?), and you want to automatically move Email relating to these projects to respective folders on the file system for later viewing.

- You have a friend with a sick sense of humor (and who doesn't?) who constantly sends you Email that is inappropriate for the workplace, even though you've told this friend to stop Emailing you at work. You can set a rule that automatically forwards Email from this friend to your home Email address (where you can later read it and laugh without having to act disgusted).

Here's how you set up rules in Mail:

1   In the Explorer window, right-click the inbox you've set up and choose Properties.

2   In the Properties window, select the Rules tab and set the appropriate rules for the inbox. Figure 32-8 for guidance.

     You may want to use StarOffice wild cards and filter characters (called regular expressions) in the Expression field. The StarOffice help system contains good information on using regular expressions.

3   If you want to add more than one rule, click the Add button after you set up a rule. This adds the rule to the list and lets you set up a new one.

4   When you're finished adding rules, click OK.

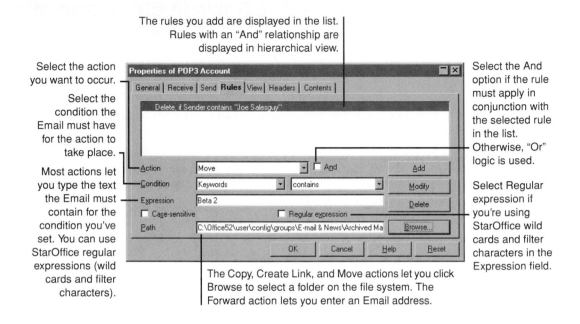

The rules you add are displayed in the list. Rules with an "And" relationship are displayed in hierarchical view.

Select the action you want to occur.

Select the condition the Email must have for the action to take place.

Most actions let you type the text the Email must contain for the condition you've set. You can use StarOffice regular expressions (wild cards and filter characters).

Select the And option if the rule must apply in conjunction with the selected rule in the list. Otherwise, "Or" logic is used.

Select Regular expression if you're using StarOffice wild cards and filter characters in the Expression field.

The Copy, Create Link, and Move actions let you click Browse to select a folder on the file system. The Forward action lets you enter an Email address.

Figure 32-8   Setting rules for an inbox

To modify a rule, select it in the list, make changes, and click the Modify button.

To delete a rule, select it in the list and click the Delete button. Email that is deleted automatically is sent to the StarOffice Recycle Bin (unless the Recycle Bin properties are set to not keep deleted items).

For information on StarOffice regular expressions, see the online help system.

Email Merge for Mass Mailings

You can set up a mail merge in an a Mail document for mass Emailings the same way you do in a Writer document. The only difference is that the mail merge is sent to Email addresses rather than to a printer or a file.

See *Merging to a Document* on page 323.

The Semi-Official Guide to Emoticons

When people communicate with Email, there's something missing. You can't see the reaction on someone's face, read body language, exchange sarcastic glances, or sense any other type of direct human reaction.

So Emailers came up with a brilliant idea to help convey emotions in Emails: emoticons. Emoticons are little pictures, usually faces, made out of characters you can type on the keyboard.

As emoticons have gained in popularity, especially in the workplace, their meanings have become more sophisticated and worthy of even Freudian analysis. The following semi-official guide, shown in Table 32-1, is presented to help shed light upon some of the deeper psychological meanings of some of the more commonly used emoticons.

Table 32-1   Emoticons and their deep psychological meanings

Emoticon	Deep Psychological Meaning
:)	What I just said was mean spirited and cruel, but I want you to feel good about it, m-kay?
: -)	Look! I can do a nose!
;)	I have colon trouble, so I had to use a semicolon.
: < (	I think I smell gas.
: p	See where I bit my tongue?
: [	My gawd, that was sour!
: I	Sorry, I'd tell you more but I can't talk right now. Got a mouth full of leftover date nut bread.
8 |	I don't care what anyone says about my glasses. I think they make me look hot.
> : (	In grade school I was subjected to daily swirlies by the sixth graders, but I let go of that YEARS ago.
:] >	My girlfriend hates goatees, and the one I grow looks pretty bad, so I'll just put 'em in my Emails instead.
: D	I'm way too happy for anyone's good, but I could be mean if I really wanted to; you know, in a nice way. : D
: #	My lips are sealed—literally. HELP! WHO PUT RUBBER CEMENT IN MY LIP BALM?!?!
: - -	I've got to get that rhinoplasty done soon.

chapter 33

Using Address Book

About Address Book

StarOffice comes with a default Address Book for maintaining your personal and business contacts. In essence, the Address Book is a database in dBase format, which means it is composed of specific database fields that contain information for each record, or contact.

You can work with Address Book in different views, as shown in Figure 31-3 on page 938 and Figure 31-4 on page 939. Address Book isn't as sophisticated as other contact management applications. But because it's a database you can make it easier to use by creating different forms and queries that let you work with it in different views. For more information on creating different interfaces for and views of databases, see 34, *Creating and Modifying Databases*, on page 987.

The term *address book* in StarOffice has a slightly more detailed meaning, because you can set any database in StarOffice as the default address book. There are, however, a couple of major drawbacks to using another database as the default address book:

- The Address Book window, shown in Figure 31-4 on page 939, is tied directly to the default address book database. If you assign another database as the default address book, the Address Book window probably won't have the exact fields necessary for working with the new database in the Address Book window.

- If you want to use any other database in conjunction with Email so that StarOffice automatically fills in an Email address when you begin typing the address or last name, first name, the address book must have the following three fields, named exactly as shown:

  FIRSTNAME, LASTNAME, EMAIL

The bottom line is that if you want to be able to edit your address book using Edit > Address Book, and if you want to use your address book in smooth conjunction with StarOffice Mail, don't delete the default address book and replace it with a dBase address book created from another application.

You can tailor StarOffice's default address book to better suit your needs by creating queries to present different combinations of fields, and by creating different forms for entering and maintaining contacts. For example, you could set up a query that displays only the first name, last name, and Email address for easy access to Email information; or you could create a form that lets you modify and view only mailing address information.

See *Creating Forms* on page 1010 and *Creating Queries* on page 1019.

Importing and Exporting Contacts

If you're going to use StarOffice for tasks that involve using contact information, such as addresses for mail merges or Email addresses for sending Email, you may need to bring existing contacts stored in another application into StarOffice.

This section shows you how to import contact information from other places, such as Microsoft Exchange or vCard files, into the StarOffice Address Book. It also shows you how to export Address Book data for use with other applications or as vCards.

About vCards

A vCard is an electronic business card. Some leading producers of hand-held organizers, software, and Web and Email systems agreed on a standard format that could be used so that people on multiple platforms could share business-card-like information. vCard technology has many uses, from allowing people to beam information between hand-held organizers, to filling out online order forms automatically, to importing contact information from an Email attachment into your address book software.

StarOffice supports vCard technology, letting you import or export contact information as vCard files to and from your StarOffice Address Book.

vCard functionality is available in StarOffice only if you installed StarOffice Schedule.

Importing Contacts

If you have contacts stored in another application, like Microsoft Exchange, this section shows you how to get those contacts into the StarOffice Address Book.

There are a couple of ways to import contacts: by converting the contacts you want to import into a dBase file and appending them to the Address Book, or by importing a vCard file directly into the Address Book.

Importing Contact Information From Another Database

You can append an external address database to the StarOffice Address Book.

This involves creating a dBase file out of the database you want to import, giving it the exact same name as the StarOffice address database, setting up a new database in the StarOffice Explorer window, and appending the imported addresses to the StarOffice address table using drag and drop.

1   Create a new folder in the `office52/user/database` folder that will contain the address database you're going to import.

You need to do this, because you're going to give the imported database the exact same name as the StarOffice address database, which means putting it in the same folder would overwrite the existing address database, which you don't want to do.

2   Turn external address database you want to import into a dBase file, and save it to the folder you created in the previous step. Name the file the exact same name as the StarOffice database file you want to append to; for example, *address*.

Refer to the other application's documentation for instructions on doing this. Some applications, such as Microsoft Exchange, let you export your contacts directly to a dBase file (using File > Export).

Other applications may not let you save a database directly to dBase format, so save or export it as a delimited text file and open it in Calc. Once in Calc, you can save the data in dBase format. For more information on this, see *Importing a Text File* on page 568.

3   Add a new dBase database to the Explorer window by right-clicking in the Explorer window and choosing New > Database.

If you need further help, see *Creating Databases* on page 992.

4   Expand (click the + sign next to) both databases in the Explorer window, as shown in Figure 33-1.

5   Expand the Tables item in the new database.

6   Modify the field names in the new table to match exactly the names of the Address Book fields for the data you want to import.

For example, if the table you want to import contains an Email field called EMAILADDR, change that field name to EMAIL to match the Address Book Email field. See *Creating and Modifying Database Tables* on page 999.

See Table 33-1 for the exact names of the Address Book fields.

7   Drag the table (for example, the *address* table) from the new database onto the Table icon of the existing address book.

8   In the Copy Table window, select the Attach data option, as shown in Figure 33-1, and click the Create button.

9   If the table you're importing has fields that don't match exactly with the fields in the Address Book table, a Column Information window displays the names of all fields that weren't imported. Click OK to close the window.

The imported data is added to the existing Address Book data.

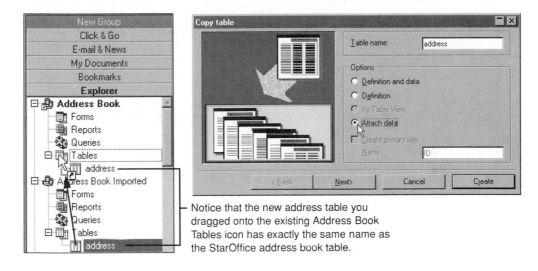

Notice that the new address table you dragged onto the existing Address Book Tables icon has exactly the same name as the StarOffice address book table.

Figure 33-1   Appending addresses to the StarOffice Address Book

After the contacts are appended to the StarOffice Address Book, you can delete the new address database you had set up.

Table 33-1 shows the exact names of the StarOffice Address Book fields, along with their data formats (in parentheses). Use this information to rename the fields in the database you want to import into the StarOffice Address Book. The fields in the table are listed in order, from top to bottom.

Table 33-1   Database fields of the default Address Book

Database Field Name (field format and length)		
PREFIX (Text, 25)	POSITION (Text, 100)	EMAIL (Text, 50)
FIRSTNAME (Text, 50)	INITIALS (Text, 10)	URL (Text, 128)
LASTNAME (Text, 50)	SALUTATION (Text, 50)	NOTE (Memo)
TITLE (Text, 50)	PHONEHOME (Text, 25)	ALTFIELD1 (Text, 100)
COMPANY (Text, 50)	PHONEOFFI (Text, 25)	ALTFIELD2 (Text, 100)
DEPARTMENT (Text, 50)	PHONEOTHE (Text, 25)	ALTFIELD3 (Text, 100)
ADDRESS (Text, 50)	PHONEWORK (Text, 25)	ALTFIELD4 (Text, 100)
CITY (Text, 50)	MOBILE (Text, 25)	ID (Text, 20)
STATEPROV (Text, 50)	PAGER (Text, 25)	CALENDAR (Text, 100)
POSTALCODE (Text, 15)	FAX (Text, 25)	INVITE (Yes/No)
COUNTRY (Text, 50)		

Importing a vCard File

vCard functionality is available in StarOffice only if you installed StarOffice Schedule. You can only import vCard files into the default address book. See *Using Another Table as the Default Address Book* on page 982. If you want to import vCard files into multiple address databases in StarOffice, take turns setting each as the default address book and importing the vCard file(s).

1   In the Explorer window, expand (click the + sign next to) the Address Book database.

2   Under the database, expand the Tables item.

3   Right click the address table, or whichever table you have set to be the default Address Book, and choose Import vCard.

4   In the Import Addresses window, find the location of the vCard file you want to import.

vCard files have a .vcf extension.

5   Select the vCard file you want to import and click Open.

The vCard data is imported into the Address Book. You can check the imported data by double-clicking the table to open it in the workspace.

Exporting Contacts from Address Book

If you need to export your Address Book contacts for use in another application, like Microsoft Exchange, of if you want to create a vCard file for one or more contacts, this section shows you how. The way you export the contacts depends on the format used by the other application.

Exporting dBase Files

If the other application can import dBase files, you can directly import the StarOffice *address* or other dBase file into that application. Microsoft Exchange even lets you map the StarOffice Address Book fields to the correct database fields in Exchange.

If you get an error message trying to directly import the StarOffice address file into an application that can import dBase files, manually save the StarOffice address file as a dBase file. See *Getting a StarOffice Database into Calc* on page 571. Once in Calc, save the database file as a dBase file. Then re-import the file into the other application.

Exporting Delimited Text Files

If the application you want to use your StarOffice contacts in can't import dBase files (or vCard files), you may have to turn your StarOffice address database into a delimited text file for the other application to import.

See *Saving to a Text File* on page 570 for information on saving a StarOffice database as a delimited text file.

Exporting a vCard File

StarOffice only lets you export an entire Address Book table as a vCard file. You can't export individual contacts as vCards, unless you create a table for an individual contact and set it as the default address book.

To create a table for an individual contact, double-click the address database in the Explorer window, select the individual record in the database, drag that record onto the Tables icon of the database, name the table in the Copy Table window, and click the Create button. The new table is displayed in the Explorer window.

vCard functionality is available in StarOffice only if you installed StarOffice Schedule.

1   Make sure the database table you want to create a vCard for is the default address book.

    To be sure, right-click the table in the Explorer window, choose Address Book, and respond to the prompt.

2   Right-click the address book table and choose Export vCard.

3   In the Export Addresses window, name the vCard file and click the Save button.

If you want to export multiple address databases to vCard files, take turns setting each database as the default address book and exporting as vCard files.

Working With Address Book

This section shows you how to add, modify, delete, and search for contacts in your Address Book. It doesn't cover procedures that involve modifying the structure of the Address Book database (which by itself is a no-no), creating queries or forms, or performing any other nasty database procedures. You can find those procedures in 34, *Creating and Modifying Databases*, on page 987, and 35, *Using Databases*, on page 1009.

Adding Contacts to Address Book

You can add contacts to the Address Book in database table view or in the Address Book window.

Adding Contacts in Database Table View

1   In the Explorer window, expand (click the + sign next to) the Address Book database.

2   Expand the Tables item, and double-click the *address* table.

The Address Book database opens in the workspace.

3   In the last empty row of the database, type in information about the new contact, as shown in Figure 33-2.

As you begin typing, a new blank row is inserted at the bottom of the table.

4   When you're finished, choose File > Save current record.

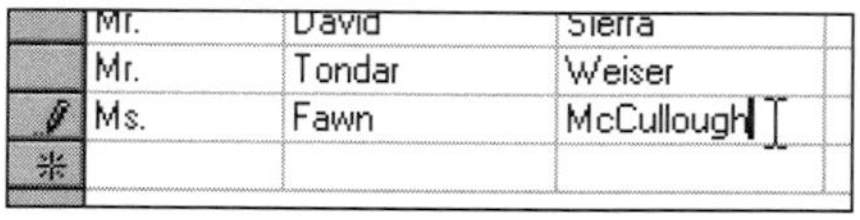

Figure 33-2   Adding a contact to Address Book in database table view

You can also add contacts to the address table by opening the Beamer window (View > Beamer), single-clicking the address table, and entering new contact information in the empty row at the bottom of the table. When you close the Beamer window, StarOffice prompts you to save your work.

Adding Contacts in the Address Book Window

If you like entering contact information in an organized graphical window, use this procedure.

1   Choose Edit > Address Book.

2   In the Address Book window, click the new button at the bottom of the window, as shown in Figure 33-3.

The fields in the Address Book window are emptied.

3   Type in the information for the new contact.

4   When you're finished adding contacts, close the Address Book window.

Figure 33-3   Adding a contact to Address Book in the Address Book window

User Information Stored on a Network (LDAP Server)

If you're working on a network, you may be able to have StarOffice detect contact information such as Email addresses for people in your organization, even though those people aren't stored in your Address Book.

Many organizations use an LDAP (Lightweight Directory Access Protocol) server to store user login, Email, and other information. If your organization uses an LDAP server, you can point StarOffice to it, effectively adding many contacts to your Address Book without actually adding them.

1   Choose Tools > Options > Internet > LDAP Server.

2   Click the New button to add an LDAP server, or select one of the default servers and click the Modify button.

3   Ask your network administrator for the information you need to set up your LDAP server connection.

The connection between LDAP servers and Email addresses in StarOffice is hit and miss. If you point to an LDAP server from StarOffice and Email addresses *don't* get filled in automatically when you begin typing them in a new mail message, you may need to populate your Address Book to get automatic Email recognition.

Editing Address Book

You can modify information about contacts by simply typing over the current information for them in database view or in the Address Book window. See *Adding Contacts to Address Book* on page 978 for information on using Address Book in database view and in the Address Book window.

Deleting Contacts

You can delete contacts from the Address Book in database table view or in the Address Book window.

Deleting Contacts in Database Table View

1   In the Explorer window, expand (click the + sign next to) the Address Book database.

2   Expand the Tables item, and double-click the *address* table.

The Address Book database opens in the workspace.

3   Click the gray square next to the contact you want to delete, as shown in Figure 33-4. The entire row is highlighted.

4   Press the Delete key, and click Yes in the confirmation window.

	Mr.	Tondar	Weiser
	Ms.	Fawn	McCullough
▶	Mr.	Scottie	Bowman
✱			

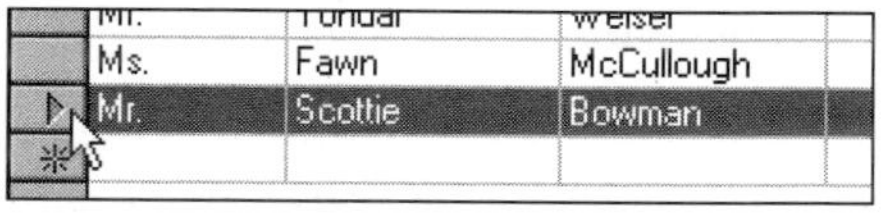

Figure 33-4   Deleting a contact in database table view

Deleting Contacts in the Address Book Window

1   Choose Edit > Address Book.

2   In the Address Book window, view the contact you want to delete.

Either use the navigation buttons at the bottom of the window, or perform a search to find the contact. See *Searching for Contacts in the Address Book* on page 981.

3   Click the delete button at the bottom of the window, as shown in Figure 33-5, and click Yes in the confirmation window.

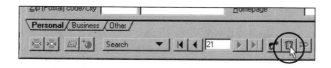

Figure 33-5   Deleting a contact in the Address Book window

Searching for Contacts in the Address Book

Because the StarOffice Address Book is a database, the information stored in it is stored in the order the contacts were entered, not alphabetically. This means if you want to view, modify, or delete a specific contact, you'll have to search for it. You can search for contacts in the Address Book in database table view or in the Address Book window.

Searching for Contacts in Database Table View

To search for contacts in database table view, see *Searching for Specific Records* on page 1030.

You can also sort fields in the table in ascending or descending order. See *Sorting Database Information* on page 1028.

Searching for Contacts in the Address Book Window

1   Choose Edit > Address Book.

2   In the Address Book window, click the Search button at the bottom of the window, and choose Address Book.

If you want to search for contents on your network's LDAP server, choose the name of the LDAP server instead of Address Book. See *User Information Stored on a Network (LDAP Server)* on page 979 for more information.

The fields in the window are cleared, and the Search button is replaced with two buttons called Start and End.

3   In one or more of the empty Address Book fields, type any information, or part of any information, you know the record contains, as shown in Figure 33-6.

For example, if you only know the first few characters of the Email address, type those in the Email field.

If you enter information in more than one field, all that information must apply to the search. So if you typed information in two fields, but the text you typed in the second field was incorrect in some way, StarOffice won't find a match.

4   Click the Start button at the bottom of the window.

If a match is found, the information for the contact is displayed in the window.

5   Click the End button at the bottom of the window.

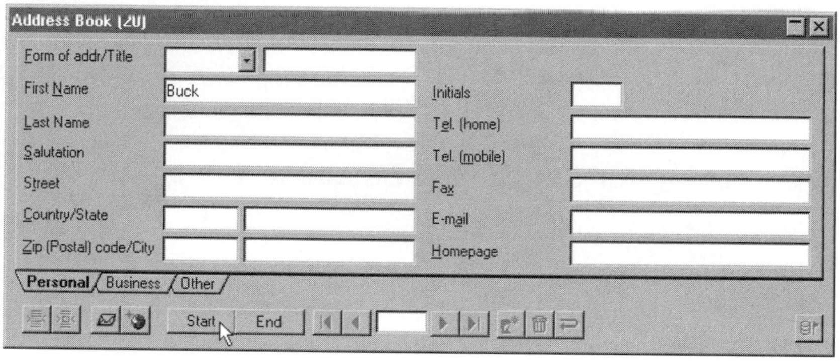

Figure 33-6   Searching for a contact in the Address Book window

Using Another Table as the Default Address Book

You can change the default address book in StarOffice to any other database in StarOffice. However, unless you're doing this for a specific, usually temporary purpose, changing the default address book could be problematic for a number of reasons. For more information on this, see *About Address Book* on page 972.

One good reason to change the default address book is if you want to export a database to a vCard file. Only the default address book can export data to a vCard file.

1   In the Explorer window, expand (click the + sign next to) the database you want to use for the default address book.

2   Right-click the Tables item and choose Address Book and click Yes in the confirmation window.

That database becomes the default address book.

Duplicating the Structure of the Default Address Book

If you want to create more than one address book with the exact same structure as the default address book, use this procedure. Duplicating the default address book structure means you can set a duplicate address book as the default and still be able to use the Address Book window (choosing Edit > Address book) and Mail functions.

1   In the Explorer window, expand (click the + sign next to) the Address Book database.

2   Expand the Tables item.

3   Drag the address table onto the Tables icon.

4   In the Copy Table window, name the new table.

5   Select the Definition option.

If you want to duplicate the data in the existing address book in the new table, rather than just insert an empty table with the same structure, select the Definition and data option.

6   Click the Create button.

The new table is displayed under the Tables item in the Address Book database.

StarOffice

Base

Creating and Modifying Databases

Quick Start

This section contains the following information to help you get started quickly:

- A checklist that points you to common tasks for quick reference
- Starting Base
- An overview of the Base work area

See 3, *Taming the StarOffice Environment*, on page 91 for general tips that can make working with StarOffice a lot easier.

Quick Start Checklist

If you need to connect to or create databases quickly, the following sections should be particularly helpful:

- Connecting to or creating a database – *Creating a Database* on page 996
- Creating forms – *Creating Forms* on page 1010
- Creating queries – *Creating Queries* on page 1019
- Creating reports – *Creating Reports* on page 1024

Starting Base

You don't launch Base like you launch other StarOffice applications. To use Base, you must first create and define the databases you're going to use. After you create a database, you can open it from the Explorer window by double-clicking any available tables, queries, forms, or reports. If the database is empty (dBase or Adabas D), you can add tables to it.

You can also view a database table or query by opening the Beamer window and single-clicking a table or query.

This chapter shows you how to create and begin working with databases.

The group containing the database must be set to hierarchical view, which lets you expand items to show available tables, queries, forms, and reports.

The Base Work Area

A database can have many different appearances, depending on what you're doing with the database. For example, if you're manually defining the fields that make up a new database, the work area is different than if you're simply entering data into a predefined database table. Likewise, if you create a more user-friendly form for entering information in a database, that work area looks different than a database table.

In the next two chapters we'll explore these different database appearances in more detail and explain fundamental database concepts.

Figure 34-1 and Figure 34-2 illustrate the basic difference between the work area for creating a database and the work area for maintaining the information stored in a database.

In Table Design mode, you can define the fields you want to use in your database, such as name, address, phone number, and so on. You can also set each field to contain a specific type of data, such as text, currency, or a yes/no checkbox.

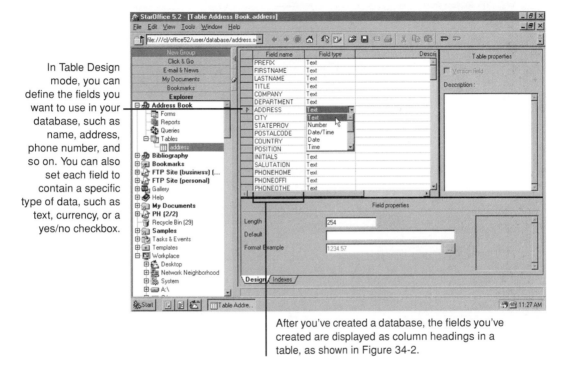

After you've created a database, the fields you've created are displayed as column headings in a table, as shown in Figure 34-2.

Figure 34-1   The Base work area, in table design mode

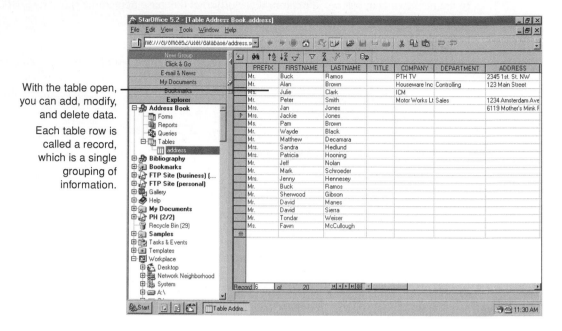

With the table open, you can add, modify, and delete data.

Each table row is called a record, which is a single grouping of information.

Figure 34-2   The Base work area with a table open

The Database Tirade

Normal people—that is, people who use rather than create software—don't mess around with databases. Most arguments for why normal people should create and use databases border on the inane: "You can keep an inventory of your household valuables." "You can keep track of your music collection." "You can run your small business." And worst of all, "It's just good to know how relational databases work."

If you're a regular person, you get a little spooked about that last statement. *Relational* databases. It implies something more than the regular ol' databases you already know next to nothing about, which already sound scary enough.

Open almost any manual on office software and you'll see a section called, "What Is a Relational Database?" But what's missing in each case is the equally important subtitle, "Who Cares?"

So who does care? Programmers, that's who. Software developers. Programmers are not "normal" people (and many programmers themselves would be the first to admit that).

Programmers build software that stores information and retrieves is back from relational databases. Relational databases are the backbone of many software products. The reason the software industry has thrived for so long is precisely the same reason that regular people in their right minds don't want to mess around with databases: Users want simplicity. Look at personal finance software like Quicken. Look at the different types of sales management software out there. Look at StarOffice Address Book.

Users want usable tools to solve their problems. They need to track sales leads. They need to run reports and statistical analyses. They need to keep contact information updated and send mass Emails, faxes, and snail mailings. But users don't want to have to build these complex tools themselves. It's difficult enough for competent programmers to build them.

Do you want to keep track of your household valuables? It's just a list of items and their values. Use a spreadsheet. Want to keep track of your music collection? Don't let people borrow your CDs who won't return them. Want to store addresses for mail merges and Emailing? Use StarOffice Address Book. Do you feel you really need to use a database tool to run your small business? Take a class and get a comprehensive book (after you've searched high and low for user-friendly, cost-effective software alternatives).

Because we don't want to decrease the page count of this book by too much (so the spine is nice and big so people will see it on the shelf), we'll talk a little about databases in the rest of this section on StarOffice Base. But we'll only present the information about databases that is most useful, especially with regard to using the StarOffice Address Book, such as creating forms and queries to help you work with databases in more manageable pieces.

Relational databases, if you haven't already guessed, are not covered in this book.

Database Basics

Say you collect business cards, and you keep them in some kind of a business card organizer (like a shoebox). That shoebox is a database. It contains a bunch of items, each of which has the same type of information on it: name, address, phone number, Email address, and so on. In database terms, each one of those business cards is called a *record*.

If you typed the information on all those business cards into the address book on your computer, it would all be stored in a database. Each card would be stored in a single row, or record, with the database columns, or fields, defining each bit of information, such as name, address, phone number, and Email address, as shown in Figure 34-3.

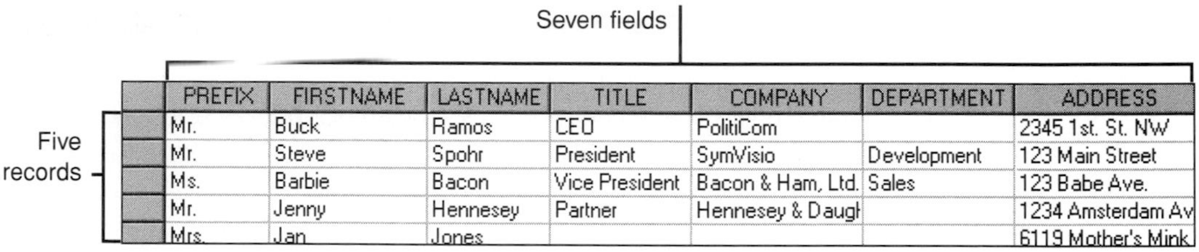

Seven fields |

	PREFIX	FIRSTNAME	LASTNAME	TITLE	COMPANY	DEPARTMENT	ADDRESS
	Mr.	Buck	Ramos	CEO	PolitiCom		2345 1st. St. NW
	Mr.	Steve	Spohr	President	SymVisio	Development	123 Main Street
	Ms.	Barbie	Bacon	Vice President	Bacon & Ham, Ltd.	Sales	123 Babe Ave.
	Mr.	Jenny	Hennesey	Partner	Hennesey & Daugh		1234 Amsterdam Av
	Mrs.	Jan	Jones				6119 Mother's Mink

Five records →

Figure 34-3   A database showing seven fields (columns) and five records (rows)

Regardless of what the address book software looks like, all the data you type in is stored in a database table, like that shown in Figure 34-3.

Databases can get complex. Just consider a company like an online book seller. They have to keep track of customer shipping information, credit card information, previous purchases, and general book preferences. They also have to store a lot of information about each book, keep track of their inventory, and store a whole host of other information. All this different type of information is stored in multiple databases, and those databases have to connect with each other, or relate to each other—hence the term *relational database*.

But that's not your problem. That's the programmer's problem. A programmer's job is to create a clean, intuitive, easy-to-use interface so that you don't have to mess around—or mess up—data in a raw database. Can you imagine trying to find a flight online by having to scroll and search through an entire database of flights for every airline, and at the same time trying to find not only flight availability, but schedules, connecting flights, seating, and prices? Don't try to imagine it. You may pass out.

In this book, we're going to keep it simple: show you the basics of how to build and modify a single database, then how to look at that database—rather, parts of it—in different ways, by creating queries, forms, and reports. By no means will this section of the book turn you into a database expert. It's just meant to give you the basics and get you up and running.

Creating Databases

In order to store information in a database like that shown in Figure 34-3, you have to create that database. This section shows you how.

Just to clarify concepts, "creating" a database doesn't mean merely entering data into it. Creating a database in StarOffice means either connecting to an existing database through StarOffice or building the structure of a database table in StarOffice so you can enter data into it.

You can create different types of databases in StarOffice. The first decision you have to make is which kind of database to create. Use the descriptions in Table 34-1 to help you decide. Many of the technologies involved (such as Oracle, DB2, ADO, ODBC, and JDBC) require specialized knowledge to use. If all you want to do is create a simple database in StarOffice, use dBase or Adabas D. (For information on installing Adabas D, see *Installing Adabas* on page 29.)

When you see the term "data source", it means one or more database tables.

Table 34-1 gives you a basic overview of the types of databases you can create in StarOffice, and it provides important factors to consider for creating each type. The actual procedure for creating a database follows this table: *Creating a Database* on page 996.

Table 34-1   Types of databases you can create in StarOffice

Database Type	Description	Factors to consider
dBase	An industry-standard database type. This is perhaps the most useful type of database in StarOffice and the easiest to use for single, non-relational databases. Not only is the StarOffice Address Book a dBase database, but StarOffice Calc can open and save to dBase files. This means, for example, that you can open a delimited text file in Calc (possibly created from something like an external address book) and convert it to a dBase file for use in StarOffice, or easily convert a dBase database to a spreadsheet file. You can create tables from scratch using the dBase format. You can't, however, create relations between dBase tables. dBase databases don't offer password protection.	dBase requires that you set a Directory location for the new database in the Type tab. The directory doesn't have to contain an existing dBase data source.

Table 34-1   Types of databases you can create in StarOffice (continued)

Database Type	Description	Factors to consider
Adabas D	Replaces the Oterro database used in previous versions of StarOffice. Adabas D is for more serious database work than what is provided by the dBase type. Adabas D lets you set up relations between tables and includes the following enhancements over the Oterro database (which are really only of interest if you're a database geek): you can specify data buffer size and data increment, view database statistics such as database size and memory usage, connect to backup files, and the database connection is shut down automatically when you close StarOffice. Adabas D databases also support password protection. To use Adabas D on a standalone system, you must install the Adabas D server separately (see *Installing Adabas* on page 29).	The Adabas software must be installed from the StarOffice 5.2 CD. To create a new data source after you've created an Adabas database (see *Creating a Database* on page 996), right-click the Adabas database item in the Explorer window and choose Properties. Then select the Type tab, enter a name for the Data Source, and click the New Data Source button. In the Create New Adabas Database window, enter an Administrator name, and click the Password button to create an administrator password. To connect to an existing Adabas data source, click the Browse button. By default, data sources are stored in the `adabas/sql` folder off of your system's root directory. When you open a data source, a traffic light icon is displayed next to the clock in the task bar. You can shut down and restart the database connection by right-clicking this icon.
StarBase	Lets you open and modify an existing StarBase database that was created in an earlier version of StarOffice. StarBase databases also support password protection.	You must point to a specific StarBase data source from the Type tab. Click the Browse button to locate the data source. You can convert a StarBase data source to an Adabas D data source by selecting the Administration tab and clicking the Convert button.

Table 34-1   Types of databases you can create in StarOffice (continued)

Database Type	Description	Factors to consider
MS Access 97	Lets you connect to an Access database in StarOffice. You can create and modify tables. But you if you plan on continuing to use an Access database in Access, know that modifying the tables in StarOffice could cause problems when you open the database in Access, particularly if it has relations. StarOffice supports password protection and other driver settings for MS Access 97 databases. You must have Microsoft Jet Database Engine version 3.5 installed on your system to use this database type. If you have Access 97 installed on your system, the Jet Database Engine is already installed.	MS Access 97 requires you to point to an Access `.mdb` file. As you create the database (see *Creating a Database* on page 996), select the Type tab and click the Browse button to select the `.mdb` file you want.
Oracle	Lets you connect to an Oracle database (version 7.3 or higher). StarOffice supports password protection and other driver settings for Oracle database connections.	In the Data Source field, enter the service name created using Oracle tools Net8 Assistant/Easy Config.
DB2	Lets you connect to a DB2 database in StarOffice. StarOffice supports password protection and other driver settings for DB2 database connections.	You must connect to an existing DB2 data source. In the Type tab, click the Browse button to locate the data source.
ADO	Lets you connect to a data source using a Microsoft ActiveX Data Objects (ADO) interface. StarOffice supports password protection for ADO connections.	To use ADO, you must have Microsoft Access 2000 or the ISGData Control for ADO (available from `www.microsoft.com/data/download.htm`) installed on your system. To connect to the data source, select the MS ADO tab and enter a URL to the data source.
ODBC	Lets you connect to a data source using Open Database Connectivity (ODBC). StarOffice supports password protection for ODBC database connections.	Your system must have the proper ODBC drivers installed to create an ODBC connection. To connect to the data source, select the Type tab and click the Browse button to select the data source.

Table 34-1   Types of databases you can create in StarOffice (continued)

Database Type	Description	Factors to consider
JDBC	Lets you connect to a data source using Java Database Connectivity (JDBC). StarOffice supports password protection for JDBC database connections.	A JDBC driver must be installed on your system to use JDBC. A Sun Microsystems JDBC driver is provided in StarOffice by default, and is displayed in the JDBC Driver Class field of the JDBC tab. To connect to the data source, select the JDBC tab and enter a URL to the data source.
Text	Lets you open a delimited text file as a database. Text databases are read-only. The only way to modify or enter data in them is in the text file itself.	To connect to the data source, select the Type tab and click the Browse button to select the data source. Text database connections are read-only in StarOffice. You must edit the text source directly to change the data. If you want to convert the text database to one you can edit in StarOffice, open the file in Calc (selecting the file type Text – txt – csv) and save it as a dBase file.

You may also have an existing database that was created in another database application, such as an address book, that you want to convert to a StarOffice dBase database. You can find that information in *Importing Databases* on page 1006.

Creating a Database

All databases in StarOffice, such as the Address Book, are accessed from the Explorer window. When you create a database, you're adding an item to one of the groups in the Explorer window. If you create a database that isn't connected to any data, or tables, it's an empty database. To get a better idea of how a database item looks in StarOffice, click the [+] to expand the Address Book item in the Explorer group, as shown in Figure 34-1 on page 989. You'll see the following sub-items: Forms, Reports, Queries, and Tables. If you expand the Tables item, you'll see a table called "address".

An empty database without any tables is a fairly useless object. Any database must have at least one table, even if it contains just one field and one record. Figure 34-3 on page 992 shows a table. Forms, Reports, and Queries merely give you different ways of working with and viewing tables, portions of tables, and the data contained in tables.

Most of the database types StarOffice supports require that you have an existing data source to connect to. In these cases, creating a database is simply a matter of setting up an item in the Explorer that lets you view and work with the existing tables. Two database types, dBase and Adabas D, don't require that you have an existing dBase or Adabas D data source. After you use the following procedure to set up a database item in the Explorer window, you can create tables for the database.

You can create a database in any Explorer window group. Any group containing a database should be in hierarchical view (by right-clicking the slider and choosing Hierarchical).

If you're going to create more than one database, consider creating a Databases slider group in the Explorer window (see page 104) to organize the databases in a central location and keep the Explorer group from becoming too cluttered.

1   In the Explorer window, click the slider of the group in which you want to create the database.

2   Right-click in an open area of the group and choose New > Database.

3   In the Properties window, type a name for the database in the General tab.

4   In the Type tab, select the database type you want to create.

To help you decide which type of database to create, see Figure 34-1 on page 993. The tabs and fields in the Properties window are different for each database type selected.

5   Enter the appropriate settings for the database you've selected.

See Figure 34-1 on page 993 for specific factors to consider in creating each type of database.

If you've entered the correct directory or URL for connecting to an existing data source, the Tables tab will contain a list of the available tables for that database type, as shown in Figure 34-4.

6   Click OK.

The database is added to the group in the Explorer window. If you created a dBase or Adabas D database that doesn't have an existing data source, your next step is to create a table for the database.

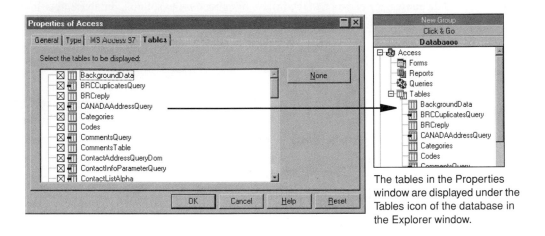

The tables in the Properties window are displayed under the Tables icon of the database in the Explorer window.

Figure 34-4   Database tables in an existing data source

After you create a database and all the tables you want in the database are available, you can view the tables and data in different ways by setting up forms, queries, and reports. See *Creating Forms* on page 1010, *Creating Queries* on page 1019, and *Creating Reports* on page 1024.

Note – Besides right-clicking in an Explorer window group to create a new database, StarOffice also lets you create databases in the following ways:

*   Start > More > Database.

*   File > New > Database.

*   From the Click & Go slider in the Explorer window (clicking the Database shortcut).

*   With a task bar shortcut (see *Adding Shortcuts to the Task Bar* on page 123).

When you create a database using one of those methods, the database is automatically put in the Explorer group in the Explorer window.

Changing Database Properties

If you ever want to change the initial settings of a database, such as changing the directory or URL, selecting or deselecting the tables you want to use, changing passwords, and so on; or in the case of Adabas D, loading a backup or changing the data buffer size or data increment:

1   Right-click the name of a database in the Explorer window, and choose Properties.

2   Modify the properties and click OK.

Creating and Modifying Database Tables

Whether you're creating a brand new dBase or Adabas D database, or creating a database to connect to an existing data source, this procedure shows you how to create a new database table in StarOffice, like that shown in Figure 34-3 on page 992.

You can create a database table with the help of the AutoPilot wizard, or manually in Table Design mode.

You can also create a table in an existing database from a Calc spreadsheet using drag and drop.

Note – Some types of databases in StarOffice don't let you add tables, such as StarBase and Text. StarBase was the relational database tool for the previous release of StarOffice. That's been replaced by Adabas D. The StarBase format exists to let you connect to a legacy StarBase database so you can convert it to Adabas D. Text databases (in delimited text files) are read-only. To add tables to a Text database, convert it to dBase (see *Importing Databases* on page 1006.

Creating a Table With AutoPilot

Using AutoPilot is a quick and easy way to build a table automatically. StarOffice guides you through the process. AutoPilot lets you create two categories of tables: business or personal. In the business category, you can choose from 21 types of business-related tables to create. In the personal category, you can choose from 9 types of tables.

1   In the Explorer window, click the [+] next to the database to show the Forms, Reports, Queries, and Tables items.

2   Right-click the Tables item and choose New > Table > AutoPilot.

3   Make the appropriate selections and settings in each of the AutoPilot windows.

    Use Figure 34-5 through Figure 34-8 for guidance.

4   In the last window, click the Create button to create the table.

After you create a table with AutoPilot, you can use Table Design mode to add, remove, and modify fields.

The table is added to the main Table item in the database.

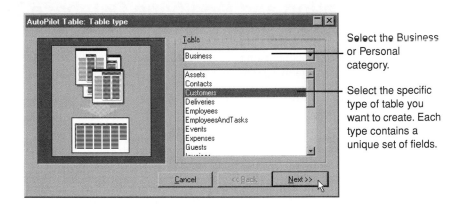

Figure 34-5   Selecting the type of table you want to create

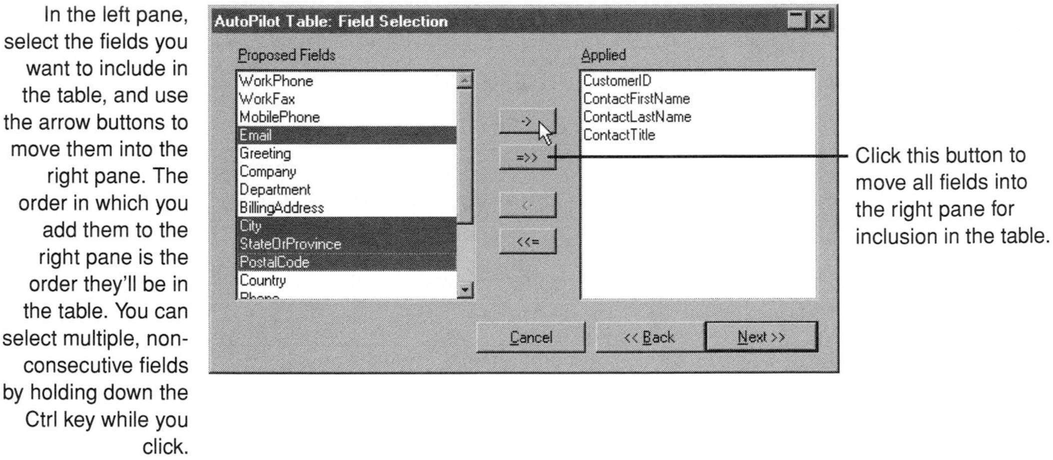

In the left pane, select the fields you want to include in the table, and use the arrow buttons to move them into the right pane. The order in which you add them to the right pane is the order they'll be in the table. You can select multiple, non-consecutive fields by holding down the Ctrl key while you click.

Figure 34-6   Selecting the fields you want to include in the table

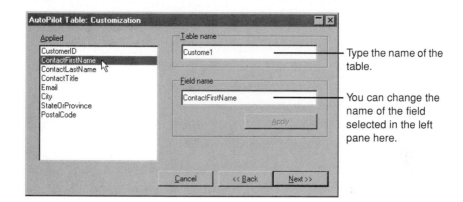

Type the name of the
table.

You can change the
name of the field
selected in the left
pane here.

Figure 34-7   Naming the table and changing the default field names

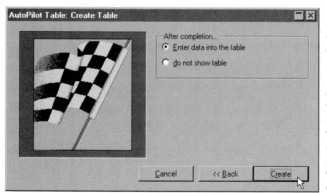

Select the Enter data
option to open the
table in StarOffice
when it's created.
Select the Do Not
Show option to
create the table
without opening it in
StarOffice. Either
way, the table is
added to the Table
item in the Explorer
window when you
click Create.

Figure 34-8   Building the table

Creating or Modifying a Table in Table Design Mode

When you create a database manually in Table Design mode, you can create any type of
table with any fields you want. Table Design works the same whether you're creating or
modifying a table.

Creating a table manually also means you can determine the type of data that each field
will contain. For example, you can set a field that will contain currency amounts to store
and display data in the Currency format; or if you want to be able to type lots of text in a
field, you can set the field to the Memo format. Table 34-2 describes these formats.

1   In the Explorer window, click the [+] next to the database to show the Forms, Reports,
Queries, and Tables items.

2   If you're creating a table, right-click the Tables item and choose New > Table > Table Design.

If you're modifying an existing table, right click the table you want to modify and choose Table Design.

Note – Make sure the table itself isn't already open in StarOffice. If it's open, Table Design will be read-only and you won't be able to modify the table.

---

3   Add or change field names or types.

Use Table 34-2 and Figure 34-9 for guidance.

4   When you're finished, click the Save Document icon on the function bar. If you're creating a new table, name the table in the window that appears. If you're modifying a table, click Yes in the confirmation window.

5   Close the Table Design window.

To check your changes, double-click the table in the Explorer window to open it in the workspace.

Table 34-2   Data types you can assign to table fields

Data Type	Description
Text	For short amounts of text whose maximum length you can determine. For long amounts of text, use the Memo type.
Text (fixed)	Similar to text. This type allows you to increment automatically to ensure each record has a unique identifier.
Number	To store numbers that are used in calculations.
Date/Time	For storing both date and time information that can also be used in calculations.
Date	For storing date information in a date format that can also be used in calculations.
Time	For storing time information in a time format that can also be used in calculation.
Yes/No	For creating a check box that you can check or uncheck. For example, in data entry, you can check the box to make sure the person in the record is invited to an event.
Currency	For currency values in a currency format. Calculations can be made on this type of data.
Memo	For creating text entries that are much longer than what the Text type provides.

Table 34-2   Data types you can assign to table fields

Data Type	Description
Image	For adding images to records. When you use this format, you can use the field only in a form you create for the table. The Form AutoPilot (page 1011) sets this field up automatically (as an Image Control). In the form, double-click this field to add an image/graphic file to a record.
Decimal	For entering decimal values. You can set the amount of decimal places.
Binary Field (fixed) and Binary Field	For storing binary data; though, unlike the Image type, there doesn't seem to be a way to add binary data to a table.

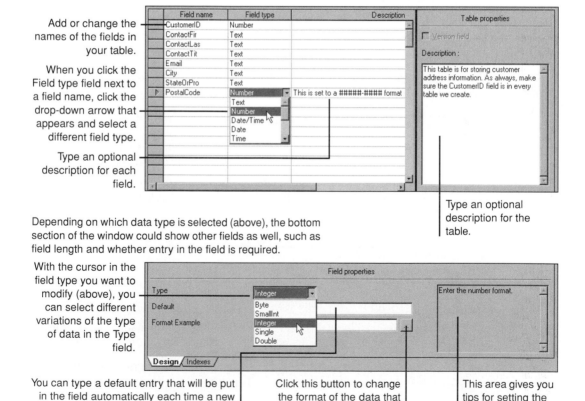

Add or change the names of the fields in your table.

When you click the Field type field next to a field name, click the drop-down arrow that appears and select a different field type.

Type an optional description for each field.

Type an optional description for the table.

Depending on which data type is selected (above), the bottom section of the window could show other fields as well, such as field length and whether entry in the field is required.

With the cursor in the field type you want to modify (above), you can select different variations of the type of data in the Type field.

You can type a default entry that will be put in the field automatically each time a new record is added to the table.

Click this button to change the format of the data that will be in the field.

This area gives you tips for setting the selected option.

Figure 34-9   Creating and modifying tables in Table Design

Troubleshooting If for some reason you can't modify a table in Table Design (if Table Design is in read-only mode), one of three things may be happening:

- The table you want to modify is open in StarOffice.

- The type of table doesn't allow changes (such as the Text the StarBase types).

- You need to click the Edit File icon in the function bar.

Assigning a Primary Key for Adabas D If you create a table in an Adabas D database, you'll need to assign a field as the primary key for that table. A primary key is a field that serves as a unique identifier for each record in a table, such as a customer ID or another type of field that will contain unique data for each record.

Assign a primary key in Table Design view by right-clicking the gray box next to the field you want to be the primary key and choosing Primary Key. A small golden key is displayed in the gray box. You can also simply close the design view window, and StarOffice will prompt you to create an automatic primary key field called ID.

Creating a Table From a Spreadsheet or a Word-Processing Table

You can create a table for any database type that supports new table creation by dragging and dropping from a spreadsheet or a Writer, RTF (Rich Text Format), or HTML table.

1 In the Explorer window, click the [+] next to the database for which you want to create a new table.

2 Select all the spreadsheet or table cells you want to include in the database table.

   The first row of selected cells will become the default heading names for the table, so if you don't have a heading for the table, you might want to add one before you select the fields.

3 Drag from anywhere in the selected area onto the Tables item of the database, as shown in Figure 34-10.

4 In the Copy Table window that appears, type a table name.

5 Select the Definition and Data option.

   You can select the Create Primary Key option and type the name of a field that will become the primary key for the table. Click Next.

6 In the Apply Columns window, move the fields you want to include in the new table from the left pane to the right pane, and click Next.

7 In the Type Formatting window, select each field in turn and set the types and options for it, or click the Auto button to have the wizard automatically set the appropriate types and options based on the data formats in the spreadsheet.

   Use Figure 34-2 on page 1002 for more information on the types of data you can select.

You can also change the names of fields in this window. Click Next.

8   Click the Create button.

The table is added to the database.

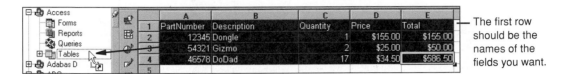

Figure 34-10   Creating a database table from a spreadsheet using drag and drop

Adding Spreadsheet or Word Processing Table Data to an Existing Database Table

You can append spreadsheet or Writer, RTF (Rich Text Format), or HTML table data to an existing database table using the same drag and drop method as in the previous procedure.

1   In the Explorer window, click the [+] next to the database for which you want to create a new table.

2   Select all the spreadsheet or table cells you want to append to the existing database table.

The first row of selected cells must match the field names in the table to which you are appending.

3   Drag from anywhere in the selected area onto the Tables item of the database, as shown in Figure 34-10.

4   In the Copy Table window, type the table name of the table to which you want to append.

5   Select the Attach Data option, and click Next.

6   In the Assign Columns window, select (click to put an 'x' next to) the fields in the spreadsheet you want to add to the table.

7   Click the Create button.

The data is added to the table.

Databases Names

This is an area of the software we want to show you just to avoid possible confusion. In the Database options (Tools > Options > Databases > Database Names, as shown in Figure 34-11), you see a list of databases. This is not a place to register databases or anything remotely practical. It doesn't even necessarily show all the databases you've created.

An entry is added automatically to the list when you open a database in StarOffice. If you move a database to a new location (such as from the Explorer group to a Databases group you create in the Explorer window), its name won't appear in this list until you open the database. If you rename the database in this window, it doesn't automatically rename the database in the Explorer window.

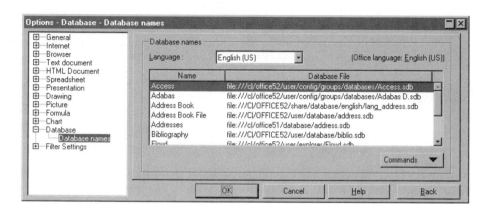

Figure 34-11   Naming databases

Importing Databases

In *Creating a Database* on page 996, we showed you how to connect to an external database using StarOffice. For data sources you can't connect to using StarOffice, use this procedure to convert those sources into a format that you can use in StarOffice.

If you want to add the data in an external address book to the StarOffice Address Book, see *Importing Contact Information From Another Database* on page 973.

1   From the application that you use to work with the external database, save the database as a delimited text file.

2   Open the delimited text file in Calc. See *Importing a Text File* on page 568.

3   Add the spreadsheet data to a database as a new table or append it to an existing table. See *Creating a Table From a Spreadsheet or a Word-Processing Table* on page 1004 or *Adding Spreadsheet or Word Processing Table Data to an Existing Database Table* on page 1005.

You can also save the spreadsheet as a dBase file by choosing File > Save As and setting the file type to dBase.

Exporting Databases

Use this procedure if you need to convert a database in StarOffice to a database in another application. This assumes that the other application can import delimited text files.

1   Move a database table into a Calc spreadsheet. See *Getting a StarOffice Database into Calc* on page 571.

2   Save the spreadsheet as a delimited text file. See *Saving a Calc Spreadsheet as a Text File* on page 570.

If the other application can import dBase files, you can also save the spreadsheet as a dBase file.

Converting to Writer, RTF, and HTML Tables

To convert a database table to a table in a Writer, HTML, or RTF (Rich Text Format) document, open the document in StarOffice, hold down the Shift key, and drag a table from the Explorer window into a document.

If you want more control over which database fields are added to the table, drag the database table into the document without holding down the Shift key. In the Insert Database Columns window, select the fields you want to include.

Using Databases

Going Beyond Tables

Databases are made up of tables, and tables are the basic containers that store data. In the previous chapter we covered creating databases and tables.

Tables, however, can get fairly large, even if they're not very complex. For example, if you open the StarOffice Address Book by double-clicking the address table in the Explorer window, try finding someone's Email address in the table. You'd have to scroll horizontally through a good many fields to find the EMAIL field; yet that's probably one of the most important fields in the table. Imagine if you had to find an Email address that way all the time. It would get old quickly.

This chapter is about going beyond tables to using databases with more efficiency and less frustration. Forms, queries, and reports let you pinpoint specific parts of a table to let you see and work with only the fields and data you want to see. Using the example of the EMAIL field in the Address Book, you could create a query that showed only the first name, last name, and Email address fields in a table. You could also create a form to enter data for only those three fields, or you could run a report showing only contacts and their Email addresses.

We'll use the Address Book as the model for these procedures, since it's the database you're most likely to use.

Creating Forms

Forms let you create a graphical environment for working with your databases. You can create forms that show all fields in a database, or you can create forms that show only specific fields. For example, you could create a form that lets you view and modify only name and Email address information for your contacts.

You can also add text and graphics to a form, making it a more pleasant and user-friendly tool for working with your data.

You can create a form for a table or a query. Since a query is only a part of a table, a form for a query really just supports the table. Creating a form for a query lets you work on smaller groupings of fields.

In the following procedures, we'll use the term "control". A control is an object on a form that connects with some field in a table or query, allowing you to enter data for that field through the form. Examples of controls are text boxes, drop-down lists, and check boxes. By default, the forms you create with AutoPilot will contain mostly labels and text boxes. The labels tell you the name of the field, and the text boxes let you enter data in the field.

To see all the controls available in StarOffice, click and hold down the Form icon on the toolbar, as shown in Figure 35-1.

Figure 35-1   The Form toolbar

Creating a Form With AutoPilot

To create any form, you must run the AutoPilot. After you create a basic form with AutoPilot you can modify it in Form Design.

1   In the Explorer window, click the [+] next to the database for which you want to create a form.

2   Right-click the Forms item and choose New > Form > AutoPilot.

3   Make the appropriate selections and settings in each of the AutoPilot windows.

Use Figure 35-2 and Figure 35-3 for guidance.

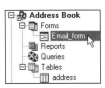

4   In the final AutoPilot window, click the Create button to create the form.

The form is added to the main Forms item in the database.

After you create a form with AutoPilot, you can use Form Design mode to add, remove, and rearrange fields, and add other elements such as text and graphics.

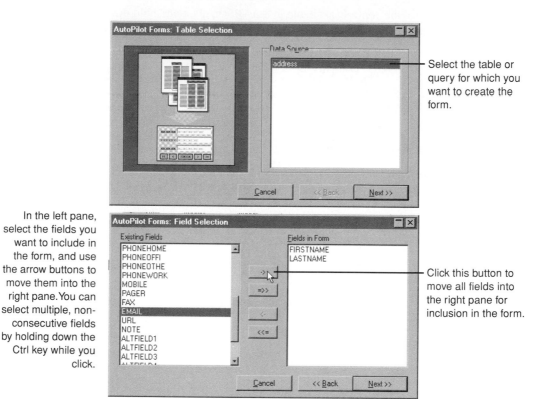

Select the table or query for which you want to create the form.

In the left pane, select the fields you want to include in the form, and use the arrow buttons to move them into the right pane. You can select multiple, non-consecutive fields by holding down the Ctrl key while you click.

Click this button to move all fields into the right pane for inclusion in the form.

Figure 35-2   Selecting the table and fields for the form

In the Field Alignment and Styles windows, set the physical characteristics of the form. You can change these characteristics in Form Design after you create the form.

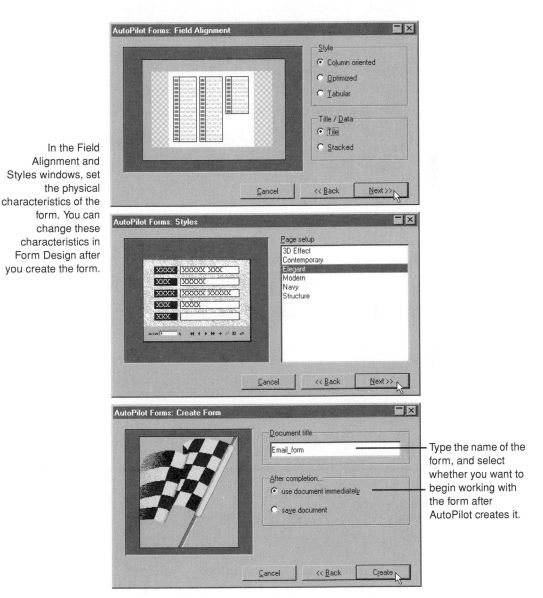

Type the name of the form, and select whether you want to begin working with the form after AutoPilot creates it.

Figure 35-3   Selecting a format and creating the form

Modifying and Enhancing a Form

After you've created a form with AutoPilot, you can rearrange, add, remove, and change the look of fields. You can also add text, graphics, and other elements to the form to make it more user friendly and attractive.

1   In the Explorer window, click the [+] next to the database containing the form you want to open, and click the [+] next to the Forms item.

2   Right-click the form you want to modify, and choose Form Design.

The form opens in the workspace in design mode, which looks similar to the environment for working with an HTML or Writer document.

The fields in the form are selectable objects that you can move and modify.

3   Arrange and add elements, such as text and graphics, using the toolbar and object bar, as shown in Figure 35-4.

4   When you're finished, click the Save Document icon on the function bar to save the modifications.

5   To begin using the form, click the Edit File icon on the function bar.

In Form Design, you have the same set of tools available as you do when working with an HTML or Writer document.

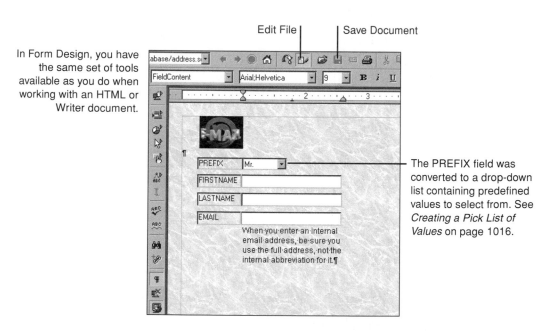

The PREFIX field was converted to a drop-down list containing predefined values to select from. See *Creating a Pick List of Values* on page 1016.

Figure 35-4   Modifying and enhancing a form using Form Design

In the example in Figure 35-4, an animated GIF and an explanatory paragraph were added to the form. To make this happen, all the controls were grouped and anchored to the first paragraph, and wrapping for the grouped object was set to None. The animated GIF was inserted and anchored above the first paragraph. The ruler was added to the workspace (View > Ruler), and the second paragraph, containing the text beneath the EMAIL field, was indented to fit under the entry box for the field.

To change the properties of the fields, select a field, right-click, and choose Group > Ungroup. This separates a field's label from the actual control where data is entered. Then select the field or label you want to modify, right-click, and choose the appropriate option. The Control option lets you change the look and behavior of the control.

Note – If you need help lining up elements on a form, use a grid. To do this, choose Tools > Options > Text Document > Grid, select the Visible Grid and/or Snap to Grid options, and change the grid Resolution (size of squares) and Subdivision (number of dots between intersections) to set the grid the way you want it.

Changing a Field's Label

By default, a field on a form uses the name of the database field it's connected to. You can change the name of the label to make it more readable, especially if the name of the field in the database is cryptic.

1   In Form Design, select the label of the field you want to change.

     If you can't select the label separately, right-click the selected field and choose Group > Ungroup.

2   Right-click the selected label and choose Control.

3   In the Properties window, change the Label field, as shown in Figure 35-5.

4   Close the Properties window.

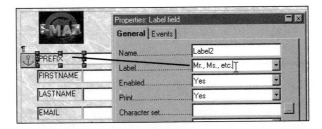

Figure 35-5   Changing a field's label

Adding Fields to a Form

After you create a form with AutoPilot, you may want to add database fields not originally included when you created the form. Here's how.

1   In the Explorer window, right-click the form you want to add to and choose Form Design.

     The form opens in the workspace in edit mode.

2   On the toolbar, click and hold down the Form icon, click the title bar of the horizontal toolbar that appears (to it floating), and click the Add Field icon, as shown in Figure 35-6.

3   In the Field Selection window, drag the name of the field you want to add onto the form, also shown in Figure 35-6.

StarOffice knows which type of control to create based on the type of field you're adding. For example, if a field format is "Image", StarOffice creates an Image control.

4   Position and modify the control as necessary.

See the text following Figure 35-6 for more information.

5   When you're finished, click the Save Document icon on the function bar.

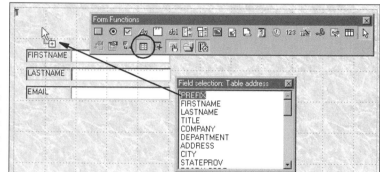

From the list of fields, drag the name of the field you want onto the form. StarOffice creates the appropriate control based on the field type.

Figure 35-6   Adding a field to a form

After you add a field, its label may not be lined up the way you want it. To move the label, select the control, right-click it, and choose Group > Ungroup. Then select the label, which is now a separate object from the control, and move it to where you want it.

Also, the label or control may not have the background you want. For example, if the other fields in the form are 3D, the new field may not be. To change that, select the new field or its label, right-click, choose Control, and change the Border or Background Color properties.

You can also change the controls used in a form. For example, you can convert a text box to a drop-down list of predefined values, letting you enter data by choosing rather than typing. See Creating a Pick List of Values, next.

Creating a Pick List of Values

One of the most useful changes you can make to a form is converting a text box control to a list box control. When you have a known set of values and data entry must remain consistent (that is, typos aren't allowed), a control that lets you select from a list rather than manually typing data is essential. This procedure shows you how to make that conversion.

1   Ungroup the control from its label by selecting the control, right-clicking, and choosing Group > Ungroup.

2   Right-click the text box control, choose Replace With, and choose List Box.

3   Right-click the control again, and choose Control.

4   In the Properties window, select the General tab, and click the List Entries field.

5   In the text box appears, enter the list of items you want in the pick list, as shown in Figure 35-7.

6   Set the Drop-down field to Yes.

7   Select the Data tab, and in the List Content field, create the same list you did in the General tab (in the List Entries field).

8   Make sure the Type of List Contents field is set to Valuelist.

9   Close the Properties window, and click the Save Document icon on the function bar.

10   To test the new field, click the Edit File icon on the function bar, which gets you out of edit mode and lets you use the form.

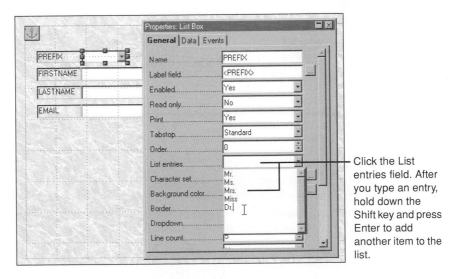

Figure 35-7   Creating a pick list of values for a field

Setting the Tab Order in Forms

Most people who do data entry don't like to take their hands off the keyboard. To move from field to field, they like to use the Tab key, which means the order in which the cursor jumps from field to field is important. This procedure shows you how to change the order in which the cursor jumps from field to field when you press the Tab key.

1   Open the form in Form Design.

    If the form is open, click the Edit File icon on the function bar. Otherwise, right-click the form in the Explorer window.

2   On the toolbar, click and hold down the Form icon, then click the Tab Order icon.

3   In the Tab Order window, rearrange the order of the fields in the list, or click the Automatic Sort button to have StarOffice set the order automatically.

4   Close the Tab Order window, and click the Save Document icon on the function bar.

Using Forms

After you've created and modified a form, you're ready to use it for managing your data.

To begin using a form, double-click the name of the form in the Explorer window. If a form is already open in edit mode, you can also click the Edit File icon on the function bar.

Figure 35-8 gives a brief description of the environment for working with forms.

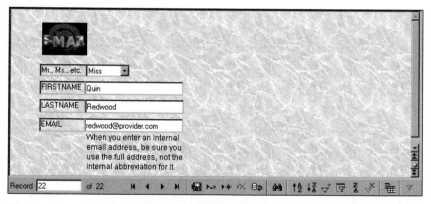

When you're using a form, there is a set of tools at the bottom of it to let you navigate between records, create and delete records, find records, and sort and filter records.

Figure 35-8   Using a form

Creating Hyperlinks to Give Others Access to Forms

If you're working on a network and you want to give others access to a form, you can add a hyperlink to the form inside a document that users can click to access the form.

1   Set the appropriate access rights to the database file.

If you need help with this, check with your system administrator.

2   Open the document into which you want to insert the hyperlink to the form.

3   Click the [+] next to the database containing the form you want to share, and click the [+] next to the Forms item to display the available forms for the database.

4   Drag the form you want to share from the Explorer window into the document at the location where you want the hyperlink to appear, as shown in Figure 35-9.

5   If you want to modify the hyperlink, select it (by clicking beside it and dragging through it), then choose Insert > Hyperlink to bring up the Hyperlink window, where you can modify its properties.

You can change the name of the hyperlink in the Note field of the Hyperlink window.

Figure 35-9   Creating a hyperlink to a form

Creating Queries

Queries look and behave exactly like tables. In fact, they're smaller sections of existing tables. They let you view only the fields and information in a table that you want to view. That means a table must exist in order to create a query based on it.

For all practical purposes, you can think of queries and tables as identical objects in terms of how you interact with them—the only difference being that queries are completely dependent on the tables from which they were created.

Queries let you focus on a small segment of your data for easier viewing and maintenance. For example, you could create up a query that shows you only the first name, last name, and Email address fields for easier maintenance of your Email addresses. Or you could create a query that displays only mailing address information to make setting up mail merges easier.

When you create a query, you can also create a form that gives you a graphical way to work with the query. See *Creating Forms* on page 1010.

When you modify the data in a query, the data in the table it belongs to is modified automatically.

You can create queries in two different ways: using AutoPilot, or using Query Design.

Creating a Query With AutoPilot

AutoPilot guides you step-by-step through the query-building process.

1   In the Explorer window, click the [+] next to the database for which you want to create a query.

2   Right-click the Query item, and choose New > Query > AutoPilot.

3   In the Table Selection window, select the table for which you want to create a query (Figure 35-10), and click Next.

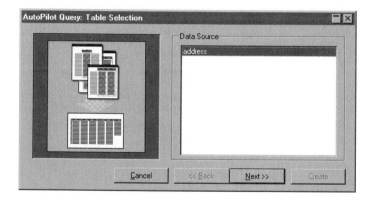

Figure 35-10   Selecting the table to create a query for

4   In the Field Selection window, move the fields you want to include in the query into the right pane (Figure 35-11), and click Next.

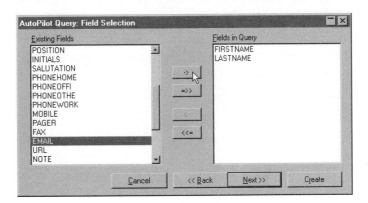

Figure 35-11   Selecting the fields the query will contain

5   In the Filter window, set any filtering options you want for the query (Figure 35-12), and click Next.

This lets you filter through the records to include only those that meet specific conditions. For example, Figure 35-12 shows a filter condition that says, "For the EMAIL field, include all records that are 'not like' %hotmail.com%." That means all records with Email addresses that contain "hotmail.com" won't be included in the query when it's built. The percent symbol (%) on either side of hotmail.com are from the SQL language, which is required for filtering in StarOffice. For more information on the SQL language, look in the online help system under "SQL commands". For more information on filtering, see *Filtering Data* on page 1030.

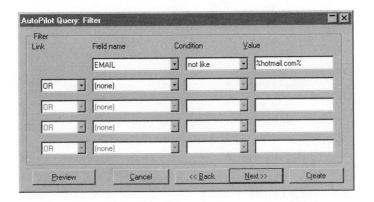

Figure 35-12   Setting filtering options for the query (optional)

6   In the Sorting window, set any sorting options you want for the query (Figure 35-13), and click Next.

This lets you order the displayed information in specific ways. For more information on sorting, see *Sorting Database Information* on page 1028.

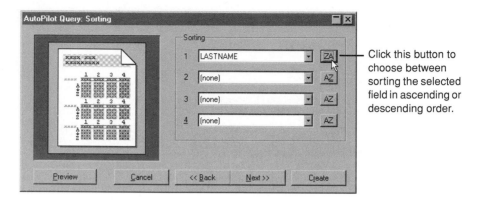

Click this button to choose between sorting the selected field in ascending or descending order.

Figure 35-13   Sorting the records in the query (optional)

7   In the Create window (Figure 35-14), name the query and select whether you want to open the query after StarOffice builds it.

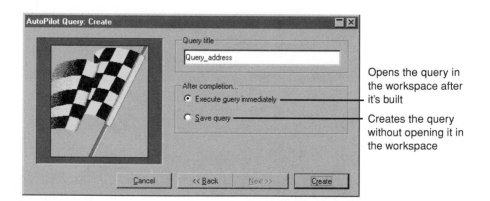

Opens the query in the workspace after it's built

Creates the query without opening it in the workspace

Figure 35-14   Naming and building the query

8   Click Create.

The query is added to the Query item in the Explorer window. If you chose the Execute query immediately option in the Create window (Figure 35-14), the query opens in the workspace. If you chose the Save query option, open it by expanding the Query item in the Explorer window and double-clicking the query you created.

You can work with a query exactly like you can work with a table.

After you create a query with AutoPilot, you can modify the query using Query Design.

Using Query Design to Create or Modify a Query

Using Query Design to create or modify a query gives you more flexibility than AutoPilot provides.

1 In the Explorer window, click the [+] next to the database in which you want to create or modify a query.

2 If you're creating a new query, right-click the Queries item and choose New > Query > Query Design.

If you're modifying an existing query, click the [+] next to the Queries item, right-click the query you want to modify, and choose Query Design.

3 Add or change the settings for the query in the Query Design window.

Use Figure 35-15 for guidance.

4 When you're finished, click the Save Document icon on the function bar.

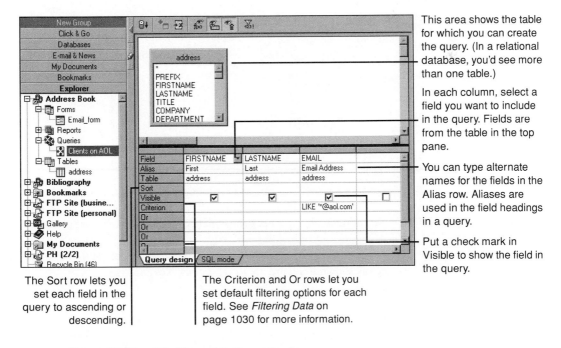

The Sort row lets you set each field in the query to ascending or descending.

The Criterion and Or rows let you set default filtering options for each field. See *Filtering Data* on page 1030 for more information.

Figure 35-15   Working with Query Design

Creating Reports

Reports let you take data from a database and display it in a formatted (though read-only) Writer document for more presentable viewing. Reports aren't static documents that you create once and don't change. Reports are items that use specific formatting information to display the current information in your database. Every time you run a report (by double-clicking it in the Explorer window), it displays the most current data in your database.

You can create reports that display selected table and query data. The only way to create a report is using AutoPilot.

1   In the Explorer window, click the [+] next to the database for which you want to create a report.

2   Right-click the Reports item, and choose New > Report. The Report AutoPilot appears.

3   In the Table Selection window (Figure 35-16), select the table or query for which you want to create a report, and click Next.

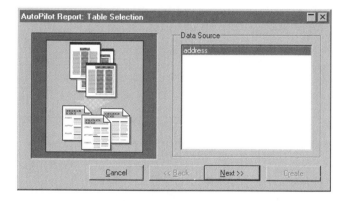

Figure 35-16   Selecting a table or query for which you want to create the report

4   In the Field Selection window, move the fields you want to include in the report into the right pane, as shown in Figure 35-17, and click Next.

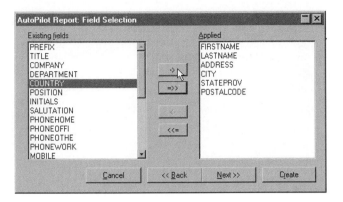

Figure 35-17   Selecting the type of data you want to include in the report

5   In the Structure window (Figure 35-18), double-click any fields in the left pane that you want to include in the heading of each record on the report, and click Next.

Any fields you select as header information won't be available to sort by in the next window.

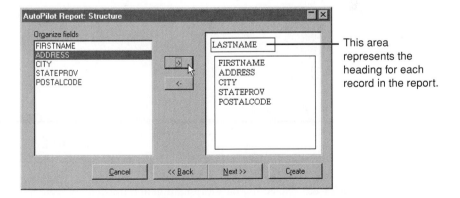

Figure 35-18   Determining which type of data will be displayed in the report headings

6   In the Sorting window (Figure 35-19), set sorting options for any available fields.

For example, if you set a sorting option for the LASTNAME field to be sorted in ascending order, the report will list records alphabetically by last name.

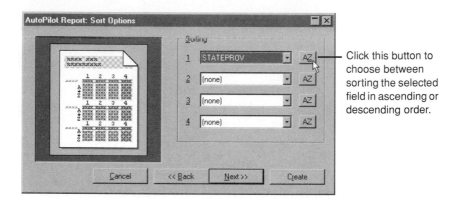

Figure 35-19   Determining the order in which records will be listed in the report

7   In the Style Selection window (Figure 35-20), select whether you want the report to be portrait or landscape, and select the style in which the records will be displayed in the report. Click Next.

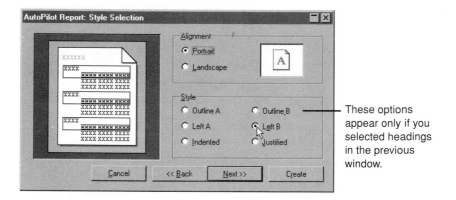

Figure 35-20   Selecting page orientation and the display style

8   In the Format Style window (Figure 35-21), select the type of template you want to use for the report, and click Next.

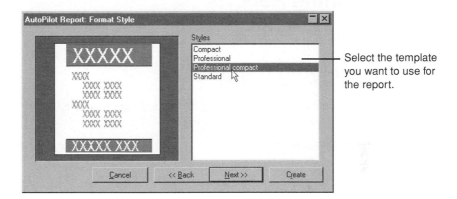

Figure 35-21

9   In the Create window, type a name for the report, select whether or not you want to
run the report after StarOffice creates it, and click Create.

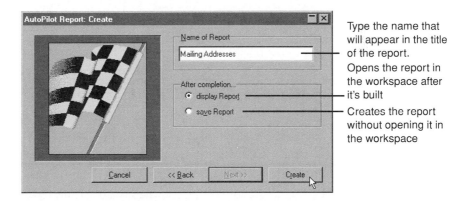

Figure 35-22

The report is added to the Reports item in the Explorer window.

If you want to add fields to a report, the best way is to create a new report using AutoPilot
that includes the fields you want.

If you want to change the look of a report after you create it, see Modifying Reports, next.

You can also save an open report as a Writer document, but the drawback to doing so is
that the document becomes static, and the information it contains isn't updated when the
information in the database changes.

Running Reports

To run a report, double-click it in the Explorer window.

Modifying Reports

Modifying a report is just like modifying a Writer template. You can change all the styles associated with the report.

1   In the Explorer window, right-click the report you want to modify and choose Report Design.

The report opens in Report Design.

2   Modify the report the same way you would a Writer document.

3   When you're finished, click the Save Document icon on the function bar.

Sorting, Searching, and Filtering

All pieces of a database, whether tables, queries, forms, or reports, let you sort, search for, and filter data.

Sorting is arranging data in ascending or descending alphabetical or numeric order. Searching is looking for specific data. Filtering is for showing only data that has specific characteristics.

When you're working with tables, queries, or forms, a set of icons gives you access to sorting, searching, and filtering tools. The following procedures give general principles for sorting, searching, and filtering that apply to tables, queries, and forms.

With reports, you set the sorting options when you create the report. No filtering options are available when you create a report, but the way around that is to create a report based on a filtered table or query. To search for data in a report, use Writer's search capability (Edit > Find & Replace).

Sorting Database Information

Sorting a table, query, or form is just a matter of sorting the data alphabetically or numerically in ascending or descending order.

There are two ways to sort data: by selecting a single field and clicking ascending or descending icons, or in the Sort Order window, which lets you sort on up to three fields simultaneously.

Sorting on a Single Field

With a table, query, or form open in data entry mode, select the field you want to sort, and click the Sort Ascending or Sort Descending icon, as shown in Figure 35-23.

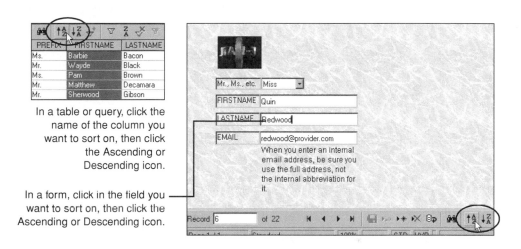

In a table or query, click the name of the column you want to sort on, then click the Ascending or Descending icon.

In a form, click in the field you want to sort on, then click the Ascending or Descending icon.

Figure 35-23   Sorting on a single field

Sorting on Up to Three Fields

1   With a table, query, or form open in data entry mode, click the Sort button.

2   In the Sort Order window, set the sort options you want.

Use Figure 35-24 for guidance.

3   Click OK.

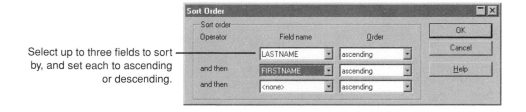

Select up to three fields to sort by, and set each to ascending or descending.

Figure 35-24   Using the Sort Order window

In the example in Figure 35-24, the logic works like this: First, sort the data in the LASTNAME field in ascending order; after you do that, put the data in the FIRSTNAME field in ascending order.

Searching for Specific Records

Searching for data in a database works on the same principle as searching for a word in a text document: you tell the search tool what you want to find, and the tool locates the next item matching the search criteria. To search for a data record in a table, query, or form:

1   Click the Find Record icon (binoculars).

2   In the Data Record Search window, set the search options.

Use Figure 35-25 for guidance.

3   Click the Search button.

From whichever record the cursor is in, the next record meeting the search criteria is found.

To find specific text, select the Text option and type the text you want to find. If you select the is Null (nothing in the field) or is not Null (anything in the field) options, you can set criteria only in the Where to Search area.

You can search all fields, or in a specific field you select.

In the position field, select whether the text you type must appear at the very beginning of, at the very end of, anywhere in, or must make up the entire field(s).

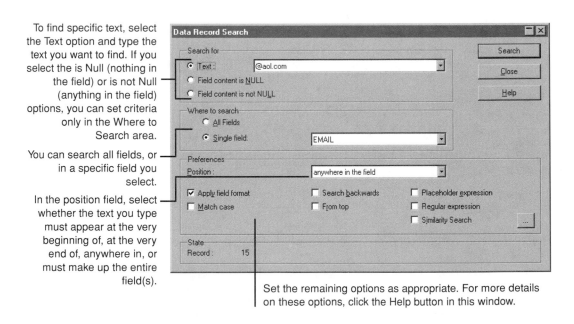

Set the remaining options as appropriate. For more details on these options, click the Help button in this window.

Figure 35-25   Setting search options

Filtering Data

Filtering data means focusing in on data that has specific characteristics. For example, you could show only the records that have "hotmail.com" in the Email address. Then, among the records that meet that criteria, you could further filter to show only the records that have a last name beginning with "J".

Much of the filtering functionality in StarOffice requires that you use the SQL language. For more information on the SQL language, look in the online help system under "SQL commands".

There are two ways to filter database information: using AutoFilter and using the Default Filter. You can use both methods in tables and queries. The Default Filter isn't available in a form.

You can't set filter options on reports. But you can create a report based on a filtered table or query.

Using AutoFilter

The AutoFilter is a great way to step through data, filtering in increments. In principle, AutoFilter works the same in tables, queries, and forms.

1   In the table, query, or form, click in a field containing the data you want to filter by.

For example, if you want to show only records of men, click in a record that has a PREFIX of "Mr.".

2   Click the AutoFilter button, as shown in Figure 35-26.

Of the records that are displayed, you can further use AutoFilter to focus in on the data in greater detail.

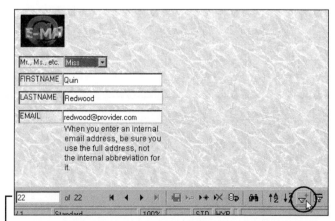

In the table above, the cursor is in the PREFIX field containing the data "Mr.". When you click the AutoFilter button, only records with a PREFIX of "Mr." will be displayed.

In this form, the "Mr., Ms., etc." field is highlighted. The data "Miss" is displayed. When you click the AutoFilter button, only records with "Miss" in the "Mr., Ms., etc." field will be available. Look in the lower left of the window to see the number of records decrease.

Figure 35-26   Using AutoFilter

To remove filtering and show all records again, click the
Remove Filter/Sort or Apply Filter icon.

Using the Default Filter

The Default Filter lets you select up to three filtering criteria for tables and queries. The
criteria you set can have "and" or "or" relationships. For example, you can determine that
the first criteria *and* the second criteria apply to the filtering, or you could determine that
either the first *or* second criteria apply, *and* that the third criteria must apply.

1   With a table or query open in data entry mode, click the
     Default Filter icon.

2   In the Filter window, set the criteria for the filtering.

3   Click OK.

The filtering is applied to the table or query. If the filtering doesn't work as expected,
double-check your criteria, especially in the Value field of the Filter window. If you need
further help setting conditions and values, click the Help button in the Filter window.

Select a column heading (Field name), a comparison operator (Condition), and the Value
the Condition will measure against. Selecting AND means that condition *must* also be
met.

Use Figure 35-27 on page 1033 for guidance.

Select a field name containing data you want to filter on; select a condition for the data; and enter a value for the data you want to filter on (with respect to the Condition setting).

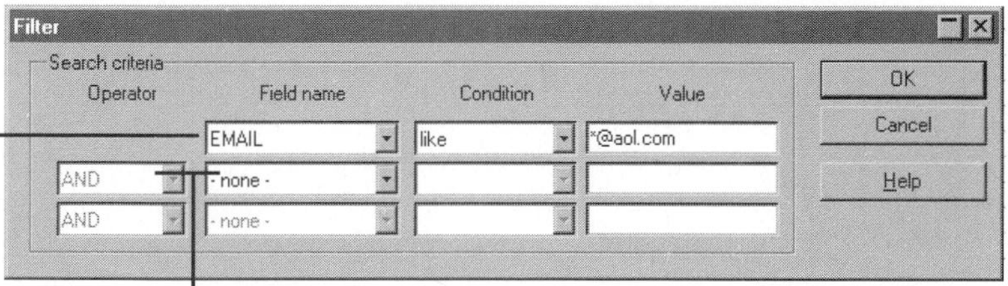

Filter					☐ ☒
Search criteria					OK
Operator	Field name	Condition	Value		Cancel
	EMAIL ▾	like ▾	*@aol.com		
AND ▾	- none - ▾	▾			Help
AND ▾	- none - ▾	▾			

To set more criteria, select another field name, select whether it has an "and" or "or" relationship to the previous setting, and set the condition and value.

Figure 35-27   Filtering data with the Default Filter

Note – Use the "*" wild card in conjunction with the "like" or "not like" options. In the example in Figure 35-27, the Condition and Value combination mean, "Filter the data in the EMAIL field to show only the data ending in ('like') 'aol.com'."

To remove filtering and show all records again, click the Remove Filter/Sort or Apply Filter icon.

StarOffice Basic

Using Macros to Automate Tasks

Quick Start

This section contains the following information to help you get started quickly:

- A checklist for quickly recording and running a macro
- Feature and macro overview
- A tutorial

See *StarOffice Writer* on page 151 for general tips that can make working with StarOffice a lot easier.

Note – Many features are available throughout StarOffice, but we don't cover them in every program's section. Check the index, or refer to *StarOffice Writer* on page 151 if you can't find the information you need in the chapters for StarOffice Basic.

Quick Start Checklist

If you have emergency macro needs right now, these are the sections to hit:

- *Recording a Macro* on page 1052
- *Running Macros* on page 1054
- *Adding a Macro to a StarOffice Document* on page 1060

StarOffice Basic Features

StarOffice Basic has two main functions: recording and running macros, and programming.

Recording and playing macros The StarOffice Basic language lets you record and play *macros*. Macros record every action within StarOffice, regardless of what application you're in. If you open a new file and type a paragraph in it, StarOffice Basic records that. The actions you perform are translated into StarOffice Basic commands, and put in a macro file. You can then play it back, and exactly the same actions will take place, automatically.

Macros can be extremely useful for repetitive tasks that don't vary much. StarOffice Basic allows you to apply formatting such as a particular font to a document. If you have a list of addresses and want the name line to appear in bold, you could record a macro that makes the first line of a file, and every fourth line after that, bold.

While you can convert some Microsoft Word macros to run in StarOffice Basic, it involves extensive research and manual editing. In our opinion, it's not feasible.

Macro/programming language Writing programs from scratch isn't included in this book; we made the assumption that most StarOffice users aren't dying to do it. You can view the API if you want to learn on your own, however; see *What You Can Do With StarOffice Basic Macros* on page 1043.

Guided Tour

This should take about ten minutes, and will give you an idea of how the program works. You can also see *Adding a Drop-Down List Box* on page 560.

1   Choose Tools > Macros.

2   Click Organizer.

3   In the Macro Organizer window, click the Libraries tab.

4   Click the New button and name the new library GuidedTour. Don't select the Attach file option.

5   Click the Modules tab.

6   Scroll to the bottom of the Module/Dialog list; the GuidedTour library and the default module Module1 are displayed.

7   Click the New Module button. Name the new module anything you want and click OK. (A module is a way of grouping macros; a library in turn groups modules.)

8   Click the Close button of the Macro Organizer window.

9   In the Macros window, scroll to the bottom of the Macro from list. Select the module you created within the GuidedTour library.

10 Get ready to record a macro by typing a new name in the Macro name field. (Type over the default name "Main" that appears.)

11 Click Record.

12 A small window will appear over the file menu; move it out of the way into the center of the work area.

13 Open a new, empty StarOffice Web file (choose File > New > HTML Document).

14 Type the following, using **only the keyboard** to move from one line to another. Don't stop if you make typing mistakes; just backspace and correct the mistake, then keep going.

```
THE OATMEAL SAGA

The Legend of the Oatmeal
The Oatmeal Annals
Fall of the House of Oatmeal
```

15 Press Enter and from the Apply Style dropdown list on the left side of the StarOffice object bar, choose Horizontal Line.

16 Press Enter and choose Insert > Fields > Date.

17 Use the mouse to select the text you typed (not the date field). Use the fields and icons in the object bar to make the text 22 point and red.

18 Use the mouse to select the bottom three lines and apply bullet formatting to them using the bullets icon on the object bar.

19 Click the icon in the middle of the small recording window to stop the recording process. (It sometimes relocates itself back to the original location over the File menu; switch back to the desktop and look for it there if it's not where you left it.)

20 Close the HTML file without saving changes.

21 Choose Tools > Macro. In the Macro from list of the Macro window, select the macro you recorded and click Edit.

22 The Basic editing environment is displayed. Review the code that your actions were translated to.

23 Click the Run icon in the macro object bar at the top of the work area.

24 Note that this doesn't work! Close the window, saving changes if necessary, and click the Macro icon on the object bar. In the Macro window, select the macro and click Run. Another HTML file containing the same text will be created.

25 Switch to the new HTML file. Note that the typing was completed but the formatting wasn't. StarOffice Basic doesn't record some mouse actions that take place in the work area (and, sometimes, doesn't record keyboard actions).

26 Close the HTML file without saving changes.

27 Switch back to the StarOffice Basic editing environment. Copy the entire macro, including the two lines for the empty Main macro.

28 Click the tab for the other module.

29 Paste the macro into the module.

30 Right-click the module tab and change its name.

31 Change the following lines:

```
Selection.Insert( "The Legend of the Oatmeal" )

Selection.InsertPara()

Selection.Insert( "The Oatmeal Annals" )

Selection.InsertPara()
```

to appear as shown:

```
Selection.Insert( "Sunday in the Park With a Bowl of Oatmeal" )

Selection.InsertPara()

Selection.Insert( "Floyd Wakes up to a Bowl of Burnt Oatmeal" )

Selection.InsertPara()
```

32 In the first line of the macro, change the macro name (the name appears after "sub").

33 Right before the "End Sub" line at the bottom of the macro, add lines to make the macro insert three more horizontal lines, separated by two blank lines.

34 Save the macro (choose File > Save).

35 Run the macro again.

The StarOffice Basic Macro Editing Window

Figure 36-1 on page 1042 shows the IDE, or independent development environment, where you can edit macros and access macro features. (Choose Tools > Macros, select a macro, click Edit.)

To switch from one library to another, select a library from the list at the left side of the macro toolbar.

To switch to a different module in the IDE, click the tab of the module you want, at the bottom of the work area.

To see a different macro, scroll up and down with the appropriate module.

Click **Object Catalog** to open the Objects window, which lets you reorganize macros and insert references to them in other macros.

Click **Macros** to open the Macro window, where you'll record macros; click **Modules** to manage modules and libraries.

Click **Save Source As** to save the macro in a specific file; it is saved by default in standard.bas.

The current **library** is shown here.

Click **Run** to run the first macro in the module.

Click **Stop** to stop the currently running macro.

Click **Single Step** to run the macro one step at a time.

The keystrokes you recorded are translated into commands. Commands are in green, values are in, red, comments are in gray, and standard StarOffice Basic commands are in blue.

Click **Breakpoint** to insert a point in the macro at which you can run the macro one step at a time.

The **library and module** are displayed here.

The **current modules** are displayed here. Each module can contain one or more macros.

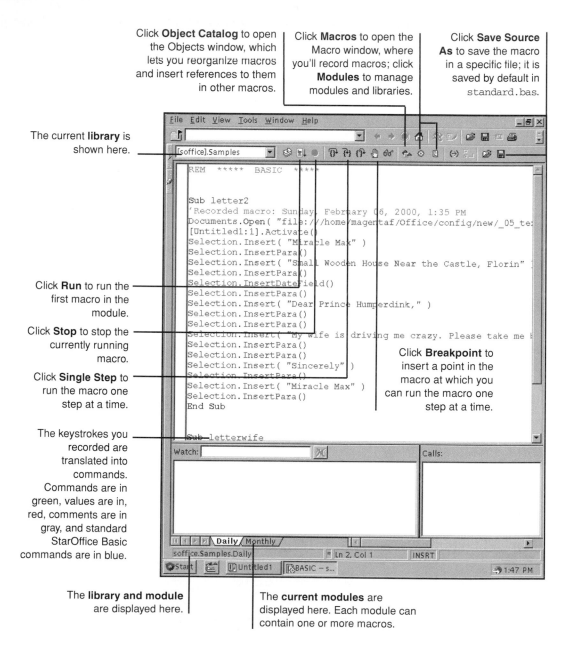

Figure 36-1   StarOffice Basic work area

What You Can Do With StarOffice Basic Macros

StarOffice Basic takes a little getting used to; read this before you start using it, and you'll save yourself some of the initial confusion that we experienced.

Macros in General

Macros are somewhat touchy; they're very literal creatures. For instance, assume you have a file, listing names, phone numbers, and birthdays.

```
Buttercup (303) 926-0614 06/24/67
Count Rugen (666) 908-2328 12/11/53
Fezzik (309) 469-9002 04/09/65
Humperdink (866) 843-7246 07/27/58
Impressive Clergyman, The (409) 943-7278 01/03/30
Inigo Montoya (303) 469-9003 04/09/65
Vizzini (206) 334-9902 03/22/58
Westley (303) 641-4514 11/26/62
```

You can't successfully create a macro that will go through an entire file and delete the phone numbers, because each customer's name is a different length. You could record the actions of moving to the end of each name on each line, then deleting the next 14 characters, but it wouldn't work because each name is a different length and can't be repeated the same way for each line.

This would work if the phone number or birthdate, or another fixed-length piece of data like a customer number, were the first item on each line.

StarOffice Basic Macros

This section will give you a sense of Basic's capabilities.

Recording Macros

The recording capabilities of Basic are extremely limited and unpredictable. Macros can be very powerful when you have a good recording tool, but Basic isn't one of those. For example, a very useful feature for macros is to search for a word or phrase and replace it with another. Unfortunately, that's another thing you can't record in Basic. It also records very inconsistently; some of the formatting you do on the object bar (with the mouse) gets recorded, and some of it is ignored.

On general principle, however, we've covered the macro recording, editing, and running features.

Writing Macros

Most programming language books take up a good 300 to 1000 pages, so we don't cover writing in Basic in this book. However, if you've got a knack for programming or writing macros, you can probably figure out a lot of it on your own. If you want to see the details of the StarOffice Basic API, go into the StarOffice Explorer, expand the Bookmarks folder, then expand the StarOffice API folder (see Figure 36-2). Then double-click the StarOffice API Overview or StarOffice API Specification bookmark. Navigate through the help to find the topics you need.

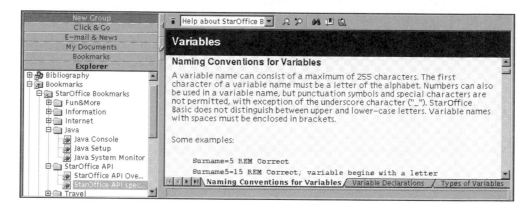

Figure 36-2   StarOffice Basic API

Adding Macros to StarOffice Documents

Perhaps the most useful thing you can do with StarOffice macros is add them to other documents, such as Web pages or presentations. StarOffice Web is full of features that let you set up hyperlinks to macros, StarOffice Basic scripts, and JavaScript. Even simple macros such as opening a new file and typing a few lines of text, or deleting lines or objects in the current or another document, or can be effective and useful within documents such as presentations and Web pages.

Note – You also can use a macro in order to create a drop-down list in a spreadsheet, so someone can select a value from the dropdown list and the selected value will appear in a cell. See *Adding a Drop-Down List Box* on page 560.

You can add macros that you create yourself and, if you're the investigative type, you can figure out what the macros are doing that are already included with StarOffice and add those to documents, as well.

The basic steps for adding a macro are covered in *Adding a Macro to a StarOffice Document* on page 1060.

Setup for StarOffice Basic Scripts

If you want to add scripts or macros written using StarOffice Basic to HTML documents, note the following setup option shown in Figure 36-3.

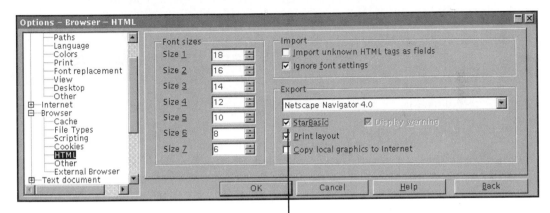

Select the StarBasic option.

Figure 36-3   Basic setup

Choose Tools > Options > Browser > HTML and select the StarBasic option. You must select this option *before* you create any StarOffice Basic script that you want to saved in an HTML document.

StarOffice Basic scripts have to be in the header of the HTML document. After you add the macro to the document, it will appear in the source text of the HTML document (in the header) with the following syntax (a "Hello World" example macro is used):

```
<HEAD>
(any additional content)
<SCRIPT LANGUAGE="STARBASIC">
<!--
' $LIBRARY: library_name
' $MODULE: module_name
Sub test
msgbox "Hello World"
End Sub
// -->
</SCRIPT>
</HEAD>
```

Organizing Your Macros

If you just want to leap in and record a few macros, go ahead and just store them in the default location (Standard); you won't need this information. However, if you'll be using more than a few, it's a good idea to read this section and organize your macros according to their function.

How StarOffice Basic Categorizes Macros

The StarOffice Basic interface and structure aren't set up very well for quick, easy macro recording. Macros are categorized in a pathname-like structure: one or more macros are stored in a module, within a library, within a file.

If you've used other macro programs, it might seem odd and unnecessarily complicated that you need to store macros in a library/module/macro tree structure, instead of just recording the macro file and storing it anywhere. We think so, too; the entire StarOffice Basic system was obviously set up with programmers in mind, not users who just want to record a macro and get out again.

However, it's fairly simple once you've got the idea. Think of the libraries simply as a closet where you keep your macros, and modules as shelves within that closet. You can store your recorded macros in modules in the Standard library, or you can create your own new libraries. You can't add your macros to any of the other libraries listed, such as CreateReport (though you can add any macros in any libraries to your documents).

Figure 36-4 shows the Macros window (choose Tools > Macro). This shows how macros that you just store within the Standard library are organized.

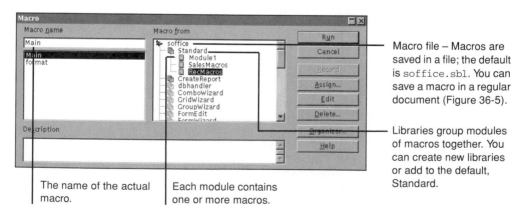

Figure 36-4   How macros are organized in the Macros window

You can also choose to store the macro in a specific document—either one you've created especially for storing macros, or the current document you're working on, in which you'll use the macro. When you scroll to the bottom of the Macro from list in the Macro window, you'll also see listed all open documents, and their macros, if any.

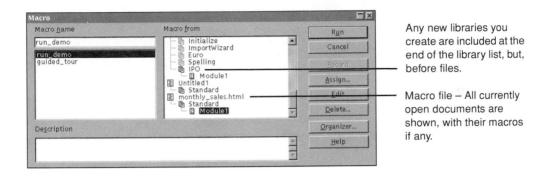

Any new libraries you create are included at the end of the library list, but, before files.

Macro file – All currently open documents are shown, with their macros if any.

Figure 36-5   Macro window, part 2

Figure 36-6 on page 1048 shows how the structures are created, and displayed in the IDE (independent development environment).

Organization Recommendations

Take note of the following StarOffice limitations.

More than one macro in a module When you use the Step and Run icons in the macro toolbar to run the macro one step at a time, only the first macro in the module is run, which may not be the one you want.

Size limit There is a limit of 64k on the amount of code allowed in one module.

Getting at a macro to add it to a document Most of the macro-insertion features in StarOffice let you insert a macro from the Standard and other libraries, and from the document you're currently in, but not any other documents you've created. Keep this in mind when you're deciding where to put macros.

Based on this, you can make your life as simple as possible by following these tips:

- If you're creating macros that a lot of people will want to use, or that you plan to run from a different document, create one or more libraries for your macros (*Creating a New Library* on page 1048). Don't just assign them to one of your own documents.

- Create a new module for each macro you want to record (*Creating a New Module* on page 1049).

soffice is always displayed, followed by the library in the title bar of the IDE. The library is displayed here.

The editing area displays the macro or macros that have been recorded or pasted in the current module.

A tab for each module in the current library is displayed here.

The category/file, library, and module are shown here. These aren't updated very well as you work; only the library and module you chose to edit in the Macros window are displayed here.

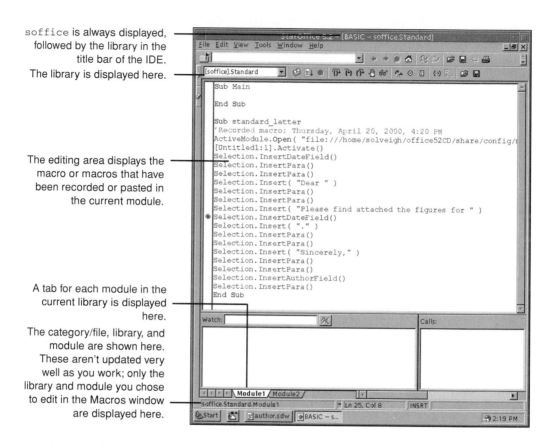

Figure 36-6   How macros are organized in the editing windows

Creating a New Library

1   Click the Modules icon on the macro toolbar.

2   In the Macro Organizer window, click the Libraries tab.

3   Click the New button to display the Macro Organizer window (Figure 36-7).

4   Enter the name in the New Library dialog.

You can select the Attach file option to create the new library as a separate file in office/basic. If you don't do so, it will be stored in the soffice.sbl file. In addition, macros stored as a separate file will not be loaded automatically after starting StarOffice, but instead must be activated manually (in the Macros window by clicking Run) or by another macro.

This isn't your only chance to save the library as a separate file; you can edit the macro, then click the Save Source As icon on the macro object bar.

5   Click OK.

6   A default module named Module1 was created and listed below the new library at the bottom of the Module/Dialog list. Click the Modules tab and select the new library. Highlight the name and rename it, based on the task that the macro you'll store in it will perform.

Note – The other libraries contain StarOffice macros you can associate with events in hyperlinks and documents. See *Adding Applets and Plugins* on page 449.

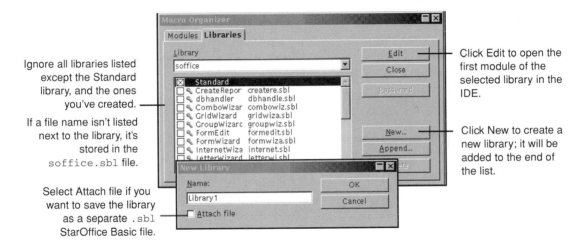

Figure 36-7   Creating a new library in the macro organizer

Creating a New Module

You can do so through the Organizer, or by opening a current library in the IDE.

Using the Organizer

1   Click the Modules icon on the macro toolbar.

2   In the Macro Organizer window (Figure 36-8), click the Modules tab.

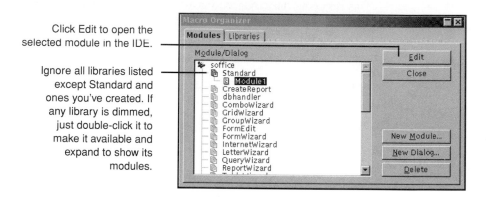

Click Edit to open the selected module in the IDE.

Ignore all libraries listed except Standard and ones you've created. If any library is dimmed, just double-click it to make it available and expand to show its modules.

Figure 36-8   Creating new modules using the Organizer

3   Select the library to add it to.

You can add only to Standard and to libraries you've created. If the library name is dimmed, double-click it.

4   Click the New Module button.

5   Enter the name, be sure BASIC is selected, and click OK.

Using the IDE

1   Click the Macros icon on the macro toolbar.

2   Select a module within the library you want to add to and click Edit.

3   Right-click on a tab of an existing module and choose Insert > BASIC Module.

Managing Macros, Modules, and Libraries

Use this information to move modules or macros around, rename, delete, and perform other similar tasks.

Moving a Module to a Different Library Using the Organizer

You can drag a module from one library to another in the organizer.

1   Click the Modules icon on the macro toolbar.

2   In the Organizer window, click the Modules tab.

3   Select the module you want to move.

Drag it to the new library; a line indicates where the module will be moved to when you release the mouse button.

4   Select the module and click Edit, then choose File > Save.

Moving Macros and Modules Using the IDE

You also can simply cut and paste macros from one module to another, in the same library or a different library.

1   Click the Macros icon on the macro toolbar.

2   Select a module and click Edit.

3   Select the macro or macros to move, then cut and paste them to a new module or library.

• To select a module in the same library, click the right tab below the work area.

• To select a new library, select it from the list in the work area upper right corner.

4   Choose File > Save to save the changes.

Renaming a Module

1   Click the Macros icon on the macro toolbar.

2   Select the module and click Edit.

3   Right-click on a tab of an existing module and choose Rename. Type the new name on the tab.

Hiding a Module

You can temporarily remove the module without deleting it.

1   Click the Macros icon on the macro toolbar.

2   Select the module and click Edit.

3   Right-click on a tab of an existing module and choose Hide.

Deleting Macros

To delete one or two macros, it's quickest to use the Macros window.

1   Click the Macros icon on the macro toolbar, then select the module and click Edit.

2   Select the correct category, library, and module, then select the macro and click Delete.

If you want to delete a lot of macros from a module, it's quickest to go to the IDE and delete the text of the macros, or delete the entire module.

1   Click the Macros icon on the macro toolbar, then select the module and click Edit.

2   In the IDE text window, delete the text of each macro. Remember that the beginning and ending of each macro is selected by the following.

```
Sub macroname
End Sub
```

Deleting Modules

Either of the following methods is quick; they just provide alternate navigation.

Use this method if you're sure you want to delete it.

1   Click the Modules icon on the macro toolbar.

2   Click the Modules tab if it's not active.

3   Select a module and click Delete.

Use this method if you want to look at the module before you delete it.

1   Click the Macros icon on the macro toolbar, then select the module and click Edit.

2   Right-click the tab of the module and choose Delete.

Deleting Libraries

If you delete a library that's stored in the `soffice.sbl` file, only that library will be deleted, not the whole file. If you delete another library, the whole file is deleted.

1   Click the Modules icon on the macro toolbar.

2   Click the Libraries tab if it's not active.

3   Select a library and click Delete.

Recording a Macro

Before you begin, see *What You Can Do With StarOffice Basic Macros* on page 1043 to get an idea of the capabilities of StarOffice Basic.

When you record, it's a good idea to use the keyboard as much as possible, and do tasks in relative, rather than absolute, terms. For instance, if you want to move to the next line in a file, press the End key, then the right arrow key, rather than moving 12 spaces to the right with the arrow key, or using the mouse to move the cursor.

When you're recording, it's fine if you make typos or mistakes, then hit the backspace or otherwise correct them. You can delete them from the macro file when you're done, or just leave them in if it doesn't interfere with running the macro.

Note – Don't overlook the options of the fields you can insert, such as date and time, which are always current no matter when the original macro was recorded.

---

1 Be sure that you're ready to start recording. If you want a file to be open when the macro begins, for instance, open it now.

2 Click the Macros icon on the macro toolbar to display the Macros window. (You also can choose Tools > Macros.)

   • If you want to store the macro in a particular module or library, select the library and module to store the macro in.

   • If you want the macro stored in the current document, scroll to the bottom of the list and select the default module.

3 Enter a macro name in the Macro name field of the Macro window (Figure 36-9), and a description if you want.

4 Each module has a default empty macro called Main; our investigations have shown it to be useless. Delete it or ignore it.

5 Click Record. A small recording icon will appear in a tiny window (shown at right) on top of the StarOffice File menu.

   Move the recording window, if necessary; the action won't be recorded.

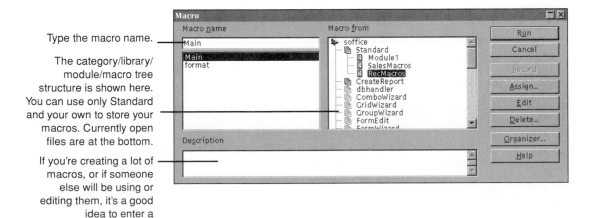

Figure 36-9   Selecting the library, module, and name of the macro

6 Complete the actions you want to record.

When selecting or manipulating text, be sure to use only the keyboard, not the mouse. Only keyboard actions are recorded as part of the macro.

7   Click the recording icon again to stop recording.

Running Macros

Running the macro, of course, is where you see whether the recording process translates into something useful.

Note – Don't be surprised if it doesn't run correctly the first time. If there are errors, see *Opening and Editing Macros* on page 1057. You can also insert *breakpoints* during macros, which stop the process at certain points. These are useful because you can examine the results of a particular step, then continue playing the macro, or play it one step at a time. See *Using Breakpoints to Stop Macros at a Specified Point* on page 1056.

Use any of the following procedures to run the macro.

Assigning a Shortcut Key to a Macro

If you'll be running the macro several times and it's not connected to a button or other element yet, it's a good idea to set up a shortcut to it, using the Configuration window. (For more information about setting up shortcut keys, see *Assigning Shortcut Keys* on page 100.)

1   Switch to the application you want to run the macro in.

2   Click the Macro button on the macro toolbar.

3   In the Macro window, click the Assign button.

4   The Keyboard tab should be in front; if not, click it.

5   In the Category list, scroll down until you see StarOffice BASIC. (The earlier list item, BASIC, lets you assign shortcut keys to functions like Add Breakpoint.)

6   Select StarOffice BASIC and, if it's not expanded to show libraries and modules, click the + icon next to it to expand it.

7   Expand the macro library, such as Standard, and select a module and macro.

8   The Keyboard lists all the preset combinations that you can use to start the macro, as shown in Figure 36-10.

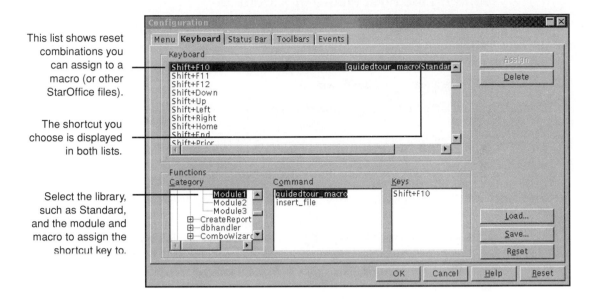

This list shows reset combinations you can assign to a macro (or other StarOffice files).

The shortcut you choose is displayed in both lists.

Select the library, such as Standard, and the module and macro to assign the shortcut key to.

Figure 36-10   Setting up a shortcut key to run a macro

You can't create your own key combination; you can only select the ones that are listed.

The shortcut key you selected will be displayed in the Keys list, when the corresponding macro is selected. If you selected a preexisting combination, the macro name will be shown next to it in the Keyboard list.

Note – If you select an existing StarOffice macro, be sure the macro's library (the category it's listed within) is activated. Choose Tools > Macros, click the Organizer button, then click the Libraries tab and be sure the checkbox next to the library is checked.

---

9   Click OK.

Running a Macro From Start to Finish

You can run a macro in the IDE or in the application where the macro will run, if the necessary conditions to start the macro are available. For instance, if the first step to run the macro is making a selection from the StarOffice File menu, you can run the macro from anywhere. If the first step is in a StarWriter document, it must be open and be the active document.

You can quickly run a macro using any of the following methods.

Running the First Macro in a Module

This works only if a macro is open in the IDE window (the icon will be dimmed if no macros are open). It will run only the first macro in the current module; only one module and library can be open at a time.

1   Open a macro in the IDE window.

2   Click the Run icon in the macro toolbar.

Running a Selected Macro

1   Click the Macros icon on the macro toolbar.

2   In the Macro window, select the library, module, and macro to run, and click Run.

Running a Macro One Step at a Time

Unfortunately, there is no debugging program for macros. However, you can run the script one step at a time to see what happens at each step.

1   Be sure the macro is the first one in the module, if there is more than one.

    Cut and paste it to move it to the top, or create a new module (right-click the current module tab and choose Insert > BASIC Module) and paste the macro into the new module.

2   In the IDE or in the application where the macro will run, click the Single Step icon on the macro toolbar.

3   The macro will run one step at a time; click the icon again to go to each new line. Click the Step Back icon to repeat the previous step.

    If an error occurs, the IDE will be displayed with an error message and an arrow pointing to the line.

4   Click the Stop icon to stop before the macro has run completely.

Using Breakpoints to Stop Macros at a Specified Point

You can add a breakpoint that stops the macro on the line you select. You can then run the macro manually step by step using the Single Step icons (see *Running a Macro One Step at a Time*).

Note – When you insert the breakpoint, StarOffice Basic checks the entire macro for errors; you can't insert one if there are any problems anywhere in the code. You might need to comment out problem lines before you can add the breakpoint.

---

1   Open the macro in the IDE.

2   Position the cursor on the line where you want to switch from automatic to manual control.

3   Click the Breakpoint icon in the macro toolbar.

4   A red circle will appear to the left of the line.

To remove the breakpoint, just click the Breakpoint icon again.

Opening and Editing Macros

You'll probably need to tweak at least half the macros you record, to fix them or to make them do something extra. In addition, if others are going to use and perhaps troubleshoot your macros, it's a good idea to add comments describing what some of the lines do.

Note – StarOffice relentlessly prompts you for a password if you try to edit the existing macros. You just can't. Which is probably just as well. You can add them, unedited, to documents using the procedures covered in *Adding Macros to StarOffice Documents* on page 1044.

Macro Code Structure

The keystrokes you record are translated into commands, shown in the IDE and in Figure 36-11. The StarOffice Basic Editor assigns colors according to the following guidelines:

- Remarks or comments (beginning with REM or a single quotation mark) are gray.
- A recognized expression such as Selection. Insert is green.
- A recognized string such as a name is red.
- A recognized Basic keyword (Print, Input) is blue.

Each macro begins with the line Sub *macroname* and ends with the line End Sub.

First line of macro; name is letter_macro.

Selection.Insert precedes most actions.

Current date was inserted.

Last line of macro.

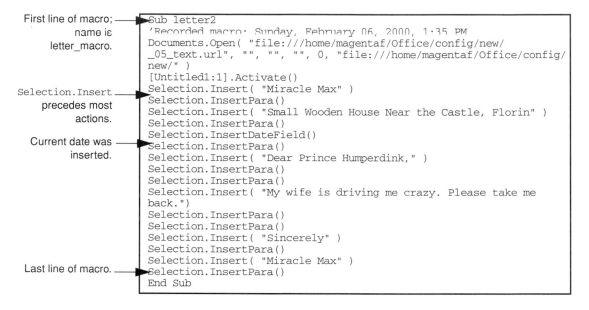

```
Sub letter2
'Recorded macro: Sunday, February 06, 2000, 1:35 PM
Documents.Open( "file:///home/magentaf/Office/config/new/
_05_text.url", "", "", "", 0, "file:///home/magentaf/Office/config/
new/" )
[Untitled1:1].Activate()
Selection.Insert( "Miracle Max" )
Selection.InsertPara()
Selection.Insert( "Small Wooden House Near the Castle, Florin" )
Selection.InsertPara()
Selection.InsertDateField()
Selection.InsertPara()
Selection.Insert( "Dear Prince Humperdink," )
Selection.InsertPara()
Selection.InsertPara()
Selection.Insert( "My wife is driving me crazy. Please take me
back.")
Selection.InsertPara()
Selection.InsertPara()
Selection.Insert( "Sincerely" )
Selection.InsertPara()
Selection.Insert( "Miracle Max" )
Selection.InsertPara()
End Sub
```

Figure 36-11   Keystrokes converted into a simple macro

The macro in Figure 36-11 would create a new file that looks like Figure 36-12:

Figure 36-12   Letter created by macro

Adding Comments

To add descriptions about what lines do in the macro, just press Enter to add a new line, and begin the line with a single quote or the letters REM in all uppercase.

```
'This line starts an animated GIF showing two
'right-handed men fencing.
Documents.Open( "file:///home/magentaf/gifs/inigo.gif")
```

Comments are shown in light gray text.

Troubleshooting Tips

When an error occurs when you're running a macro, an error message will appear and StarOffice Basic will point to the line containing the error.

Pinpointing problems If you're having problems, always use the Single Step feature to run the macro one step at a time (see *Running a Macro One Step at a Time* on page 1056). If the error occurs late in the macro, add a breakpoint.

Comment out lines that are creating problems. If it's optional, add a single quote mark in front of it to "comment it out". The text will turn gray and the macro will run without that line. You can use this technique to pin down the source of errors.

Macros that create new files For macros that create new files, you might need to edit some of the macros. The following lines are generated when you create a new StarWriter file, for example:

```
Documents.Open( "file:///home/magentaf/Office/config/new/
_05_text.url", "", "", "", 0, "file:///home/magentaf/Office/
config/new/" )
[Untitled1:1].Activate()
```

If you already had an untitled document open, though, the line will be recorded as **Untitled1:1** instead and you'll get an error when you run the file. StarOffice likes all the untitled files it opens to be titled **Untitled1**. Change this line if you encounter errors.

You can't edit the file name so that it's named "Annual Report" or whatever you're going to save the document as; StarOffice will complain and give you an error.

StarOffice Web has a feature that lets you create hyperlinks that open new files. You might want to use it instead, if appropriate for your project. See *Linking to a New Empty File* on page 438.

Adding a Macro to a StarOffice Document

Once you've recorded a macro, or found an existing StarOffice macro you want to use, you can add it to any document. You can do this in a number of ways, most of which can be done in all StarOffice documents. Table 36-1 summarizes the ways you can add macros to documents, and where to find that information.

Table 36-1   Adding macros to each type of StarOffice document

Feature	Where to go to find the information
Interaction	*Adding Actions Using Interaction Effects* on page 694
Form functions	*Attaching Actions to Form Controls* on page 455 *Adding a Drop-Down List Box* on page 560
Hyperlinks	*Linking Macros and Scripts to Graphics* on page 454 *Using Macros, Scripts, and Events* on page 451
Shortcut keys	*Assigning a Shortcut Key to a Macro* on page 1054

Note – Most of the macro-insertion features in StarOffice let you insert a macro from the Standard and other libraries, and from the document you're currently in, but not from any other documents you've created. If you're having trouble finding the macro you want, it's probably in a separate document. You'll need to cut and paste it into a module in the Standard library, a new library, or create a module for it in your current document.

Index

Symbols

! 522
in cells 501
$ (absolute cell reference marker) 530
) 523
) in formulas 523
.cfg files 99, 102
= ^ * / + - = 522

Numerics

0 values, hiding 510
1/2 to .5, changing 494
1/2, 1/4, 3/4 139
1st, 2nd, 3rd, 4th 139
3D
   3D effects window 769
   attributes, applying changes 769, 770
   conversion options 792
   conversion using Effects tearoff menu 794
   conversion, example 791
   converting polygons to 793
   converting text to 675, 776
   geometry, modifying 770
   objects, creating 768
   objects, merging 768
   rotation object, converting curves to 793
   See also converting
3D charts, rotating 558
3D clipart 105
3D Controller icon, finding 692

45-degree lines, drawing 741
45-degree rotation of image 825

A

absolute cell references 530, 484
absolute paths
   relative paths display absolute in tool tips 432
   setting up 379
Accept option
   cookie setup 363
Accept or Reject Changes window (Calc) 594
Accept or Reject Changes window (Writer) 343
accepting
   document changes (Calc) 593
   document changes (Writer) 342
access
   among Schedule Servers 859
   missing access rights message 362
   to others' calendars 855
Access 97 995
access level for events 887, 891
Account field, FTP setup 402
accounts
   Email, setting up 943
   News, setting up 943
Acrobat, Adobe 352
   See also PDF
Action at mouse click field, interaction 695
Action performed event, defined 458

Action started event 458
Active Server Pages WebCast options 718
ActiveX Data Objects 995
Adabas D 994
   assigning a primary key 1004
   installation 29
ADD (Writer task bar) 171
Add Holidays to Calendar window 869
adding
   attachments to Email 962
   AutoText categories 169
   cells quickly 525
   colors to the palette 127
   columns (Email) 957
   contacts to Address Book 978
   dictionaries for spell check 144
   Email addresses 966
   floating frames (Calc) 565
   floating frames (Writer) 250
   forms to databases 1010
   items in sliders 104
   notes to documents (Calc) 594
   notes to documents (Writer) 344
   queries to databases 1019
   reports to databases 1024
   sheets to a spreadsheet 488
   signature to Email 965
   sliders to Explorer 104
   tables to databases 999
   text boxes (Writer) 249
   your own stuff to Gallery 107
adding (+) in formulas 522
adding a custom format 606
Address Book
   about 972

Z

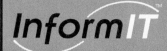

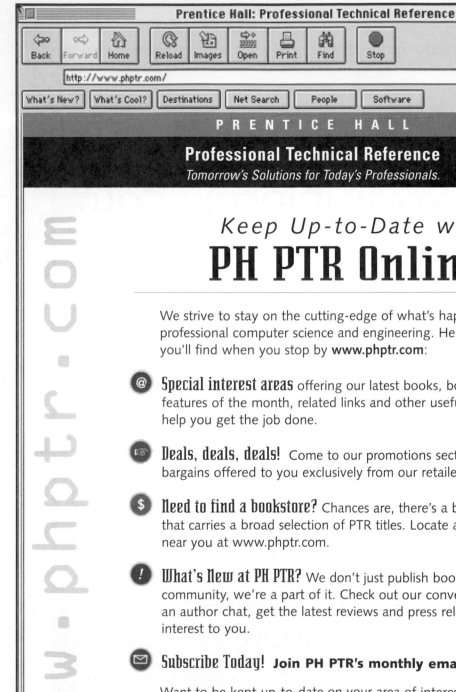